Captain Roy Brown

A True Story of the Great War, 1914-1918

by Alan D. Bennett
and Margaret Brown Harman
with major contributions by Howard Morton Brown
and Denny Reid May

Brick Tower Press
Habent Sua Fata Libelli

Brick Tower Press
1230 Park Avenue
New York, New York 10128
Tel: 212-427-7139
bricktower@aol.com • www.BrickTowerPress.com

All rights reserved under the International and Pan-American Copyright Conventions. Printed in the United States by J. T. Colby & Company, Inc., New York. No part of this publication may be reproduced, stored in a retrieval system, or transmitted in any form or by any means, electronic, or otherwise, without the prior written permission of the copyright holder. The Brick Tower Press colophon is a registered trademark of J. T. Colby & Company, Inc.

Library of Congress Cataloging-in-Publication Data

Bennett, Alan D.
Captain Roy Brown, A True Story of the Great War, 1914-1918

  Volume I
  ISBN-13: 978-1-883283-56-8, Trade Paper

  Volume II
  ISBN-13: 978-1-883283-89-6, Trade Paper

   I. World War I—Biography, 2. World War I—The Red Baron, 3. Aviation—Military I. Title

Copyright © 2011 by Alan D. Bennett

First Trade Paper Edition
January 2012

Captain Roy Brown

A True Story of the Great War, 1914-1918

Volume I

Biography of the First World War Canadian Flight Commander who never lost a man in combat or left one behind in enemy territory, even during the bloodiest days of 1918

By ALAN D. BENNETT

and MARGARET BROWN HARMON with major contributions by
HOWARD MORTON BROWN and DENNY REID MAY

Captain Arthur Roy Brown,
Distinguished Service Cross and bar, in Royal Air Force uniform, 1918.

CONTENTS

Volume 1 of the ebook edition
Volume I of the print edition

Dedications	7
Foreword	9
Acknowledgements	13
Authors' Prefaces	25
Introduction	33

PART ONE

Captain A. Roy Brown	37
Chapter 1: "Come with me and I'll show you what a Camel can do."	38
Chapter 2: Roy Brown's Early Life	45
Chapter 3: The Wright School of Aviation	70
Chapter 4: RNAS Chingford	126

Volume 2 of the ebook edition

Chapter 5: Dover Patrol, Part 1	212
Chapter 6: Dover Patrol, Part 2	319
Chapter 7: Home Leave & a Secret Mission	402

Volume 3 of the ebook edition

Chapter 8: The Ludendorff Offensive	420
Chapter 9: Rest, Crash and Demobilization (1918 to 1928)	563
Chapter 10: General Airways (1929 to 1939)	677

Volume 4 of the ebook edition

Chapter 11: Early Family Memories (1919 to 1939)	740
Chapter 12: Lisnaclin Farm and the RCAF, Women's Division (1939 to 1944)	755
Chapter 13: Second World War and the Provincial Election (1939 to 1944)	764
Chapter 14: A Quiet Departure (1944 to 1965)	786
Chapter 15: Epilogue	789

PART TWO

Volume 5 of the ebook edition
Volume II of the print edition

THE RED BARON AFFAIR   793

Chapter 16: 21 April 1918   795

Volume 6 of the ebook edition

Chapter 17: 22 April 1918 to 31 July 2005   971
Chapter 18: 1998 to 2006, The Investigation   1080
Chapter 19: Who Did Kill the Red Baron?   1137

APPENDICES
A. Summary of Roy Brown's Military Career   1140
B. Roy Brown's Combat Successes   1144
C. Allied Military Organization in North East France   1147
D. Bibliography   1149
E. List of Illustrations   1155
F. Index   1182

DEDICATIONS

To the late Howard Morton Brown, the youngest brother of Captain A. Roy Brown, DSC and bar, and the official historian of the Town of Carleton Place, Ontario, Canada. Without his personal archives and prodigious memory this biography would lack much important detail.

Howard Morton Brown

AND

To Arthur G. Harmon, the late husband of Captain Brown's elder daughter, Margaret, who although seriously ill himself, invited co-author Alan Bennett to their home and spent several days locating and helping to copy family records and precious photographs.

Arthur G. Harmon

FOREWORD

By Denny Reid May

During my travels in northern Canada I often had the thrill of sitting on a river bank or standing on a snowy hill, watching aircraft coming and going. There are few sounds that cause the hair on my neck to stand up, but the sound of a bush plane coming in over the trees is indescribable— a sound that was common in the days of bush flying, one that brought hope to those on the ground. During the First World War the sound of a rotary engine approaching an airfield brought a different kind of hope. Roy Brown brought hope to many, both as a First World War pilot and later with General Airways aircraft.

This book is a detailed that is not intended to answer the question "Who shot the Red Baron?" to rewrite history or to denigrate the works of others; it tells the long-lost story of Roy Brown. A lot of documentation and new information has come to light thanks to Alan Bennett's efforts during the past seven years and they allow the story of Roy Brown to be understood within the context of the times.

My wife, Margaret, and I (with our son David and his wife, Kimberly) had the pleasure of spending a week in France with Alan Bennett during the late spring of 2000. He took us to visit the places where Royal Air Force 209 Squadron was active in April 1918. We flew the route along which the Red Baron had chased my dad on 21 April 1918; we stood on the spot where the Red Baron had crash-landed and died. We visited Bertangles and Fricourt cemeteries and found the locations of the field hospital near Bertangles village and the railway siding between Bertangles and Poulainville airfields. Finally we paid homage to the brave soldiers and airmen from all armed forces who fell during that terrible war so many years ago.

During my active participation in the production of this book I was impressed by the quantity of research necessary to complete such a task. Working with Alan Bennett has been a learning experience for me, and his research skills and determination to get the facts have proven invaluable. Together with Alan in France, we located the original base of the Sainte-Colette brick-factory chimney, marking where it stood in 1918, and met individuals who confirmed this. They showed us the previously unknown precise, final resting place of the red triplane and the direction travelled by Manfred von Richthofen during his landing approach. We were introduced to people involved with keeping memories alive in the Somme. This truly was an experience not to be missed.

There is no doubt in my mind that had it not been for the care Roy Brown had for his pilots—the careful tutoring and guidance, many would not have returned from their first combat flight, including my dad, were it not for the courageous action of Roy Brown, who dived down after the Red Baron Wilfrid (Wop)Reid May on 21 April 1918, my dad would have been No. #81 on the list of those who fell to the guns of Manfred von Richthofen, and I would not be writing this introduction.

We would like to thank Margaret Brown Harmon for coming to visit us a few years back, and for her enthusiasm in working with Alan Bennett in writing this biography.

The effort has been tremendous, the results impressive and the story well told. I know you will find this book a most worthwhile resource and a tribute to a great man.

Denny R. May

Alan Bennett's Biography

In the 1930s as a child I lived about three miles from Hendon RAF Aerodrome in NE London. I was enthralled to watch the silver biplanes pass overhead; one helmeted head meant a Hawker Fury fighter, two meant a Hawker Hart day bomber. I became air-minded. The annual Hendon Air Pageant always coincided with the family summer holiday, but I could still borrow books on aviation from the local library - Biggles was my hero. The war came and I joined the Air Training Corps where in 1945 I was selected for a glider pilot training course. In 1952, as a lecturer at the Brazilian Air Force Institute of Technology, I began learning to fly powered aircraft at the university flying club. Upon moving to north-eastern Brazil, I completed training and gained my licence. I spent six years in the Amazon River region where every little town had a dirt runway for light aircraft and navigation between them was by map, watch and compass; just as in World War I. From Brazil I travelled to Thailand where I was fortunate to meet a Royal Thai Air Force Wing Commander (Lt.-Colonel) who arranged for me to join the Bangkok Flying Club. The club flew the RTAF De Havilland Chipmunk training aeroplanes on Sunday mornings and I was given training in aerobatics. In the USA I was able to fly the biplanes of the 1930s, which brought me back to Biggles. After 62 years and with pilot's licences from four countries in my pocket, illness put an end to flying.

In 1995 I took a guided tour of the Royal Flying Corps and the Royal Naval Air Service aerodomes in northern France. We also visited the village of Vaux-sur-Somme near where Captain Roy Brown attacked Rittmeister Manfred von Richthofen on 21 April, 1918. We also saw the field at Sainte Colette where the triplane came down and were given previously published descriptions of the event to read. As an experienced pilot of aircraft of the same speed and weight as a Fokker Triplane and a

Sopwith Camel, I had grave doubts as to the veracity of some parts of the story - aeroplanes do not behave in the manners described. One thing led to another, and with time now available, I obtained 1918 British Army maps, current French maps and returned to France. Many people, whose parents or grandparents had been witnesses, helped me, and the eventual result was a book on the subject, THE RED BARON'S LAST FLIGHT, written in conjunction with Norman Franks and published in 1997 by Grub Street. After plentiful information from readers, Captain Roy Brown's family and Lieut. May's son, plus three more trips to France, a considerably different picture of the entire event and Roy Brown's life emerged. The new book, CAPTAIN ROY BROWN, tells the story.

ACKNOWLEDGEMENTS

Chapter 1

For the information from reports and letters written by Ronald Sykes, the authors are indebted to Bradley King of the Imperial War Museum and author Norman Franks.

The photographs are by courtesy of the J.M. Bruce and G.S. Leslie collection, the late Theodore Crayston and the Captain A. Roy Brown family collection.

Photographs by courtesy of the J.M. Bruce and G.S. Leslie Collection.

Chapter 2

Permission to publish Roy Brown's letters, currently in the Canadian War Museum, Ottawa, Ontario, was given by his late brother Howard M. Brown.

Roy Brown's gold pocket watch is currently in the Canadian Military Heritage Museum, Brantford, Ontario, and it authorities' kindly permitted photography.

Family photographs and documents are from the Brown family collection currently in the care of Howard Brown's daughter, Carol Nicholson. Information on the Chicago Air Meet was provided by Lynn Stough.

The early documents and photographs are from the Brown family collection.

The winter 1998/9 photographs were taken by Alan Bennett.

Chapter 3

Photographs of activities at the Wright School of Aviation are from the Brown family collection. The photograph of Wright Brothers' field on Huffman Prairie was taken by Alan Bennett and Ronald Sager in 2004.

Photographs taken at the Stinson Flying School were provided by David, Hugh and Peter Alexander and by the late Theodore Crayston.

The reproduction of Roy Brown's Royal Aero Club file card is by courtesy of the RAF Museum, Hendon, London.

William Melville Alexander's Aviator's Certificate appears by kind permission of his sons, David, Hugh and Peter.

The photographs of historical aeroplanes are by courtesy of the J.M. Bruce and G.S. Leslie collection.

The photographs of Huffman Prairie and the Wright Brothers Monument Park were taken by Alan Bennett and Ronald Sager in 2004.

The replica Wright Model B was photographed by Alan Bennett and Ronald Sager at the Dayton-Wright Brothers Airport, 10550 Springboro Pike, Miamisburg, Ohio, in 2004 by kind permission of the Wright "B" Flyer Organization for inclusion in this book.

The FAI. document comes from the Brown family collection.

Bret Stolle, Reference Archivist, National Museum of the United States Air Force, Dayton, Ohio.

Chapter 4

Roy Brown's letters, currently in the care of the Canadian War Museum, Ottawa, Ontario, were made available by his brother, the late Howard M. Brown.

The majority of the photographs depicting complete aircraft were kindly provided by Mr. Stuart Leslie from the J.M. Bruce and G.S. Leslie collection.

The sketch of an aeroplane in a tree at Chingford is from the W.R. May collection.

Most of the detail photographs of B.E.2 aeroplanes were taken at the Royal Air Force Museum, Hendon, England, and at the National Aviation Museum, Rockcliffe, Canada, with the most helpful co-operation of the authorities at those two institutes. Simon Moody (Hendon) and Stephen Payne (Rockcliffe) deserve the authors' thanks for time spent in answering their letters.

The photograph of Roy Brown's RNAS Aeroplane Pilot's Certificate was supplied by the Canadian Military Heritage Museum, Brantford, Ontario, where it forms part of a display (2005).

Much of the background material on RNAS Chingford was found in documents kindly provided by Simon Moody of the RAF Museum, Hendon.

The photographs of instruction on the Vickers machine-gun and "Walking the Plank" are by courtesy of H. Gower and C.C.I.

The photograph of Alice Pickup in her nurse's uniform was kindly offered by her daughter, Mary Baxter.

The other photographs were provided by the late Theodore Crayston.

The photograph of the lesson on a Lewis automatic gun is via H. Gower by courtesy of Cross and Cockade International.

The photographs of a Gnôme aircraft engine are by courtesy of the late Theodore Crayston.

The photographs of Maurice Farman S7 No. 146 and Lieutenant. Warneford's Morane were provided by the J.M. Bruce and G.S. Leslie collection.

The photographs of the skeleton B.E.2C are included by kind permission of the National Aviation Museum, Rockcliffe, Ontario, Canada.

The photograph of the B.E.2C with the wireless telegraph transmitter is by courtesy of A. Thomas.

The information on Henry Muddle's farm was provided by Mr. Andrew Mussell of the London Borough of Barnet, Local Studies and Archive Centre.

Chapter 5

The photographs of complete aircraft in this chapter were most kindly provided by Mr Stuart Leslie from the J.M. Bruce and G.S. Leslie collection.

The detail photographs were taken at the RAF Museum, Hendon, England, and at the National Aviation Museum, Rockcliffe, Ontario, Canada, by the generous permission of the respective authorities.

The photograph of the fully "leathered" British pilot was contributed by Warrant Officer A. Schnurr of the Canadian Army.

The photograph of an RFC pilot's anti-frostbite headwear is by courtesy of Mr. J.P. McSherry.

Mr. Peter Wright of Cross & Cockade International provided the solution to the meaning of the term "YPatrol."

Clarification in many areas was made by Simon Moody, Curator of Documents, and his colleagues at the RAF Museum, Hendon.

Mr. Chad Wille, who flies a rotary-engined replica of an F1 Camel at air shows, kindly explained how Clergêt, Le Rhône and Bentley rotary engines were controlled by pilots.

The photograph of the lower part of the cockpit of a Sopwith Triplane was taken at the National Aviation Museum at Rockcliffe, Ontario, Canada, with the aid of the authorities there.

All other aeroplane photographs are by courtesy of the J.M. Bruce and G.S. Leslie collection.

The photograph of the Maxim LMG 08/15 machine guns was provided by J.P. McSherry.

Warrant Officer A. Schnurr of the Canadian Armed Forces most generously provided photographs of items from his collection of British airmen's flying clothes.

The Great War Flying Museum at Brampton Aerodrome, Ontario, kindly permitted the airman's mitten/glove and the Rotherham fuel tank air pump in its collection to be photographed by Denny May and Alan Bennett.

Chapter 6

The photographs of complete aircraft in this chapter were kindly provided by Mr. Stuart Leslie from the J.M. Bruce and G.S. Leslie collection.

The photo of a Sopwith Camel's cockpit interior was supplied by Mr. Bain Simpson.

Some detail photographs of British aircraft were taken at the RAF Museum at Hendon, England, with the kind permission of the authorities there.

The photographs of the aeroplanes of the German Naval Air Service are from the album of Leutnant Friedrich Hoepkin, who flew them in action. He was Alan Bennett's neighbour and kindly permitted Ronald R. Sager to copy his collection. The prints were provided by Ronald R. Sager.

The Vickers machine-gun ammunition belt was supplied by Mr Peter Franks, LLB.

The 1917 British Army 0.303inch Mark VII rifle bullets and the disintegrating link belt were part of the collection of the late Mr Theodore Crayston.

The documents and photographs related to Captain A. Roy Brown are from the family collection.

The photograph of Captain Oliver LeBoutillier was contributed by Mr. Dale Titler.

The Sutton Harness shown is part of the collection of Warrant Officer A. Schnurr of the Canadian Armed Forces.

Roy's hospital record cards were kindly provided by the RAF Museum at Hendon.

Summaries of the confidential reports submitted on Roy by his commanding officers were provided by the Fleet Air Arm Museum at Yeovilton, Somerset, England.

Roy's log book was kindly provided by his son Denny.

The two-seater Sopwith Camel photograph was provided by Bain Simpson.

Chad Wille, a pilot who flies replica Great War aeroplanes at air shows, generously provided help on many points.

Stephen Payne at the National Aviation Museum, Rockcliffe, Canada kindly arranged permission for Alan Bennett to photograph its Sopwith Camel.

The other photographs are by courtesy of the J.M. Bruce and G. S. Leslie collection, Bruce Robertson and the late Theodore Crayston.

The combat reports are from Captain A. Roy Brown's own documents and papers.

Chapter 7

Additional information concerning home leave at Carleton Place was provided by Larry Gray, Service Officer, Royal Canadian Legion, Carleton Place; Sandy Docker, Historian of St John's Lodge #3 A.F. & A.M.; and Brian Costello, Mayor of Carleton Place.

The photographs connected with the home leave are from Captain A. Roy Brown's family collection.

Gerald A. Nash, son of Flight Lieutenant Gerald Ewart Nash, provided the information on his father's poker games.

Tami Davis Biddle, Historian United States Air Force, Washington, D.C., kindly offered information on the work of the Bolling Commission.

The information on the McLaughlin car was kindly provided by the late Theodore Crayston.

The photograph of Horace Brown with Alice Pickup was made available by her daughter Mary Baxter.

The friendly poker game story was told by Gerry E. Nash's son, Gerry A. Nash.

The 1917/18 British airman's helmet and goggles are part of the collection of genuine Great War aviators' equipment at the Great War Flying Museum, Brampton, Ontario . Photography by Denny May, with permission of the Museum.

Chapter 8

The photographs of most complete aircraft and details of the RFC's order on aircraft markings were most kindly provided by Mr. Stuart Leslie from the J.M. Bruce and G.S. Leslie collection.

The photographs of Roy Brown, his colleagues, their aeroplanes and aerodromes are from the Brown family collection.

The photograph of the S.E.5A in flight and the F.K.8 are by courtesy of Mr Bain Simpson.

The photographs of Wilfrid May were supplied by his son, Denny Reid May.

The photograph of the Eastman Vest Pocket Kodak is published with the kind co-operation of the Royal Canadian Military Institute in Toronto.

The photographs of the 41 Field Hospital and the wrecked R.E.8 were contributed by Geoffrey Hine.

The aerial depiction of Bertangles and Poulainville aerodromes was assembled by Owen Brierley from three overlapping photographs.

The diary of Lieutenant Warneford was kindly provided by his son John B. Warneford.

Squadron Commander Butler's confidential reports were made available by the Fleet Air Arm Museum at Yeovilton.

Information on artillery batteries in the area and their equipment was provided by Colonel (retired) Andrew Pinion via Colonel (retired) David Storrie.

The description of "night-life" at Bertangles and Poulainville aerodromes in April 1918 was taken from the diaries kept by Air Mechanic First Class Morris Waldron and Air Mechanic Second Class Thomas Spencer of RAF 65 Squadron at Bertangles and by Lieutenant Walter Warneford of AFC 2 Squadron at Poulainville. The originals of the first two diaries and a copy of the third are in the RAF Museum Archives at Colindale, near Hendon, London, where they are available by appointment for study.

The photographs of the machine-gun timing marks and the cable synchronized Maxim LMG 08/15 twin machine guns are published by courtesy of the Royal Air Force Museum at Hendon.

The photograph of the R.E.8 struck by a passing artillery shell was supplied by Air Vice-Marshal Peter Dye of the Royal Air Force.

The photographs of the other aircraft in the Endnotes were most kindly provided by Mr. Stuart Leslie from the J.M. Bruce and G.S. Leslie collection. Mr. Leslie also provided the information on the Constantinesco-Colley hydraulic machine-gun synchronizing system.

The photograph and memoirs of Mel Alexander were supplied by his sons David and Hugh. The extract from Lieutenant W.R. May's Pilot's Flying Log Book, his Royal Flying Corps Acton Training School group photograph and the machine-gun instructor photograph are by courtesy of his son Denny.

The aerial photographs and combat reports are from Captain A. Roy Brown's documents and papers.

Author Dale Titler generously provided a copy of the air to air photograph for this book.

Chapter 9

Larry Gray for permission to quote from his book We Are the Dead, published in 2000 by General Store Publishing House, Burnstown, Ontario, Canada.

Hugh Alexander for information on his father, William Melville Alexander, and for the photograph of Clara Monypenny before she became Mrs Alexander.

The Board of Directors of the Royal Canadian Military Institute, Toronto, for access to the Roy Brown display and for the aid of the museum curator, Gregory Loughton, in taking the photographs.

F.A. Beardmore for the photographs of Marske-by-the-Sea Aerodrome.

Phil Philo, Old Hall Museum, Kirkleatham, for information on aerodromes in the area of Marske-by-the-Sea.

Michael J. Charteris for extensive newspaper research in Australia.

W. Brian Costello for photographs of pilots from Carleton Place.

Lambis Englezos for the correspondence between C.E.W. Bean and H.A. Jones.

Stuart Leslie for photographs of aeroplanes and aerodromes.

Stewart Taylor for information on the Canadian Comrades Association.

Leslie K. Redman of the Canadian War Museum, Ottawa, for locating the J. Horace Brown file, his service record and the notes he took during his flying training course.

Margaret Bell, RN, historian, for providing a list of the Great War military Hospitals.

Sarah Paterson, Imperial War Museum, for showing the way to learning about the Great War military hospitals in the north of England.

Patricia Sheldon, Newcastle City Library, for advice on whom to consult on the Great War military hospitals in the area.

David Tyrell, Teesside Archives, Middlesbrough Borough Council and Elizabeth Rees, BA, DAS, Tyne and Wear Archives, for providing information on the role of the hospitals in the area during the Great War.

R.L. Barrett-Cross, MRSH, RAMC, for identifying the Middlesbrough hospitals involved in treating Roy Brown after his crash at Marske-by-the-Sea.

Dr. Geoffrey Stout, MB, ChB, for detailed information on the history of the hospitals in the Middlesbrough area and on the effects of the injuries suffered by Roy Brown and Stearne Edwards.

Terry Gilder, "Remember When" column, Middlesbrough Evening News, for seeking information from the general public on Roy Brown's hospitalization.

Ian Marsh, BSc, FIDiagE, engineer and aviation enthusiast, for information on the fuel systems employed with rotary engines.

Stuart Leslie for aviation history and photographs of aeroplanes.

Chad Wille, pilot of a Sopwith Camel with a 160hp Gnôme rotary engine and a Nieuport 11 with an 80hp Le Rhône rotary engine.

Gordon Leith for help from the Royal Air Force Museum Archives, Hendon.

Mrs. Mary Baxter for information and photographs of her mother, Alice Pickup.

Frank Mcguire for information on his visit to the Royal Air Force Historical Branch in 1961.

Chapter 10

The information on air transport in Canada in the 1920s and 1930s was derived from Roy Brown's papers and Denny May's knowledge of Canadian airlines, supplemented by extensive research on aeroplanes of the period made by the late Theodore Crayston.

Thanks are given to Mr. Owen A. Cooke for his help in locating the Department of Defence file on the accident to No. CF-AOL.

The photographs are from Roy Brown's personal album, except where otherwise indicated.

The photographs are from Roy Brown's personal album, except where otherwise indicated.

AUTHORS' PREFACES

During research into the aspects of airmanship, ballistics and forensic pathology involved in the death of Rittmeister (Cavalry Captain) Manfred Albrecht Freiherr von Richthofen, I was impressed by the paucity of information available concerning the Royal Naval Air Service and Royal Air Force ace fighter pilot Captain Arthur Roy Brown. Happenstance brought my efforts to the notice of the well-known aviation author Norman Franks, and my research then became part of a project upon which he had been working for some time. The result was a co-authored book entitled the Red Baron's Last Flight. However, I remained intrigued because no biography of Captain A. Roy Brown, DSC and bar, unlike most of the well-known airmen of The Great War (1914-1918), appeared to have been published.

Captain Brown seemed to spring into history on the morning of 21 April 1918 and then disappear on the evening of 22 April; yet, he had twice been awarded the Distinguished Service Cross. The operative word in the name of this particular award is "Service". The DSC is not conferred for a single event, no matter how brave; there are other awards, such as the Military Cross and the Victoria Cross, for those occasions. The award of a DSC is in recognition of a series of actions, each one of notable leadership or bravery. Therefore, a fighter pilot who held two such crosses must have had an unusually eventful career aloft, spanning some length of time. However enquiries made at major aeronautical museums, exhibitions and public airshows where the encounter between Roy Brown and the Red Baron was featured produced little intelligence on the subject. When I did make some headway, I was surprised to discover a similarity with the story the Red Baron's demise; namely, a surprisingly large part of the information, both previously and currently being presented to the public, is incorrect. The story of Roy Brown has been derived, albeit quite sincerely, from stories written for the principal purpose of thrilling the reader, from inaccurate or incomplete data and sometimes from outright fabrication.

Having been told, as newspapers suggest, by a usually reliable source that the only close relative of Roy Brown still alive was his son, who lived at an unknown address in the United States, I was surprised to learn that on 9 April 1997 reporter David Brown of the Ottawa Citizen had published an interview with Howard Morton Brown, the youngest brother of the late Captain A. Roy Brown. Further enquiries revealed Howard Brown, at that time 93 years of age, to be still alive and enjoying good health. It was not difficult to obtain his address and thence to learn that those said to be long ago dead were still in the land of the living, and vice versa.

Knowing how Roy Brown had always shunned publicity, I took a chance and wrote to Howard Brown explaining my problem. By return post I received a most courteous answer inviting me to his home where he would be pleased to show me a scrap book relating to his late brother's life. On this occasion he and his wife, Constance, invited me to a family reception at their home and to be their guest at the Carleton Place, Ontario, Armistice Day Parade on 11 November 1997.

—ALAN BENNETT

Carleton Place War Memorial. The central column is the original portion and contains the names of the young men who died in the Great War, 1914–1918. Counting from the bottom, the ninth name is Lieutenant John Horace Brown a younger brother of Roy Brown. The eleventh name is Captain Stearne Tighe Edwards, Roy Brown's closest friend.

The two minutes' silence was first observed on 14 May 1918 when the Bishop of Pretoria, South Africa, suggested a prayer be offered at noon for the safety of the boys serving in the armed forces. When the armistice came, the period of silence was included in the annual tribute.

After the parade there was to be an unveiling ceremony for a new plaque, inscribed in English and French, honouring Captain Arthur Roy Brown, DSC and bar. It was a replacement for the weather-damaged, original plaque erected in 1969. Both the new plaque and the ceremony were in great part the initiative of His Worship the Mayor, W. Brian Costello.

The replacement plaque immediately following the unveiling on 11 November 1997. Left to right: Margaret E. Brown Harmon (Captain Brown's daughter), Howard Morton Brown (Captain Brown's brother), W. Brian Costello (Mayor of Carleton Place).

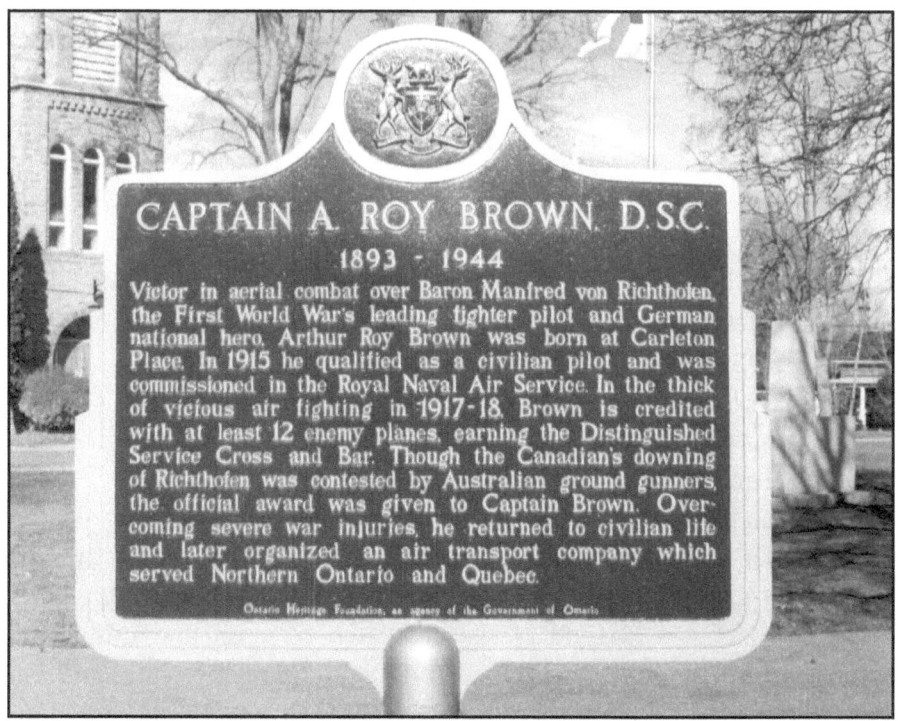

The English text side of the plaque.

At the reception I was introduced to Mrs Margaret Harmon, née Brown, Captain Roy Brown's daughter, and our conversation on the lack of a biography of her father developed into a project to co-author such a book.

It is with great surprise that I find myself sitting at a computer terminal trying to decide what to write as a preface for this book. My co-author and friend, Alan Bennett, could not have chosen a less likely collaborator.

As I look back on the events that have led to this unexpected assignment, I realize that even my first meeting with Alan might well never have occurred but for the kindness of my family and friends. I was invited to attend a ceremony on November 11th, 1997 honouring my father in his birthplace, Carleton Place, Ontario. Though I was proud of my father and pleased to be invited, my time and thoughts were greatly occupied with my husband's ongoing battle with cancer. At that point in time he was being treated with aggressive and debilitating radiation, and as his principal caregiver, I felt there was no way I could leave his side. However, my son Jim, who lives nearby, and our dear neighbours exerted their considerable influence on me (and demonstrated abundant good will in the process), so with my husband's blessings and encouragement, I was able to attend after all.

I left my home in sunny Sun City West (a retirement community near Phoenix, Arizona) and made my way to Pennsylvania where I acquired three travelling companions, my daughter Sue, her daughter Patti and her son Jeff. What better way for them to understand their grandfather and great-grandfather's historical contribution. The three of us trekked to Carleton Place where we were united with yet a fourth generation, my father's brother Howard, and bore witness to the impressive and gracious tribute to my father, Captain Arthur Roy Brown, by the town's eminent mayor, Mr. Brian Costello.

The trip was a complete success, but as it turned out, only the first step in the journey that has brought me to this unexpected effort. I met Alan Bennett and learned of his dedicated research and unflagging interest in the events that had led to that proud moment in Carleton Place. His initial proposal for me to join him in this effort was met with even greater doubt on my part than the trip itself, but once again my initial misgivings were outweighed by the enthusiastic encouragement of my crack staff (read family).

So here we are. I must say that Alan brings much more to the table than I in this undertaking, and I am grateful to him for including me. By delving into dusty, old archives on two continents and with the enthusiastic help of friends around the world, he has found documentation and data on my father's post-war business life, which I had long believed lost. He also located over sixty of my father's wartime letters, which I had never seen, and he obtained copies for me. He is the historian and I am just his conduit to history. Some of what has been written, not only in this book, but in others, has long been regarded as controversial, and more knowledgeable experts than I will undoubtedly continue to agree to disagree. However, I am happy for the opportunity to co-author this book and pleased to offer my slight efforts in the desire to see my father remembered as a good and a brave man.

—MARGARET E. BROWN HARMON

Captain Roy Brown

Left to right: John Nicholson, husband of Carol Nicholson; Diane Sample, Roy Brown's grand-daughter; James Sample, husband of Diane Sample; Howard Morton Brown, Roy Brown's youngest brother; Heather Nicholson, daughter of John and Carol Nicholson; Susan Carlson, Roy Brown's grand-daughter; Margaret Brown Harmon, Roy Brown's daughter; and Carol Nicholson, Roy Brown's niece. Kenneth Hibbert, husband of Ann Brown, was not present.

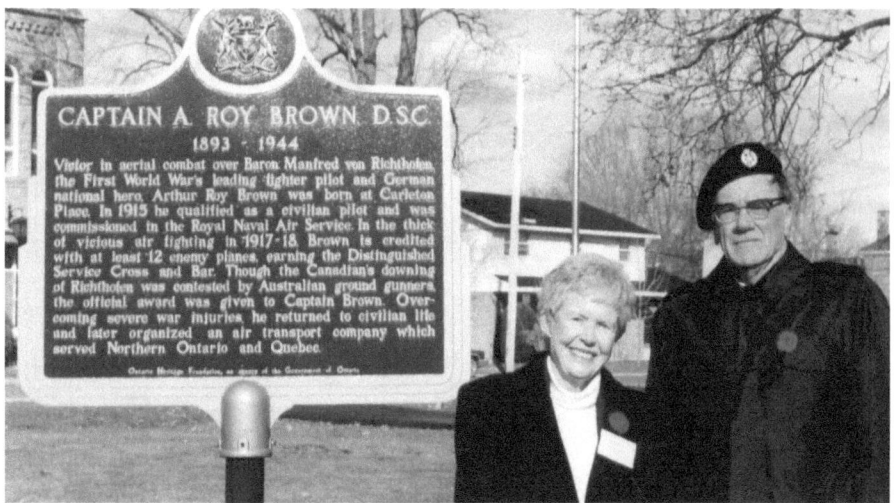

The authors

INTRODUCTION

In the gathering and verifying of the information contained in this book, a serious problem has been the existence of widely differing—nay, totally contradictory versions of situations and events starting as far back as Roy Brown's family history. Even his true name was disputed. Distinguishing truth from fiction became a major task and is the direct cause of this book taking seven years to write. In the case of Roy Brown's encounter with Rittmeister Manfred Freiherr von Richthofen, several visits to the sites where the actions took place, plus studies of the surrounding topography, caused light to dawn: namely, some long-accepted accounts had described the landscape incorrectly and/or included events that the so-called eye-witness could not have seen from his particular vantage point. In certain instances, a similarity of phrasing or the repetition of an error in an account made it possible to identify the source of the addition—a previously published article which contained more imagination than fact.

Fortunately a large number of letters written by Roy Brown, some by his relatives, and two by his best friend, Captain Stearne Edwards, had been kept by Roy's youngest brother, Howard. These letters resolved many of the gaps and contradictions between 1913 and 1919, but their greatest value has been to make it possible for the authors to arrange for Roy to tell his own story. Over the three years 1916 to 1918, the letters are accompanied by the respective entries from Roy's First World War pilot's flying log book. The information concerning his post-war career is drawn from his relatives, government reports, newspaper articles and several local historians.

At the 1999 annual general meeting of the Cross and Cockade Society held at the Royal Air Force Museum at Hendon, England, Norman Franks introduced Margaret Brown Harmon and Alan Bennett to Stuart Leslie. Stuart, who together with Jack Bruce had assembled the J.M. Bruce and G.S. Leslie collection of Great War aircraft photographs, advised the authors that the collection contained photographs of some 50 percent of the actual machines flown by Captain Roy Brown, and he most generously offered to provide prints. The offer was gratefully accepted. The resulting combination of letters, log book entries and photographs brings Roy's story to life. Stuart Leslie and his wife even went so far as to visit the museum near the site of the wartime Marske-by-the-Sea Aerodrome to obtain information and photographs taken during Roy's time there.

In the mid-1990s a number of letters and personal diaries written in April 1918 quite unexpectedly came to light. In addition, official files which had been closed to the researchers of the 1960s were by then open. All these sources helped considerably, but as of this writing, some discrepancies still remain unresolved.

The material in the chapter which covers Roy Brown's encounter with Rittmeister Manfred Freiherr von Richthofen (later to become known as the Red Baron) is derived from statements made by some of those who participated in the events or watched them from nearby. Information from stories written by people who neither witnessed the events nor communicated with those who did has not been included. This exclusion also encompasses stories published under bylines and/or source attributions phrased in such a manner that the reader might believe Roy Brown had written them.

Mr Peter Franks, a ballistics expert, kindly arranged the test firing of a 1917 water-cooled Vickers machine gun on an official range. It had the same barrel as the air-cooled version used on British aeroplanes in the Great War. Ammunition containing the same powder charge, bullet nose shape and weight as employed in 1918 was used.

In the year 2000, M. Jean-Pierre Delarue of the Aero-Club of Picardie provided an aeroplane and pilot for Denny May to overfly the route of his father's adventure with a certain red Fokker Triplane. Aerial photographs taken by Denny May and Alan Bennett on that occasion illustrate parts of the story.

The director of the Historial de La Grande Guerre, the French Great War Museum at Péronne, M. Jean-Pierre Thierry (now retired), spent two days helping with the historical and geographical aspects of the fighting in the Somme Valley. M. Michel Delaplace, the mayor of Vaux-sur-Somme in the year 2000, spent an afternoon showing M. Thierry and Alan Bennett where the red Fokker Triplane was first sighted and the exact location of its landing by the dying pilot later. Thanks to the efforts of M. Thierry, an official Somme Valley tourism plaque has been placed at the edge of the field not too far from the exact spot.

The names of others whose interest was aroused by situations within their expertise and who kindly volunteered their services in the cause will be revealed as events unfold.

Yet another claimant to having shot down "The Red Baron" came to our attention. The tale is worthy of inclusion and contains an interesting final twist.

The authors and the specialists who helped have made every effort to be factually correct, to shun sensationalism and to avoid attempting to force their judgements and opinions upon the reader. Many of the events which occurred during Roy Brown's service life can only be really understood if the military situation at that time is appreciated. Therefore, the necessary background is given in detail and much that was previously obscure becomes clear. The tireless help provided in this area by historians Frank McGuire and Stewart Taylor has been of immense value.

The Acknowledgements contain the names of contributors the people and organizations which kindly provided photographs from their collections or allowed exhibits to be photographed for this book.

PART ONE

Captain A. Roy Brown

Roy Brown's life, in part or whole, has already been included in several First World War stories, but in some areas, including his character and scholastic studies, the material presented has diverged considerably from the truth. Even his middle name has been changed.

As the story of Roy's wartime service as a fighter pilot unfolds, the basics of air fighting in the 1914-1918 era are presented herein as background. Copious examples taken from the memoirs of respected Allied and German airmen are given on the tactics they employed, the capabilities of their machines and the weapons they carried. Thus, when aerial combat situations occur, the reader will already have in mind the reasons for Roy's actions and, in some instances which he graphically describes, relive the event.

Over the years the public has been treated to several different versions of "the truth" concerning Roy Brown, but with his life story now placed into proper context and supported by letters from his friends and contemporaries, it should not be difficult for the reader to reach his or her own conclusions.

Several of the items and explanations given in this section were deliberately included to prepare the way for a proper understanding of the events described in Part 2, The Red Baron Affair. Although several good, honest and accurate books have already been published on that subject, some have been overshadowed by stories which began in the late 1920s and apparently followed the maxim "Sensation means sales". Once again, the reader who is aware of the manner in which the war in the air was conducted should have little difficulty in deciding the truth.

CHAPTER ONE

"COME WITH ME AND I'LL SHOW YOU WHAT A CAMEL CAN DO"

In September 1917, Flight Sub-Lieutenant Ronald Sykes of the Royal Naval Air Service (RNAS) completed his aeroplane pilot gunnery and bombing training and he was posted to Naval 9 Squadron in France. The squadron was equipped with Sopwith Camels. The most successful Allied fighters of the war, credited by the Royal Air Force (RAF) with the destruction of 1,294 enemy aircraft.

Upon arrival at Leffrinckoucke aerodrome Ronald Syke reported to Squadron Commander Theophilus Chater Vernon who allocated him to A Flight and introduced him to commander. He cautioned Sykes that this officer was a highly experienced pilot whose advice was worthy of particular attention and must be carefully heeded; Sykes's very life might well depend upon it. The Flight Commander could see from Sykes's log book that his flying school experience, which totalled fifty-six hours, included a few hours in Sopwith Camels. However, there was a distinct difference between scholastic achievement and what he was about to encounter at the front: as he became familiar with his aeroplane and his work, there would be people shooting at him.

Three Sopwith BR1 Camels of RNAS 9 Squadron in late January 1918. The broad stripes painted around the fuselage and on the top wings of the nearest one were pale blue with white borders and served to identify the pilot.*

The most dangerous period of a fighter pilot's life occurred when he was fresh from training school, and there was a good chance that a new arrival's first and last encounter with the enemy might be one and the same. Therefore, once Sykes had settled in, the A flight commander took him to one side and gave him some counselling. He reminded Sykes that a Camel gave virtually no warning of an impending stall, and said, "Keep up plenty of speed near the ground. Don't bother about loops, and when you do a spin, make sure that you are out of it before you are down to 1,000 feet above the ground." The flight commander then explained how to use the structural strength and flight characteristics of a Camel to his best advantage in aerial combat.

Flight Sub-Lieutenant Ronald Sykes wearing RNAS khaki overseas service uniform. Note the single ring on his sleeve indicating his naval rank, and the "bird" above it signifying RNAS.

Surprise, the light commander explained, was the key to success and was best achieved by first climbing to a high altitude, positioning one's aircraft between the sun and the enemy aeroplane, and then diving on it at an angle which maintained that relationship. It was essential to maintain a steady speed so that the gunsight deflection angle would remain stable. Guns were not to be fired during the dive as this would alert the enemy, who would swiftly take evasive action. With surprise, the enemy would be flying straight and level when close range was reached. This was the real objective of the exercise. A short burst of fire would then do the trick.

The Flight Commander allocated Sopwith F1 Camel No. B3906 to Ronald Sykes and said to him "Come with me and I'll show you what a Camel can do." In 1970, Ronald Sykes, who ended the war as an RAF captain credited with six victories (including shared), described what happened shortly afterwards.

"I went up as part of his flight, and we climbed at a very steep angle up to the lines, 10,000 feet or more. Then, by previous arrangement, as soon as we ran into some archie [German anti-aircraft fire] and the shells began to burst around us, another pilot led me away from the main group which, carried on with the offensive patrol. He took me round and into a steep dive to introduce me to just how much a Camel could stand. He went over fairly quickly, down, nose first. I was following him. Very soon we were going down vertically with the engine full on. The airspeed indicator was round to its maximum of 180 knots [207 mph], and everything was making a terrific din—the wires, the wind in the struts. We went down for thousands of feet like that in a steep dive. Everything was shaking and howling—tremendous noise. Then I noticed that he was coming out of the dive: first of all, his speed dropped slightly; that was when he throttled back the engine. I throttled mine back, and my speed dropped a little. Then, moving the stick backwards just about an eighth of an inch at a time, we came out of the vertical. With every movement you could feel the centrifugal force pushing right down into your shoulders and your body down on the seat. When the speed dropped back to 150 knots [173 mph], the Camel handled quite well and we continued to pull out. It seemed that above 150 knots it had to be handled in a very sensitive way otherwise the canvas and wood would break up."

After lunch on 20 December 1917 A Flight Commander led his five Camels on an offensive patrol over Ostend in Belgium. He noticed a solitary German two-seater aeroplane flying along below. Being wary of "the Hun in the sun" he squinted upwards to the south, carefully searching for specks in the sky. Despite all precautions, he failed to see the two-seater's companions waiting upstairs for a "customer" to come by—a clear example of how effective a baited trap can be when it is properly executed. Their leader, who had been watching A Flight approaching, had mentally been calculating the interception angle, to be ready should the Camels take the bait. They did.

Four Albatros D.Vs gently eased into a dive. Three of them held station behind their leader to protect him while he paid strict attention to his flight path. It was a gentle downward curve, carefully chosen to maintain position directly between the sun and the eyes of those who were not going to be particularly grateful for what they were about to receive.

Typical Albatros D.V.

The Albatros pilots either opened fire too soon or aimed poorly, for upon hearing the first shots, four of the Camels successfully took immediate evasive action. The fifth, flown by Sykes, delayed a little. This was the fatal, slow reaction of a novice; probably due to looking around to see where the "Rak-ak-ak" sound was coming from, or even wondering what might have come loose on his aeroplane and make such a noise. Hesitation was often the prelude to a rapidly descending spiral of thick, black smoke, marking what, moments earlier, had been a man and his machine.

Ronald Sykes continued the story from his perspective:

"Flying at 10,000 feet over the Belgian coast, we attacked a German two-seater and were dived on by four Albatros scouts. Our flight commander's guns iced up so he led us into climbing turns, but before I could join the others, bullets came into my cockpit and grazed my back. The engine stopped, and petrol squirted all over my leather coat and sheepskin boots. Immediately the flight commander came down, and although (as I learnt afterwards) his guns were jammed, he half-rolled and stall-turned above the four Germans, who, apparently impressed by his display of skill, left me alone. Then the sky cleared. The Germans had disappeared. They had gone away. I was left to do a long glide back, more or less in peace, without anybody shooting at me."

The flight commander was Flight Lieutenant A. Roy Brown. The Albatros D.V scouts belonged to Jasta 2, named Boelke after the deceased German ace, and the fight took place at 1510 hours over Ramskapelle, Belgium. Ronald Sykes was the fifth victory of Unteroffizier (Corporal) Paul Baümer, who survived the war and with an eventual, impressive total of 43 victories.

Leutnant Paul Baümer (left).

Due to the intense cold at 10,000 feet in December, the lubricating oil on the moving parts of Flight Commander Roy Brown's machineguns had solidified. Despite this, and with total disregard for his personal safety, he had gone speedily to the rescue of one of his men. A study of Roy Brown's service record shows that he had done so before and would do so several times again. Official records show that no member of his flight was ever left behind in German-held territory, and as in the case of Major Edward (Mick) Mannock, VC, DSO and bar, MC and bar (61 victories including shared), his subordinates were always confident he would come to their aid if they were in a tight corner.

Sykes force-landed in no man's land on the German side of a canal, finishing the ground run with his Camel upside down in a water-filled shell hole. Emerging, covered in mud, from his ruined aircraft but still with his wits about him, he detached the watch from the instrument panel, jumped into the canal and swam to safety. For a pilot to return without his aeroplane was a case for sympathy, but without the watch, be it wet, dry or smashed, he was in deep trouble. This was not a case of official pettiness; the many-jewelled, shock-resistant timepiece had a high value on the French civilian market.

"That same evening," continued Ronald Sykes, *"Captain Brown and the rest of his flight, off duty, toured in the squadron tender behind our lines and found me in a casualty clearing station, still under the cheerful influence of hot whisky given me by some helpful Scottish troops near whose trench I had crash-landed."*

The was just one episode in Roy Brown's eventful life.

CHAPTER TWO

ROY BROWN'S EARLY LIFE

Arthur Roy Brown was born on 23 December 1893 at Carleton Place in the province of Ontario, Canada, the eldest son of Morton and Mary Brown (née Flett).

Birth Certificate of Arthur Roy Brown.

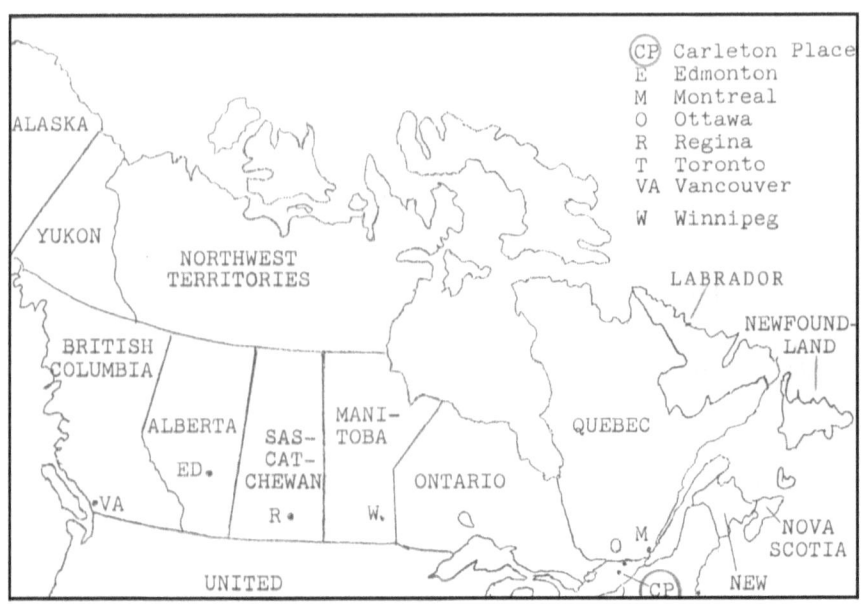

The location of Carleton Place, Ontario (Map of Canada 1900).

Morton was the major shareholder in the family business, H. Brown & Sons, possibly the most prosperous company in Carleton Place at that time. Among its principal tangible assets was a large flour mill, and also owned the Carleton Place Electric Light Company, which was personally managed by Morton.[1]

146 Judson Street where Roy and his siblings grew up. Taken in 1997, the photograph shows the later additions to the side of the house.

The bearded man in the centre, James E. Willis, owned the local photographer's shop. To his right, Mary Brown is holding baby Roy. In 1894 during a picnic at the summer camping site of James Caver's family at Lake Park.

Morton Left to right: Mary Brown with baby Horace on her lap; children Margaret (Reta), Bessie and Roy, and Brown. Photograph taken in 1900, shortly before Roy started school.

The records of Roy's primary education have been lost to antiquity, but fortunately in 1999 Howard Brown, Roy's youngest brother, remembered that Roy attended Carleton Place Public School from age 6 to 13, which would be from 1900 to 1907, and found a photograph of one of his teachers.

Miss Florence Ewing, Roy's school teacher, with whom he maintained a correspondence during his years as a fighter pilot in the Great War. Beside her is Mr. Elwood Lawson whom she later married.

In 1908 and 1909, Roy attended Carleton Place High School where he was prominent in athletics, baseball and ice hockey. He was involved in the usual schoolboy tricks including playing truant. The old school building stood beside the river, and some of the seniors would take their bathing costumes (as they were known in those days) along to school. At times when their absence would not be noticed, they would jump from a ground-floor window and head for the river. The absences from classes could not remain unnoticed forever, and one day a vigilant teacher caught the boys departing through the open window. On the basis that one might as well be hanged for a sheep as for a lamb, Roy and his friends fled to the river, had a swim and then returned to face the music.

A family photograph circa 1910. Left to right: the rear, Horace, Margaret (Reta), Bessie and Roy; in the front, Mary Brown, son Howard, and Morton Brown.

Instead of completing high school in Carleton Place, Roy transferred to the Willis School of Business in Ottawa. The Willis family had for many years been the owners of a business college and were known to the Browns. Roy studied business from age 16 to 18 (1910 to 1912), living during the weekdays with his uncle, Clarence H. Brown, MD, and his aunt, Mary Edith (n_e Frost), in Ottawa. Mary, who was known to all as Mamie, had been widowed early in life. Her daughter, Alice Louise Pickup, who never changed her surname to Brown, lived there also.

In August 1911 Canadian participation in the Chicago Air Meet captured the attention of major newspapers. They carried stories about the exciting performances of daredevil aviators from various countries and their new-fangled flying machines. By chance, a fortnight before the

Air Meet, Roy's uncle Clarence had travelled to San Francisco to attend a medical conference. On his return journey he stopped for a few days in Chicago, where he read the newspaper's daily special reports on this great event. Although it was billed as the world's first, it was actually the third; it was, however, the first in Chicago. Uncle Clarence sent an Air Meet picture postcard to his nephew Howard, but the best was reserved for Roy—stories of the air races and the crashes. He was an eager listener, and the seed of an interest in aviation was planted.

Picture postcard sent from Chicago by Dr. Clarence Brown to his nephew Howard.

The young Howard Brown with his dog, Teddy.

Roy's weekend trips home from Ottawa allowed him to keep his status as a resident of Carleton Place, and he was invited to join the town's baseball and hockey teams.

Carleton Place's, 1912 baseball team. Roy Brown is fourth from right.

Carleton Place's 1912–1913 hockey team, The Independents. Roy Brown is second from left in rear row.

According his brother Howard, Roy, who was anything but shy, was "quite a ladies' man," and several of the local girls had their eyes on him. In mid-February 1913 Roy suffered a hockey accident in which he injured his left knee so badly that he was forced to use crutches. One of the ladies sent him a picture postcard inscribed with a message that was guaranteed to accelerate his recovery.

An encouraging 'Get Well' card. Note the simple address used in those times.*

Roy was not particularly interested in the young lady in question, and Howard revealed that whenever Roy's siblings wished to dissuade him from doing something, they would threaten to tell her where to find him. The knee injury in question never healed properly, and in letters home during his war service Roy mentions it as bothering him from time to time.

Roy's prowess in hockey came to the notice of a talent scout for a first-class Ottawa team, The Senators. For Roy, this was an attractive opportunity, but his father, who took the long view, refused to consent to a trial game. He insisted that professional hockey, although both exciting and glamorous, was neither a stable career nor likely to be a long one. The "on crutches" episode mentioned in the get-well postcard story may have had some connection with this.

In early 1913 Roy, having graduated from business school, decided to return to high school to complete the syllabus and obtain his diploma. With this in hand, he would try for acceptance at McGill University, Montreal, to study for a degree in business management. However, the death of his grandmother, Harriet Brown, changed the direction of his life. At her funeral held at Carleton Place in April 1913, Roy met his uncle William (his father's brother) who lived in Alberta. Roy listened eagerly to his uncle's descriptions of life out there in the west and the excellent reputation of Victoria High School in Edmonton. A diploma from such a renowned school as this, he was told, would be a major asset in the selection process at McGill University.

Some years earlier Uncle Will and Aunt Blanche had moved out west where the economy appeared to be booming. They had hopes of converting their inheritance from Will's father, Horace, the founder of H. Brown & Sons, into a fortune by dealing in real estate. However, as the expression goes, Will lost his shirt and now had a less exciting, but more stable, position in the government civil service. Will and Blanche had no children and took great interest in their nephews and nieces. The outcome was an invitation for Roy to stay with them at 10033 108th Street in Edmonton, and complete his high school curriculum there. His uncle did not tell him that his aunt Blanche was quite strict, would tolerate no nonsense and would keep his nose to the grindstone—all for his own good, of course.

Left to right: Roy Brown, unknown, and Uncle Will at Carleton Place

Many of Roy's letters home have been preserved. The earliest available one from Edmonton is dated 2 November 1913. After describing how he had caught a cold at school and given it to his aunt and uncle, he continued:

I played in a football match last Saturday against Strathcona in defence of the Rutherford Cup which our school holds. We won with a score of 2 to 1. There will be no more football this fall but we will have to defend the cup in spring again. Skating will soon be starting out here in the Pavilion at the Exhibition grounds.

Friday night last Hallowe'en I was at a party. We had a very nice time, danced and played cards.

A letter to his sister Bessie, dated 21 December 1913, continued in the same happy tone:

It is snowing today for the first time this winter. I wish it would snow enough that we could have a sleigh ride for Christmas day but I do not think it will.

Have got a job for Christmas holidays. It is to measure the windows at the Grand Trunk Railway Hotel here for bronze screens.

On the same day he wrote to his sister Reta, mentioning that he was obeying his father's orders, enforced by his aunt Blanche, not to play hockey, but was playing basketball instead. He also attended Sunday school, and there is no prize for guessing at whose behest. The winter term at Victoria High School began the next day.

Spring was late in coming in 1914, and there not being too many distractions, Roy studied hard and achieved an 82 percent average at the end of term examinations. The Easter term was equally successful. Unfortunately his uncle's summer holiday period did not coincide with the term break at school, so to avoid missing classes during the first three weeks of September and to escape for a while from his aunt's well-intentioned discipline, Roy did not accompany them. Somewhere about this time he became friends with a slightly younger student who would re-enter his life somewhat dramatically fourteen years later: Wilfrid Reid May.

War against Germany and Austria-Hungary was declared in August 1914, and Roy's younger brother Horace, who for some time had been a member of the Carleton Place (Officer Training Corps), immediately gave up his summer job and volunteered for overseas service. His sisters, Reta and Bessie, became heavily involved in collecting comforts for the Canadian troops in France, and the wartime song "Sister Susie's Sewing Shirts for Soldiers" reflected the activities of the times.[2]

In a letter to Roy's mother, dated 4 October 1914, Blanche chastised her for not exerting a firm hand over her five children and gave vent to her thoughts on Horace, Roy and the war:

The last blow, Horace's enlistment, is the most terrible to us all. It seems strange that a boy of 18 could be let to do just as he wanted and cause so much trouble for us all. Had you let him come to us two years ago, I'm mighty sure he wouldn't have got his own way in everything and would have looked at things in as sensible a light as Roy does now. Roy has the extra two years of better judgment. He certainly is a good youngster and, as I told him last year when he got the hockey bug, he would have sense enough not to want to plunge headlong this year into every fool thing that came along. We all laughed when Reta said that she thought Roy took a right view of the situation for it was the first time that they have agreed on anything. Roy has no desire to plunge headlong to the front to be aimed at like a dog by the cruel; Germans. Well, I hope they may never see active service but things look pretty long drawn out just now. To think of overcoming an army by starvation is pretty cruel, also those dreadful mines blowing our ships to pieces without a vestige of warning.

The well-known stories of the German atrocities to babies in Belgium had Blanche in deep distress over human nature. She would have been even more distressed had she learnt that after the war the Belgian prelate, Cardinal Mercier, held an enquiry into the matter but found no evidence whatsoever to substantiate a single authority.[3]

The people in Edmonton were worried that with so many Canadian soldiers out of the country, Americans of German descent might convince the U.S. Congress to make a second attempt to annex Canada.[4] In 1812 the first attempt had failed due to the presence of mind of a farmer's daughter named Laura Secord. She had overheard some American officers discussing plans for a surprise attack on the morrow, and pretending to be driving a cow out to pasture, she slowly passed through the area to alert the local militia. On the following day, the surprise at the battle of Lundy's Lane did not belong to the Canadians.

Aunt Blanche, although alarmed by the possibility of another invasion from the south, seemed to be more upset by a government decision to allow Wet Canteens to be established on Canadian Army bases and camps. Surprisingly enough, her opposition to tobacco, beer and "the demon rum" stemmed not from her religion, Presbyterian, but from her strong opinions.

By 1 November 1914 Aunt Blanche had realized that Roy was only six months away from receiving his diploma and making his application for matriculation at McGill University.⁽⁵⁾ She wrote to his parents:

I don't know how I'll get along without Roy —he is such good company. I hope the rest of the year will pass slowly instead of quickly as when he gets his matric he will be gone from us forever, likely.

Roy's 1914 Christmas present from his parents was an engraved gold pocket watch.

On 27 December 1914 Roy wrote to his mother:

Before going any farther I want to thank you and papa ever so much for the watch. It is a beauty and I am more than pleased with it. I did not expect or deserve anything so good and I most surely appreciate it. It is something that I will always have and be proud of. It was too much to give me but I thank you both very much for being so good.

Aunt Blanche was now heavily involved in the local chapter of the Daughters of the Empire. On 28 March 1915 she described her activities to Roy's mother as follows:

Everything here is patriotic teas, they seem to draw the greatest crowd. Last week our Chapter had a "socks tea". Admission was one pair of socks or as many more as you felt like giving to go direct to the Edmonton men in France. Also tobacco, cigarettes, chocolate, etc. I will not do anything for the tobacco line as it would be a good thing to break some of the young lads of the habit.

One can imagine her standing at the entrance to the tea, collecting the admission fee, with Roy beside her carefully placing the "baccy" and booze into a separate box. That Roy, two years later, discovered he was the only pilot in his Royal Naval Air Service squadron who did not smoke, which may well be attributable to his aunt's iron hand. When patrolling at altitudes of 15,000 to 20,000 feet, where oxygen is rare and the smallest movement becomes hard labour, non-smokers definitely held an advantage.

Surrounded by a plethora of local patriotic activity and receiving frequent news of his younger brother Horace, who was sneezing while freezing in temporary sub-standard army accommodations on Salisbury Plain in England, Roy began to feel that his brother should not suffer alone and that he should wait no longer to begin preparing to do his bit. On 11 April 1915 he wrote to his father:

Dear Papa,

Am enclosing this note to you and you can do whatever you think best about reading it to Mamma but I do not think it any use worrying her unnecessarily until the time comes. I found out this week that there was not going to be any course given in military training at Calgary this year as the government has set aside no money for that kind of work. It comes under the Cadet branch.

I have never said so before but my reason for wanting the military training was to go to the war. I have thought it over a long time and have come to the conclusion that it is my duty to go. This is no sudden burst of patriotism or a thirst for adventure or as you used to say, "fightin' and killin'" and things." This war is a terribly serious thing and if we are to win we have to get large numbers of men to enlist and to do it voluntarily. We do not want any conscription if it can be avoided. Of course, I am only one but everyone is needed. I know what this is going to mean to you at home and have considered what it will mean to myself. But where things like this are concerned, self has to be put aside and we need to look a little wider and broader.

I would like if possible to get a commission but, if not I would go without it, but I feel I would be of more use if I had the training than I am now, without it. For this reason I wish you would keep on the watch for some course of training along this line. You know some of the military men in Ottawa and they would be able to tell you what would be best for me to do. I would sooner take the training in the east anyway and leave from there, when it is not convenient for me to get it here.

I cannot write down all the way I feel about it but I wish you would think it over carefully and write me your advice. Of course I am not thinking of letting this affect my school work at all and will not start anything till after June but from the way things look now I do not see much use in me wasting my time here after June.

Your son
Roy

Typical recruiting poster.

The answer from Roy's parents was not particularly favourable to his ideas, and a further exchange of letters took place. On 25 April, Roy wrote:

Received your letter with Horace's enclosed and was of course glad to get it but sorry to know that you and Mamma are feeling so badly, but of course you cannot help it. It means so much but the cause is worth it and I am quite willing to give whatever I can. I hope you can find some short course being given in Ottawa because I would prefer to go from the east.

On 22 April, Horace was sent to Rouen hospital to be treated for a minor infection. By good luck he was still there on the 24th when his company, mainly from Carleton Place, suffered terrible casualties at Saint-Julien in the second battle of Ypres, most being killed, or seriously wounded and then captured. The battle news reached Carleton Place first, and Horace was not listed among the survivors. To put it mildly, this had a negative effect on Roy's request. Upon receiving the news from home, he replied on 2 May:

I hardly know how and what to say about my going to the war. I think in view of the way you feel it is perhaps better for me not to go for a year… If the war situation does not improve within a year, I will go and do my little share.

Then news arrived that Horace was safe, and the climate on the home front improved a little. Roy, who had not forgotten the Chicago Air Meet, indicated he would like to become an aviator, but as Howard Brown told Alan Bennett, their father had heard exaggerated tales of the casualties being suffered by the Royal Flying Corps, which was part of the British Army, and would not allow Roy to even think of joining that organization. Morton Brown initiated enquiries among his friends in Ottawa for something in aviation but a little less dangerous, and he found a promising lead. The Royal Naval Air Service which was encharged with aerial defence of the British Isles against German airships and aeroplanes and was not involved in the slaughter in France and Belgium, needed officer pilots. Candidates were required to have a good knowledge of mathematics, geometry and trigonometry, essential for the learning of navigation. Proven ability to fly an aeroplane to the standard required by the Federation Aeronautique Internationale was also a requirement.

The Royal Naval Air Service (RNAS) had established recruiting centres in Canada, and Admiral Kingsmill, Director of the Canadian Naval Service, would shortly be interviewing applicants in Ottawa, Toronto, Vancouver and other major cities.

Successful applicants would be offered commissions as temporary probationary flight sub-lieutenants and then sent to England for officer training. This would be followed by a course in the active service operation of the latest military aeroplanes. The icing on the cake was that when an applicant fulfilled the educational requirements but had no Aviator's Certificate, as the FAI—The Federation Aeronautique Internationale—Private Pilot's Licence was then known, the RNAS would accept him provisionally while he learned how to fly at his own expense. Upon receipt of his certificate, the candidate presented himself again to the recruiting office, where his tuition fee would be refunded and his appointment confirmed. This was not discrimination against Canadians but merely a copy of the approach used by the British Army's Royal Flying Corps in its first years. Apparently their lordships of the Admiralty did not wish to finance an Atlantic crossing for someone who might turn out to be all fingers and thumbs when seated in a flying machine or might suffer from vertigo.

The requirement for an FAI Aviator's Certificate unfortunately created a sellers' market for flying schools in Canada and the United States, and the result was not exactly what had been intended.[6] However, upon arriving in England, the Canadians who had acquired the certificate were found to be of such high quality that by 1917 the requirement was dropped.

On 27 May, Roy's brother Horace, now a corporal, received a flesh wound in the right arm, but he was back with his battalion within a week.

With Roy now aware that his parents were not opposed to his taking up the sword, or a "winged trident," the remainder of the term passed swiftly—too swiftly for his aunt and uncle. Shortly after the graduation ceremony at Victoria High School, Roy returned to Carleton Place where three weeks later, together with Stearne Edwards, Murray Galbraith and Walter Sussan (who had journeyed up from Florida), he was interviewed by Admiral Kingsmill at Naval Service Headquarters in Ottawa. The Admiral accepted their educational qualifications and promised that if they could demonstrate aptitude for flying an aeroplane (some said "driving a flying machine") by obtaining civilian FAI Aviator's Certificates, he would refund their tuition fees and confer upon them the officer rank of temporary probationary flight sub-lieutenant in the Royal Naval Air Service. Upon successful completion of their advanced training in England, they would become probationary flight sub-lieutenants, the RNAS equivalent of a Royal Navy acting sub-lieutenant. (In peace time it would take several years for a Royal Navy officer entrant, a cadet, to be promoted to acting sub-lieutenant. This rank is equivalent to a second lieutenant in the army and to an ensign in the U.S. Navy.)

The reader who recall's an oft-published, completely different version of Roy Brown's pre-war activities and attitudes may, with justification, be wondering whether the story above can possibly be true. The late Howard Brown, without doubt, was the authority on the matter, and when asked to clarify it, he handed Alan Bennett a book on Canadian air aces, published in 1990; it contained the other version and the following annotation in his own handwriting: "All totally false."[7]

Endnotes to Chapter 2

(1) THE FLOUR MILL.
The flour mill dated from 1869 and had been owned by the Brown family since 1880 when Horace Brown, Roy's grandfather, purchased it outright. He named the company H. Brown & Sons.

The eldest son of Horace Brown was James Morton Brown, born in 1863. In 1892 he purchased the Robert Raine Electric Light Company, which he reconstituted as the Carleton Place Electric Light Company, with himself as manager. Both the mill and the electrical generators were driven by the water flowing down the Mississippi River.

With the increasing importance of H. Brown & Sons in the business life of the community, Morton Brown at various times held office as a town councillor, school trustee, public utilities commissioner, chairman of the health board and treasurer of the church. He belonged to the Masonic and Oddfellows lodges.

For fifteen years the business prospered; then slowly and inexorably the commercial situation of H. Brown & Sons began to change as the technological advances around the turn of the century became standard practice. By 1900 the large-scale prairie wheat farming no longer needed the services of the community miller. He could still survive if his mill, like the one at nearby Almonte, was directly beside a major railway, since he could contract with a distributor to receive prairie grain in bulk, mill it and then ship the flour to its ultimate destination. Being beside a strong flowing river was no longer the prime necessity of a mill; electric power from a major supplier and a strategic location between producer and consumer had become the criteria for success. The grinding of grist for feeding livestock had also declined because the availability of electricity now enabled individual farmers to produce their own feed. H. Brown & Sons began investing in other businesses as the demand for local milling decreased.

In 1919, when Roy Brown would return from the war, he would find H. Brown & Sons being run by his father and his uncle Alexander (Morton's brother). The other sons of Horace had, one by one, withdrawn from the partnership to follow various careers. Around that time, a plan for linking the individual municipal electrical companies of Ontario into one contiguous system came before the Provincial Legislature. H. Brown & Sons, seeing the writing on the wall, decided that a board or commission with powers for the compulsory purchase of private electrical companies would eventually materialize, and that a publicly owned company would be able to negotiate with such a commission from a far stronger position. The Carleton Place town council agreed with Morton, and towards the end of the year it purchased the Carleton Place Electric Light Company for $100,000.

During Christmas 1998, Roy's brother Howard recalled to Alan Bennett how as a teenager he had helped to unload grain from railway wagons and then load it into sacks to be carted to the mill two blocks away. After the grinding, the carting process then had to be reversed. Until then, Howard he had had no idea what the men discussed whilst working, and he learned quite a number of new words from them. Unfortunately, with the reduced amount of grain then being received for grinding, there was no suitable position for Roy Brown to fill after he was demobilized in late 1919. He would have to make his own way in the world.

Until Morton Brown's death at the age of sixty three in November 1926 (the eventual result of a fall from a ladder while he was checking the amount of ice on a church roof), Morton and his brother kept the mill in operation, supplying flour, grist and oatmeal to the retailers, bakers and consumers in Lanark County. In truth, it was a public benefit gesture under break-even conditions to provide employment for the remaining workers. The intensification of the Great Depression made it impossible to continue even that type of operation, and in February 1927 Alexander Brown placed the entire mill on the market for $15,000, but without result. In 1929 he was forced to close the flour mill section. Nathan McCallum, the H. Brown & Sons company accountant, operated the grist-grinding section for a year but was defeated by the continuing business depression. In negotiations conducted by Roy Brown, the Ritchie Feed and Seed Company purchased the building, but early in the morning of 7 February 1938 it caught fire, and eventually became derelict.

In 1977 the building was converted into luxury riverside condominium apartments, but the original facade was maintained. Howard Brown's parting gesture was to excavate an original millstone and have it placed in front of the building.

(2) SISTER SUSIE'S SHIRTS.
The remaining lines of the first verse of the 1914–1918 wartime, tongue-twisting song "Sister Susie's Sewing Shirts for Soldiers" are:

"Such skill at sewing shirts our sly young sister Susie shows / Some soldiers send epistles that they'd sooner sleep in thistles / Than the saucy, soft, short shirts for soldiers sister Susie sews."
(Now read it outloud quickly.)

(3) GREAT WAR ATROCITY STORIES.
The so-called evidence which had convinced the public had been artists' lurid pen and ink illustrations of the alleged misdeeds to Belgian babies.

In 1918 an Australian soldier, Albert Sloan from Rainbow, Victoria, met the Mayor of Brussels socially and to satisfy his curiosity, he enquired about the baby-associated atrocities in that city. The Mayor shrugged his shoulders and commented; *"True or false, the stories generated a lot of recruits for the army."*

In the case of the British Isles, post-war revelations that the authorities had knowingly and deliberately released concocted stories to the newspapers resulted in a loss of public confidence in the printed word. Alan Bennett recalls hearing his grandmother say more than once just prior to the Second World War, *"It must be true. I heard it on the BBC news."*

(4) THE US ARMY'S PLAN TO ANNEX CANADA.

A document released by the U.S. Government Archives in November 2005 revealed that the concern of the inhabitants of Edmonton over an American invasion actually had a sound basis. Towards the end of the nineteenth century the U.S. military had formulated a plan, which they updated every twenty years or so, for the "liberation" of Canada via an assault from the west, with the capture of Winnipeg as the initial aim. The final revision of the plan was dated 1942, during the darkest days of the Second World War.

(5) ROY'S SCHOLASTIC ACHIEVEMENTS IN EDMONTON.

Fortunately, the late nineteenth and early twentieth century records of Victoria High School have been preserved, and in 1998, Denny Reid May (the son of Lieutenant Wilfrid May, RFC/RAF) was able to obtain a copy of some pages. They indicate that Brown, Arthur Roy, was present for the academic years of 1913/1914 and 1914/1915, during which he completed Grades 11 and 12. At that time he was aged 19 to 21, and the results of his annual medical examinations indicated his health as being excellent.

(Denny may also discovered that whilst his own father had sometimes chided his son for poor examination marks in French, the old school records indicated that Wilfrid May's progress in French had been equally bad, if not worse.

The descriptions of Roy's excellent health, plus his hockey, basketball and football activities at Victoria High School, all diverge considerably from what, is still being peddled as fact. However, it is possible that note 6 below has some involvement in the matter.

(6) A SELLERS' MARKET FOR FLYING SCHOOLS.

With the Royal Flying Corps and the Royal Naval Air Service both considering an FAI Aviator's Certificate as a prerequisite for a passage to England, a sudden demand was created in North America for flying training. One entrepreneur, who shall be nameless, purchased an aeroplane, then depending solely upon his belief in his own capabilities and the native wit of his son, started a business which he termed a flying school. To finance the endeavour, he collected prepayment from those who wished to be students and he used their labour to assemble the aeroplane. His son, whom he had presented as a qualified instructor, lost control of the machine on his first attempt at flight and thereby re-asserted the old saw that most flying accidents happen very close to the ground. The son was not seriously hurt, but his father, who had spent half of the prepayments to purchase what was now a jumble of twisted wood and metal, had to face the demands for refunds.

(7) IDENTICAL NAMES.

The origin of a totally false version of Roy's parentage and youth has long been a puzzle; it seemed odd that someone would have invested so much time and effort in concocting it. The surprising answer appeared quite accidentally during a check into the war service record of Brown, John Horace, Regimental Number 8404. Also listed was a Brown, Arthur Roy, Service Number 2250678.

The service number was a crucial discovery for, as historian Frank McGuire pointed out, in those times service numbers were not allocated to naval officers. Roy had been a direct entrant into the Royal Navy as an RNAS officer, therefore he should not have had one. The files for Wilfrid May and Horace Brown contain service numbers because Wilfred and Horace both served initially in the ranks of the Canadian Army, but upon becoming officers they surrendered their numbers.

The file for Brown, Arthur Roy, service Number 2250678, was thereupon requested, and his birthdate was found to be 4 August 1896. He came from Eden Grove, Ontario, and gave his trade or calling as bushman. He served in England in 1916 and in France in 1917 and was demobilized in June 1919. The dates and places are close enough to mislead one unfamiliar with the precise details of Captain Arthur Roy Brown. The entries on a document deep down in the file for Brown, Service Number 2250678, indicate that he was a private in the Canadian Army and that his parents were John and Maggie Brown.

The guilty party was the unknown person who several decades earlier had seen the first page of the file and apparently had assumed that it referred to the RNAS pilot Arthur Roy Brown. The result was a completely fictitious human-interest story on how success and fame came to a poor Prairie wheat farmer's timid and sickly son who, to steal a phrase from Gilbert and Sullivan's comic opera *HMS Pinafore*, "cleaned the windows and swept the floors" to earn money to pay for flying lessons. It is a pity that the words concerning "polishing the handle of the big front door" were not included, as some alert person with a musical bent might have suspected something was amiss with the tale.

As a point of interest, it has recently come to light that at one time a student at the Wright School of Aviation did indeed fetch, carry, clean, sweep floors and perhaps polish door handles in exchange for flying lessons. It was Edward Stinson, the brother of the well-known aviatrixes Marjorie and Katherine.

CHAPTER THREE

THE WRIGHT SCHOOL OF AVIATION

Unfortunately for Roy and his colleagues when they went looking for flying training. They found that Canadian flying schools were already full. Finally they found places at the Wright School of Aviation at Huffman Prairie near Dayton, Ohio. Roy told his father that for $250 dollars, paid in advance, the school would provide him with four hours of flight instruction, which should be more than adequate to pass the FAI's internationally recognized test. The test would be administered and judged by an official of the Aero Club of America, 297 Madison Avenue, New York. The prospectus issued by the Company for the Wright School of Aviation (Dayton) and for the Wright Flying School (Hemstead Plains and Mineola, Long Island, New York) made the course duration appear more impressive by describing it as 240 minutes.

Roy was unaware that despite their impressive names, the Wright schools were no longer among the worlds leaders in aviation instruction. After Wilbur Wright had died in 1912, his brother Orville had managed both the factory and the schools, but his heart was not in the tasks. In mid-1915 he was actually trying to sell the entire Wright Company, and as a result, there had been no movement into more modern aeroplane designs. The only progress made was in refinements to the box-kite basis of the original Flyer.

Since 1913 Glenn Curtiss in the United States, and others in France, England and Germany that development of the box-kite layout had reached a dead end. Indeed, in 1915 the world's speed record for an aeroplane, 125 mph, was held by a sleek, beautifully streamlined French

Wright School of Aviation airfield. One of the white flags marking the south boundary today is clearly visible above the tree-tops in the foreground; three north boundary markers can be seen along the far side. Photograph taken in 2004, looking north from beside the monument to the Wright brothers on the nearby hill.[1]

monoplane, designed in 1913 by Louis Béchereau and built by Armand Déperdussin, the founder of the Société pour les Appareils Déperdussin (SPAD, an acronym that became famous during the Great War). This speed record was impressive when compared with the 60 mph maximum flying speed of the Wright Company's fastest product in 1915, the machine designed for the U.S. Army.[2]

On 1 September 1915 Roy and his colleagues arrived at Wright Brothers Field on Huffman Prairie, which lies between Dayton and Fairborn, Ohio. They lodged in the school hangar with the Wright Model B flying machine for company, and a lady who lived nearby provided board.

Within a few days, they all learned a little about paying careful attention to the exact wording and the fine print of a contract. Admiral Kingsmill's pledge to refund tuition expense covered precisely that, nothing more. Travel, lodging, meals, damage to a flying machine, aspirins, iodine and bandages were not included in his largesse.

One of the three hangars built by the Wright Brothers during their tenancy on Huffman Prairie. The hangar in which Roy slept, if not this one, was of the same draughty construction.*

The "gang" at Dayton, September 1915. *Left to right:* Walter Sussan, Murray Galbraith, Stearne Edwards and Roy Brown.

Until recently, the Wright Company had been building flying machines with the two-stick control system used on the original Flyer. To turn left, the right hand stick had to be pushed forwards, moving the rudder to the left and simultaneously warping the wings to bank the machine in that direction. To turn right, the right hand stick had to be pulled backwards. The turn and bank part of the Wright two-stick control system was not instinctive. Pupil Fred Southard killed himself in May 1912 when, moments after takeoff, he forgot whether to push or pull the right hand stick to correct a swing to the left.

The U.S. Army, which was purchasing aeroplanes from several different manufacturers, decided that one type of control system, and one only, should be adopted for military use. The control column system, which was a stick with a wheel on top, was chosen, thereby forcing the Wright Company to adopt some of its rivals' ideas.[3]

Marjorie Stinson at the wheel of a 1915 Wright Model B with the Wright two-stick and the Déperdussin wheel control systems. The bar under her feet is a fixed foot rest. Turning the wheel flexes the wingtips and moves the rudders; pushing or pulling the wheel moves the elevators.

The U.S. Army also insisted upon a wheeled undercarriage, so the Wright system of a monorail for takeoff and skids for landing also had to be changed. The most obvious design improvement over the original *Flyer* was the removal of the four long booms which projected out front to carry the elevator. The elevator was moved to the rear behind the twin rudders. A Wright Model B, powered by a 30hp Wright engine. The object in front of the crew's seats is a side view of the two control wheels mounted on a column. The twin counter-rotating propellers, barely visible, are on the rear end of the two shafts which can be seen through the wings. This machine was one of four built under licence in England by an American named Beatty who used them during 1914 and 1915 in his flying school at Hendon, London.

A Wright Model B flying machine of the type used by Roy. It was powered by a 30 horse power Wright engine.

The enforced standardization greatly benefited Roy and his friends, for they received all their flight training using a type of control system and an undercarriage fairly close to those they would encounter in the RNAS. Fortunately, most of Roy's highly descriptive letters home during his stay in Dayton, have survived and enable him to tell his own story of the training.

Apart from the deletion of an occasional sentence referring to personal family matters or simply repeating something written earlier, the letters, his thoughts late at night after a hard day's work, are exactly as Roy jotted them down. His weariness is indicated by the deterioration of his handwriting, punctuation and spelling as the letter continues. For easier reading here, the spelling slips have been corrected and some missing punctuation has been added where the meaning of a long chain of words would otherwise be unclear. From the improvement in the handwriting and syntax, the reader can identify which letters were written after a relaxed breakfast on a Sunday. Only one letter has been edited, and the reason given.

Wright Hangar
Sept. 3/15

Dear Papa,

Well, now we are nicely settled down to work here I will let you know exactly how we are getting along. There are 14 men in our class, 13 of us all starting together and one man with only about 2 hours more to put in.
We expect to have a lady enter our class next week. She has already taken a course and is now going to take a second one. Two of the boys have taken about 100 minutes at Toronto school but left there as they were getting along too slowly. One chap told me that he had waited two weeks without flying and then quit. He said there were too many for one machine and then there was always something going wrong with it.
I had my first flight yesterday evening which was just a passenger flight. He just gave us a ride around the field, above it of course, without our touching the wheel at all. This morning I received my first instruction flight. I was up 8 minutes, driving all the time I was up. We do not make landing or take off until we are up for a couple of hours. Of course I kept making mistakes all the time I was up. Every time I do something wrong he corrects us by a little touch of the wheel or rudder. I can hardly explain how the machine is guided in a letter as it would take too long but I will be able to tell you when I come home. We had our first accident this morning but as one of the boys put it, it was not really an accident. An accident is when somebody gets smashed up.
This was only a slight mishap. He was landing as usual when a wheel or a wing caught on something, a small weed or stick or something which

retarded one side. The machine swung right around, twisting two of the wheels all around and bending one axle very slightly. However, we fixed it in a few minutes and got going again. There are two Americans taking the course, all the rest are Canadians and all naval men. One of the Americans may enlist with us if he can. He is writing Mr. Pinsent today to see if by swearing allegiance to the King, he can be admitted. I do not think he can because he is a Pennsylvania Dutchman although it is 100 years back. He is of mixed German and English descent. He seems a very nice chap.

I have to go to town today to get my picture taken. We are to have it for our licence. We are to write immediately so as to have all arrangements made when the time comes. I would have Hammond send me some but I am going to see if these will be any better. We make a formal application and send five dollars as our fee, also two photographs. One photo is placed on the pilot's certificate when you get it and the other they retain to identify you at any time.

Oh yes, another thing I forgot to mention is that they have no facilities here for water flying, it is all land work. Our instructor Mr. Rinehart is a very decent chap and is awfully nice to tell us anything we ask him. He is anxious to have us all get through at the same time or as near as possible. It would be fine if we all got on the same boat to England. Three weeks I think will see us finished if we have good weather. The idea they have in flying without wind is that then the conditions are always the same and you are better able to correct your own mistakes. If you were flying in windy weather you could not tell whether you were causing the machine to move the way it was going or whether it was just the wind that was doing it. It is a good idea as you learn much quicker. The class is divided into two squads, one takes lessons in the morning and the other in the evening. I am on the morning squad just now but the squads change each week so I will have evening next week. We have to be present no matter whether we are flying or not as we profit by the other fellows' errors.[4]

Roy Brown's photograph for his FAI Aviator's Certificate.

The fourteen members of the class, plus one instructor. Roy Brown is third from the left. The man on his left resembles Stearne Edwards, and the man wearing hat and goggles in the middle looks like Howard Rinehart.

The 40hp, slow-flying Wright Model B was a relatively safe training aeroplane. For a student to be hurt beyond cuts and bruises in a mishap or seriously injured in a crash was rare. The instructors' policy of only flying when there was no wind certainly minimized damage during takeoff and landing. Aircraft accidents tend to occur very close to the ground and to be weather-related and mainly in the vicinity of an airfield.

"There goes another piece of bark!" Roy applies a bandage to a scrape on his leg.

The fly in the ointment for Roy, Murray Galbraith, Walter Sussan, Stearne Edward was that the RNAS aeroplanes used on active service by mid-1916, and some of those in flying schools, had landing speeds that were faster than the top speed of the Wright Model B. This was vividly brought to Roy's attention when he arrived in England. However, the Wright Model B, which performed simple manoeuvres extremely well, inspired confidence in the minds of the pupils, and very few fell by the wayside.

Unfortunately the projected course length of three weeks was to prove well short of the mark. To reduce expenditure, several other students moved their belongings into the hangar and slept there on camp beds.

Roughing it.

Wright Hangar
Sept. 14/15

Dear Mamma,

Time surely does fly here. Several of the fellows have bad colds. Stearne has had one ever since the first night we slept in the hangar. I think they are caused by our being in damp shoes all day caused by walking through the wet grass, and our bed clothes seem to be damp the majority of the time. The roof leaks pretty badly but my bed is in a dry place so I am not too badly off. I have not caught a cold yet and I hope to escape. I feel great and eat much more than I did at home. Don't you pity the woman who is boarding me?

I am going to town today to have a good Christian bath at the YMCA. I have not had one since the day we arrived and as the hangar is dirty and the work is dirty, you can imagine what we feel like. As far as dirt goes the soldiers have nothing on us right now but we don't mind it. We all have a good time.

We have two new students in our class now. One a Scotsman and the other an American. They are both older than we kids. Scotty is about fifty something and the Yank is about 30. Our lady student will not be here as her mother is ill.

I think October should see us in Carleton Place if we have good luck at all. We are to have a new machine and instructor this week. I mean a second machine. We will have a spare engine here all the time so we should get on much faster then. I like flying very much. In fact the fellows are all crazy about it and all eager for their turn to come round. Will close now as I want to get the car for town.

The new instructor was probably Walter R. Brookins, an internationally known Wright Company pilot and the first intrepid birdman anywhere in the world to exceed one mile (5,280 feet) in altitude; in July 1911 he had coaxed a Wright biplane to 6,234 feet over Indianapolis, Indiana.

Roy Brown is in the student's seat on the left side of the aeroplane. The instructor sits between him and the engine, at the centre of balance of the machine. Thus, when a student flies solo, the machine will not be unbalanced. Photograph taken on 15 September 1915.

Wright School
Dayton
Sept. 21/15

Dear Mamma,

  We do not seem to be doing very much now that is interesting to write about. We seem to be in more routine work now. It seems as if I have told you all about what we are doing. We should be finished here somewhere in the first week of October, at least that is when we all expect it and that is what our instructor says. We have had our altitude flights. I was up to about 800 feet, cut off my engine and volplaned down. It is a great sensation to feel the earth coming up at you and know that you are going to land just wherever you wish. That is the greatest sensation in the whole game. It is the safest part of the flight, though. The machine is much easier to control with the engine off. We are having real cool weather here now. Last night it turned cool during the night and some of the fellows thought they were nearly frozen. The hangar is not much of a place to sleep in when it is cold. (5)

Watching a flight. Roy is third from the left.

With the second aeroplane and instructor, the school began accepting more and more students. The members of Roy's class gradually understood that they were being taught how to drive a flying machine rather than to fly one and were not receiving very much instruction in aerodynamics, airmanship or navigation. However, at just about this time the Wright Company realized that in the protection of its patents concerning flying machines, it had been outmanoeuvred legally by its competitors. It was time to stop throwing money away in legal actions and to take a new approach.

Wright Hangar
Sept. 23/15

Dear Papa,

> I received your letter yesterday, it was the first one I have received from home for a long time. We are getting along very slowly here now as our class is so large and the weather is not at all good. It is quite cool here now. I have, like the rest of the fellows, a little touch of cold. It does not amount to anything and will be gone in a couple of days.
> It looks now as if Stearne Edwards will be through first as he has been lucky enough to get his flights at shorter intervals than we have. When we came down here we all thought that he would be finished last but mechanical knowledge is not the least advantage to get through quickly. Anybody with the necessary confidence can learn in a short time. I will have some snaps to bring home and will be able to tell you all about our type of machine, at least all I have learned. We do not get any of the techniques at all, in fact I do not know if we ever shall.

The novelty is obviously wearing off, and in Roy's next letter, it appears that grim realities are starting to sink in.

Dayton
Sept. 30/15

Dear Mamma,

Received your letter with Howard's enclosed. This is a very damp place here. Our bed clothes always have a clammy feeling. If it rains, it comes through the roof and all over us. I put on more clothes when I am in bed than when I am up, wear all my clothes but they do not do me any good because they are damp. It is good practice for what I'll get in the trenches. It cannot be doing us much harm for we are all getting fat on it. I weigh more than I ever did in my life.

Things are going very slowly here. I have given up trying to say when I'll be home. It is no use. Some of the fellows may finish Saturday but they will not let us go up alone unless the weather is perfect and it has been very bad lately.

I am enclosing a snap one of the fellows gave me showing our machine against the sunrise. It looks like moonlight and I think it is very good. It is exactly the way we look when we are up. This would be a beautiful picture to enlarge, it is so clear.

I hope that the pajamas that you are making are heavy as I'll not have any use for them unless they are, that is if I have to sleep in a place like this.

On Saturday, 2 October, a day with good flying weather, a reporter from the Dayton Sunday News visited the flying school. His story, a masterpiece of description, appeared the following day.[6] Unfortunately the weather changed, the sky in the Dayton area began to darken, the winds became too strong for flying, and even with Roy's previously careful spending, the bottom of his purse became visible.

A Wright Model B at sunrise.

The Algonquin
Dayton's largest and best hotel

Oct. 8/15

Dear Papa,

    I am still here and if the weather stays like at present, I am apt to be here for an indefinite period. Two days good weather and I will be finished, but the weather bureau says a big storm is coming so things do not look very promising.

Stearne and I came to town to sleep tonight as it turned so cold this afternoon.

The way things look now, papa, I think I will need some more money before I go home. I have enough to last me until Wednesday or Thursday and leave enough for my expenses home, but if I have to stay longer than that I will need some. I wish you would send me $25.00 which should get here Wednesday. Then if I am away by that time, it will be returned to Carleton Place and no harm done. All I am afraid of is being finished and having to wait for money to take me home. Stearne is ready to fly his tests as soon as he gets favorable weather and there is only one man between us, so it is simply a matter of weather now.

Flying in some ways is very easy but it is quite a nervous strain on anyone who is at all nervous. Some of the boys had quite a time when they started but they are all improving except one poor chap who is up against it pretty badly.

I hope that this will be my last letter from here.

A break in the bad weather allowed Stearne Edwards to take the FAI flight test on 13 October 1915, and he received Aero Club of America Certificate Number 350.[7]

He returned home to Carleton Place to await the arrival of Roy. Their respective parents wished them to follow family traditions and proposed them for membership of St. John's Masonic Lodge at Carleton Place. Due to the proximity of their expected departure for England and the war, a special meeting of the lodge was convened for 29 October.

Stearne Edwards in the left seat of a Wright Model B. The instructor, beside the engine, is probably Walter Brookins.*

On 15 October, Orville Wright signed the papers transferring ownership of the Wright Company to a consortium of businessmen. He agreed to stay on for one year as a consultant.

The Algonquin Hotel
Dayton
Oct. 16/15

Dear Papa,

Received your letter with Bessie's and the money enclosed on

> **St. John's Lodge, AF&AM**
> No. 63, G. R. C., IN ONT.
>
> Mt. Wor. Bro. S. A. Luke. Ottawa, G.M.
>
> Harry Cox. Renfrew, Ont. D. D. G. M.
>
> Wor. Bro. H. W. Dummert, Worshipful Master
>
> Carleton Place, Oct. 22nd, 1915.
>
> Dear Sir and Bro.,
> You are hereby summoned to attend a Special Meeting of this Lodge, to be held in the Masonic Temple, on Friday, Oct. 29th, 1915, at at 7.30 p.m. sharp.
>
> By order of the W.M..
>
> Yours fraternally,
>
> A. T. HUDSON,
> SECRETARY.
>
> Your dues to Dec. 27th, 1915, are $........
> If any change of address please notify Secretary at once.
>
> **BUSINESS**
>
> To initiate Stern Tighe Edwards and Arthur Roy Brown.

St. John's Masonic Lodge Convocation Card.

Thursday. I was very glad to get both letters and money as I was just about out. This hanging around with nothing to do is awful. Some of the lads do not know how they are going to last financially as it runs away with money very quickly.

I am all finished with my course and have been for a week. I have to wait, though, till we get weather suitable for flying for my Pilot's Certificate, which means perfect weather. As a rule, there is absolutely no wind here both morning and evening but it has only been calm once all week. The chap who was taking his test made a mess of it and has not finished yet. He still has his altitude test to go. I am next on the list. One good evening would put me through but no one knows when we will get that. There is a sore bunch of fellows around here now but surely our bad luck cannot hold much longer.

The complications resulting from the new ownership, plus the bad weather, combined to drag out the progress of the flight training programme. Unfortunately, worse than that was in store for Roy when

Mr L. Luzern Custer, the examiner from the Aero Club of America, came to observe his flight test two days later.

Roy in solo flight position for his test.*

Roy's next letter has been edited a little as he was still in shock when he wrote it. The handwriting in the original is shaky, some words are missing from sentences and the thought sequence is disjointed.

Dayton
Oct. 18/15

Dear Dad,

Well I am here yet and apt to stay here for some time as I did a stunt today which will keep us here for a couple of weeks at least. I started up this morning to take my test and there was something the matter with the throttle which would not let it work properly. As a result I had a very bad fall from about 50 feet high, smashing the machine all to pieces. Everybody thinks I was *wonderfully lucky to get out with my life and so I was. I was all ready to leave for home this morning and as a result tore my only suit all up. I was thrown out of the machine on my head and got a little cut on the forehead. Tore the right leg of my trousers and scraped the leg pretty badly bruising the right knee. That is not my old sore one. As a result I had to spend the money that was to take me home on a new suit of clothes and had to borrow some from Murray Galbraith. We have an extra $10.00 to pay to the observer for our test so I will need some more money. I guess I'll need about $75.00 at least as it will take about two weeks to fix up the machine. I don't want this mentioned to mamma at all please as she would only worry without necessity. Do not say anything to anybody as Murray does not want his folks to hear about it for the same reason.*

I cannot tell exactly how I got out of it alive but I am still here. I cannot explain at all by letters but will be able to tell you all about it when I get home if we ever get finished here. I hope you will not think of this too seriously because it may never happen to me again. We are having a rainy season here now. Sunday is the only day we do not seem to have bad weather and we do not fly on Sunday.

The Wright Company has sold all its rights to a body of Eastern capitalists who are going to rush things forward in favour of the Allies. The school is going to be moved south as soon as the fellows get out of here. I am trying to talk and write at the same time so this is very disconnected.

Exactly what had happened to Roy cannot be determined because those who were watching at the time are long departed. A landing accident can be eliminated, as all the trainees had been taught, by switching off the engine, and gliding in. If the loss of power had occurred during take-off, it is certain Roy would have said so. A novice is in a difficult situation should a strange thing occur in flight since he does not have the experience to foresee what may well happen next. It would appear that engine power began to fluctuate as Roy was positioning the aeroplane for the low-altitude manoeuvring tests. Not having been trained to handle such situations, he failed to put the nose down immediately for an emergency landing. Whatever the cause of the engine problem, the failure of the instructors to give their students a good grounding in aerodynamics was a shortcoming which, like a bird, had come home to roost.[8]

Roy and Stearne still had hopes of reporting together to the RNAS recruiting office in a week or two and thus being able to train together in England; however, the Wright Company had already reported Stearne's success to the RNAS office, which thereupon sent him an invitation he could not refuse.

Dayton
Oct. 20/15

Dear Dad,

    I was sorry to hear that the RNAS office has asked Stearne to go but I wrote him telling him he had better not wait because it will be easily the end of next week, and most likely the week after, before I get through here as they are very slow in making their repairs. That may leave me in time to catch the November meeting of the lodge. I do hope that they do not need to call a special meeting for Stearne and then go and call a second special meeting for me.

    I have come to the conclusion that there is no use counting on anything in this game, we are so dependent on the elements that you are sure of absolutely nothing. I am sorry I am missing all your nice autumn weather as I would have liked very much to see the maple trees in their fall colours once more. You might as well forward my mail for at least another week. There is not a thing of interest to write you as we are doing nothing.

The new owners of the Wright School of Aviation apparently decided that its business motto would no longer be 'You bend them; we mend them,' and they dropped the first shoe on Roy.

    It should be noted that all solo flying at the Wright schools took place with an instructor on board as a passenger. The first time a student genuinely flew alone occurred when he made his FAI test flight. Due to the light weight of the Wright Model B, the absence of the second person's 160–180 pounds had a noticeable effect upon the glide ratio, namely, the number of feet travelled forwards for each foot of altitude lost. Assuming the student was at his normal, accustomed height above the ground at the beginning of the landing approach, the absence of the instructor's weight thus would create a major difference in the point where the aeroplane would contact the ground. Instead of touching down in the usual place at the usual speed, it would "float" along in the air and appear to have a mind of its own. This has unnerved many a student, who thereupon has attempted to put the aeroplane onto the ground instead of allowing it to continue floating until it settled of its own accord. The usual result is a bounce back into the air, which, if uncorrected, often leads to a series of noises from the aeroplane along with cuts and bruises to the pilot and his bank account. Again we come back to the lack of instruction about flight and aerodynamics, plus the danger accruing from always piloting a machine in fair weather and with the same gross weight.

Dayton
Oct. 25/15

Dear Dad,

      Received your letter with draft enclosed this morning. I have more bad news to give. Mr. Wright demands a $500.00 bond in case of breakage before I can fly my test. I do not blame him in the least because he has already lost money on me, and business is business. One of the other boys, an American, has a similar bond to put up. It is a new rule they have that anyone who makes a bad flight on the test is not allowed to fly any more test flights until he puts up a $500.00 bond.

      I am sending a telegram to you tonight regarding this as it will save time and hence money. I am very, very sorry to have to ask you for this because $500.00 is a lot of money and, of course, there is always the slim chance that I lose out. My lesson on my last flight was pretty severe and I'll not make that kind of mistake again. Mr. Rinehart, my instructor, tells me not to worry a bit about it, he says I shall not have the least trouble. I am taking 30 more minutes to get used to the new machine which means $30. It surely is an expensive game. But I am not so badly off as if I had gone to Toronto or any other school where you have to put up a bond when you start and pay for all breakages during the course. If Mr. Rinehart had any doubt about my getting through, I would not dare risk it but he has said from the very first that I would make a good flyer and he is not the kind of man that says yes when he means no. He tells you exactly what he thinks of you and says some wild things sometimes. He told one of the boys, Saunders it was, regarding his flying that if it were not so pathetic he would laugh. That is typical of him.

Well, I am going to the hangar and have no more time to write at present but I hope you will be willing to back me for this though I know it is a lot to ask. I'll be very careful as it means all or nothing now.

The new owners of the Wright Company now dropped the other shoe.

The Algonquin Hotel
Dayton
Oct. 26/15

Dear Dad,

Well, things seem to be getting worse and worse all the time. One of the fellows in flying his test today smashed a machine again but very slightly. His was due to poor flying so he has no one but himself to blame. He was afraid to dive steeply enough on his altitude descent, which resulted in a pancake landing, i.e., settling straight down instead of in a curve.

The result is that everyone, before taking a test flight, must put up $500 in cash in the Wright Co's Bank, which is entirely too much and unfair. All they should require is the signing of a bond but they demand $500 in cash from everyone. There surely is a sore bunch of Canadians in Dayton. I am trying to get out of taking my test at all. I wired the Naval Secretary tonight asking him if a certificate from my instructor assuring him that I was a competent flyer would be acceptable as a Pilot's Certificate. I should receive a reply from him tomorrow. We are trying to make some better arrangements among ourselves, better than putting up $500 as it is impossible for some of the fellows to finance it after paying so much for the tuition and living expenses here which are very high. The average is about $30 a week which is a lot of money. How it is going to end up we cannot figure but we are hoping for the best. Stearne was lucky to get out and Murray may get out of it too as all his arrangements are completed with the observer for his test. The Wright Company are going back on what they promised in their school calendar ,but of course we can only hold them to what is in the contract and there is no mention of test flights as they do not guarantee to have a man pass. It looks *a worse muddle every way you look at it but all's well that ends well, so here's hoping.*

There was no flying except part of a test this morning, and none whatever this afternoon, which means another day wasted. Some of the boys have been here a month without a flight and they have no prospects of making an immediate start. This is almost as bad as the Toronto school. There are six fellows here writing letters similar to this.

I hope things are better at Carleton Place than here.

Roy was apparently unable to explain aerodynamically what had caused the pancake landing; namely, the student had failed to maintain adequate engine-off flying speed. As a result, the aeroplane had glided in to land in a semi-stalled condition and at a high rate of vertical descent. As soon as the student tried to raise the nose to slow the descent, a full stall began but was terminated by contact with the ground before it could develop into a spin. The root cause of the accident was the student's failure to recognize a partial stall and his lack of knowledge of how to correct it. Such omissions from the training syllabus could be dangerous to a student's health.

Dayton
Oct. 27/15

Dear Papa,

Received your letter of Sunday this morning. I suppose you will be nearly disgusted with me and have come to the conclusion that I cannot make good. I had my first flight in the machine this morning since my smash and flew practically perfectly my instructor said. He tried to make me nervous or perhaps to see if I was nervous by slowing down the motor on me, but every time the power decreased I dove the machine, so he was pleased. I have not the least doubt that if I get a chance and the machine holds together, I will have the least trouble in getting my certificate.

We had a peculiar break in the motor this morning while in the air. I was not up at the time. One of the connecting rods broke and smacked a hole in the crankcase that you could slip your hand through. A new motor was put in this morning but it was not set up properly and as a result there was no flying on that machine this afternoon. Murray would have tried his test if we had not had that motor trouble.

   I am very glad that you are busy in the mill. I had a reply from Pinsent and he says test flights must be made. I will not be able to go with Stearne and I am very sorry but if things go O.K., we'll see each other across in England. I am telling you frankly about test flights and do not want either you or Mamma to worry about me.

From the letter above it can be seen that instructor Howard Rinehart was belatedly teaching Roy how to recognize and react to the first signs of an engine failure.

Howard Rinehart is in the instructor's seat beside the fuel tank. Lieutenant. Smith is in the student or pilot's seat.

   In response to Roy's request, Morton Brown arranged for the Bank of Ottawa to place a bond for $500 as Roy's guarantee money. This was communicated to the Wright Company.

The Algonquin Hotel
Dayton
Oct. 28/15

Dear Dad,

Received your letter this morning and I cannot tell you just how I felt when I knew you were so willing to trust me with the money. I surely appreciate it and I will never forget how good you were but I have to impose upon you again as The Wright Company are not satisfied. In my telegram I thought I had said cash but I must not have because they demand that I deposit cash at their bank here. They are most unreasonable about it and as I am in no position to dictate, I have to take what they say. They heard from the Bank of Ottawa but would not pay any attention to it. Wright himself is no business man at all and the complete management of the school is in the hands of a girl in the office who has one idea in her mind which she thinks is the only one. The management has changed and Mr. Wright has no power now, so we have no real authority to go after to try to get any satisfaction. It makes me angry to think how unreasonable the Company is. The bond is just as good as the money when it is guaranteed by The Bank of Ottawa.

The boys are all sore at the school now. There is only one thing good now —the instructors. They surely are fine fellows, could not be nicer and will do anything they can for us. If it was not for them, I would not have stayed here.

To give you another idea of the way management does things. You remember they asked for a $50.00 dollar deposit to reserve a place before the course started. Several of the boys did not bring $200 cash with them. Murray (Galbraith) was one and they would not allow any student to take one minute in the air until he had paid them the full $250. No chap would come here to study aviation if he had not enough money behind him to pay his tuition fee but they are very peculiar.

Poor Murray is in hard luck too. He took one test flight this morning and missed his mark by over 400 feet.

I guess I had better get back to my room and go to bed as 4.30 is not far off. [9]

A warmly dressed Murray Galbraith climbing into the pilot's seat. One of the few photographs showing the control column of a Wright Model B fully forward.

On Friday, 29 October, the day for Roy's and Stearne's initiation into St. John's Lodge at Carleton Place, Roy was still in Dayton. In view of Stearne's imminent departure for England, the ceremony took place for him alone.

The Algonquin Hote
Dayton
Oct. 30/15

Dear Dad,

    Received your letter of the 27 today. I surely needed your advice because the way things were going was beginning to get on my nerves. There seems to be a hoodoo on our machine as it is always in trouble. Murray was to take his test this morning but the Aero Club of America observer never showed up. Then when he did come out this afternoon the engine was not running properly. By the time they had another engine in, the instructor would not let Murray take his test as, I guess, he wanted to make some money. Murray surely was angry but it does no good as they do not care whether you get your certificate or not. They consider their part done when they teach you how to fly. Allowing you to use a machine of theirs for your test is an extra favour they are granting you.

    The machine was repaired alright. One is hardly ever broken so badly that it cannot be of some use, that is when its pilot is still alive. I had an altitude flight this morning and I got on pretty well. We were up about 1,000 feet when our engine started to give trouble and our instructor had to cut it off and we came down just fine. When the engine begins to miss it, often gets the machine vibrating with it so that allowing it to run would really shake the whole thing to pieces. Diving down from a great height certainly is great stuff and I like it fine.

    I will not write a letter tomorrow as there is no flying on Sunday and there will be nothing to write about but I shall try and write you on Monday.[10]

News of the presence of a large number of Canadians at Huffman Prairie Field had reached the press, and on Sunday, 31 October, the Dayton *Sunday News* published a well-written, factual article in which the absence of hyperbole and sensationalism is both notable and commendable. By comparison the headline above this well-crafted Article, "Thirty Wealthy Canadian Men Taught Aeroplane", was oddly lacking in clarity and obviously not composed by the same person.

In his next letter Roy describes how, for many students, success had been just around the corner for too long and that some had decided to stop throwing good money after bad.

The Algonquin Hotel
Dayton
Nov. 1/15

Dear Papa,

Received your letters with both bank drafts enclosed today. Also received your telegram on getting back the bond. I will make arrangements with the company tomorrow. There was no flying at all today. I don't see how they can keep the school open here much longer as the weather seems to be getting worse and worse all the time. There are more students coming each day and nothing doing. I may get my test at the end of this week but do not think so the way the instructors are acting about them. Murray, had he been allowed, could have tried for his certificate Saturday evening but they would not let him. This waiting is certainly hard on a fellow's nerves and we are all getting worse and worse every day. There have been four leave so far with no certificate, and the mother of one of the boys arrived here yesterday so he expects he will leave without his. They will go to England and take a course there.

I am very sorry for mamma because I can easily understand the strain under which she is, but I cannot help it in anyway. If I only could, I would do it quickly enough. The more I think of the war, the more foolish it seems but we cannot alter facts, we must go no matter what the cost is. Somebody must do the dangerous work.

In a letter written the following day, Roy provides the following news, which shows good sense in a difficult situation:

There is a promoter here trying to start a new flying school in the south where the weather is better. I believe quite a few of the fellows are going to leave and go south with them if they prove they are going to produce the goods. I hardly know what to say but guess I had better let it go a few days longer, surely we will have a change in a short time one way or the other.

I did not go to the factory today as I will not put up any money till I see when I am going to get my test.

On 3 November, Murray Galbraith made his test flight and earned his certificate, Number 356. With the arrival of funds from his father, Roy moved to a hotel that had opened the week before.

Hotel Miami
Dayton
Nov. 5/15

Dear Dad,

Well I had one flight today but there was only one test which was flown in the morning. There is one more before I fly mine. That means next week at least. The weather was fine this morning and two tests could have been flown if the instructor had allowed it. It was too windy this evening to fly a test and there was a very windy looking sky when the sun went down.

I sure wish the war was over but it looks less like a successful finish now than ever. All we get is pro-German news in our papers here as this place is strictly German and they are not ashamed of it.

I suppose you will have seen Murray by now. I hope he does not have to go before I get finished here.

"That was a close one!" Instructor Rinehart was flying the machine when the main wing warping cable on one side suddenly parted. *Left right:* Stearne Edwards, Roy Brown, unknown, unknown & Howard Rinehart inspecting the damage. He was unhurt.

The dates given in Roy's next letter home should interest the North American reader who, at the beginning of the twenty-first century, is accustomed to an airmail letter from the United States to Canada, and vice versa, taking four to seven days.

Hotel Miami
Dayton
Nov. 7/15

Dear Dad,

Received your letter of 4th yesterday and it did me a lot of good. I hope you do not think I am the only one who is disgusted with the way the school is mis-managed here but everyone is.
Saturday was too windy for a test again but they were able to do some flying with the instructor. Sussan is next to take a test on our machine and I

am to follow him. I am going to take a flight every day now till I take my test so as to keep from getting rusty. I will not need any more money as I can pay for it out of the five hundred when I get it back.

What do you think of this note paper? They put it on the desks only on Sundays as a special attraction. The reason we all like it so well is that it is much nicer and very much cheaper than getting some of our own.

This is a busy town now as the National Cash Register Company are holding a convention here. The hotels are full to overflowing.

Serious competition with the Wright schools was now appearing. Eddie Stinson, who had recently earned his certificate there, had opened a flying school in San Antonio, Texas, where his sister Marjorie, a highly experienced pilot although still in her teens, was the instructor. William Melville (Mel) Alexander from Toronto, who appears later in this story as an RNAS ace fighter pilot (twenty-three victories including shared) and was awarded a Distinguished Service Cross, achieved his FAI Aviator's Certificate at their school. As Roy noted in his next letter, the Stinsons had "two Wright machines, the same as we are using and they also have two fast machines. The boys who get time on the fast machines will have a big advantage over us fellows who only have experience on the slow ones."

Mel Alexander at the wheel of a Wright *Model B* at the Stinson Flying School. This photograph is obviously posed, note where he is seated. Refer to the photographs of Murray Galbraith and Roy Brown a little earlier in this chapter.

The Wright Company's new owners regarded the Wright flying schools as being strictly business. They really could not do otherwise if the schools were to remain solvent, but to implement a financially sound policy in a manner that resulted in a group of disgruntled—nay, hostile trainees—could hardly be considered good advertising. The FAI test situation moved from bad to worse.

Hotel Miami
Dayton
Nov. 9/15

Dear Dad,

Today there was one test run off on our machine which means I should get mine very soon, weather permitting.

My, the fellows are sore here. The National Cash Register people are holding a convention here, as I told you before, and one of their events is an aeroplane flight around their factory by Walter Brookins, one of our instructors, of which moving pictures are to be taken. The result is that our instructor flew the machine to town this morning, kept it in town all afternoon and brought it back tonight too late for the evening flights. He will take it there again tomorrow morning.

To make it worse, Brookins has decided he will not fly any more in the morning as it is too cold. The result is that many of the fellows expect that if they remain here, they will never get through and are going to leave as soon as they can. Once you get your course finished, the company does not seem to care any more.

I expect you have read the letters in the Toronto papers on the way students feel about the things at the school there.

We received a telegram from Pinsent saying that he expected we would have to go to England to finish our training the way things look to us now.

"Who done it?" Photograph taken at San Antonio, Texas by Mel Alexander.

Canadian Naval Service Headquarters in Ottawa was now becoming sated and wearied with the Toronto, Dayton and Long Island flying schools. Pilots were urgently needed by the RNAS and the RFC, and soon some of the more enthusiastic candidates would give up, owing to the endless frustration of their ambitions and the waste of personal money which would not be refunded. The last straw was Mr. Pinsent's realization that the Stinson Flying School at San Antonio was following the same path as the others.

Hotel Miami
Dayton
Nov. 10/15

Dear Dad,

Another windy day gone and no test. We have received word from Pinsent that we can expect to be ordered to England at any time to complete our training, the same as the army (RFC) men. I hope, however, that I shall have passed my test first.

As if the bad weather were not causing trouble enough, bad luck now lent a hand.

Hotel Miami
Dayton
Nov. 11/15

Dear Dad,

I suppose you wondered when you opened this letter what tale of woe and hard luck was inside it.
This morning when we got up there was a warm south wind blowing and as usual we drove out to the hangar but it was much too windy for flying. The instructors had made arrangements between themselves that if it was too windy to fly to the National Cash Register factory, the machine would be taken there by motor truck. We dismantled the machine and put it onto the trailer behind the motor truck and started for the NCR factory. They got it right out to where they make the turn to the hangar when the wind picked it right up bodily off the trailer and threw it into the ditch, smashing it all to bits. All that was left of it that was any good was one propeller and the engine. There will be no tests until the machine is repaired so I am here for that much longer. Two more fellows are leaving this week without their tests as a result of this.
It is raining here this evening so there should be good flying in the morning for the other machine. This is enough woe for one letter.

During the afternoon of 12 November, the sky over Dayton began to brighten and the wind decreased. It was calm enough for instruction in the evening but still not suitable for a test. The morrow dawned calm and clear; however, the students were not comforted, as the machine used by Roy's class would be out of service for at least a week, and moreover, it was the thirteenth day of the month. Fortunately for Roy, in 1915, 13 November was a Saturday, not a Friday, and to his great surprise that morning, the new school manager allowed him to use the other group's machine, the only serviceable one remaining, for his test. That afternoon a telegram was delivered to his long-suffering parents.

Roy returned home on Monday, 15 November, and wasted no time in reporting to the Canadian Naval Service office, where he was accepted as a temporary probationary flight sub-lieutenant in the Royal Naval Air Service, effective from that day. The confirmation of his temporary commission would be subject to the satisfactory completion of his training in England for active service.

In the evening of Monday 22 November, Roy attended a special meeting of St. John's Lodge to be initiated as an apprentice mason. At the end of the ceremony he received a certificate in English, French and German. The emphasis placed upon Roy and Stearne becoming Freemasons before going to war derived from the hope of their respective parents that if they were captured, they might encounter a German officer who was also a Mason, and thereby might receive less harsh treatment. The false stories in the 1914 newspapers of German army atrocities to Belgian women and children, and to anyone else who failed to obey the soldiers' orders, had clearly produced the intended effect.[11]

On 24 November, Roy received notice that Aero Club of America Certificate Number 361, dated 13 November 1915, would be issued in his name and posted to him in the near future. The granting of an Aviator's Certificate to Roy was communicated to the F_d_ration A_ronautique Internationale in France. The Royal Aero Club of Great Britain was advised of his intention to join the Royal Air Service

Roy's file card at the Royal Aero Club of Great Britain.

ENDNOTES TO CHAPTER THREE

(1) WRIGHT BROTHERS FIELD AND MONUMENT AT HUFFMAN PRAIRIE.

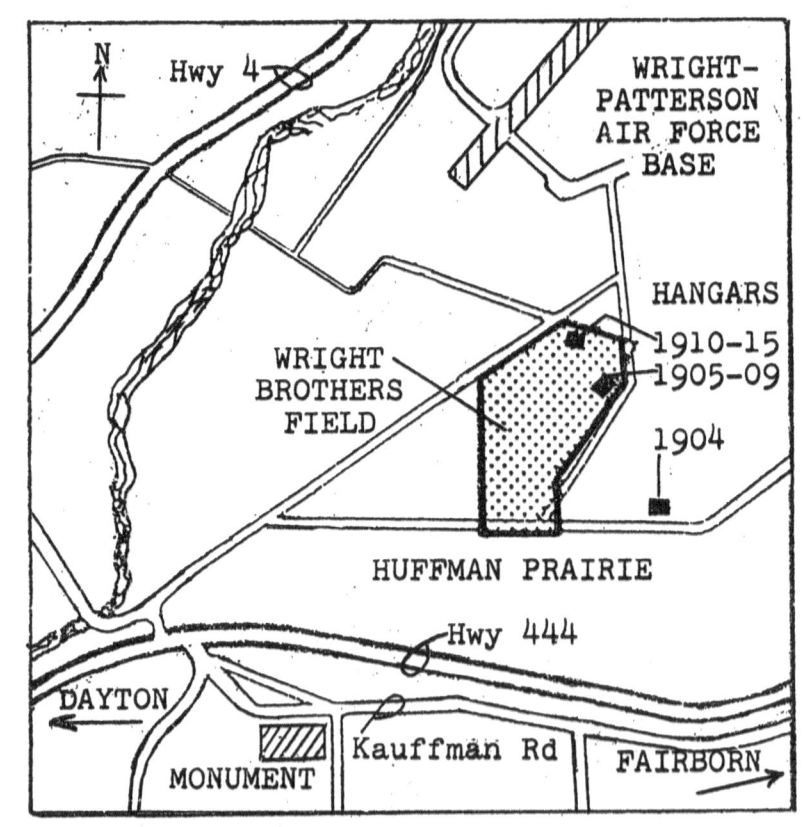

The location of Wright Brothers' field, museum and monument near Dayton, Ohio.

View to the southeast from the site of the hangar, built in 1910, where Roy Brown and his colleagues lived until the weather closed in. The two lengths of concrete on the left are the remains of the foundation of the hangar used between 1905 and 1909. The building in the distance is on the location of the 1904 hangar, and it is used to shelter a Wright Model B look-alike it has been flown in from the Dayton-Wright Brothers Airport museum, and airfield, Miamisburg, for public demonstration and joyrides.

View to the southwest from the site of Roy's hangar. The airfield (note the white flag) is within the approach pattern for the northeast runway of Wright-Patterson

U.S. Air Force Base.
The look-alike Wright Model B is fitted with a two-way radio, rudder pedals, ailerons, seat belts and a modern engine, thereby complying with current (2005) regulations for small aeroplanes.
It is permitted to fly in that area and carry a passenger.

The monument at the Wright Brothers Memorial Park.

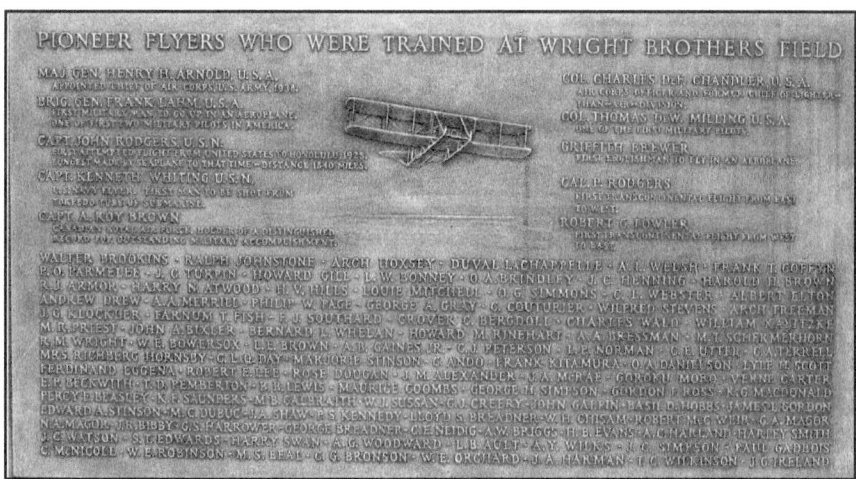

The plaque on the wall of the Wright Brothers Memorial Park honouring those who learned to fly at the Huffman Prairie school.

(2) AEROPLANES IN USE IN OTHER FLYING SCHOOLS IN 1915.

Louis Blériot's 1909 tractor monoplane layout would eventually prove to be the shape of things to come. Photograph [AN3-9] shows a more powerful and generally improved version of the aeroplane in which Louis Blériot made the first crossing of the English Channel on 25 July 1909. In January 1916 it would come as a surprise to Roy and his friends were surprised to see stylish French aeroplanes, such as this, being used at flying schools in England—and then they were shocked to learn that the planes were no longer employed against the enemy; they were obsolete.

Blériot XI-2 Tractor Monoplane, RNAS No. 3218, with 80hp Gnome rotary engine, arrived at Chingford on 30 July 1915 and was in use there during Roy's time. It was deleted on 22 April 1916.

Glenn Curtiss had realized that although the box-kite layout flew well, it was a dead-end design. His 1912 flying boat was a neat-looking machine and augured well for the future if he could avoid infringing the Wright Brothers' lateral control patents.

Single-engined Bass-Curtiss Airboat. Photograph taken in June 1914 after a rebuild at White & Thompson Works.

In 1912 Germany, aeroplanes with a dove-shaped layout, known as *Tauben*, became highly successful once proper lateral control was added. The version produced by the Etrich factory, known as the Etrich (dove)Taube, was good looking and flew well. A Taube dropped primitive bombs on Paris in 1914. By the time Roy arrived in England its use over France had long ceased.

Etrich Taube. Pylons at the wing-tips supported the wires which twisted the rearward tip extensions up or down to provide lateral control.
This arrangement was known as wing warping.
The tailplane, out of picture, was a long, graceful narrow triangle.

By 1913 the Wright Company had produced a new and more powerful flying machine, the Model C. Their basic design, which was perfectly sound at the weights and speeds up to the last version of the Model A, had reached its plateau with the Model B on which the forward elevator had been moved to the rear. Although this improvement increased the speed, it changed the balance and altered some of the flight characteristics of the earlier A series.

In most aeroplane designs, the power from the engine tends to raise the nose. This means that to fly level, the pilot has to trim his machine nose down. Thus, an engine failure will automatically lower the nose, often by a greater amount than is required to maintain flying speed. This provides a good safety margin if the pilot fails to react immediately. Apparently the design of the Wright Model C did not include this feature. The U.S. Army purchased six, and they all crashed, five instructors being killed. It was later learned that the chief instructor, one of the victims, had written to Orville Wright the day before he was killed, saying the Model C was badly out of balance and dangerous in a glide.

The Wright single-seater Scout, a 1913 design based on the Model D flying machine, had only half the speed of an equivalent European military aeroplane and the pilot still sat on the front of the lower wing. Even worse, the maximum flying speed of the Wright Model D was 20 miles per hour slower than the landing speed of the 1912 Déperdussin Racing Monoplane.

The harsh truth is that in late 1915, the Wright Model B on which Roy learned to fly belonged in a museum, not in a flying school. In December 1916 the Wright Company's new owners ceased building box-kite flying machines. After a brief flirtation with aeroplanes laid out in the Blériot style (the Model K and Model L biplanes), they chose the manufacture of aircraft engines as their staple industry. A merger of Wright Company and Wright Flying Field, Inc., with Glenn L. Martin Company, Simplex Automobile Company and General Aeronautic Co. of America took place in September 1916. The newly constituted Wright-Martin Company obtained a contract from France to build Hispano-Suiza aeroplane engines. In 1919 Glenn Martin dissolved the merger and restarted his own company. Orville Wright formed Wright Aeronautical Company, retaining the licence to manufacture Hispano-Suiza engines. In 1929, Wright Aeronautical Company merged with its old rival, Curtiss Aeroplane and Motor Company, and together they finally put an end to the patent infringement lawsuits which had seriously impeded aircraft development in the United States. The famous series of Curtiss-Wright aeroplane engines was a direct result of the merger.

Progress from success to disaster happened several times in the history of aviation as attempts were made to improve the performance of a successful type of aeroplane by installing engines of ever greater power. A dangerous imbalance of weight or applied force then occurred, and the type, which (to use a twenty-first century term was originally "user friendly"), could quite unexpectedly become exactly the opposite under certain combinations of speed, load and attitude. Louis Blériot was one of the designers who fell into the trap, and American pioneer aviatrix Harriet Quimby paid the price with her life. The powerful Sopwith Camel, derived from the Sopwith Pup (a delightful aeroplane to fly), is reputed to have killed as many pilots in accidents were the enemy pilots in battle. Roy Brown came very close to being one of its victims.

(3) OTHER CONTROL SYSTEMS FOR AEROPLANES.

Armand Déperdussin's idea of a single stick to control the elevators and the ailerons, and a foot-operated swivelling bar to control the rudder, was a great leap forwards. It had been popularized in Europe by Louis Blériot and had already crossed the Atlantic. Being instinctive, the system was rapidly gaining in popularity, but unfortunately Blériot used wing warping instead of ailerons, and infringement of the Wright brothers' patents was difficult to deny. Blériot later acquired Déperdussin's company and renamed it Société pour l'Aviation et ses Dérivés, thus maintaining the acronym SPAD, which would become famous during the 1914–1918 war.

The Déperdussin control system could be described as a stick supported by a bell-shaped swivel at the bottom. When the pilot pushed the stick forwards, the elevators would pivot downwards and raise the tail of the aeroplane. Pulling the stick backwards would raise the elevators and lower the tail. In a similar fashion, moving the stick sideways would cause the aeroplane to bank towards the side selected. The rudder was controlled by a bar pivoted in the middle and fitted with toe straps at each end so the pilot's feet would not slip. This arrangement had a painful disadvantage; the rudder bar, as it was known, would swing round sharply in a crash and frequently the toe straps either sprained or broke the pilot's ankles. The change from a centrally pivoted bar to a pair of pedals cured this defect.

Two variations on Déperdussin's basic system were also used. One had a small non-turning wheel or a spade grip at the top of the stick for the pilot to hold. This variation was often used in fighters as it provided an convenient place to mount the machine-gun trigger(s). On aircraft fitted with rotary engines, the magneto cut-out button for stopping the engine was also fitted there. On the other variation, the wheel turned, and the stick, now known as a control column, only moved backwards and forwards. This variation was used on multi-engined flying boats and bombers. The wheel had a reduction ratio to reduce the force required from the pilot's in order arms to move the large ailerons needed to bank such heavy aeroplanes.

All three versions of the Déperdussin system are in use today.

The Wright Brothers made one improvement to their two-stick system. A short handle, hinged to the top of the right hand stick (the turning stick) and enabled the pilot to modify the amount of rudder deflection (provided by the linkage to the wing-warping system) as he banked into a turn. The two-stick system could not be used in training schools where the pilot and pupil sat side-by-side; therefore to make total control available to the instructor, a three-stick system was installed. The elevator control stick on the pupil's left side was duplicated on the instructor's right, which meant that the instructor's left hand was on the pupil's right hand stick and his right hand was on the extra left hand stick.

A Wright three-stick flying machine.

The Wright Company's solution to the confusion was to add a fourth stick so that, regardless of where the pilot or trainee sat, his left hand controlled level flight and his right hand controlled turns. In all fairness, it must be stated that the Wright Company's Model A and Model B flying machines, when flown within their limitations, performed better and were safer than most of the competition on both sides of the Atlantic Ocean. However that as flying and landing speeds increased, the limitations began to bite.

A Wright four-stick flying machine.
The instructor is Max Lillie and the pupil Katherine Stinson.

Glenn Curtiss employed ailerons mounted halfway between the upper and lower wings and coupled to a harness worn around his shoulders. By leaning his body to one side, he could move them to match the angle of bank to the radius of a turn. He hoped that this arrangement would shield him from a patent-infringement law suit, but, it did not.

(4) Harold Charles Frank Pinsent of the Royal Navy, whose rank was staff paymaster, served in the office of the Department of Naval Service in Ottawa.

The lady intending to join the class was one of the Stinson sisters who wished to take a refresher course.

The word *Dutch* in the term *Pennsylvania Dutch* used in the letter above is an ancient mistranslation of *Deutsch*. A large group of Germans settled in Pennsylvania around the year 1800, and their descendants continue to be known as Pennsylvania Dutch.

(5) Like many aviation terms, volplaning, meaning "gliding," is French in origin.

(6) THE DAYTON SUNDAY NEWS 3 OCTOBER 1915 ARTICLE ON THE TRAINING COURSE AT THE WRIGHT SCHOOL OF FLYING.

THIRTY WEALTHY CANADIAN MEN TAUGHT AEROPLANE:

INSTRUCTORS WALTER BROOKINS AND HOWARD RINEHART GET $1.05 A MINUTE WHILE IN THE AIR WITH PUPILS: THREE MONTHS TRAINING IN EUROPE NEXT

Twisting and turning about in the azure sky above Wright Station, the training grounds of the Wright company, original inventors and manufacturers of the aeroplane, thirty Canadian youths are putting in their time here in a six weeks' course in the art of flying. Numbered among these future air raiders who may fly for the Allies in the European struggle and who are said to be paying their own expense in the school, are sons of some wealthy citizens of Montreal, Toronto, Winnipeg, and other Canadian cities.

The majority of the Canadians here, who are taking the course in aeroplane flying and who will be granted pilot's licenses before leaving Dayton, are expected to enlist, if they have not yet done so. Most of them are anxious to get through so that they may get back to Canada and join the next Canadian contingent for Europe, where they will be required to undergo a four months' course of military observation and manoeuvres before getting into actual service.

Aviators Walter Brookins and Howard Rinehart, leading aeroplanists for the Wright company, are instructing the members of the class in manipulation of the air craft. Wright aeroplanes, equipped with the Wright control, standard the world over, are being used. The Canadian youths learning to fly are B.D. Hobbs, Sault St. Marie; M.C. Dubuc, Montreal; L. Breadner, Ottawa; M.B. Galbraith, Carleton Place, Ont.; W.H. Chisam, Edmonton; A. Y. Wilks, Montreal; L.C. Angstrom,

Toronto; P.L. Kennedy, Montreal; J.C. Stinson, Guelph, Ont.; Gordie Falkner, Toronto; O.J. Creery, Vancouver; A.R. Brown, Carleton Place, Ont.; G.S. Harrower, Montreal; A.G. Woodward, Victoria, B.C.; R.M. Wier, Toronto; J.R. Bibby, Toronto; O.M. Nicoll, Montreal; G. Magor, Montreal; N.A. Magor, Montreal; C. Bronson, Ottawa; J.A. Shaw, Edmonton; Wallace Orchard, Montreal; D. Gordon, Montreal; J. Galpin, Ottawa; and J. Harmon, Uxbridge, Ont.

There are three Americans in the class. They are E. Stinson of Texas, a brother of Katherine Stinson, famous American woman aeroplanist who loops the loop in exhibition flight; A.N. Hall of Lansing, Mich., who is learning the game from the manufacturers standpoint, and W.J. Sussan of Jacksonville, Fla.

The Wright training grounds are located about five miles east of the city. Many of the youths from the dominions are gathering plenty of experience at sleeping out, for as many as can be accommodated have cots in the hangar and never leave the grounds, except to walk up the road to a nearby farm house at meal times. Others are living in the city and go out to the grounds every day by traction [tram or street car].

The course provides for a training of 240 minutes actually in the air. For this course, reasonably expected to take six weeks, the student pays $250. At this rate the cost to the student is $1.05 for every minute in the air. Straight flying, turns, dips, spiral glides, and other manoeuvres are taught by the instructors, as they gradually familiarise the men with the use of the aeroplane.

The men are given regular turns accompanying the instructors into the air, but practically all are to be had on a moment's call, as they are eager to complete the course. Two aeroplanes are being used.

Saturday was a splendid day for flying and all afternoon Brookins and Rinehart were kept busy taking their pupils into the air. Taken in regular turns, the men don heavy sweaters and gloves for protection from the wind, reverse their caps in aeroplane fashion, and after taking their seat beside the instructor, apply the power. The machine trundles along the ground for a couple hundred yards and then rises gradually from the earth.

Soaring back and forth continually, forming the figure eight, the aeroplane is never allowed beyond a certain altitude during the progress of the instructions. The roar of the engine precludes the possibility of the instructor indulging in any oral explanations and suggestions, but actual operation of the machine, under the careful guidance of the trained aviator at his side, is enough to impress upon the student various lessons of control and operation.

The machine remains in the air only a few minutes and then descends when other students flock about and hear a short talk on experiences gained during the flight just completed. As one machine descends, the other is taken aloft on its canvas wings, the idea apparently being to have only one machine in operation at a time.

Every student, before he has gained his pilot's license, must take the entire course of 240 minutes in the air and then pass the aviators' test, which demands certain knowledge and ability to successfully operate the machine alone. The coveted pilot's license is awarded only after the student has displayed a certain degree of perfection in three distinct branches of aeroplane flying. Figure eight flying, rising to an altitude of more than 300 feet, spiral gliding with the power shut off, and finally, the making of a proper landing, are the determining factors in the awarding of the license to fly.

L. Luzern Custer, son of Dr. N. E. Custer, representing the Aeroplane Club of America, goes to the training grounds and witnesses the tests before passing on the application for the issuance of the pilot's license. Custer was at the grounds Saturday afternoon to witness the test flight made by M. B. Galbraith of Carleton Place, Ont., who had finished his course and was in readiness for the final proof of his eligibility.

Several of the Canadians expected to finish the course in a week or so and, within a month's time, after returning to Canada, they hope to be enlisted in the British aerial service, well started on the four months' course of military observation and training, which is demanded before the aeroplanist is allowed to begin actual military duty.

"Although we have our own licenses," one of the Canadians said Saturday, "we are not, by any means, aviators when we leave Dayton to return to Canada. We will have acquired the fundamental principles, it is true, but it is not until we have gone through the longer and more thorough course in store for us that we consider ourselves aviators in every sense of the word, equipped to pilot an aeroplane into the clouds.

Throughout the provinces of Canada now, it is the ambition of thousands of young men like ourselves to get into the aerial service. Not in the Canadian aerial service but in the British service. We are among the fortunate ones who are able to obtain sufficient money to pay for the course and our expenses while taking it. Of course, this money is returned to us when we obtain our pilot's licenses and become a part of the Allies' aerial fleet."

This man, a typical Canadian, who dreams of the time he will be at the steering wheel of one of the powerful British aeroplanes, with bombs exploding all about him, said he hopes to be able to distinguish himself. Coming to Dayton and taking the Wright course has already cost him about $600, he said.

AERO CLUB OF AMERICA

CONTEST COMMITTEE,—297 MADISON AVENUE, NEW YORK

INSTRUCTIONS GOVERNING THE CONDUCT OF TESTS FOR AVIATORS' CERTIFICATES OF THE
INTERNATIONAL AERONAUTIC FEDERATION

1. Candidates must accomplish the three following tests, each being a separate flight:

A and B. Two distance flights, consisting of at least 5 kilometers (16,404 feet) each in a closed circuit, without touching the ground or water; the distance to be measured as described below.

C. One altitude flight, during which a height of at least 100 meters (328 feet) above the point of departure must be attained; the descent to be made from that height with the motor cut off. A barograph must be carried on the aeroplane in the altitude flight. The landing must be made in view of the observers, without restarting the motor.

2. The candidate must be alone in the aircraft during the three tests.
3. Starting from and landing on the water is only permitted in one of the tests A and B.
4. The course on which the aviator accomplishes tests A and B must be marked out by two posts or buoys situated not more than 500 meters (547 yards) apart.
5. The turns round the posts or buoys must be made alternately to the right and to the left so that the flight will consist of an uninterrupted series of figures of 8.
6. The distance flown shall be reckoned as if in a straight line between the two posts or buoys.
7. The landing after the two distance flights in tests A and B shall be made:

(a) By stopping the motor at or before the moment of touching the ground or water;

(b) By bringing the aircraft to rest not more than 50 meters (164 feet) from a point indicated previously by the candidate.

8. All landings must be made in a normal manner, and the observers must report any irregularities.

The issuance of the certificate is always discretionary.

The responsible representative of the Contest Committee is charged with the supervision of the tests and is responsible for the preparation and accuracy of the reports which should be dated, signed, and returned to the Chairman of the Contest Committee as soon as practicable after the completion of the test. A separate blank must be made for each test.

The responsible representative must see that the posts about which the aviators turn are located at a distance not greater than 1640.4 feet (500 meters) apart, and shall note in the report the way in which the distance between the posts was measured, whether by chain, steel tape, metallic tape, etc., etc.

An observer must be stationed in the close vicinity of each post to see that the turns are made in the proper order, direction and number.

The applicant shall be required to designate in advance a landing point and when his machine comes to rest it must be less than 164 feet from this point. The location of the landing points must be indicated in the report.

The aviator shall be instructed that in each of his distance tests he must make a minimum distance of 16,404 feet without touching the ground in the manner set forth in the Regulations of the F. A. I. printed on the report.

The distance made in flight is governed entirely by the distance between the posts, for example:—if the posts are exactly 500 meters apart he must make five complete figures 8.

To determine the number of complete figures 8 that an applicant must make, in case the posts are other than 1640.4 feet (500 meters) part, divide 16,404 by twice the distance in feet between the posts. The quotient in general will not be a whole number but an improper fraction consisting of a whole number and a decimal. If the decimal is less than .5 the aviator should, in addition to making the complete figures 8 indicated by the whole number, turn the next post. If the decimal is greater than .5 the aviator should complete an additional figure 8.

The aviator should be advised in advance as to the number of turns around each post in order that he may make the minimum distance of 5 kilometers (16,404 feet).

The number of figures 8 performed by the aviator must be noted in the report.

While extremely desirable it is not necessary that all the tests should be made on the same day.

Under the heading of "Remarks" (see page 3 of this blank) the time of day and weather condition should be noted and the comment of the responsible representative as to the manner in which the applicant handles his machine.

The blanks on the fourth page are not to be filled out by the responsible representative.

(7) ROY'S COPY OF THE F.A.I. AVIATOR'S CERTIFICATE FLIGHT TEST INSTRUCTIONS.

(8) POSSIBLE CAUSES OF ROY'S ACCIDENT.

When one considers the little knowledge obtaining at that time on the effects of rainy weather and overnight temperature changes on aeroplanes, two possible causes of the accident may be suggested: water in the fuel or the formation of ice around the butterfly in the carburettor. Water in the fuel would be created by the overnight condensation of humid air inside an almost empty fuel tank. Droplets of water would form on the inside walls of the tank, and the next day, with the motion of the aeroplane in flight, they would sink to the bottom. Eventually the water would be carried to the carburetor where it would disturb or even interrupt the flow of fuel through the jets. Today it is a golden rule in aviation to fill the fuel tanks before an aeroplane is put to bed for the night. Most carburetors use air pressure drop to suck fuel through the jets and onwards into the cylinder heads. When humid air is subjected to a pressure reduction, droplets of water condense and rapidly turn into ice. The ice sticks to the inside of the carburetor, causes a reduction in engine power and most likely jams the throttle control. The entire process can occur rapidly, even at air temperatures well above freezing point. Once the nature of the problem was understood, a supply of hot air, which the pilot could turn on and off as needed, was added to the carburetor air intake.

(9) The girl in the office was probably Mable Beck, Orville Wright's secretary who, we are told, was a tough nut to crack and had been specially selected by him for that reason. He needed peace and quiet to deal with the business arrangements and the legal manoeuvring involved in the sale of the company.

Murray Galbraith's experience is not surprising. It was his first landing glide without the extra weight of the instructor on board. It was to his credit that he kept his head and controlled the aeroplane in its float until it gently touched down.

(10) Although the religious persuasion of the Wright family was definitely involved here, flying on a Sunday was considered in several U.S. communities to be in violation of municipal Lord's Day

Observance statutes. Hilarious stories abound of how local police in cars chased aviators who had dared to fly on such a sacred day and how the ingenious efforts of the fliers' faithful friends helped to foil the fuzz. To some with a vivid imagination, the happenings resembled scenes out of a Mack Sennett film featuring the Keystone Kops.

(11) THE ANTWERP CHURCH BELLS, OR THE PROGRESSION FROM FACT TO FICTION OF ONE PARTICULAR BELGIAN ATROCITY STORY.

When the German army, using special seige guns, captured the fortified Belgian city of Antwerp (Anvers), church bells were rung throughout Germany in celebration of the achievement. The newspaper *Kölnische Zeitung* (Cologne News) reported *"When it was learned that Antwerp had fallen, church bells were rung."* In France, *Le Matin* (The Morning News) informed its readers: *"According to the Kölnische Zeitung, when the city of Antwerp was captured, the priests there were forced to ring the church bells."* In England, *The Times* told its readers that the news from France was, *"The Belgian priests at Antwerp who refused to ring their church bells have been sentenced to hard labour by the Germans."* In Italy, *Corriere della Sera* (Evening Mail) repeated the story from London.

Le Matin told its readers that reports from England and Italy had confirmed its original story.

The final version, which was believed by many, read as follows: *"The brave Belgian priests in Antwerp were given a barbaric punishment for their refusal to obey German orders. They were hung upside down in the belfries of their own churches and their heads used as clappers to ring the bells."*

Something similar would happen to the facts of Roy's heroic adventures in an air battle on 21 April 1918, and what really happened would become lost in a sea of falsehood, fantasy and fiction. The final truth concerning some of the events was only learned in the years 1998 to 2005 when several 1918 letters, diaries and a long-lost document came to light.

(12) THE FINAL PRODUCTS OF THE WRIGHT COMPANY.

CHAPTER FOUR

RNAS CHINGFORD

Roy Brown arrived home during the afternoon of Monday, 15 November 1915, to find that his good friend Stearne Edwards had sailed that morning from New York bound for London. Mr. Pinsent, the secretary in the Naval Service Office in Ottawa, gave Roy his papers, his instructions and a first-class steamship ticket. Temporary Probationary Flight Sub-Lieutenant Arthur Roy Brown was to sail from New York on 2 December on the SS Finland of the American Line.

His sister Reta was working at a hospital in Troy in the State of New York, and some time earlier Roy had promised to interrupt his journey and pay her a visit if time permitted. He left Ottawa on Monday, 29 November, and travelled on the overnight sleeper express to New York. The train made a stop at Troy just after midnight. From that point onwards he had a troubled day.

Nov. 30/15
[Tuesday]

Dear Mamma,

Arrived safely in Troy on time early this morning. Went to the hospital immediately, spent the rest of the night in a guest room there and met Reta in the morning. I was all morning looking through the hospital and after lunch we only just caught the train to New York. After it had started I found I had forgotten my suitcase, so Reta and I got off at Albany and now we are in Troy again with my suitcase. Did this by local train.

Now we are on a local for Albany. Will get there at 3.30 and take a train at 3.57 for New York, getting there at 7.20, so I do not lose very much by it.

The aviators I expected to have for company from Ottawa to Troy were not on board but I met another Brown from Ottawa so I had company. He was a son of the Mr. Brown papa and I were introduced to at the Grand Trunk Railway station in Ottawa.

This is terribly rushed but I will have more time in New York.

Love to all
Roy

The SS *Finland* passenger list for Thursday, 2 December 1915, gave noon as the departure time, and in the wake of the Titanic disaster only three and a half years before, passengers were comforted by the proclamation in bold capital letters that the SS *Finland*, and all others of the line, were fitted with the Marconi system of wireless telegraphy. Among the first-class passengers were Brown, Mr. Arthur R. Sussan, Mr Walter J.; and Dr M.B. Galbraith. Somehow the D in D.M.B. (Daniel Murray Bayne) Galbraith had gained an R.

S.S. "FINLAND" New York
Thursday 11.00 morn
Dec. 2/15

Dear Mamma,

I am writing this on the boat just before we sail. The boat seems to be a very small one, not much bigger, if as big as the boat I came down the lakes on this summer. It is snowing this morning here and windy so we are ready for a rough voyage. So I'll see whether I am good and sea-sick, but such is life. My stay in New York seemed very short.

The gangways were removed, the ropes released, the tug boats huffed and puffed, and the SS *Finland* was soon underway.

The following letter, started in the evening of 2 December, covers several days. As each one passed, there became progressively less to write about. Substance was gradually replaced by idle chit-chat as Roy watched the horizon go up and down, and his companions wished they could order the captain to hold the ship still.

S.S."FINLAND"
Thursday evening 10.45
Dec. 2/15

Dear Mamma,

 Well, I am on my way to England at last and so far am enjoying my trip very much but that will not last long I am afraid, for we shall soon get off the Newfoundland Banks. We are told it then becomes very rough and that is the time we will be real sick. Our boat, however, is supposed to be a very good sailer, so here's hoping. I am also.
 I had really better tell you more about my trip from Ottawa. When we arrived in New York I got my room, then Reta and I went to see Montgomery and Stone in Chin Chin. They were very funny but I could not keep myself from thinking how peculiar the world was. Here was New York at the very height of pleasure and luxury and the people not realising that if the Allies lose in Europe, their life style will change radically.

Saturday morning 10.15
Dec. 4/15

 The next morning I met Murray and Walter at the train. They took their room and then together with Reta we spent the morning seeing as much of New York as we could. We went to the Aero Club on Madison Ave but not one of our certificates was ready. We are having them sent to us C/O the Admiralty. Then we did a funny stunt. We decided to walk back to the hotel. We walked and walked and then becoming tired we decided to take a subway train for the rest of the way. We got on and told the conductor where we wanted to go and he floored us by saying that that was the name of the station where we had boarded his train. We had walked right past our hotel and had not recognized it. After dinner we took our bags to the wharf and boarded the boat ready to sail next morning.

Monday morning 10.45
Dec. 6/15

We are getting it really rough now, I can hardly sit on the chair to write. The meals are quite good. One of the boys has only had two meals in the dining room since we left. Sussan has dropped out now but Murray and I have not missed one yet. The ship's doctor, who sits at our table, told us we could expect to be sick soon but he might just be kidding us.

Tuesday afternoon 3.30
Dec. 7/15

This surely is rough, you would almost wonder how the boat holds together. The attendance at table has dropped remarkably but I am still feeling fine. Everybody on the boat seems to be pro-allied and a southern lady is trying to teach me some French to help me if I have to go to France.

Thursday morning 10.45
Dec. 9/15

The sea has been so rough that instead of travelling 350 miles per day we have averaged about 280 only. We shall be late arriving.

Sunday afternoon 2.00
December 12/15

The sea is much calmer now, yesterday we travelled 295 miles. I don't think I shall be sea sick now.

Monday evening 6.25
Dec. 13/15

We are now in the danger zone. The life boats were swung out and provisioned then the name and the large flags painted on the sides of the ship were illuminated by special lights. We can see the Scilly Islands lighthouse. The weather is clear and cool and we shall dock tomorrow. We expect a naval officer might come to meet us.

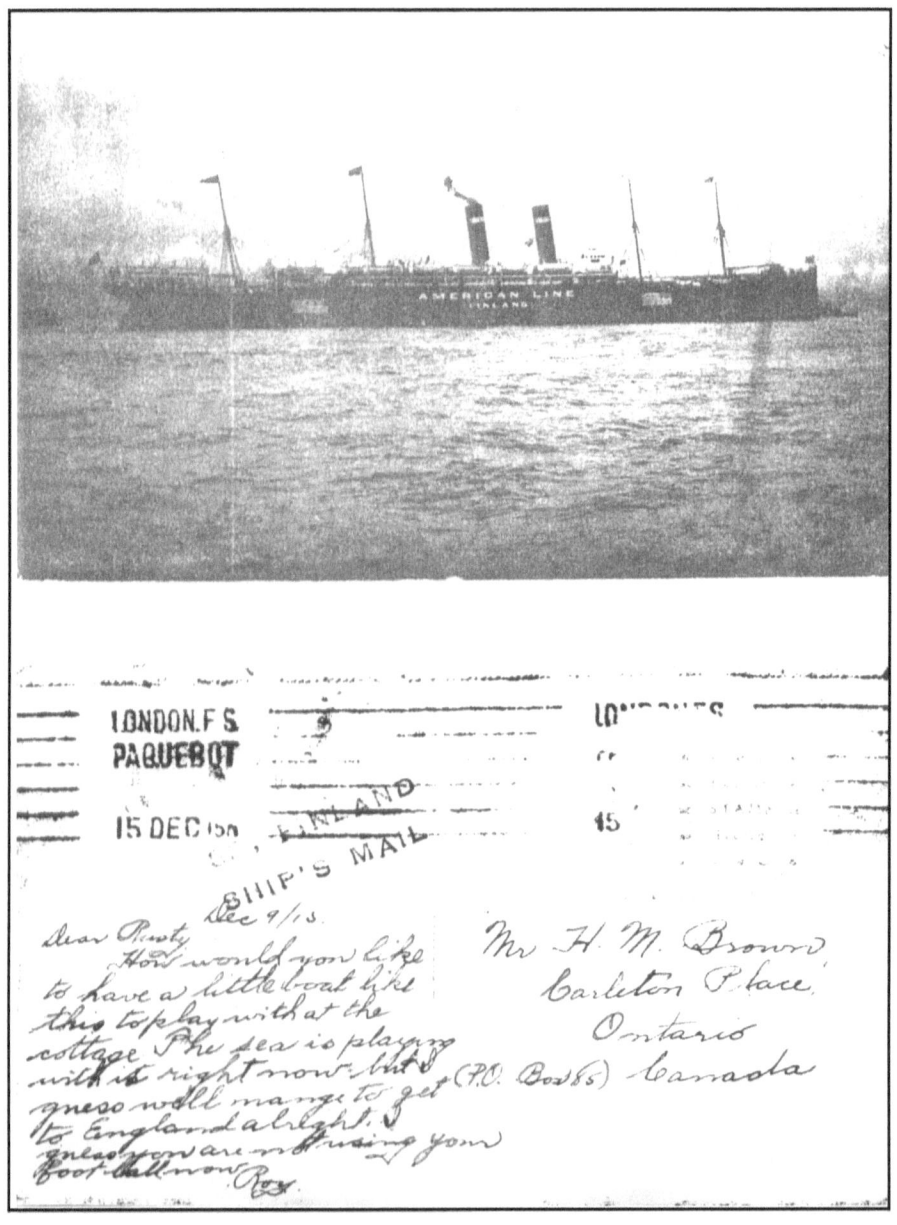

SS *Finland*. Postcard addressed to Roy's youngest brother, Howard.

Hotel Cecil
Strand, London

December 15/15
[Wednesday]

Dear Mother,

     As you see above we are now here in London and a dark, dreary but busy-looking place it is.

     We dropped anchor in the harbor at Falmouth about a few minutes before midnight Dec 13. On the morning of Dec 14 we were inspected by the Alien Officers, who find out and decide whether or not you are admitted to the country, then we had our baggage go through the Custom's Officer. We just showed our naval papers, told him everything was OK and he never said a word.

     The trains seem somewhat peculiar to us but are really much more comfortable than at home and travel much faster. Their dining service is not nearly so good but it is somewhat cheaper.

     We reported to the Admiralty this morning and were sent immediately to buy our uniforms and told to report as soon as we got them, which will not be for several days. They did not give us any money, so I am glad I have some and will need it all before I get my pay and expenses from them. They are terribly busy there.

     London is fearfully dark at night on account of the danger of Zeppelin raids. No blinds are left up on windows. Cars have only the dim little side lights. How there are not accidents all the time I do not understand. The gas lights in the streets have the upper half darkened and are turned low to reflect as little light skyward as possible.

     We do not know where we are to be sent yet but expect it is a flying school. Send mail C/O the Admiralty until I advise different.

Roy's Royal Navy education was about to begin, and although at Dayton he and his colleagues had been big fish in a little pond, a temporary probationary flight sub-lieutenant in the Royal Naval Air Service was someone who had yet to reach the first rung on the officer ladder. First, as a temporary, he had to prove he could find the ladder; then as a probationary, stand on the rung; and after receiving his commission as a flight sub-lieutenant, climb higher by merit alone.

Strand Palace Hotel
Strand, London, W.C.

December 19/15
[Sunday]

Dear Dad,

> *We have moved to a cheaper hotel so as to cut down our expenses. We have found out several not too pleasant things about our branch of the service and as a result we are going to economize all that we can. We shall not be so well off as we expected but I do not mind as I expected it in a way.*
> *We are to get our uniforms tomorrow evening and I will be very glad as I feel most uncomfortable going around in wartime London in civilian clothes. Then we report the next day when we get our orders. I have only bought barely what I need and it cost about 25 pounds more than we are allowed. I shall need to get some more things as soon as I get some pay, which will not be for nearly two months. I am glad I brought what money I did.*
> *Will write to you Tuesday as soon as we know where we are going.*

Roy, Walter and Murray spent the waiting time in London expanding their cultural horizons. During the daytime they visited the museums, art galleries and historical buildings which they had read about back home. In the evenings they went to the theatre where surprisingly enough, given wartime conditions, some of the best-known musicals and plays were running; the quality of the productions equalled and occasionally surpassed what they had seen in New York.

Strand Palace Hotel
Strand, London, W.C.

Dec. 23/15
[Thursday]

Dear Dad,

 Today is our last day in London for some time I expect. We are to report in Chingford tomorrow morning. That is the same place as Stearne is and, of course, we are glad to be with him again but they have not a very rosy story of the manner in which they are treated. Such is life though and that is what is to be expected anyway. We are not to get any pay until February 1st so I see where we must do some close figuring in the meantime.

 I am much better off than lots of the boys who have been throwing away their money expecting more to be waiting for them here as soon as we arrived. Our uniforms cost 21 pounds which was 6 pounds more than we were allowed. We get another 15 pounds later when we complete our training but then we have to buy a stack of leather clothes for flying.

 I will give a list as nearly as I can of what we have bought so far. One coat, one vest and pair of trousers, one overcoat or British warm as it is called, one pair of shoes special for the navy & they are awful looking things, 4 pairs socks, 4 flannel shirts, 1/2 dozen white collars, 2 black ties, gold braid for coat sleeve rings, and birds [aviator's badge] for coat sleeves etc. I shall send some birds home for mamma and Bess as soon as I get some pay. The fellows who are spending so easily now will want to borrow before very long. I am going to have some pictures taken now.

Address - - - - -
C/O The Admiralty
Dewar House
Haymarket
London
England

Chingford aerodrome was 12 miles due north of central London, located between the towns of Enfield and Chingford, and half a mile from the Ponders End railway station. The Chingford reservoir was close to the north boundary of the aerodrome, and although it was an excellent landmark, it was a little too close to the flying field for the comfort of those trainees who could not swim. There were also some tall trees on one side where crows had built their nests.

"How much rent shall we charge him?"

Roy wrote home on 27 December and to his sister Reta on 30 December. The letter to Reta is essentially a summary of the letter home, but it does include some pertinent extra details have been inserted in the letter home where applicable.

RNAS Chingford
Dec. 27/15

Dear Dad,

I have been here now since Dec. 24 but we really have not got down to business as everything is demoralized from Christmas and New Year's leaves. We have really done nothing yet as a result of this. I am very glad as it has given us an opportunity to become accustomed to surroundings and pick up ideas. As officers, we are expected to know everything regarding Naval etiquette, etc. We Canadians are absolutely ignorant of anything and everything naval so we are rather at a disadvantage in that respect but we pick up everything much quicker than the average Englishman.

One thing I am very glad about is that our C.O. is a very fine fellow and thinks the world of all Canadians so we must work hard to live up to his ideas. He has one Canadian officer on his staff.

We cannot get Canadian newspapers over here. If you would send me the STANDARD, the Saturday edition, I would like it very much and so would the boys whom I might wish to show it to.

I wish you would go to the attic where my books are that I brought from Edmonton. I want the one with my trigonometry notes. Take out the pages with the notes and send them to me. Please do this as soon as you get this letter.

The weather is abominable at this season and I hope it is not the same every one. Rain and wind and fog, in fact everything to stop flying. The ground is covered in water. I have not had a flight yet but, of course, we have many duties and things to learn besides flying. There are plenty of machines of different types and lots of mechanics to keep them in order.

Someone borrowed my pen and never returned it which accounts for this peculiar writing.

I cannot tell you what an ordinary day is like at the ship, as we call our flying station, which, by the way, has over 80 officers and 300 men and is the largest in England, because due to the Christmas and New Year's leaves, we have not had an ordinary day since I came.

As a rule we get up in the morning, if there is no early flying, at 6.45. We have divisions at 7.15, i.e. we form up in ranks and answer the roll call. Then there is physical drill for half an hour and breakfast at 8. At 9 we have physical drill again for an hour and then there is a lecture on something such as engines, navigation, naval etiquette and law, trigonometry, carpentry, Morse code or something along those lines. We have lunch at 12.30. We have more lectures and drill in the afternoon till 4.30 then tea. Leave till 8.00

when there is dinner. Our meals are very fair but they are always the same and everything tastes alike. Leave can be obtained 3 nights in 4 which allows you to go out till 11.30, and late leave which allows you till 7.15 next morning can be obtained twice a week, I think. I am not sure as I have not asked for it yet.

Our quarters are very fair, considering. Some fellows are billeted out but I am not. I am in a room (here we call it a cabin) to myself. It is quite small, only about 6 feet by 8. I have only a bed and two chairs as yet but I shall get a chest of drawers and a wash stand. It is not heated so it is not too comfortable that way but it is like all English places except that they have fireplaces.

Dec. 28

We have had a very busy day. There was lots of flying but our instructor is ill so I am not having any but am busy enough. Had lectures all morning and this afternoon was on a shooting party to some ranges about 7 miles away. I am not a very good shot but did not do so badly as lots of the others.

The Englishmen who are training there do not think much of we Canadians but our C.O. has said very nice things about us. When we reported, Sussan, Murray and I, he said he had had many men and many classes of men pass through his hands but, generally speaking, never had he handled such fine men as Canadians. Of course, there are exceptions, in fact several have been dismissed from the service in this station.

The training here may take anything up to a year as this station is greatly overcrowded and getting worse all the time. One Canadian, Evans, the man who told me about the Wright school, has been ill for about three weeks and is really no further ahead than we are.

I am not going to write anything about our flying machines and the accidents, our letters may be censored and there might be trouble. I did not buy a Kodak as pictures are not allowed in the grounds. I do not care to run the risk of losing my chance of a real commission.

I have my civilian clothes all packed and shall keep them till I get well started here for I might get rejected like some of the others. As long as you are respectful to officers   in authority and make fair progress you will get on OK.

The regular navy men are somewhat jealous of the R.N.A.S. for this reason. It takes a man about 8 of the most miserable years to get the curl, as it is called, which is the gold braid ring with a loop in it on the sleeve for the rank of Sub-Lt. We just take our ticket or Pilot's Licence and get it in a few months, so naturally they resent it and rightly I think. We should be a separate branch of the service but of course we do not mind as we get the advantage.

We get two mail deliveries a day from London but nothing has come for me since I arrived here. The Admiralty has not much of a system so perhaps the trouble is there.

We do not get any leave for New Year as we have not been on duty long enough. Stearne has gone to London for his 4 days.

The leave boat going ashore.

As Roy partially explained in his letter, the RNAS used naval terminology for all activities. To leave the station, which was officially "a ship", he had to request permission to go ashore.

The lectures on navigation and on assembling aeroplane frames required knowledge of geometry and trigonometry, hence Roy's request for his high school notes to be sent from Canada. In recent years the Royal Flying Corps and the Royal Naval Air Service had been criticised for only looking among the upper classes for pilots. However, given that most, but not all, of the working class only had schooling up to age fourteen, where else were young men with knowledge of algebra, geometry and trigonometry to be found? In the early days of the war, when an officer with maps sat in the front seat of an observation aeroplane and told the person, whom he called a driver, which way to go, pilots, both in England and Germany, were corporals or sergeants. With the advent of single-seater scouting machines the requirements changed. A prerequisite for pilot training became sufficent knowledge of geometry and trigonometry to be able to learn to navigate, plan an interception course and estimate a deflection angle. The offer of a commission was required to attract such people, but the artillery and the navy seemed to have first pick, hence the recruiting drives in Canada by the RFC and the RNAS.

Chingford, Essex Co.
Jan. 4/16

Dear Dad,

We are having no flying here on account of bad weather but we are very busy just the same. Yesterday we had two very interesting lectures. One in the morning by one of the staff officers on flying without formulae. Another by Major ———, I forget his name, who had just returned from the front, on fighting in the air. It was fine and he gave us a lot of information regarding machine-guns and also the relationship between the German and British airmen. The men have a very great respect for the Germans in some parts of the front but in other parts they do not care anything for them. That is, some places they have real good fliers and other places they are neither fliers nor gentlemen. He also told us why it was that the British required so many more men to hold a trench than the Germans. In the war in South Africa machine-guns proved to be a failure because the men did not understand them, so they were considered useless. As a result, when the present war started, each English regiment only had two machine-guns whereas the Germans had a machine-gun to about every twenty men and all knew how to manage it perfectly. The trouble with the British machine-gun is that it is so delicate an instrument, I am speaking of the Lewis gun now, that it requires expert handling but when it is properly taken care of it is a beauty. I had some work with a machine-gun this morning. It is very interesting and a good experience.

Roy's remarks cover two types of machine guns: the 1914 Vickers 0.303 inch belt-fed machine-gun and the Lewis 0.303 inch drum-fed automatic gun. It was not long before the Lewis gun would also be called a machine-gun. [1]

Chingford
Jan. 10/16

Dear Everybody,

We seem to be progressing very slowly if at all. We fellows who took our ticket in Dayton are much better off than any of the other new men. We are at the head of our list now for flights. However, for the sake of the war and in order to have us finished and away, it would be much better to have more instructors.
I had word from Horace on Jan 5. He was misdirected to Chelmsford instead of Chingford. The C.O. at Chelmsford phoned here and found me. Horace came here the next day, arriving about 1.00 P.M. He looks very healthy and strong but much older. Anyone who has come through what he has cannot help but look older. He does not seem very enthusiastic about the treatment the soldier receives from the officer, in fact he said he would have applied for a commission before this if it were not for the fact that the officers were such a rotten bunch. I am going to try to persuade him to take a commission and then transfer to the Royal Flying Corps.
We are having some very good lectures now on navigation. They are

very interesting and very useful to us in our flying work. I have not had one flight since I have been over here. It is windy and rainy the majority of the time and when not that, it is foggy. I have had a rotten cold ever since coming here but every one else has one so nobody minds you coughing all night to keep them awake.

During 1915, Roy's younger brother Horace had seen hard fighting in the Ypres area trenches, where he had received the minor wound described earlier, but fortunately he had not been in the front lines during a poison gas attack.

The next letter shows how the authorities were tightening the screws on the officer trainees so they would learn to react to the unexpected, whether it be a bomb or a visiting admiral, and by the time they advanced to active service, they would be accustomed to the standard naval routines and strict discipline. The amount they were required to learn about the Royal Navy and its way of doing things may seem strange, but it was precisely their lack of experience and knowledge in these areas which created the resentment and hostility they were encountering. To distil the situation to thimble size: by coming from rich families which could finance the high cost and expense of 240 minutes of pilot training, the Canadians had leapfrogged right over the heads of others who had to suffer eight years of "jump to it or else" service as midshipmen or chief petty officers before reaching the same status. Not only that, but they were now at the head of the list for flying lessons. Money did not merely talk; it apparently shouted.

The first entry in Roy Brown's Royal Naval Air Service Pilot's Flying Log Book states: "Obtained Licence from Aero Club of America in 270 minutes. 50 minutes solo. Nov. 13, 1915. Total time in the air, 5 hrs 20 min."

Chingford
Jan. 17/16

Dear Dad,

I had my first flight yesterday. It was just a "Joy flip," that is a flight just as a passenger but that is a start anyway and I am very glad of that.

We are getting down to real business here now and the station is beginning to be run in a most thorough and business like way. I am very glad as we are here to work and learn all we can and as quickly as we can. One of my old Dayton chums is now flying alone on a certain type of machine, the first type we fly. There are about seven, no eight different types of machines which we have to fly before we get out of here. As you see, there is a lot to learn. After you are a good flier on all those, you are sent on active service. I hope I have some luck when I start because if you smash too many machines, you are kicked out. They do not hesitate very long unless you have shown yourself to be exceptionally brilliant along other lines besides the flying, then you are given a little preference. We will all be able to sleep with an easy conscience when we have our Probationary status lifted off but that will not be for about six months for us yet.

I am to be Duty Officer tomorrow and it is a stiff job. Everybody has to do it once and after that you are only given it as a punishment. You are up and on duty for 48 hours at a stretch with only a few winks of sleep you happen to snatch. You have to know everything that is happening on the whole station. You are on dead jump, inspecting men, making rounds plus meeting all the high officials who come to the station by car or in aeroplanes and then seeing them off. In fact being as busy as it is possible to be. There are a hundred things you are responsible for and if you make a mess of it, you get it from the C.O. good and proper. I hope I get along alright and do not make any mistakes. I have been A.D.C.—Assistant Duty Officer—twice and got along alright both times. That gives you an opportunity to pick up information as to what you should do when you are D.O. I am not worrying, everybody else does it, so I can too. Sometimes you are unlucky and have some exciting things happening, then you do have to move fast.

We have just heard today that all our letters are going to be censored. I would not mind in the least having my letters censored by someone who did not know me and whom I did not know, but ours are to be censored by officers on the station. Some of the officers do not like it at all as it really is not necessary. Some of the officers are billeted and can write whatever they wish. They are to be put on their honour not to write anything that would be of real importance to the service. I am not sure what has caused the change but I have a very good idea. We should not be made to suffer for someone's foolish mistake.

The weather here continues to be very bad but I do not mind at all as I am learning lots of valuable things which will be most useful to me if I ever get so far as active service. There were some officers from foreign active service here on the station yesterday. They wore a uniform more like the military and I like it better, I think, for our daily work, although for a dress uniform, I prefer the navy uniform.

I should have some photographs to send you pretty soon but have not got them from the photographer yet.

I surely am glad I brought over what money I did as it would have been rather awkward without it. I have not received any pay yet and it is more expensive here than in Canada. We are not like the men, we have to pay for our meals and have mess fees, which nobody knows where they go to, but have to be paid before anything else.

On that very day an instructor had taken Roy for a flight in a French aeroplane, Maurice Farman S7 Longhorn Serial Number 3006, and they flew for seven minutes at 2,000 feet. The name Longhorn meant it had a second elevator mounted way out in front on long booms, which gave it a diamond shape when viewed laterally. The Maurice Farman S11 Shorthorn was a later version without the front elevator. The Farman crew sat in tandem cockpits with the engine and propeller behind them. Aeroplanes with the engine and propeller at the rear were known as *pushers*. The Remarks column in Roy's log book states that it was his first flight at Chingford and he flew as a passenger.

The rear position of the engine and propeller on the Farman flying machines had its advantages. Royal Naval Air Service ace fighter pilot William Melville (Mel) Alexander, described flying a Maurice Farman as sheer bliss, and added, *"There was no slipstream from the propeller or castor oil from the engine to hurt the eyes, and the forward visibility was excellent at all times."*

Maurice Farman S7 Longhorn NO. 3006, flown by Roy on 16, 24, 26, 27, 28, 29 and 30 January 1916. Note the second elevator mounted in front.

It may seem strange that Stearne, Roy and the others, who had already received their FAI licences were not given aeroplanes to fly upon arrival but were sent back to school. The simple reason for this was that most elementary training aeroplane at Chingford, the Maurice Farman, with short or long horns, had considerably more power than the Wright Model B, and had its landing speed was about the same as the Model B's flying speed. In addition, the directional control of all the aeroplanes at Chingford required a combination of foot action on a rudder bar to turn, and hand action on an aileron wheel, or a joystick, to bank. The two actions had to be co-ordinated so the aeroplane would neither slide inwards nor skid outwards as it turned. On the Wright brothers' designs the aileron wheel also moved the rudder, and the pilot's feet did nothing. This basic simplicity, so useful for pleasure flying, denied the rapid manoeuvrability required in combat.

The Maurice Farman type of flying machine was nicknamed the *Rumpty* or *Rumpety* becuase of the "rumpety-rumpety-rumpety" noise produced by the wheels as the aeroplane took off or landed on turf. In his book Winged Victory, pilot V.M. Yeates compared flying one to *"sitting inside a birdcage whilst playing a harmonium."* Flying at Chingford was not restricted to calm weather, which was probably more important than the control differences between the Wright designs and the *Rumpty*. Four years before, Claude Grahame-White had demonstrated that a flying machine with a hand-and-foot control system and enough power to fly 50 percent above stalling speed could be flown safely on windy days. Grahame-White had also flown long distances at night, navigating by IFR. In the present jet age these initials mean Instrument Flight Rules, but in 1912 they could be said to have meant "I Follow Railways" or "I Follow Rivers".

In a nut shell, the Canadians had to qualify on aeroplanes that were considerably more complicated and powerful than the Wright Model B they had flown at Dayton, and to do so under adverse weather situations. To survive such conditions required a good knowledge of aerodynamics, airmanship, meteorology and navigation— four subjects not included in the syllabus at the Wright School of Aviation.

Chingford
Jan. 24/16

My Dear Mother,

Received your and Bessie's letters this week and it surely is good to get letters way over here but I do not yet appreciate them as much as I will when I get separated from my old Dayton chums. One of them, Simpson from Toronto, is sick with a cold now and I do not wonder for this is a terrible place. Originally it was a swamp but it has been drained and filled in somewhat, so it is very low and damp and therefore   quite unhealthy.

Yesterday we had the worst fog I have ever experienced. You could not see the width of an ordinary street. It was a real London pea-souper but was purely local, just over the low place around the aerodrome. Murray and Stearne are both well. Stearne should be flying "solo"; i.e. alone, very soon and then it will not be long before he gets into real work. It will be much longer for Murray, Sussan and I as the school is very over-crowded. I had a beautiful flight today, I enjoyed it more than any I have ever had before. The country around here looks perfectly wonderful when it is all flattened out about 3,000 or 4,000 feet below you. Today was so clear and bright that I could see much farther than ever before.

Like every one of the Canadians here I have had my attack of cold. It was really a bad one for a while. Every morning it was a debate whether I should get up or not but I would say to myself perhaps this would be a flying day and I would miss a flip, so up I got.

Until Roy arrived in England, the only gnome he had even seen was a small statue in a garden, and he had only seen castor oil used for medicinal purposes, but now, immersed in a new world, Roy and his chums were about to encounter the Gnome aircraft rotary engine, designed and built in France and lubricated with castor oil.[2] They would also enjoy their first taste of what plentiful horse power could do for a flying machine. As we have learned from Roy's letters, his favourite lectures were those on engines. This was all to the good because his life would depend more upon them than any upon other aspect of flying.

Between 24 and 30 January Roy made twelve flights in Maurice Farman 3006, totalling two hours and five minutes, during which he made steady progress in maintaining a straight course in the air and making takeoffs and landings. The big difference between flying at Dayton and at Chingford was that he now had to cope with the effects of winds up to Force 3 on the Beaufort scale of wind velocities, a naval system of estimating wind speed based upon observation of ocean waves or of bushes and trees on land. In civilian terms, Force 3 was a gentle breeze from 8 to 11 mph. The instinctive reactions needed to fly safely on a windy day could only be acquired through practice.

Chingford
Jan. 30/16

Dear Dad,

We are being worked real hard here now and it is about time, for around Christmas and New Year things were much too slack. They are making up for it now though. I have been getting quite a bit of flying now. I am not on solo work yet but should be as soon as we get suitable weather. It is very foggy here now which makes flying very dangerous for fear of collision in the air.

We Canadians get along splendidly with the English now. We each know the other's peculiarities and make allowances for them. Then, of course, there is always the other kind but everyone treats them the same.

Had my first daylight leave this afternoon since coming here. Sussan, Saunders and I went for a walk through the country as we wanted very much to see it when we got the chance. It is beautifully quaint country around here, funny old cottages all covered with ivy, thatched roofs, queer looking old chimneys and everything to make them look old. Reta would rave about this country for the rest of her allotted span of life. I would like to have the chance to take a trip through it in the summer when it must be splendid.

I have sent my picture home in Royal Naval Air Service uniform. I hope you receive it and like it alright.

Chingford
Feb. 4/16

My Dear Bess,

Received your and papa's letter with the newspaper clippings enclosed. I laughed when I thought how proud Ottawa would be to see old Wright Model B's flying over them. They are a joke compared with a decent machine but what people do not know does not hurt them. I wish I had never seen a Wright machine. Any machine is better to take a licence on than that one.

So far I have only received one Standard, although you say that you send them regularly. I cannot get accustomed to the newspapers here, they do not seem to have any news in them at all.

We are having a regular epidemic of measles particularly but also colds, etc. on the station. This is my first day out of bed since Sunday but I am better now. I had influenza quite severely and this is surely no place to be sick. Nobody to look after you practically at all and the food is rotten. Everything is cold and dirty. Kicking does not do any good, I got better on it so I should worry. Hope I don't get it again, that is all. For two days I could only whisper. Yesterday is the first day since getting it that I had a bite to eat in my mouth.

Just now everyone is lazy as they are all expecting to get a dose of the measles. Some poor beggars are darn sick when they have it too. They all get rushed off to an isolation hospital as soon as it develops.

I received my first pay, 44 pounds. It seems quite a bit but when I start paying for my clothes it will look pretty small. They charge something fierce over here. They tell us it is only since the war began though.

Roy Brown in Royal Naval Air Service uniform.

The reference above to the antiquated Wright Model B used in some flying schools in Canada and the United States is not being completely fair to the aeroplane itself. Despite the shortcomings of the Model B, it had enabled Roy to acquire the ability to leave all his cares behind him on the ground while he communed with the birds in the sky. Then after such enjoyment he could return whence he came at a time and place of his own choosing. That, plus the confidence he could do so safely, was the Wright School's contribution to his future.

On 8 February Roy spent twenty minutes of dual instruction making take-offs and landings in Maurice Farman S7, RNAS No. 2983, which in Chingford parlance would have been "circuits and bumps in a Rumpty." Flight Lieutenant F. Warren Merriam, a well-known pre-war aviator, thereupon approved him for solo flight. Roy's log book informs us he flew solo that afternoon in a west-southwest wind blowing at Force 3 in Maurice Farman S7, RNAS No. 146. [3]

Maurice Farman S7, No. 146 flown by Roy on 8, 9 and 10 February 1916. Although resembling a Shorthorn, it was actually an early S7 Longhorn modified by the removal of the forward elevator and fitted with a 70hp Renault inline engine. Note the Longhorn in the background. Photograph taken in March 1914 at Yarmouth with Commander Charles Rumney Samson in the cockpit.

Chingford
Feb. 11/16

Dear Dad,

I am feeling fine now, never felt better in my life. I weigh about 170 pounds now and don't see how the machines ever get me off the ground.

We are getting more flying here now. I am flying solo, i.e., alone, and got in a couple of hours from Sunday to Wednesday, half as much time as I had in two and a half months in Dayton. It surely is fine when the weather is half decent here. I would not be at all surprised if we are sent away from here pretty soon. We are all in a hurry to see where.

I had a dandy flight yesterday morning. I was up about 3,000 feet when the sun rose and it was beautiful to see it from there. It was a perfectly steady day so I did not have to bother much with the machine but was able to enjoy looking around the country. You certainly have to work hard when there is good flying weather but I am only too glad to do it because we feel we are getting ahead and really doing something.

I was in London yesterday having a new jacket fitted. I guess that is my last time this month as I am broke as far as cash goes. I have opened an account at The Bank of Montreal and as soon as my commission is confirmed and I get settled at my new work, I shall send home what money I can and have you look after it for me.

Naval officers had to know their ship inside out, for in battle, when others had either been killed or disabled, the survivors had to fight the ship. Roy may have been in the air arm, but naval tradition and regulations still applied. He had to learn his "ship" in detail and due to this extra training and knowledge, the pilots in the Royal Naval Air, rightly or wrongly, considered themselves better trained than those in the Royal Flying Corps, which was part of the army. Certainly, in 1917 when the RFC, under fierce onslaught by the Germans, requested help from the RNAS over the trenches, the survival rate of RNAS pilots who had come straight from an aerial combat training school was much higher than the rate of those who had not.

On 12 February Roy moved forwards to the advanced training

stage. The machines he would now fly had the engine and propeller at the front and were therefore known as *tractors*, which meant that the propeller pulled the aeroplane through the air instead of pushing it. He began with Avro 500, 504B and 504C two-seaters. At one time these types had been in front-line military service. One Avro 500, Serial Number 939, was the machine in which Flight Lieutenant. E. Bentley Beauman tried to find Zeppelin LZ38, commanded by Hauptmann Erich Linnarz, over Southend on the night of 9/10 May 1915. This venerable aeroplane had come down so far it would no longer go up more than a few feet and was merely used for trainees to learn how to taxi a tractor aeroplane; it was definitely not for flight. Once trainees could steer it straight, they moved on to making takeoffs followed immediately by landings, all without leaving the field. These short hops into the air were termed 'straights' and the worn-out No. 939 had been nicknamed The Hopper.

German Army Zeppelin LZ38. Note the machine-gunners on top at the front end. A forced-air duct diverted any escaping hydrogen.

Chingford
Feb. 17/16

Dear Everybody,

    I have been having a beautiful cold and have been coughing badly the last few days. There has been no flying this week except Sunday as it has been fearfully windy especially yesterday when it reached 50 to 60 knots.
    We are busier than ever though as they are making us pass all kinds of examinations before we get out of here. I have to pass exams in Engines, Morse code, Semaphore signalling, Navigation, Armament, which is a big subject, Aeroplane construction and I don't know what else. All are pretty stiff examinations so you can see what we are up against. This is the only station which is conducted this way. We are really very lucky in a way because we will know something worth while when we get out. There is a rumour current around here now, but I do not put much faith in it, that all the officers in this service who do not go onto seaplanes will be transferred to the Royal Flying Corps, which is the army flying service. I am not at all keen about seaplanes or the work which they are given, I want something with more activity. Seaplanes may be sent to some old coast station and left on patrol work for the rest of the war, I surely would not like that. I would much sooner go to France and do work over the trenches. Although that is much more dangerous, I would prefer it. I guess it will be rather a nervous job with 8 inch high explosive shells breaking under you but very few machines are brought down by anti-aircraft guns.
    It is nearly impossible to write with all this row going on around me. There are seven officers here all around the table talking and laughing so I can hardly think and will have to give up.

There was something behind the rumour, but it was not quite what the trainees were hearing. The Lords of the Admiralty had earlier realized that seaplanes could no longer be used for protecting the cross-channel troopships and for attacking enemy installations along the Belgian coast. Seaplanes, with their bulky floats, could not manoeuvre rapidly in the air and were now being faced with the latest German high-performance landplanes. Reports ending *"The seaplane failed to return"* were becoming far too frequent. The answer seemed to be for the RNAS also to use high-performance landplanes. This was not quite so suicidal as it first appears since most of the work took place near ships, and with the low landing speeds of the era, a glide down onto the water in a landplane that would float for a while generally limited resulted in an easy rescue. Then be a sopping wet pilot would be dripping dirty sea water onto the squeaky clean deck of a ship, while muttering imprecations on the mechanics who had maintained his engine and the engineers who had designed it. Roy and many of his colleagues were going to test the new philosophy.

In Roy's next letter we see how his reflexes, which had been conditioned to the obsolete control system used at Dayton, nearly dumped him in the soup, or a most watery version thereof.

Chingford
Feb. 21/16

Dear Mother,

I have not written anywhere for quite some time for we have been having a rather bad time of it and everyone is feeling in the blues. I cannot tell you what has been happening but it was not pleasant. War is hell alright.

I did a stunt today that should never have been done. I was flying a machine which is only supposed to go 10 to 20 feet off the ground as her engine is very poor. By the time I got 20 feet off the ground in her I was so far down the field that if I had landed it, it would have been in a large pond which the heavy rains have put there. So I went up and made a circuit in her, just getting her high enough to miss the trees. It was a close call but I got away with it alright. This machine has a different system of control from what I have been used to, that is why we have to be very careful when trying to control her. Another thing is that it is a tractor and I have always flown pushers. There is a very material difference between the two. Straights are very hard for me because I never did any in my life. By straights I mean taking off on the first part of the field, flying straight along just above it and then landing before the end. I would much sooner do circuits as that is what I am accustomed to do. The trouble with straights is that everything has to be done in so short a time that it makes it very difficult. We all have to learn though. We do it without an instructor which makes it much better for us as we get all the experience ourselves.

This weather does not seem to agree with me. It is so damp that when it gets cold it seems to go right through you. I never seem to get cold in the air except my feet which get cold both mentally and physically quite often.

Murray and Stearne are both well and getting along fine. All the boys except one who trained with us at Dayton have done very well so far. I touch wood when I say it. I hope we continue to get along well as the other Wright pupils who came over before us did not give our school a very good name. Of course, we are at a very great disadvantage learning on the type of machine we did but we are making the best of it.

Some time ago you sent me some newspaper clippings about the Stinsons starting a school in Ottawa to train with old Wright 'B's. If the officials ever wrote to some of the Wright pupils who trained on them and then came over here and had to start again, I believe we would convince them of the absolute futility of trying to train pilots for war purposes on that particular type of machine. I hope for the country's sake and for that of the men who train, they do not decide to open a school of Wright 'B's.

My eyes are very sore tonight from flying and oil getting on my face. Guess I shall slip off to bed.[4]

Roy's log book entry tells us that the machine in which he just missed the trees was "The Hopper", Avro 500, No. 939, and that he hopped it thirteen times between 12 and 29 February. The instructor appeared to have been somewhat displeased by the unauthorized solo flight on his fifth hop, and the remarks column in Roy's log book for 21 February states: *"Circuits & straights, very crude."*

Surprisingly enough, one of the most difficult things to learn on an aeroplane with a tail skid or tail wheel is to "drive" it in a straight line on the ground. Airfields, in those days, were nearly always square in shape so that takeoffs and landings could be made directly into the wind. This helped the aeroplanes to run straight because they did not have brakes or a tail wheel to assist with directional control when the airflow over the rudder was insufficient for steering. Therefore, at takeoff time, ground crew members of that particular flight would run alongside, guiding the wingtips until the aeroplane had gained enough speed for the pilot to obtain directional control. Upon landing, ground crew would run out to catch hold of the wing tips as speed was lost. Whether those detailed for this duty were exempted from the morning physical training sessions is unknown.

Strangely enough, it was the need for such physical exertion which lay behind the use of coloured canvas discs to cover the wheel spokes. In most squadrons each flight used a different colour and when an aeroplane was seen coming in to land, the first thing all duty ground crew members did was to look at the undercarriage and try to discern the hue of the wheel covers.

As an aid to learning how to control the taxiing speed via the engine cut-out button and to steer the aeroplane at the same time, the French l'Armée de l'air used worn-out old Blériots with time-expired engines and a couple of metres sawn from each wing tip; they were nicknamed *Penguins*. On the first day of taxiing lessons for a new group of officer students, every rigger, fitter or mechanic who could sneak away from his duties for a little while would find a vantage point from which to watch the fun and the occasional collisions. It was the best comedy show in town, and better still, it was free.

Flying straights was a serious business, for takeoff and landing accidents were almost as frequent as combat losses. The Air Service's ace fighter pilot, Flight Commander Robert Alexander Little, DSO and bar, DSC and bar (47 victories including shared), was once "congratulated" by his Commanding officer for having destroyed five aeroplanes in one week; two of which belonged to the enemy.

"The Hopper", Avro 500 No. 939, in which Roy unintentionally made a circuit on 21 February 1916

Chingford
Mar. 4/16

Dear Dad,

    I am taking a special armament class now. Can see nothing but bombs and darts and guns around me all the time. I like the armament work very much. It is very interesting and very useful. Outside of the flying, it is the most interesting study we have. Engines are good too but we do not get enough of them.
    I believe this is the start of the rainy season here now. It is raining nearly all the time. Our field was completely covered with water yesterday and today, by evening, it will be the same again.
    You can change my address now to,

Randvol House
34a Charing Cross Road
London W.C.
England

In a letter of even date to his sister, Reta, Roy added the following:

> *This morning they did try flying one of the machines but when it landed it stuck in the mud and turned right upside down. Luckily the pilot was not hurt. We have all kinds of accidents here but very few fatalities. I have only seen one. I cannot tell you about it though.*

The fatality which Roy saw was probably the accident to a Maurice Farman S7 Longhorn which occurred while he was at Chingford. The aeroplane was flying along quite happily with an instructor and a pupil on board when suddenly the propeller broke. A flying blade cut through one of the tail booms and jammed the controls. The aeroplane immediately nose-dived to the ground killing the instructor, Flight Lieutenant Louis Morgan, and his pupil, Flight Officer Randolph Seed. Here we possibly have the explanation of the *"everyone is feeling in the blues"* remark at the beginning of Roy's letter of 21 February.

The letter to Reta also contains the following addition: "Stearne is with me on the armaments work so we do our studying together and argue everything out so that we learn far more and learn it more thoroughly."

Beginning on 12 March Roy received dual flying instruction from Flight Lieutenant Hayward in Avro 504Bs No.1030 and 1044.

Avro 504B No. 1030 flown by Roy on 12, 18 and 19 March 1916.*

On 19 March Flight Lieutenant John Stanley Mills released him for solo flying on Avro 504s—intentionally this time. Roye flew several times to Hainault aerodrome where he practised circuits and bumps. The Avro 504Cs used were No. 1479, 1480, 8596, 1032 and 1481. Roy describes this type of machine as a fast scout, which indeed it had been in 1915, but it was now outclassed in combat by the latest German designs. However, being a well-designed, docile and reliable aeroplane, it had won a new life as an advanced trainer. After the war the type was downgraded to the role of basic trainer and, with several updates, served in the RAF as such until 1928.[5]

Chingford
Mar. 12/16
Dear Dad,

Everybody is wild on this station now over the way engines are taken care of. It is a crime to ask a chap to take up a machine with its engine in the condition some of ours are in. Everybody has been fairly lucky so far but there will be a smash someday with someone landing in the reservoir. This is a poor field for learning in one way but in another it is very good. Because it is so hard to land, it makes a chap a better flyer.

I was in London last night and have found a splendid place to go to when I am in town. It is the Royal Automobile Club which makes all overseas officers honorary members. They have a beautiful pool, oh in fact, everything you could wish for. You can get away from the rush and have a quiet time.

The hours of service obtainable from a particular type of engine, between overhauls, varied considerably: some required complete dismantling every twenty-five hours; others would run for seventy-five hours. The situation is reminiscent of the engines of German and British jet-propelled aeroplanes used at the end of the Second World War; in both cases, deferred maintenance on the ground meant problems in the air.[6]

Chingford
March 19/16

Dear Dad,

Things are going much better here now. I have had a bad cold on and off ever since leaving home but I am getting acclimatized now. The last few days we have had some really decent weather and if it lasts a couple of weeks more, I will be away from here. For a while I thought I was never going to learn to fly and wondered what was going to become of me but I feel different now and am getting my confidence back again.

Logically, it is when I feel all right physically that I fly the best. Of course, I am no stunter. Do not know whether I shall ever loop or more. Don't see much use in it myself except that it must give a fellow confidence. About all I do is make steep turns. It feels funny to look at your machine and see how it is turned way up on one wing. I started solo on the first real machine we fly at this station today. No use giving the name, it would not mean anything to you anyway. They are a tractor and certainly fly beautifully. The reason is they are built much more precisely and are of a much better design than those I have been on up to the present. A pusher bobs about no matter how you fly it but these, oh they are beautiful. You bank them for a turn and they stay exactly where you put them until you change the position of your controls again. The others require the use of the controls all the time in a turn.

I had a funny sight before me today. I was clipping along about 80 miles an hour when a poor gull got in front of me. The way that poor bird struggled to get out of the way was funny. I almost imagined I could see a scared expression on its face the way it fluttered and seemed so excited. It lost its head completely but managed to stay out of the way alright. I was more pleased than it was, as it is very dangerous. The bird is liable to be struck by the propeller, which would of course break, and then there would be trouble in bunches. What I find the most difficult is to judge my descent properly to come into the field to land. It requires that you know exactly what your machine will do and how strong the wind is to come down from four or five thousand feet with your engine off. I always come short of my field but that is so much better than the other way as then you can come in alright by turning your engine on again. Don't know whether all this junk will be interesting or not or whether I have put it so that you can make sense out of it.

Actually Roy was acquiring a very bad and dangerous habit. In the case of engine failure, there would be no correction available for a short approach. The type of machine he now flew, the Avro 504, was perfectly capable of making a sideslip to lose height rapidly; therefore, to err on the high side was the safe way.

One of Roy's friends from Carleton Place, Douglas Findlay, was following in his footsteps. He was at the Stinson Flying School in Texas. Roy received another letter from Douglas Findlay in which he said,

Katherine Stinson was out at the field one day and looped the loop and flew upside down but she used a machine of her own, not the old boats that

we use. *She also flew at night with fireworks attached to her machine and made a big S-A for Stinson Aviation in the sky.*

Katherine Stinson in her 1916 Partridge-Keller Looper exhibition machine.

It would not be too long before Roy would be flying a machine capable of doing the same.

By now some idea of Roy Brown's character has become apparent from the correspondence. He had absorbed a great deal of morality and uprightness from his parents, plus the willingness to work hard to achieve a particular goal. His Aunt Blanche's strong views along the same lines had reinforced his home training. It has been remarked that aeroplane pilots with bad characters are few and far between, apparently because the self-discipline and the patience, as well as the amount of studying required to fly safely, do not appeal to those who prefer to do things in a lazy or haphazard manner.

The local newspaper in Carleton Place had carried a report on his brother Horace's experiences in the army, which caused Morton and Mary to feel that news of Roy's progress would also be of interest to the community. So, with the best intentions, they submitted the photograph of Roy in his RNAS uniform as a patriotic news item. Unfortunately, photographs of Stearne Edwards and Murray Galbraith, who were equally deserving, were not printed, which proved more than a little embarrassing to Roy.

Chingford
Mar. 22/16

Dear Mother,

I want to do what they call "strafing" over here about something you have done. Please do not ever again give my photograph to any paper for publication. I do not like it and as it is me who is made to be discussed, I should have some say in the matter.

Things are going much better at the station now and I hope they continue so. They do not treat us like they did before but treat us now as if we do know a few things and did not merely come over here for a pleasure trip. I am flying a fast scout machine alone now and it certainly is beautiful. There is not likely to be any flying for a while now as we have had more rains again and our field is practically under water. All I need now is two weeks of good weather and I should be finished here.

At last I am in billets in Chingford at a very nice home. Two ladies are here whose husbands are both at the front. It certainly is a change from all the dirt down there to such a nice place as this with all the comforts. They treat me just like one of the family and I certainly appreciate it. I will be sorry when I have to leave.

Roy Brown outside his billet in Chingford.

The following week, the powers that be on earth decided to fool those upstairs who send the rain for the farmers; they should have known better than to try.

Chingford
Mar. 26/16

Dear Dad,

They are doing their best to hurry us forward now but the weather will not give them a chance. On Friday the weather was good so, our field still being flooded, they decided to take   some machines to a good field about 10 miles from here. It was a very hard place to pick out from the air and everyone seemed to get lost or have engine trouble. I did not fly over but went in a car. We got lost for nearly an hour but finally got there. When we did, there were no machines for us to fly so after waiting for an hour we came back. It was like going to a picnic and I enjoyed it very much. Saturday morning I was told to fly one over but as things turned out I did not have to as the weather got bad and we did not go. I sure was glad, for the machine I was to take had a bad engine and it is no fun flying when you are wondering at what moment your engine is going to stop.

Stearne and I have just about the same time in and we are trying to work it so that we will finish up together and be moved away together.

I have this Saturday afternoon and Sunday off. I went to town last night, had a swim & went to a theatre. Slept in this morning & it surely felt good. Am going out for a walk with Edwards now.

The most common engine ailments at that time resulted from the young technology in certain areas[7]. As additional complication, aircraft engines and their fuel systems had to be capable of being operated on their sides or backs and had to be lightweight in construction.

Chingford
Mar. 29/16
[Wednesday]

Dear Dad,

Our field is flooded again but Monday I got in nearly two hours flying. It was a very bumpy and windy day, the worst I was ever up in. Did not know for a while how I was going to get down but I did after some weird manoeuvring. It was very peculiar, as a rule the higher you get, the less bumps there are but Monday it was the very opposite. At 3,000 feet it surely was awful.

I guess the next day there is flying I will have a cross country flight as our field is not or will not be suitable for flying for some time. Murray is being moved to another station in the northern part of England, Cranwell is the name of the place. He is to report there April 1st. Our Dayton bunch is quickly becoming broken up. It is a good station Murray is going to. He may be a little longer getting sent on active service but that is all the more advantage for him as he will have had that much more experience. Every time I go up I learn something new.

While RNAS pilots under training at Chingford were suffering under these make-shift arrangements, an improved training station was being built at Cranwell in Lincolnshire with good accommodations and an excellent airfield.

On 31 March at 12.45 Roy flew Avro 504B No. 1032 down to Hainault Aerodrome with instructor Mr Mills on board. The following day he again flew to Hainault but in Avro 504C No. 1480.

"Our field is flooded again." The RNAS version of walking the plank.

Avro 504B No. 1032, flown by Roy on 31 March 1916. Note the hoops beneath the ends of the lower wings to protect the ailerons and wing tips should the pilot lose directional control on the ground.*

This later version of the 504 did not have hoops under the wings, and Roy had his first landing mishap in England. In the Remarks column of his log book he wrote: *"Broke king post on aileron by landing too fast and having to turn on ground."* This was probably caused by the fact that Roy had recently been flying in Force 4 winds (moderate breeze, 12 to 16 mph), but on that morning the air was perfectly calm. Having become accustomed to landing into strong winds, he forgot that his groundspeed would be much faster without them. When he saw the that Avro would not stop before striking the boundary hedge, he deliberately made a rapid U-turn, known to aviators as a *ground loop*. Roy's quick thinking saved the propeller and the engine, but the outside wing tip touched the ground as the Avro leaned over in the turn. This resulted in minor damage to the aileron mounting. Had he been flying an Avro 504B, it is highly probable that no damage whatsoever would have occurred.

Another view of Avro 504B No. 1032 flown by Roy on 31 March 1916. The protective hoop beneath the lower wing tip stands out well.

On 2 April Roy was on his way to Woodford in Avro 504C No. 8596 when engine trouble occurred. In the Remarks column of his log book he wrote: *"Engine stopped 2,000 ft over Woodford. Landed in field which appeared alright but had 3 inches water under grass. Broke one wheel otherwise alright. Came down fast to get into field."* A side slip would have enabled him to lose height without gaining speed. [8]

On that same day Roy began dual instruction on the B.E.2C. This tractor aeroplane had a stationary engine; namely, the crankcase and cylinders were fixed to the aeroplane, and the propeller was fixed to the crankshaft. It had a true carburetor with proper throttle control from idling speed to full power; therefore an engine cut-out switch, also known as a *blip switch*, was not required. It also had a derisory nickname: *The Quirk.* [9]

A typical B.E.2C., a contemporary of the Wright Model C design. This particular B.E.2C, No. 8496, was stationed at RNAS Manston until it was destroyed in an accident there on 2 November 1917.

On 5 April, after twenty-five minutes of circuits with Flight Lieutenant Fowler in B.E.2C No. 967, Roy was released for solo flight on a B.E.2C. The short period of dual instruction, coupled with the major differences between the Avro 504 and the B.E.2C, tells us all we need to know about Roy's progress as a pilot.

Later on the same day he flew circuits at Chingford in B.E.2Cs No. 1193 and 1122. He then practised bomb dropping from No. 1107.

On Thursday, 6 April, an early morning flight in B.E.2C No. 1107 ended unhappily after sixty-five minutes in the air.

Chingford
April 8/16
[Saturday]

Dear Dad,

I had quite an experience Thursday and as a result I am laid up in my billet with a sore back. Thursday morning I was told to go up and see how high I could get. I left at 6.45 and had not got up to 500 feet when I struck clouds. They were fairly thin and went to 1,000 feet. At 2,000 feet I ran into great heavy ones going up to 3,000. Above that all was clear but I could see absolutely nothing as far as the earth was concerned. I did not feel very comfortable as I knew I should get lost, so I did not go so very high. Went up to about 6,000 or 6,500 and decided I had better see if I could find where I was. I came down below the upper clouds and could see through the others very little distance but could not see any place I knew, so I began to look for a suitable place to land. Was just looking around when the engine began to go bad. I was told by one of the mechanics when I went up that I had enough fuel in my lower tank for two hours but I knew by the sound that I was out of fuel. This type of machine has two tanks and you have to pump from the upper to the lower one. I started to pump but the pump would not work so my engine finally stopped.

I did not come out of the clouds till about 500 feet and of course had practically no chance to pick a place to land. The fields under me were not bad but I could not make the first one because I was too high but the second one was just about right. I looked around the front to see that everything was alright and saw I was going straight for a tree so I had to turn quickly. In doing so I lost so much height that I hit the hedge with my landing chassis and dove down on my nose and of course had a rather bad smash. I walked to the nearest place to find a telephone and got a motor truck and a carpenter party to come. It was just four o'clock when I got back to Chingford. I felt alright till I got out of the truck and then I could not straighten up. My back had apparently been strained so I was sent here to my billet and went to bed. It feels some better to-day. I have been downstairs but do not feel like walking about much. Will be O.K, soon though, I hope. Do not worry as, if you have not received a cable, I will be alright before you get this. The head of my flight was very nice to me and exonerated me from any blame. To use his own word, "Damn hard luck" is what he said because I really did not have half a chance to get out of it. Such is life though.

You need not bother sending me anything as I am treated like a prince here in this billet. Stearne has been sent to another station, he leaves tomorrow. We had it all fixed up so we would be sent together but my getting hurt has spoiled that. I am going to try and be sent to that station if I can.

Must get off to bed now as am tired sitting up.

From 500 feet above the fields of Stoneyfields Farm, about ten miles west of Chingford, there was not much time for Roy to think or room for him to manoeuvre without engine power. [10]

On Friday, 10 April, the commanding officer went to Roy's billet to see how he was doing. Roy really appreciated his kindness; the commanding officer of a station that size was perforce a very busy man.

The pre-flight procedures at Chingford in April 1916 are unknown, but composed with today's training something was clearly amiss. Nowadays it is drummed into a pilot that he must accept no-one's word as to the quantity of fuel present in any tank; he must open the filler cap(s) and see for himself. He must personally check any fitted fuel pumps by operating them while observing the fuel pressure gauge.[11] Whatever the routine at the time, Roy appears to have taken off in B.E.2C No. 1107, trusting someone else's word concerning the quantity of fuel on board. It is doubtful he repeated that mistake.

A B.E.2C pilot with his hand on the manual fuel pump. Note the electrically operated Holts flare for night-time landings, which is mounted beside the protective hoop beneath the wing tip, and the bomb rack beneath the fuselage. The front seat is for the observer.

In early 1916, German airships began another series of raids over various cities of England. One of the intentions, possibly the main one, was to create a public outcry. The German hope was that the British government would then be forced to recall some of its best aircraft squadrons from the battle in France and employ them in England for home defence. This tactic apparently met with some success as there was an outcry in the newspapers, demanding that the government put a stop to the German attacks. In truth, considerable effort had been expended by the Royal Flying Corps and the Royal Navel Air Service, during which a surprising discovery had been made. Although airships at night might be clearly visible from the ground against a starlit sky, they were most difficult to find from the air unless the glow from their engine exhaust gases was sighted. Unfortunately, only too often the glow seen by an RNAS pilot seeking a reported German airship came from an RFC aeroplane on the same quest, and vice versa. Worse still, neither pilot had known the other was airborne.

One night, a lost RNAS pilot searching for an aerodrome—any aerodrome to land on—had triggered air-raid alarms over a wide area along the south coast. The reason was extremely simple: the RFC, when queried, had denied having any machine airborne over that part of England, and the authorities immediately telephoned an order to every aerodrome in the area to extinguish all lighting, to foil an imminent enemy attack.

To stop this dangerous and confusing duplication of effort, during the hours of darkness the RNAS was made solely responsible for attacking airships over the sea and the RFC for those over the land. Therefore, for a commanding officer to send up aeroplanes to attack a Zeppelin cruising over his own station was strictly forbidden. In addition the sole result of sending up some of his worn-out training machines, probably without cockpit lighting or landing flares, would most likely be two or three injured or dead airmen. During fruitless standing patrols at night, the losses in aeroplanes and pilots due to engine failures, lost pilots, landing accidents and the ilk had been unacceptably high, and the idea of training school participating in air defence was abandoned.

Sopwith Pup B849 of 198 (Night) Training Squadron at Rochford on the morning after the night before.*

The plain truth was that until aircraft that were properly equipped for night fighting and able to climb fast enough to respond to a sighting came into service, the game was not worth the candle.

In the case of the RNAS Flying Training School at Chingford, for valid security reasons the commanding officer had not explained the situation to the trainee pilots. Nor had he told them their training would continue until up-to-date aircraft, currently under construction, became available to the RNAS squadrons for use against the enemy. Experienced pilots could recognize distant danger and knew when to fight and when to run; thus, they could still perform useful work with outdated equipment. Newly trained pilot's between, stood little chance; their lives would simply be thrown away.

Chingford
April 17/16

Dear Dad,

I don't want this letter shown to anyone because I am going to write something I really should not, even if nearly every other member of the RNAS agrees with me. I got a letter from Alice [Pickup] in which she says she had heard from many that the RNAS never gets into active service. Have you heard that also? For if you haven't, I will say it now that to a large degree what she wrote is true. Stearne and I had a long talk yesterday and as a result I am writing to you today to ask what you would do in my place.

It seems very funny, nobody can understand it here nor even advance a theory that explains it, but the fact remains that the authorities in charge of the RNAS do not want to allow the pilots to do anything, not even when the Zeps come over. All the incidents I am going to tell you are facts that I have either seen myself or heard from an authority that could not be questioned.

At Eastchurch, which is a very large station on the Isle of Sheppy at the mouth of the Thames, a Zep came over there and stayed there for at least 20 minutes. No pilot was allowed to go up after it though they simply begged their C.O. to let them for they would have had a good chance of getting it. This is a typical incident.

But what interests me more: They hurry us through our training here as fast as they can and then send us to another station where we are given exactly the same stuff over again. Then they send us to a war station on the coast somewhere and there we remain. There are fellows who came over as the very first graduates of the Curtiss school who have never been able to get an opportunity to do a thing. They fly every day that the weather is fit but they just tour around to keep themselves from forgetting how. This is not the case with everybody but it is what usually occurs.

I will tell you of another peculiar case concerning a fellow who was a consulting engineer to a big firm in Russia and who is now a Sub-Lieut.RNAS. He was at our station a short time ago just doing nothing. He had come from being C.O. of a small station not far from here. He is an exceptionally clever chap and a good pilot having done night flying with a machine loaded with bombs, etc., to try for Zeps. Now that officer is at Eastchurch sitting in lectures under a Chief Petty Officer being told how bombs work. Edwards and Beasley are in the same class and so would I be if it were not for my back.

Do you wonder that all the probationary officers are getting tired of the service? We may go months and never even be confirmed in our rank. At the first of the war when a chap did not have half the experience I have, he was sent to the front and now we do nothing. I hope against hope that there will be a change soon but it has been that way as long as I have been over here and seems to be getting worse instead of better.

When I have passed all my exams for the second time I shall go to the Admiralty and ask to be allowed to do something useful. If they send me off to some war station in England where I can get no chance of doing anything, I shall resign. If I cannot do anything else, I can enlist as a private in the army and do something that way.

I realize fully that somebody has to stay here and defend England against Zeps but it is no defence to have machines, bombs and pilots and not to allow them to leave the ground when the enemy comes.

Enough of that. My back seems to be very slow in coming around. It tires very easily and leaves me all in. It feels pretty decent when I get up in the morning but before I am dressed it begins to get weak and sore. I surely am not going to fly again till I feel all O.K. as there is no use taking any chances.

The above letter, posted off the station, was unsigned. If the civilian overseas mail inspector saw it, perhaps he agreed with the content and read it in a Nelsonian manner—with a blind eye.

On the assumption that the date of the Eastchurch sighting was the night of 5/6 March, the airship would have been the Zeppelin L13 commanded by Kapitänleutnant Heinrich Mathy. We now know that he was hopelessly lost and was circling around at about 10,000 feet, trying to identify a decent landmark. Nothing which he saw below resembled his map, which is not surprising; he was about 150 miles south of his calculated position. The Zeppelin and Schutte-Lanz airship captains were learning the hard way that the winds at high altitudes are very strong and often blow in the reverse direction to those at ground level.

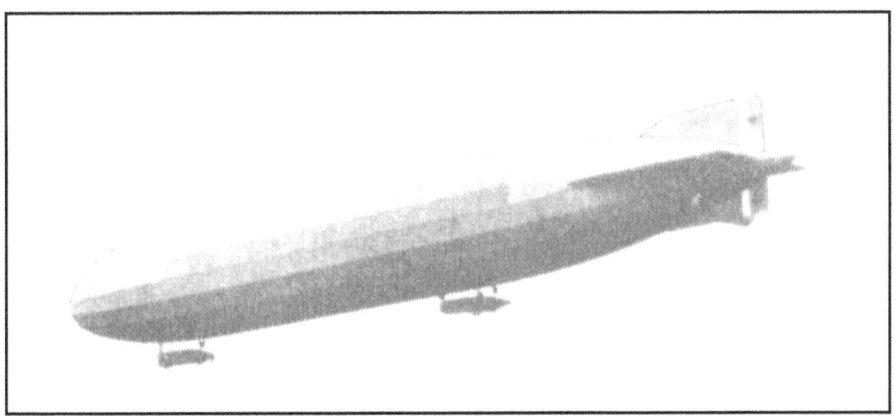

German Navy Zeppelin L13.*

Actually the commanding officer at Eastchurch had allowed Flight Sub-Lieutenant. C.C. Wyllie in B.E.2C No. 987 to hunt the airship that night, but by the time the worn-out aeroplane had struggled to 7,000 feet, Kapitänleutnant Mathy, 3,000 feet higher, had finally realised why a river, which until then he had believed to be the Humber, resembled the Thames to a most remarkable degree, and he had departed for home.

Fortunately for Wyllie and the commanding officer who had disobeyed orders, B.E.2C No. 987 returned safely.

The daily, monotonous but highly successful work of the RNAS in its principal home waters task of keeping the eastern half of the English Channel safe for Allied ships did not make newspaper headlines. Its days of fame over the western front were yet to come.

Chingford
April 19/16

Dear Dad,

You speak about me getting my picture taken again. That kind of thing costs money and at the moment I have just enough to scrape by. If I am sent out of England, I shall have to get a khaki uniform and then I will get another picture taken, full figure. Stearne and I have discovered that by not going to town too often and by being careful, we can get along on our pay.

I have not been back on duty yet but hope and expect to be there the first of next week. I have missed very little flying as the weather has been typical of their April over here, all rain and wind.

On 2 May, Roy was admitted to Chatham Hospital for "treatment to a back injury."

Chatham Hospital
May 3/16

Dear Dad,

I am in hospital for the first time in my life. I hope mother will not worry too much. I will be well looked after here although it will be rather monotonous and somewhat lonesome. It is just as I told you, a strain of the muscles of the back. I feel it most in the small of my back.

I will be here about a month I expect as nobody ever gets out of here in less no matter what is the matter, so don't worry.

Royal Naval Hospital
Chatham
May 11/16

Dear Mother,

They are treating my back with radiant heat as well as massage. The heat tries to make a rib roast out of me but it has not yet. It seems to be a little better but very slightly.

I saw Howard's name in the papers which, by the way, have been coming more regularly. Give him my congratulations, he has the brains for all of us.

R.N. Hospital
Chatham
15/5/16

Dear Dad,

On May 9 they took an X-ray of my back, little expecting that it would show anything. The Fleet Surgeon gave his opinion yesterday and I am writing this to let you know what he said, no more, no less. The vertebra of the backbone have little pieces of bone sticking out each side. One of those pieces on the left hand side just at the small of my back seems to be broken. It is a green break and not very serious as far as permanent injury is concerned but it will take a long time to get better. In fact they told me it would be 3 or 4 months after I get up and out of here before I will be ready to fly. One of the stewards brought my X-ray plate to me (which is against orders) and it shows quite plainly this little piece of bone twisted the wrong way. Tell mother not to worry as it is getting better and seems to be responding to the treatment.

While Roy was in hospital at Chatham, Douglas Findlay and Stearne Edwards were frequent visitors. When he received the official medical diagnosis, he asked Findlay to send a cable to his father:

31 May 1916

Mortimer Brown
Carleton Place
Ontario Canada

    Muscles torn, transverse process twisted, two months hospital minimum, home leave impossible, Brown.

The hospital also began treating rheumatism in Roy's left arm: the result of the cold accommodations he had lived in at Dayton and Chingford, plus sometimes having to sleep in a damp bed. He had became quite bored with having nothing to do all day, every day, but his situation was about to improve.

R.N. Hospital
Chatham
16/6/16

Dear Dad,

    The Fleet Surgeon came in with the Surgeon General, a Rear Admiral, to have a consultation. They examined my back and then we had a talk. They asked me if I wanted to fly any more. Of course you see what that meant. If I had said I wasn't over keen about it, they would have invalided me out. I told them I liked flying very much and that as soon as I was fit I wanted to get back to it. The result was that he recommended three months' leave.
    My back is much better now than it was, I can walk much straighter than I did. I will cable you when I leave hospital and send details by letter.
    I have just received the refund from the Admiralty for my tuition fee at Dayton and am O.K. now for money.

By 4 July, Roy had improved enough to begin planning where he would go for his discharge leave, which had been reduced to one month and would be followed by a status review. His first idea was for Horace to apply for leave over the same period. If he were successful, Horace would purchase a motorcycle with a sidecar for them to tour the English countryside and historical places, and then sell it before returning to France.

The big push at the Somme had begun on 1 July, and Stearne had just left for "somewhere in France." The talk was that the war would be over by autumn, and Roy was apprehensive that it might end before he had a chance to do his bit. Then horrendous casualty lists began to appear and everyone realized that although the attack had relieved the German pressure on the French at Verdun, it had failed to break through the German defences in the Somme River area. Roy would get his chance after all.

After the war, German sources revealed how close to success General Kitchener's New Army had before when the arrival of the rainy season turned that part of the front into a sea of mud, and further progress against the German positions became impossible.

On 11 July Roy was discharged from Chatham Hospital, and he sent a telegram to his parents:

CANADIAN PACIFIC RAILWAY COMPANY'S TELEGRAPH

Marconi
London, Jul 11/16.

LCO. M. Brown,
Carleton Place, Ont.
Canada.

Left hospital today, leave, letter.
Roy Brown.
4.43 p.m.

In the meantime, 13 June, Horace, by this time promoted to sergeant, had been standing in an unsheltered position when he heard a whizzing sound. On the valid assumption that a German projectile nicknamed a *whiz-bang* was heading his way, he decided not to wait for the second act but ducked forthwith into a shell hole. Unfortunately a discarded rifle with bayonet affixed stood right where he landed; the bayonet first cut his knee, then penetrated deeply into his chest. Horace was immediately sent to the thirteenth Stationary Hospital in Boulogne, where his life was saved, and on 23 June he moved across the Channel to Nottingham General Hospital in England to recover from loss of blood.

Roy's plan for taking Horace on a tour of England thus came to naught, but fortunately he had a "Plan B". He had become friendly with a navy sub-lieutenant, Skeet, who had been badly injured by a hand grenade at Tenedos during the Dardanelles campaign. Skeet invited Roy to spend a week with him at his cottage on the banks of the River Thames, far up in the countryside. Good fortune struck again when a lady named Edith Hirsch, who had heard about Roy's accident from a friend in Carleton Place, invited him to her home for the remainder of his leave. She lived in Leeds, not far from Nottingham, and it seemed as though the brothers would have a chance to meet. Roy's plan again came to naught: Horace was transferred to the Canadian Convalescent Hospital at Bushy Park, London, on 19 July. There was, however, some light at the end of the tunnel because Bushy Park was not too far from Chingford, and Roy would soon be back there.

Roy tells the story of his leave in the following letter written from Edith Hirsch's home. Note the simple address and telephone number used in 1916.

Tel. 564 Weetwood Grove, Headingley, Nr. Leeds

July 25/16

Dear Dad,

Just arrived here last night after spending two most enjoyable weeks with my friend Skeet on the river. I have not enjoyed anything in the amusement line so much since coming to England. I am nearly fit again so when I go to London for a survey at the Admiralty a week from to-day I should be able to get back to duty again. I would sooner be sent to another station but should not be very long at Chingford anyway. I have not seen Horace, he had recovered and been sent south. I will visit him next Saturday.

This is a beautiful English country home here and the Hirsch family are very nice to me, doing everything to make me fit again. They have beautiful grounds and everything one could wish for. I am so glad Horace is going home on leave and will be getting a commission. It will be funny for him to make speeches for recruiting and patriotic activities around home, won't it?

Mrs Edith Hirsch wrote to Mrs Brown on 31 July with the good news that Roy was not pretending; he had indeed almost fully recovered. He had played tennis on their court on the Wednesday and Friday—the latter occasion in a most energetic manner. His recovery had accelerated beyond expectations, and he had only stayed there one week. While on sick leave, Roy was on half-pay, which was an understandable incentive to return to duty.

Chingford
Aug. 6/16
[Sunday]

Dear Dad,

I saw Horace and spent a few days with him. I reported for survey at the Admiralty Wednesday Aug 2 and was sent back to Chingford to complete my training. The station has improved greatly in the way it is managed. Of course I have got very much behind as the course was changed while I was in hospital. The staff have been very good and are giving me every possible advantage to catch up in my work. My back bothers me very little and my nerve seems still good. I am considered to be alright in flying but I have to work hard at the book work and pick it up again. Most of the chaps I knew here have gone and I am much too busy for fun. I had some interesting experiences on my first solo flight but they will keep. Horace will be able to tell you about things when he gets home.

Roy's log book shows him having received dual instruction at Chingford from Flight Lieutenant Mills in Avro 504B No. 9825 at 8.35p.m. on 2 August. The usual strong, gusty winds would have died down by that time, and with the August twilight lasting until late in the evening, such a flight would be truly enjoyable. Bright and early the next morning he flew dual with Flight Lieutenant Hayward in Avro 504B No. 9825. At 6.00 in the evening he went up for solo practice in Avro 504B No. 1039, and although he was not looking for trouble, trouble found him. The Remarks column in his log book states: *"Spiralled to land, went up again to avoid S. A. Henry. Shut petrol off and engine back-fired starting fire. Landed and put out fire with my hands."*

On the following day, Avro 504B No. 1002 misbehaved after fifteen minutes in the air. The Remarks column blandly states: *"Engine failed."*

Avro 504B No. 1002, flown by Roy on 4 August 1916.

Chingford
Aug. 14/16
Dear Dad,

It has been pouring rain all to-day but the weather has been splendid the last few weeks, just like the weather at home.

I have bought a Rudge Multi motorcycle. It is for running me down to the aerodrome and saves time splendidly. I got it for 35 pounds. I may take a run on it to see Horace on Sunday   if I can. I am alone in my billet, the people have gone for a holiday to the south coast.

On 15 August at 6.10 p.m., instructor Flight Lieutenant Hayward gave Roy twenty minutes of takeoff and landing instruction in Avro 504B No. 9825 in a force 6 wind (strong breeze, 22 to 27 mph). Roy must have handled the machine well, because immediately after landing he was sent aloft in Avro 504B No. 1019 to practise solo. This Avro must have been a new arrival at Chingford, with a good engine and tightly rigged, for Roy wrote in the Remarks column: *"Best machine I ever flew."*

Roy flew Avro 504Bs Nos. 1045 and 9825, and 504Cs, Nos.3313, 3314 and 8596 until 27 August, and then he changed to B.E.2Cs Nos. 983 and 9898. On 30 August, B.E.2C No. 1170 attempted to give him a ducking after five minutes of flight. The Remarks column states: *"Engine failed over reservoir. Just got over sheds. Landing good."*

Having avoided "The Sailor's Farewell" courtesy of B.E.2C No. 1170, he made thirty-five minutes of circuits and bumps in B.E.2C No. 980 on 31 August, a very misty day.

On 2 September the chief instructor recommended that Roy, who now had a total flying time of 39 hours and 46 minutes, be awarded his certificate. He was given four days' leave, with orders to report to gunnery school at RNAS station Eastchurch on 7 September. Roy shook the dust, or perhaps one should say scraped the mud of Chingford from his flying boots and departed for London.

On 6 September the commanding officer issued RNAS Aeroplane Pilot's Certificate No. 163 in Roy's name.

![Roy Brown's RNAS Aeroplane Pilot's Certificate]

Roy Brown's RNAS Aeroplane Pilot's Certificate.

The Wing confirmed Roy as a probationary flight sub-lieutenant RNAS effective 11 November 1915, the date Admiral Kingsmill accepted him in Canada. He had finally shed the prefix "Temporary."

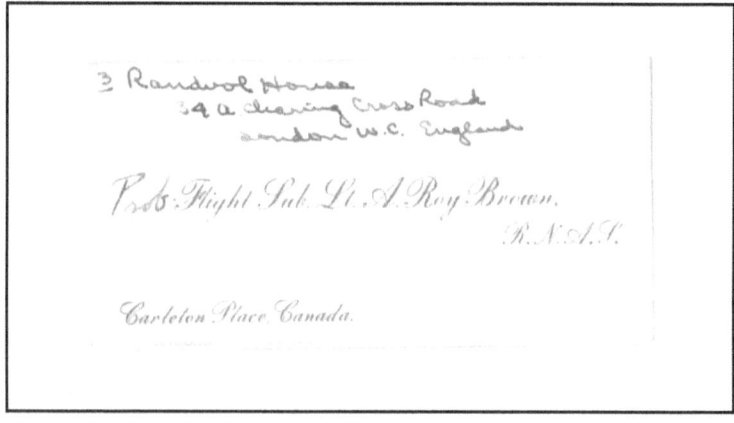

Roy's Visiting Card (printed with an eye to the future).

The key to victory in the air was marksmanship, or gunnery as it was known in the navy. It is no coincidence that the aces on both sides were marksmen of the first order, and when one appreciates that aerial combat means firing a moving gun at a moving target in untold different combinations of relative positions, all of which may be changing simultaneously, the complexity of what is termed "deflection shooting" becomes apparent.

By this time, it was quite well known that with a machine gun mounted directly and not too sturdily above a vibrating engine, only the first two or three shots fired would go exactly where intended. The rest spread out wildly as the barrel jumped around; therefore, a long burst of fire was a waste of ammunition. It was also an open invitation to an overheated breechblock which could cause the gun to jam. Some pilots believed the only way to be sure of success was to close the range to 25 yards or less before opening fire. With such courage, it is not surprising they soon became aces. There are plenty of stories of aces, on both sides, who returned from shooting down an enemy aeroplane and were found to have fired only ten shots—namely, a mere half-second burst from twin machineguns.

For various reasons, mainly the terrible weather, Roy was not to fly again in 1916.

In late August, Horace had been granted sick leave in Canada, and on 5 September he sailed for Quebec on the SS *Olympic*. He telegraphed his parents, the news flashed around Carleton Place and a reception was planned for him at the Town Hall. He reached Quebec on 11 September and Carleton Place five days later. The reception took place on 20 September.

R.N. Air Station
Eastchurch
Sept. 13/16
[Wednesday]

My dear mother,

I saw Mrs Galbraith and Molly in town Sunday when I was coming through London on my way down here. It is nice to see someone from home. If Horace comes over here again, you should come with him and bring Alice with you. I could get leave to meet you. Poor Horace, he has my sympathy. The idea of a reception in the Town Hall gives me cold feet.

I am to take a three-week gunnery course before being put on a war station somewhere. I hope it is France and I think I have a pretty good chance of getting over there.

Ask Horace to give the Zeppelin souvenirs, which I sent home, to Alice but you keep a piece of the gasbag.

Mrs Galbraith and Molly (Murray Galbraith's mother and sister), accompanied by Mrs Findlay, had come to England to visit Murray, Douglas Findlay, several relatives and friends.

It was a time of great patriotism, and ladies of all ages were doing what circumstances allowed to help the boys at the front. Roy's sister Bessie had become a registered nurse, and both sisters were now working in hospitals away from home. His brother Horace had resigned from the 2nd Battalion and then joined the 240th Battalion with a commission.

Second Lieutenant Horace Brown.*

He had not yet recovered sufficiently from his wound to return to France, so the army sent him to help with recruiting drives around Ontario. This meant that there was no close family member of suitable age to accompany Mary Brown on a voyage to England, hence Roy's suggestion of Alice Pickup.

Horace with Alice Louise Pickup, step-daughter of Uncle Clarence.*

Alice was also doing her bit for the war. She had joined the St. John Ambulance Brigade, a volunteer organization which still exists today and performs paramedical work.

Alice Pickup (step-daughter of Uncle Clarence) in her
St John Ambulance Brigade uniform.

Even in late 1916 a voyage from the United States to England on an American passenger liner was still reasonably safe because such ships were not being attacked by German submarines. The huge *Lusitania*, which had sunk surprisingly quickly with great loss of life on 7 May 1915 after a single torpedo strike from the German submarine U20, was a British ship. Many now believe, from a long line of debris on the ocean floor that the torpedo explosion ignited coal dust in an empty bunker and, with what passengers described as a long, loud rumbling noise which occurred a few seconds after the big bang, blew out part of the ship's bottom.

R.N. Air Station
Eastchurch
Sept. 29/16

My dear Bess,

The weather has turned bad again so now it blows or rains most of the time. I passed my exams on the ground work of our course yesterday. All the rest is air work and until we get some reasonably good weather we will have nothing to do. The whole course here does not matter very much as up to the present nobody has ever failed.

The Royal Navel Air Service and the Royal Flying Corps were later to revise their views on the gunnery importance of air work, and in 1917 officers with special training were sent to the aerodromes in France to explain to pilots and observers that German scouts and bombers were not armoured, and that the problem was their own poor shooting.

On 29 September Roy received a posting to RNAS Dover. The weather improved, and no longer feeling any pain in his back, he simply did too much. On 8 October, for his own good, he was sent for a rest to Sheerness Sick Quarters near Dover, and his posting was cancelled.

R.N. Sick Quarters
Sheerness
Oct. 19/16

My dear Reta,

My back is getting better again. They say I am run down but I am not and hope that a week or two will see me on duty again. It is not sore, just weak. All I do is loaf around in a hospital. I'll be a raving lunatic soon if I was not always one. Give my love to all,

Roy tried to talk his sister Reta into making a voyage to England in the spring of 1917 when the countryside would be beautiful. He planned to ask for leave when she arrived and then they would have a good holiday together. The Scottish poet Robbie Burns would prove to have the last word there; something about the plans of mice and men....

R.N. Air Station
Eastchurch
Oct. 29/16

Dear Dad,

    Back on duty again but have not had an opportunity to do any flying as the weather is awful. Stearne tells me that there is mail for me at his station in France. It seems to be going everywhere except to here.

    I often wonder what I shall do when it is all over. It will be a fairly long time before I will have become useful in a business way as my experience is very short. Horace and I had a talk over here one day, so if you ask him, he will tell you about it.

As far as the flying was concerned, all through November and for most of December the seagulls were following the rivers and the crows stayed close to the railways.

R.N. Hospital
Chatham
Dec. 25/16

Dear Dad,

    As you see I am in hospital again, This time nothing serious, only tonsilitis which came as a birthday present. It was lucky that I was still here and not in France.

    I had some menu on Christmas day! For breakfast the steward asked me whether I would like a cup of tea or a glass of milk. There will be a splendid Christmas dinner menu for me consisting of a cup of beef tea and a glass of milk.

    Last night there was a choir which went around the wards singing carols at about midnight.

    I hope you are all enjoying your Christmas in Ottawa. Perhaps I shall be there next year.

Royal Naval Barracks
Chatham
Dec. 29/16

Dear Dad,

I am out of hospital again and have been sent here for appointment to a station. I hope I am not sent back to Eastchurch again. My throat feels nearly O.K. now so I do not expect it will bother me any more.
I had a letter from Stearne this morning saying that he has asked his Wing Captain to get me out there and he has consented to do his best. If that gets to the Admiralty before I am appointed, things should be alright. I will let you know as soon as I get definite news.

This time, although Roy did not totally get his wish, he had at least finished with Eastchurch and Chingford. With his officer's rank confirmed, he was on his way to an advanced training station in preparation for active service.[12]

ANNEX TO CHAPTER FOUR

(1) MACHINE-GUNS.

The Imperial German Army Air Service equivalent of the RFC and RNAS special air-cooled 0.303-in. (7.696-mm) Vickers machine gun was the 0.312-in (7.92-mm) LMG 08/15; both were versions of the original Maxim gun. In each case, the Maxim breechblock had been redesigned to accept the standard infantry rifle ammunition in use by that army at the time, which, in layman's language, means both German and British machine guns fired rifle bullets. It must be emphasized that in documents and reports of the era, the term *rifle bullet* refers to the type of cartridge employed, not to the weapon which fired it.

In the year 1910, Lieutenant-Colonel Isaac Newton Lewis of the U.S. Army had a good idea: design a rifle which automatically reloaded and fired as long as firm pressure was maintained on the trigger. Unfortunately, the Board of Ordnance and Fortifications of the U.S. Army had already adopted an early version of the Hotchkiss automatic gun and did not wish to introduce a second type. In 1913, Lieutenant-Colonel Lewis, now retired from the army, had an even better idea, and he packed his bags and sailed to Europe with a sample. His invention was tested in Belgium and England and found to be exactly what the Belgian Army and the RFC needed. The British Army, especially gunners with a musical ear, liked it also; an expert Lewis gunner could play a tune with the sound of his weapon.

"How's your father? All right" [- .-. - -]
"Shave and a hair cut, two bits" [- ..-. - -]

are examples.

Learning the operation of a Lewis gun, Mark 2.
The ammunition drum has not yet been fitted.

The Lewis automatic gun was later adopted by the U.S. Army.

(2) ROTARY ENGINES.

On a radial engine (sometimes called a *round engine* in the U.S.) the crankcase and the cylinders are stationary, as one would expect; the crankshaft rotates, carrying the propeller with it. However, on a rotary engine the exact opposite obtains: The crankshaft is stationary, and the crankcase, together with the cylinders, rotates around it. This arrangement originated in France as a star-shaped petrol engine which fitted inside a bicycle wheel. The rim (carrying the tire) was bolted to the cylinder heads, and the crankshaft was bolted to the bicycle frame. The original idea of using an engine of this type in an aeroplane came from the Australian inventor of the box kite, Lawrence Hargreaves. His engine had only three cylinders and the base of a propeller blade was attached to the head of each cylinder. The idea was simplicity itself, but the stresses and strains imposed upon the cylinders by the blades were unacceptable. The concept was capable of development, and a more practical layout soon appeared: the crankshaft was fixed to the aeroplane (as per Hargreaves's idea), but the propeller was made in a single piece and bolted to an extension of the crankcase.

Mr Henri Farman (wearing a cap) and one of his aeroplanes with a Gnôme engine (stopped).

A Gnôme engine running on a test bed, probably a gun carriage. The crankshaft (at the rear) is stationary, and the cylinders are rotating around it, carrying the propellers with them.

The rotary engine presented four advantages over the earlier radial engines: by spinning around like the blades of an electric fan, the cylinders were cooled easily and equally; lubricating oil did not collect in the lower cylinders; the absence of a float chamber in the fuel system enabled the engine to run equally well on its back, its side or upside down; and its-power-to weight ratio was merely 3.6 lbs per horsepower—almost unbelievable for those days. Like a fairy-tale gnome, it was small and powerful.

Unfortunately, all was not quite that simple. With a rotary engine supplying the power to the propeller, the pilot also had to be an engine driver. Aircraft rotary engines had no carburetor as it is understood today; they had a mixing chamber for the air and the fuel. No throttle existed on the early models made by the Gnôme company; the only power settings were Full or None. The pilot was required to set and then maintain the correct air-to-fuel ratio to keep the engine running sweetly at full power.

When low power was required, the pilot had to continually switch the ignition off and on by pressing and releasing a button known as the blip switch because of the characteristic noise of the engine being so tortured. The sparks for ignition were provided by a high-voltage electrical generator called a magneto. The magnets was basically an ignition coil in which the primary coil was energized by a powerful rotating magnet; no battery was required. In the 1910s, a magneto was a high-tech device, the only truly reliable ones being manufactured by Bosch in Germany. A somewhat crude manner of providing controllable engine-power reduction, was later achieved by making the ignition timing retardable from the cockpit.

Later rotary engines, such as the Le Rhône, Clergêt and Bentley, were fitted with individual levers to control the amount of fuel and the ratio of air fed to the engine. A pilot on the ground would first set the engine to a fast idle, about 800 rpm, by adjusting the two control levers and would blip this power setting for taxiing. He then had to reset the two levers to obtain full power for takeoff. Landing required the use of the blip switch, otherwise even at the lowest practicable engine power setting, the thrust from the propeller would not permit the aeroplane to lose speed quickly enough to land inside a small field.

(3) MAURICE FARMAN S7, No. 146.

The original owner of No. 146 was the Marquis Jules de Lareinty Tholozan, who sold it to the RNAS in 1913. It was modified and sent to Chingford on 11 August 1915. Roy Brown and Leonard Henry (Titch) Rochford (29 victories including shared) were among the future ace fighter pilots who had received primary instruction in it. This slow and gentle *Rumpty* was retired on 1 November 1916 after a flying life of almost five years, a record for those times.

Maurice Farman S7, No. 146, in early civilian life when it was still a Longhorn. The photograph, taken in 1912 or early 1913, provides a good view of the original 80hp De Dion Bouton inline engine fitted to this historic aircraft.

(4) THE DIFFERENCE BETWEEN THE FRENCH AND BRITISH AEROPLANE CONTROL SYSTEMS.

In Roy's letter dated 21 February 1916, he mentioned that he had to be careful because the Avros had a different kind of control system from the Maurice Farmans. The differences encompassed both the flying and the engine controls, and in the latter case were serious.

THE FLYING CONTROLS

For flying controls, all the Avros had a pure joystick, as first used by Armand Déperdussin in France and later adopted by Louis Blériot.

There was no movable wheel on top nor was the rudder coupled to the ailerons as in the Wright system. What appeared to be a small wheel on some aeroplanes are actually a fixed, circular handgrip. In some cases this was shaped like a spade handle, and the device, whatever its shape, soon became known as a spadegrip.

An Avro pilot could move the joystick in any direction, including forwards and sideways simultaneously, or backwards and sideways simultaneously, in independent proportions. Once the aeroplane was trimmed at flying speed, only the finger and thumb were needed to hold the stick, and gentle pressure, rather than movements, would produce a gradual change in the attitude of the aeroplane. With pressure to the left, the aeroplane would incline (or bank) to the left, and if pressure from the left foot were also applied to the rudder bar, a gentle turn to the left would begin. If the pilot felt wind on the right cheek, he or she knew that the aeroplane was skidding outwards and that more pressure to the left was required on the joystick. The Déperdussin system was so amazingly simple and logical that one wonders why it had not been invented right at the beginning of aviation. A trained pilot would react instinctively to wind on the cheeks and to the pressure of his or her posterior against the seat, and thereby control the flying machine in a most elegant manner.

The Maurice Farman had a control column which moved in one sense only—backwards and forwards to raise or lower the elevators. At the top of the column was a wheel which the pilot turned to one side or the other to move the ailerons. The pilot's feet operated the rudder bar.

Both the Déperdussin and the Farman flying control systems are in use today, the former in small single-engined aeroplanes and the latter in large single - and multi-engined aeroplanes. The only serious improvements to these systems over ninety years have been the replacement of the rudder bar with two pedals and the addition of individual wheel brakes, one coupled to (or built into) each pedal.

To increase the power of an aeroplane built in France, the pilot pulled the throttle lever backwards, that is, towards himself. In the case of an aeroplane built in England, the pilot pushed it forwards. The expression built in is used intentionally, for French-designed aeroplanes built under licence in England worked the English way. There was, however, a joker in the pack: many of the French-designed aeroplanes in service in England had been imported from France.

Standardization was eventually achieved but there were a few hair-raising moments; for example, a British pilot, trying to park his newly issued French-built Morane Parasol monoplane, found it charging towards a brick wall instead of slowing down.

Morane Parasol, Type L. The name is derived from the manner in which the monoplane wings are attached to the fuselage. This machine, No. 3253, was flown by RNAS Flight Sub-Lieutenant Reginald Alexander John (Rex) Warneford when he stalked Zeppelin LZ37, commanded by Oberleutnant van der Haegen, for one hour on the night of 6/7 June 1915. He brought it down at 7,000 feet over Ghent by dropping a string of six 20 lb. Hales bombs. For this successful flea-versus-elephant contest, the first of the war, he received the Victoria Cross.

In October 1999 the historian and author Dale Titler told Alan Bennett that Roy Brown's wartime colleague, Captain Oliver Colin LeBoutillier (10 victories including shared), had mentioned to him in the late 1960s that the lever which controlled engine power on the Maurice Farmans at Chingford operated in the reverse direction from the British aircraft used there. LeBoutillier, known to his fellow pilots in 1917 and 1918 as "Boots," also commented that from one day to the next the trainees never knew which type of aeroplane would be used for their next flying lesson. Another complication was that English - and French-designed engines rotated in opposite directions. This meant that during take off, when the tail skid lifted from the ground and the torque from the propeller would try to swing the tail to one side, the direction of the swing depended on the nationality of the engine. It all made for an interesting time.

(5) POSTWAR USE OF THE AVRO 504 VARIANTS.

The Avro 504, mainly the later "K" variant, with the rear cockpit modified to carry two, sometimes four, passengers, formed the backbone of the "joyride" industry in England after the war.

Joyride ticket purchased by Alan Bennett's parents in the 1930s.

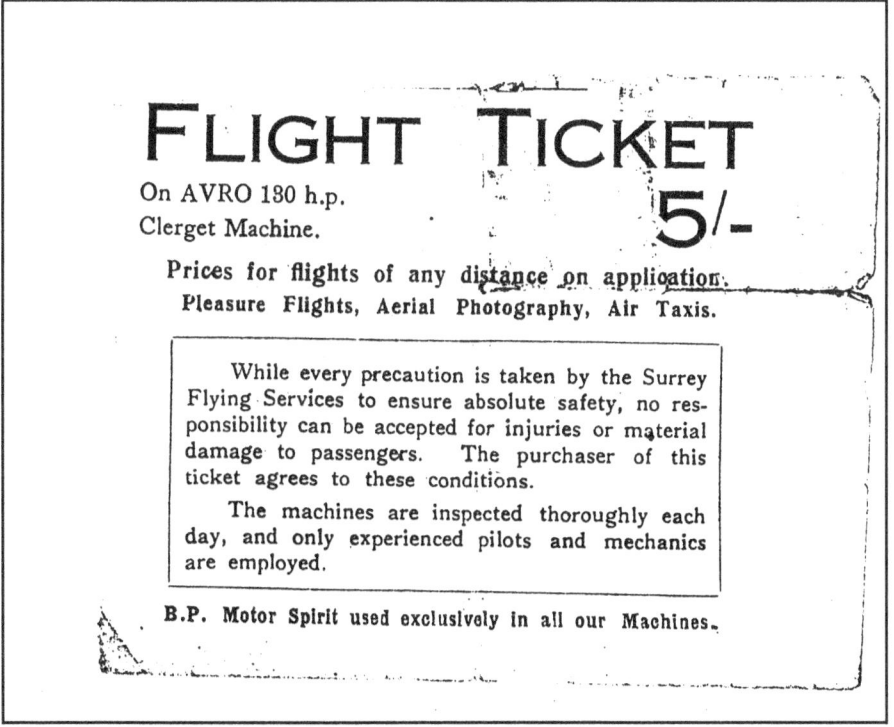

Apparently not all Clergêt rotary engines had been replaced yet.

Several Avro 504 reproductions are still flying at airshows today. An American pilot owns two: one is fitted with an original 110hp Le Rhône rotary engine; the other has an up-to-date 225hp seven-cylinder radial engine. In 1997 he told the late Theodore Crayston of Ontario that the plane with the Le Rhône rotary engine could fly rings around the other with the modern, low maintenance, fuel-efficient engine. The apparent contradiction comes from the different methods employed in for rating the engines and from the torque available from a large propeller turning at 1,200 rpm versus a small one at 2,400 rpm.

The builders of the replicas used in the film Those Magnificent Men and Their Flying Machines discovered that to obtain the performance of the original aeroplanes they needed to install modern engines rated at two and a leaf or three times the horsepower of those fitted in 1910.

(6) AIRCRAFT ENGINE MAINTENANCE INTERVALS.

The early Gnôme rotary probably had the shortest life of all engines between maintenance intervals, owing to the severe operating conditions of the inlet valve in the piston crown. The rotary was a four-stroke, seven-cylinder engine with the exhaust valves in the cylinder heads. During every second downstroke of the piston, the pressure differential would cause the inlet valve to open to admit the fuel-air mixture from the crankcase. Every ten hours of running time, each of the seven inlet valves had to be ground into its seat in the piston and the seven return-spring tensions equalized. The later single-valve (*monosoupape* in French) Gnôme engines overcame this problem by using transfer ports in place of the inlet valves. Brass piston rings were employed to accommodate the cylinder distortion which occurred at normal operating temperature; they had to be replaced every twenty five hours.

The nine-cylinder Le Rhône rotary, used in the Avro 504B, was also four-stroke but had both the inlet and exhaust valves in the cylinder head. Like the Gnôme, it also used brass piston rings, and major maintenance was required every twenty five hours.

The Renault and Royal Aircraft Factory inline engines used on the B.E.2C aeroplanes at Chingford in 1916 had major maintenance intervals of about seventy-five hours.

If engine mechanics had been removed from Chingford to support the battle in France, a crisis situation could indeed have occurred.

The late Cole Palen, founder of the Old Rhinebeck Flying Museum in New York State, stated that for each hour's flying time of the Great War aircraft in his collection, fifteen man-hours of maintenance were required. To give an idea of the progress achieved since those days: Alan Bennett's 1961 Champion 7FC with a 95hp engine, an aeroplane of equivalent weight and power to a Sopwith *Pup*, requires but one man-hour for every ten flown. In fifty years, the maintenance man-hours have decreased by a factor of 150.

(7) COMMON ENGINE TROUBLES WITH MAGNETOS AND VALVES.

Prior to the war, the sparking plugs and magnetos used in British aeroplanes and airships had been imported from Germany. Logically this importation ceased in August 1914, and local suppliers had to be found. The local sparking plugs were satisfactory, but the magnetos were not; the insulation of the high-tension winding was inadequate for the operating conditions. Airships carried one or two spare magnetos, and there are many hair-raising stories of flight engineers hanging by their finger-nails from the rigging and holding tools in their teeth while changing a magneto, sometimes two, during a long patrol over the sea. When engines with twin ignition systems (two magnetos and two sets of sparking plugs) came into service, airmen felt a strong sensation of relief.

In 1914 the art of tempering steel alloys for use in high heat zones was in its infancy, and broken engine valves or collapsed valve springs were the cause of many engine problems. Today we find it strange that in those days the engine exhaust-valve stems and springs were exposed to the dirt in the air—for cooling.

(8) SIDESLIPS.

During a landing, normal or emergency, once the recommended gliding speed for a given type of machine has been established, a pilot must immediately hold his head still and note whether, relative to the nose of his machine, the chosen field appears to be moving away from him or towards him. That will indicate to him whether he is too low or too high (in that order) to reach it under the wind conditions of the occasion. If he is too low and the engine has stopped, there is no safe remedy; lifting the nose to prolong the glide will increase the vertical rate of descent and will most probably result in expensive bending noises on the wrong side of the boundary fence. If he is too high, a smart sideslip will enable the aeroplane to lose height rapidly without gaining forward speed.

A sideslip to the left is made by applying left aileron and right rudder; this is known as cross-controlling. The prerequisite for a sideslip is lowering the nose of the aeroplane, and then the pilot must maintain adequate flying speed during the entire manoeuvre, otherwise the old saw, that most aircraft accidents happen very close to the ground, will once again be demonstrated.

Roy had learned to fly in the Wright Model B on which the wing-tip twisting (it did not have ailerons) and the rudder were mechanically linked together. Turning the wheel to the left moved the rudder to the left and twisted (warped) the wing tips to bank the machine to the left at the same time. Turning the wheel to the right did the opposite. The linkage prevented the cross-controlling required for intentional sideslips; therefore, the latter would not have been part of the syllabus. It may not have occurred to Roy's instructor at Chingford, who had never flown a Wright Model B, that there was such a dangerous gap in his pupil's knowledge.

The legacy of the 240 minutes' instruction at Dayton was proving to be dangerous.

(9) THE STORY OF THE B.E.2C, OR HOW AN EXCELLENT 1912 DESIGN WAS KEPT IN SERVICE FAR TOO LONG.

The original B.E.2, a contemporary of the Wright Model C, was designed as a reconnaissance machine at the Royal Aircraft Factory. Geoffrey de Havilland (of post-war fame) did much of the design work, and the B.E.2 is said to have been the first military aeroplane in the world that could be termed "user-friendly". The "C" version of the B.E.2 was such a good machine for its time that hundreds were ordered. However the Royal Aircraft Factory, too small for wartime production, had been transformed into mainly a research and design centre. Therefore, the army began placing orders for the construction of the B.E.2C directly with outside contractors, such as Beardmore, Bristol and Austin Motors, and they, in turn, subcontracted the wooden airframes to peacetime piano and furniture factories where skilled there were abundant woodworkers.

The B.E.2C was so nicely balanced aerodynamically and mechanically that once the desired altitude had been reached, the pilot could adjust a trimming wheel, a spring coupled to the joystick, and the aeroplane would fly level indefinitely; he merely had to steer it gently with his feet. Furthermore, if it slipped to one side, the wing design would cause it to automatically level itself. Therefore, if a pilot became spatially disoriented, for example inside a cloud, all he had to do was release the controls, and the aeroplane would sort him out gently and safely. For this reason B.E.2Cs were frequently used to intercept German bombers and airships at night.

General arrangement of the B.E.2C middle fuselage section. *Left to right:* the pilot's metal seat, joystick, trimming wheel and spring, compass, and the main fuel tank beneath the observer's wicker seat at the centre of balance of the aeroplane. Thus, the balance of the aeroplane was not affected by the quantity of fuel in this tank or the absence or presence of the observer.

Detail of the B.E.2C trimming wheel for spring-loading the joystick. When properly adjusted, this feature made flying a pleasure instead of fatiguing work. Note also the inclinometer which had an air bubble inside the curved tube. This would confuse today's pilots because the bubble moved in the opposite direction to the steel ball in today's slip or skid indicators.

By early 1916, the B.E.2C, had already been outclassed at the front, so both the RNAS and the RFC started using it at training schools. For some reason, the army was unable to cancel existing B.E.2C production orders, and RFC squadrons in France continued to receive them until the early summer of 1917.

A 1916 *"Quirk"* with an early type wireless telegraphy transmitter mounted at the centre of balance. The transmitter and the many-cell lead or acid storage battery weighed so much that the observer was often left behind.

As military aviation developed, so did the need for a machine that could turn quickly. The original B.E.2 had been designed with the exact opposite in mind, and although it initially provided yeoman-like daytime service in the war, by late 1915 the B.E.2C crews were receiving a rough time from the state-of-the-art, faster and more manoeuvrable German aeroplanes.

(10) STONEYFIELDS FARM.

Henry Muddle, the owner of a butcher's shop in High Street Edgware, raised his own cattle and pigs on Stoneyfields Farm, a rented property about a mile to the north. The farm was bounded in the west by Edgwarebury Lane, in the south by Hale Lane, and in the east by Stoneyfields Lane. The farmhouse, where Henry Muddle lived, had a telephone.

In the late 1920s, when Highway A-41 (Edgware Way/Watford Way) was built, it passed through the northernmost fields of Stoneyfields Farm. Over the following years the farmland was gradually sold for housing. In 1931 the farmhouse was demolished to make way for an institute for crippled people, know as John Groom's Crippleage, which exists today.

Under the municipal dividing lines, as they stood in the year 2005, the place where Henry Muddle's farm used to be is close to the northern boundary of Greater London and lies within the Borough of Barnet.

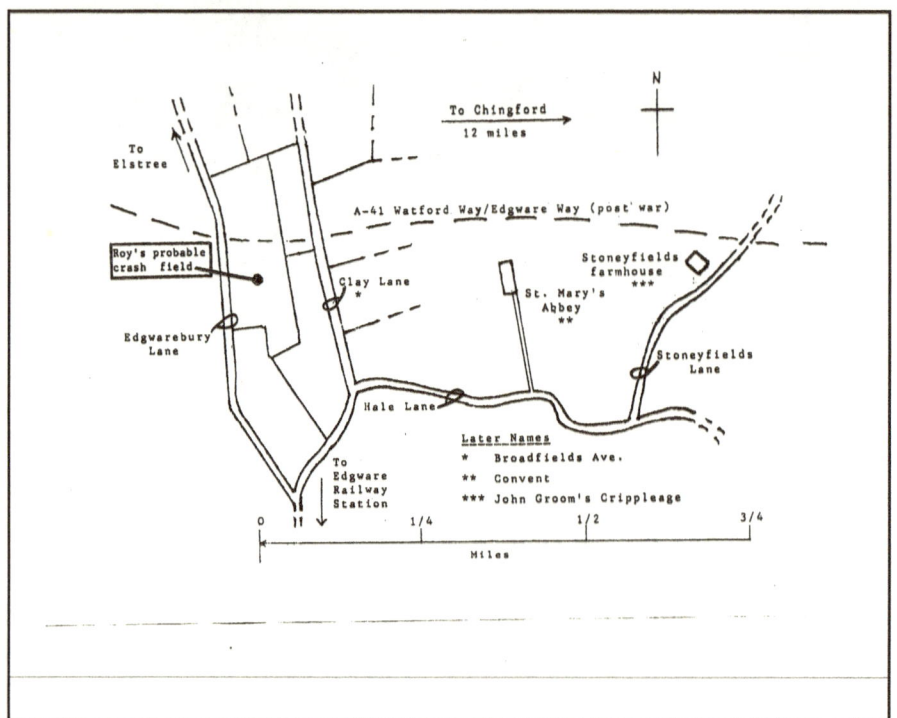

Stoneyfields Farm. With reference to the municipal maps of the era, the indicated field on the west side of the farm near Edgwarebury Lane would have been a good choice for a forced landing.

Following his crash, Roy extricated himself from his upturned "Quirk" and walked either to St. Mary's Abbey or to Mr. Muddle's house, where he requested the use of the telephone. Upon examination at Chingford, B.E.2C No. 1107 was declared uneconomical to repair and was struck off charge on 24 April.

In the days before the 1916 naval service records were made public and Roy's letters were released by his family, the precise nature of the injury to Roy's back and the damage to the aeroplane were unknown. A description of the accident, imagined some forty years after the event by someone who had not been in the RNAS or even in England at the time, authoritatively stated that the "Quirk" had caught fire and Roy had been crippled for months.

(11) THE FUEL SYSTEM OF THE B.E.2C.

Roy was still in shock when he wrote the letter about his accident, and it appears that he accidentally reversed his explanation of the purpose of the manual fuel pump. The RAF Museum at Hendon kindly provided a treatise by J. M. Bruce on the standard B.E.2C fuel system. It informs us that the fifteen-gallon fuel tank, located high up in the fuselage between the engine firewall and the front cockpit instrument panel, is a header tank which feeds the carburetor by gravity. The eighteen-gallon main tank is located beneath the observer's seat and is pressurized by an engine-driven air pump to force fuel up to the header tank. There is an air pressure gauge and an air pressure regulating valve inside the pilot's cockpit. A manual air pump is mounted outside the fuselage on the port (left) side within the pilot's reach and is for use before starting the engine or in the event of engine pump failure. Logically, if Roy's main tank were empty, the manual pump would give the impression of being defective.

(12) COMPARISON OF RNAS OFFICER RANKS WITH OFFICER RANKS OF THE RFC AND TODAY'S RAF.

RNAS	RFC	RAF
Flight Sub-Lieutenant	Second Lieutenant	Pilot Officer
Flight Lieutenant	Lieutenant	Flying Officer
Flight Commander	Captain	Flight Lieutenant
Squadron Commander	Major	Squadron Leader
Wing Commander	Lieutenant-Colonel	Wing Commander

1. From 25 July to 28 September 1917, RNAS Squadron No. 9 was stationed at Leffrinckoucke on the French coast between the towns of Dunkirk (Dunkerque) and Bray-Dunes the latter being close to the Belgian border. The squadron was one of five sent to France that year in response to a government decision that the navy should help the army's (RFC), which was being hard-pressed in air battles over the land. (In reports and documents the unit designation is normally abbreviated to 9 RNAS, Naval 9 or 9(N).)

When Ronald Sykes arrived, Naval 9 was attached to 14 Wing RFC and equipped with Sopwith F1 Camel single-seater scouts. A French 130hp Clerget 9B rotary engine powered the F1; the armament was twin synchronized, air-cooled, Vickers machine guns. Later on, the F1 Camel was replaced by the BR1 version with a 150hp Bentley rotary engine. Towards the end of the war, the term "scout" was changed to "fighter".

2. Until mid-1916 the emphasis in the Great War had been upon avoiding dogfights, not seeking them. The principal role of the scout was to prevent enemy aircraft from observing, photographing and bombing ground installations. Enemy aircraft only became desirable targets when they were engaged in trench or road strafing, a euphemism for the indiscriminate slaughter of men and horses.

Dogfights, in general, resulted in a waste of highly trained men and expensive machines to the detriment of the overall strategic objective. This explains the large number of two-seater photographic reconnaissance aeroplanes shot down by many of the aces, for these planes were the real enemy. Major James Byford McCudden, VC, of the Royal Flying Corps and Royal Air Force specialized in quietly stalking them and then making a quick surprise attack from the most favourable position possible.

In 1917 Thomas Sopwith specially designed an aeroplane for this type of operation, the 5F.1 Dolphin high-altitude fighter with a 200hp Hispano-Suiza engine. In addition to having a pair of Vickers machine guns for normal work, it was intended to carry two Lewis automatic guns which pointed upwards at an angle of 45 degrees, but in practice, to decrease weight and to thereby be able to climb even higher, pilots always removed one before takeoff. The angled Lewis gun eliminated a problem which had foiled pilots attempting a sneak attack from below on a German two-seater or Zeppelin flying at 15,000 feet or higher. The instant the pilot lifted the nose of his fighter to aim at the enemy, the thin air at such altitudes would cause it to stall and spin. The wings and the cockpit of the Dolphin were arranged for visibility forwards and upwards; the pilot's eye level passed above the upper wing, and a stout crash bar looped over his head.

Typical Sopwith 5F.1 Dolphin.
The backward stagger of the wings made it easy to identify.

The golden rule for aerial combat was aptly and concisely phrased by Major McCudden; "*An attack must not be allowed to degenerate into a gunnery contest.*" The Sopwith Dolphin was a significant step in this direction.

The corollary to Major McCudden's dictum was stated by the German ace Hauptmann (Captain) Oswald Boelke (40 victories): "*Foolish acts of bravery only bring death.*"

3. The furthest Camel, No. B7195, was flown in Naval 9 by Roy Brown on 2 February and 3 of February 1918.

The middle one, NO. B5749, was flown by Ronald Sykes on 12 August 1918 when as a flight commander with RAF 201 Squadron he shot down two Fokker D.VII fighters.

The closest one, No. B7202, was flown extensively in Naval 9 by Flight Commander Oliver LeBoutillier.

4. In general, even with a steady target directly ahead, tolerably accurate shooting could only be expected at ranges of 150 yards or less. Assuming a dive at 150 mph upon an enemy flying at 100 mph, there was not much time to aim and fire became the closing speed would be 50 mph, or 25 yards per second. If one pressed the trigger at 150 yards' range, only a four-second burst of fire would be possible before separation from the target would be down to 50 yards and a mid-air collision become a distinct possibility. Fortunately, a two-second burst (40 rounds, 20 from each gun) was more than ample to destroy the enemy if the aim was accurate. Surprise produced such results.

The post-war stories of Allied airmen who returned from captivity in Germany indicated that over half of them had not seen the approach of the German aeroplane that shot them down. An impressive number of those taken by surprise were observers in two-seater aircraft, some of whom had failed to see "*the Hun in the sun*". Others had even failed to see one close by. Unlike their pilots, they did not have cockpit flight instruments to scan from time to time, and their eyes had become set in distant focus and somewhat de-sensitized by searching the bright sky above. Consequently they had failed to notice the second principal danger, an enemy aeroplane creeping up beneath them. The masters at the art, such as Hauptmann (Captain) Max Immelmann (15 victories) and Hauptmann Oswald Boelke, would creep up as close as 25 yards and then fire a half- to one-second burst. They rarely missed. "Get in close and shoot them down" was another dictum of aerial warfare.

Quite often, on both sides experienced pilots worked in pairs. One distracted the enemy observer by opening fire prematurely while his colleague dived from the sun or slipped underneath from the other side. In such cases the victory was usually shared.

A sneak attack from below, or a properly executed diving attack from above, would certainly provide surprise, but what if the shots missed their target? The diving attack method provided the better chance of escape because the enemy aeroplane would require time to gain speed in order for its pilot to respond.

In 1917, unless the enemy fighters were Halberstadt D.IIIs, which could outdive anything the Allies had, a power dive was frequently a good escape tactic for a Camel pilot. Such dives were rarely demonstrated in RFC and RNAS advanced training schools, in part became their Camels had seen far better days.

5. The airspeed indicators fitted to RNAS Camels were calibrated in the naval manner, in knots, and the speeds cited in Sykes's diving lesson are not exaggerations. The powerful engines available by the middle of 1917 had ended the era of lightweight construction and apart from occasional lapses in workmanship rather than design, Allied fighter aircraft were very strongly built indeed.

If a pilot has no visual reference except the ground below, dive steeper than 60 degrees from the horizontal may well appear to be vertical. At more than 70 degrees, the horizon can no longer be seen and all perception of diving angle and direction is lost. It then becomes easy, quite unknowingly, to progress through the vertical into an inverted dive, from which a novice may be unable to recover. For this reason Camel pilots were taught that the best indicator of the recommended diving angle, 70 degrees, was airspeed.

An April 1917 Royal Aircraft Factory report entitled The Terminal Velocity of the S.E.5, which was a contemporary of the

Sopwith Camel, stated the following:

The terminal velocity of the SE5 at 10,000 feet is 265 mph indicated with the engine on and 255 with it off.

The report continued by pointing out that when corrections for altitude and temperature were applied to the indicated speeds, the true airspeeds would be about 290 mph and 280 mph respectively.

6. Many reliable wartime memoirs by fighter pilots state that to hesitate or look around upon hearing shots or seeing holes appear in the wings is tantamount to committing suicide. They generally add that if a novice survives the first occasion of doing that, he has just been granted the opportunity of remembering not do it again. Immediate evasive action in any direction is required since the slightest delay allows the attacker to correct his aim. With twin machine guns firing a total of fifteen to twenty shots per second, the chances of survival are slim for a target which remains steady for an extra second or two.

7. Flight preparation involved checking the wind strength, the wind direction, and the distance to be covered to the destination, and noting any useful landmarks. Then, based upon the cruising speed of the type of aeroplane involved, the flight commander would make a calculation of the elapsed time required to fly from landmark to landmark. One of the duties of the other members of the flight was to guard the commander against surprise attack while he gave his full attention to the navigation.

Staying with round numbers and assuming: a typical west wind of 30 mph, a target 60 miles away to the east, a cruising speed through the air of 90 mph, the following example of navigating to and from the target illustrates the method used and the importance of the dashboard watch as a navigational instrument.

A west wind blows from west to east; the aeroplane is flying to the east at 90 mph, supported by an air mass that is moving in the same direction at 30 mph. The two speeds, when added together, produce a ground speed of 120 mph, which is 2 miles per minute. The elapsed time to fly the 60 miles from the pilot's aerodrome to the target would therefore be 30 minutes.

The difference, if any, between the calculated elapsed time to the first landmark and the time shown on the cockpit watch, would tell the flight commander his true speed over ground. He would then remake his miles-per-minute calculation. He had to be precise on the way out; otherwise he would not find the target. Therefore, even if cloud cover were present, he could not hide above it the entire way.

The return journey would be less complex. An Allied pilot only needed to cross no man's land by a few miles to be safe from German fighters; the exact location did not matter because there were plenty of available aerodromes where he could land and ask directions. The calculation, however, was different, and herein lay the peril. His aeroplane would still be supported by an air mass moving east at 30 mph (the same west wind), but with his 90-mph aeroplane now heading west (into the wind), its speed over ground would only be 60 mph, or 1 mile per minute. The 60-mile return journey would therefore take one hour and require twice as much fuel as the outward one. The pilot would look at his compass and his watch, climb above the clouds if he wished, and head west for one hour, not knowing precisely where he was, or possibly even caring. There would be plenty of time for that after the hour had elapsed provided he kept a sharp lookout for the opposition along the way and did not run out of fuel.

One lost RFC pilot who had landed to ask for directions was happy to be waved in by a friendly mechanic in overalls. Then, as he taxied past a hangar with open doors, he noticed the aeroplane within wore black crosses. Fortunately there was enough open space remaining on the airfield for a hurried departure.

Becoming lost was very easy indeed. It was even easier if persistent enemy attacks had to be beaten off.

End of Volume 1 of 6 volumes, ebook edition.

CHAPTER FIVE

DOVER PATROL, Part 1
(1 January to 31 July 1917)

A Royal Naval Air Service greeting card.

The role of the Royal Navel Air Service in guarding the fleet during the Great War has not received much publicity or fame; nevertheless, the success of the destroyers which escorted the leave boats and supply ships across the English Channel depended principally upon their companion RNAS airship spotting and signalling the presence of a waiting or approaching U-boat just below the surface. But how were the highly vulnerable airships protected from attack by

German aeroplanes? The answer is simple— a combined sea and air organization named the Dover Patrol.

The entire area covered by the ships of the Dover Patrol lay within the range of land-based aircraft from both sides of the Channel. The sky over the western half was kept clear by the French Armée de l'Air; the eastern half was kept clear by RNAS high-performance, land-based aeroplanes stationed on both sides of the Channel, as well as by RNAS seaplanes operating from Westgate and Dover (Marine).

To the north, the area was defined by the coverage of the Harwich force of destroyers and light cruisers, and the big flying boats from Yarmouth and Felixstowe. They patrolled according to a plotting system which, when drawn on a map, looked like a spider's web and soon became known as such. The Spider's Web was centred on the North Hinder light vessel, and its western limit touched England from Harwich to Lowestoft. The eastern limit covered Zeebrugge, and the Dutch coast and could be stretched as far as Heligoland Bight. The patrols were mainly concerned with the arrival and departure of U-boats from Ostend and Zeebrugge but they also watched for German airships and seaplanes reconnoitring the North Sea or on their way to raid England. The position of German naval or air forces was transmitted in Morse code to Harwich as a bearing and distance from the North Hinder light vessel.

It was not necessary to risk battleships or heavy cruisers in bombarding Zeebrugge, Ostend and other targets on the Belgian coast when a pair of battleship-calibre guns mounted on a shallow-draught monitor could perform the task equally well. Such monitors and the aircraft to protect them were supplied by the Dover Patrol.

Depending upon the source of the data, the official grand total of military personnel carried safely from one side of the Channel to the other during the war years lies somewhere between sixteen million and eighteen million. This achievement in itself is the perfect tribute to all those who sailed or flew in the Dover Patrol. [1]

Although Roy may not have realized it at the time, on completion of his training he was destined to become part of the patrol.

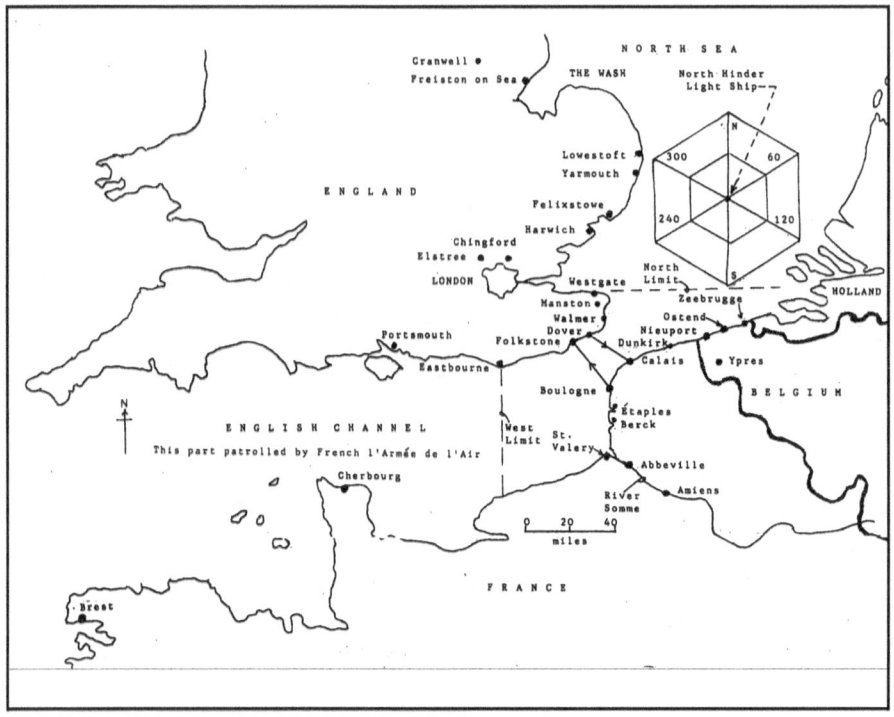

The area covered by the RNAS Dover Patrol,
showing its relationship to the Spider's Web.

On 1 January 1917 the commanding officer at Chingford decided that Roy could handle an Avro 504 and a B.E.2C well enough to move on to the next stage of his training: learning how to attack ground targets from the air and how to judge the deflection angle when shooting against moving targets. Roy was posted to the new RNAS training school at Cranwell, known as His Majesty's Ship *Daedalus*. The prefix *HMS* was for administrative purposes only; the ship comprised buildings on land, and the nearest smell of the sea came from the shellfish stall in Cranwell on market day.

After a week at HMS *Daedalus*, Roy was sent to the east coast to enjoy the healthy ocean air at RNAS Freiston on Sea, on the northwest side of the Wash. The station, which should have been named "Freiston on Mud," was a lonely, isolated aerodrome where the airmen had only the seagulls for company, but the nearby mudflats formed an ideal place for ground attack training.

As before, we shall let Roy tell his own story, and from this point onwards, Roy's log book entries are transcribed verbatim, except for some abbreviations which are given in full for clarity.

Jan 12 - NW1 - BE2C R.A.F. 8423 - 70 mins - 3,000' - Over mirror.

NW1 is the wind direction and speed; decoded, it means that the wind is blowing from the northwest at Force 1 on the Beaufort scale, viz., at two to three miles per hour, which is defined as light air movement.[2]

The abbreviation "R.A.F." means that B.E.2C No. 8423 was fitted with a Royal Aircraft Factory engine instead of a Renault. The "mirror" was a device on the ground to help a pilot learn when to pull the bomb-release toggle so as to hit the target.

"*Sorry, but I didn't want to be late for tea.*" B.E.2C No. 8423, photographed at Cranwell in 1916. After repair it was sent to Freiston on sea, and flown by Roy on 12 January 1917.

R. N. Air Station
Freiston, Lincs
Jan. 13/17

Dear Dad,

As you see I have been moved to a new station. I am here to have some bombing and Lewis gun work and then I am pretty sure of foreign service. At least, I was inoculated for typhus which only happens when you go on foreign service. My arm was pretty sore for a few days but I am O.K. now. My throat is a little sore at times but nothing to speak of.

I had a nice time on New Year's leave. Saw some very good theatres, Harry Lauder in Three Cheers and some others. Was out to Chingford to see the people with whom I was billeted. It is rather funny eating meals in town now. You can only have so much and pay so much. It keeps you figuring to get enough in one restaurant. Some of the chaps go from one to the other like we used to go from Uncle Will's home eating a meal each place.

I have not received any mail. The last letter was in December. I cannot understand it. Some other chaps are the same but others get all their mail.

We get no leave at all here. I would have liked to see Mrs. Hirsch but will not get a chance.

Our aerodrome here is just on the shores of The Wash near Boston. I was out over it yesterday. It is all mud banks around the shore where we are.

The weather is very bad here but we get a chance once in a while. I had a nice flip yesterday.

Please write soon.

Food rationing had not yet been introduced in England, and supplies were becoming short. The situation became critical later when the Germans realized what was happening and decided to lend a hand.

Jan 17 - N3 - BE2C R.A.F. 8433 - 45 mins - 1,200' - Dropping dummy bombs.

Wind Force 3 on the Beaufort scale means a gentle Breeze, eight to eleven miles per hour.

Typical B.E.2C fitted with a type C bomb rack for twenty pound Hales bombs, the type dropped by Roy. Note the manual fuel pump within easy reach of the pilot, Lieutenant A. T. Wilson, in the rear cockpit. Photograph taken in Egypt.

Jan 18 - 3.25 PM - N4 - BE2C R.A.F. 8722 - 35 mins - 2,000' - live bombs - Rainy and cloudy. Did not drop bombs.

Wind Force 4 means a moderate breeze, twelve to sixteen miles per hour.

R. N. Air Station
Freiston
Jan. 18/17

Dear Dad,

Have just received a lot of old mail. In fact they sent me a small mail sack of it. One old letter was from Helen Latimer telling me that she was getting a couple of weeks' leave and asking if I could get leave and see her in London. It is rotten getting mail like that. Please send me Reta's address so that I can explain to her.
I should be away from here very soon now but do not know where I am going so do not send mail to this station.

I have a bothersome cold at present, just enough to make me feel rotten. I don't know how I got it. Unless it is the kind of place we have to sleep in. The walls go up about seven feet and then are open to the roof with big ventilators open to the outside above. The wind whistles around you all the time. I would sooner sleep in a tent.

The weather here is pretty bad but we manage to get a little flying time in. One more good day or so and I will have all the practice I need.

At present we are in quarantine for spotted fever. I did not mention it before till I was sure everything was alright. They took swabs of our throats and all were negative so it is alright now. We are to be out of quarantine tomorrow. The chap who got it is getting better.

Had an awful flight this afternoon. Went up with some bombs to drop and ran into a rain and hail storm. It was anything but comfortable the way I felt full of cold and headache. Such is life.

B.E.2C No. 8433 is the middle aeroplane, flown by Roy at Freiston on sea on 17 and 22 January 1917.

Jan 22 - 11.00 AM - E2 - BE2C 8722 - 35 mins - 1,800' - Live bombs.

- 2.40 PM - E2 - BE2C 8433 - 10 mins - 150' - Firing at target.

A few days later, on 24 January, Roy was sent again to RNAS Dover, and this time the posting would stick for a while.

R. N. Air Station
Dover
Jan. 25/17

Dear Dad,

I have not written lately as I have been waiting to see what I am going to do. We are now down here on a war flight and will go across to Dunkerque in two or three weeks to be sent somewhere in France from there. We do not know but it is most likely to be the Somme. I got my first look at France today. We could see the coast quite well from here this morning. I came down here by train last night and as I have not been off this station or in the air I have seen nothing of Dover yet. I am on the sick list at present with a beast of a cold but it is somewhat better tonight and I will try to do some work tomorrow.

This is much the nicest station I have been on yet as far as accommodation goes but the aerodrome itself looks pretty bad. From the ground it looks as though engine trouble would about finish you. It very nearly did with one chap this morning.

Murray is stationed here but I have not seen him yet as he has gone to get a machine somewhere or is on leave. I do not know which.

The letter you wrote to Eastchurch has not shown up yet.

I shall be going on khaki leave in a few days time as I have never got it yet. If I can, I will have a picture taken in it before I go across.

"Khaki leave" meant leave to travel to London to purchase two sets of the khaki uniform worn by RNAS officers on foreign active service. As usual, things did not happen quite as quickly as Roy expected.

Jan 31/17 - 2.10 PM - N1 - Avro 504C 1459 - 15 mins - 2,000' - Local - Engine cut out. Landing carriage removed and propeller broken.

The Avro 504C production line at the Brush Electric Factory.
No. 1459 is the first in the row and has yet to grow wings.

Standard RNAS procedure called for a promising trainee pilot who had been able to walk away from an accident to be immediately sent aloft again in another aeroplane. Roy's instructor took him over to a single-seater type he had never flown before and ordered him to fly it around the field for a while.

Jan 31/17 - N1 - Bristol C 3034 - 15 mins - 1,500' - Local - Liked Bristol very much.

On 26 October 1916, 8 RNAS Squadron, commonly known as Naval 8, had been attached to the Royal Flying Corps and sent to France. The result was promising, and on 11 December, the Lords of the Admiralty had agreed to supply four more RNAS squadrons by spring 1917 to help the hard-pressed Flying Corps. On 1 February 1917, Naval 3 Squadron relieved Naval 8. Most Naval 8 pilots were sent back to England for a rest period, but some were ordered to remain at the RNAS pilots' pool at Saint Pol Aerodrome to form the nucleus of a new squadron—Naval 9 under Squadron Commander Henry Fawcett.

As new RNAS pilots graduated from Chingford and Cranwell and completed their gunnery and bombing courses, many were posted to the four new squadrons. Once formed, these were to be equipped with the latest types of scouts and give a surprise to the Germans. Roy's training programme was part of the plan, and it is easy to see why the Admiralty did not wish to waste pilots in nighttime crashes while they were on wild Zeppelin chases.

It was also on 1 February 1917 that Germany began unrestricted submarine warfare against the British Isles. Any ship of any nation, coming or going, was liable to be attacked without warning by German submarines. Admiral Tirpitz believed the threat of starvation would force the British government to ask for peace terms by the end of April. The RNAS would be busy helping the fleet to foil his intent.

Feb 10/17- 11.20 AM - E5 - Bristol C 3045 - 10 mins - 1,400' - Local - Wind got under wing landing and I crashed. Not landing into wind.

Roy had learnt that in a Force 5 wind (fresh breeze, seventeen to twenty-one miles per hour), a Bristol Scout was not quite so user friendly as an Avro 504 or a B.E.2C.

The cockpit of a Bristol C Scout.
Note the simple joystick and the manual fuel pump.

On 13 February 1917, Roy began instruction on the types of aeroplanes used against the enemy. As preparation for flying rotary-engined French Nieuport single-seater scouts, he was first given dual instruction in the Nieuport two-seater Types 10 and 12, then sent solo in winds up to Force 6. Three of the landings left depressions in the turf, which is not surprising as Force 6 is a strong breeze of twenty-two to twenty-seven miles per hour. In such conditions the aeroplane would not need much distance to take off and land, but the gusts, which tended to swing in a somewhat different direction from the basic wind, would have made him work hard.

There might have been another difficulty for Roy to manage since it is unknown whether these Nieuports had been built in England or purchased directly from the French factory. As mentioned before, on aeroplanes built in France, of which the RNAS and the RFC had many, the lever which controlled engine power operated in the reverse direction from that of the almost identical machines built in England.

Feb 13 - 10.15 AM - E4 - Nieup 10 3967 - 20 mins - 4,000' - Local - Bounced a little but slow landing.

Nieuport 10AV No. 3967 two-seater flown by Roy at Dover on 13 February 1917. The suffix "AV" stood for the French word "avant", meaning that the observer sat in the front *(avant)* seat. Note how the interplane struts formed a V at the bottom because the narrow chord lower wing had only one spar.
Photograph taken at Chingford in early 1916.

At this point the Dover Station's recording officer apparently requested that henceforth Roy enter all log book dates in the regulation RNAS fashion.

13.2.17 - 2.10 PM - E5 - Nieup 12 3928 - 20 mins - 3,000' - Local - Landing called good. Clouds low but visibility good.

14.2.17 - 10.20 AM - E5 - Nieup 12 3928 - 10 mins - 3,000' - Local - Clouds 1,000'. Landing fair.

- - - - E6 - Nieup 12 3928 - 10 mins - 3,000' - Local - Slow landing. Bumpy.

Typical Nieuport 12 two-seater.
The narrow chord of the single-spar lower wings stands out clearly.

Roy also had to be judged proficient on single-seater Nieuport Scouts.

R.N. Aeroplane Station
Dover
Feb. 15/17

Dear Dad,

As you see above I am still in England. I have not had my khaki leave yet as they have been unable to let me go due to a temporary scarcity of pilots on the station. I was told yesterday that I am to go next week. I would have liked it this week as Stearne is on leave now. He came down here to see Murray and me. He just left a few minutes ago. He looks very well and seems to like his work very much. He has a dandy job bombing in that region.

Murray is fine. He is kept busy taking machines to France. Murray has a bar to his DSC which is the only one in the RNAS. Pretty good, eh?

What did you think about Sir Douglas Haig's speech about the war? I did not like it at all. It looked too much like playing to the gallery. Perhaps he was ordered to do so. It matters not a lot what anyone thinks, it will go on just the same.

We are pretty busy here as there are so few pilots on the station at present. Although our work does not matter any, it has to be done. It looks like eye-wash for the public but it is experience. None of that kind of stuff when we go across to the other side.

Sir Douglas Haig had just returned from a conference with the French commander-in-chief, Général Robert Nivelle, who had recently replaced Général Joseph Joffre and was planning a major attack in the Chemin des Dames area. Haig promised that the British forces would assist the French by making simultaneous attacks at other parts of the front to occupy the German reserves. Hopes were high within the French and the British general staffs that the combined effort would bring the war to a successful conclusion. Unfortunately French security was rather leaky, and it has been reported that the plan of attack, which became known as the Nivelle Offensive, was published in a Swiss newspaper. Whatever the reason, the Germans were completely ready to face the French, made mincemeat of them and were poised to send plentiful forces to take care of General Haig's attacks.

The Royal Flying Corps situation in France and Belgium was not much better. Major-General Hugh Trenchard, the commander-in-chief of the RFC, was well aware of German technical progress in the air. In December 1916 he had warned the Air Council in London, and in January 1917 had taken the matter up directly with the director of air organization, Major-General Sefton Brancker. General Trenchard wrote,

"You are asking me to fight the battle this year with the same machines as I fought it last year. We shall be hopelessly outclassed."

Unfortunately, a government spokesman contradicted Trenchard and assured the public that the RFC had complete mastery of the air in France. Trenchard's requests for more and better aeroplanes were met by further production of the same types which had proven so successful in 1915 and 1916. This was both cheap and convenient as the tools and jigs still existed, but it also reveals that the extremely rapid progress of aerial technology was not appreciated by some of those who worked in offices; in addition, Trenchard was considered to be an alarmist.

The British government spokesman, had been confusing quantity with quality. Although the Imperial German Army Air Service was outnumbered in northern France, 350 of the 900 Royal Flying Corps' aeroplanes in use there were hopelessly obsolete. A further 200 were obsolescent and could only engage in battle on favourable terms. The RFC squadrons were thus equipped with a frightening percentage of out-of-date aircraft and would soon have to support the army in what would become known as the Battle of Arras. The aircrews, in performing their allotted tasks, would be up against German fighters in steadily increasing numbers.

Fortunately, some wiser heads existed, and as the navy had done some time ago, the army now placed orders for modern aeroplanes with the Sopwith Aviation Company and the SPAD factory in France. Roy Brown and his colleagues fly the new types of scouts and give the Germans a surprise. One revolutionary innovation was a triplane, the work of Herbert Smith, chief designer for Thomas Octave Murdoch Sopwith. [3]

The Sopwith Aviation Company's triplane scout prototype, Naval Order No. N500 (the prefix "N" stood for "Naval"), was placed into the tender hands of Naval 8 from 16 to 26 February 1917 for evaluation, but it would appear that not enough attention was directed to its high centre of gravity. On its first day there, Flight Sub-Lieutenant Reginald Rhys Soar (12 victories including shared) made one of those landings which guarantee an interview with the squadron commander.

Lesser pilots achieved the same attitude of a duck dabbling by merely taxiing N500 without sufficient attention to the wind speed and direction. Ten days later Flight Sub-Lieutenant Soar did it again, but this time he received commendations for quick thinking and expertise when the engine caught fire during takeoff.

"Not quite Naval 8 standard, you know, old boy."*

Flight Sub-Lieutenant R. R. Soar's emergency landing in Sopwith Triplane N500 on 26 February 1917 on rough ground. Note the high and forward centre of gravity created by the top wing.

After repairs, N500 was sent to France for evaluation by the RNAS squadrons stationed there. It received acclamation from those who tested it and production orders were placed immediately. [4]

Gerrard 4343
Savoy Hotel
London
20.2.17

Dear Dad,

    I am on my last leave now before going to France. At least that is what is on the books now and I hope it comes all O.K. I am in khaki now and if possible I shall get my picture taken tomorrow.
    I have just come back from Leeds an hour ago. I stayed with Mrs. Hirsch last night and to-day. I could not stay longer as I have such a lot to do and am going back to Dover on Friday. Their youngest son is pretty badly crocked up. His leg was broken by a shell and it is now two inches shorter than the other one. He was only in the trenches 3 days and then lay in front for four days so is pretty lucky to be alive. They are very nice people and I appreciate their being so good to me. Their other son has been in France 12 months and has not been wounded yet.
    I have a rotten cold. It seems as if I just get rid of one and pick up another.

R. N. Aeroplane Station
Dover
4.3.17

Dear Dad,

    I am enclosing the proofs of some photographs I had taken when I was on khaki leave. If you will mark on the back what you want, I will get them for you. Let Alice see them too, please, and ask her to do the same.
    The weather has been very bad here so I have missed very little by being on the sick list. It now depends upon the weather and the doctor when I go across to France.
    Murray has been sent to another station.

A. Roy Brown in RNAS khaki uniform for active service overseas 1917.

In an earlier letter, written at Chingford and dated 14 August 1916, Roy had said that he had bought a Rudge Multi motorcycle which he would sell before crossing to France, but he did not mention this vehicle after leaving Eastchurch. On 7 March 1917 he made note that he and another chap had taken a bus to Folkestone; therefore it seems probable that he no longer possessed it. Margaret Brown Harmon recalls her father telling of a motorcycle accident which resulted in a broken bone, and it seems possible there may be a connection between the disappearing motorcycle and some of his inactivity in the air between

1 September 1916 and 12 January 1917. Certainly, Roy did not tell his parents he had progressed from bending aeroplanes to bending a motorcycle.

On 9 March the chief instructor accompanied Roy on a progress evaluation flight.

9.3.17 - 10.05 AM - S4 - Nieup 12 8510 - 20 mins - 4,000' - Local.

Roy's log book contains the Royal Navy Dover Aeroplane Station date stamp for 9 March 1917 releasing him for service with an active squadron. Also included were the following remarks from both the chief instructor and the commanding officer: *"Total time in air 45 hrs. Fairly ready for active service. More practice required."*

On 10 March, Roy travelled with his kit by sea to France and thence by land to the RNAS pilots' pool at Saint Pol Aerodrome, just inland to the east of a seaside village named Saint-Pol-sur-Mer. Upon arrival he was posted to the newly formed Naval 9 Squadron, a No. 1 Wing unit. He did not have far to travel; Naval 9 was stationed at Saint-Pol Aerodrome.

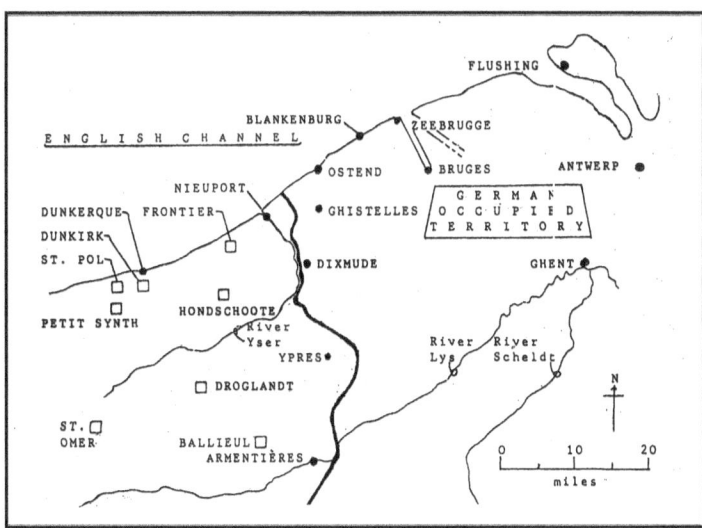

Aerodromes and towns mentioned in Roy's log book and letters from 10 March to 31 July 1917. The RFC pilots' pool was located at Saint-Omer Aerodrome.

Naval 9 was equipped with various types of last year's successful RNAS aircraft, mostly 80hp Le Rhône rotary-engined Sopwith Scouts. A reduced version of an earlier Sopwith two-seater fighter, the Scout had immediately been nicknamed *Pup* which soon became it's official name. It was fast (by 1916 standards), nimble and pleasant to fly, and pilots liked it.

Typical Sopwith Pup. Note the pet name *Mildred H* painted below the cockpit of N6183, and the "parking brake" tied to each wing.

There were also a few Nieuport 11 biplanes, with 80hp Gnôme or 80hp Le Rhône rotary engines, which were scaled-down single- seater versions of the Nieuport 10 two-seater and aptly nicknamed *"Bébé"* by the French. The RFC and RNAS called them *Baby* Nieuports. The pilots soon learned not to dive them too fast—one of the lower wings would tear off.

11.3.17 - 12.00 PM - E2 - Baby Nieup 3993 - 25 mins - 4,000' - Local - Heavy handed going off but saw mistake. Dove about 1,000' and my stomach began to rise. Landing a little bumpy.

Typical Nieuport 11 Bébé. The narrow lower wing and the V struts are apparent. No. 3977 was flown by B Squadron, RNAS. The aeroplanes inside the hangar are B.E.2Cs.

11.3.17 - 2.35 PM - E1 - Nieup. 17bis 8751 - 25 mins - Height 4,500' - Local - Clouds 4,000', misty, rain. Machine tends to stall left & nose down. Right swing on landing. Walters and I chanced each other in a huffing match.

"Huffing" is a term borrowed from a variant of the game of draughts, known as checkers in the United States. In today's parlance, it means that Roy and Walters played "Chicken" in mock attacks upon each other.

This was the last occasion on which Roy entered the aerodrome wind conditions in his log book. Training was now definitely over.

On the strength of Naval 9 there were several of the somewhat streamlined Nieuport 17bis single-seater biplanes with a 130hp Clergêt rotary engine. The suffix "bis" was the French equivalent of Mark 2. Despite the high power, they were heavy and their performance was disappointing; therefore, the final RNAS order for one hundred aeroplanes from the British Nieuport Company was cancelled.

Typical Nieuport 17bis. The size of the engine, compared with the rest of the machine, gives an idea of the power the pilot had at his command.

That evening, after his flight in Nieuport, Roy wrote to his brother, Horace, who was still at home on convalescent leave.

R. N. Aeroplane Station
No. 1 Wing, No. 9 Squadron
G.P.O. London
11.3.17

Dear Horry,

Left England yesterday so I have put in one day on active service, foreign. Not very active as yet for me though. We cannot write anything about machines, work or where we are, so   you can tell Dad and Mother to expect very little news.

I was sore as a boil after my first flip here. I did not pull my goggles down over my face on going up so that when I went to pull them down they had been blown off and of course lost. I had just bought a new fur mask so I was pretty sore.

Our quarters here are very comfortable and we have a good mess. Cannot get a bath on this station but can go into town for one. Pretty good bunch of fellows so everything is O.K. Have got rid of my cold at last, I think, and hope it stays away.

To-day has been beautiful and warm, the first one for months. Doors open and sitting outside so we certainly enjoyed it. Stearne will be near us pretty soon and for a few months we will be able to see each other every few days if we last.

To avoid exercising the censor, Roy did not give Horace the reason why a well-fitting, good quality fur mask with goggles was essential. The truth was that frostbite was an open-cockpit pilot's most insidious enemy; even in summer, the air could become bitterly cold at high altitudes. A scarf was another essential item, and to permit a pilot to continually search the surrounding sky without rubbing his neck raw, the best available material was silk. He could also use the ends of the scarf to wipe the castor oil from his goggles as it worked its way back from the engine.

Naval 9's primary role was to protect Dunkirk and its harbour from the attentions of German bombers. Its secondary task was to defend the British Isles against attacks by German aeroplanes or airships. After dark, the RNAS alone were responsible for the seaward side of the coast, and Naval 9 was well-positioned to do this.

Another Naval 9 duty was to act as fighter escort to Naval 2. This squadron was mainly employed in spotting the fall of the huge battleship-type shells which were fired from miles out at sea by the shallow draught-monitors of the Dover Patrol. Targets were the German-occupied harbours on the French and Belgian coasts where the U-boats, which had already caused such destruction in the Atlantic, had their bases.

The aircraft flown by Naval 2—from which the Pup had been derived—were the single-seater and two-seater versions of the long obsolete Sopwith One and a Half Strutter, another nickname which had quickly become official. The W shape of the struts which attached the upper wings to the fuselage were called half-struts. When combined with the full-length struts out near each wing tip, they formed the origin of the well-known nickname. One and a Half Strutters were officially listed as RNAS Type 9700. Strange as it may seem today, the single-seater Strutters (as they became known) were bombers, and the two-seaters were fighters. This sound concept allowed a low-powered aeroplane to carry a useful load of bombs; after the bombs were dropped, the bomber version, now the lighter of the two, flew faster than the fighter. Unfortunately, progress in German aircraft design was such that by early 1917 the Strutter fighter, so successful in 1916, could not even protect itself, and Naval 9, equipped with Nieuport Baby and Sopwith Pup scouts, was obliged to escort the Strutter bombers.

In addition to bombing, Naval 2 had the task of photographing German installations along the French and Belgian coasts as far as the Dutch frontier. The pilots of the escorting scouts from Naval 9 had to monitor their fuel consumption carefully on such long flights over enemy territory.

The Strutter fighter and bomber were equipped with a Scarff-Dybovsky synchronized Vickers machinegun for the pilot. In addition, the fighter carried a Lewis gun mounted on a swivelling hoop, for the rear gunner who, in RNAS naval terminology, was called a gun-layer. The hoop carrying the rear gun was referred to as a Scarff ring, named after its inventor, Warrant Officer Frederick William Scarff.[5]

Typical Sopwith One and a Half Strutter single-seater bomber. It carried four 65pound bombs suspended vertically in an internal compartment, so positioned that their presence or absence did not change the fore and aft balance of the machine.

The basic design of the One and a Half Strutter was good, and as mentioned above, a reduced version was developed in 1916 as a nimble, fast, single-seater scout. The Sopwith Pup's agility and docile behaviour made it highly successful in service despite its being equipped with only one machine gun. Roy began flying Pups later in March 1917, but unfortunately this was just about the time that, as Trenchard had predicted, German aeroplanes with superior performance to the Pup, and carrying two machineguns, began to appear on the Western Front.

13.3.17 - 12.15 PM - Baby Nieup 3993 - 30 mins - 5,500' - Local.

This flight in a Nieuport 11 Baby enabled Roy to become familiar with the area around Saint-Pol. He would have placed emphasis on any prominent landmarks which would indicate the whereabouts of the aerodrome, when clouds were low or visibility poor.

13.3.17 - 4.30 PM - Nieup 8750 - 30 minutes - 5,000' - H.A. Patrol to Nieuport. Clouds too low to carry on. Saw shells but not fired at me.

This day saw Roy's first hostile action of the war. He had attempted what was known as a hostile-aircraft patrol, but the low clouds prevented him from climbing above 5,000 feet. The flight of Nieuport aeroplanes reached the similarly named town of Nieuport where they found the weather had deteriorated appreciably.

Part of the town that once was Nieuport. Being just inside territory held by the Allies it was susceptible to destruction.

The weather remained bad, but improved a little during the afternoon of 15 March. Roy was ordered to have a "look-see", but his report was discouraging:

15.3.17 - 3.10 PM - Baby Nieup 3993 - 10 mins - 1,100' - Clouds 900 feet, visibility bad. Stood by all morning for patrol to Zeebrugge. Bad weather, nothing doing.

On Friday, 16 March, Roy tried his hand at a Sopwith Pup and flew it once around the aerodrome. His log book does not contain the serial number of the unfortunate Pup or the time of the flight, but the Remarks column tells the story:

16.3.17 - Sopwith - 10 mins - 2,000' - Local - Turned over on landing. Tried to land like on a Nieuport.

According to information kindly provided by historian R.C. Sturtivant, the identity of the machine involved is revealed by the maintenance record of Sopwith Pup No. N5182. It states that, after a flight with Naval 9 on 16 March 1917, No. N5182 had to be sent to Dunkirk Aircraft Depot (RNAS code name "ADD") for repairs.

A Sopwith Pup looked rather like a Nieuport Baby, but there the resemblance ended. During landing, as soon as the broad lower wings of a Pup became subject to what is now known as ground effect; they gained extra lift and the wheels seemed to have an aversion to meeting the ground. Nieuport Babies, with their narrow lower wings, behaved differently: they suddenly stopped flying, touched down with a thump and stayed down.[6]

Typical RNAS Sopwith Pup with its broad lower wings at RNAS Dover. The aeroplanes in the background are Sopwith Triplanes. (7)

The following letter from Roy to his father suggests that he did not escape unscathed in the accident to Sopwith Pup No. N5182. Although "other conditions" which kept him on the ground for a month.

R.N.A.S.
23.3.17

Dear Dad,

I have not been doing much lately due to the weather and other conditions. You asked about my back. To be perfectly frank, ever since I hurt it, it has bothered me more or less but not enough to stop me carrying on duty. When I get on leave I will be able to write a decent letter. I intend to spend my first half-day writing. We get leave every three months or are supposed to. It will not take very long for that to slip around. Stearne and I are quite close together though not in the same squadron. He was over to our mess for dinner on Wednesday night. He is getting some leave very soon.

At about this time, Roy's sister Reta slipped on a wooden platform in the rain, fell awkwardly and incurred a complicated leg fracture.

R.N.A.S.
2.4.17

Dear Dad,

There is practically no news as the weather is rotten. We had a young snow storm to-day.

Stearne has left for England to-day on leave. He surely is lucky about his leave. He had a letter from Doug Findlay a couple of days ago. Doug seems to be kept busy and doing good work.

I hope Reta's leg does not give her a permanent limp as might result from such a serious break.

Although Roy did not yet know what was in store for the Royal Navel Air Service and the Royal Flying Corps, the period that became known as Bloody April had begun the day before. Roy's sprains and bruises from the overturning of Sopwith Pup N5182 kept him earthbound for the entire month of April 1917, which was possibly the greatest piece of good luck to occur in his entire adult life. Of the 912 RFC and RNAS airmen who supported the army in the Battle of Arras that month, 316 were posted as either killed or missing. The additional number of those wounded in action or injured in crashes is unknown. Roy, who was well aware of the situation, obviously did not wish holes to be cut in his letters by the censor's scissors, thereby causing anxiety to his parents.

The increasing number of surprise attacks by German U-boats upon neutral passenger ships approaching or leaving the British Isles was causing concern. Equally deadly were the minefields which each side had carefully sited to block the other's sea routes and harbours. Ships of the Dover Patrol swept the channels every day, weather permitting, but the mine anchor cables, weakened by age and violent winter storms, could release their charges at any hour, day or night. From the beginning to the end of the war, over 3,500 mines, both Allied and German, were destroyed in the English Channel by British and French minesweepers, many of which disappeared without trace in the process.

Although the number of British ships lost to German U-boat warfare was being made public, their tonnage was not. In the month of

March, very few people, outside the government and the Lords of the Admiralty, knew that stocks of food and munitions were becoming dangerously low; sufficient imports from overseas were simply not arriving. Admiral Tirpitz had not achieved his beginning of April 1917 date for ending the war, but he was running close to it.

On 6 April 1917 Admiral Tirpitz lost his gamble: America declared war on Germany, and U.S. Rear-Admiral William Sowden Sims was sent to England to begin organizing naval help. On 4 May a flotilla comprising six US destroyers arrived at Queenstown naval base in Ireland, where Royal Navey Vice-Admiral Sir Lewis Bayly was in command. Every fortnight another flotilla arrived until Rear-Admiral W.S. Sims had a total of 100 US destroyers in action. When they combined with the Royal Navy's 200 destroyers, sufficient strength became available to escort merchant ships across the Atlantic in convoys. With supplies once more reaching England, the fortunes of battle slowly began to turn against Germany, Austria and Turkey.

Towards the end of the year, a plan would be made for part of the U.S. destroyer force to blockade the German U-boats and destroyers in their bases at Zeebrugge and Ostend on the Belgian coast. The Dover Patrol was to provide protection from the air.

The transatlantic voyage would then become safe enough for U.S. General John Joseph Pershing's army to be transported to France, where it would be armed and trained.

The part played by the U.S. Navy in changing the fortunes of the Allies is relatively unknown on both sides of the Atlantic Ocean; in those days there was not much room for newspaper reporters or cinema newsreel cameras on destroyers. There is little mention of those who deserved a large portion of the credit for overcoming the U-boat menace—those who served in the U.S. Navy's destroyer fleet under Rear-Admiral Sims.

US Navy Rear-Admiral William Sowden Sims.

During the air war in France, Murray Galbraith had seen much "work" with Naval 8, including several combat successes, between July and late November 1916 and was in need of a well-earned rest. Accordingly, he was sent back to the "Home Establishment" (the term covering all aerodromes in the United Kingdom) to pass on his knowledge and expertise to others. By the end of 1917 he was an advanced flying instructor at Manston in Kent, and in 1918 Murray was posted to the Italian theatre of war on anti-submarine operations.

Captain Murray Galbraith, DSC and bar (6 victories), standing beside Sopwith F1 Camel No. B3996, *Happy Hawkins*, at Manston, Kent.

The Admiralty intended to raise Naval 9 to a full complement of eighteen pilots and to replace the Bristol Cs, Bristol Ds, Nieuport Babies and Sopwith Pups with Sopwith Triplanes. The new squadron was then to relieve Naval 3, which was due for a rest. Throughout Bloody April about 240 British and about 55 French aeroplanes had been lost in action. Surviving Imperial German Army Air Service records list its losses in the region of 80 and are probably correct, thereby showing the German superiority even at that stage of the war.

The chorus of a 1917 aircrew song, which was sung to the tune of "Do You Ken John Peel?" went as follows:

> *For a batman woke me from my bed,*
> *I'd had a thick night and a very sore head,*
> *And I said to myself, to myself I said,*
> *Oh we haven't got a hope in the morning.*

Very few Sopwith Pups or Triplanes were lost, but the Royal Flying Corps photographic reconnaissance crews in their B.E.2Cs and F.E.2Bs were slaughtered. These two types of aeroplane were simply too slow and unmanoeuvrable for the 1917 conditions. Whatever the odds and no matter how heavily armed they were, once detected they had to stay and fight. (8)

The injuries which Roy had incurred in the accident on 16 March aggravated the old problem with his left knee. It did not respond to local ministrations as hoped, so on 8 April he was sent for treatment to England on the hospital ship *Liberty*, a yacht owned by Lord Tredegar. He arrived at Chatham Hospital on 13 April having travelled with a Canadian from Ottawa, an old friend from the Wright Brothers School at Dayton, Flight Lieutenant James Alexander (Ally) Shaw of Naval 5, who had a similar injury. The story of this adventure is to be found later in a letter written to his sister Reta, on 6 May, ten days after he had returned to duty. Roy's absence was unfortunate because he missed the chance to try out two Sopwith Triplanes which arrived at Saint Pol on 24 April.

R.N.A.S.
15.4.17

Dear Mother,

Just received your letter of March 13 this morning. It certainly takes a long time to get mail.

About sending things over to me: It is hardly necessary as we can always go to town to buy anything we need. Although what the shops have is not so good as you could send, it is not worth while in the present state of shipping.

You wrote a long time ago about coming over this summer. Stearne said that his mother had mentioned it too. Much as I should like to see you, I do not want to have you come as the risk is too great. There are too many floating mines being laid by the Germans and there are too many submarines around. They have to pay a heavy toll for the shipping they get but I do not think a visit is worth the risk. Stearne does not want his mother to come either.

Reta will be very sorry about missing her chance to come over but the way the Huns are carrying on now, it is just as well, for nurses on a hospital ship are just as apt to get it as not.

There is lots of work going on with us now. I have been doing some but have not really got going yet. It surely is no fun in France. Our station is right near Dunkerque at St. Pol. We have a dandy C.O.

Murray Galbraith is still at the same place. He surely has a good job now and he deserves it. I am feeling fine again and may get some leave before long as it is over a month since I left for France.

On 23 April Roy was discharged from hospital, and on the 28th he was posted to Walmer. This new RNAS aerodrome, a satellite of Dover, lay between Dover and Deal on the south coast of England. It was to be a key aerodrome of the Dover Patrol. In his log book Roy wrote: "*Stationed at Walmer. New station for protecting ships in the Downs from aerial torpedoes.*" The RNAS was making preparations to protect the warships which were shortly to intensify operations against the German U-boat bases.

On 30 April Roy took Bristol Scout D No. 8963 for a flip around Walmer. Apparently his belongings had not yet followed his unexpected posting to Walmer, for there is no entry in his Log Book concerning this flight. However, an Aircraft Damage Report does exist, telling what he did to the unfortunate Bristol: he crashed upon landing and wrecked it. Roy was unhurt in the accident, but later events suggest that the badly bent biplane displeased someone in authority.

On 2 May, in the morning, Roy flew some practice circuits around nearby Manston aerodrome where the RNAS War School was located. His log book entry reads:

2.5.17 - 11.45 AM - 80 HP Bristol Scout C 3055 - 10 mins - 2,000' - Local at Manston.

Typical Bristol Scout C with a Lewis gun fitted
by the RNAS to fire over the propeller.

There are two further log book entries for 2 May, but these refer to a Bristol Scout D. This later type had a Gnôme monosoupape engine but, unlike Scout C, Scout D had left the factory already equipped with a Lewis gun.

2.5.17 - 4.00 PM - Mono Bristol Scout D 8958 - 10 mins - 2,500' - Local at Manston.

- 5.00 PM - Mono Bristol Scout D 8958 - 20 mins - 5,000' - Manston to Walmer.

On the morning of 3 May some work was performed on the engine and the rigging of Bristol D Scout No. 8959. Roy took it up for a test flight in the afternoon; his log book does not state the takeoff time.

3.5.17 - Mono Bristol 8958 Scout D - 30 mins - 6,000' - Local at Walmer - Testing machine and engine. Flies right wing down.

A slight alteration to the rigging of the wings would have easily corrected that fault.

Deal, England
May 3/17

Dear Dad,

I expect you will think I am dead or at least a prisoner of war but nothing like that. In fact, as far as service matters go I am one of the luckiest boys.
Shaw, a chap from Edmonton, and myself had bad knees. He twisted his playing football and I also hurt my old one. They sent us from France to hospital and have now given me a job in England on a new stunt which I cannot write about. We will do lots of flying and should do lots of good if we have any luck.
How long we shall be here I don't know but we were very lucky to get a job out of France as our casualties there are pretty heavy.
Perhaps you will see in the papers a lot of criticism of the R.N.A.S. but the public doesn't know anything about it. If they did, it would be a different tale but the navy lets them think what they like and goes on just the same. Some of the criticism is justified but the majority is written by men who do not know what has to be contended with and only look at a row of figures in their office chairs.
My knee is O.K. now and I hope it will stay that way. I am as tanned as an Indian now and, here, it is just like living at the cottage on the lake so we will surely be healthy if surroundings can do anything for us.
I have not had a letter from you for a month but I suppose my mail is still going to France.

Roy still had a weak left knee from the pre-war hockey injury in Canada and had apparently hurt it again. He does not specify what had happened, but one can speculate. Tension-relieving games in the mess after a drink or two sometimes resulted in several sprains and bruises, plus much broken furniture. The worst occasions were "Guest Nights" when another squadron paid a visit and the competition was at its highest. On the morning following one particular Guest Night at a certain RFC aerodrome, expected bad weather did not occur, and each of the four morning patrol pilots of the guest squadron had a mishap during takeoff. Major Tom Algar Elliott Cairnes, investigated the scene of the crime, but could take no action because the host squadron's morning patrol had proceeded normally. Its wily commanding officer had not permitted its four pilots, whose *"batmen woke them from their bed,"* to stay beyond dinner.

Roy made one more test flight in Bristol Scout D 8958. It turned out to be his last flight at Walmer.

5.5.17 - 3.45 PM - Bristol Scout D 8958 - 20 mins - 3,000' - Local at Walmer. Testing engine.

Apparently the rigging adjustment had been successful.

R.N. Air Station
Walmer, Nr. Deal
Kent
May 6/17

My dear Reta

I was very pleased to get your letter as it was the first one you had written to me since going to Salem. I thought you had nearly forgotten I was alive.

As you see above I am not in France now but have a lovely job in England which should last for about three months with luck. My old knee went bad on me in France and they sent me to hospital in England. Our hospital ship was held up on the French coast for about a week so that by the time I got to hospital I was nearly better. I was in ten days then sent to the Admiralty and then down here.

This is a beautiful place. It is on a hill overlooking the sea and the healthiest place I have been since coming over here. I feel like a fighting cock already and sleep like a log as soon as my head touches the pillow. At present we are sleeping in a hotel in Walmer with one night in three in a tent on the aerodrome. We are in tents and outside all day except when we are up, so *with the sea breeze, you can understand how healthy it is.*

There are not very many of us here but when we get things running properly we should have a very good time. That is the big advantage of the air service. Your work is more a nervous strain than anything else and while it is on there is plenty of it but it does not last long and the rest of the time you have more or less to yourself. Of course you spend a lot of time seeing the mechanics keep your machine in proper condition as all engines require very delicate care. After each flight a machine has to be all washed down with petrol and coal oil, then the engine is all washed with petrol and the sparking plugs taken out and cleaned. They surely do everything to make us sure of having our engines in good condition but even then there are lots of things that are missed.

I was very sorry to hear about your accident but our family has all the luck. I surely hope you will not have a permanent limp. Do you remember old "Limpy" Logan with the wooden leg? You can get married to him if you do.

Write and tell me how you get along with the house-cleaning in the hospital and how you get things working.(9)

The sea traffic between England and France was intense: an average of thirty cargo or troop ships per day crossed the Channel from 5 August 1914 to 11 November 1918. If vessels of all types, from the largest to the smallest, of the Royal Navy and the mercantile marine are included, the daily average rises to ninety-five. However, due to the efforts of the British and French naval and air units of the Dover Patrol, it was extremely rare for a vessel to be lost due to enemy action. Both Roy Brown's letters and the war experiences of Captain William Carpenter Lambert (18 victories including shared) described in his book Combat Report, indicate that travel from England to France was routed from Dover to Calais, and the return voyage from France to "Blighty" routed from Boulogne to Folkestone, to reduce the risk of collision in fog.

According to the Belgian fighter ace Willy Omer François Coppens de Houthulst (37 victories including 34 balloons), leave boats crossed the Channel in pairs, escorted by two destroyers and an RNAS airship. The airship's crew usually were the first to see a periscope and would use an Aldis lamp or semaphore flags to signal the submarine's position to a destroyer. On calm, sunny days the airship's crew could often see quite clearly the dark shape of a U-boat below the surface of the water. It had been unexpectedly discovered early in the war that a German U-boat would break off an attack on a ship and dive very quickly if an Allied aircraft approached—hence the introduction of organized air protection. The effectiveness of the system depended upon the ability of the Dover Patrol to prevent German aeroplanes from attacking the airships.

When one hears of airships, one tends to think of the German Zeppelins and Schutte-Lanz rigid types. It is little known that from 1914 to 1918 over two hundred airships, mainly non-rigid "blimps", were employed by the RNAS, a larger number than were used by the Germans.

Two destroyers escorting a leave ship as it departs from Boulogne on its way to Folkstone. Photograph taken from their guardian airship.

Logically the Lords of the Admiralty did not wish the Germans to learn how heavy the cross-Channel traffic really was, so the Royal Navy and it's Air Service worked in silence. One ship sunk was news; one thousand ships having crossed safely was a deep, dark secret. The Royal Flying Corps was shooting down German aeroplanes, which made weekly headline news; the RNAS was successfully protecting ships and airships, but that could not be divulged. The remark made by Alice Pickup, mentioned in Roy's letter home dated 17 April 1916, that *"from what she heard, the RNAS never gets into active service"* was actually a glowing tribute to the tight security around the vital work of "The Silent

Service", as the Royal Navy sometimes called itself. It was certainly far superior to the secrecy of the plans for Général Robert Nivelle's French Army offensive earlier in the year.[10]

An idea of the success achieved by the Dover Patrol ships, aeroplanes and airships may be gleaned from the following two statistics: Only one cross-Channel steamer, the *Sussex*, was torpedoed by a U-boat during the entire war, whereas forty-two German U-boats are known to have been lost in the area protected by the Dover Patrol. The 24 March 1916 attack on the *Sussex* was not a complete success; although the prow was blown off, the ship limped across to Boulogne where it was successfully beached.

An RNAS airship, Type SS (Submarine Scout), on patrol in the English Channel. The crew sat in a B.E.2 aeroplane fuselage slung beneath the envelope. To provide better comfort, the later type SSZ had a housing which looked like a motorboat.

Roy had used the previous weekend to pay a visit to Mrs Edith Hirsch at Weetwood, near Leeds. On Friday evening, 4 May, he had gone up to London and from there filled in a telegram form at the hotel desk, advising her that he would arrive "tomorrow" on the evening train. Later events suggest that he had not been generous enough with the tip!

[letter undated]

Dear Mrs. Brown,

 About three weeks ago we had the pleasure of a visit from your son. We were very disappointed about the bother he had but it was just an accident. He gave a telegram to the hotel Hall Porter to send to me and the stupid man did not take it to the Post Office until the next day so of course we hadn't gone to the station to meet the train. He had great difficulty getting a taxi and then the driver lost his way - it was a terribly dark night - and poor Roy had nearly half an hour's walk up hill with his heavy hand bag. The worst was that he had a most terrible cold and cough and ought to have been in bed. He could only stay here one night. His visit gave us all great pleasure. My Frank, who was wounded six months ago, was at home and he was delighted to meet Roy. How the two talked!!!
 Roy seems to be very happy and was looking forward to his trips abroad. A letter from him yesterday says that he has already gone but he can tell us nothing, only that his cold is perfectly better. He was in khaki and I think it becomes him well.
 If he has leave again we are hoping to have him for longer.

With kindest regards,
I am yours very sincerely,
Edith Hirsch

When Roy returned to his squadron at Walmer, he was greeted with disturbing operational news. The Germans now had large numbers of their latest twin-machine-gun fighter, the Albatros D.III, in service at the front in France, and the situation of the Allied air forces was deteriorating rapidly. The Albatros designers, in what appears to be an attempt to keep down the weight of this fighter with its heavy water-cooled engine, had used a single-spar lower wing. Then, as with the Nieuport Bébé, one of the narrow, lower wings would sometimes tear off in a high-speed dive. From this it may be deduced that the cause was not bad workmanship or weak material but some mysterious aerodynamic phenomenon. Many German, French and British pilots were to die before the phenomenon was identified and a cure implemented.

Typical Albatros D.III. This particular machine, D.2015/16, was forced down and captured by 29 Squadron RFC on 4 June 1917. Note the V struts between the wide upper and the narrow, lower wings.

Below 15,000 feet the performance of the new Albatros D.III fighter was better than that of the Sopwith Pup, and RNAS casualties were increasing. The RFC was in an even worse situation: its D.H.2 and F.E.8 pusher fighters were hopelessly outclassed, and even after the Battle of Arras, experienced pilots continued to be lost at an alarming rate. By this stage of the air war, about the only positive thing one could say about the rotary-engined pusher fighters was that their pilots' goggles remained absolutely free of castor oil.

An Airco D.H.2 scout of the RFC visiting an RNAS aerodrome.

Royal Aircraft Factory F.E.8 scout of the RFC, one of a formation of nine belonging to 40 Squadron RFC, which encountered eight Albatros D.IIIs led by Baron von Richthofen on 9 March 1917. In the one-sided battle, four F.E.8s were lost and the rest were badly shot up. This scout was forced down near Pont à Vendin on the German side of the front.

Another view of an F.E.8 scout. Note the flight commander's pennants attached to the interplane struts, and the single Lewis gun.

One of the songs heard in the messes of RFC Officers these obsolete pusher fighters went as follows:

The young aviator lay dying
As beneath the wreckage he lay.
To the ack-emmas around him assembled
These last parting words did he say;
"Take the cylinders out of my kidneys,
The connecting rod out of my brain,
From the small of my back take the crankshaft
And assemble the engine again."

(It was sung to the tune of "Columbia, the Gem of the Ocean.")

"Ack Emma" was Great War phonetic code for "a.m.," but in this case it stands for "aircraft mechanics." The code for "p.m." was "Pip Emma".[11]

Hope for the Royal Flying Corps lay with the anxiously awaited delivery of large orders of the Triplane from the Sopwith Aviation Company, the Spad S-VII from Louis Blériot's factory in France, and the new S.E.5 fighter from the Royal Aircraft Factory.

The shape of things to come. Flight Lieutenant Edward Thomas Newton-Clare, RNAS 5 Wing, examines a visiting Sopwith Triplane from Naval 12.*

"*Anyone for tennis?*" A visiting French pilot arrives in great style in his Spad S-VII on the tennis court of RNAS 5 Wing at Petit Synthe.*

Typical Royal Aircraft Factory S.E.5 scout.
Note the pilots protection against the elements.

    The S.E.5 had a 150hp Hispano-Suiza V-8 engine, and while production had begun in March, this formidable new fighter scout had not yet reached the front. The standard pilot's windscreen was taller, and a transparent roof and sides had been added to provide protection against frostbite. This semi-enclosure was promptly nicknamed the "greenhouse" and were removed immediately by pilots because it interfered with visibility and safe flying: they could no longer distinguish by wind pressure on their cheeks whether their aeroplane was slipping inwards or skidding outwards in a turn, which could lead to takeoff and landing accidents.

    Slipping and skidding are not restricted to improperly banked turns; they can also be caused by use of the rudder alone to maintain direction. Accurate shooting from the Great War single-seater fighters required that the guns be moving towards the target in exactly the same direction as the muzzles were pointing, that is i.e. with no slipping or sliding occurring. Wind pressure on the cheeks, or rather the lack of it, gave this information to the pilot.[12]

A Spad S-VII scout. Shown here on his 1917 visit to a British aerodrome in the Dunkirk area, No. 1613 was flown by French pilot Lieutenant Raymonde of Escadrille SPA 3 (Les Cigognes). The "9" on the upper right wing is the pilot's individual identification mark.

Both the army (RFC) and the navy (RNAS) wanted thei orders of the Triplanes and the Spad S-VIIs first, which created problems with the manufacturers. The RNAS had a particularly pressing problem—the immediate need to bring Naval 9 up to strength in France and send it into battle.

Hotel Burlington
Dover
May 10, 1917

My dear Mother,

  I sent a cable to dad this morning to change my address again. My nice work at Walmer did not last very long as I am going back to France this morning. I did not expect to be sent back so soon as I was told I was at Walmer for the summer but they changed their minds in a hurry.
  I shall be near Dunkerque for the time being. If I am moved south, it will mean the Somme front and west will mean Belgium. I shall write and let you know that way. My letters will seem to be mailed on board a ship from the stamp but they will be mailed in France. Each station is run like a ship as far as possible. Hence the stamp on the letter "H.M.S.———."

My address will be:

No. 9 Squadron R.N.A.S.,
G.P.O. London.

    I wrote Horace telling him what I thought about his transferring to the R.N.A.S. I am sorry that he has done so, for his work in the army will count for nothing in this service. I am sure he will get along alright but it seems a shame to throw away all the work he has done in the army without doing himself any good.
    Must close now as the destroyer leaves in a short time and I have some passes to get.

On 10 May, Roy reported to Naval 9 at Saint Pol, and the next morning he was in action for the first time—at 16,000 feet in a Sopwith Pup escorting Airco D.H.4 two-seaters. Such formations normally flew high to avoid anti-aircraft fire, but in this case there was a better reason: above 15,000 feet a Sopwith Pup, with its lighter wing loading, could outfly the higher powered, but heavier Albatros D.III. In Roy's log book entry below, the letter 'N' before the serial number of the Pup indicates that the purchase order to the Sopwith Aviation Company had been placed by the navy.

11.5.17 - 9.45 AM - Pup N6167 - 95 mins - 16,000' - Blankenburg - Escorting photographic reconnaissance. Visibility fair. A.A fire poor.

The Airco D.H.4 was a fast bomber and reconnaissance two-seater; Roy would not need to fly his Sopwith Pup at reduced speed to maintain station. Service experience revealed that in the D.H.4 the pilot and the observer were too far apart for good co-operation. Even more troubling, between them lay the fuel tank—exactly where enemy bullets would strike when aimed at the crew.[13]

Typical Airco D.H.4, No. F5706 of C Flight, 202 Squadron Note the raised, swivelling Scarff ring upon which the observer's Lewis gun is mounted. The object under the fuselage streamlined around the protruding lens of a high-resolution vertical camera. Other D.H.4s had a similar shaped appendage—to carry baby incendiary bombs (B.I.B's).

[Address cut out by censor's scissors]

13.5.17

Dear Dad,

I certainly have been changing around the last few days. I have been moved south from where I was before. I came here two days ago but have not started work here yet.
I was over Hunland before I came down here. They shot quite a bunch of archie up but they did not hit me at all. Some of them were pretty close.
My address is changed now. I hardly know what to say about my mail, they change us around so often we can never be sure two days in succession:

No.3 Squadron R.N.A.S.,
attached 22nd Wing R.F.C.,
B.E.F.

I am with Lloyd Breadner now, and two of the boys who

were in Dayton with me are also here.

The day I wrote to you from Walmer saying I had received no mail for such a long time was followed the next day by fifteen letters but only one from you. I was surprised to hear from Horace that he had joined the R.N.A.S. He knows what he wants to do though.

We have a lovely place here for our mess, in a bush under lovely big trees. We are very comfortable here considering - much better than I thought it would be. Must close now, I am going ashore for a run.(14)

Roy's sylvan idyll did not endure; his turn for leave in England came around but the exact dates are unknown. From his log book it may be gathered he left Naval 9 somewhere around 14 May. His orders were to return to France on 3 June and report to Naval 11 Squadron at its new location Hondschoote Aerodrome.

22.5.17 My dear Mother,

Just received dad's letter of April 26 and was surely pleased to get it. I hope he is feeling perfectly well again but he should be very careful of himself for some time.

Things are very quiet here at present for us as the weather has been bad, cloudy and rainy but that is what we call good weather. After the war we shall all want to stay in bed unless the sun is shining, we have all become so accustomed to doing it in the service.

I saw Stearne about a week ago. He is feeling fine but rather fed up with where he is at present but he will not be there very long. They certainly shift us around a lot. There may be another move in store for me very soon. One thing is that you see lots of places, and things never get a chance to become monotonous. I will be sorry if I have to move from here. I have not got my khaki uniform pictures from England yet but should have them very soon.

Are you going to the lake this summer and is Reta coming home to go with you? I surely would like to have a week or two there but not this summer and perhaps not next if the Russians chuck their hand in.

Roy's father, Morton, had suffered a severe high-voltage electrical shock in the switchyard of the Carleton Place power station early that month.

He had been holding a strong, sharp knife in his hand, and the blade, with the cutting edge facing towards him, was on the far side of an electric cable. The blade touched the cable. By what can best be described as a miracle, the violent muscular contraction in Morton's arm from the electric shock caused the sharp edge of the blade to cut the cable that was electrocuting him. He was badly burned and was considered fortunate not to have been killed.

On 3 June Roy arrived at Hondschoote, having accomplished total flying time to date of 50 hours and 15 minutes, of which only five hours were on active service, and the commanding officer of Naval 11, Squadron Commander Herbert Stanley-Adams, placed him in charge of a flight. On the RNAS organizational ladder that position was intended to be held by a flight commander; Roy was but a probationary flight sub-lieutenant, three ranks lower. This early increased responsibility indicates that serious casualties had been incurred by the RNAS in the recent weeks and that among the replacement pilots Roy was considered to be one of the better trained. However, the situation could not be considered permanent; Squadron Commander Adams would either have to promote Roy to acting flight lieutenant or ask RNAS Headquarters to send him a more experienced and higher ranking officer to command the flight. Meanwhile Roy was very busy. He was now in charge of the maintenance and repair of five aeroplanes plus the discipline and welfare of their mechanics. He had to lead the flight in the air, which meant he would need to train his pilots to maintain formation and to follow his signals while he took care of navigation and decision making. The key to combat success was working together, each pilot keeping an eye on the sky behind his neighbour in case an enemy pilot was positioning his aeroplane for a surprise attack. Roy's permanence as commander of a flight would depend upon how quickly he could grow into the position and its accompanying responsibilities.

No.11 Squadron
[undated but posted 4 June]

My dear Mother,
        Just got back from leave yesterday. I had a very nice time. I was up

the river with Skeet again the same as last year. Not quite the same though as he is married now. He has a lovely wife. Surely is a lucky boy not to be crippled any worse than he is and to be out of it all with a good position.

I had some nice baths in London town while I was there. I t surely is good to just soak away after going more or less without a real bath for so long.

Murray was in town when I was there but we missed each other and as he did not leave his address I could not find him. I believe he is coming out here again very soon.

It is nearly a month since I have had any mail at all. That is because I have been moved around so. It tries to chase me but seems to miss me all the time.

The weather out here is beautiful now. Much too good for flying as there is too much work.

My best wishes to Horace and Howard on their birthdays.

Skeet, was a friend who lived in a house on the banks of the River Thames and had been invalided out of the army.

The date on which a pilot's leave could begin was rather fluid; it depended upon casualties, the weather and coming events. That being so, it was quite normal for Roy to be unaware that Murray, who was from a different squadron, was also in London on leave. To circumvent the situation, the boys conceived a plan which they named the "Five O'clock Standby." Whenever possible, all RNAS pilots who were on leave in London were to direct themselves to the bar at the Savoy Hotel at 1700 hours, where they would wait until 1800. After a drink or two and a general exchange of news, those who had gathered there would go to dinner at Simpson's-in-the-Strand, where excellent roast beef with Yorkshire pudding was served. Then, for those who had no previous engagement for the evening, it would be time for the second house to begin at the London theatres and music halls.

Back in the technical world an unexpected problem had arisen. During the previous months, the triplane built by Tommy Sopwith's company had not exactly met with an enthusiastic reception at the top level of the Royal Flying Corps. Its landing speed of 55 to 60 mph was considered to be dangerous; B.E.2Cs, F.E.8s, Pups and Strutters all landed at 40 to 45mph. Furthermore, instead of the farmers' fields used by the earlier machines as aerodromes, the triplane required longer and smoother surfaces. The task of providing such surfaces was not welcomed by those in the army who had to supply the labour for the RFC. The cause of the high landing speed was the narrow (high aspect ratio) wings, which were so efficient at normal flying speed. Engineering-wise, one can rarely obtain something for nothing.

As the RFC and the RNAS both had Spad S-VIIs and Sopwith Triplanes on order from the same suppliers, competition between the respective purchasing officers for priority on deliveries had became a real problem. In February 1917 agreement was reached that all the Spads on order would go to the RFC, and all the Sopwith Triplanes would go to the RNAS.

3.6.17 - 11.15 AM - *Pup N6184 - 65 mins - 9,000' - to Calais & return.*

- 7.25 PM - *Pup N6199 - 25 mins - 7,000'*

4.6.17 - 7.15 AM - *Pup N6167 - 40 mins - 7,000'*

- 11.35 AM - *Sop. Triplane N524 - 25 mins - 8,000'*

The flight in Sopwith Triplane No. N524 was made to familiarize Roy with this new type in preparation for his ferrying one from Dunkirk Aircraft Depot in the afternoon. Nothing is written about either Triplane in the Remarks column of his log book which is rather unusual. When most of the aces first flew a Sopwith Triplane, they had high praise for its pleasant flight characteristics, excellent manoeuvrability and fantastic rate of climb. In a wide climbing left turn, thanks to the gyroscopic effect of the rotary engine, it could escape from any German aeroplane in front-line service at that time. These benefits more than compensated for the high landing speed.

4.6.17 - 3.00 PM - *Nieup Baby N3994 - 20 mins - 2,500' - to Depot Dunkirk - very bumpy. Could hardly control machine.*

- 5.15 PM - *Sop. Triplane N5351 - 15 mins - 3,000' - Depot to Hondschoote - Prop broke on landing. Must have been a stone thrown up.*

Sopwith Triplane No. N5351. Note how close the tips of the large-diameter propeller would be to the ground if the machine were at a level attitude. The control wire coupling together the three port ailerons stands out quite well.

On the Sopwith Triplane the upper-wing-bracing wires starting from the top of the fuselage at the rear of the engine cowling, and those starting from the bottom of the fuselage between the landing gear struts, would cause of accidents on some of the later, mass-produced models.

5.6.17 - 10.30 AM - Pup N6192 - 75 mins - 10,500' - Boulogne & return - Practice in leading a formation.

- 7.20 PM - Pup N6184 - 80 mins - 12,500' - H.A. Line Patrol Ypres to Ploegsteert - Leading Patrol. No A.A. or H.A.

The morning practice on 5 June, prior to the afternoon patrol, shows that Roy was taking his new duties seriously. As well as extra work, commanding a flight brought benefits; namely, when he led his flight in an attack, he was accompanied by two aircraft whose prime duty was to protect his tail from those who would like to shoot it off. Thus, he need not keep turning his head to guard his rear and could concentrate on navigation, stalking distant dots in the sky or staying between the sun and the enemy. In short, he now stood a much greater chance of surviving the war. From the offensive point of view, the absence of distraction in a diving attack would allow him to judge the distance and the deflection angle accurately. When the range was close enough he would open fire and his subordinates would take their cue. Surprise could be maintained until the last moment, which made the system highly effective. Unfortunately, in Allied war stories, German flight leaders are often accused of cowardice for using a pair of tail guards.

Sopwith Pup No. N6192 flown by Roy on 5 June 1917. Photograph taken on 15 August 1917 after a member of Roy's flight had made an unhappy landing on the sands at Saint Pol. The large letters on either side of the roundel signify that aircraft "C" belonged to "A" Flight.

6.6.17 - 7.30 AM - Pup N6184 - 10 mins - 2,000' - To Bray Doones [sic] *to No. 4 Squadron.*

Roy's destination would have been Middle Aerodrome located near the village of Bray Dunes and sometimes called by that name.

Sopwith Pups of Naval 4 Squadron at Bray Dunes. "ANZAC" is No. N6185. Note the condition of the field where the aeroplanes are parked.

6.6.17 - 1.50 PM - Pup N6184 - 110 mins - 16,000' - Escort Belgian spotting machine. Other two of escort lost spotting machine and I had to stay alone. Little A.A. but saw no H.A.

The Belgian Air Force used a somewhat improved version of the B.E.2C for artillery spotting. It had a 150hp Hispano-Suiza engine, the pilot occupied the front cockpit, and the observer had a tall mounting, designed by Albert Étévé of the French Technical Section of Aeronautics, for his twin machine guns. Despite the increased power and the improved crew positions and armament, this type of aeroplane (whose basic design came from 1912 when stability, not manoeuvrability, was the requirement) would certainly have needed a strong escort in mid-1917. The wireless telegraphy transmitter was mounted internally, and the Morse code key was sometimes mounted on the outside of the fuselage where the observer could comfortably flex his wrist.

Typical Belgian B.E.2C artillery spotter.

A two-hour flight atan altitude of 16,000feet without heat and oxygen was not good for the health, and after the war many pilots died young from heart and lung ailments. The most common effect upon the lungs was listed by the authorities on service records as "Flying Sickness D." Today it is called tuberculosis.

6.6.17 - 4.20 PM - Pup N6184 - 10 mins - 2,000' - Return to Hondschoote.

On 8 June Roy was sent by car to Dunkirk Aircraft Depot to ferry the prototype Sopwith Triplane back to Hondschoote for pilot evaluation.

8.6.17 - 2.30 PM - Sop. Triplane N500 - 15 mins - 1,500' - Engine fault. Returned to ADD.

Shortly after takeoff the engine had begun to run roughly, so Roy had turned back immediately. The mechanics found that the stems of three exhaust valves had become tight in their guides.[15] Roy finally departed for Hondschoote late in the afternoon.

The prototype Sopwith *Triplane* N500. Flown by Roy on 8 June 1917. Note the bracing wires from the fuselage to the upper wings which were mentioned under 4.6.17 Log Book entry for *Triplane* N5351.

8.6.17 - 6.00 PM - Sop. Triplane N500 - 15 mins - 4,000' - Dunkirk to Hondschoote.

Eventually, on the Western Front, three RNAS squadrons (1, 8 and 10) were fully equipped with Sopwith Triplanes (fifteen machines plus three spares), and three more squadrons (9, 11 and 12) received some. A few Triplanes were sent to the Middle East.

The Sopwith *Triplanes* of Naval 1 Squadron at Ballieul neatly lined up for inspection, the one with the white fin belonging to the squadron commander. Photograph taken in mid-1917.

A flight (five) of Sopwith *Triplanes* of Naval 10 at Droglandt Aerodrome in Belgium in 1917, where Mel Alexander was stationed.

Unfortunately, it was not to be long before a Sopwith Triplane in northern France fell almost intact into German hands.

In their Triplane design, Tom Sopwith and Herbert Smith, to use an ancient phrase, *"had builded better than they knew."* When the Germans filled its fuel tank with the synthetic petrol used by the German Air Service and then tested this six-winged dragon that was running rings around their best aeroplanes, they were astonished at its performance. The best petrol supplied to the RFC and RNAS at this time was about seventy octane and was destined to become even worse. Manfred von Richthofen complained to his superior, General Ernst von Hoeppner, that the British were just toying with his pilots, who despite their best efforts could do nothing about it. The solution for the Germans seemed to lie in building triplanes, preferably even better ones. Accordingly, instructions were issued to the major German and Austrian aeroplane manufacturers to urgently design a triplane fighter. (16)

The standard Sopwith Triplane was equipped with one Vickers machine gun which, like the gun on the Sopwith Pup, fired somewhat slowly. The German scouts now carried two Maxim LMG 08/15 machine guns, both of which fired rapidly. The need for rapid-firing multiple machine guns lay in the very short time that a pilot could hold an enemy aeroplane steady in his gunsight. Investigation had shown that unless the enemy pilot was a novice or was foolishly watching one of his own victims going down, the attacker had a maximum of three seconds in which to aim, press the trigger(s) and finish firing. When this very short period was coupled with the behaviour of a machine gun mounted on a wooden airframe—namely, only the first three shots went where the pilot intended and the rest spread out in a cone—the value of having twice as many bullets heading directly for the target needs no explanation.

Only in the minds of some film directors and writers who add imagined details to enhance Great War air combat stories does a neat row of bullet holes stitch its way along the wings or fuselage of an aeroplane. In reality, the scatter makes the damage resemble the work of a shot gun.

A close encounter of the real kind—four genuine Great War air-to-air combat 0.303inch calibre bullet holes (enhanced for clarity). The Albatros pilot who escaped by an inch or two is Oberleutnant Ernst Udet. With 62 officially credited victories and one parachute jump in combat, he survived the war as Germany's second-highest scoring-ace fighter pilot.

9.6.17 - Pup 9899 - 10.05 AM - 10 mins - 1,000' - Tried to do formation flying but too cloudy.

- Pup 9899 - 11.40 AM - 35 mins - 3,500' – Formation flying leading. Engine vibrating.

Formation flying with a Le Rhône or Clergêt rotary engine presented no difficulty; engine power could be adjusted smoothly between idling and full power by co-ordinated use of the Tampier control, which regulated fuel and air, and the fine mixture lever.

Roy's comment on engine vibration dealt with a serious matter: pieces of the engine could work loose, or the shaking could cause a fuel leak, an invitation to a fire. Depending upon the severity of the problem, the remedy was to either reduce power and head for home or switch the engine off and make a forced landing.

Sopwith Pup No. 9899 flown by Roy on 9, 11 and 13 June 1917. Note the large pet name painted onto the fuselage, and an "N", which signifies Naval Purchase Order, incorrectly added before the serial number. Photograph taken in March 1917 at 4(N) Squadron.

The four to six weeks' time needed for Roy to receive a reply from Carleton Place to his letters was apparently causing some confusion. Although Horace had joined the RNAS, there had obviously been some discussion that the RFC might have been a better choice. The latter, being part of the British Army, would have accepted him as a sergeant from the first day.

No. 11 Squadron
June 9/17

Dear Dad,

I have just received two letters from home dated May 8 and May 15.

Before I say another thing, if you can possibly help it in any way, please don't let Horace get into the R.F.C. If he is bound to fly, let him join the R.N.A.S. Not that I have anything against the R.F.C. but the machines they have to fly, well, all I can say is I surely take off my hat to the work they do but they have to lose so many in doing it.

Stearne was here to dinner about three or four nights ago. He is well and everything is going all O.K. with him. He is in charge of a flight now and so am I here. We are a long way apart now but he says he expects to move very soon as he has put in for it but of course may not get it.

I am feeling fine now, have not felt better for a long time. All the chaps whom I have not seen for a long time tell me I'm getting fat again.

*Address mail to me at
R.N.A.S. Mail Office,
Moorgate Hall,
Finsbury Pavement,
London E.C.*

P.S. Tell Horace not to go to Camp Borden. I know what kind of instructors were sent over and I don't want him practised on.

Roy's persistence in formation practice was rewarded, and he finally succeeded in obtaining a good formation flying session with his flight.

11.6.17 - 3.20 PM - Pup 9899 - 30 mins - 3,000' - Formation flying leading.

The following day, Roy learned how unpleasant Mother Nature could be:

12.6.17 - 5.30 PM - Pup N6184 - 15 mins - 3,000' - Hondschoote t o Bray Dunes - In thunderstorm. Awful bumps.

No return flight is recorded.

The air war now began to heat up. To discourage aerial observation and photography of the occupied Belgian seaports, the Germans brought in a number of large-calibre anti-aircraft guns together with some particularly good gunners. What used to be a milk run was about to have exciting moments.

A German heavy anti-aircraft gun and its crew.
Note the two range finders on tripods beside it.

On 13 June Roy was sent to Naval 4 Squadron at Bray Dunes while Naval 11 moved to another location. The commanding officer of Naval 4 was Squadron Commander B. L. Huskisson.

13.6.17 - 2.15 PM - Pup 9899 - 20 mins - 4,000' - Hondschoote to Dunkirk & Bray Dunes while No. 11 moves.
(Roy's Log Book says 9989, but that was a B.E.2C)

\- *7.05 PM - Pup N6184 - 75 mins - 17,000' – Nieuport to Dixmude Patrol - Chased H.A. over lines but could not get high enough. Some A.A.*

14.6.17 - 5.05 PM - Pup N6184 - 100 mins - 19,000' - Ostend - Nothing to report. Machine bumped about by A.A. & hit in left wing.

The last two entries above were the daily routine evening patrols. To use civilian measurement, the height at which such patrols were flying, 19,000 feet, is 3.5 miles. At such altitudes, without oxygen, the smallest control movements were hard labour and the intense cold eventually penetrated the thickest of clothes. It was not uncommon for the ground crews having to lift pilots bodily from the cockpit after they had taxied in.

The Archie hit in the left wing at 3.5 miles altitude on the 14th indicates that the expert German anti-aircraft gunners knew their business and were in good practice.

19.6.17 - 7.35 AM - Pup N6184 - 105 mins - 18,500' - Offensive Patrol, Ostend to Ghistelles - Followed leader of 4 Albatros scouts but he did not press attack as he thought his flight had not followed. Formation poor as my engine was dud.

The word *"offensive"* means that the patrol was conducted on the German side of the front line. In current parlance, the task would be called a Combat Mission, but whatever the term used, the true meaning would be 'looking for trouble'.

The German flight leader was quite correct in declining combat with the Sopwith *Pups*. At 18,500 feet the Albatros D.III had an inferior performance, but if the encounter had been at 8,500 feet, he most likely would have been happy at the prospect of a fight on favourable terms. The break-even point was 15,000 feet, and therein lies the main reason for the patrol's high altitude. The British ace Major James Thomas Byford McCudden, VC (57 victories including shared), strongly recommended never engaging the enemy when the latter held the advantage. Four ace pilots who made a habit of disregarding such advice—Albert Ball (England, 44 victories including shared), Georges Marie Ludovic Jules Guynemer (France, 53 victories including shared), Werner Voss (Germany, 48 victories) and Frank Luke (USA, 18 victories)—eventually fulfilled Oswald Boelke's prediction and became dead heroes. Incidentally, Frank Luke's memory is kept alive by Luke Air Force Base in Arizona, The world's largest fighter base.

Albatros D.III, No. D.2015/16, taken at Dunkirk Aircraft Depot while the aeroplane was on its way to England for flight testing as a prize of war G-42.

An additional reason for patrolling at such a high altitude would be to set a trap. If some Albatros D.IIIs happened along lower down and did not spot the Pups up high, Roy could then place his flight between the sun and the enemy and launch a surprise attack. Obviously this situation could not continue indefinitely; the Sopwith Triplanes were urgently needed.

Roy flew Sopwith Pup No. N6184 until 13 July 1917, and his log book entires are listed as follows:

23.6.17 - 10.20 AM - Pup N6184 - 105 mins - 17,000' - O.P. [Offensive Patrol - Dove on Hun two-seater to 8,000' but could not catch up to him. Also on kite balloon but lost sight of it in cloud over Ghistelles.

Forcing down the kite balloon was Roy's first combat success. For him to make an unprepared attack on an observation balloon was an indication of his inexperience. It would have been heavily defended from the ground and often from the air as well. Success in encouraging the observer to make a "brolly hop" usually required making arrangements in advance for one or two companions to distract the defences while the attacker dived in from the sun or hedge-hopped over the fields and then zoomed up. If the balloon were set on fire, it counted as one enemy aircraft destroyed; i.e. that is a combat victory. There was a tacit agreement between both sides not to shoot at the helpless observer as he descended beneath his parachute. A few pilots on both sides violated this convention, but their colleagues were not happy about it.

25.6.17 - 6.45 AM - *Pup N6184* - 45 mins - 11,000' - O.P. attempted - Clouds at 4,000', 7,000' & 11,000'.

- 1.15 PM - *Pup N6184* - 10 mins - Gun jambed.

- 1.30 PM - *Pup N6184* - 15 mins - Gun jambed.   Defective extractors and feed block.

- 5.50 PM - *Pup N6184* - 75 mins - 17,000' - Nieuport to Dunkerque - D.P. - Nothing to report. My head went dud coming down.

"D.P." meant a defensive patrol, viz. on the Allied side of the lines. The term "*dud head*" refers to the splitting headache which often developed while pilots descend after having spent more than thirty minutes without oxygen in the intense cold above 12,000 feet.

Although Roy had not led his flight to any victories in combat, he had worked hard and, as far as weather permitted, successfully completed all his missions and brought all his men home. In the month-end confidential report on personnel, Squadron Commander Adams evaluated Roy as:

"A fair officer."

This was to improve dramatically when Roy got into his stride.

The time for Roy's weekly letter home came around. The change of subject would be what is known in Brazil as "mental hygiene";

The presence of so much trivia indicates the strain he was feeling.

No.11 Squadron
June 29/17

My Dear Mother,

I expect just about now you are getting ready to go to the lake. What are you going to do with all the fowl? Will it be a case of "Who will feed the chickens" every night like it used to be? I wish I could be there to do it or rather forget to do it. That was always my strong point. Dad will not need Mrs McLeod to look after him any more now he is almost completely recovered from the accident. Will the car be quicker to go to the lake than the motor boat? Bess should learn how to run one or the other as it would be very nice then. I guess Howard is about ready to do that now. I expect I shall hardly know him when I get back if this game over here lasts as long as it seems to be going to do. Stearne's brother wants to enlist and he is in favour of it though it will be very hard on his mother. I feel very old when I think of some of the little chaps who are joining up. Percy Moore, whom I see is missing, was the mascot of the baseball team when I played at home. Stearne and I were just talking about it the other night. We are very close together now and will be on the same aerodrome very soon which makes it very nice. He certainly is a fine fellow and is liked by everyone.

Must go to bed now, mother, so good-night.

P.S. Just received my photos. Will send them as soon as I get something to protect them in the mail.

Roy's reply to a letter from the Reverend Dobson, the minister at the Presbyterian Church in Carleton Place, tells much about his daily life in action. In July 1999, his brother, Howard, remembered the minister giving excellent sermons in church and conducting wonderful summer camps for the young folks of the town.

July 2/17

Dear Mr. Dobson,

I was very pleased to receive your long interesting letter. Father has mentioned you very often in his letters to me saying how much he enjoyed your addresses.

My knee is quite better again and I hope will give me no more trouble.

I am very sorry to think conscription has to come in force at home. We did so well for such a long time without it. If we could have kept it up and proved that conscription was not needed to conduct a war it would be a great thing for Canada. I suppose all the willing ones are in uniform now and the remainder will have to be driven. Our work over here is very interesting and also exciting but it is rather risky at times. When you think about it afterwards you get afraid but at the time you are too busy to be afraid or anything else but concentrate on the work in hand.

I fly a fighter machine, a single seater. They are very fast compared with other methods of locomotion. We have to fly very high at much too great a height for comfort. It is an impossibility to keep warm no matter what clothing you wear. When you get over 16,000' you begin to feel it and the higher you go the worse it becomes. Summer or winter makes but a very slight difference. One of the chaps got his face very badly frost bitten last week at 18,000'. It has all swollen and broken out in a very nasty sore. The unfortunate part is he is going back to England on leave to-day with it at the very worst.

The Germans are not at all keen to fight with us in the air. I have never had one attack me at all. They never do unless they outnumber our machines and have the advantage of position. When we attack them they run for home as hard as they can go. It is hard to get near them at all. (I don't know how much of this the censor will allow. I have never written anything like this before but there is really nothing in it that can do the enemy any good so it should go through.)

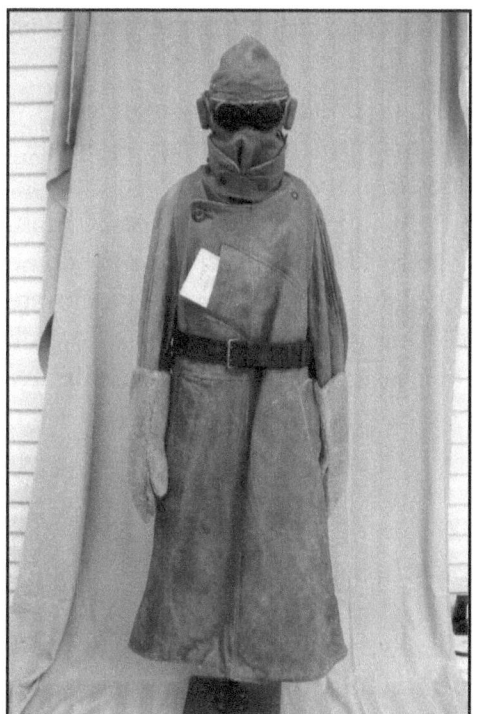

Wishing you great success in your very useful work.

I remain
Yours sincerely
A. R. Brown

British airman's leather flying clothes with handy map pocket. (16)

The attitude of the German fighter pilots towards air combat was actually sound strategy on their part because of the frequent occurrence of engine failure in those early days of aviation, together with the British wish to keep German aviators as far east of the Allied front line as possible. German pilots in trouble could land and telephone for help; British pilots would become involuntary "guests of the Kaiser". Another factor was the wind direction: it normally blew from the west and, on some parts of the front, quite strongly, which meant that many of the RFC and RNAS cases of engine failure could not glide their way back to friendly territory. Rittmeister Manfred Freiherr von Richthofen's oft-repeated dictum, *"Let the lords come to us,"* was good advice. If the Allies wished to present aeroplanes and pilots to the Germans as gifts, why should the latter risk their own just to extract the enemy from the sky a little sooner? The French emperor Napoleon had won many battles by encouraging a superior enemy to do something foolish. The strategy was as old as the hills; the Imperial German Army Air Service had simply given it a new twist. Roy obviously knew this, but he could not say so and have it pass the censor. This German strategy was one of the factors which cost French ace fighter pilot, Capitaine René Fonck, recognition of his claim to be the highest scoring ace in the Great War. (17)

Another effective and purely psychological German aircrew tactic, was to tempt Allied fighter pilots into chasing their aeroplanes (generally two-seaters) as far as possible to the east. Assuming an airspeed both ways of 90 mph and the wind from the west at 30 mph, the difference in ground speed is 60 mph. Therefore, a six-minute chase in an easily direction (ground speed 120 mph) becomes a twelve-minute return west (ground speed 60 mph). Unfortunately for those who took the bait, aircraft fuel consumption at cruising speed goes by the minutes flown, not by the miles covered over the ground, and they would often end up landing in enemy territory.

3.7.17 - 3.00 PM - Pup N6184 - 100 mins - 18,000' - D.P. - Lead to plug came off and I left the patrol. Had headache but not a bad one.

Roy was wise to return home immediately, because a non-firing cylinder would throw petrol into the engine cowling. It would then be blown backwards along the fuselage, carrying with it the danger of fire, and many pilots had lost their lives that way. He would need to put the nose down, reduce power to lessen vibration, and head for Allied territory in a semi-glide.

4.7.17 - 8.15 AM - Pup N6184 - 120 mins - 17,000' - H.A. Patrol - For raiders returning from England. Nothing to report past Flushing in Holland.

Roy's hostile aircraft patrol was in response to a telegraphed report from England on the night of 3/4 July that eighteen Gotha G.III heavy bombers were attacking Felixstowe and Harwich. These heavily armed and unexpectedly large machines were not easy to shoot down from the air; most night fighter pilots misjudged the range and fired at them from too great a distance. Captain R. A. Little (47 victories including shared), a night fighting expert of RAF 203 Squadron (previously Naval 3) did the opposite: he approached too closely and was mortally wounded by air gunner Vize-feldwebel Ehmann of Jasta 47 on 27 May 1918.

Typical Gotha G.III.

Around this time, someone in authority took a dislike to the mild expression "Hostile Aircraft;" furthermore, its abbreviation, "H.A.," could be confused with "High Altitude ". A new, more emphatic term was proposed: "Enemy Aircraft" (E.A.). The change was accepted and would become obligatory on 1 August.

4.7.17 - 4.10 PM - Pup N6184 - 5 mins - Bray Dunes to Frontier aerodrome. New No. 11 drome.

The five-minute flight at 16:10 hrs was Roy's return to duty with Naval 11 Squadron. The next day Squadron Commander Huskisson, the commanding officer of Naval 4, sent a good report to the Wing on Roy's.

6.7.17 - 5.40 PM - Pup N6184 - 55 mins - Local - Practising formation leading.

- 8.30 PM - Pup N6184 - 20 mins - as above

9.7.17 - 8.45 AM - Pup N6184 - 10 mins - Engine test.

9.7.17 - 6.05 PM - Pup N6190 - 15 mins - Depot Dunkirk to No. 11.

11.7.17 - 9.50 AM - Pup N6184 - 130 mins - 15,000' - Y Patrol - Nothing to report. Cloudy over lines.

Sopwith Pup No. N6190 which had wheels when it was ferried from Aircraft Depot Dunkirk to Frontier aerodrome by Roy on 9 July 1917. This photograph was taken in mid-1918 during trial landings on a dummy aircraft-carrier deck. The friction from the skids produced a worthwhile braking effect.

On that part of the front, the dividing line between the opposing armies was the canalized River Yser, which ran from Nieuport via Dixmüde to Ypres; hence the term "Y Patrol."

12.7.17 - 3.20 PM - Pup N6184 - 65 mins - Y Patrol - Centre section cross bracing wire broke. Came down.

13.7.17 - 3.20 PM - Pup N6184 - 120 mins - 19,000' - Y Patrol - All flight except Buckley did not follow. Patrol carried out by the 2 of us. Saw 10 huns over Ostend but we both turned away at same time. Smoke seen off Middlekerke.

14.7.17 - 7.50 AM - Pup N6174 - 25 mins - Y Patrol attempted - Rain falling so patrol washed out.

Roy performed well as commander of a flight, and Squadron Commander Adams decided to regularize his position. On 15 July he recommended Roy for promotion to local acting flight commander. This was three steps up from probationary flight sub-lieutenant and rather a large jump at one time.

No.11 Squadron
July 15/17

Dear Dad,

I am afraid I am rather overdue in writing home but the truth is I have been so busy that I have not had a minute to myself. I have been put in charge of a flight and as we are just getting started it means absolutely no end of work for the time being. I have about twenty-five men under me, mechanics to keep the machines in order, and I am responsible that they are in order.
Then I have to lead the flight in whatever work we are doing. I do not know how long I shall hold the position but the C.O. told the Wing Commander he did not want a Flight Commander to take my place so I may keep it. I shall know in a week or two. It means a lot of work but all very interesting and I hope I keep it. You are in trouble about things the whole time but it's all in a day's work.

You have never mentioned anything about the electrical power station, I have seen mention of it in the home papers. Burgess seems to have a great time talking his head off. It would pay him to talk less and to do more.

In the Royal Naval Air Service, wing commander, squadron commander and flight commander were official rank designations. They corresponded, in the same order, to the army ranks of lieutenant-colonel, major and captain.

Mr Burgess was the owner of a small hydro-electric generating station at Arklan, near Carleton Place. He had made a proposal to the Carleton Place town council to supply electricity for the street lighting at a lower price than that of the Carleton Place Electric Company, which belonged to H. Brown & Sons. He obtained the contract but was later bought out by H. Brown & Sons.

15.7.17 - 9.00 PM - Pup N6184 - 20 mins - Test.

16.7.17 - 4.05 AM - Pup N6184 - 65 mins - 1,000' - O.P. attempted - Low clouds. Flight did not stay low to pick me up.

- 11.40 AM - Pup N6184 - 140 mins - 15,000' - O.P.- Dunkerke to Ostend - Nothing to report.

- 4.30 PM - Pup N6184 - 20 mins - H.A. Pursuit - Engine mis-firing.

17.7.17 - 9.45 AM - Pup N6174 - 145 mins - 17,000' - Saw Huns above us but they did not attack.

- 5.50 PM - Pup N6174 - 105 mins - 15,000' - O.P. Ostend - Saw our A.A. south-east of Nieuport. Went to see what they were firing at. Dove on 6-8 Albatros Scouts. Opened fire on one, got one burst in and he went down in a spin. Gun jambed, cleared and opened fire on another. Got about 50 rounds right into him and he went down out of control. Gun jambed again. Hun opened fire on my tail. Side-looped, clearing jamb going over, and came out under his tail and got 25 rounds into him and he went down spinning. No more Huns left. A.A. very severe coming back as I was low. Machine hit in upper right plane by A.A.

With the drowning of the Albatros D. III over southeast Nieuport, Roy was officially credited with this first victory. Unfortunately, the Wing did not agree to something so radical as a three-step promotion, but it did agree to two steps, one of which was permanent in nature.

On 18 July 1917 Roy's promotion from probationary flight sub-lieutenant to local acting flight lieutenant was announced, and his substantive rank was raised to flight sub-lieutenant. Furthermore, the commanding officer request that he remain in charge of the flight had been approved. At last Roy was on the way up.

That evening he wrote a detailed and thrilling description of his victory to his sister Bessie.

No. 11 Squadron
18/7/17

Dear Bess,

We had a great time yesterday. On our patrol I saw some of our anti-aircraft guns firing on some Huns so went down to see what was on. We ran right into about eight of their scouts. I was right in the middle of them before I knew it. I opened fire on one and just got a few rounds off when he went down in a spin and my gun jambed. I cleared my jamb and opened fire on another one. I got a lot of lead into him and he went out of control immediately. He went down side-slipping every way but the right way. Then my gun jambed again and a Hun got under my tail, i.e. the back of my machine, and opened fire on me. I side-looped immediately and came out of the loop right on his tail and got about 25 rounds into him when he went down in a spin also. My gun jambed again, which I cleared, but there were no Huns left to fight with as they were all driven down by that time. I was quite low then and came back across the line dodging their anti-aircraft fire at me. They must have fired 75 shells at me but I stunted all around and got away alright. They only put one piece of shell into my wing so I was pretty lucky.

That is what a fight in the air is like in a brief way. It is the greatest sport you can imagine. That is the first scrap this squadron has had so we did pretty well. One of the other chaps got one too. I was glad it happened as it did because that is the first time I have been in charge of the patrol so I have got in pretty strong with my C.O. It surely is exciting while it lasts but I was scared stiff coming back through their archie. It was much too close for comfort I can tell you.

I cannot write a letter like this very often so I hope this one gets to you alright.

How is the lake this summer? Are many of the cottages occupied and what kind of a time are you having? I expect it is rather quiet. I don't know how I shall ever settle down again after the exciting time we are having over here.

I am going to try to get out of this for the winter and get a job in England. I wish I could get leave to go home but there is a war on and pilots are pretty useful at present and will be, so all are needed.

It is interesting to note that Allied anti-aircraft shells were filled with smokeless powder, and the bursts appeared white against the sky; German shell bursts were black. In addition to the normal hostile intent, the Allies used a particular shell burst-pattern to call any fighters in the area to the aid of colleagues under attack.

Concerning marksmanship ("gunlaying" to those in the RNAS) one can see that in a properly executed surprise attack, there was time to aim with the required deflection and to wait until the range was close before opening fire. Once the turning and twirling began, there was a maximum time of three seconds during which the enemy could be held in a gun sight. Therefore, the twenty-five-round burst fired by Roy, at a speed in a Sopwith Pup of about six rounds per second, indicates that he aimed at the target for only one second longer than the effective period. This was one mark of an expert pilot.

A Sopwith Pup carried only 500 rounds of ammunition, and despite what one finds in adventure stories, no pilot wishing to survive the war would make a long dive *"with guns blazing."* To do so would invite a jam caused by an overheated breechblock, long before he came into effective range—assuming that by then the enemy had not heard the "Rak-ak-ak" sound of bullets passing by at double supersonic speed or seen the smoke trails from the tracer. Wasted ammunition or a serious jam could easily leave the pilot defenceless on his way back to the Allied side of the front.

20.7.17 - 5.45 AM - Pup N6174 - 120 mins - 13,000' - O.P. Ostend - Visibility very bad. Up to Zeebrugge no E.A.

- 1.40 PM - Pup N6174 - 105 mins - 17,000' - O.P. Ostend - Nothing to report.

The flight times for 17 June and 20 June indicate that Roy had spent around four hours in an open cockpit at high altitude on each of those days. The result was pure physical exhaustion, known today as combat fatigue. The duration and altitude of what Roy called *"the work"* shows the miserable, health-ruining conditions which pilots and observers had to suffer in 1917 and 1918. This does not include living in tents, or in huts made from aeroplane packing cases, and enduring Spartan (albeit. Fortunately, the standard of food served in the RNAS officers' messes was good.

The reason for Roy's 5:45 a.m. departures was to make use of the sun as it rose above the horizon in the east. The strategy was for the Allied patrol to take off, cross the lines into German-held territory and wait high up for any German Gotha or Staaken bombers to return from raids over France or England. The enemy would be tired, thinking of home and heading directly into the sun's rays—not a felicitous combination for longevity. At the same time, the patrol could take a look at the activity of the U-boat bases in the German-occupied Ostend and Zeebrugge harbours.

21.7.17 - 2.15 PM - Pup N6174 - 130 mins - 16,000' - O.P. Ostend - Observed batteries with smokescreen in front. No E.A. on our patrol. Ordered not to attack E.A. far from our patrol.

Note the commanding officer's admonition not to be enticed deeply into Hunland.

22.7.17 - 8.00 AM - Pup N6174 - 120 mins - 18,000' - O.P. Ostend - Nothing to report.

- 6.15 PM - Pup N6174 - 120 mins - 16,000' - O.P. Ostend - 7 E.A. dove on flight just over Nieuport. All my flight followed. I climbed into sun but Huns carried on towards south of Ostend.

Another view of what was once the town of Nieuport.

In Germany, on 22 July, the prototype of the Fokker F.I Triplane, factory Serial Number 1697, made its first test flight and outperformed all its rivals. An order was placed by the Imperial German Army Air Services for fifty.

23.7.17 - 10.45 AM - Pup N6180 - 40 mins - 8,000' - O.P. attempted - Returned owing to bad weather conditions.

24.7.17 - 4.55 AM - Pup N6174 - 65 mins - 13,000' - O.P. - Returned owing to bad weather conditions.

25.7.17 - 12.55 PM - Pup N6468 - 135 mins - 17,000' -Defensive Fleet Patrol - Nothing to report.

The intense work of June and July, including the many flights at sub-zero Fahrenheit temperatures and physically exhausting high altitudes, took its toll, and Roy had to report in sick.

No.11 Squadron
July 29/17

Dear Dad,

I have been on the sick list for a couple of days with my stomach. I feel O.K. again to-day though. My C.O. is as nice to me as he could be. Comes in and talks to me as if I were his own son. Scolded me for getting up too soon and yesterday, every time he saw me, he chased me off to my cabin.

He recommended me to Head Quarters for promotion to Acting Flight Commander. They have made me a Flight Lieutenant though. If all goes well, I should be made a Flight Commander in the September promotions. I would have it now if he could get it for me. I have been in charge of a flight for two months now. This is a rather unhealthy service to be in here at present but I am as careful as I can be. The trouble is when you are on the ground you make all kinds of good resolutions about how careful you will be but when you get in the air you feel altogether different and forget about them. The trouble is stunting too near the ground. The number that are killed that way is awful and that is one thing I never do under any circumstances as I have seen too much of that. Sid Ellis who was at our home when he was a little kid was killed that way.

Mother asked about Murray Galbraith. The last I heard of him he had a job instructing in England. I do not think he will be back to France for some time anyway. Stearne is on leave in England now. I am the only one in France now out of the boys I started to train with in Dayton. Stearne will be back with me very soon I expect. I wish he was coming to this squadron but it seems we cannot get together again. We have certainly tried often enough but it never has worked. Stearne is going to have a try at it this time. He certainly is a fine fellow. They don't make them any better than he is.

As soon as I get an opportunity I will send home a souvenir to you. I shall explain later what it is exactly when I send it.

P.S. Re address:
I am not attached to the R.F.C. at present. That comes off the address.

Murray Galbraith was the first member of the RNAS to be awarded the distinguished Service Cross twice, and after having been in the thick of the fighting for six months with Naval 8, he was now enjoying a rest period in a quieter place.[19]

A period of bad weather helped Roy to take a rest, and he did not fly again until 10 August.

Roy's comment that *"this is a rather unhealthy service to be in"* most probably refers to the out dated Sopwith Pups with which the squadron was equipped. They could not stay forever above 15,000 feet, and while climbing or descending, they were easy prey for the mid-1917 German fighters. The hopes of the Naval 11 pilots to receive the promised triplanes would never be realized. Good as the Sopwith Triplane was in dealing with the Albatros D.III, the Germans already had better machines on the drawing board. Twin, rapid-firing machine guns and a higher, safe diving speed were required for Allied fighters.[20]

Technology had progressed so quickly that by the time the Sopwith Triplane was in production, Thomas Sopwith already had his mind on its replacement: to obtain a fast diving speed, a biplane or a monoplane was required. He and Herbert Smith started work on a completely new design which incorporated the necessary features and capabilities and was named the F.1 Super Pup.

The prototype Super Pup more than met the needs of the hour. Its performance, structural strength and manoeuvrability were so good that the decision was taken to build no more triplanes. One of the new features designed into the Super Pup was heating for the twin fast-firing machine guns. Hot air from the engine flowed into a housing where the warmth prevented the breech-block's lubricating oil from congealing. This housing arrangement somewhat resembled a hump, and the Super Pup quickly gained the nickname of *"Camel"*. Which soon became official.[21]

Six Sopwith Triplanes were built in 1917 after the order to suspend production was received. With Serial Numbers N533 through N538, they had been on the Clayton & Shuttleworth factory shop floor in a well-advanced state. They were delivered to the RNAS armed, as planned for the *Super Pup*, with twin Vickers machine guns and an improved synchronizing system. Sopwith *Triplane* No. N533 was issued to Naval 10 on 21 July, and Raymond Collishaw (60 victories including shared), the senior flight commander, first took it into battle on 24 July.

He found that the doubled rate of fire more than compensated for the slightly longer takeoff run and the slightly lower ceiling caused by the extra weight of the second machine-gun. A second Sopwith *Triplane*, No. N536, with twin machine guns was received on 28 July and flown by Flight Commander Alfred William (Nick) Carter, DSC (16 victories including 2 shared). When Raymond Collishaw went on leave to Canada on 3 August, he "bequeathed" N533 to Flight Lieutenant William Melville (Mel) Alexander, who was most happy with his inheritance.

The distinctive shape of the Sopwith Triplane helped to reduce accidental attacks on it by other Allied aeroplanes and anti-aircraft gunners. When a "Flying Venetian Blind" appeared in the distance an Allied observer would tell his pilot, *"Relax, it's one of ours."* In October 1917, those words were to cost several lives.

ENDNOTES TO CHAPTER FIVE

(1) THE HISTORY OF THE ROYAL NAVAL AIR SERVICE AND THE WORK PERFORMED BY THE DOVER PATROL.

For detailed information on the RNAS and the work of the Dover Patrol, see Brad King, *Royal Naval Air Service 1912-1918*, ISBN 0-9519899-5-2, ([U.K.: Hikoki Publications] 1997), fully illustrated, and covering in detail the equipment and activities of the RNAS; and Roy Humphines, The Dover Patrol 1914-1918, ISBN 0-7509-1967-1, ([U.K.: Sutton Publishing Ltd.], 1998), well illustrated and describing the daily work of the ships and aircraft, in the form of stories told by those who participated, including their German adversaries.

(2) THE BEAUFORT SYSTEM OF WIND STRENGTH MEASUREMENT.

In 1806, when wind-speed measuring equipment had not been invented, Admiral Sir Francis Beaufort devised a means of determining wind strength by observation of the surface of the ocean, which can vary from smooth as glass to huge waves. His system was later adopted by the army which observed the effect of the wind from the movements of leaves right up to the uprooting of large trees.

The wind strengths were given numbers from 0 (calm) to 12 (hurricane).

(3) THE ORIGIN OF THE SOPWITH TRIPLANE.

Mr. Thomas O. M. Sopwith, who died in January 1989 at the age of 101, had listened to pilots' complaints about the four broad wings of the 80 hp Sopwith *Pup* interfering with forward visibilty, and his designer, Herbert Smith, replaced them with six narrow wings. This corrected the problem in a novel manner, and he turned a biplane into a triplane.

Surprisingly enough, the total wing area of the Triplane (231 sq. ft.) was only 90percent of that of the *Pup* (254 sq. ft.), but the narrow wings, were far more efficient at flying speed. Herbert Smith also provided considerably more power— the new 130hp Clergêt rotary engine.

The cumulative effect of the two improvements was dramatic. The six narrow wings provided high lift with low drag, and when they were coupled with the extra power, the result was a machine that could outclimb anything in service at the time, Allied or German. In level flight, the prototype Sopwith *Triplane*'s maximum speed was measured at 117 mph. This was accomplished with the 130hp engine in brand new condition and unwrinkled fabric on the airframe. Such pristine conditions would not remain for long once the machine was in service against the enemy.

The prototype Sopwith *Triplane* N500. The purpose of the cutout in the middle wings shows up well, and the position of the top wing creates a high centre of gravity. Some of the officers are still wearing blue naval dress uniform. Photograph taken at Saint-Pol RNAS Depot in France.

(4) THE COCKPIT OF A SOPWITH *TRIPLANE*.

In the cockpit of a Sopwith Triplane, the single Vickers machine gun pokes through the windscreen, partially hidden behind the crash pad for the pilot's face. The blip switch is in the middle of the cross bar of the triangular spade grip at the top of the joystick. The lever, which the pilot pulled upwards to fire the machine gun, is situated between the ignition switch and the compass. The second ignition switch is obscured by the crash pad. The handle to tension the spring, which drives the take-up spool for the empty ammunition belt as it leaves the gun breech, is located to the left of the triangular spade grip and below the ignition switch. The sight glass to monitor the flow of castor oil to the rotary engine appears on the left of the handle.

Detail of the upper part of a Sopwith *Triplane* cockpit. Both ignition switches for the twin magnetos on the Clergêt 130hp rotary engine are visible . They are standard household type electric light switches, and both are in the Ignition Off position. The tiny propeller on the upper right strut drives the air pump in front of it to pressurize the main fuel tank in flight.

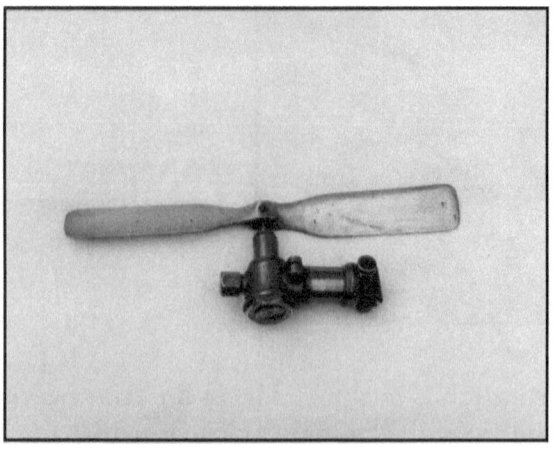

The Rotherham Company manufactured this standardized airpump design for many different types of aircraft.

Detail of the lower part of a Sopwith *Triplane* cockpit. *Left to right*: blip switch on spade grip; altimeter 0 to 20,000 feet, main fuel tank level sight glass; and hand pump to pressurize the tank for starting. Note the large tailplane trimming wheel beside the seat.

During the war 149 Sopwith Triplanes were built. A genuine *Triplane* was built by nonagenarian Thomas O.M. Sopwith and associates in the 1980s, and now belongs to the Shuttleworth Trust; it flies regularly at Old Warden Aerodrome near Biggleswade in England. Tommy Sopwith termed it "late production" and it raised the grand total to 150.

(5) SCARFF/DYBOVSKY MACHINE-GUN SYNCHRONIZING GEAR.

Lieutenant Commander V.V. Dybovsky of the Imperial Russian Navy had conceived the idea that if he could make an aeroplane engine fire the individual bullets from a machine gun one by one and at the proper time, he could mount it behind the propeller. His idea was to attach a cam to the propeller shaft and connect it to the firing mechanism in the breechblock via a system of rods, pivots and levers.

In 1916, naval business took Dybovsky to the Admiralty in England where he met Warrant Officer F. W. Scarff who had invented the Scarff ring, a fully flexible mounting for one or two Lewis guns. (It can be seen in photographs of R.E.8s, D.H.4s, Bristol F.2B fighters and twin-engined Handley Page bombers). Dybovsky had the method, Scarff had the need, and the Admiralty had the money. Several propellers later, they produced a design which successfully synchronized a standard British Army Vickers Mark 1 machine gun with a French rotary aircraft engine. The first type of aeroplane to be equipped with their system was the Sopwith One and a Half Strutter, followed later by the Sopwith Pup and the Sopwith Triplane. The rate of fire produced by the Scarff-Dybovsky gear was five or six rounds per second depending upon the engine's revolutions per minute.

The pilot fired the machine gun by pulling upwards on a handle which stuck out from the instrument panel. This action engaged the Scarff-Dybovsky gear, which thereupon began providing timed pushes to the Vickers gun firing lever. A cam on the engine initiated each push just as the trailing edge of the chosen propeller blade was about to clear the gun muzzle. The firing lever received the push from an arm with an adjusting screw at the end. The latter device resembled a bird's head and was immediately nicknamed the "pecker".

The Pecker, in the lower left corner of the windscreen, on the Sopwith *Pup*.

German engineers employed an ingeniously simple method of enabling the propeller to signal the Maxim gun. They eliminated the friction and the inertia of pivots and rods by using a flexible drive cable similar to that used for car speedometers. The improvement was such that a Maxim LMG 08/15 could safely fire ten rounds per second, and the Albatros D.III had two of them.

The factories producing versions of the Maxim machine gun were principally located in the industrial town of Spandau, and this name features prominently on most weapons manufactured there. The abbreviation "MG" means *Maschinengewehr* (machine gun); "LMG" means *Luftgekühltmaschinengewehr* (air-cooled machine gun) and "08/15" stands for Type 8 introduced in 1915. Although the Maxim MG 08/15 (German Army) or the Maxim LMG 08/15 (air-cooled version for the German Air Service) are often called *Spandaus*, that designation is actually the equivalent of calling a Vickers machine gun a *Birmingham*.

A pair of Maxim LMG 08/15 machine guns and the flexible drive cable.

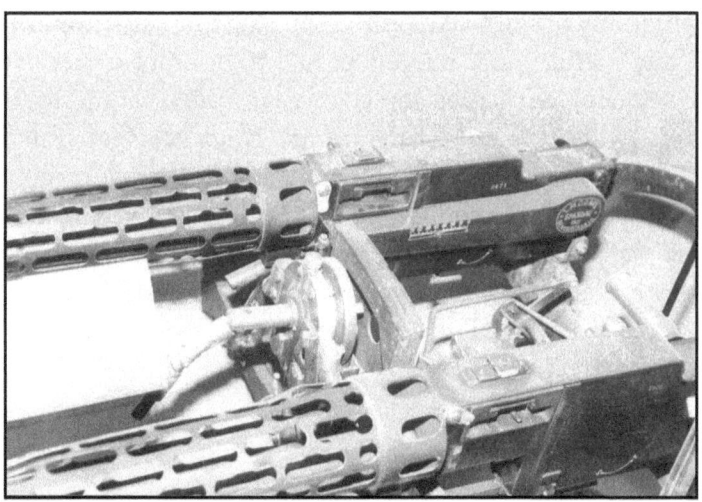

Note the nameplate at the rear of the upper breechblock.

Mel Alexander of Naval 10 once said in a recorded interview, that when he pulled up the firing handle his Sopwith *Pup* went "*pop-pop-pop*", where an Albatros would have gone "*woosh*." At altitudes below 15,000 feet, it took much courage for an RNAS pilot under such a handicap to tackle an Albatros D.III, and great skill to defeat one.

(6) LANDING A SOPWITH *PUP*.

The extra lift created by the proximity of an aeroplane's wings to the ground is known technically as "ground effect." The broad lower wings of a Sopwith *Pup* were particularly susceptible to this phenomenon, and instead of landing, the aeroplane would continue flying or "floating"; the pilot had to exercise patience and wait for the airspeed to bleed away. When the wings cease producing lift (the technical term is "stall"), the wheels and the tailskid should touch down gently. If the pilot tries to force the wheels onto the ground, the aeroplane will bounce back into the air, taking the wings out of "ground effect" but the sudden loss of lift creates a dangerous situation. The pilot must immediately apply power from the engine to increase the airflow over the wings and then make another landing if there is enough space ahead; otherwise he must go around again.

A bounce during a night-time landing on an airfield marked (not illuminated) by oil lamps produced a difficult situation. The unlighted ground would suddenly disappear from sight, and the pilot, without any useful visual reference, had to attempt corrective action. After many accidents, plus some uncomfortable moments by highly experienced nighttime fighting pilots, Brigadier General T. C. R. Higgins, the commander of the Home Defence Brigade, recommended that the use of the Sopwith *Pup* at night be discontinued. It was replaced by the Sopwith F1 Camels, which landed like a Nieuport, and the S.E.5a. Both types had a far higher weight per square foot of wing area (wing-loading) than *the Pup* and therefore did not float.

(7) THE COCKPIT LAYOUT OF A SOPWITH *PUP*.

The cockpit of a Sopwith *Pup* with the machine gun removed. Pointing downwards across the inclinometer, the handle to fire the machine gun is clearly visible between the single ignition switch and the compass. The blip switch is the push button in the middle of the crossbar of the triangular spade grip at the top of the joystick. The small battery on the floor at the front left of the pilot's seat and the wires across the top of the panel illuminated the instruments for night flying.

It has often been inaccurately written that pilots hammered the breeches of machine guns with their fists to clear a jam. The only reason for a pilot doing such a thing could be an attempt to restore circulation to his frozen fingers. The hammering or beating action upon which this "canard" is based is explained as follows:

> Pilots carried a wooden mallet to beat the cocking handle down into the firing position if a deformed cartridge case caused a jam. Unfortunately, about the only available space to stow the mallet was down on the floor near the compass, and any misguided soul who took a *metal* hammer aloft was likely to find himself writing letters home with German postage stamps on the envelopes.

The cockpit of a Sopwith *Pup*.
The pilot's padded windscreen and single Vickers machine gun, with deflection sights, are in place. Note the geared cocking handle fitted to the machine-gun breech.
The synchronizing gear and the cover over the ammunition belt where it disappears into the "used box" have been removed. The take-up spool inside the used box was equipped with a powerful spring, which had been wound up by an armourer when the ammunition belt was installed. The spring tensioning handle is just out of picture in the lower left corner.

(8) THE B.E.2C AND THE F.E.2D AEROPLANES.

In order to give some defensive power to the ultra-stable B.E.2C, Lieutenant (later Captain) Louis Arbon Strange of 5 Squadron designed a variety of Lewis gun mounting posts which could be permanently attached to the fuselage. The observer had to move his Lewis gun from one mounting to another as the situation dictated.

Not unexpectedly, the posts became known to airmen as "*strange mountings*".

The success of the B.E.2 in 1912 cast a long shadow, and in 1917 the C version of this relic from a bygone era sent many a brave airman to his grave. Some, more outspoken than others, called it murder.

A Royal Aircraft Factory B.E.2C with the swivelling rearward-firing Strange Mounting in use.

In the photograph note the thin ammunition drum on top of the Lewis gun; this type held forty-seven rounds in two layers (twenty-two in the lower and twenty-five in the upper) and was known as a single drum. Below the gun is the catcher bag for the empty cartridge cases. The manual pump to send fuel from the main tank to the header tank is on the outside of the fuselage, beside the pilot's cockpit.

A B.E.2C with the right side forward-firing Strange Mounting post in use. The Lewis gun is minus an ammunition drum. The rearward-firing mounting post is behind the observer's head. Further behind is the left side forward-firing post.

The Royal Aircraft Factory F.E.2B, a 1915 design, was reliable and easy to fly. From the start it was intended to carry machine guns and serve as a fighter its prey being German observation, photography and bombing aircraft. However, with the arrival of the synchronized machine gun, the F.E.2B became obsolete overnight. More than 1,000 had been built, and they were used in photographic reconnaisance squadrons and bombing squadrons, of both day and night varieties. The F.E.2B could carry a heavy load of bombs and remained in service as a night bomber until the end of the war.

The F.E.2D, a higher powered, heavily armed version produced in 1917, was a tough nut to crack by a single German fighter. However, It was an easy victim to a well co-ordinated attack by two German pilots. For defence against an attack from above and behind, the pilot would apply full power and lift the nose into a semi-stalled condition while the observer stood on his seat and used the upper Lewis gun.

When a flight of F.E.2Ds was attacked by a pair of German fighters, the 'Fees' would form a defensive circle in which each pilot covered the other's tail while the observers could bring a considerable weight of fire against the attackers. The defensive circle would become a continual series of horizontal loops as the 'Fees' edged their way to friendly territory. It was in such an encounter that Manfred von Richthofen was shot down on 6 July 1917, and he never recovered fully from the head wound received on that day.

Typical F.E.2D. Note the pilot's own Lewis gun and the observer's camera. All three Lewis guns have thick ammunition drums designed to hold 97 rounds in four layers (22, 25, 25, 25), known as double drums.

Historian Stewart Taylor told Alan Bennett that double drums were more prone to jamming than were single drums, but that in practice fewer jams occurred if the upper layers were loaded with fewer rounds, for example, 22, 23, 24, 24. As a result smaller totals of 93, 94 and sometimes 95 rounds were often given for a double drum.

(9) THE DIRTY EXHAUST FROM ROTARY ENGINES.

Coal oil is known today as lamp oil, paraffin oil or kerosene. The navy liked things to be clean; it was good for morale and therefore for discipline. Unfortunately, however rotary engines did not have exhaust pipes, and each cylinder spewed products of combustion and partially burned castor oil through its own short stub of pipe. The oil and carbon collected inside the engine cowling, and air pressure forced the mixture through joints in the sheet metal. The slipstream then smeared the mixture along the sides and bottom of the fuselage. Some castor oil vapour found its way into the cockpit, and there were few pilots who complained of constipation. To add insult to injury, the dust from aerodrome surfaces then stuck to the mess as the pilots taxied in. At this point, another benefit was derived from the fact that each flight in a squadron used a different colour for wheel covers: the ground crew for one flight was able to avoid accidentally cleaning an aeroplane that belonged to another.

(10) THE ACTIVE SERVICE PERFORMED BY THE ROYAL NAVAL AIR SERVICE.

Roy could hardly tell Alice Pickup the methods by which the RNAS protected the battleships, cruisers and airships of the Silent Service as they went about their business. Nor could he tell her the great success of the work of his squadron in protecting the supply vessels and the troop ships crossing the English Channel and in preventing the Germans from learning the intensity of the traffic. Although Roy was not involved in the protection of warships hundreds of miles from land, he had many friends who were, and the situation which they had to face was daunting.

As soon as Germans suspected that part of the British fleet had left port, high-altitude Zeppelins would attempt to locate it and determine where it was heading. The German naval headquarters would then begin planning attacks by U-boats, surface ships and/or seaplanes. A special squadron, designated T-Staffel and equipped with Gotha WD11 and Brandenburg GW twin-engined seaplanes capable of carrying a torpedo, was stationed at Zeebrugge for those attacks. The only effective defence against then these was high-performance RNAS land planes which were launched into the air when the enemy was sighted, which could be hundreds of miles out to sea. Two primitive aircraft carriers existed, but until this type of vessel could be perfected, other means had to be employed.

During Roy's time in the RNAS, Sopwith *One and a Half Strutters*, *Pups* and 2F1 *Camels* were launched from platforms built over the upper forward gun turret of cruisers and battleships, or from lighters towed far enough behind destroyers to avoid the wake. With the vessel steaming at full speed into wind, the airflow over the wings of the fighter was only a little less than minimum flying speed; after a short run at full power, it was airborne. After chasing away a Zeppelin or searching for the plume of a periscope, the pilot then had to worry about the other end of his flight, which although definitely well-organized, tended to be rather damp.

Sopwith 2F1 *Camel* No. N6623 departing from a lighter and beginning a curve to its left. Before lifting off, the *Camel* had slid over the edge of the deck, and the pilot, Lieutenant-Colonel C. R. Samson, took a bath.

The Sopwith 2F1 *Camel* was a naval version of the F.1. The fuselage was hinged immediately behind the fuel tanks, thus allowing the tail to be folded against the wings for storage aboard ship. The hinged part contained flotation bags, which made both man and machine recyclable.

The hinged rear portion of a Sopwith 2F1 *Camel*, showing the flotation bags fitted inside.

Sopwith 2F1 *Camel* departing from a platform built over X gun turret on HMS *Ramillies*. The platform was folded back when not in use. Note the single Lewis gun mounted above the wing; absolute minimum weight was required for the *Camel* to reach the heights at which the Zeppelins flew.

Sopwith 2F1 *Camel* No. N6789, supported by the flotation bags inside the fuselage, waiting to be retrieved by a crew from HMS *Malaya* to fight another day. The figure in heavy clothing in the rowing boat is probably the pilot, Flight Lieutenant Remnitz, a Canadian.

When the German naval airship command finally discovered how Sopwith *Camels* were able to appear hundreds of miles out to sea, the next step of the perfidious English was ingenious. A full-size Sopwith *Camel* and its shadow (most important) were painted on the deck of each lighter. From 15,000 feet altitude and above, where the Zeppelins flew, the artwork gave the impression that the real thing was still there. On 11 August 1918, Sopwith 2F1 *Camel* No. N6812 was launched from a lighter towed behind HMS *Redoubt*. The pilot, Flight Lieutenant. Stuart Douglas Culley, climbed to 18,700 feet near Heligoland Bight, where he stalked a Zeppelin L53 and shot it down. The L53 had been shadowing his ship and its several companions while reporting their position by wireless telegraphy. Sopwith 2F1 *Camel* No. N6812 was retrieved, wrung out and dried, and now hangs in the dome of the Imperial War Museum in London.

Woe betide the Zeppelin captain who believed what he saw.

(11) DISTINGUISHING BETWEEN FLIGHTS AND INTERPRETING FLIGHT COMMANDERS' PENNANTS.

The following table lists the colours of the aeroplane wheel covers and the locations of the pennants (sometimes called streamers) flown by the three flight commanders of Naval 1. Other squadrons used different arrangements, particularly for wheel-cover colours; for example, B flight of Naval 10 used black.

Flight   Wheel Covers   Commander's Pennant(s)

A	red	1.–attached to the rudder
B	white	2.–one attached to each elevator
C	blue	2.–one attached to the middle of the outer, rear interplane strut on each side

(12) THE S.E.5 AND ITS LATER VERSIONS.

When the Royal Aircraft Factory's test pilot climbed out of the cockpit after the first flight of the S.E.5 prototype, he joyfully exclaimed, *"We've got a pixie here!"* the aeroplane was responsive to the pilot's touch, had no tendency to wander if he removed his hands from the controls, and was not difficult to land. The intention had been to install a 200hp Hispano-Suiza engine, but only the 150hp version was available at the time. Even with 50 hp lacking, it was fast and climbed well. The much maligned Royal Aircraft Factory had produced a winner.

The armament of the S.E.5 was well chosen—a synchronized Vickers machine gun mounted on the fuselage in a location which did not obstruct the pilot's vision, and a free-firing Lewis gun on a curved rail above the top wing. Although, like the Vickers, the Lewis normally fired straight ahead, the pilot could pull it back to a 45-degree position on the curved part of the rail, sight it and fire upwards into the belly of an enemy two-seater or airship. With the Lewis pulled right back, he could clear a jam or fit a new drum of ammunition in flight. The S.E.5 had a tailplane-angle-adjustment wheel in the cockpit, enabling the pilot to trim the aeroplane for level flight before taking both hands from the controls to service a machine gun. If the aeroplane began to bank or turn, he could give the joystick a gentle nudge with his knee.

There was one shortcoming to the drum-changing system. If thick flying gloves caused the pilot to fumble the operation, the empty drum could fly off and give him a crack on the head, one that would remind him to be more careful next time. C. E. Lambert described how such an incident knocked him unconscious, and he only recovered his senses at a much lower altitude. One wonders how many similar events caused S.E.5 pilots to fly into the ground for no apparent reason.

The Lewis gun rail on an S.E.5. The extra thickness of the double ammunition drum stands out clearly.

The cockpit of an S.E.5. Note the triggers for the Vickers and the Lewis guns at the bottom of the round spadegrip on the joystick. Note also the empty hole at the top; the stationary Hispano-Suiza engine had a carburetor with throttle control from idle to maximum power and therefore did not require a blip switch.

As the 200hp Hispano-Suiza engine was being licence-manufactured in England by the Wolseley Company under its own name, it was not long before supplies became available. Thus, the S.E.5A was born.

S.E.5A No. E5968 with 200hp Wolseley Viper 1750rpm direct-drive engine and two-bladed propeller. Note the angle of the blades.*

Many S.E.5A fighters were fitted with a 220hp Hispano-Suiza 2200rpm engine manufactured in France. The increased power had little effect upon the maximum speed of this blunt-shaped aeroplane, but it did wonders for the rate of climb and operation at high altitude. An engine of this power required a four-bladed propeller; therefore a step-down gearbox was employed to place the final output revolutions per minute in the range for 1917 propeller technology.

The 220hp propeller rotated in the opposite direction of the 200hp propeller. A pilot who switched from a 200hp to a 220hp engined S.E.5A (or vice versa) and failed to remember this difference could easily have a takeoff accident if he applied correction the wrong way against tail swing.

S.E.5A No. B4867 with a geared, French-manufactured, 220hp Hispano-Suiza engine. Note how the gearbox raises the position of the four-bladed propeller.

(13) THE AIRCO D.H.4 DAY BOMBER.

The D.H.4 aeroplanes escorted by Roy would have belonged to Naval 2 or Naval 5, which had recently received them as replacements for their obsolete Sopwith One and a Half Strutters. Although the D.H.4 had originally been designed as an unarmed fast bomber, was found to be eminently suitable for photographic reconnaissance work.

When fitted with a Rolls-Royce Eagle VIII 375hp engine, the D.H.4 reached maximum speed of 143 mph, which made it only vulnerable to surprise diving attacks or to anti-aircraft artillery. When flying without a bomb load, the D.H.4 was faster than all the scouts in service in 1917 and most of 1918. This meant that on their way to the target, the D.H.4 pilots were unhappy because they had to slow down so that their protectors could keep pace with them. Once the mission was accomplished, it was the scout pilots' turn to be unhappy: the D.H.4 pilots would look at watch and compass, add or subtract the wind and then depart at full speed towards Allied territory for the requisite number of minutes. The unfortunate scouts then had to handle the hornet's nest which the D.H.4s had stirred up.

(14) Hunland meant not only Germany, but also the areas of Belgium and France occupied by the German Army. Archie, which meant "anti-aircraft fire," is said to have been derived from comedian George Robey's music-hall song, *"Archibald, Certainly Not!"*—the inference or the hope of the airmen, being that the German gunners would not manage to hit them.

If we recall a previous letter in which Roy wrote that *"everything is run like a ship,"* the meaning of *'going ashore'* becomes clear. When he later returned to the aerodrome, he was *'coming aboard.'*

(15) OPERATING A ROTARY ENGINE.

As explained earlier, rotary engines did not have a carburetor; fuel and air were fed into a mixing chamber. On early engines the pilot controlled the amount of each ingredient via two levers; one for fuel, the other for air, and operated both with his left hand. On later rotary engines, such as the Le Rhône, Clergêt and Bentley designs, the Tampier control (invented by Claude Tampier) exercised simultaneous control over the quantity of fuel and the quality of air being fed to the mixing chamber; The mixture lever provided a fine adjustment.

The easy way to cause exhaust valves to stick was to overheat them by feeding too lean a mixture to the engine. Incorrect use of the mixture lever by mechanics on the ground during testing or by the pilot in the air would do precisely that, and sometimes the fault only revealed itself the next time the aeroplane was flown. It was an easy trap to fall into because flights which covered long distances required careful control of the fuel supply, and too rich a mixture could cause the need for a refuelling stop in an area where French francs would not be acceptable payment.

(16) THE SURPRISING PERFORMANCE OF THE SOPWITH TRIPLANE.

General Hoeppner was not the only person to be surprised by the performance of a Sopwith *Triplane*. One of the last order built by Oakley & Co, Ltd., Sopwith *Triplane* N5912, used at Marske-by-the-Sea School of Aerial Fighting, managed to avoid the post-war scrapyard. With more suitable fuel in the tanks than available in 1918, it was flown in the 1936 Hendon Air Pageant where its climbing abilities astounded the spectators who had been watching far more modern aircraft perform. As of this writing, N5912 is on display at the RAF Museum, Hendon.

(17) AN RFC/RNAS/RAF AIRMAN'S FLYING LEATHERS.

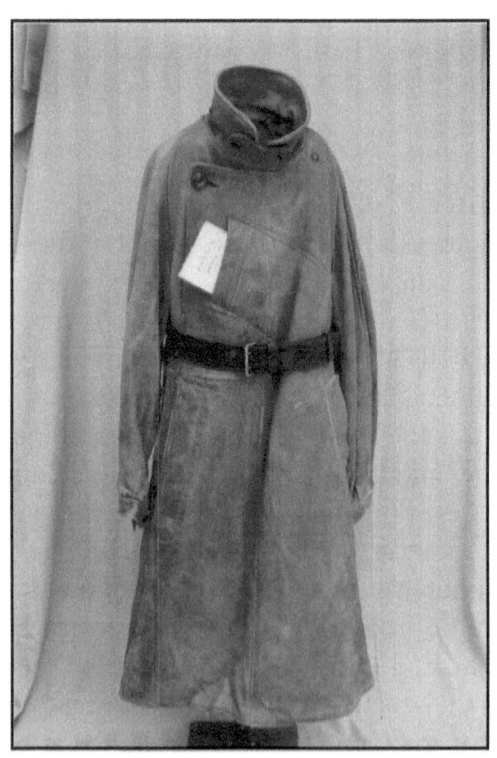

Typical leather flying coat with handily positioned map pocket.

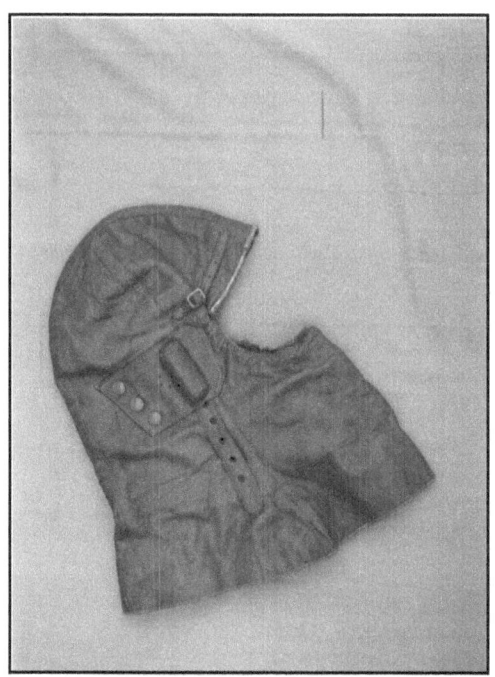

Adjustable-size helmet with face and neck mask.

Goggles with tinted lenses.

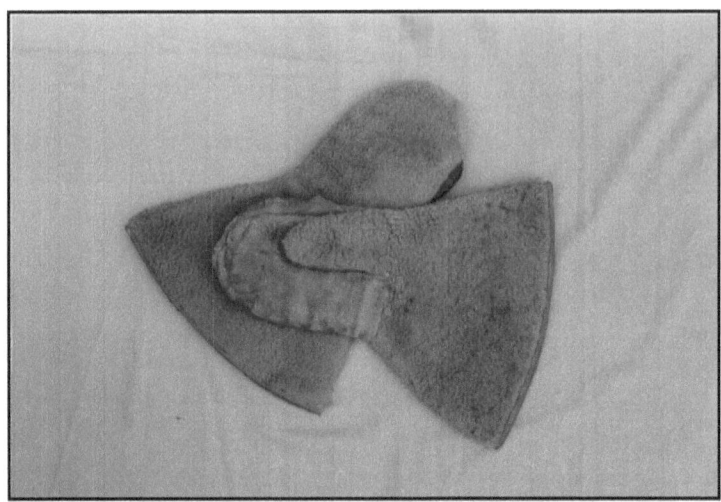

To unfold a map or change a Lewis ammunition drum would not have been easy wearing sheepskin mittens like these.

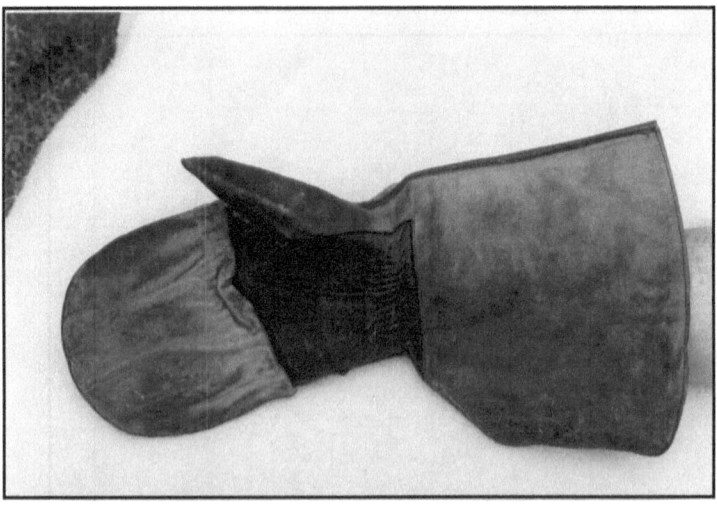

A right hand mitten/glove used by aircrew, arranged as a mitten.

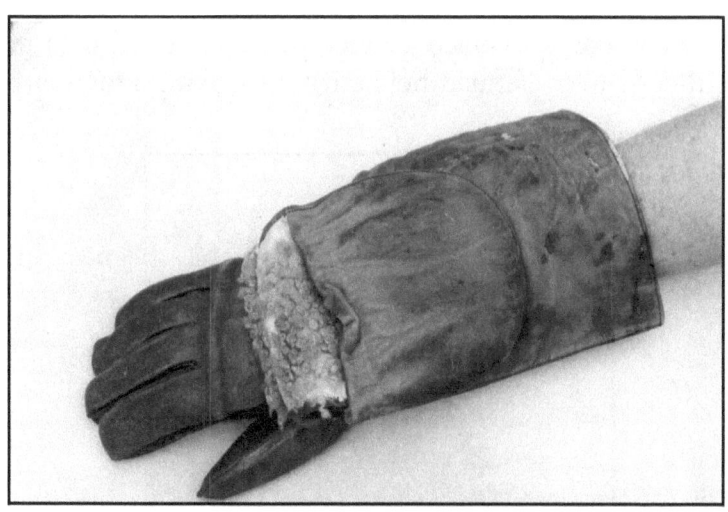

The same mitten/glove arranged as a glove.

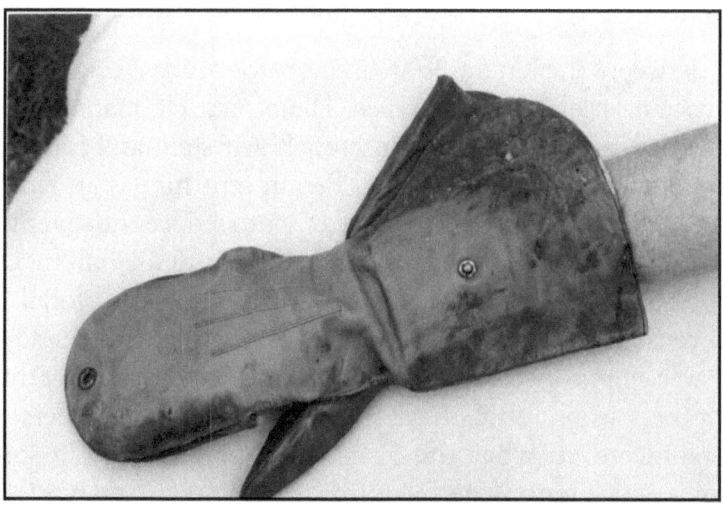

How the conversion was made.

(18) CAPTAINE RENÉ FONCK.

Captaine René Fonck claimed 75 victories over Allied-held territory and a further 52 over German-held territory, making a total of 127.

Le Capitaine René Fonck.*

Between the Great War and the Second World War, René Fonck became friendly with ex-ace, Hauptman Hermann Göring. By 1939 Fonck was a colonel on the French Air staff, and following the defeat of France in 1940, Maréchal Pétain sent him as an emissary to Generalfeldmarschall Göring in an attempt to reduce the severity of the demands made by the German Armistice Commission. In October 1944, after the liberation of Paris (25 August 1944), Colonel Fonck's mission caused him to be charged for collaborating with the Germans, and he was imprisoned awaiting trial. He was released together with several others whose only crime had been to obey the orders of their superior officers, in what the French now refer to as le soi-disant gouvernment de France (the so-called Government of France). He died in 1953, aged 59, in relative obscurity.

(19) REST PERIODS FOR PILOTS.

Both the RFC and the RNAS entertained a system of pilot rotation between service at the front and "rest periods" as combat instructors at advanced training schools in England. The latter were known as postings to Home Establishment (HE). Rest periods were nominally by the calendar, but the squadron or wing medical officer could advance the date if he noticed a pilot was beginning to show symptoms of strain, often from long flights at high altitudes in extremely cold temperatures rather than from combat with enemy aircraft.

Even though instructors' aeroplanes were usually painted white, some who sat in them considered it far safer to be shot at by experienced Germans than to engage in mock combat with pupils who could not foresee what was going to happen. Strangely enough, the two serious accidents which Roy suffered in 1916 and 1918 were both at training schools.

Eventually, when the powers-that-be decided that a particular pilot had risked his life enough for his country, he was sent to a quiet area back in England or given an administrative job. If he was a particularly good leader and organizer, he would be promoted and placed in charge of a squadron. By 1918, commanding officers were discouraged from leading their squadrons into battle; that was the duty of the senior flight commander.

The Germans did not employ a rotation system, and apart from regular leaves, the Jasta pilots flew until they were either crippled or killed—the reason so few of their aces survived the war. On one occasion when Baron von Richthofen was at home on leave, his mother picked up a photograph of him with a group of his pilots and began asking about their health and recent adventures. After an attempt at changing the subject, he finally said; *"Mother, please let's not talk about them. They are all dead."*

(20) THE STRUCTURAL STRENGTH OF THE SOPWITH TRIPLANE.

Pilots in combat usually fly their aeroplanes well beyond the designer's intended limits. Logically, Herbert Smith had included a "fudge factor" in the triplane design, but occasional structural failures began to occur. According to Mel Alexander, who flew a Sopwith *Triplane* named *Black Prince* in Raymond Collishaw's B Flight (with black wheel covers) of Naval 10 Squadron, investigation revealed that a certain contractor, with the best of intentions, had improved upon the ordinary 5/8" wide streamlined steel bracing wire for the wings. He had used an excellent quality 3/8inch wide high-tensile steel, which was both lighter and stronger. However, the "hi-tech" metal quite unexpectedly fatigued when subjected to vibration in the low temperatures at high altitudes, and in a high speed dive, the wings on some of the triplanes made at his factory folded back when a bracing wire parted.

In a 1970 recorded conversation with his wartime colleague, Nick Carter, Mel Alexander described how the report that Flight Commander John Edward Sharman (8 victories including shared) had received a direct hit from an anti-aircraft shell was incorrect. Mel had watched the wings of Sharman's *Triplane* fold back as he dived on an enemy aeroplane. As a corrective measure, even though it reduced the top speed in level flight, Naval 10 mechanics added stranded cables to the wings in key places to provide the necessary strength. This led to another problem: pilots, now being able to dive safely, dived even faster than before. Unfortunately, the force needed to hold the nose of a Sopwith *Triplane* down in a dive increased with speed, and the stresses on the tailplane trimming mechanism passed well beyond its design limits. Tailplane failures began to occur, and like the pirates who dug the holes for their captain to bury the treasure, few lived to tell the tale.

The advantages presented by streamlined high-tensile-strength steel had occurred to more than one engineer. Anthony H. G. Fokker in Germany had used it on some of the E series monoplanes and the result had been identical. He was forced to replace the streamlined wires with stranded steel cables like those which Mel Alexander added to his Sopwith *Triplane*, and to accept the speed penalty incurred. The solution came in the form of an idea inspired partly by Professor Hugo Junkers, with whom Fokker had co-operated for a while, and partly by a Swedish engineer named Forssman, whom Fokker had met in Russia while trying to sell his early designs before the war. The idea was revolutionary: use thick wings in place of thin ones, and make the internal structure so strong that no external support whatsoever would be required, even under the violent loads of air combat. Anthony Fokker used this idea on his triplane and most of his later designs. The cantilever wing, as it is now known, is the normal method of construction employed today, except on some light aircraft.

The Sopwith *Triplanes* of Navel 10's B Flight were named as follows: Raymond Collishaw, *Black Maria*; Mel Alexander (23 victories including shared), *Black Prince*; John Edward (Ted) Sharman (8 victories including shared), *Black Death*; Gerald Ewart (Gerry) Nash (6 victories including shared), *Black Sheep* and Ellis Read, *Black Roger*. The fuselage from the engine cowling to the cockpit was painted black as were the wheel covers; hence the nickname "The Black Flight." All the pilots named above were Canadians.

From one point of view, Flight Lieutenant Percival Beasley of Naval 13, who flew an aeroplane named *Black Bess*, could be said to have been a magician: he had changed Dick Turpin's famous horse into a *Camel*, No. B6399.

(21) THE SOPWITH F.1 *CAMEL*.

In parallel with the triplane production, the Sopwith company had been developing the F1 *Super Pup*, later renamed the F1 *Camel*. It was intended to be stronger, extra powerful, faster and more manoeuvrable than any previous scout, Allied or German. The Camel's armament was twin Vickers machine guns controlled by the factory's own synchronizing system, the Sopwith-Kauper Type 2 gear. Pushrods and cranks were again used, but there were fewer than on the earlier Scarff-Dybovsky system—a simplification which reduced the inertia, thereby increasing the rate of fire per gun. The firing handle was replaced by two short trigger levers mounted in the V of the joystick, just below the blip switch. A Bowden cable from each trigger lever engaged the firing mechanism of the associated machine gun. The "Sopwith" part of the system's name represented the involvement of aircraft designer Harry Hawker in the production and testing; the "Kauper" part represented Harry Alexis Kauper, the foreman fitter in the Sopwith factory. Both were Australians. Harry Hawker's name was later immortalized by the Hawker *Hurricane, Typhoon* and *Tempest* fighters used in the Second World War.

To strengthen the tailplane, Sopwith abandoned the in-flight adjustable feature which had made long-distance flying a pleasure on the *Pup* and the *Triplane*. To make a *Camel* fly level, riggers had to adjust the tailplane on the ground. This was not so simple as it sounds, since unlike that of the B.E.2C and the D.H.4, the fuel tank was not at the centre of gravity; it was behind it, and furthermore, the ammunition boxes were ahead of the centre of gravity. As a result, was the balance of the machine revolved around the relative amounts fuel and ammunition on board at any given moment.

According to Ronald Sykes, the tailplane was normally (but not always) set so that with a full load of fuel and ammunition the aeroplane was tail heavy. Therefore the pilot had to apply forward pressure on the joystick to fly level at cruising speed. The amount of pressure needed would progressively decrease as fuel was burned, until after about one hour of flight the machine would fly level of its own accord. During the next hour, assuming no ammunition was fired, the pilot would have to apply gradually increasing backward pressure. In such cases, one way to relieve aching arms was to indulge in some trench strafing from a safe altitude before leaving Hunland behind. Pilots found the *Camel* tiring to fly on a two-hour patrol, and its late-1918 replacement, the *Snipe*, was given a much strengthened, adjustable tailplane.

The production version of the Sopwith F1 *Camel* met all expectations of speed and manoeuvrability, and its structural strength enabled the aircraft to dive safely at up to 180 mph. Given pilots of equal ability, only a Fokker Dr.I *Triplane* could outmanoeuvre a *Camel*, and only a Halberstadt D.II was able to outdive it.

From the flying log books of the RNAS aces, it is noticeable that the number of victories scored per month increased as the pilots changed from Sopwith *Pups* to *Triplanes*, and then it took a dramatic jump after they moved to *Camels*.

CHAPTER SIX

DOVER PATROL, Part 2
(1 August 1917 to 10 November 1917)

The development of the means to operate high-performance landplanes from lighters towed behind destroyers and the commissioning in mid-1916 of the aircraft carrier HMS *Furious* did not alter the situation in the English Channel.[1] The entire area was adequately covered by Dover Patrol units stationed along both shores, and the work of the RNAS fighter squadrons on the French side of the Channel remained unchanged.

HMS *Furious* was a converted cruiser, with the takeoff deck at the bow and the landing deck at the stern. Note the three screens to protect parked aircraft from propeller blast.

The physical exhaustion from the living conditions in that battered part of France and spending three to four hours each day at altitudes of 15,000 to 19,000 feet without oxygen or heating, plus the attendant headaches, had upset Roy's entire digestive system. The sympathetic commanding officer of Naval 11 at Frontier Aerodrome, Squadron Commander H. Stanley Adams, allowed Roy to spend a quiet fortnight just taking care of the maintenance and supply needs of his flight. This was a good move because a flight commander who was not fully alert in the air constituted a hazard for himself and his subordinates. The Remarks column in Roy's flying log book contains the following entry:

"Been sick & weather bad for all of time - 25.7 to 10.8/17."

On 10 August it was back to the grind. However, an event of future significance took place at another aerodrome that day. Naval 6 had just been disbanded, and Stearne Edwards, who was on its strength, had requested a posting to Naval 11 where his old chum Roy was serving. His request had been denied, and on 10 August he was sent to Naval 9 which needed a flight commander. In the long run, this proved to be fortunate for it facilitated their eventual reunion. Ignorant of what the future held, a disappointed Stearne Edwards reported to Squadron Commander T.C. Vernon at Leffrinckoucke Aerodrome that afternoon. Meanwhile, Roy was back in the air:

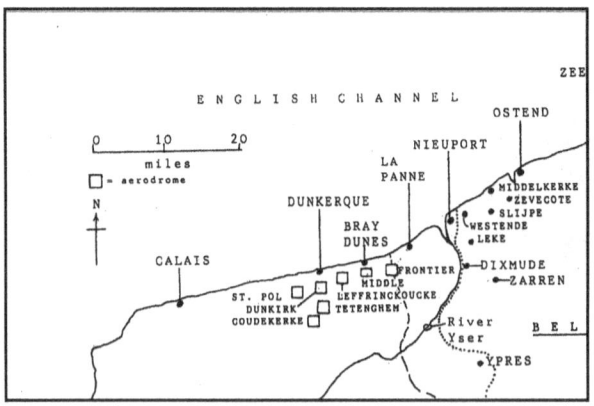

The coastal aerodromes and towns in northeast France and southwest Belgium known to the Dover Patrol.

10. 8.17 - 6.45 PM - Pup N6468 - 15 mins - Gun jambed - Links jambed in chute causing double feed.

7.10 PM - Pup N6469 - 85 mins - 17,000' - O.P. Ostend - Nothing to report. Hit - twice by A.A. in right lower plane. Stunted around in A.A. to make them sore.

The use of the word *"links"* in Roy's description of the Vickers machine gun jam in No. N6468 reveals that metal ammunition belts composed of disintegrating links were now being used by his squadron.[2] The earlier canvas-webbing belts absorbed moisture and would freeze as stiff as a board at high altitude. When the pilot pressed the trigger, the gun would fire the round in the breech and then lapse into total silence.

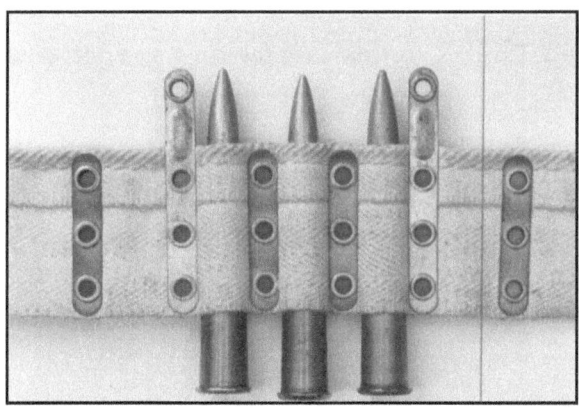

Early RNAS, RFC and army canvas webbing ammunition belt. Note the incorrect positioning of the middle cartridge which would cause a misfeed; the tip of its nose is not level with the tips of the alignment tabs. The pilot would then have to operate the cocking handle to extract the cartridge and insert the next one. Pressing the trigger would start the gun firing again.

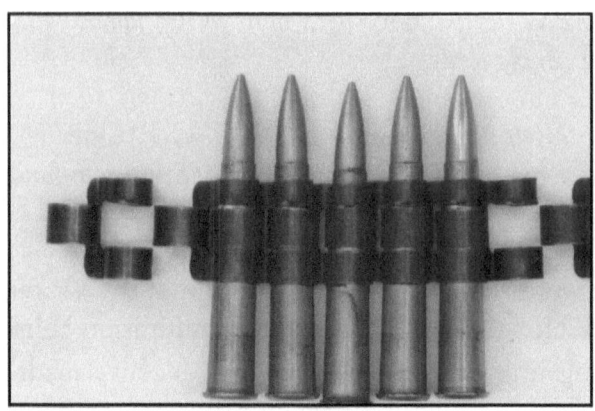

Disintegrating link belt as used by Roy. Each cartridge had to be inserted until its shoulder butted firmly against the lower edge of the upper ring, which was smaller in diameter than the other two and acted as an alignment stop. The middle cartridge is improperly positioned and would cause a misfeed.

See (2) in the ANNEX to this chapter for more information on link belts.

12. 8.17 - 12.50 PM - Pup N6468 - 105 mins - 17,000' - Defensive Fleet Patrol - Fleet 20 miles to sea between Ostend & Zeebrugge returning to base. No E.A.

13. 8.17 - 10.40 AM - Pup N6468 - 145 mins - 16,000' - Defensive Fleet Patrol - Nothing to report. Squadrons of fleet from Nieuport to Zeebrugge.

4.40 PM - Pup N6468 - 140 mins - 17,000' - Defensive Fleet Patrol - Fleet returning to base. Did Line Patrol between Dixmude & Nieuport. No E.A.

The Defensive Fleet Patrols mentioned above involved flying several miles out over the sea for between 90 and 120 minutes in a single-engined aeroplane with one magneto only. Even worse, the magneto had been made in England or France.

Line Patrols were normally distinguished by "Outer" or "Inner." outer Line Patrols were conducted on the German side of the front at high altitude; Inner Line Patrols were conducted on the Allied side at lower altitude to catch any enemy aircraft which had slipped through. In 1917 Nieuport was in Allied hands, and Dixmüde was in German hands; so the kind of line patrol Roy's flight conducted along the canalized Yser River is open to speculation.

14. 8.17 - 7.45 AM - Pup 6468 - 140 mins - 15,000' – Defensive Fleet Patrol - Johnston's engine failed, landed by fleet. Followed him down with engine misfiring but got back O.K. Engine failed at last.

These comments read just like a run-of-the-mill patrol with a minor mishap at the end, but there was more to it than that. The error in the day's date at the head of Roy's letter home that evening suggests that he was still a little tense.

No. 11 Squadron
Aug. 13/17

My dear Mother,

Just received your letter of July 29 and am getting busy immediately. I am about as tired tonight as possibly can be. I never, as the saying is here, had the "wind up" so high in my life before as I had today.
We are doing patrols now to protect the fleet on land machines, and the fleet, of course, is miles out in the North Sea. Today my engine was misfiring badly all the time and the climax came when one of my flight had his engine quit, and I had to go right down to 300 feet off the sea to make sure the fleet picked him up. He was picked up alright and I thought I should have to crash in the sea too but I got back alright. I nearly crashed on landing as once I shut my engine off I could not get it to start again. I was all in when I got down again as I was so scared. It's no fun, I can tell you. That is why I do not like writing about what we do as it is all done with too narrow a margin. This letter will be mailed in England.
I am very glad you liked the photos. I have another one which you will like better when you get it but I cannot send it till I go on leave. Unfortunately all leave is stopped for this month which means I get no leave till October at the earliest. Stearne is all O.K. again and back on duty. He tried to get to No. 11 squadron but could not manage it. I am very sorry as I wish he could

have got here.

The weather, as I told you in my last letter, has been very bad for nearly a month. All rain and miserable. The result is our drome is all under water and, where there is no water, there is mud.

The chap that fell in the sea has just got back. He is pretty lucky as it was hard for him to swim with a big leather coat and great hip fur boots on. They picked him up so quickly though as he was only in the water for about 8 minutes or so.

I must get to bed now as I have to be up at 5 something in the morning, so good-night.

Roy is strongly exhibiting the qualities of a leader of men. A member of his flight had been in peril, for unlike the later 2F1 *Camels*, a naval *Pup* did not have flotation bags inside the fuselage; once the Pup had sunk, it would not be easy for anyone on a ship's deck to see a head bobbing up and down in the waves against the dark background of the sea. Probably, the only thought in Roy's head at the time was to go to the aid of his subordinate. Then, hoping that his own misfiring engine would not cause him to join Johnston in the drink, he dived down and circled overhead to give his colleague confidence, while marking the spot. What Roy did on that day was the instinctive reaction of a brave man; courage came the next morning when he took off at the break of dawn to lead his flight over the North Sea once more.

"Where there is no water there is mud." On the left is Navel 9's Sopwith *Camel* No. B6327 flown by Flight Sub-Lieutenant Harold Francis Stackard of B Flight; his personal markings are on the wings and fuselage. The Camel behind the reflecting puddle is No. B3884 flown by Flight Sub-Lieutenant Arthur William Wood.

15. 8.17 - 6.45 AM - Pup N6468 - 40 mins - 10,000' - Defensive Fleet Patrol attempted - Returned due to clouds. Clouds very beautiful this morning.

1.50 PM - Pup N6468 - 80 mins - 14,000' – Defensive Fleet Patrol - Very cloudy but found our fleet.

16. 8.17 - 10.45 AM - Pup N6468 - 45 mins - 12,000' - D.F.P. attempted - Returned owing to clouds.

That night Roy's tonsils became inflamed once more and he reported sick in the morning. The medical officer, realizing the underlying cause was lack of resistance due to physical exhaustion, sent Roy to hospital in England. Squadron Commander Adams, the commanding officer arranged for Roy to receive a week's leave to complete his cure after treatment.

On 24 August 1917, Adams included a confidential report on Roy Brown in his monthly returns to the Wing, commenting: "Recommended for promotion."

Waldorf Hotel
Aldwych, W.C.
[London]

Aug. 29, 1917.

Dear Dad,

Just a note to let you know I am on leave. I am due back in France Sept. 1.
All our leave was washed out but I had an attack of tonsilitis so managed to get my leave advanced due to that; December was too far away.
I am having a pretty good time. I have been up the river with Skeet until yesterday. I have 7 days altogether and am staying in London for the remainder of the time. I am going to   send you a piece of a propeller with a photograph mounted in it. It is off the original triplane which is the fastest machine we have. It goes about 125 knots and climbs to 10,000 feet in about 6 to 7 minutes. The prop split in the air with me in France. We break a great many props in landing and shoot through a lot more due to defective tracer ammunition. I have packed it pretty well so you should receive it in good condition.
My next letter will be from France. We are just on the Belgian frontier about 2 miles from the sea. We fly over Ostend and Zeebrugge every day that the weather is suitable. It is no fun as they have pretty good archie around there.

Sopwith *Triplanes* had a far higher centre of gravity than did *Pups*. If the surface of the aerodrome were muddy or rough, they had to be landed with the tail well down in order to place as much weight as possible behind the wheels. On the first occasion that Mel Alexander flew one, he failed to do so and was rewarded with an unusual view of the surrounding landscape. The Sopwith *Triplane* had a tendency to nose over.

Sopwith *Triplane* No. N5386, supplied to the French l'Armée de l'air, after a less-than-perfect landing by Quarter master Malvoisin in a Wheatfield near Coudekerque on 17 July 1917. F13 is the French l'Armée de l'air number.

31. 8.17 - 4.45 PM - Pup 1818 - 20 mins - Frontier Aerodrome to depot.

Some aerodromes had odd names—*Frontier* and *Middle* are two examples. The depot would be the Naval Aeroplane Depot (NAD) at an aerodrome near Dunkirk.

    To Roy's surprise (or had Stearne been pulling strings?), upon his discharge from hospital, instead of being instructed to report back to Naval 11 he was posted to Naval 9 at Leffrinckoucke. After reporting to the commanding officer, Squadron Commander T.C. Vernon, he was greeted heartily by his old chum Stearne Edwards, the temporary deputy leader of C Flight.

    Roy's previous position as flight lieutenant in charge of a flight at Frontier Aerodrome had only been local acting, so upon leaving Naval 11 he reverted to his substantive rank of flight sub-lieutenant. He would have to begin a new climb up the ladder.

    The posting to Naval 9 brought Roy a new challenge: he had no combat experience in the type of aeroplane with which the squadron was equipped; even worse, he had never flown one. They were 130hp Clerget-powered Sopwith F1 *Camels*, a type which many pilots refused to fly at that time.[3]

    With a distinct view of the cockpit of a Sopwith *Camel*, one can see the manufacturer's nameplate which states, "Designed by Sopwith Aviation Co. Ltd. Kingston-on-Thames, Built by: RUSTON PROCTOR & Co. Ltd, LINCOLN." The circular clamp above the nameplate and the hole in the windscreen beyond are the front and rear supports for an Aldis Tube gunsight. Note the convenient positioning of the long cocking levers for the Vickers machine guns. The instruments and devices from left to right in the upper row, are engine rpm indicator 0-20 [2000]; magnetic compass; airspeed indicator 0-160 mph, and fuel tank pressure gauge 0-5 psig, with manual pump directly below. The lower row comprises left and right magneto switches in the Off position; T-shaped magneto information plate (the crossbar at the top reads Contact, the bottom of the leg reads Off); altimeter Height 0-28 [28,000] feet; inclinometer 20-0-20 degrees; and the removable watch clamped in place. Mounted on the triangular "spade grip" are the blip push button and the two separate triggers for the twin machine guns.

Cockpit of a typical Sopwith F1 *Camel*.

The view forwards from the pilot's seat of typical Sopwith F1 *Camel*. This machine has a ring sight for the guns. The hole in the decking behind the cockpit is the filling point for the reserve fuel tank.

Among the pilots of Naval 9 was Flight Sub-Lieutenant Oliver Colin LeBoutillier, an American volunteer. He had scored four victories in Sopwith *Triplanes* in sixty days, the last being on 29 July. Three of the victories had been over Albatros fighters with twin fast-firing machine guns. One had been a D.V, the latest design just coming into service. LeBoutillier had converted to *Camels* when Naval 9's remaining Sopwith *Triplanes* had been sent to Naval 1 as replacements on 4 August. Nicknamed "Boots," he later became well known for his adventures with RAF 209 Squadron in 1918. Other familiar names will shortly start to appear as Roy settles in at Naval 9.

Flight Sub-Lieutenant O. C. LeBoutillier standing beside his Sopwith *Triplane* No. N5459. Note the Aldis Tube gunsight, the single machine gun and the wind-driven Rotherham pump to pressurize the main fuel tank.

Reflections on a *Camel*. Machine No. B3884 was on the strength of Navel 9 from 4 August 1917 to 13 January 1918 and was flown by Flight Sub-Lieutenant Arthur William Wood. The dihedral angle of the lower wings and the level upper wings stand out clearly.

A Sopwith *Camel* had a mind of its own— or rather, it did not have one at all. A *Camel* pilot could not let his attention wander; otherwise he would end up in the aerial equivalent of the ditch. According to the late Cole Palen, the owner and operator of the First World War flying museum at Old Rhinebeck Aerodrome near New York, Sopwith *Camels* were not difficult to fly, just different. The trick, he said, was to learn how to handle the differences before one of them killed you.

Unfortunately, it was only in mid-1918 that two-seater *Camels* were built; prior to that, the cemeteries near training schools collected far too many pilots who had been killed in low-level accidents. It is a documented fact that, although the Sopwith *Camel* was the most successful British fighter, it killed as many Allied pilots in accidents as it killed opponents in battle. The official total of German aircraft shot down by Sopwith *Camels* between June 1917 and November 1918 stands at 1,294—a far higher number than credited to any other type of Allied fighter.[4]

Unlike the B.E.2C and the *Pup*, which both floated for a while above the field before losing enough speed to land, the *Camel* was much heavier and its wheels would hit the ground hard if the pilot misjudged his height by two or three feet. However, a pilot who had flown Nieuport Bébés and was accustomed to the precision required by their sharp stall would find landing a *Camel* to be "duck soup".

The first verse and the chorus of a 1917 *Camel* pilot's song, to the tune of "Oh Where, Oh Where Has My Little Dog Gone?" went as follows:

> *The Camel is a noble bird,*
> *Complete with wings and a hump.*
> *It flies about like any scout*
> *And then it comes down with a bump.*
>
> *Oh where, oh where have my two wheels gone?*
> *Oh where, oh where can they be?*
> *They're not around upon the ground,*
> *They're up in the air, don't you see?*

Naval 9, on attachment to the Royal Flying Corps, was part of 14 Wing. In 1917, the headquarters of this wing were at the château on the northeastern outskirts of Bertangles village, about five miles due north of the big city of Amiens.

The Château at Bertangles, headquarters of RFC 14th Wing.

The 14 Wing was part of the 4 Brigade RFC which, in turn, was part of the British 4 Army. In other words, Roy had been posted to one of the RNAS squadrons on loan to the army. He was temporarily off the Dover Patrol and stood a better chance of keeping his feet dry. He was allocated to C Flight, which was commanded by Flight Lieutenant Frederick Everest Banbury, another Canadian. Banbury's heart had been strained by high-altitude flying, but as he had not mentioned sometimes feeling weak to the medical officer, he continued doing his duty. While Roy was in this posting, his ultimate superior officer was the Commander of the Fourth Army, General Sir Henry Rawlinson, which meant that any commendations earned or any medals won would be awarded by the army, not the navy.

3. 9.17 - 10.45 AM - Camel B3896 - 75 mins - 14,000' - Local - First flip on Clerget Camel. Do not like them.

3.15 PM - Camel B3896 - 155 mins - 15,000' - O.P. - Middelkerke & Slijpe - Flight shot observer in two-seater but Hun got away. Dove on two 2-seaters but E.A. above so could not go down. Did not get any Huns down.

4. 9 17 - 4.45 PM - Camel B3897 - 135 mins - 15,000' - O.P. - Hun dove on my tail and opened fire. I spun away. One hit in centre of right wing.

In this combat success a German scout had taken Roy by surprise from behind, and to escape Roy had used the ease with which a *Camel* could be made to spin. It is worthy of note that after this episode he no longer complained about Camels.

5. 9.17 - 6.10 AM - Camel B3818 - 135 mins - 15,000' - O.P. - Dove on 12 E.A. near Middelkerke. Guns jambed. Hun followed me back but I got away with 1 bullet hole and two archie holes. Cleared one jamb and went back then it jambed again so I came home. One hun seemed to be finished.

The combat report of 5 September 1917 submitted by Stearne Edwards, who led the flight, provides details of this action.
    The other members of the patrol were O. M. Redgate, A. W. Wood and F. E. Banbury. Roy was officially credited with his second victory.[5]
    Roy's service experience to date, supported by his fourteen months at various RNAS pilot-training schools, had saved his life. He knew how to respond to hearing shots from a surprise attack by a Hun in the sun—*'Take immediate evasive action. Don't waste time looking round'*—and had quickly learned how to use the low-level enemy-killing characteristics of the *Camel* to his own high-level benefit.

5. 9.17 - 10.40 AM - Camel B3818 - 150 mins- 15,000' - O.P. - Chased spotters. Forced down kite balloon. One hun on my tail but I got away alright.

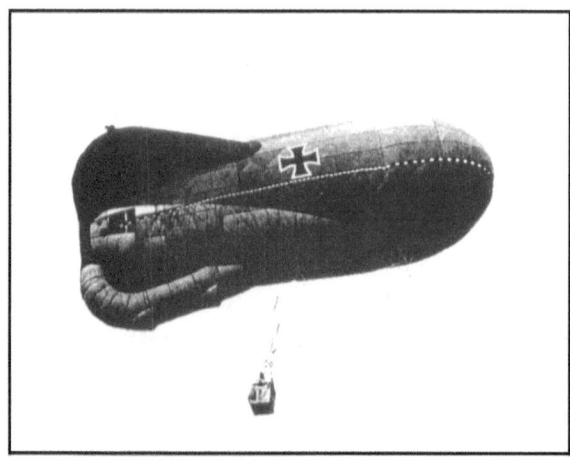

German Drachen (Dragon) kite balloon. The observer's parachute is inside the container fixed to the outside of the basket. It is said that five hops meant a week's leave, but not many observers seemed to be in a hurry to earn it.

A German kite-balloon winch.

No. 9 Squadron
Sept. 5/17

Dear Mother,

Just a note this evening as I am pretty tired and want to turn in.
As you see above I have been moved to another squadron. Stearne and I are together again and we are very glad. It has been a long time since we have been this way and surely is very nice.
I had a pretty good time on leave. The weather was very bad when we were up the river so that we did not have as enjoyable a time as we otherwise would have had. I saw a few theatre shows in town and had some good nights' sleeps which were the big item as I did not seem to be able to keep awake.
We are attached to the RFC in this squadron and have lots of work to do. It is of a different nature from our work in No. 11 Squadron.
I have not had any mail from home since before I went on leave. Please write soon.

The heavy rain which had fallen during the summer of 1917 was quite unusual. In England, people blamed it on the gunfire in France which could be heard from across the Channel on days when the wind blew from the southeast. This belief persisted for many years, and in the late 1920s, when there was a drought, people clamoured for heavy artillery to be fired at clouds to shock them into releasing rain. Some people in the 1930s claimed to remember having heard the guns being fired for that purpose, but it may simply have been rumour.

6. 9.17 - 5.15 AM - Camel B3897 - 75 mins - 14,000' - O.P. - Uneventful. Returned due to weather conditions.

On this same date, 6 September, Squadron Commander Vernon recommended to the Wing that Roy be awarded a Distinguished Service Cross. If approved, the recommendation would be forwarded to the British Army general headquarters responsible for that part of France, where approval would again be required. This would take some time.

At Naval 9 in Leffrinckoucke, Flight Lieutenant A. T. Whealy, a Canadian fighter ace who commanded A Flight at the time, went on leave that week and then was posted to the Home Establishment. Where he would serve in England for a while in a home defence squadron or a training unit. Squadron Commander Vernon had a good replacement at hand, a proven flight commander from Naval 11 named Roy Brown. The icing on the cake for Roy was that on the 9 September he was allowed to take over Whealy's *Camel*, No. B3893, which was in far better shape than No. B3897.

In June or early July, a pilot on leave in England had brought back some posters advertising the latest London play, a review called Zigzag. It featured George Robey, the well-known comedian, whose response to affronted dignity had soon had the audience in tears of laughter. Robey's head was cut from the posters and doped onto both sides of the fin of *Camels* Nos. B3810, B3880, B3881 and B3893 of A Flight. This unusual flight identification symbol was still in place in August, but it is not known whether No. B3893 still sported "George Robey" when flown by Roy Brown. This kind of excess triggered General Trenchard's August 1917 ban on decorative personal, flight or squadron identification markings in the Royal Flying Corps, which General Salmond attempted to impose on the RNAS squadrons in France as soon as they were incorporated into the Royal Air Force in April 1918.

Sopwith F1 *Camels* of A Flight, Naval 9, with posters of George Robey. Roy's fifth to eleventh combat successes were achieved in No. B3893, the second from the left. The different-shaped white bands around the fuselages are pilot identification markings. Photograph taken on 4 August 1917 by Flight Lieutenant A.T. Whealy.

9. 9.17 - 4.00 PM - Camel B3893 - 135 mins - 14,000' - O.P.- Dove on 2 Hun two-seaters, lost them in mist south of Middelkerke at about 4,000'. Dove on two-seater spotter. Observer's fire silenced and Hun glided down as if to land on beach. Seemed to be naturally stable machine.

In Roy's fifth combat success, on 9 September, the enemy observer in the two-seater was killed or disabled, and there was possible wounding of its pilot and/or damage to the aeroplane.[6]

Roy's mention of natural stability recalls the B.E.2C. There had been occasions upon which a B.E.2C had been seen flying steadily along in a strange direction, ignoring everything around it. A curious pilot had flown alongside and discovered that both crew members were dead. In two documented cases, a B.E.2C "flown" by a dead crew had made a good landing after running out of fuel—one in a field and the other on the beach near Dunkerque. However, unlike the B.E.2C, the Camel did not have a wheel which its pilot could adjust to fly level with "hands off," and it would soon be in a descending turn at an ever-increasing speed; eventually the fuselage would leave the wings behind.

10. 9.17 - 3.55 PM - *Camel B3893 - 130 mins - 13,000' - O.P. - Uneventful. Observed 5 TBD's outside Ostend and 2 going out.*

The port of Ostend was deep in enemy territory and the Admiralty liked to know how many German U-boats and torpedo boat destroyers (TBDs) were stationed in port. Attempts were made to learn the whereabouts of those which had sailed, by using Felixstowe flying boats and/or airships for aerial searches.[7] If a particular search was to be carried out within range of German land planes or Brandenburg high-performance seaplanes, protection by RNAS scouts was required. In this matter the RNAS held the advantage as British single-seat fighters held fuel for two and a half hours of flight, whereas the German machines only had tankage for one and a half hours.

Typical *Felixstowe* F.2A flying boat, a development of the Curtiss twin-engined flying boat of 1914.

Typical Brandenburg W.12 seaplane, designed by Ernst Heinkel, who started his own company after the war. It followed the same philosophy as the Bristol F.2A *Fighter*: the pilot flew the aircraft as a fighter while his colleague guarded the tail. The inverted rudder provided an exceptional field of fire to the rear.

On 11 August 1917 the Ottawa Citizen had published an article somewhat loosely based upon a letter allegedly written by Roy's RNAS colleague, Flight Lieutenant Walter Sussan, to some unnamed friends. The introduction told of a letter home *"in which he tells of some of his hair-breadth escapes and thrilling experiences, winning several promotions for his successful efforts in the Royal Flying Corps."* (The last three words did not auger well for the accuracy of what was to follow.)
Morton Brown sent the article to Roy.

No. 9 Squadron
Sept. 10/17

My dear Mother,

Just received your and Dad's letter of Aug. 12 with that newspaper clipping of Sussan's enclosed.
You said something about wanting to publish some of my letters. I wrote once about that kind of thing when there was something in the Citizen and I feel more strongly against it now than I ever did. If you have noticed, it is the chaps who do nothing that put those in. They are all talk. Some chaps hoodwink their C.O.s and even get decorations out of it but I don't want

anything at all if I have to do that to get it.

When I write letters home they are for the family only. I do not care a rap whether people think I am doing anything or not. I did not come over here for that. I came because I felt I should come. I am doing my best and can do no more. I have been some help in this war and if anything happens to me now, I have done some work anyway. If I am satisfied within myself that I have done as well as I can, that is all I care about. I am striking out what is not true in Sussan's letter and sending it back. He just came out to France about a week and a half ago and is going back again he told me.

I am going on patrol in an hour so I have to get lunch now.

Although Roy had by now joined his colleagues in drinking and smoking, it can be seen from his letter that he still maintained his integrity and original ideals.

11. 9.17 - 12.55 PM - Camel B3893 - 135 mins - 12,000' - O.P. - Dived on 1 DFW Aviatik, 1 Aviatik & 1 Albatros Scout. Fired 200 rounds but was too far behind the lines to carry on. 3 Shrapnel holes.

The Aviatiks mentioned above were two-seater observation aeroplanes. Note Roy's attention to the squadron commande's warning against chases deep into Hunland.

11. 9.17 - 5.20 PM - Camel B3893 - 70 mins - 14,500' - O.P. with Pups - Engine cut out on pressure. Came home on gravity tank. Pressure pump not working.

Roy was referring to the pressure provided by a wind-driven Rotherham pump If the hand-operated pump had not provided pressure either, the pressure-control valve may have been at fault; instead of venting excess pump pressure, it may have jammed or frozen open. With Roy's *Camel* at cruising speed, the engine would have ceased producing power but continued turning, in a mode that is called "windmilling"; that is, the propeller was driving the engine. Roy would have had to change to the gravity tank and wait for fuel to reach the mixing chamber before the power was restored. He was lucky the problem had occurred at a height where he could afford to lose 1,000 feet in a glide. [8]

12. 9.17 - 12.20 AM - Camel B3893 - 140 mins - 14,000' - O.P. - Dived on Albatros scout. Fired about 150 rounds but both guns jambed. Came home in clouds.

14. 9.17 - 1.00 PM - Camel B3893 - 30 mins - 12,000' - O.P. - Engine cut out on pressure.

1.40 PM - Camel B3906 - 90 mins - 14,000' - O.P. - Uneventful. Very strong wind, 70-80 MPH up top.

On 14 September, this day, Flight Commander Joseph Stewart Temple Fall (DSC with two bars), Flight Sub-Lieutenant A. C. Campbell-Orde and Flight Sub-Lieutenant C. A. Narbeth were surprised by two Albatros scouts which dived on them from the Allied side of the front. While Fall was shooting one down, the other shot down Campbell-Orde. He came down in no man's land, where Belgian and German Red Cross personnel ran to his aid. The Belgians, seeing the Germans coming, bandaged his leg and claimed that he was wounded, which by the rules of the day, enabled them to take him back to their first aid post. Orde's *Camel* was only slightly damaged, so that evening Squadron Commander T C Vernon led a party to salvage it. However, the Germans were expecting their retrieval attempt and had prepared an ambush. Vernon was severely wounded as he worked on the *Camel*. Members of the Belgian Red Cross came to help, and two of them were wounded as they carried him back to the front-line trench. Subsequent events, beginning 30 September, suggest that Roy was a member of the salvage party and received a leg wound during the fracas. Vernon died of his wounds the following day in La Panne hospital and was replaced by Acting Squadron Commander Ernest William Norton, DSC (who also held three French and Belgian decorations.)

15. 9.17 - 11.30 AM - Camel B3893 - 120 mins - 14,000' - O.P. - Dove on 2 DFW Aviatiks. Engine failed on pressure. Dove on 2 DFW Aviatiks & 3 Albatros scouts. Dog fight for about 30 minutes. One I was firing on went out of control, spun on his back and I lost sight of him. Confirmed by flight. Two others, perhaps 3, got by flight.

Roy was officially credited with this victory over a DFW two-seater above Westende-Zevecote.[9]

Typical DFW (Deutsche Flugzeug Werke *Gesellschaft*) C.V. This particular machine was forced down by Navel 3 Squadron on 12 September and flown to England by Captain L.H. (Tich) Rochford.

Obviously, Roy was using expertise and prudence. By diving on the enemy aeroplane, most likely from out of the sun, he was assured of surprise as well as the time to position the target in his gunsight and judge how far ahead he should aim. With both hunter and hunted moving steadily in the same direction, he only had to apply deflection in one geometrical plane. Once he had fired, he had the choice of diving away or returning to fight. An expert only returned to the fray if the odds were still in his favour. *"He who fights and runs away lives to fight another day"* was a combat rule well worth following.

Roy had also refused all invitations to chase his quarry deep into 'Hunland' as the RFC and RNAS called enemy-occupied territory. Assuming no catastrophic engine or structural failure, he had acquired sufficient combat experience to stand a reasonable chance of surviving the war. Contrary to the theme of the 1917 airman's song, he did have a hope in the morning.

By this stage of the war, many of the aces had become tired of the blood-letting. Once the twin techniques of diving out of the sun and shooting with accurate deflection were mastered, it was all too easy to down an enemy pilot. You simply shot him in the back before he even knew you were there. It was sickening to some pilots on both sides; Major James McCudden, VC, described himself as *"a hired assassin"*. Note that he did not say *"killer"*, but *"assassin"*. Some pilots, instead of inflicting the coup de grace, began to allow a disabled enemy aeroplane to land, provided it did so on their side of the lines. There had been an incident near Croiselles on 13 July 1917 when Leutnant Huppertz, the observer in an Albatros two-seater who had been taking photographs of Mont St Éloi Aerodrome, had become hopelessly tangled up in the belt of his Parabellum machine gun (it had escaped from the pouch), and he was unable to hold off an attacking Sopwith *Triplane*. The German pilot, Leutnant Neumuller, made a good emergency landing, but the victor, RNAS Flight Commander Robert Alexander Little, who wished to take the crew prisoner, caught a wheel in a shell hole and turned over. Guess who had to rescue whom! (Flight Commander Little, DSC and bar, DSO and bar was the highest scoring pilot from Australia in either the RNAS or the RFC.)

The epitome of success was forcing an enemy pilot to surrender in the air, as well as capturing the aeroplane intact. Since German strategy, except for reconnaissance, was to let the Allies come to them, not many German airmen fell into the bag that way. The German ace Karl Allmenröder and his brother Willi each succeeded in convincing more than one British pilot that a riotous night in a German officers' mess was preferable to a hero's death hero. The last surviving German Great War pilot, Otto Roosen, who flew Rumpler two-seaters and in 1997 died in Canada at close to 103 years old, said he had been told by pilots in Richthofen's flying circus that towards the end of the Rittmeister's career, he gave some of his opponents a chance to surrender if he could do so without endangering himself. It counted as a victory, so why kill the man? An examination of the Rittmeister's combat record, specifically victories Nos. 61, 62, 64 and 66, indicates that Otto Roosen's assertion has foundation; such victories did not derive from good luck or shooting an unsuspecting enemy in the back but were definitive proof of a master at his craft.[10]

16. 9. 17 - 4.00 PM - Camel B3893 - 135 mins - 14,500' - O.P.- Dived on 2 DFW Aviatiks & 1 Albatros scout. Fired about 100 rounds but too far behind lines to carry on. Dived on Kite Balloon and forced them to haul it down. E.A. above but could not climb up.

The pressure-relief valve problem had now been cured. In Roy's attack on the observation balloon, good luck was on his side; apparently the defending German aeroplanes above had not seen him approaching. Captain A. H. Cobby of 4, gave a good description in his post-war memoirs, High Adventure, of the strength of observation balloon defences: *"One day, just for the hell of it, I tried my hand at shooting one down. It looked so easy; it was just floating so peacefully up there in the sky."* Unfortunately, the balloonist's associates on the ground objected to Cobby's presence. His aeroplane acquired forty bullet holes, one of which cut a control cable, and he only just managed to return home. *"The balloon,"* wrote the chastened Cobby, *"continued to float up there, bobbing in the breeze as though nothing whatsoever had happened."*

Captain Arthur Henry Cobby, DFC, DSO, the highest scoring Australian ace serving in an Australian Air Force squadron.

No. 9 Squadron
Sunday, Sept. 16/17

My dear Bess,
    I was very pleased to get your long newsy letter. We are very busy here at present and have been doing pretty good work the last few weeks. We have the huns in our sector scared stiff. They run as fast as they can whenever we turn towards them. They have been losing too many just lately. We have just been congratulated by the Divisional General on our good work. Everyone is feeling tired out and I hope we are able to carry on.
    Mother is not thinking of putting any of my letters in the paper, is she? She mentioned something about it but if it   ever happens, I don't know exactly what I would do. I would not forget it for a long time and would be about as angry as I could be over it. I hate that kind of thing and do not want to acquire the same name as the fellows who have done it.
    By this time you will have the cottage all closed up. What are you going to do this winter? Are you going to be at home? I wish I was. This is the first bad cold I have had for some time, and it will be a nice rest. Nearly everyone is off the station today and I am in charge. What do you know about that?
    There really is little more that I can write. I wish I could tell you all that happens.

The Germans, now being faced with Sopwith *Camels*, S.E.5As and Bristol F.2B two-seater *Fighters*, were finding the boot decidedly on the other foot and were being cautious. In 1916 the Admiralty had done the same thing when Roy's class at Chingford was held at the Home Establishment until the latest types of aeroplane became available.
    The German Army on the Western Front had been fighting defensively with great success from behind strong natural positions since early 1916, in the east it had knocked Russia out of the war. By the spring of 1918 the German high command would work out the details of a plan to attack in the west, and when the time came, the Imperial German Army Air Service would need experienced pilots to lead the trainees. It was believed that the latter, flying newly designed, highly manoeuvrable triplanes would easily be able to sweep the Allies from

the skies and allow the army to win the war.

The latest version of the Albatros single-seater scout, the D.V, now began to appear over northern France in quantity. It preformed better than the D.III, but like the earlier version, one or both of the lower wings could tear off during a high-speed dive. The cause was finally discovered: the single spar was allowing the outer panels of the lower wings to pivot around the point where the V-shaped interplane struts were attached. A correction was devised: the addition of a small reinforcing strut which ran forwards and downwards from the front arm of the V strut to the leading edge of the lower wing. However, much time would elapse before wind tunnels demonstrated the mechanics of what was actually happening.

Today the phenomenon is termed "wing flutter."

Typical Albatros D.V. Oliver LeBoutillier had shot down one of these on 17 July. Look carefully at the lower portion of the front arm of the V strut, then compare this photograph with that of an earlier Albatros D.V in Chapter One.

17. 9.17 - 7.00 AM - Camel B3893 - 130 mins - 12,000' - O.P. - Clouds rolled up, so did protective patrol over RE8s below clouds. No E.A. Landed in rain.

18. 9.17 - 4.00 PM - Camel B3893 - 105 mins - 4,000' - O.P. - Low clouds down to Ypres. Returned due to rain.

20. 9.17 - 4.40 PM - Camel B3893 - 140 mins - 13,000' - O.P. - Middelkerke to Zarren - *Dove on 5 Albatros scouts east of Slijpe. Fired about 250 rounds into one. He went out of control and onto his back. Falling onto his back while I was firing. Then guns jambed and I saw him disappear in clouds still on his back. He was dark on top and sky blue underneath. Saw 4 huns on Sykes's tail. Dove on them without guns and they cleared off. Saw 3 huns on Bramhall's tail. Dove on them and they cleared off. Sykes wounded. Landed in no man's land but got away alright.*

In this action on 20 September Roy was credited with his fourth official victory, over an Albatros DV above Leke.[11]

That evening Squadron Commander E. W. Norton recommended to 14 Wing that Roy receive an award for his oft-times demonstrated personal bravery and the string of successes achieved by A Flight during the month. The recommendation had, in turn, to be approved by the RFC fourth Brigade and Fourth Army headquarters For Roy's leadership and motivation of his men, the squadron commander decided to promote him at the first opportunity.

Around this time, Roy Brown sent home two photographs of his colleagues and their accommodations. The presence of Flight Sub-Lieutenant W. Ingleson, who was taken prisoner on 26 September, a fortnight before the squadron moved to middle Aerodrome, suggests that it was Leffrinckoucke Aerodrome.

Left to right: John Playford Hales, Harold Francis Stackard, A. Roy Brown, C. A. Narbeth and Harold Edgar Mott at Leffrinckoucke.

Standing: Frederick Everest Banbury. Seated, *left to right*: Oliver William Redgate, Ingleson, Herbert James Edwards, Bramhall and A. Roy Brown at Leffrinckoucke.

21. 9.17 - 6.55 AM - Camel B3893 - 145 mins - 14,000' - O.P. - Never saw so many Huns up last hour of patrol, solid fighting. Camels and Bristol Fighters left us. In circling match one Hun I was firing on side-slipped and went into nose dive. E.A. on my tail but I got away. All formation broken up. Crossed trenches at 500'.

Although Roy engaged in successful combat on 21 September, he did not see the enemy crash, nor did he have a witness.

Typical Bristol F.2A *Fighter* with Rolls-Royce Falcon I, 190hp engine. Although No. A7115 belonged to RFC 48 Squadron, based at Leffrinckoucke, it was not one of the four which accompanied Roy.
Being lower powered than the later F.2B, it was used as a station "hack."

21. 9.17 - 10.45 AM - Camel B3893 - 135 mins - 14,000' - O.P. - Uneventful. Lots of archie.

2.30 PM - Camel B3893 - 145 mins - 15,500' - O.P. - Uneventful. Low clouds.

23. 9.17 - 10.40 AM - Camel B3893 - 125 mins - 11,500' - O.P. - Uneventful. Low clouds. Flew around trenches at 50'

3.45 PM - Camel B3893 - 125 mins - 15,000' - O.P. - Uneventful. Low clouds.

25. 9.17 - 1.55 PM - Camel B3893 - 135 mins - 16,000' - O.P. - Uneventful. Very misty. 3 destroyers out of Ostend. Flew down coast and back.

26. 9.17 - 12.5 PM - Camel B3893 - 35 mins - 4,000' - O.P. - Returned due to weather conditions.

The activities of the German fleet at Ostend and Zeebrugge were a constant worry to the Admiralty, and German destroyers at sea meant work for the Felixstowe flying boats and Short Brothers seaplanes. The safety of the cross-channel shipping depended upon the keen observation of the RNAS aircrews, and whenever weather permitted, Naval 9 alone flew three patrols per day.

Typical Short Brothers seaplane, Type 184, which featured a tail float. The radiator was constructed so the pilot could see through it.

On 26 September Squadron Commander Norton sent a confidential report regarding Roy to the Wing and he described him as "a very good pilot and fearless flight leader, with good command of the flight."

No. 9 Squadron
Sept. 26/17

My dear Mother,

Received your nice letter of Aug. 30. That was a pretty piece of maidenhair fern you enclosed.
You were worrying about me flying over the North Sea. I have not been doing any of that since coming to this squadron. I don't think it worried you any more than it did me at the time. I try not to think of it any more than I can help.
Abbott is alright and getting along O.K. He is in England now, in some hospital there. Stearne has written the Abbotts so I do not need to. He did very good work in the time he was out here.
I want to ask you to do something which I expect you will think foolish but I do not. I wish you would not read my letters to everyone who comes to see you. My letters home are for whom they are written to and I don't like the idea of everyone hearing them. I have good reasons for it, so please do it.
The work is going on much as usual here. The weather is still much like summer but should change pretty soon and give us a rest. Our squadron has been doing very good work lately and receiving congratulations from all the high and mighty. I have shot down four huns since coming here. Not bad for a thing like me, is it? I have not had a pilot killed in my flight yet and I hope I don't.
I am looking forward to a rest soon. I don't know what I can get yet. I will know in another month or two.

Lieutenant Robert Franklyn Preston Abbott (nicknamed "Skimp") from Carleton Place had joined the Royal Navel Air Service on 7 November 1916. He trained at Chingford, then Cranwell, and served with Naval 3 at Dunkirk. On 17 August 1917, he had been surprised by a German fighter as he approached his aerodrome and was severely wounded in the left thigh. He landed successfully and was immediately taken to a hospital in Calais.

The *"good reasons"* to which Roy refers derive from his having been a shade outspoken on RNAS matters in several letters, and sometimes having by passed the censor by posting letters in England. If even a hint of this reached the RNAS office in Ottawa, it would probably be reported to London, and that would spell trouble.

27. 9.17 - 7.30 AM - Camel B3893 - 115 mins - 13,000' - O.P. - No E.A. Lots of archie.

28. 9.17 - 12 noon - Camel B3893 - 100 mins - 12,000' - O.P.- No E.A. Returned due to weather conditions.

The RNAS was short of replacement pilots, and following the destruction of the Royal Flying Corps engine repair shop at Aircraft Depot Dunkirk by enemy action, the Corps was short of engines. The Fourth Army could now only supply three of the four RNAS fighter squadrons on its strength, so at the stroke of midnight on 28 September, Naval 9 was withdrawn from loan to 14 Wing of the RFC fourth Brigade and allocated to RNAS 4 Wing.

Squadron Commander Norton, now back under the direct jurisdiction of the RNAS, could act more independently. He requested that 4 Wing agree to Roy's promotion from flight sub-lieutenant to flight lieutenant. The wing commander must have been impressed by Norton's recent confidential report on Roy, and he agreed, but it had to be done in two steps. On 29 September Roy was promoted to acting flight lieutenant.

The squadron continued to operate from Leffrinckoucke while the workshops, stores and support services were being moved and set up again at Frontier Aerodrome.

29. 9.17 - 2.55 PM - Camel B3893 - 135 mins - 17,000' - Escort Zeebrugge - Returning dived on 3 E.A. over Middelkerke. Guns jambed. Fired 150 rounds into two-seater which went down.

As Roy did not see the enemy air craft crash, and there was no witness, he was not officially credited for this victory, his tenth combat success.(13)

The experienced German two-seater pilot, Otto Roosen, who had been the victim of such a diving attack, said that his observer was taken completely by surprise. The attacker had come from above, behind and out of the sun. Otto's first intimation of trouble was the bullets striking all around him. The engine stopped, and when he looked behind, he saw that his observer had collapsed. The scout which had done the damage flashed past and did not return. It was a classic Billy Bishop–style attack–one precise pass and then away.

30. 9.17 - 12 noon - Camel B3893 - 130 mins - 12,000' - Defensive Fleet Patrol - Fleet 40 miles to sea off Zeebrugge.

2.00 PM - Camel B3893 - 120 mins - 12,000' - Defensive Fleet Patrol - Fleet 60 miles to sea off Zeebrugge.

The mole which protected the entrance to the Zeebrugge Canal. The German seaplanes stationed there constituted a serious danger to the fleet. Four can be seen out of the water; a fifth one is taking off. The two batteries of heavy guns, four 4inch and two 6inch, sited on the mole itself, are in action. This photograph was taken by 202 Squadron in April 1918.

Typical German Brandenburg NW seaplane.

Walking a Friedrichshafen FF.33B seaplane into the water.

Roy's medical records show that on 30 September the medical officer sent him to the military hospital for treatment of a gunshot wound in his right leg. This procedure would have been followed if the wound had failed to respond as expected from the ministrations at Leffrinckoucke. Roy returned to duty the same day and did not mention wound in his log book, which suggests it had been received not in the air but during the ambush on the night of 14 September when Squadron Commander T.C. Vernon was fatally wounded.

1.10.17 - 9.00 AM - Camel B3893 - 15 mins - 500' - Leffrinkoucke to Frontier Aerodrome.

On 1 October, the wing commander authorized the second step, and Roy was promoted to substantive flight lieutenant. From this date onwards, when he was posted to another squadron, he maintained that rank.

No. 9 Squadron
Oct. 3/17

Dear Dad,

I have no letter to answer or any news but this will let you know I am still on the right side of the earth.
We have moved since I last wrote and we are now under No. 4 Wing RNAS. I do not like our work now as well as I did under the army. It is the same work now as I did when I was   with No. 11 Squadron. It does not give you as many chances to get Huns either.
Today is the first day the weather has been unsuitable for flying for over a month. It is clearing up now and we may have a patrol yet.
We may be getting back to England for a rest this winter. I have no idea how soon but I do not think it will be for a month yet. It certainly would be a nice change if it happens. It will not take long for the time to slip around. Time goes very quickly out here.

Roy's "weather eye vision" was 20/20, and in the mid-afternoon he was airborne, leading A Flight.

3.10.17 - 3.00 PM - Camel B3893 - 125 mins - 12,000' - O.P. - No E.A. Archie holes in machine.

Reaching 12,000 feet, over two miles high, those German specialist anti-aircraft A.A. crews had certainly not been partying the night before.

Naval 9 was not to remain at Frontier Aerodrome for long; in fact, unpacking proved to have been hardly worth while.

No. 9 Squadron
Oct. 4/17

My dear Reta,

Just received your letter of Sept 12. It is not very often I get a letter from you now. I suppose that is partly why I enjoy them so much when they do come.

This is a day off for me, in fact for everyone, as it is raining and low clouds. I hope it keeps up for a week. This is the kind of weather everyone likes to see.

There has not been very much excitement the last few days but I have already had enough to last me the rest of my life. We have left the R.F.C. now and are under No. 4 Wing R.N.A.S. We just moved four days ago and we will be moving in another three days. That is a thing I do not like. Your stuff gets all smashed up and everyone is out of humour.

This is very short, but I have to go over to our new place with the C.O. now so must close.

The commanding officer was Squadron Commander E.W. Norton, and on the next day, he recommended that Flight Lieutenant Roy Brown be given a further promotion to acting flight commander, which was equal to an army honorary captain. Confirmation quickly arrived from the Wing, but the effectivity was local only. The *"new place"* referred to was Middle Aerodrome, located near Bray Dunes. Roy did not go there immediately; the leg wound still troubled him, and that same day he was admitted to hospital for treatment. He returned to the squadron in time for the move to Middle Aerodrome on 8 October.

8.10.17 - 9.00 AM - *Camel* B3893 - 5 *mins* - *Frontier to Middle Aerodrome*.

At the time of the move the squadron was composed of the following pilots and Sopwith *Camel* aircraft:

# Flight Commander	J.S. T. Fall	B3992
# Flight Sub-Lieutenant	M.S. Taylor	B5652
#* Flight Sub-Lieutenant	H.F. Stackard	B3883
#* Flight Sub-Lieutenant	C.A. Narbeth	B3905
# Flight Sub-Lieutenant	A.W. Wood	B3892
Flight Commander	S.T. Edwards	B6217
* Flight Sub-Lieutenant	O.W. Redgate	B3818
* Flight Sub-Lieutenant	J.P. Hales	B3832
* Flight Lieutenant	A.R. Brown	B3893
Flight Sub-Lieutenant	W.E.B. Oakley	B3880
Flight Sub-Lieutenant	F.J.W. Mellersh	B3830
Flight Sub-Lieutenant	E.M. Knott	B6356
Flight Sub-Lieutenant	N. Black	B5653
#* Flight Commander	F. E. Banbury (absent)	B6230

Spare Camels bore Nos. B3897, B5651, and B6358

* Pictured in the group photographs in the chronology between 20 and 21 September 1917.

Naval 9 Pilots
Front row; from *left to right*: Arthur William Wood, Merril Samuel Taylor and dog, unknown, unknown, unknown, Joseph Stewart Temple Fall.
Rear row; *left to right*: unknown, C. A. Narbeth, Harold Francis Stackard, Frederick Everest Banbury.

Sopwith F1 *Camels* of Navel 9, B Flight, at Middle Aerodrome. Each machine displays its pilot's personal markings.

On 10 October 1917 General Sir Henry Rawlinson, Commander of the British Fourth Army, promulgated the immediate award of the Distinguished Service Cross to Acting Flight Commander A.R. Brown and to Acting Flight Commander S.T. Edwards. General Rawlinson's signature on the certificate sent to Roy makes it quite clear where the final authority over Naval 9 lay in that part of France.

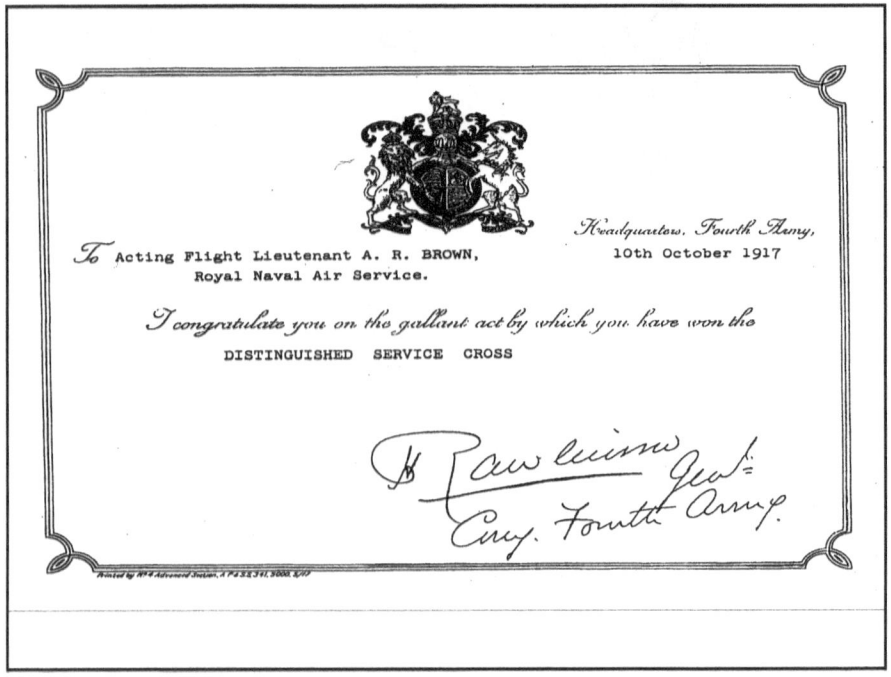

Roy Brown's Award Certificate for his first Distinguished Services Cross.

Army Orders, 10 October 1917. The Field Marshal Commanding-in-Chief would have been Sir Douglas Haig.

11.10.17 - 2.00 PM - Camel B3893 - 120 mins - 15,000' - O.P. - No E.A. - Fired into trenches.

13.10.17 - 8.40 AM - Camel B3893 - 45 mins - 6,000' – Hun Wireless Spotter - Dived on spotter but cleared off; scouts above. Climbed into clouds and dived again over Middelkerke. Followed back to 1,000 feet over Ostend. E.A. smoking & out of control. Confirmed as going down in flames.

Roy's fifth officially credited victory—over a DFW two-seater above Ostende. He had used Major J. McCudden's recommended tactics: just when the crew of the DFW (Deutsche Flugzeug Werke) observation aeroplane had thought they were safely home and let down their guard, he took them by surprise.[14]

Major James Thomas Byford McCudden, VC, DSO and bar, MC, MM, Croix de Guerre, killed in a crash following engine failure at takeoff in an S.E.5A from Auxi-le-Château on 9 July 1918.

14.10.17 - 8.15 AM - Camel B3893 - 90 mins - 8,000' - O.P. - Dived on two-seaters. Guns jambed. Dived on second two-seater but did not get him. Guns jambed and I could not see through sight.[15]

1.45 PM - Camel B3893 - 15 mins - W.S. - Engine trouble.

2.05 PM - Camel B3893 - 30 mins - 12,000' - W.S. - No E.A. observed.

The German wireless spotter (ws) was a two-seater aeroplane equipped with a wireless-telegraphy (Morse code) apparatus. The observer spotted the fall of artillery shells and transmitted in Morse code the location of their landing. The gunners then made the necessary corrections.

For such spotting and observation the Germans were sending over high-flying Rumpler C.IV two-seater aeroplanes with a special high-compression Maybach engine. Despite the use of good quality German synthetic petrol, full power could only be employed above about 18,000 feet, otherwise detonation, instead of smooth combustion, would occur. (Detonation is familiar to car drivers as the "pinging" sound which occurs on hills when cheap petrol is used in an engine requiring a more expensive variety.) The extra performance enabled pilots to evade the Allied scouts by climbing above them. The design of the aeroplane was so good that at 20,000 feet the Rumpler still responded well to its controls, whereas the few Allied types that could climb that high, albeit far more slowly, would stall and lose height if the pilot attempted to out turn the German. The Rumpler C.VII was even better: its absolute ceiling was 24,000 feet (4.5 miles or 7.3 kilometres).

The Rumpler crews wore electrically heated gloves and electrically heated mid-calf length boots. Oxygen fed by tube into Thick face masks, kept them both mentally alert and physically strong. In short, above 18,000 feet they held all the advantages. Some months were to pass before similar equipment was issued to British D.H.4 crews.

A captured Rumpler C.VIII No. 12212/18, which was a 1918 improved version of the prior year's C.VII.

Major McCudden found a simple counter-strategy against aircraft that could fly higher than his: he stayed at a lower altitude and shadowed the unsuspecting Rumplers while they worked; he then followed them back towards their bases and made sure of success by not attacking until they had descended to an altitude where their performance was inferior to his. Sometimes he waited until, after a long flight, the tired crew finally had their home aerodrome in sight and were relaxed enough to let down their guard. The method might be "dirty pool," but as the French said, "*C'est la* guerre."

No. 9 Squadron
Oct. 14/17

My dear Mother,

I was very pleased to get your letter and Howard's this morning. It is a very long time since I have had one from Howard. I wish he would write often but I expect he likes to write just as much as the rest of us.

No mother, I did not go to see Mrs Hirsch when on leave at the end of August. I went over with a chap from Coppercliff so I could not very well go away and leave him to go up there. I wrote to them explaining but as yet have received no answer.

I was appointed an Acting Flight Commander today. As it is just acting it does not mean very much. I lose it as soon as I go out of this command. It is just local unless it appears in the Gazette, *which these do not. You do not need to change the way you address my letters at all.*

I heard from Uncle Harry yesterday. He is in France now. I should very much like to see him but it is impossible as he is too far away from me.

You ask about my getting home this winter. Well, there is just a chance that I might. I wish Stearne and I could get home together but there is not the least chance of that. They would not let two flight leaders from one squadron be away at the same time. We have been trying to get it but it will not come though. That would be too much of a lucky thing to happen to me.

Things are going along much the same as usual. This weather is terrible to have to live practically outside but we are having huts put up now and we shall be very comfortable then. I have my tent pretty comfortable now but it leaks pretty badly.

I am pretty tired tonight so shall go to bed.

Uncle Harry was Roy's mother's brother, who had joined the Canadian Army, John Henry Flett, the *Gazette*, to which Roy refers, the supplement to the *London Gazette* in which all promotions and awards were promulgated, thus making them public, official and substantive.

Roy spared his parents dismay by not revealing how the huts were to be built—from the used plywood of aeroplane packing cases. The degree of comfort obtained depended heavily upon the occupant remaining at the same aerodrome for a while. Royal Flying Corps captain (later major) Gilbert Ware Murlis-Green, MC and two bars, DSC and bar, stayed long enough at one location to erect a two-roomed residence which had electric light, running water, a telephone, a kitchen range and a small garden in which his wife kept a flock of chickens.

Fortunately, it was just about this time that the U.S. Navy confidentially requested two RNAS officers with great experience in the successful protection of warships from aerial and submarine-torpedo attack, to give advice in Washington on the aircraft types and tactics best suited for the task. Two such officers, who also had a legitimate reason for a transatlantic journey, were not difficult to find—Roy Brown and Stearne Edwards. The wheels of the Admiralty began to turn—or perhaps one should say "the propellers."

16.10.17 - 8.30 AM - Camel B3893 - 45 Mins - W.S. - Nothing to report.

- 10.05 AM - Camel B3893 - 40 mins - W.S. - Dived on E.A. No spotter observed.

By the end of 1917, wireless telegraphy (W/T) in aircraft had advanced considerably, but so had counter-measures. The British Army established a network of direction-finding (D/F) stations, and when Morse code transmissions from a German aircraft were detected, the system swung into action. A bearing taken on a wireless telegraph signal by two direction-finding stations would give an approximate idea of the spotter's location. Three bearings would place the latter inside a triangle known as a "cocked hat". British Army telephones buzzed, a klaxon sounded at the aerodrome nearest the cocked hat, and the duty pilots, together with their ground crews, began preparations for immediate departure.

The German Army artillery's ground observation officers knew that within a certain elapsed time Allied scouts would arrive, so telescopes, binoculars and range-finders were trained on the distant skies to the west. The German artillery men could not arrange clouds on demand, but they could fire a pre-arranged pattern of shells near the spotter aeroplane as a warning to the crew that trouble was heading their way.

Generally, as can be deduced from Roy's log book entries, by the time the scouts arrived at the requested map reference point of the German wireless-equipped spotter, its pilot had moved to greener pastures or had hidden inside a cloud. This was a new variation of the old game of hide-and-seek.

However, the direct objective was not to shoot down the spotter but to drive it away. If the spotter was shot down, so much the better, but it had to be quick, since a chase deep into Hunland was not a good idea. Apart from the spotter's friends, who could be waiting up there in the sun, the usual, strong west wind at altitude meant the risk of running out of fuel on the return.

17.10.17 - 9.25 AM - Camel B3893 - 105 mins - O.P. - Dived on large E.A. formation but could not get to close quarters as too few of us. E.A. dived on one of our formations. Dived on them and drove them off. Dived on third formation but guns jambed. Fired about 350 rounds.

This entry on 17 October was Roy's first report of both sides adopting layer tactics as a mean of better defence. [16] There was an occasional disadvantage to the method, however in one documented instance, on 5 June 1918, a 24 Squadron patrol dived on a German Halberstadt two-seater observation aeroplane. A formation of Albatros D.Vs, the first layer, dived down to its rescue. The second layer of Albatros D.Vs mistook the first layer for the attackers, and the astonished RAF pilots had a ringside seat for a lively fight between the two German formations. Quite unsportingly, the RAF patrol left before the end of the show and without paying.

The foregoing once more demonstrates clearly that it is not so easy, as one would imagine, to distinguish friend from foe when a rapid glance through cloud or into the sun requires an immediate decision, and any hesitation could mean death. The inability of a pilot to describe the aeroplane which had attacked him an hour earlier does not detract from the veracity of his tale; indeed, it could be said to enhance it since at the time he had other things on his mind than noting his attacker's artwork.

From a distance, most aeroplanes appear to be greyish dots against a brighter background. To aid in telling whether the approaching dots were friend or foe, many flight commanders carried a pair of low - or medium powered-binoculars. High-powered binoculars were rarely used as the relative motion and the air bumps made it difficult to hold the subject in view long enough for identification.

Sub Lieutenant R.W. Gow of 1 Wing at Dunkirk, preparing to board his Nieuport. Note the binoculars on a sling around his neck, and the helmet and goggles in his left hand.

18.10.17 - 11.10 AM - Camel B5653 - 30 mins - Testing Clayton - Flies left wing down.

Sopwith *Camels* were manufactured by various contractors; No. B5653 was built by the firm of Clayton and Shuttleworth. The *"left wing down"* fault could easily be rectified by adjusting the tension of the cross-bracing wires between the wings, which would change some angles by a whisker or two. During combat, these wires were subjected to heavy loads, often under conditions which might make a modern-day metallurgist shudder—stress, vibration, low temperature and the metals composition.

19.10.17 - 1.30 PM - Camel B3893 - 30 mins - O.P. - Returned due to bad weather conditions.

2.45 PM - Camel B3893 - 60 mins - O.P. - Visibility bad. No E.A. observed.

20.10.17 - 9.30 AM - Camel B3893 - 120 mins - O.P. - 15,000' - Dived on E.A. Lost them in mist. Dived again but guns would not fire.[17]

3.00 PM - Camel B3893 - 30 mins - O.P. - 9,000' -Returned due to mist.

Machine guns, which shot holes in the propeller or did not fire at all, continued to be a serious problem. Only too often, when tested on the ground, they worked perfectly. Some pilots took to wrapping the target area of the propeller with adhesive tape so that if, the blades were struck, they would not splinter. The pilots could then reduce power to ease the strain on the weakened propeller and fly slowly to safety.

A jam caused by defective ammunition was something else again. Of the four types of jam which could occur to a Vickers machine gun, only two could be cleared in the air. The others required an armourer on a stepladder, with a screwdriver in his hand (and other tools in his pocket), to open the outside panel which gave access to the breechblock. He also needed a helper to hold the ammunition belt in place, otherwise when he opened the breechblock cover, the belt would be released and immediately disappear back into the ammunition box inside the fuselage.

Pilot's Report on Vickers Gun Trouble, it was soon discovered that the intense cold at high altitudes caused the metal rods of the Sopwith-Kauper synchronizing gear to contract. The change in length, compounded by mechanical wear at the many pivots and links, upset the delicate adjustments required. Fortunately, a far better system was about to be introduced, one which worked hydraulically and used a non-freezing oil.

21.10.17 - 6.15 AM - Camel B3893 - 50 mins - 8,000' - O.P. - Returned due to engine trouble.

10.30 AM - Camel B3893 - 130 mins - 8,000' - Defensive Fleet Patrol - Monitor in action.

22.10.17 - 1.30 PM - Camel B3893 - 140 mins - O.P. - Cross bracing wire broken.

23.10.17 - 3.15 PM - Camel B3893 - 30 mins - 12,000' - O.P. - Returned due to bad weather.

The Dover Patrol had a monitor, a small, strong shallow-draught warship, generally armed with a gun turret similar to that found on a cruiser.

The monitor *Raglan* firing shells at German installations on the Belgian coast.

Four of its monitors were of a more powerful type. Named *Marshal Ney, Marshal Soult, Erebus* and *Terror*, they were armed with a battleship turret containing two 15inch guns. From close inshore these huge guns could fire shells weighing one ton each into German-occupied territory for more than twenty miles, or they could bombard a port from twenty miles out to sea. However, any type of monitor would have been within easy range of German torpedo-carrying seaplanes, so the RNAS high-performance fighter squadrons came into the picture. These fighters also served to protect the escorting RNAS airship while the members of its crew were busily scanning the sub-surface of the ocean for any sign of a U-boat.

No. 9 Squadron
Oct. 23/17

My dear Bess,

Just received your letter of exactly a month ago and one from Jean in the same mail. It is the first I have had from home for some time.

I was very pleased to know that Horace has joined the R.N.A.S. and is coming back. He is sure to make good. I am due for leave in a month from today and he should be over here by then. I hope that he is, for I can give him a few tips which will help him.

I expect poor mother will be lonesome with everyone away again. I should like very much to get home this winter and have been trying. I have been sat on every time, so I do not suppose I shall get it.

If I do get home, you and Reta shall have to try and get leave at the same time.

You must look pretty nifty in your new fur coat. I wish I had a good fur coat out here as it is pretty cold above 10,000 feet now. I shall get one soon, I think.

Things go along much the same as usual. I have been doing a fair amount of work lately. It is pouring rain now and coming straight through the roof onto my bed. Such is life. C'est la guerre, as the French always say.

Stearne and I saw Eva Wilson a few days ago. She looks well and seems to be enjoying her work very much. She is very busy.

Fur coats and hip-length boots with a fur lining were highly sought by pilots of both sides. A captured airman could expect to surrender these items to his victor. There is a story (possibly apocryphal) known to historian Stewart Taylor of a well-to-do Allied pilot who had outfitted himself with the warmest of socks, shirts and underwear, plus the best quality fur-lined outer clothing. His captor first stripped him stark naked, then handed him some well-worn German Army clothes—hardly a fair exchange.

Eva Wilson was related to the lady who had sent a get-well postcard to Roy four years earlier.

24.10.17 - 9.30 AM - Camel B3893 - 130 mins - 9,000' - O.P. - Dived on E.A. but lost them in clouds over Middelkerke.

1.15 PM - Camel B3893 - 65 mins - 12,000' - O.P. - Returned due to bad weather conditions.

The fracturing of a cross-bracing wire, which had occurred on 22 October, had been a warning that the service life of some highly stressed components of Roy's *Camel* might be coming to an end; therefore No. B3893 was scheduled for a complete inspection later that week. The diagnosis was "general fatigue". No. B3893 was withdrawn from service, and Roy was allocated *Camel* B6317, which had left the factory in mid-September and been delivered to Naval 9 on 19 October. Being a flight commander (even an acting one) provided useful benefits in addition to mere privileges. (On 1 November No. B3893 was sent to the Naval Aeroplane Depot at Dunkirk Aerodrome where it spent two months being overhauled. It was subsequently issued to Naval 8 minus the posters of George Robey on the fin.)

26.10.17 - 9.35 AM - Camel B6317 - 15 mins - test

28.10.17 - 11.30 AM - Camel B6317 - 120 mins - 12,000' - O.P. - Dived on 7 E.A. scouts - One on my tail, got into a spin and was thrown out of seat. Got under control at about 4,000 feet. Met E.A. scout on our side of the lines and shot him down in floods. Confirmed by Belgian observation post. Banbury got an E.A. Confirmed by Bristol Fighters.[19]

The *"floods"* were the low-lying region of Belgium that had been flooded to impede the German advance.

Roy was officially credited for this victory, his sixth, over an Albatros DV above Pervyse. The Remarks column suggests that Roy's seat belt, known then as a Sutton Harness, was not sufficiently tight at the time. It is probable that in making a tight right-hand turn to escape from his attacker, he had applied just a fraction too much backpressure on the joystick and the *Camel* snapped into a high-speed stall. Being cross-controlled at the time (that is, turning right with the rudder to the left to counteract the torque of the rotary engine), it flicked onto its back and entered an inverted spin. Other pilots, trapped in such a position, have afterwards said that they worked the joystick with their feet to right the aeroplane and then promptly fell back into the seat, grateful for having been high up when it happened.

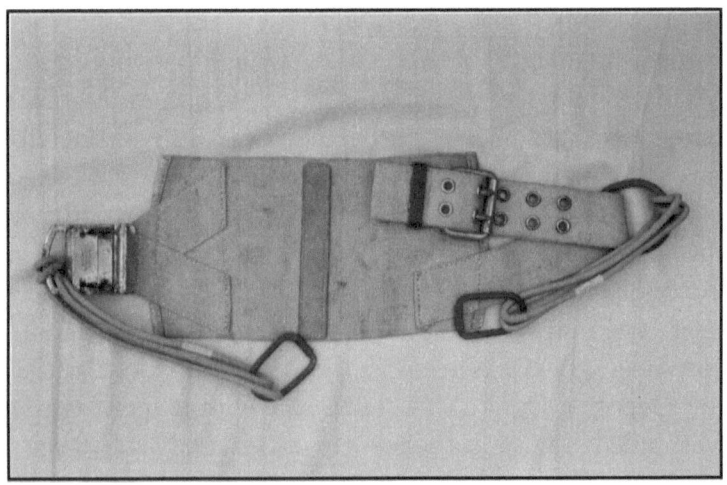

A British pilot's Sutton Harness. Bungee cords at each end prevented the wearer from suffering abdominal injuries in the event of a crash. The inscription reads "Sage & Co., Peterborough, Pat. No. 1019/16."

On the ground, the leaking roof of Roy's hut and the bad weather took their toll. His log book between 29 October and 3 November states, *"Sick with cold."* While Roy was indisposed, Sir Henry Rawlinson's "In the Field" immediate award of the Distinguished

Service Cross was promulgated in the *London Gazette* on second November 1917usually reprinted the more exciting announcements, and from one of them Mrs Hirsch learned about Roy's DSC.

The KING has been graciously pleased to approve he award of decorations to the under mentioned officers of the Royal Naval Air Service:

Act. Flt.-Lieut. (now Flt.-Lieut.) Arthur Roy Brown, R.N.A.S.

For the excellent work he has done on active service.

On the 3rd September, 1917, he attacked a two-seater Aviatik, in company with his flight. The enemy was seen to dive down vertically, the enemy observer falling over the side of the fuselage shot.

On the 5th September, 1917, in company with formation, he attacked an Albatross scout and two-seater, driving them away from our lines. One machine was observed to go down apparently out of control.

On the 15th September, 1917, whilst on patrol, he dived on two Aviatiks and three Albatross Scouts, followed by his flight. He fired several times and picked out one enemy scout, firing about 200 rounds, when the enemy machine went down out of control, spinning on its back.

On the 20th September, 1917, whilst leading his flight, he dived on five Albatross scouts. Flt.-Lieut. Brown picked out one enemy machine and opened fire. One of his guns jambed, but he carried on with the other. The enemy machine went down out of control and over on its back, and remained in that position for about thirty seconds, whilst Flt.-Lieut. Brown continued firing until his other gun jambed. The enemy machine then disappeared in the clouds, still on its back.

Another officer of the same patrol was followed by four enemy machines, as he was separated from the formation. Both Flt.-Lieut.

Brown's guns were jambed, but he dived on the enemy machines and drove them off, thus undoubtedly saving the pilot's life.

Note that the decoration was awarded for four events which took place over a period of time; that is distinguished service. In the paragraph above concerning 15 September, note that the officer who drafted Roy's recommendation used "when" in the sense of "whereupon" in the second sentence. This usage, common in 1917-1918, has caused occasional mis-interpretation of other documents in modern times.

9.11.17 - 2.10 PM - Camel B6317 - 30 mins - E.A. pusuit - Could not get near E.A.

The arrangements between the Admiralty and the U.S. Navy had been completed, and on that same day, 9 November, Roy and Stearne Edwards were granted three months' home leave; they both had to relinquish their local acting rank of flight commander and revert to their substantive rank of flight lieutenant, which in turn meant a reduction in pay. On 10 November, Squadron Commander E. W. Norton gave them each a certificate of service, just in case they encountered an over-inquisitive military policeman in London or at the quayside; then he bade them on their way.

On 11 November Roy and Stearne first travelled from France to England on the leave boat accompanied as usual by two destroyers and an airship. They were to collect their leave passes in London.

Roy Brown's Certificate of Service.

A leave boat travelling from Boulogne to Folkstone, photographed from its guardian airship.

The SSZ6, one of the airships which regularly guarded the leave boats. The lorry carries the cylinders of hydrogen used to replenish the charge in the envelope which had been "valved off" at the previous landing. Photo taken at No. 2 shed, Polegate, four miles northwest of Eastbourne, England, in June 1917.

While in London they made certain not to miss the "five o'clock standby" at the bar of the Savoy Hotel. Remembered his family's earlier request for a photograph, and wearing neatly pressed uniform and shining boots, Roy visited a professional studio.

Roy's medical records show that on 13 November 1917 the medical board of The Prince of Wales Hospital at Staines (situated beside the River Thames about sixteen miles upstream from central London) declared him unfit for general service for three months due to a severe gunshot wound in the right leg. He was also restricted to light duties for six weeks. A sea cruise would just be the right thing. Roy and Stearne sailed on 17 November, and it appeared that unbeknownst to them, the liner was also carrying a letter from Mrs Hirsch to Mrs Brown. The letter conveys the quiet fortitude of a mother in the face of adversity in those difficult times and illustrates how Roy's letters and visits had caused her to grow fond of him.

Flight Commander A. Roy Brown, DSC, wearing RNAS Active Service khaki uniform in 1917. Note the RNAS wings above the left breast pocket and that he has not yet begun wearing his DSC ribbon.

The Grove
Weetwood
Nr Leeds

9-11-17

My dear Mrs Brown,

 I fear time has jumped far more than I intended since I received your letter. But it is easy to put off until tomorrow - for letters. But now I want to write very particularly as I saw your dear son's name in the paper yesterday and he was so highly praised for all his bravery that I just have to send you our heartiest congratulations and pray he may soon be home - I mean this war over.
 I wish he might take great care of his precious self. These brave lads seem so often to be utterly careless of self & seem - to me - to take risks which shouldn't be allowed. For these brave priceless lives are great treasures of the nation and we simply cannot afford to lose them or be careless with them. If the nation could only realise this -
 The news from Italy and Russia is most depressing just now and it is hard to see any gleam of sunshine. But I still think that perhaps we have not all the news from these two Allies & it may be a little better than we fear.
 It is a long time since we heard from Roy. I am always hoping to have a wire that he is coming to see us. But I believe all the airmen are very, very busy and have little time off, although it seems to me that those men need a change more than others. I hope that you are all well and continue to receive happy letters from Roy.
 My son Frank is at Cambridge studying. He is wonderfully better and can walk quite nicely with the aid of one stick & is enjoying his work. It keeps his mind well employed.

With kindest regards
I am yours sincerely
Edith Hirsch

The time for the monthly confidential reports arrived, and on 28 November Squadron Commander Norton recommended Roy for promotion to substantive flight commander. On 31 October while Roy was away on home leave, he described him as "a very good officer and pilot with good command of his men."

On the other side of the front lines, the German plan to build a large number of super triplanes and thus regain mastery of the air had received a setback. At the end of August a small number of the mass-produced Fokker design, known as the Dr.I, had appeared at another part of the front, but the rainy summer weather had caused the dissolution of the glue used in the construction of their wings. Thus, after a brilliant beginning, they were withdrawn from service during the first week of November. The Albatros *Triplane* showed no performance improvement over the D.V and did not enter production. The Pfalz *Triplane*, with its "hi-tech" engine, performed impressively when the engine ran properly, which was far too infrequently for squadron service.[20]

ANNEX TO CHAPTER SIX

(1) HMS FURIOUS.
While there were no problems with taking off, the smoke and the steam from the centrally positioned funnel caused poor visibility during the approach to the carrier, and the airflow disturbed by the bridge and tall superstructure created heavy turbulence across the landing deck. To operate any of its aircraft, HMS Furious would steam into the wind. The ship was taken out of service to be rebuilt with an uninterrupted flight deck from stem to stern and with the funnel exiting from one side and discharging downwards. Making these changes to HMS Furious and the other aircraft carriers under construction delayed their entry into service, and none was commissioned until after the armistice. Of the seven aircraft carriers serving with the Royal Navy at the start of the Second World War on 1 September 1939 HMS Furious and her 1919 companion, HMS Argus, were the only ones not sunk during the war.

(2) DISINTEGRATING LINK AMMUNITION BELTS.
In April 1916 a Fokker Eindecker (monoplane) was captured by the French, who quickly discovered how Anthony H. G. Fokker had managed to squeeze two LMG 08/15 machine guns into the space previously occupied by one—by eliminating the take-up spool. The ammunition belts were made of metal links which were "pinned" together by the cartridges, and as each cartridge was extracted from the belt and fed into the breechblock, the preceding link became detached and dropped into a chute which emptied into space. An additional benefit was the elimination of jams due to frozen canvas belts.

The Germans also developed a type of re-usable belt which would feed ammunition to the observer's swivelling machine gun(s) in damp, freezing weather. An individually manufactured canvas pocket held each cartridge securely, and the pockets were linked together into belt form by helix-shaped coils of wire. The same method is used today to hold pages together in a notebook. The pockets could freeze stiff, but the belt would still bend. It was a narrow belt, about half the overall width of the Vickers canvas belt.

German helix linked belt.

W. DeCourcey Rideaux copied the German disintegrating link idea, and improved upon it by providing a positive stop inside each section, which would align the cartridges perfectly as the belt was assembled. The elimination of the take-up spool box enabled the Sopwith F1 *Super Pup*, soon to be renamed *Camel*, to be designed with twin Vickers machine guns as the standard armament. An early version of the Sopwith twin-machine-gun design for the *Super Pup* was ready just in time for use on the last six Sopwith *Triplanes* manufactured during the war.

(3) THE SOPWITH *CAMEL* AND ITS ARMAMENT.

The 130hp Clergêt engine fitted to Roy's Sopwith F1 *Camel* included twin magnetos, and each cylinder had two sparking plugs; that is, there were two independent ignition systems. This removed much of the hazard of flying over the sea beyond the gliding distance to shore. Another useful feature was the Camel's vastly improved armament—twin Vickers machine guns with a fast-firing synchronizing system.

The F1 *Camel* was usually equipped with two Vickers machine guns synchronized to the propeller by version (Type 3) of the Sopwith-Kauper mechanical linkage that had been used on the last six Sopwith *Triplanes*. Although better on paper than the Type 2, in service the Type 3 still suffered from rapid wear, and a perforated propeller decorated many an officer's cabin. Countless patrols were wasted and lives lost when machine guns failed to function in the air; Mel Alexander's flying log book lists case after case. Too often, no discernable reason for the mal functions could be found when the guns were later examined and tested on the ground.

When the mechanical linkage worked properly, a *Camel*, like the last six Sopwith *Triplanes*, could shoot at any Albatros D.III or D.V which came by.

The disintegrating link belts for the *Camel* contained 400 rounds, were ten yards long, weighed 27 pounds and could only be installed on the ground. An armourer and a helper were required for the task. After the access panel on the outside of the fuselage had been opened, the helper supported the weight of the belt while the armourer folded it into the storage compartment. Then, with one holding the loose end in position in the breechblock, the other closed the breechblock cover. If either one fumbled his part, the loose end of the heavy, loaded belt would immediately disappear into the storage compartment. Finally, the outside access panel had to be closed and locked shut. It has been described as an operation requiring two men, a step ladder and a dog and was certainly difficult for one man to perform even when accompanied by a well-trained, four-footed helper.

In the following photograph, the major part of the new link belt is piled on the pilot's seat out of sight. The armourer has removed the access cover and is preparing the Vickers machine gun to receive the belt. Note the square opening (beside his pocket) in the large oval, metal panel which is the chute for the discharge of the loose links from the starboard gun belt. The empty cartridge cases from the starboard gun joined those from the port gun and exited via a common chute on the port side. The round tube protruding to the left of the oval panel is part of the air intake system to the fuel-air mixing chamber. The large round hole in the top of the fuselage, just behind the loose ends of the belt, provides access to the filler cap of the main petrol tank. The reserve tank filler cap is out of sight beneath the belt.

An armourer working on a Sopwith *Camel*.

Some special RNAS *Camels* were equipped with a different arrangement of weapons. The 'hump' would be eliminated, and the starboard Vickers machine gun replaced with an upward-firing Lewis gun. The pilot could approach an enemy night bomber from below, sight carefully and open fire.

Detail of a special RNAS Sopwith *Camel*, starboard side. This version still has two

fuel tanks, and the position of the cockpit has not been changed. The starboard air intake tube to the fuel-air mixing chamber is clearly shown. The small square, metal panel with four twist-locks, seen directly above the oval panel, would be opened by the armourer to load the belt into the port Vickers machine gun.

Detail of the port side of a standard Sopwith *Camel*. The upper chute discharges the loose links from the port Vickers machine gun. The lower chute discharges the empty cartridge cases from both the port and the starboard Vickers machine guns.

A special Sopwith *Camel* for high-altitude night fighting was developed for the Royal Flying Corps. Surprisingly, the 110hp Le Rhône rotary engine was found to produce more power than the 130hp Clergêt in the rarified air above 18,000 feet. Pilots had complained that the flash from the Vickers guns blinded them at the critical moment, so two Lewis guns mounted on rails were attached to the upper wing. The "upstairs" Lewis guns were lighter than the Vickers, and the muzzle flashes were no longer in the pilot's line of sight. With the hump for the Vickers guns removed, the pilot had a clear view to the front in level flight; he no longer needed to look along the side of the fuselage.

It became possible to improve the pilot's upward view by deleting one fuel tank and moving his seat eighteen inches to the rear. To aid the pilot in keeping the enemy in view when using the Lewis guns to fire upwards, the fabric was removed from the centre section of the upper wings. Unexpectedly, this made a night-fighting *Camel* much easier to land than a standard one. Apparently, at landing speed the downwash from the covered centre section reduced the effect of the elevators when the joystick was pulled back. At the 20,000 feet altitude where the Rumplers flew, the much-modified *Camel* was still responsive to the controls and had no tendency to stall and spin during turns. In the inevitable manner of the time, these much-modified *Camels* were nicknamed "Comic Camels", or simply "*Comics*".

In the *Comic Camel* pilot's cockpit the semi-conical structure behind the pilot's head was for streamlining, not comfort. Anything that reduced wake turbulence would thereby decrease parasitic drag by a useful amount, which meant a further increase in operational ceiling. Beneath each wing tip was an electrically ignited Holts flare the pilot lit one of them on his final approach and looked at the ground on the opposite side to avoid being blinded by the glare. After two missed approaches, the easier landing of the night-fighting *Comic* became more difficult.

Night-fighting Sopwith *Comic Camel* No. B2402 of RCF 44 Home Defence Squadron stationed at Hainault Farm. A flight leader's streamer is attached to the tail, and only the blue part of the roundel remains on the fuselage.

Some night-fighting *Comics* were further modified for attacks on high altitude Zeppelins. They were lightened as far as possible since every pound removed meant greater height could be reached; one pound was said to equal one hundred feet. For this reason the *Comics* carried just one Lewis gun and only one 47-round drum of exploding, incendiary ammunition. Forty-seven such rounds, carefully aimed to concentrate the shots in one place, were ample to start a leak and then ignite the escaping hydrogen after it had mixed with atmospheric oxygen. Towards the end of a flight in the wee hours of the morning, a pilot at 16,000 to 18,000 feet would often witness an usual phenomenon: he would see the sun rising unexpectedly early, then as he descended, he would watch a glorious sunset; shortly after landing, he would see the sun rise again.

(4) FLYING A SOPWITH CAMEL.

The syllabus at Chingford had covered the gyroscopic effect which a rotary engine could have upon an aeroplane, but the Avro 504, the Sopwith *Pup*, and the Sopwith *Triplane* had not exhibited that phenomenon to any disagreeable extent in flight. The Sopwith *Camel* was different. The short fuselage, in which all the heavy items were concentrated at the front, helped to provide rapid response to control movements. An unfortunate side-effect of this principal was that when combined with a heavier, more powerful engine, it resulted in a product considerably more sensitive to gyroscopic forces.

According to the memories of Air Vice-Marshal Arthur Gould Lee, Major Christopher Draper and others, a proficient, experienced pilot who had flown a Nieuport Bébé would be converted to a *Camel* by being shown how to work the fuel system and then told to take off and climb straight and level until he reached 3,000 feet; at that altitude, if he accidentally allowed the *Camel* to spin, he would have ample height to recover and would be surprised how easily and rapidly it would do so. He was then to make very gentle 90-degree right and left turns, noticing how the nose of the *Camel* would try to drop on the right turn and rise on the left. When he had become accustomed to this phenomenon, he was to return to the aerodrome using right turns only, make a landing and take off again—this time to climb as high as was comfortable and to practise medium turns, steep turns, spins and combat manoeuvres to the left and right.

The first part was meant to create confidence, and the second part to learn how to handle the beast as would be required in action. The unusual feature was the manner in which sharp turns had to be made: a sharp, steeply banked turn to the left required almost full left rudder all the way round not just the amount required to keep turning.

A sharp, steeply banked turn to the right also required almost *full left* rudder all the way round. To use the rudder in this manner was not instinctive, but it had to become automatic via a learning process, which tended to be either rapid or fatal. The RNAS ace Major Alfred William (Nick) Carter, DSC, said that the pilot of a *Camel* would begin a right turn and then change his mind.

It is well known that a spinning gyroscope exerts force to remain in the same plane; it is not so well known that if a spinning gyroscope is prevented from doing so, it exerts force in another plane. The technical name for this effect is "precession." A rotary engine is in effect a gyroscope, and when a pilot begins a turn, he is changing the plane in which his engine is rotating. The direction of rotation of a Clergêt engine was such that if its axis was turned to the right by the pilot, as in a right turn, force would be exerted towards the ground; hence the need for left rudder to hold the nose up. Insufficient left rudder would result in a shallow, diving turn, from which a novice could easily straighten out; hence the advice given to a trainee *Camel* pilot before his first solo, *"Make all your turns to the right."*

As soon as a *Camel* pilot began thinking about a turn to the left, he had to begin countering the force about to be exerted in the other plane by the disturbed gyroscope (the engine), otherwise the nose would lift and his machine would begin to climb. The correction was to apply more left rudder. In the case of a trainee who did not notice he was losing speed and allowed the climb to become really steep, his left turn could rapidly progress into a stall immediately followed by a spin to the right. A surprised, or frightened, low-time pilot could easily fail to notice the spinning direction and apply correction the wrong way. Near the ground such a mistake only too often led to eternal repose. Roy Brown's advice to trainee Ronald Sykes was, *"Keep your speed up in turns."*

As if the foregoing were not difficult enough, there was one more complication. The application of correction to nosing up or nosing down during a turn also changed the plane of the engine's rotation. Precession would occur once more, and the *Camel* would try to turn to the right or the left. Correcting the turning created further nose-down or nose-up precession, ad infinitum. A novice could over - or under-correct for quite a while before getting the hang of things. The secret was to apply gentle pressures to the controls, rather than movements, so as not to initiate strong, processive reactions. Once decided on his target, a proficient *Camel* pilot could close the range without wandering around in the sky and then position his victim-to-be in his gunsight for the necessary three seconds.

After the technique of turning right with the application of left rudder had been learned, the next step was to bank almost vertically to the right with full left rudder and the joystick pulled back as if to climb steeply. Before the pilot could say "*Jack Robinson,*" his *Camel* would be in an extremely tight right-hand turn. If an Albatros was on his tail when he began the turn, by the time the German pilot started wondering where the *Camel* had gone, it would already be on his tail. Unfortunately this did not work with those Albatros pilots who had met the manoeuvre before and survived; as soon as the *Camel* disappeared, they suddenly remembered an urgent appointment in another part of the sky. Only a Fokker Dr.I *Triplane* could make a tighter turn than a *Camel*, and Lieutenant D. G. Lewis was to learn this the hard way on 20 April 1918. A few moments after opening fire on Rittmeister Baron Manfred von Richthofen's bright red triplane right in front of him, he became that pilot's eightieth and last combat victory.

At high altitude an experienced pilot could use gyroscopic precession in a left turn to escape from the enemy. The trick was to begin a left turn and then pull the joystick back hard. The *Camel* would immediately snap into a spin to the right.

In active service *Camel* squadrons, even the most highly experienced pilots always made shallowly banked turns to the right after takeoff. If for some reason a pilot did not apply sufficient force on the rudder pedal to obtain full correction for his machine's desire to nose down, it would gain speed until he did, and speed meant safety.

However, all was not negative in the *Camel* world. Although the compensation applied by the pilot for the gyroscopic forces of the engine caused a *Camel* to fly slightly sideways in a straight line, such behaviour thoroughly confused the enemy's high-altitude anti-aircraft gunners. They would carefully measure the speed of a *Camel*, note the direction in which its nose was pointing, allow for the wind and then aim precisely at the place where the aeroplane should be when their shells reached that height. They would more often than not miss the target since they had actually fired where the *Camel* was not going. When asked his opinion of the flight characteristics of a Sopwith *Camel*, the Australian fighter ace A.H. Cobby said that when flying a Camel, he was only sure that it was not moving through the air in the direction its nose was pointing.

By late 1917 the situation had improved. Roy's schoolmate from Edmonton, Wilfrid May, serves as an example. He began Royal Flying Corps pilot training on 27 October, and his log book shows that he soloed in a Caudron 141-50 after 3 hours 59 minutes of dual instruction on the type. He moved on to Avro 504s, which he flew for 28 hours 40 minutes, he learning aerobatics, formation flying, and navigation (cross-country) and practising engine failures. He moved on to Sopwith *Pups*, which he flew for 11 hours 50 minutes, learning to perform the same manoeuvres, plus aerial gunnery, in a machine with a better performance. He then moved on to Le Rhône 110hp and Clergêt 130hp *Camels*, where he spent 10 hours 40 minutes, essentially repeating the same syllabus but now on high-powered, state-of-the-art fighters. On 9 April 1918 and with a total flying time of 55 hours 9 minutes, he reported to RAF 209 Squadron in France, where he first had to learn again to do most of the same things, but this time in a Bentley-engined 150hp *Camel* on windy days and while someone was shooting at him.

By December 1917 the number of trainee and low-time *Camel* pilots killed in simple flying accidents was causing concern to the Royal Flying Corps, but as has been alleged, the cause was not that the *Camel* was a brute to fly. The shortage of pilots after heavy losses during the year had brought about a change in the RFC pilot-training courses in England. The intermediate stage between basic training in, for example, a gentle B.E.2C and training to handle a high-powered fighter was considerably reduced. Unfortunately it was precisely the intermediate stage on Sopwith *Pups*, with their sedate Le Rhône 80hp rotary engine which ran like a sewing machine that gave confidence to trainee pilots. Once their reactions had become automatic and they could tell from the feel of the aeroplane when they were doing something wrong, they could be converted to *Camels*. Even so, this was a big step since *Camels* had double the power of *Pups* and everything happened within a much shorter time frame. For low-time pilots who had not had a proper intermediate stage on *Pups*, Nieuport Bébés or Bristol Scouts, the much louder engine and more rapid response of a *Camel* relative to a B.E.2C or an Avro 504 created a distracting situation. The results were inevitable, and although *Camels* were credited by the Royal Air Force with the destruction of 1,294 enemy aircraft, they are said to have killed about the same number of their own pilots.

Within six weeks of Wilfrid May's graduation, two of the four *Camels* which he had flown in the well-planned training course described above were damaged beyond repair in "stalling and spinning" accidents at low altitude; Second Lieutenant T.C. Attewell was killed in No. B4640 on 8 May and Second Lieutenant G.F. Williams in No. B9328 on 26 May. Accidents such as these, despite the hours their pilots had spent on *Pups*, provided the impetus for a useful step to reduce casualties. In mid-1918 several flying training schools made their own local conversions of standard F1 *Camels* into two-seaters. The removal of the machineguns made it possible to reposition the pilot's cockpit a few inches forward, and there being no need to carry fuel for flights of two and a half hours, smaller tanks were installed, thus releasing space for an instructor's cockpit at the rear.

A documentary film made in 2001 showed a replica F1 *Camel* dancing around on the ground and, in a computer simulation of Roy Brown attacking a red triplane, quite incorrectly led viewers to believe a *Camel* flew in such a manner. The truth is that when the engine is operated on the ground, the slipstream from the propeller is deflected upwards from the surface below onto the underside of the wings, thus creating lift. When the engine is accelerated to normal flying power, the lift is so great that the aeroplane dances around. Obviously, this situation does not occur when the machine is airborne. Once a *Camel* was anywhere between normal flying and diving speeds, and its direction of flight and attitude had been established by the pilot, it was as steady as a rock in the air and an unsuspecting target could easily be held in the gunsight.

(5) The lettering on some of Roy Brown's combat reports was unfit for reproduction, and in these cases, they have been retyped exactly. Roy's three-step promotion from substantive flight sub-lieutenant to acting flight commander during the months of September and October is clear proof of his abilities.

(6) Combat report of 9 September 1917 Acting Flight Lieutenant Brown led the flight. The comment in the left margin is *"indecisive"* abbreviated.

(7) THE *FELIXSTOWE* FLYING BOAT.

Even during the Great War lawsuits over the violation of patents were still keeping the U.S. aviation industry behind Europe in the design of fast land planes and seaplanes. However, Glenn Curtiss, who had found an arguable but not absolutely certain way around some of the legal restrictions, was far ahead with flying boats. From his successful 1914 single-engined flying boat, he developed a twin-engined model named the America. A long-range version of the America was built for a transatlantic attempt (which was postponed due to the war), and for want of a name, it was referred to as the Large America. The type performed so well that it caught the attention of the Admiralty. Glenn Curtiss was approached, and with the aid of a Royal Navy officer named John Porte, he designed a military version of the *Large America* for purchase by the RNAS.

The RNAS Curtiss Large Americas had a crew of four—two pilots and two gun layers, the RNAS term for an air gunner. Each gun layer operated twin Lewis guns. The *Large Americas* carried enough fuel for six hours of patrol flying, plus a pair of homing pigeons to bring help in case of engine failure. The reluctance of some pigeons to leave the comfortable inside of a downed flying boat, in favour of the cold, rainy and windy skies outside, spawned several hilarious tales of the crews' efforts to change their feathery minds. One mercenary-minded bird turned around, came back, sat on a wing and looked at them; it only departed for good after the crew threw coins at it. During the Second World War, Mrs Maria Dickin, founder of the People's Dispensary for Sick Animals, financed a bronze medal for animals which saved human life at grave risk to their own. In the case of pigeons, the green, dark brown and light blue ribbon of The Dickin Medal was displayed on their cages.

Active service experience revealed the need for stronger hulls to withstand the rough waters around the British Isles, but the extra weight of the new hull, plus goodly supply of anti-submarine bombs (the forerunners of depth charges), meant that more powerful engines were required. John Porte set to work, and the result was a new hull grafted onto Curtiss wings and tail. Two Rolls Royce Eagle engines were installed, and the new flying boat was named "Felixstowe" after the place in England where the hull had been designed. The *Felixstowe* was a huge success, and several versions were built in quantity during the war for the RNAS and the U.S. Navy. Eleven examples of an even larger version were also built and immediately received the nick name "*Porte Baby*". They had a third engine, mounted directly over the fuselage, with the propeller at the rear, and could carry one ton.

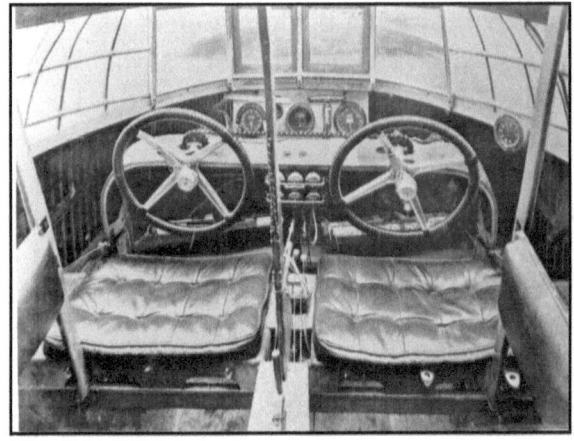

The spacious and luxurious pilots' cabin of a *Porte Baby* in early 1918. Note the Déperdussin-style control columns with a wheel to operate the massive ailerons via a step-down chain drive, and the foot bars to control the huge rudder.

The patent issue was put to rest in late 1916 when Orville Wright sold his company and a general legal settlement within the United States took place. Glenn Curtiss was then able to market an excellent two-seater training aeroplane, the Type JN-4, better known as the *Jenny*. The RAF purchased many for use at flying training schools in England.

(8) SOPWITH *CAMEL* FUEL SYSTEM.

There were two separate fuel tanks, located one above the other, behind the pilot's seat. The lower,(main fuel tank) was pressurized with air supplied by two separate systems—a manual pump for starting the engine and a wind-driven pump (made by the Rotherham company) for flying. The latter was mounted within the propeller slipstream, sometimes on an undercarriage leg, sometimes on a wing centre-section strut, and began pumping as soon as the engine was started. A relief valve limited the pressure inside the main tank to somewhere between 2 and 3 psi above the outside atmosphere. An air-pressure gauge was provided in the cockpit to enable the pilot to monitor the system.

The upper, reserve or gravity fuel tank operated by gravity alone and had to be selected manually by the pilot.

The purpose of pressurizing the main fuel tank was to provide a reasonably constant flow to the fuel valve, whether the main tank was full or almost empty. In level flight the upper two-thirds of the fuel in this tank flowed to the mixing chamber by gravity, assisted by the air pressure; the lower third needed to be "pushed" at all times. The term "fuel valve," for the lever which the pilot moved with his left hand to control engine power was only used with rotary engines. On stationary engines, such as those in the B.E.2C, S.E.5A and R.E.8, it was known as the "throttle lever." On cars it takes the form of a pedal and is called the accelerator.

Obviously both air pumps were functioning at the beginning of Roy's flights, and a repeated double failure is not very likely. Clearly it was not easy to find the cause on the ground since the problem returned three times at high altitude before being finally diagnosed and solved. From Roy's description, the loss of air pressure seems likely to have been caused by misbehaviour of the relief valve at sub-zero temperatures.

There are two additional points worthy of mention. First, to start a rotary engine, the pilot closed the fuel valve and used the manual pump to pressurize the main fuel tank to the prescribed value. A mechanic then primed the cylinders and swung the propeller. As soon as the engine fired, the pilot cracked open the fuel valve and took control of the revolutions per minute. Secondly, although Clergêt rotary engines came with an engine-driven air pump, for standardization purposes a wind-driven pump was used.

(9) At the time of this combat report on 15 September 1917, Roy Brown had reverted to his substantive rank of flight sub-lieutenant but retained his position as flight leader.

> Army Form W. 3348.
>
> ### Combats in the Air.
>
> Squadron: Naval No.9.
> Type and No. of Aeroplane: Sopwith Camel B 3893.
> Armament: Two Vickers Syn. Guns.
> Pilot: F. S. L. Brown.
> Observer: -----
> Date: Sept. 15th 1917.
> Time: 1.5 p.m.
> Duty: O. P.
> Height: 8,000-3,000 ft.
>
> Locality: WESTENDE TO ZEVECOTE.
>
> Remarks on Hostile machine:—Type, armament, speed, etc.
>
> 2 Aviatik D.F.W. and 3 Albatross Scouts.
>
> Flight Leader's Report.
> —— Narrative. ——
>
> With my flight, I dived on two two-seater Aviatiks at 12.15 pm. when my engine cut out, and I had to leave, but it picked up just over lines, and I rejoined flight, but E.A. were lost in mist.
>
> At 1.0 pm. I dived on 2 Aviatiks and 3 Albatross Scouts followed by flight. Dived several times on Scouts, then picked out one and followed him. Got about 200 rounds into him and he went down out of control, spinning on his back going down and I lost sight of him.
>
> Continued diving with F.S.L.Oakley who was firing on another two-seater which went down out of control.
>
> ----------------
>
> *Confirmed by F.S.L. Hales.*
>
> I was flying at 10,000 feet when F.S.L. Brown dived. I followed him for 2,000 ft. and then pulled out of dive when I saw enemy machines above me. Kept watching enemy machines and my flight.
> When our flight was about 4,000 feet I saw F.S.L. Brown and F.S.L Oakley attacking Albatross Scouts. Later an Albatross Scout was seen to fall over on its back and fall apparently out of control.
> Owing to haze and the enemy machines above I was not able to keep my eye on enemy machine until it crashed.
>
> (Sd) J. L. WALSHE.
> Lieut. R.N.V.R.
> Records Officer.

(10) THOSE KNOWN TO HAVE SURRENDERED IN THE AIR TO THE RITTMEISTER.

According to under the *Guns of the Red Baron* by Norman Franks where the complete stories may be found, following are the names of those who surrendered in the air to the Rittmeister:

Victory 61, 3 September 1917: Lieutenant Algernon Frederick Bird, Sopwith *Pup* No. B1795.

Victory 62, 23 November 1917: Lieutenant James Alexander Vazeill Boddy, D.H.5 No. A9299.

Victory 64 - 12 March 1917: Second Lieutenant Henry James Sparks (pilot) and second Lieutenant Leonard Cyril Frederick Clutterbuck (observer), Bristol F2B *Fighter* No. B1251.

Victory 66, 18 March 1918: Second Lieutenant William George Ivamy, Sopwith *Camel* B5243

Following are disabled or downed opponents whom he did not attack further:

Victory not claimed, 13 March 1918: Second Lieutenant. C. Allen (pilot), Lieutenant N. T. Watson (observer), Bristol F2B *Fighter* No. B1207.

Victory 65, 13 March 1918: Lieutenant Elmer Ernest Heath, Sopwith *Camel* No. B2523

Victory 80, 20 April 1918: Second Lieutenant David Greswolde Lewis, Sopwith *Camel* No. B7393.

The above list contradicts the Allied propaganda stories that the Rittmeister only attacked obsolete or clumsy types of aeroplanes. With the exception of Victory 62, the D.H.5, all were the best the Allies could put in the air at the time.

(11) Combat report of 20 September 1917 for flight led by Sub-Lieutenant Brown.
[document AN6-3]

(12) Combat report of 21 September 1917:
[document AN6-4]

(13) Flight Sub-Lieutenant Brown's combat report of 29 September 1917:
[document AN6-5]

(14) Combat report of 13 October 1917 submitted by Roy Brown who had been restored to the rank of acting flight lieutenant:
[document AN6-6]

(15) Combat report of 14 October 1917 by Flight Lieutenant Brown led the flight.
[document AN6-7]

Captain Roy Brown

(16) Combat report of 17 October 1917 by Roy Brown, the flight leader, who had been promoted to acting flight commander:

```
                    COMBAT      REPORT.
                    ---------   ---------
         No. 9 Squadron.           October 17th 1917.
         Locality.    Ghistelles.  Height.   10.000 feet.
         Duty.    Offensive Patrol. Time.    9. 50 a.m.
         Pilot.   Flt.Cmdr. Brown.

                  Albatross Scouts and D.F.W.Aviatiks.

              Dived on enemy formation of about 10 - 15 machines followed
         by three of my flight.    Could not get to close quarters as
         the formation of H.A. was too large to pick one out and stay
         with him.   We drove them down by diving, firing and turning
         off then diving again.
              I saw a flight of E.A. dive on four Camels so we dived on
         the former and they cleared off.
              We dived on a third formation but both my guns jammed so
         I came home, having fired a total of 350 rounds.

                                        [signature]

         Indecisive.           Squadron Commander.R.N.(act)


         Retyped 12 March, 2002
```

(17) Combat report of 20 October 1917 by Flight Commander Brown, who led the flight.
[document AN6-17]

(18) REPORT FORM FOR JAMMED VICKERS MACHINE-GUNS.

PILOT'S REPORT ON VICKERS GUN TROUBLE

Date. *8th December, 1917*   Type of Machine   *Sopwith F.1*

No. of Machine	*B 4270*	Type of Engine	*130 H.P. Clerget*
Port Gun	*C 2357*	Type of Gear	*Sopwith Kauper*
Starboard Gun	*C 4611*	Type of belt	*Bare 111 Links*

(QUESTION)   (ANSWER)

What Type of Jamb (1,2,3 or 4)? *No. 1*
(If No. 3, only answer questions that apply.)

What height were you when trouble occurred? *Between 17,000 and 6,000 feet*

Did you fire the guns before you reached this altitude? If so, how many rounds (approx) and at what altitudes?
Made attempts to fire every 5 or 10 minutes

Did the guns fire directly you pushed the levers on the joy stick   *No* or did you have to hold them pressed for an appreciable time before the Gun fired? (This is important.) *Yes*

When the Gun would not fire, what did you do? *Cleared the jambs in the usual way of clearing jambs*

Did the same trouble occur again? *Yes and recurred many times*

Did the Guns fire slowly at first or at normal rate of fire? *Single shots only*

Was a thermometer carried by your flight at the time, if so what was temperature at altitude trouble occurred? (If no thermometer, would you consider it colder than usual?) *No*

Did the Guns get covered with white frost during Patrol? *No*

Did the Guns fire O.K. when you reached a lower altitude? *Yes*

Were you diving, climbing or on even keel? *On my back. No one ever scraps in any one given position, either diving, climbing or on an even keel. (God help him if he does.)*

Pilots must do their best to remember exactly what happened, as only by reliable and clear reports can the cause of the trouble be traced.

Armament Officers are to give pilots any assistance they may require with this report, but the original is to be in the pilot's own handwriting.

    [signed] *J.S.T. Fall*
    Acting Flight Commander

There is a pencilled comment on the bottom of the report which indicates some higher authority did not appreciate the "God help him if he does" remark.

(19) 28 October 1917. Flight Commander Brown led the flight.

```
                    COMBAT     REPORT.
                    -------------------------

        No. 9 Squadron.            October 28th 1917.
        Locality.  Near Pervyse.   Height.  12.000 feet.
        Duty.  H. O. P.            Time.  12. 20 p.m.
        Pilots.  Flt.Cmdr.Brown
                 & Flt.Lt.Banbury.


                    7 Albatrose Scouts. D 5's.


            Dived on formation of 7 E.A. near Pervyse, followed me
        down but could not get sights on him as I was diving past vertical
        and thrown out of seat.  A second E.A. followed me and he was
        followed by Flight Lieut. Banbury who fired about 100 rounds into him
        but broke away owing to engine trouble.  I did not open fire until
        at about 4.000 feet and followed him carrying on firing until about
        50 feet over floods.  I fired 300 rounds into him and then
        broke off combat owing to two No. 3 jambs.


                                          [signature]
                                          for Commanding Officer.
                                              (on leave)
```

One E.A. certainly destroyed

Confirmed by 48 Squad. R.F.C.

(20) THE FOKKER F.I & Dr.I *TRIPLANES*.

Of the surprisingly large number of triplane designs submitted by German and Austrian aircraft manufacturers (fourteen are known, but according to Paul S. Leaman there were more), two were chosen for production—those by Fokker and Pfalz. The Pfalz *Triplane* encountered serious problems with its new design engine and was not built in quantity. The first three Fokker F.I *Triplanes* (German Army Orders Nos. 101/17, 102/17 and 103/17) were built by skilled workmen. No. 101/17 was tested to destruction by the authorities at Adlershof to determine exactly what loads the wings would withstand before collapsing or breaking. The answer was eight times the weight of the machine.

A triplane had a higher centre of gravity than a biplane and therefore tended to tip onto its nose when landing on a soft field or if the wheels hit a rut during the taxiing. Such accidents resulted in considerable damage, and sometimes the pilot was badly hurt. Fokker's designers had already invented a system to reduce the number of serious landing accidents caused by wheels striking an obstruction and had used it on some previous types of aeroplane. It was based upon the premise that far less damage to man and machine would occur if the sudden, severe stress on the undercarriage caused the entire assembly to break free of the fuselage; the aeroplane would then sit down and slide along on its belly, suffering little more damage than a broken propeller and some torn fabric. The idea was simple, and he employed it again on the F.I: the undercarriage struts were attached to the fuselage by soft metal pins that would break under severe stress. Such pins have many applications in today's industry and are now known as *"sheer pins"*.

In late August 1917, Fokker F.I *Triplane* No. 102/17 was sent to Jasta 11 where it was successfully used in combat by Manfred von Richthofen. He went on leave and passed it to the acting commanding officer Oberleutnant Kurt Wolff (Pour le M_rite and 33 victories), who was shot down and killed in it on 15 September by Flight Lieutenant N. M. Macgregor. Triplane No. 103/17 was delivered to Jasta 10 where it was used in combat by Werner Voss (Pour le M_rite and 48 victories); whilst in a dogfight against impossible odds, he was shot down and killed in September, thus fulfilling Oswalde Boelke's prediction that foolish acts of bravery only bring death. During the twenty-four days in which

Werner Voss had flown his F.I, he had downed 21 Allied aeroplanes. The phenomenal success of these two triplanes greatly impressed the German authorities, and it was only much later that the real reason for the success was discovered: most Allied pilots did not know a German triplane existed, and as a result, they took no defensive precautions whatsoever at the approach of what they believed to be an RNAS Sopwith *Triplane*.

Production of Anthony Fokker's apparent aerial wonder, renamed Dr.I (*Dreidecker* [triplane] Type 1), began under an accelerated timetable. The demand for deliveries was great, but quality control on the production line was poor. The weather in October 1917 was bad, and when it was not raining, the air was damp and the sky dreary. By the middle of the month some of the triplanes had reached the front, and when the weather improved a week later, two ace pilots decided to try out their new toys. As soon as Heinrich Gontermann had acquired confidence in the behaviour of his machine, he tried some aerobatics—nothing rough, just some properly executed loops and rolls. The aileron attachment points failed on one of the top wings; he lost control and crashed. Günther Pastor simply flew his around the aerodrome for a few minutes, and then as he came in to land, an aileron came adrift and he also crashed. Both pilots were killed.

Inspection of an undamaged Fokker Dr.I revealed that during manufacture, the glued joints of the wooden structure inside all six wings had been poorly made. In addition, the multiple coats of varnish required to waterproof the wood and the glue had been skimped. The list of defects of workmanship was long. All Dr.I's were immediately grounded, and a proposal was made to Anthony Fokker that he could not refuse. For future deliveries, a return to the quality of the three protoypes was required, plus a few improvements. Furthermore, all Dr.I *Triplanes* built to date were to be upgraded and provided with new wings at Fokker's expense.

Properly built Fokker Dr.I *Triplanes* began to appear at the front in October 1917, and the same misidentification promptly happened, but this time in reverse. An Albatros D.V pilot saw one of those "British flying Venetian blinds" he had heard about, stalked it and shot it down. It was Dr.I No. 113/17 of Jasta 11 flown by Sergeant Major Josef Lautenschlager. Like Erich Loewenhardt who shot down Otto Roosen, the victor, also no novice, had failed to see the large black crosses displayed on his victim's machine. The position of the sun, plus the angle from which he approached No. 113/17, may have caused his error.

The Fokker *Triplane*, which had no dihedral angel whatsoever on any pair of wings, was the only aeroplane that could turn more tightly than a Sopwith *Camel*. It could also climb faster, which was often useful for escaping. In level flight, it was probably the slowest fighter in service in the last part of 1917 onwards, but as Anthony Fokker wrote, *"It was so agile that it was some time before the Allies realised how slow it was."* Like the Sopwith *Camel*, the Fokker *Triplane* had neutral stability and no elevator trimming wheel to facilitate level flight; its pilot had to pay constant attention to the horizon or he would soon be wandering around the sky.

By the beginning of 1918 the Dr.I was obsolescent, and its successor, the superb Fokker D.VII biplane, had been selected for production. In May 1918 the Dr.I was declared obsolete and gradually withdrawn from service at the front.

The Fokker Dr.I *Triplane* and the Sopwith *Triplane* did not see simultaneous service in France. In the Middle East, where the Sopwith *Triplane* also saw action, there were no Fokker *Triplanes*. As a result, there is no known encounter of one with the other.

CHAPTER SEVEN

HOME LEAVE AND A SECRET MISSION
(11 November 1917 to 29 January 1918)

The precise date upon which Roy and Stearne reached Carleton Place is unknown. Apart from a number of family photographs and four letters, there is little first-hand information available covering the period from 11 November 1917 to 29 January 1918. Howard Brown was away studying most of the time, and the file copies of the relevant issues of the two Carleton Place local newspapers, *The Central Canadian* and *The Herald*, were lost before microfilming began. Considering that they sailed on 17 November 1917, and Roy's outward ocean crossing on the SS *Finland* in December 1915 had taken twelve days, they should have arrived in Carleton Place somewhere around 30 November, Unfortunately Horace was not there to greet Roy because after recovering from his June 1916 encounter with a discarded bayonet, he had been accepted for pilot training by the RNAS and had sailed for England two months prior to his brother's arrival.[1]

Bessie, however, had arranged a few days off from her work as a registered nurse at the Presbyterian Hospital in New York so that she could spend some time in Carleton Place with him. Roy and Stearne's "secret mission" upset this plan.

Carleton Place
9 Dec. 17

Dear Bess,

I am very sorry you are unable to get home before the 17th as Stearne and I expect to leave that day for a short trip on business. We are going to Washington and will be home before Christmas. Could you not make arrangements so that we could come back from New York together? I would change my plans if I could but it is impossible. Perhaps you are in the same position as I am. If so, it is just hard luck and cannot be helped, but have a try if you can. Let me know as soon as possible what you are going to do.

The British public was unaware that from the beginning of 1917 the Allies had been losing the war. The Russian army was a spent force and the British offensives at Arras and Ypres (the third battle, also known as Passchendaele) had resulted in little beyond huge casualty lists; the most significant achievement was the capture of Vimy Ridge by the Canadians. The French offensive at Chemin des Dames, from which so much had been hoped, had failed and a large part of the French army would not obey any further orders to attack; the soldiers would defend their positions but absolutely refused to charge into entrenched machine-gun fire and be slaughtered. The Italians were not doing any better.

On the bright side, thanks to the combined efforts of Royal Navy Vice-Admiral Bayly and U.S. Rear-Admiral Sims, the danger to the Atlantic lifeline had been reduced. In June 1917 a commission of six civilian and military experts, headed by Senator R.C. Bolling, had been sent to Europe, and by the end of August had completed its recommendations concerning the best way in which U.S. industry could contribute to the war. It specified the types and quantities of aircraft, aircraft engines, tanks and guns, etcetera, which should be manufactured. A De Havilland D.H.4 fast day bomber and a Bristol F.2B *Fighter* were shipped to the United States for a manufacturer to modify both airframes to accept the 400hp Liberty engine which was just leaving the production lines. This specially designed engine was lighter than the 275hp Rolls Royce Eagle normally fitted and the combination of more power and less weight was expected to confer a significant increase in performance. The clock now began to tick against Germany and her allies.

The U.S. Navy, for its part, wished to use a portion of its fleet to blockade the German naval bases on the Belgian coast, and air cover would be required to protect the ships from attacks by German seaplanes armed with small torpedoes. Technology never remained still, and a German twin-engined seaplane able to carry a large torpedo was expected to come into service in the near future. The fighter squadrons of the Dover Patrol were going to be busy.

Washington consulted the Admiralty in London, and as it turned out, RNAS 4 Wing had the requisite experience and success in that protecting ships. It also had two fighter aces who knew the Belgian coastal area very well—Stearne Edwards and Roy Brown. The seeds of the Zeebrugge attack on St. George's day (23 April) 1918 and the later attack on Ostend had been sown.

Before Roy left England he had written a letter to Squadron Commander Norton at Middle Aerodrome, greeting him formally. There is really nothing odd about this as mail to France was often censored and a familiar greeting to a far senior officer might cause trouble. Norton's reply was addressed to Carleton Place, and from the hearty greeting we learn Roy's nickname in Naval 9. Roy incurred thirty-two fractured bones during his life, ninety percent of them in Europe, and probably as a result of some horseplay in the mess he had been living for a while with a finger or two in splints.

No. 9 SQUADRON
29 Nov. 1917
RNAS

Dear Old Fingers,

Many thanks for your letter, should have replied to it sooner ere this, only have been putting it off, etc.
Well how's the town using you both? Having a hell of a time I expect, photographs in the local papers! You shall see the ones we have when you

return, so that's that.

Fall has just got a bar to his D.S.C. and, given a bit of luck, I hope Banbury will get a decoration soon. By Gad, you know I wish that I were with you both, the place is damn quiet without you.

Give my love to all the priceless little girls, your own sisters, and other fellows' sisters. Best of luck.

*Yours always
Ernest W. Norton*

P.S. Don't call me Squadron Commander in letters and off the station, you know.

P.P.S. When you both return, if I am still here there will be a place for both of you in this squadron.

"Fall" is a reference to Flight Commander J.S.T. Fall.

Squadron Commander Norton's P.P.S. requires explanation. When an RNAS pilot went on leave or for a long stay in hospital, he was replaced by another from the RNAS pool at Saint Pol-sur-Mer. Upon returning from his absence he first had to report to the pool for assignment. A squadron commander could place a request that a particular pilot be reposted to his squadron, but there was no guarantee it would be granted; he could also request the contrary.

Squadron Commander Ernest William Norton, DSC, Belgian Order of the Crown, Belgian Croix de Guerre and French Croix de Guerre (nine confirmed victories).

With Stearne Edwards away as well, the Naval 9 officers' mess would indeed have been "damn quiet." Although Stearne was a non-smoker and teetotaller, he was fond of rough and tumble indoor games and could keep the place lively when the cards came out for a game of poker. Some years after the war, Raymond Collishaw described the poker games in the RNAS 3 Wing officers' mess at Luxeuil in the spring of 1916. Stearne Edwards and Mel Alexander had both been there at the time. There were three poker "schools". The first had a five-franc limit, the second a twenty-franc limit, and the third no limit. Stearne Edwards had learned the game well in his pre-war employment on the railways, and his long experience had turned him into a shrewd player; he was only to be found at the no-limit table. Players at this table had long ago exhausted their finances, so they made their bets in the form of IOU's; thus, the pot mostly contained sheets torn from toilet rolls and inscribed, for example, *"I.O.U. 100 francs."* Stearne, through his expertise, had amassed a wad of them, which he prudently kept in his tunic pocket in the daytime and in his pyjamas when he slept. If he survived the war and his debtors were both alive and solvent, he stood to be quite comfortably off. Collishaw thought it possible that some pilots had included Stearne in their nightly communication with the Lord, praying that he might be caused to make a forced landing behind German lines and that the contents of his pockets would be confiscated and burned. Gerry Nash, also a good poker player, was forced to land in German-held territory but his captors did not relieve him of his wad of toilet paper IOU's. He amassed more in the prisoner-of-war camp and took them all back to Canada after the war. In view of the circumstances in which most returned pilots found themselves, he decided it would not be gentlemanly to try to collect the debts and burned the IOUs; over ten thousand dollars' worth.[2]

Back in Carleton Place, Canada, Morton and Mary's family gathered at their home for Christmas. From nearby Ottawa came Morton's brother, Dr Clarence Brown, together with his wife, Mamie, and his step-daughter, Alice. One must assume that Roy's sister, Bessie, was unable to change her days off as she does not appear in any of the photographs taken on the occasion.

Roy with his mother, standing at the junction of Judson Street and Mill Street on a snowy day. The Mississippi River is just off picture to the right, and the mill can be seen between Mrs Brown and the tree.

In this portrait of Roy, the town hall tower in the background stands out well. The shadows show a military cap and a lady's hat, which suggest that the photographer was Stearne Edwards, but who was the lady?

Alice Pickup and Roy.

Roy with his sister Reta (Margaret).

Stearne Edwards (wearing heavy flying gloves), Howard Brown (age 11) and Morton Brown. This photo was apparently taken on a different day; the snow is deeper and more widespread.

Roy in his flying leathers—A somewhat unusual item to take home on leave unless he had been instructed to do so.

On Monday, 17 December, Roy and Stearne (both Apprentice Masons) attended meeting of St John's Lodge at Carleton Place where in a special combined ceremony they passed to the second degree (Fellow Craftsmen) and were then raised to the third degree (Master Masons). The Masonic documents identifying their new standing were printed in English, French and German a sound idea for members who were serving in Europe.

Immediately following the meeting, Roy and Stearne set off for Washington, D.C. with their flying clothes packed in their baggage. When they returned at the end of the week, neither said anything about the trip, other than that it was a military secret. The time frame suggests that the trip may have had a connection with information which the U.S. Joint Army and Navy Technical Board needed concerning the war in the air, the performance of German aircraft, and the quality of their crews.

On some presently unknown date and location in the United States, Roy made a flight in a Curtiss Jenny. The flight is not recorded in his log book and whether he was pilot or passenger is unknown.

Roy and an unknown U.S. Army officer beside a Curtiss JN-4 *Jenny*. In Roy's handwriting on the rear of the print is written,
"Just before taking off. The engine is running."

Another reason for the journey to Washington could have been the U.S. Navy's plans to provide formidable assistance in the air bombing of the German U-boat bases along the Belgian coast. The U.S. Marine Corps was also trying to get a foot into the military aviation door and saw itself as providing fighter escort for the navy bombers. The logical questions for Roy and Stearne would concern their first-hand experience with the defences of Ostend and Zeebrugge against air attack. Concomitant with Roy and Stearne's visit to Washington, Major Alfred A. Cunningham of the U.S. Marine Corps was in France visiting French and RNAS aerodromes in the Dunkirk area.

In those days, navies tended to think in terms of seaplanes and flying boats. However, the proposed bombing attacks on the German U-boat bases would place such aircraft within easy range of the latest German high-performance land plane fighters, whose capabilities Roy and Stearne were able to describe. In any encounter the chances of survival for the slower and less manoeuvrable U.S. naval aircraft would not be great, which meant that the U.S. Navy and Marine Corps would have to use land planes, like it or not. The information provided by Roy, Stearne and Major Cunningham would help these U.S. services to decide on the specific features for the aeroplanes that were to be designed and built for them. A fast bomber, such as the Liberty-engined D.H.4, would be needed, together with good fighter protection. The Liberty-engined Bristol F.2B *Fighter* was an obvious choice for that second task.

At the time these discussions were taking place, the Royal Navy had already made a decision on the best use of land planes at sea. Three aircraft carriers had been ordered and were due to enter service in late 1918. Like the Sopwith 2F1 *Camels* the aeroplanes on board would be fitted with internal flotation bags in case they were forced to ditch.

On 23 December 1917, U.S. Brigadier-General Benjamin D. Foulois submitted a report on the best ways to implement the Bolling Commission's recommendations on the development of military and naval aviation. One plan was the use of RFC and RNAS expertise in the advanced training of pilots. Initially graduates of existing primary flying training schools in the United States would be sent to England for advanced training. Later, graduates received their advanced training in the United States, and a number of experienced combat instructors were "borrowed" from the Royal Flying Corps to establish a syllabus suited to operations in France.[3]

All good things must come to an end, and by the second week of January 1918, Roy and Stearne were saying their goodbyes.

Halifax Hotel
Jan. 10, 1918

Dear Mother,

We arrived here between 4 and 5 this morning. Reported, and we go on board the S.S. Justicia today. She sails within   two days, so we are told. I expect, however, it will be longer than that. She is a comfortable boat I believe, and as there are several fellows I know going over on her, we should have   a good trip.
This is for dad about the sleeping berths to Halifax. I did not receive my checks at Carleton Place, so I had to pay for the berths on the train. If the checks are obtained at the station and sent with the enclosed receipt to the address on the back of it, the money will be refunded. Will you please do this, as there is no use in them having the money.

Surprisingly enough, the convoy did weigh anchor on the 12 January.

White Star Line
S.S. Justicia
Jan. 17 1918

Dear Dad,

This our fifth day but I do not think we can be half way across yet. We are held up by one ship in the convoy which is so very much slower than the rest. She should never have been in the convoy at all. There are nine of us in all. I do not know what the others are. We are the largest ship in the convoy. The Justicia weighs 32,000 tons and will do 18 knots, that is 21 MPH. We have 5,000 Chinamen on board who are going across as labour companies.

I went down below to have a look at the engine room. It certainly is immense. She has 12 boilers with six fires to each boiler. She has turbine engines and three propellors. The propellor shafts are immense, each section weighing 28 tons, and there must be ten or twelve sections for each propellor. It would be a bad business if a shaft was slightly out of line.

I cannot understand how people take an ocean voyage for pleasure in peace time. There is only eating, sleeping and doing nothing to occupy time, so it is very slow in passing.

I shall mail this letter from England. You will know by the postmark what date I landed.

It is likely that the SS *Justicia* arrived at Liverpool or Falmouth around the 25 January. This would have given Roy and Stearne a day or two in London and the opportunity to attend the five o'clock stand-by at the Savoy Hotel Bar to see who was in town, before heading back to France.

Flight Commander A. Roy Brown, DSC. This well-known photograph is normally dated 1918, but the dimples around the brim of Roy's cap are identical to those in the November 1917 photograph taken in London just before he embarked.*

Roy's Flying log book and 209 Squadron's records show that Roy and Stearne arrived back at Middle Aerodrome on 29 January 1918.

ANNEX TO CHAPTER SEVEN

(1) HORACE BROWN.

When Sergeant Horace Brown returned home in September 1916 to recover from the bayonet accident, he took his discharge from the army; after some rest, he applied for and was granted a commission in the 240th Battalion.

Second Lieutenant
John Horace Brown.

Horace Brown and Alice Pickup outside the Ottawa house of his uncle, Dr Clarence Brown.

Initially Horace was put in charge of a recruiting campaign in the Kingston area of Ontario, and his father purchased a McLaughlin motor car to help him travel around. The McLaughlin was actually a Buick manufactured in Canada by the McLaughlin Carriage Company, which claimed that the parts were fitted together with tender loving care, as distinct from being merely assembled. As a result, it was quite an expensive vehicle and had an excellent reputation.

Morton Brown in the McLaughlin touring car.

In September 1917, Horace applied to the RNAS office in Ottawa for pilot training. By this time the requirement that applicants must hold an FAI pilot's licence had been dropped. His transfer from the army was accepted, and he became an acting flight sub-lieutenant. On 8 October 1917, he sailed for England on the SS *Justicia*.

RNAS pilot training had been re-organized for the better since Roy's time, and Horace was sent to the Royal Naval College at Greenwich for the classroom studies. In early December he was posted to Vendôme Aerodrome in France to begin flying training, and by the time Roy and Stearne arrived back at Middle Aerodrome, Horace was practising "circuits and bumps" with an instructor. He made his first solo flight on or about 7 January.

Acting Flight Sub-Lieutenant J. Horace Brown. Note the RNAS "bird" on the left sleeve of his Royal Navy uniform.

(2) BRITISH AVIATOR'S HELMET AND GOGGLES c. 1917/18.

The helmet and goggles shown below are identical to those carried home by Roy.

British airman's goggles towards the end of the war, identical to these carried home by Roy in 1917. The clear lenses can easily be replaced with tinted ones to suit the weather and the type of work to be performed.

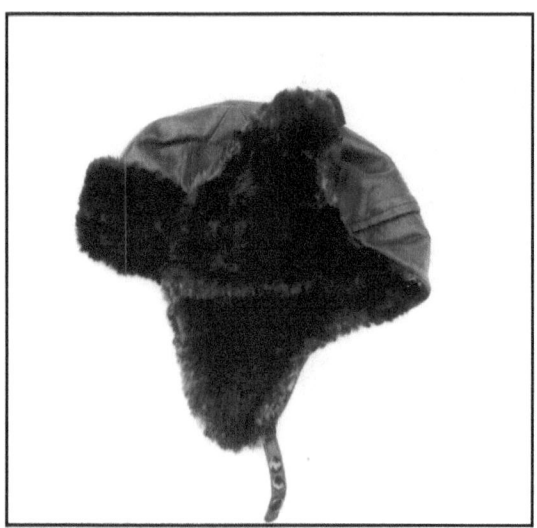

British airman's flying helmet without face mask. Roy presented one to his brother Howard after the war and he wore it every winter when he went hunting.

(3) THE US AIR FORCES IN EUROPE.

Following the deliberations in Washington, the U.S. Navy decided to send squadrons of bombers and fighters to France, which became known as the Northern Bombing Group. The D.H.4 bomber project proceeded well, and large numbers were shipped to Europe. The U.S. version of the Bristol F.2B *Fighter* was unlucky: a bureaucratic wrangle developed over control of the design and the manufacture and the project died. The single-seater fighters chosen for U.S. production were the S.E.5A and SPAD S-XIII, both to be powered with an 8-cylinder version of the 12-cylinder Liberty engine. However, fighter design was evolving so rapidly that the project was abandoned after one S.E.5A had been built, and the device was made to purchase the latest types as they left the production lines in England and France. French Breguet bombers were also purchased.

By the end of the war the Northern Bombing Group had grown to 112 aeroplanes, and the grand total of enemy aircraft claimed to have been destroyed by the U.S. Army, Navy and Marine Air Forces in Europe was 624. This number probably included "driven down, apparently out of control" or "last seen in a spinning nose dive," since German records indicated a much lower number, less than half.

End of Volume 2 of 6 volumes, ebook edition.

CHAPTER EIGHT

THE LUDENDORFF OFFENSIVE
(March, April & May 1918)

While Roy and Stearne had been in Canada on leave, the weather in northern France had not been good; consequently there had not been much aerial activity on either side. They first reported to the RNAS pilots' pool at the Naval Aircraft Depot at Saint Pol Aerodrome, where both were pleased to find that Squadron Commander E.W. Norton's request for them to be reposted to Naval 9 had been granted. Upon arriving back at Middle Aerodrome, they learned that Flight Commander Fall had scored six more victories, bringing his total to thirty-six; he had received a second bar to his DSC and been posted to England for a rest. The squadron had suffered no losses, but leave, promotions, hospitalization and rest periods had caused quite a shift around of pilots throughout the RNAS establishments on both sides of the Channel.

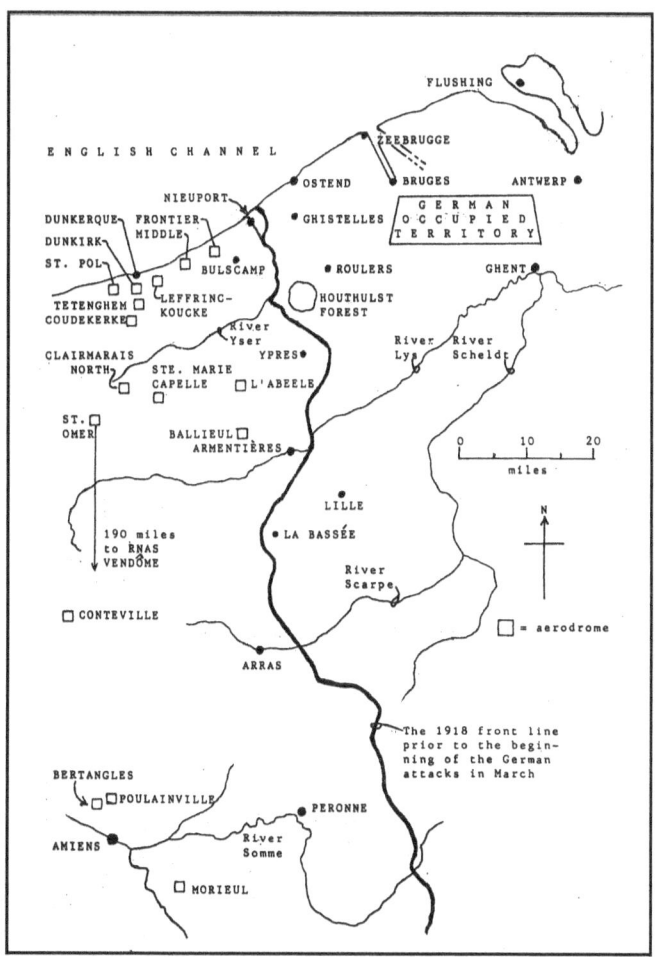

Towns and aerodromes on the French side of the English Channel. Saint-Pol and Saint-Omer were the RNAS and RFC main aircraft depots, respectively.

Roy and Stearne were happy to find that Naval 9 had been equipped with the latest version of the Sopwith *Camel*, powered by the new 150hp Bentley BR1 rotary engine and fitted with recently developed hydraulic actuating gear for its twin machine guns. These two major improvements could easily mean the difference between life and death in a tight corner. First, the additional 20hp provided an increased rate of climb, which, due to W.O. Bentley's improved methods of engine construction, could be maintained for long periods without the pistons and cylinders overheating. Second, the hydraulic connection between the engine and the machineguns eliminated the problems of thermal contraction, friction and wear that had plagued all the previous mechanical systems. Perforated propellers and mysterious jams could be a thing of the past, provided the ammunition had been properly manufactured and carefully loaded by the armouries into the disintegrating link belts.[1]

30.1.18 - 10.45 AM - BR1 Camel B3781 - 35 mins - practice

The arrival of the Sopwith BR1 *Camel* in France at that time was fortuitous. The Fokker Dr.I *Triplane*, now with properly constructed wings, was being issued to some of the German fighter squadrons, although a month would pass before it appeared in the north of France.

No. 9 Squadron
Jan. 30/18

Dear Dad,

Just arrived back here yesterday and had my first flip today. Got along O.K. It did not feel the least bit peculiar as I expected it would. My old C.O. Squadron Commander Norton has left and as yet we have not got a new one. Norton has gone to Cranwell in England. That makes a lot of difference as he was the best friend I ever had as a superior officer. The result is I have had my acting rank taken away from me. Whether I shall get it back under the new C.O. remains to be seen. Stearne had his confirmed. I am very glad he got it. We may be in England again in a few weeks. I shall let you know as soon as we do, if it does happen. The old squadron is very much changed. There are only four fellows here I know now.

We had a very narrow squeak coming over. The last day out a Hun U-boat tried to torpedo us and only missed by a few feet. The torpedo was so close to our stern that the wash from the propellers threw it out of the water.

I saw Horace in town. He has finished at Vendome and was passing through London on his way to Cranwell to finish his training. He looks fine and is getting along very well. I spoke to some of the instructors he will have about him, which should help him along some.

I was out to Skeet's last Sunday for lunch. My namesake is a fine, healthy looking baby boy. The situation in England at present looks pretty serious and unless there is a change, it looks as if there could be trouble. The labouring classes will not stand for it. I expect it will come out alright in the end. The British nation always blunders along some way and finally gets there.

I will know more about what is going to happen when our new C.O. arrives. The RNAS and the RFC are expected to unite before very long. I do not know exactly what that will mean. My next letter may be from England.

Roy's comment on the situation in England refers to the war-weariness that was setting in. Conscription had been decreed in 1916—something previously unheard of there—and food rationing was in force. The latter was a good move since rumours in late 1917, such as, *"There is going to be a shortage of potatoes,"* had caused panic buying and made the prediction come true. There were also rumblings of discontent in Germany. Food was short, and there was a rumour that meatless weeks were about to be decreed. In some cities, protest strikes against the continuation of the war were occurring.[2]

On both sides, the euphoria of glory and a quick victory had vanished; stark reality was setting in as the casualty lists steadily grew longer. Hardly a single family had escaped the wounding, gassing or loss of a father, son or close relative. In the year 2000, the Canadian playwright R.H. Thomson told of his five maternal uncles who had enlisted in Toronto to do their bit in the war: two were killed, two were badly gassed and only one was able to resume normal life upon returning home.

31.1.18 - 11.00 AM - Camel B3781 - 90 mins - H.O.P. - Nothing to report.

The new commanding officer for Naval 9, Squadron Commander C.H. Butler, arrived that afternoon. He had flown Sopwith *Pups, Triplanes* and *Camels* in twenty-nine sorties, both day and night, against heavily armed Gotha bombers in tight formation that were attacking England. He had destroyed or badly damaged about six and forced many others to abandon their target. His combat-success total is unsure because he never followed his victim down but pressed on with the task of ensuring that as few Gothas as possible returned to base. He was now being given a well-earned rest in an administrative position. Unlike E.W. Norton, C.H. Butler was a strict disciplinarian and followed superiors orders to the letter.

The new commanding officer rapidly decided that Stearne Edwards, who had been promoted to flight commander on 31 December 1917 while on home leave, should continue to lead the squadron in the air and that Flight Lieutenant Brown should continue leading A Flight. He advised the Wing of his decisions. Upon Butler's endorsement of E.W. Norton's earlier judgement, the wing commander promoted Roy to acting flight commander with effect from 2 February and informed higher authority. Although Roy was still acting flight commander, he was no longer local acting, and the promotion would become official throughout the RAF when it was published in the London Gazette.

Squadron Commander Charles Henry Butler, DSO and bar, DSC. Photograph taken in late 1914.

2.2.18 - 1.30 PM - Camel B7195 - 90 mins - Offensive Sweep - Dived on 2 two-seater Albatros. Members of flight not used to each other, so did not get any.

A co-ordinated attack was the key to success and revealed the abilities of a flight commander. While one or two members of the flight distracted the enemy, another one shot him down. In such cases, the victory would be shared. From Roy's comment it is fair to assume that a discussion on tactics soon followed. (3)

3.2.18 - 2.20 PM - Camel B7195 - 60 mins - 10,000' - Defensive Fleet Patrol - Nothing to report. Bad weather conditions.

The Wing decided that Naval 9 was due for a rest and refit in England, but their 150hp BR1 *Camels* should stay behind and contribute to the battle. Accordingly, on 4 February, Naval 9 and Naval 10 exchanged machines, which meant that Naval 9 reverted to flying the earlier F1 *Camels* with 130hp Clergêt 9B engines.

4.2.18 - 3.00 PM - Camel B6299 - 10 mins - Engine test - Clergets again. They seem poor after BR.

Sopwith F1 *Camel* No. B6330 with 130hp Clergêt engine used by B Flight of Naval 9 from 4 February to 19 March 1918. The Sopwith *Triplane* in the background belonged to Naval 1.

5.2.18 - 10.05 AM - Camel B3919 - 15 mins - Test - O.K.

02.15 PM - Camel B3919 - 45 mins - Offensive Sweep Returned due to clouds and mist.

6.2.18 - 10.00 AM - Camel B3919 - 60 mins - Defensive Fleet Patrol -

Dived on 3 aeroplanes. Drove them right to Zeebrugge harbour. Guns jambing all the time, so did not get them.[4]

When both his machine guns jammed during a diving attack, a pilot was in a difficult situation; not only had all the effort to position an unsuspecting enemy in his gunsight been wasted, but his intended victim had been alerted. The pilot then had to use the speed gained in his dive to zoom above the enemy and attempt to clear the jam while keeping an eye cocked for danger. To dive for home was not recommended unless the enemy aeroplane was slower than his.[5]

At the time Roy wrote his next letter home, he had not yet received the news that the Wing had confirmed his promotion to acting flight commander.

No. 9 Squadron
Feb. 7/18

My dear Mother,

Just received the Christmas parcel you sent. I also received several other ones. I passed them around the mess last night and everyone had a feed.

We have just dropped back into the same old stride since coming back. I have not managed to get a Hun yet, but have had a couple of pretty fair scraps.

The squadron is going back to England for a month to refit. Stearne and I are very fortunate to be going back with them as that means a month away from the war. We should go tomorrow if the weather is fit. It has been good weather till today but now it is raining and blowing great style, and getting colder. Yesterday it was just like summer.

We are to go to Dover and are supposed to have two weeks' leave while we are there. I do not know whether I shall take it or not as I do not want leave at present. It is just a matter of spending a lot of money and not having such a wonderful time; nothing like as good as I had at home, anyway.

I have been given a flight again. I am sure of keeping it as long as I can stay in France, so that means getting confirmed eventually. I wish confirmation would come soon.

There was a second advantage to confirmation in an acting rank—an increase in pay.

No. 9 Squadron
Feb. 15/18

My dear Mother,
As I wrote to you about a week ago, we were to go home to England for the squadron to refit on Feb 8. We have been waiting over a week now and have been unable to get away due to bad weather. I do not remember a spell of weather when we could not fly which has lasted as long as the present one. All our kit went to England on Feb. 8, so you can imagine the state we are in now without a change of any kind. I bought a pair of socks yesterday and feel quite clean now. This weather cannot last very much longer.
I have received no mail since coming back but I expect it is waiting in Dover for me. Everything stopped on Feb. 8 with us. As you can expect, we are pretty fed up with it all.
I saw a picture taken at Dayton when we were training which one of the boys has. It was taken after Stearne left. There were 37 fellows in it. Out of them all, there is only this chap in No. 3 Squadron and myself who are in France now. About 10 have been killed. Three have been out to France and gone back to a soft job, and the remainder have never been out at all. Two out of 37 still carrying on is a very small percentage.

Life in a front-line squadron was distinctly "roughing it," and it seemed that after the refit, Roy's reward for having successfully toughed it out for six months and scored six victories was going to be a further six months of the same living conditions. In view of the constant moving, the mess officer was having difficulties with food supplies and facilities. There were many complaints; one being that the whole place was dirty, but the dirt which got into the food was even dirtier. In 1958, Oliver LeBoutillier told author Dale Titler the story of one evening that he and

Flight Lieutenant Francis Mellersh found a shop in town which had a tray of freshly baked cakes on the counter. Mellersh wanted to purchase the entire tray, but the shoplady demurred; she would certainly sell him a cake, but one only. Mellersh made a sign to LeBoutillier to distract her, and while she was looking the other way, he seized the tray and hared out of the shop. LeBoutillier dumped enough French money onto the counter to pay for cakes and tray and joined Mellersh in flight. They ran helter-skelter down the road towards their motor transport while the shop lady stood in the doorway angrily screaming and waving her arms at them.

A happy group on its way to town in a Crossley tender, "the leave boat." Roy is second from right.

A genuine 1916 "French Postcard" from a series specially printed for British soldiers to send home to their pals; the grubby edges are genuine 1916-1917 fingermarks.

15.2.18 - 09.15 AM - Camel B3919 - 45 mins - Middle to Dover.

18.2.18 - 10.05 AM - Camel B3919 - 25 mins - Dover to Manston.

11.25 AM - Camel B3919 - 25 mins - Manston to Dover.

19.2.18 - 03.00 PM - Camel B6225 - 30 mins - Dover to Manston-Delivering machine to War School.

21.2.18 - 02.15 PM - Camel B3919 - 25 mins - Dover to Manston.

03.00 PM - Camel B3919 - 25 mins - Manston to Dover.

Sopwith *Camel* No. B3919 with Clergêt 130hp engine, flown by Roy on 5, 6, 15, 18 and 21 February 1918. After this Camel's delivery to Dover, its career steadily downwards, and it was finally scrapped at Chingford.

The RNAS operated a combat training unit at Manston known as the War School, and there *Camel* No. B3919 began its descent from fame to oblivion. Most current types of aeroplanes were to be found there, plus a few of the previous generation. Roy's chum from Carleton Place, Murray Galbraith, who had been awarded the DSC twice and the French Croix de Guerre, was serving as an instructor at the school during a well-earned rest from combat duty. Lloyd Breadner, also from Carleton Place, was among those who had passed through recently.

left to right: Lloyd Breadner, Murray Galbraith and A.B. Shearer beside Sopwith *Triplane* No. N5910 at Manston War School. In the background are two Sopwith *Camels*.

While Roy was at Dover, he was shown the Admiralty's newest toy—a Sopwith 5F1 *Dolphin* 200hp high altitude fighter. The pilot looked over the top wing and thus had a clear view of a target in front or above. It was such a formidable aeroplane that there were numerous reports from *Camel* and S.E.5A pilots such as follows: *"We were attacked by a large number of Albatros D.Vs and were being given a hard time. A flight of Dolphins came along and the Huns cleared off."* In most cases the *Dolphins* did not just happen by; their leader had seen a "help needed" signal in the distance, a coded pattern of white anti-aircraft bursts fired by alert Allied ground gunners, and decided there might be some trade around.

Sopwith 5F1 *Dolphin* No. C3785 was one of two purchased by the Admiralty to test type's usefulness. The shark's jaws and eyes painted on the nose would have displeased RFC Colonel John Salmond.

Waldorf Hotel
Aldwych, W.C.2
Feb. 28/18

Dear Mother,

As you see above, I am on leave again. How long I shall have I do not know, it just depends on how soon I get tired of it.

I went to a theatre last night and had a good laugh. I was at a couple of dances at Walmer before coming on leave and had a very nice time. Even though I cannot dance, I had lots of fun trying.

Stearne has had his leave and had a very good time.

I saw Murray at Manston. He had just had a slight accident, hurting his knee. It did not amount to anything and he is better again. He looks quite well and is trying to get back to France again.

We are to go back to France sooner than we expected; it just depends on when old man Hun starts his push.

I heard from Alice that Bess is coming over. I am sorry to hear that as I would much sooner she had stayed at home.

Just going out to tea now, so must close.

Murray Galbraith never did return to France. After his rest he was sent to the Italian front where he flew anti-U-boat patrols.

On 10 March, Allied daylight-saving (summer) time came into force and all clocks were advanced by one hour. Allied time was now the same as German time and would remain so until 16 April.

On 13 March, Squadron Commander Butler submitted a confidential report on Acting Flight Commander Roy Brown: "Recommended for promotion. Performs his duties as a Flight Leader with great skill and dash. Most efficient officer with very good control of men." Major Butler was recommending Roy for promotion to the substantive RNAS rank of flight commander (equivalent to an RFC captain). From there, the next step upwards would be acting squadron commander (equivalent to an RFC honorary major).

The German army in the West was deeply dug into heavily fortified positions on the high ground, and with but few exceptions, attempts at dislodging it had resulted in utter failure together with horrendous casualty lists. Economic warfare was now being tried, since without imports from abroad, Germany would eventually run out of food and material to supply its needs. 1918 was the time for the Allies to wait and build up their strength while the enemy weakened.

The USA had defined itself as a co-belligerent, not as an ally of France and Britain. By fighting as a separate entity, the USA would be able to make a separate peace with Germany if need be. This point caused some confusion in Germany later in the year when President Woodrow Wilson offered a basis for peace negotiations.

A new attempt to breach the German defences was being planned for spring 1919, in which 2 1/2 million fresh American troops of fighting age were to be added to the four million battle-weary French and British. In 1918, the priority was to transport the American soldiers to France, then to provide a temporary supply of French and British weapons and start their training there. Time was not critical; the Allied planners expected no final victory until spring 1920.

Like the US plans for building aeroplanes, the permanent weapons for the US Army, including several hundred French licence-built Renault two-man tanks, were to be manufactured in the USA and shipped to France over the winter of 1918/1919. The first half-dozen tanks arrived in France just after the Armistice was signed. All further shipments were immediately halted and production was terminated. At least two of these tanks are on public display as of this writing (2005). One is in the Eisenhower Museum at Abilene, Kansas; the other can be seen in action under its own power at the World War One Aerodrome, Old Rhinebeck, New York state, on flying days.

US-built Renault two-man tank engaging the enemy at Old Rhinebeck Aerodrome.

No. 9 Squadron
Dover
Mar. 15/18

Dear Mother,

  I have not written to you for some time as I have been on the sick list with a beautiful cold in my head. I just got up today at noon and still feel fairly rotten. It is on the mend now, though. I have a couple of beautiful, big cold sores on my upper lip and a red nose. Taking it all around, I am very, very ill and not expected to live through the night. I had a splendid time on leave but cut it short due to my cold.
  We are going back to France on Wednesday to the same place we were. I expect we shall only be there a short time then we shall move south to a more lively part of the line. This new Royal Air Force is making everyone sore. There are going to be a good many resignations as a result. I do not know what I am going to do yet. I shall wait and see how things go before I make any move. I shall have very little chance of ever getting a squadron now, though. I think I shall leave France some time next summer. What I shall do, I do not know yet, but I am not going to stay on in France. Someone else can give it a try for a change.
  I had a letter from Uncle Harry the other day. Everything seems to be going on alright with him.

The amalgamation of the Royal Flying Corps with the Royal Naval Air Service was to come into effect on 1 April. The RNAS was full of rumours, and no-one knew how his seniority would be affected in this new Royal Air Force. The highest RNAS rank was wing commander (equivalent to an RFC lieutenant-colonel), which meant all ranks above that level in the new Royal Air Force (colonels, Brigadiers and generals) would be ex-RFC personnel. The RNAS personnel feared that the ex-RFC "top brass" might be inclined to give preference to their own kind when a new commanding officer was required for an RAF squadron or wing. In some instances, that fear proved to be valid.

  Uncle Harry, Marion Brown's brother, was serving in Europe in the Canadian Army.

17.3.18 - 10.30 AM - Camel D7245 - 30 mins - Local - Test.

03.10 PM - Camel D7272 - 20 mins - Local - Test.

18.3.18 - 03.35 PM - Camel B3326 - 25 mins - Test - Controls had wire jambing them, intentionally or otherwise. Noticed it fortunately.

Roy's comment *"intentionally or otherwise"* may raise an eyebrow, but opposition to conscription and the continuation of the war was starting to manifest in several countries. Acts of what appeared to be sabotage were being noticed in the armed forces in England: and even the U.S. Navy was suffering. Rear-Admiral Sims describes how the inhabitants of Queenstown, Ireland, were told by political agitators that the American sailors on the naval base were to blame for the local food shortage; the truth was that all U.S. Navy food supplies came from America. One day an Irish official who should have known better complained to Sims; *"You Americans are eating us out of house and home."* Finally, after a number of assaults on his men, to which they responded in kind, Sims was forced to declare Queenstown out of bounds.

In France, soldiers of the Australian Imperial Force, while taking up positions to defend a village, were surprised to find the inhabitants rather hostile to them. The villagers' position was quite simple and most logical: their houses would not be damaged or destroyed if the Germans passed through without hindrance. In another village, the inhabitants encouraged their would-be defenders and their horses to depart, by removing the handles from the water pumps. To understand the local inhabitants' attitude, one needs to comprehend that more than one farmer in that region of France had already seen their homes destroyed twice, first in 1870 and then in 1916. According to M Jean-Pierre Thierry, Director of the Historial de la Grande Guerre in Péronne for many years, a particular farmer must have been born beneath a black cloud; his family home was destroyed for a third time in 1940.

No. 9 Squadron
Dover
Mar. 18/18

Dear Dad,

Received your letter of Feb. 5. You speak about the food shortage in England. The rations allowed are quite sufficient for anyone. I had not the slightest difficulty in obtaining food while on leave. The situation seems to be made out to be a great deal worse than it really is. Everything is terribly expensive, but you can get quite enough.

From what I read in the home papers of the first council meeting, it certainly does look as though you will have to sell the power house. It seems too bad now that it is on such a good basis. There is not much use in trying to do anything else, as I suppose whatever they say will happen eventually, anyway.

Abbott flew over here today to see Stearne, but he was on leave. Abbott is not going back to an active service squadron at present. He is wise not to do so as he is really not fit for it.

We are going through big changes over here at present as I suppose you have noticed in the newspapers; i.e. the RNAS and the RFC being amalgamated into the Royal Air Force. This is actually to take place on April 1. One thing it means is that I shall never again have as good a chance of receiving a squadron. In the new service I shall not be known at all and shall practically have to start all over again.

Please send me some films for a VPK Eastman. It is impossible to obtain them over here. I bought a Kodak when on leave and intend to take some snaps in France. There are plenty of interesting things to photograph.

I had a bear of a cold for a few days but it is nearly better now.

The pilot Abbott, was Lieutenant Robert Franklyn Preston Abbott from Carleton Place. In a letter home on 26 September 1917 Roy had written that Franklyn Abbott had been wounded. By March 1918 he was back with his squadron, Naval 3, but he was not really fit; extensive high-altitude flying had affected his lungs. He died in March 1932 from what was officially known as "Flying Sickness D," alias tuberculosis.

The letters "VPK" stood for Vest Pocket Kodak, a camera which used roll film. It produced twelve 2-by-3 inch negatives and, when folded, was small enough to fit into a pocket. This last feature was rather useful as it was totally illegal for anything in a military area to be captured on film, except by official photographers.

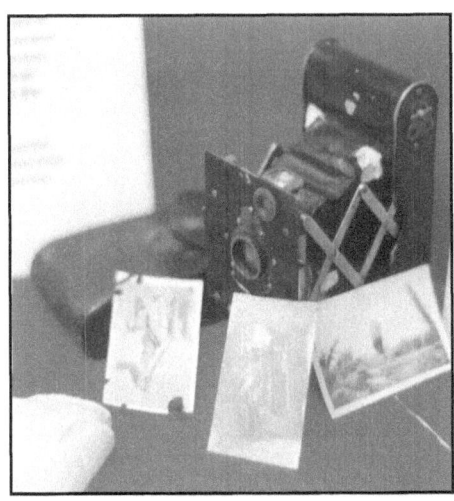

Typical Eastman Vest Pocket Kodak with carrying case.

One of the changes to which Roy referred was that many, if not most, Royal Flying Corps regulations and procedures would replace the familiar ones of the Royal Navel Air Service, Royal Flying Corps Order 1693.G, dated 15 August 1917, defined RFC aircraft colour schemes. Part One of this order stated that only khaki-coloured paint was to be used on all aeroplanes. Part Two, dated 18 August 1917, stated:

"Only the following identification marks will be permitted:

(a) National markings.
(b) The squadron mark on the fuselage.
(c) The machine number on the rudder.
(d) The flight mark, which may be either a single letter or a number.

Gaudy colours on wheels, cowlings etc., will not be allowed."

The final comment was a sore point as it restricted the individuality to which the RNAS pilots had become accustomed, and in the case of Naval 9, also prohibited their "trademark"—the distinctively painted engine cowlings. A Flight used cherry red; B Flight, light blue; and C Flight, black.[7]

Oliver LeBoutillier of Naval 9 standing beside his pride and joy, F1 *Camel* No. B3883 with a Clergêt engine, in August 1917.
Note the brightly polished cherry-red engine cowling and forward section of the fuselage and the two-coloured wheel covers.

In preparation for returning to France, where it was again to be attached to the Royal Flying Corps, Naval 9 received twelve BR1 *Camels*. Six were to come later, bringing the squadron to full strength (fifteen plus three spare machines). The twelve *Camels* were allocated as follows:

> B7273 Squadron Commander C.H. Butler
> B7199 Flight Commander S.T. Edwards
> B7270 Flight Commander A.R. Brown
> D3332 Flight Commander O.C. LeBoutillier
> B7245 Flight Lieutenant F.J.W Mellersh
> B7250 Flight Lieutenant O.W. Redgate
> B7247 Flight Lieutenant F.E. Banbury
> D3326 Flight Sub-Lieutenant A.R. McAfee

B7249 Flight Sub-Lieutenant W.N. Cumming
B7200 Flight Sub-Lieutenant M.S. Taylor
B7272 Flight Sub-Lieutenant M.A. Harker
D3328 Flight Sub-Lieutenant A.P. Squire

19.3.18 - 10.10 AM - Camel B7270 - 10 mins - Test - Engine cut out on pressure.

Roy's comment meant that once again a failure had occurred with the system of maintaining pressure in the main fuel tank. Provided a *Camel* pilot kept the nose down to maintain air speed, the wind force on the propeller would keep the engine turning while he changed over to the reserve fuel tank, which was mounted high enough to feed the engine by gravity. As explained earlier, apart from staying calm, success depended upon having sufficient altitude above ground to glide for eight to ten seconds.

As far as the war was concerned, there were ominous signs that the expected German attack was about to be launched. Russia had dropped out of the war and Germany had transferred huge forces, said to be a million men, to the Western Front to the point that Germany now held a considerable numerical advantage in divisions over the Allied armies. According to historian Sir Basil Liddell Hart, the German strength at one time reached 208 divisions. To oppose them, the French had 99 divisions and the British 58. There were also four and a half divisions of the American Expeditionary Force in training. Each American division held twice the number of men as a European division; therefore, their total force could be counted as having the value of nine divisions.

From spring 1915 to February 1918, the German army in the west had mainly been on the defensive while a decision was forced in the east. The battles of the Somme (1916), Chemin des Dames, Arras (1917) and the third battle of Ypres (1917), also known as Passchendaele (1917), were major Allied attempts to break through the German defences; all were costly failures. Although the Germans had been heavily outnumbered on those occasions, they had held the high ground and had been deeply dug in.

Naval 9 was ordered to wait at Middle Aerodrome until the

Royal Flying Corps decided where its presence was best needed.

20.3.18 - 03.10 PM - Camel B7270 - 75 mins - Dover to Middle Drome - Shelled by destroyers during fight off coast. 4 enemy destroyers sunk.

In 1917, the French and British had suffered such heavy losses in futile assaults on the German defences that towards the end of the year, both governments agreed that the best strategy would be to use 1918 to gather strength while the blockade weakened the Central Powers; then, in the spring of 1919, they would mount a combined French, British and American offensive. In accordance with this plan, the British government retained the newly formed divisions of conscripts in England, a decision which would cost Lieutenant-General Gough his command and almost lose the war.[8]

The German high command was well aware that shortages of material and food were sapping the country's strength; the longer the war continued, the more likely Germany would lose. It was decided to stake all on one throw of the dice, and in order to obtain sufficient food for General Ludendorff's armies in France, the government further reduced civilian food rations, which caused much public discontent and also created great hardship for prisoners of war. It has been said, and ex-prisoner-of-war Flight lieutenant Gerry Nash swore it was true, that flour used for baking bread in Germany was adulterated with sawdust to make it go further. This may explain the post-war belief held by some in England that "ersatz," was German for "sawdust." The word actually means "substitute."

At dawn on 21 March 1918, during a dense fog, forty German divisions sallied out from their strong defensive positions. They advanced onto the plains and attacked the sector of the front held by Lieutenant-General Sir Hubert Gough's Fifth Army; in doing so, they sowed the seeds of their own defeat. Maréchal Foch and General Haig reckoned that if the Allies could blunt the assault and then hold the German troops in exposed and therefore difficult-to-defend positions, the boot would be on the other foot. This time the Allies would hold the high ground, thereby making it possible to defeat the German forces and end the war that very same year.

Unfortunately, Hubert Gough had but fourteen divisions with

which to oppose them, and his reserves would take three days to arrive. If the Germans reached Amiens, the big city on the River Somme through which the railways from Abbeville on the coast and from Paris carried supplies and reinforcements to the armies under Field Marshal Sir Douglas Haig's command, the consequences would be grave. Not only would the British Expeditionary Force and the Australian Imperial Force be cut off from their supplies, but they would also be separated from the French Third Army on their south by a deep wedge of German troops. Maréchal Foch recognized the danger, but could the French reserves reach General Gough in time? If Foch failed, the British Fifth Army would be forced to retreat along its supply lines back to the ports on the English Channel, and the Dunkirk evacuation of the Second World War could have happened twenty-two years earlier. In his book Memories General Ludendorff describes the hope that such a victory would open the way to a satisfactory negotiated peace before the Allied naval blockade caused food and raw materials in Germany to be exhausted; otherwise, all would be lost.

For the Allies, the general situation was also grim. Despite the adoption of the convoy system and American naval help, shipping losses were still heavy, and the British Admiralty had warned the government that unless the submarines, destroyers and seaplanes of the German Navy could be cleared within a month or two from Ostend, Zeebrugge and other places on the Belgian coast, severe shortages of food and munitions would start to occur. The French Army was still recovering from the mutinies which had followed the disastrous Nivelle offensive at Chemin des Dames the year before, and to find troops to help the British, Maréchal Foch would need to "rob Peter to pay Paul." General Pershing, whose directive was to assist the French (the British were not mentioned), was unwilling to go beyond his instructions and send a division or two of his untrained troops to be slaughtered by experts. The Allies were running very close to losing the war, although this did not become known outside tight government circles until the official documents of the time were released fifty years later.

21.3.18 - 03.10 PM - Camel B7270 - 20 mins - Gun test - O.K.

Shortly after Roy completed testing his guns near Middle Aerodrome, the advancing German troops tested theirs. Unfortunately the German guns were 24 centimetres (9.5 inches) in calibre and were pointed his way.

2 1.3.18 - 05.00 PM - Camel B7270 - 15 mins - Middle to Tetenghem 10(N) - Shelled out of drome. Twelve .5" shells fell in drome.

The strength of Naval 9 was temporarily divided between Naval 1 and Naval 10 at Tetenghem while 4 Wing gathered its thoughts. There was not much time as the Fifth Army had asked for all possible airborne help to slow the German advance. The RFC and RNAS were given orders to attack anything German, stationary or moving. The day bombers, protected by fighters, attacked the German guns and supplies. Fighters were hastily fitted with bomb racks, and when they were not needed to protect bombers and observation aircraft, they were employed in bombing and strafing the German troops.

Sopwith F1 *Camel* No. B2516 (code letter "I") of 46 Squadon loaded with four 20-lb. Cooper bombs. Note B Flight commander's pennants attached to the elevator-bracing wires; one is mainly hidden by the tailskid.

The term "strafing" tends to hide what really transpired—the merciless slaughter, with small bombs and machine-gun fire, of marching or resting men and also the horses which drew their baggage carts and guns; during the Great War a trained horse was considered to be a legitimate military target. Many fighter pilots on both sides were sickened by this type of "work" and after the war they refused to talk about it. Roy was one of them.

Rapid re-arming of Sopwith *Camels* in between strafing flights. The trolley contains loaded machine-gun belts and Cooper bombs.

Operational difficulties prevented the German Air Service from interfering to any great extent. German fighters only carried fuel for ninty minutes' flight, and each advance made by the army left their bases further away from the front. To provide effective troop coverage, the German squadrons needed landing fields with refuelling facilities close to the action. Levelling the recently acquired shell-holed fields and removing hedges between others would require a few days, and this work had only just begun.

The German officers in charge of the advancing troops soon learned that an enemy aeroplane which followed a predictable path was an easy victim for a practised machine-gunner, and as a result the losses incurred by the Allied fighter squadrons from groundfire were heavy. After the war Roy Brown sold to Liberty magazine the idea for a story, which described how eleven Bristol F.2B *Fighters* were shot down in such attacks. A.H. Cobby of 4 Squadron, Australian Flying Corps, wrote in his memoirs how a 20 Squadron Bristol F.2B *Fighter* with a Canadian crew had been so badly shot up while ground strafing that it had to make a most unusual landing at his aerodrome. Most of the wires which bore the weight of the wings when the aeroplane was parked had been shot away, and as the *"Brisfit"* lost speed after touchdown, *"it collapsed like a wounded duck."* On one occasion Cobby's seat supports were shot away, and he had to fly his *Camel* home in a standing position. To use the rudder pedals for landing, he hung his left arm over the edge of the cockpit and supported himself by his armpit. He managed to land without overturning.[9]

In a recorded interview in the 1970s, Captain Mel Alexander of Naval 10 Squadron described the work performed in late March 1918 as follows

> *That was the craziest business. Ground strafing was all right behind the German lines, but when they were advancing in 1918, we were ordered out to ground strafe the trenches where they were coming forward. That was why we lost so many machines in such a short period. Behind the lines, yes, where the Germans were assembling, but right at the lines, that was terrible. We lost a lot of machines. I was on it; I got badly shot up. The same with my flight, so we pulled out. I led them back about a mile and a half where we found bunches of German troops. We caught them without their machine guns ready. They were assembling, you see. The ground strafing of the line was just plain crazy. It was just throwing pilots away. I have never forgotten that. The losses were awful there.*

A pilot's skill or experience mattered little; flying low down in a straight line earned a wooden cross for so many. Another danger came from the artillery shells passing horizontally through the space in which the fighters were flying. More airmen were killed by such shells than was realized at the time because an explosion nearby occurred when it happened; the aeroplanes involved appeared to have suffered structural failure in flight.[10]

22.3.18 - 02.45 PM - Camel B7270 - 85 mins - Escort to DH9s - Could not keep up with DH9s so did O.P. Met 7 E.A. two-seaters over Houthulst. Dived on two, and got about 100 rounds in one when he went down vertical and burst into flames. Confirmed by flight. One bullet hole in my machine.

Roy was officially credited for this, his seventh, victory, over an unknown type of two-seater northeast of Houthulst Forest.

The steep dive described by Roy usually signified that the pilot had collapsed over the joystick and his body had pushed it forwards. The dive would continue with the engine turning ever faster until mechanical failure caused a fire or the wings tore off.[11] The aeroplane which Roy identified as D.H.9s would probably have been D.H.4s belonging to Naval 5 or Naval 6. The D.H.4 was faster than a 150hp Bentley-powered *Camel*; the D.H.9 was not.[12]

Note Roy's use of the word "when" "in the sense of "whereupon". He will do that again one month later in a log book entry which will become the subject of much contention.

On the same day RFC Headquarters issued Part Four of Order No. C.R.F.C. 1693.G to commanding officers of the first, second, third, fourth and fifth Brigades, 9 Wing and the headquarters of the RNAS. This part established the identification marks to be used by all fighter squadrons in preparation for the coming amalgamation of the RNAS and the RFC into the RAF. Naval 9 was one of the thirteen allocated a bar code; its mark was to be *"three vertical white bars; one in front and two behind the national markings."* The order, effective immediately, was explained as follows:

There is no objection to the change being spread over two or three days in each single-seater fighter squadron in order not to interfere with operations, but not less than one flight should be changed on any one day.

Not every squadron commanding officer considered this order particularly urgent; there were far more important things to do. Major Raymond Collishaw ignored it altogether.

23.3.18 - 02.45 PM - Camel B7270 - 60 mins – Photographic escort - Escorted French Caudron to Ghistelles. A.A. severe.

Typical Caudron G.VI of the French l'Armée de l'air.
Photograph taken at Bray Dunes in 1917.

23.3.18 - 05.05 PM - Camel B7270 - 10 mins - gun test - Started to go to lines without orders to look for Hun. Gun gear went out of commission and would not stop firing. Shot one blade nearly off.

It was fortunate that the station medical orderlies had been co-operative when Roy had requested a couple of yards of wide adhesive tape for the propeller fitted to his *Camel*.

24.3.18 - 02.00 PM - Camel B7270 - 90 mins - 16,000' - H.O.P. - No E.A. Piston seized causing terrible vibration. Thought machine going to break up. Glided back down from 1 mile west of Roulers, landing near Bulscamp. Boots landed to help me and crashed in a ditch.

Roulers was ten miles into Hunland and fifteen miles from the nearest Allied haven, Frontier Aerodrome, so from 16,000 feet altitude Roy might just have been able to glide that far. "Boots" was the American volunteer pilot, Oliver LeBoutillier, and seeing Roy's stationary propeller he had stayed nearby just in case a roving German pilot saw an easy victim. They both crossed into Allied territory safely, but Roy "ran out of sky" and had to put down in a field near the village of Bulscamp. Roy's landing was uneventful, but Boots would never forget his own.

Margaret, Roy's daughter, remembers her father telling how furious Boots had been at the time. Roy's *Camel* successfully rolled to a stop in a farmer's field, but Boots' *Camel* caught a wheel in an unseen hole, swung round, tipped over, and decanted him into a nearby drainage ditch. Boots was soaked to the skin and plastered from head to toe with slimy, smelly mud. Roy had to help clean him up the best he could before they removed the watches from the instrument panels and trudged off to find a telephone. Help arrived, probably from Naval Air Depot Dunkirk, and Roy's *Camel*, No. B7270, was pronounced repairable where it stood. Oliver LeBoutillier's *Camel*, No. D3332, was dismantled and transported to 4 Aeroplane Supply Depot at Guines. He received No. D3338, fresh from a rebuild there, as a replacement. Rebuilt No. D3332 was issued to 204 Squadron one month later.[13]

Meanwhile, at Sainte-Marie-Capelle the Wing had found a half-finished aerodrome intended for Handley-Page Types 0/100 or 0/400 heavy bombers. The aerodrome was "borrowed" for Naval 9, even though the landing field had not been completed to anywhere near its planned length. The worse part was the accommodation—filthy shacks used at one time to house construction workers. Roy, thanks to his involuntary stopover at Bulscamp, arrived there a day late.

Typical Handley Page 0/100 heavy bomber, No. 3116. The difference between the 0/100 and the 0/400 was mainly in the type of engines fitted.

25.3.18 - 01.45 PM - Camel B7270 - 15 mins - Bulscamp to St. Marie Capelle - Very short take off in field but got away all O.K.

The final four BR1 *Camels* arrived, and Naval 9 now had its complete establishment of aeroplanes and pilots.

26.3.18 - 05.10 PM - Camel B7270 - 80 mins - H.O.P. - No E.A. lots of A.A.

On 26 March, Naval 9 was allocated to the Second Brigade of the Royal Flying Corps. A brigade would be close to what is known as a group today. The Second Brigade allocated Naval 9 to 11 Wing, which decided to station the squadron at Bailleul. On the same day, Moreuil Aerodrome was overrun by the Germans, who had advanced far in five days. The RFC's 24 Squadron, equipped with S.E.5A fighters, departed in a hurry and found temporary shelter at Bertangles.

Also on 26 March, the British, French and Belgian governments decided that Maréchal Foch should assume supreme command of their armies on the Western Front. Field Marshal Sir Douglas Haig, who had been receiving conflicting instructions from government ministers and his superior in the War Office, was happy with the new arrangement and stated, "*I can deal with one man, but not with a committee.*" General Pershing's army was not included in the arrangement; the U.S. Congress had defined America's role in the war as a co-belligerent, not as one of the Allies.

No. 9 Squadron
C/O G.P.O.
London

Mar. 27/18

My dear Mother,

I am sorry I have been unable to write home as often as I should but we are working very hard at present, and when I have any time I am too tired to write. It will be worse from now on as after tomorrow we will be in it up to the eyes. You will know what I mean when you read the newspapers. What they will be saying when you receive this, I wish I knew now. Time and work alone will tell. I wish I could write to you what is going on. Needless to say, we have had some exciting times.

After April 1 this will be 209 Squadron and the address will be G.P.O. London, B.E.F. France. I shall no longer be a Flight Commander R.N. but a Captain in the Royal Air Force.

I shall write just as often I can. Do not worry if you do not hear from me as, if anything serious happens, you will receive a telegram.

All leave is cancelled indefinitely and likely to remain so until the big show is over.

Within the Fifth Army, organization was returning, considering the means at his disposal, Lieutenant-General Gough had achieved a virtual miracle. On the German side, an unexpected difficulty had surfaced for General Ludendorff—too much food and drink. His soldiers, who had tolerated their miserable rations in the belief that the British and French were worse off then they were, suddenly found cellars filled with wine, and shops and houses filled with far more food than they had imagined in their wildest dreams. The German soldiers tarried in the towns and villages, "liberating" sustenance, and nighttime drunkenness produced serious problems in the mornings. The hours wasted daily in getting the men onto their feet and moving again, plus the delays imposed by the efforts of the RFC and the RNAS, placed the German advance about two days behind schedule and gave the defence time to harden. Reinforcements from England and the French divisions sent by Maréchal Foch were able to move into position. Further German advance against the Fifth Army was stopped—for the moment.

On 28 March the battered Fifth Army, now reinforced, was reorganized as the Fourth Army under the command of General Sir Henry Rawlinson.[14]

28.3.18 - 09.15 AM - Camel B7270 - 75 mins - Ste. Marie Capelle to Bailleul - Squadron moved again. Attached to 11 Wing RFC.

The German big guns still had Naval 9 within range, so on the night 28 March the squadron moved its impedimenta, probably not yet unpacked, to a quieter location; the *Camels* were left behind till daylight. What Roy did not tell in his next letter home was that, having become accustomed to sleeping through the noise of guns firing and shells exploding, he did not discover until the cold, clammy, pre-dawn air awakened him that one wall of his sleeping quarters had been sucked down by the blast of an exploding shell.

Quite apart from the empty chairs in the mess resulting from casualties in action against the enemy, simple flying accidents accounted for twenty percent of the RFC, RNAS and RAF aircraft lost during the war. An ever-present spectre which haunted all pilots was the sight of colleagues injured, killed or roasted to death in accidents on their own aerodrome. A stomach-churning example occurred as the S.E.5As of RFC 24 Squadron shook the dust of Bertangles from their wheels after spending but two days there. All the aircraft had been fully loaded with fuel and ammunition to ground-strafe the advancing German forces in the north east, before turning for their new home at Conteville, twenty-five miles away to the northwest. After taking off, Second Lieutenant James Arthur Miller from Kona, Hawaii, a replacement pilot who had been but five days with the squadron, was circling the aerodrome, preparing to form up on his flight commander, when his S.E.5A No. C1789 suffered engine failure. During his attempted forced landing, which (judging by the events which followed) was crosswind, he lost control of his machine and crashed badly. Fuel escaping from the tanks caught fire, and then the ammunition on board began exploding. With cartridge cases and bullets flying in every direction, the ground staff were unable to approach close enough to help him. When it became safe, they removed what remained of Lieutenant Miller's body and buried it in one of the woods beside the airfield.[15]

On an S.E.5A fighter the reduction gear raised the centre line of the four-bladed propeller, and one could identify the engine, a 220hp French-manufactured Hispano-Suiza. The Lewis gun above the top wing was fitted with a thin ammunition drum holding forty-seven rounds. The fighter had a uniform application of dull khaki-coloured paint, the squadron bar code, and the flight identification letter, all as per General Salmond's instructions to the RFC.

No. C1752 a typical S.E.5A fighter of 1918, with Captain J. S. Smith in the cockpit. The four-bladed propeller meant it had a 220hp engine. One of the two pennants, which in RFC 41 Squadron denoted A flight commander, can be seen tied to the left rear interplane strut. This machine was usually flown by Lieutenant Frank Harold Taylor, MC, a Canadian from Toronto. Photograph taken at Bertangles on 28 March 1918.

29.3.18   11.00 AM - Camel B7270 - 30 mins - Bailleul to Clairmarais Nord - Shelled out of Bailleul last night.

Sometimes a typical crater on an aerodrome was not caused by a heavy artillery shell but by a bomb, such as the 250-Kg bomb dropped during an ingenious night attack on St Pol by a Gotha bomber in October 1917. With its port and starboard wing-tip lights shining, an unidentified aeroplane approached the aerodrome at an altitude and in a manner which suggested it intended to land. The majority of the aerodrome ground crew took it to be a large French bomber with some kind of problem, but one or two were suspicious; the beat of the engines was not quite right. Then came a whistle followed by a loud bang as a bomb landed beside Naval 2's tent hangars. Even so, some still believed a French bomber had mistaken their aerodrome for one occupied by the Germans and two French aviators came to investigate.

"Things that go bump in the night."
RNAS Squadron Commander John Foster Chisholm is seated centre stage near the edge of the water, accompanied by some of his officers and ratings.
The two not wearing naval uniforms are the French investigators.

30.3.18 - 12.15 AM - Camel B7270 - 110 mins - Reserve Patrol - Houthulst Forest to La Bassee - Very cloudy and misty. Came back in rain storm. Nothing to report.

31.3.18 - 10.15 AM - Camel B7270 - 115 mins - Reserve Patrol - Nothing to report. Very cloudy.

04.15 PM - Camel B7270 - 25 mins - Reserve Patrol - Returned due to rain storm.

At 2359 hours on 31 March 1918 the Royal Naval Air Service ceased to exist, and it is at this point that Roy's first Pilot's Flying Log Book ends. His summary of the flight time and combat victories while he was with the RNAS is entered in his own hand as follows:

Total Time in the Air: 231 hours.

Date	Aeroplanes Claimed Shot Down	Two-Seater Observers Disabled	Kite Balloons, Forced Down	Officially Confirmed Victories
23 June 1917		1		
17 July 1917	1		1	
3 September 1917				1
5 September 1917	1			
9 September 1917		1		1
15 September 1917	1			1
16 September 1917			1	
20 September 1917	1			1
21 September 1917	1			
29 September 1917	1			
13 October 1917	1			1
28 October 1917	1			1
22 March 1918	1			1
Total	9	2	2	7

Roy's summary shows thirteen successes in aerial combat, including a pair of two-seaters sent packing with the observer killed or wounded and two kite balloons forced down. Of this total, seven were officially confirmed by the RNAS as victories.

Observation kite balloons were so heavily defended by ground gunners that brave airmen flinched when detailed to attack one. For that reason, each balloon shot down counted as a confirmed combat victory, but one balloon which its crew was forced to pull down did not.[15]

On 1 April 1918 the *London Gazette* announced Roy's promotion to acting flight commander, and with Squadron Commander Butler's most favourable confidential report of 13 March in his file at the Admiralty, he was now firmly on his way up the naval ladder. There was, however, one complication: he was no longer in the navy.

Roy's second Pilot's Flying Log Book begins by defining his new position. The RNAS rank of acting flight commander was the equivalent of an army or RFC honorary captain; therefore, he describes himself as Captain A. Roy Brown of the Royal Air Force, belonging to 209 Squadron, stationed at Clairmarais Nord (Claire Marie North) Aerodrome. The squadron belonged to RAF 11 Wing, part of the Second Brigade. (Squadron Commander Butler's title changed to Major.)

There was going to be another change for the ex-RNAS land plane squadrons which had been helping the RFC: as they had ceased doing naval work, the Royal Navy would no longer provide their food;

they would henceforth be supplied by the army, which had a lower standard.

John Salmond, who had by now been promoted to general, was placed in command of the RAF in northern France.

This long-awaited opportunity to do something about his aircraft artwork had arrived, and he immediately issued an instruction that RFC Order No. 1693.G now applied to all squadrons in his command, and that only the red, white and blue roundels, the squadron bar code, and the aircraft serial number and flight number or letter should be displayed. To cover all cases, he let it known that only the official khaki paint was permitted to be applied to any part of an aeroplane and that all proscribed colours and/or works of art were to be removed forthwith, if not sooner. The ex-RNAS personnel did not see much urgency in obeying what looked like typical "office bumph" from a new commander; in their innocence, they did not expect the new broom would personally check that a clean sweep had been made.[17]

Sopwith BR1 *Camel* of B Flight, Naval 9. In that particular flight, the engine cowling and part of the metal sheeting behind it were blue. The broad blue stripe, with white edging just discernable in the photograph, continued around the other side of the fuselage. Khaki only would soon be the order of the day. Photograph taken at Middle Aerodrome in January 1918.

Marie Claire North. No. 209 Squadron. No. 11 Wing R.A.F.

1.4.18 - 08.40 AM - Camel B7270 - 130 mins - Reserve Patrol - Ypres to La Bassee - Nothing to report. A.A. on our side of the lines.

Roy's patrol had obviously encountered some nervous anti-aircraft gunners to whom any aeroplane approaching from the enemy side of the front was automatically hostile. Manfred von Richthofen wrote that he dealt with trigger-happy gunners by painting his Albatros a bright red and so advising the troops on the sector of the front where his *Jasta* (squadron) was stationed. According to Alexander Freiherr von Richthofen in 2002, Manfred had chosen red because that was the colour of the First West Prussian Uhlan (lancer) Regiment to which he belonged. Other reasons have been suggested for the colour. Would an aeroplane painted bright red be more intimidating than one painted bright green or bright blue? Support for Alexander's contention comes from the dominant yellow colour found on the aeroplanes flown by Manfred's brother Lothar; Yellow was the regimental colour of the Fourth Silesian Dragoon (heavy cavalry) Regiment to which Lothar belonged. At the request of Alan Bennett, German historian Dr. Ing Albert Niedermeyer verified the regiments and colours concerned. Dr. James S. Corum, Professor of Comparative Military Studies at Maxwell U.S. Air Force Base, provided the additional information that Manfred's distant cousin, Wolfram, painted his aeroplane predominantly brown; the regimental colour of the fourth Silesian Hussars (light cavalry) to which he belonged.

Distinguishing between different types of distant aeroplanes is not so simple as is generally believed. If the background is bright, the human eye will close down and the dot being studied becomes less distinct. After the war, it was remarkable how clearly some people claimed to have seen distant aeroplanes on a particular day, and ten or more years later they could recall both type and colour and could even name the pilot, but by that time one or more stories which included the event had been published.

On 1 April the symptoms of a strained heart, which Flight Commander Banbury had bravely been ignoring, finally caught up with him. He collapsed at the controls of his *Camel* about five minutes after takeoff and was found dead in the wreckage.

2.4.18 - 02.45 PM - Camel B7270 - 120 mins - Reserve patrol - Nothing to report.

3.4.18 - 08.45 AM - Camel B7270 - 95 mins - Reserve patrol - Clouds in layers 500 to 9,000' - A.A. and machine-gun from ground.

A major RAF base at Saint-Omer was only thirty miles from the halt of the German advance and was now within easy reach of German bombers; the letter could be well on their homeward way before the responding fighters reached their height. Even worse, Saint-Omen was within range of German heavy artillery. Planning was initiated to send most of the squadrons to aerodromes further west and to move the main RAF hospital for that part of France (9 Stationary) to Étaples, fifteen miles south of Boulogne.

On 3 April, Lieutenant Walter John Warneford, the equipment officer of the Australian Flying Corps 3 Squadron, was performing the preparatory tasks for a move south from Abéele Aerodrome, twelve miles east of Saint-Marie-Capelle, to Poulainville Aerodrome, four miles north of Amiens. He had completed a pilot's training course, but due to his flair for organization and things mechanical, he was found to be more valuable on the ground than in the air. His diary, which is quoted frequently in part two for this book, aids the understanding of the events of early April 1918, and in particular the entries for 21 and 22 April settle a couple of points that have been in doubt for decades. Walter Warneford was related to Flight Sub-Lieutenant R.A.J. Warneford, VC, who successfully attacked a Zeppelin LZ37 on 6/7 June 1915.

Lieutenant Walter John Warneford of the Australian Flying Corps before he gained his pilot's wings.

Walter Warneford's squadron was equipped with R.E.8 two-seater aeroplanes used for photographic reconnaissance and night bombing. The first version of the Reconnaissance Experimental "user hostile," and it is rumoured that some factory ferry pilots had refused to fly it to the supply parks. In single-seater fighter squadrons, some with a sense of humour said that R.E.8 pilots were afraid to stress their aeroplane for fear that the long upper wings would fold back and box the observer's ears.

Typical R.E.8 aeroplane used for photographic reconnaissance and night bombing. A wireless telegraphy transmitter for artillery-spotting duty could also be carried. Note the huge air scoop required to cool the engine. The object attached to the side of the fuselage between the engine and the pilot is a Vickers machine gun.

Detail of the Vickers machine-gun mounting on an R.E.8. The output of a Vickers at 10 rounds per second was calculated at 20 hp power; hence the strong horizontal bar to prevent the angled metal support strips from bending. The muzzle flash suppressor is clearly visible.

The R.E.8 was a development of the B.E.2E, in which (unlike the B.E.2C) the pilot occupied the front seat. Its centre of balance reflected its origin, hence the warning on both sides of the fuselage. Note the twin Lewis guns on a Scarff mounting.*

Using cockney rhyming slang, the R.E.8 was soon nicknamed the *"Harry Tate"* after a well-known comedian of the time who often featured in music hall (vaudeville) sketches in which his hopeless incompetence provoked utter disaster.

The fears of RNAS officers that once the RAF was formed, they would be swamped by RFC personnel and lose seniority turned out to be a tempest in a teacup, as Roy explains in his next letter home.

No. 209 Squadron R.A.F.
C/O G.P.O.
London
B.E.F.
France

April 3/18

Dear Reta,

Received your letter of Feb. 27 about a week ago but have been unable to answer it till now. We have been working hard and I have had very little time. We are more or less settled down now. Today has been rainy and we have had a chance to get things straightened away.

As you see my address has changed and also my rank. I am now a Captain in the Royal Air Force. The change has taken place quite smoothly, all things considered. Everyone has trifling grievances of their own which will be smoothed out in time.

We have been having some excitement here lately as you will have noticed in the papers. It looked quite serious for some time but the situation has greatly improved now.

I was rather surprised to hear that you have been toboganning again. I should think that you would have had enough of that. I guess I am getting older now myself. I never fool around in the squadron with the boys the way I did.

I have been pretty well since coming back and have not had cold feet at all as I expected I would. I don't know how soon I shall get them again though.

Stearne is quite fit and got a couple of Huns yesterday. I have got one since coming back.

On the morning of 5 April it was raining cats and dogs, and at 1030 hours Lieutenant Warneford set out by road from Abeele to Poulainville Aerodrome.

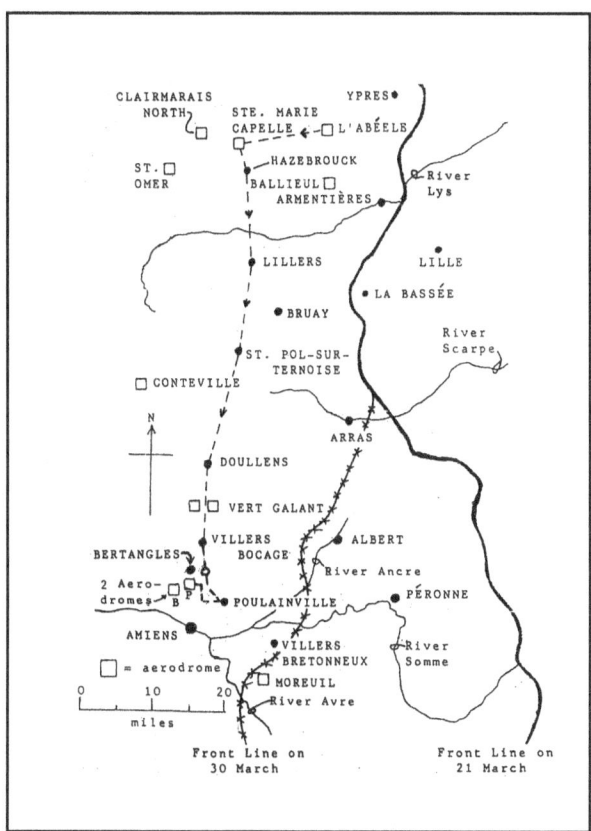

Lieutenant Warneford's journey from Abeéele to Poulainville.

The rain descended steadily as he passed by Sainte Marie-Capelle Aerodrome and then turned south onto the road for Hazebrouck. He wended his weary way through Lillers to Saint Pol-sur-Ternoise and then onwards to Doullens. From there he continued south through the big aerodrome at Vert Galant, which lay on both sides of the highway. An hour later he drove around the traffic circle at the exit for Bertangles and, ignoring the road which led west to the village and the aerodrome there, he continued south. A mile further on, he turned left (east) off the highway onto the sideroad to the village of Poulainville. In his diary he remarks, *"Terrible job to find our new aerodrome."* The difficulty is not surprising for Poulainville Aerodrome was nowhere near Poulainville village; it was situated on the west side of the highway directly beside Bertangles Aerodrome and had earlier been known as Bertangles East.

When Bertangles West and Bertangles East had been separated for administrative reasons, the apparently strange choice of name for the latter had been made because part of the east airfield lay within the municipal boundary of Poulainville. Warneford had actually driven past the exit for Poulainville Aerodrome, a narrow rough sideroad to the right (west) which looked like a cart-track, some minutes before he turned left (east) for Poulainville village. He eventually arrived there at 1830 hours, having travelled only sisty-five miles in eight hours.

Geographically speaking, Bertangles Aerodrome was five miles north of Amiens. It was one mile southwest of the village of Bertangles and lay along the west side of the railway which links Amiens to Doullens. Poulainville Aerodrome was on the east side of the same railway, and both aerodromes used the Bertangles railway halt, with its three sidings and unloading facilities, as their main supply source. The two aerodromes were employed by the squadrons stationed on them as well as by various other squadrons based in the Dunkirk area as advanced landing grounds. Aircraft would re-arm and refuel at Bertangles or Poulainville during the day and then fly home in the evening. The Germans soon discovered this and began to pay due attention.

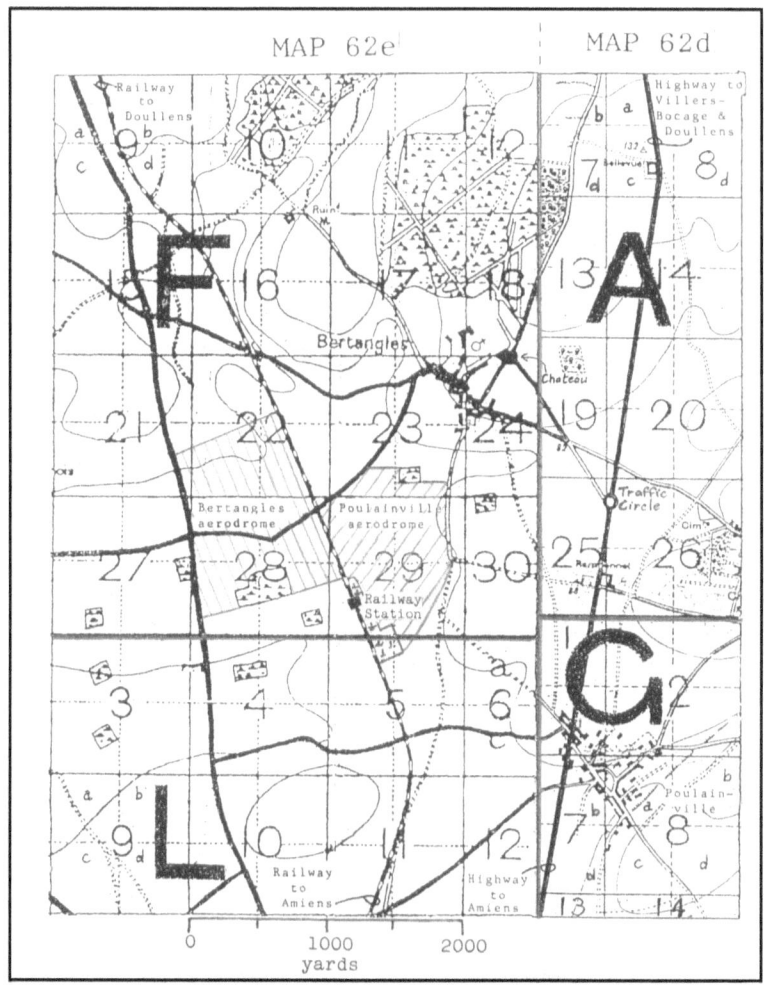

Portions of army maps Nos. 62E and 62D, juxtaposed to show the locations of Bertangles and Poulainville aerodromes in Squares F22, F 28 and F 29.

No. 209 Squadron R.A.F.
C/O G.P.O.
London
B.E.F.

April 5/18

Dear Dad,

Just received your letters of Feb. 24 and March. 10. So we are really going to lose the power plant at last. If they gave you $10,000 it would not be so bad. What are you thinking of investing in when you do sell?
We have had a rainy and cloudy day. It has been a blessing as we have a lot of work to get caught up on in the flight, so today has given us the chance we desired.
We shall have some scraps after this dud day as everyone gets a rest and is then full out. The more Huns around, the more there are to shoot down, if you are lucky.

Roy's daughter, Margaret, recalls one of the few stories about the war which her father told his family. There was a pilot in his flight who around that time suddenly seemed to be uneasy about flying. Roy asked him what the trouble was and finally understood that the fellow was afraid of his *Camel*. The pilot claimed, "At any little bump, even in level flight, the wings flap like a God-damned bird." To give the pilot confidence, Roy promised to keep an eye on his machine on the next patrol and was astounded by what he saw; the wings did indeed *"flap like a God-damned bird."* To have been able to eavesdrop on the subsequent discussion between Roy and the sergeant rigger of his flight would have been worth a weekend leave pass.

At the crack of dawn on 7 April the Germans attacked along the River Lys and in the Bassée Canal area. General Salmond decided to send 209 Squadron to Bertangles. From there the pilots could fly north to the Lys or south to the Somme as required by the military situation.

On a misty day with low clouds, an easy way for a pilot to find Bertangles Aerodrome would be to fly to Amiens, look for the single-track railway heading north to Doullens and follow it. After two or three minutes' flight, the woods on the east side of the railway should come into view. Then as he drew nearer, he should see Bertangles and Poulainville aerodromes directly below. Bertangles belonged to RAF 22 Wing (commanded by Lieutenant-Colonel Felton Vessey Holt), and Poulainville was on the east and belonged to RAF 15 Wing (commanded by Lieutenant-Colonel Ivo Arthur Exley Edwards). Both formed part of RAF fifth Brigade (commanded by Brigadier-General Lionel Evelyn Oswald Charlton), which was attached to the British Fourth Army (commanded by General Sir Henry Rawlinson).

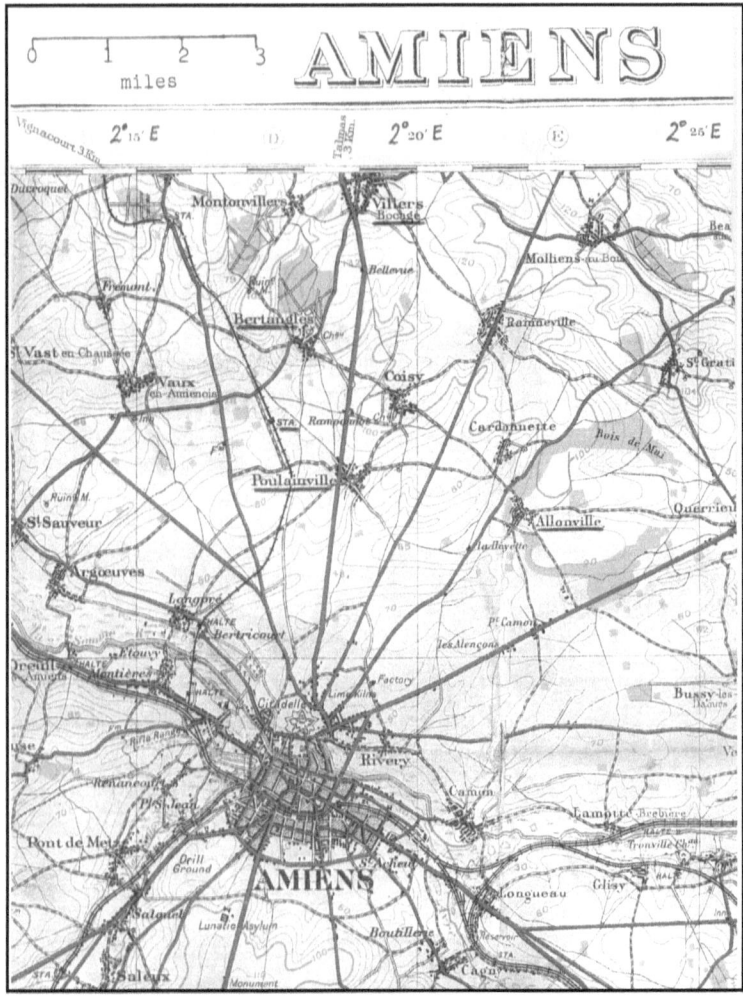

Portion of army map No. 17 which Roy carried in the cockpit. It was printed in five colours on a scale (1:100,000) suitable for pilots.

7.4.18 - 09.20 AM - Camel B7270 - 50 mins - Clairmarais Nord to Bertangles - Squadron attached to 22 Wing. Big push on by Hun. Guns firing day and night. Dud weather, misty low clouds.

When Roy arrived at Bertangles, there he found RAF 65 Squadron (Sopwith *Camels*), commanded by Major Jack Armand Cunningham, DSO, and 84 Squadron (S.E.5As), commanded by Major William Sholto Douglas (Lord Douglas of Kirtleside), MC, already in residence.

Typical S.E.5A. In flight photographs of that era are rarely so clear. This beauty, No. D6391 of 32 Squadron, was taken by Flight Commander Captain Callender. Note the position of the propeller boss, halfway up the radiator, indicating the presence of a 200hp engine and a two-bladed propeller.

At Poulainville RAF 23 Squadron (Spad S-XIIIs), RAF 35 Squadron RAF (Armstrong Whitworth F.K.8 *Big Acks*) and RAF 48 Squadron (Bristol F.2B *Fighters*), commanded by Major Keith Rodney Park, MC and bar, DFC, French Croix de Guerre, were in residence. The hangars of Australian Flying Corps 3 Squadron (R.E.8s), commanded by Major David Valentine Jardine Blake, had been erected and personnel were arriving; the aeroplanes were flown in later that day.

Typical Armstrong Whitworth F.K.8 *(Big Ack)* reconnaissance bomber fitted with a 160hp Beardmore engine. Serial Number B5751 belonged to RAF 2 Squadron.

The Amiens-Doullens railway passes diagonally from the lower right corner to the middle left margin, and Bertangles railway halt and the manoeuvring area for motor vehicles stand out clearly in the lower right corner. The "spear head" at the north end of the railway is actually chalky rock ground beneath a viaduct which goes over a road and a valley. The vertical support columns for the viaduct are visible on its left (west). The seven tent hangars used by the Bristol F.2B *Fighters* of 48 Squadron are at the middle right margin, arrange in groups. The tent hangars of 209 Squadron. at Bertangles Aerodrome are along the east side of the road in the lower left corner of the photo; the area immediately in front of them is devoid of grass. The southwest part of Bertangles Aerodrome is out of the picture, along the lower edge. What looks like an aeroplane, between the 209 Squadron hangars and the six hangars against the east side of the railway on Bertangles Aerodrome is actually a well-used practice air-to-ground firing target cut through the turf into the chalky subsoil.

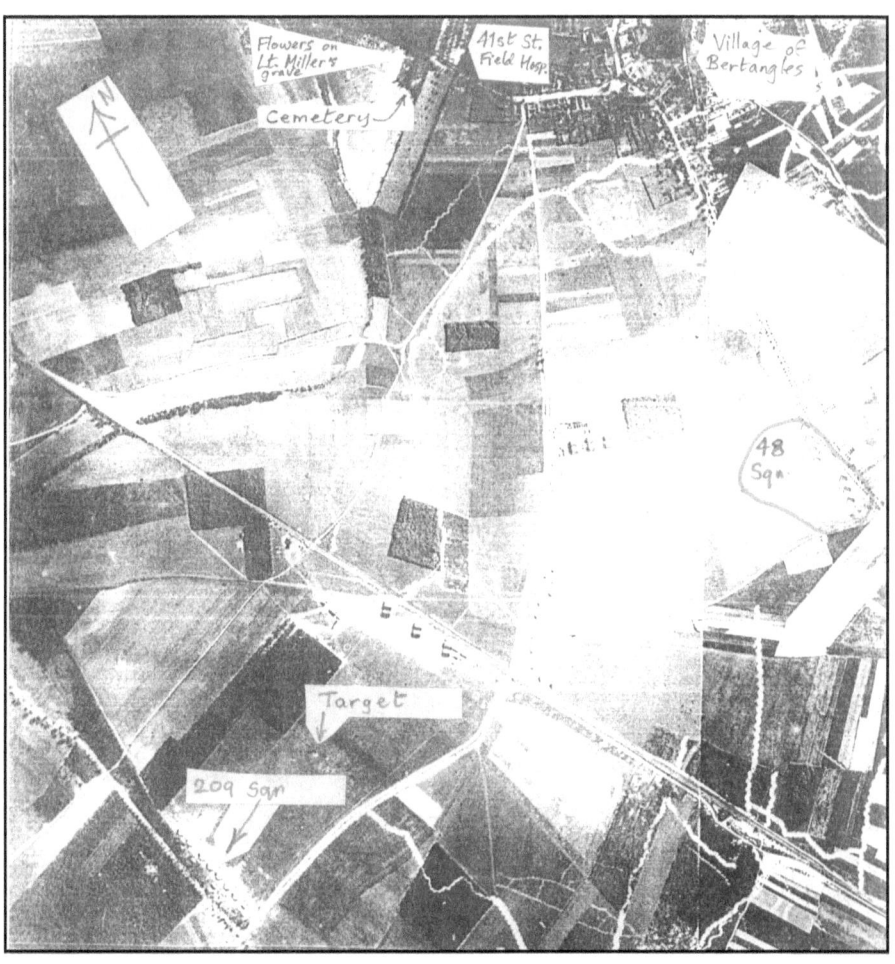

Bertangles (lower left) and Poulainville (middle and upper right) aerodromes in April 1918.

Bertangles Aerodrome, with hangars alongside the roads which form its east and west boundaries; 209 Squadron can be identified. Most of Poulainville Aerodrome is also shown, as indicated by the grouping of the seven tent hangars of 48 Squadron in the upper right corner.

Lieutenant Walter Warneford's diary records that the Germans heavily bombed Poulainville Aerodrome that night, and started a big fire. The purpose of the bombing was as much to keep the pilots awake all night and thereby lessen their effectiveness the next morning, as it was to destroy their equipment. Roy was to suffer many disturbed nights that month.

8 April 1918.

The distant thunder of heavy guns and the night bombing were the beginning of the second phase of General Ludendorff's plan—a dawn attack through the heavy mist north of the Bassée Canal. If his army could capture the town of Bruay, they would cut off seventy percent of the coal supplies to the French munitions factories. The Germans achieved great initial success: the Portuguese Expeditionary

Force was routed on the 8 April, and the British divisions in the area began a fighting retreat the next day. The situation was grave, for according to information received by Field Marshal Haig, the coal stocks on hand in France would only last five days.

At Poulainville aerodrome, despite the heavy rain which fell all day, personnel of AFC3 squadron erected most of their canvas hangars and tents.

9 April 1918.

On 9 April there occurred one of those cases which throw doubt on official records. An RFC Training Transfer Card made out in the name of "May W.R., Lieut. R.F.C. G.L." (General List, that is, no regiment) contains a departure stamp from 2 Auxiliary School of Aerial Gunnery at Turnberry in Scotland dated 31 March 1918. Turnberry is fifteen miles south of Prestwick. May spent a couple of days in London and then crossed the Channel on the leave boat, arriving at Saint-Omer Aircraft Supply Depot on 5 April (about right for his journey from Scotland to France). He was booked out of Saint Omer on 10 April and is listed as having arrived at 209 Squadron that same day. However, W.R. May's Pilot's Flying Log Book states, *"Reported to 209 Squadron on 9 April."* As if that were not bad enough, his Transfer Training Card, which he had to present upon arrival at Bertangles, shows him reporting for duty on 11 April.

Some twenty years after the war, Wilfrid May, whose nickname was "Wop," presented an explanation: he and the sergeant who drove him down from Saint Omer had stopped for "refreshments" and had become involved in a party; as a result, he had reported for duty two days' late. The authoritarian Major Butler, who did not want such an undisciplined officer in his squadron, declined Lieutenant May's services and ordered him to return to the RAF pilots' pool at Saint-Omer (formerly the RFC pilots' pool). On his way out of Major Butler's office, the chastened Lieutenant May had met his old school chum Roy Brown, who thereupon used his influence to persuade the commanding officer that May was a good type and could be straightened out. May's documents, which showed he had been an exceptional student at pilot training school, to the degree that he had graduated as a first lieutenant, may have helped.

Due to the conflicting dates, some have cast doubt on Wilfrid May's post-war story, but it quite accurately conforms to the personal characters of all three parties involved, and thus has the ring of truth. The two dates provided by Saint-Omer to RAF Records were most likely scheduled dates, whereas the Bertangles dates represented reality.

Allowing for lapses of memory and for embellishments to make the story more amusing, the dates do fit if Lieutenant May left Saint-Omer on the date entered in his log book, that is on Thursday, 9 April rather than on the scheduled date, Friday, 10 April. The availability of transport could have been the reason. He and the sergeant left Saint-Omer in the afternoon, and like Lieutenant Warneford who came from Abeele, they would have joined the highway to the south at Hazebrouck. Lieutenant May, unlike Lieutenant Warneford who was delayed by heavy rain, would have made better time, but it was still a slow journey with so much military traffic on the road, and they would have arrived at Bertangles too late for dinner. A possible scenario could be that Lieutenant May left his kit at the officers' quarters, intending to report to the orderly officer after he had found something to eat, and they then drove back two miles to Villers-Bocage where they had seen some open restaurants as they passed through. Apparently, in addition to food they found congenial company, and the meal turned out to be rather a long one. After all, May was not expected at Bertangles until late on Friday, which would mean no duty until the morning of Saturday, 11 April.

It has often been written that Lieutenant May and his driver spent two days in Amiens, but this would not have been possible because, due to the constant German bombardment, the city had been evacuated and a special pass was required for entrance. Furthermore, Wilfrid May said, *"On the way down."* Amiens lay five miles to the south, that is, beyond Bertangles.

Congenial entertainment for brave soldiers and airmen. Another 1916 French postcard sold to British forces, with genuine 1916-1917 grubby fingermarks around the edges.

In any care *Camel* No. D3340 was allocated to Lieutenant Wilfrid May, and he was placed in Captain Roy Brown's flight.

Historians have been plagued by another error in Wop May's military documents, which began when he joined the Canadian Overseas Expeditionary Force on 8 February 1916. On Attestation Paper No. 231048 his first Christian name was misspelled, and the error was copied onto all subsequent documents, including his Army Pay Book. Occasionally his second Christian name was also misspelled. Knowing the ways of the military and legal professions, he probably had to misspell, and his own name on official receipts in order to have it accepted as correct. On all his civilian documents, beginning with his birth certificate, his name is Wilfrid Reid May.

Lieutenant Wilfrid Reid May in Sopwith *Camel* No. B6398. The crash pads on the machine-gun butts and the Aldis tube gunsight stand out well. This photograph, from Lieutenant M. S. Taylor's album, is dated May 1918.

Second Lieutenant George Duerdin, a new pilot recently posted to 65 Squadron, obviously had not received so much training on *Camels* as had Wop May. At 1435 hours on the day of May's arrival, he made his first flight from Bertangles to practise circuits and bumps. Fifteen minutes later, watchers were horrified to see him fall into a spin at 1,000 feet and crash. He died in hospital that evening.

Roy's new area of operation from 9 April to 25 April. Only rivers

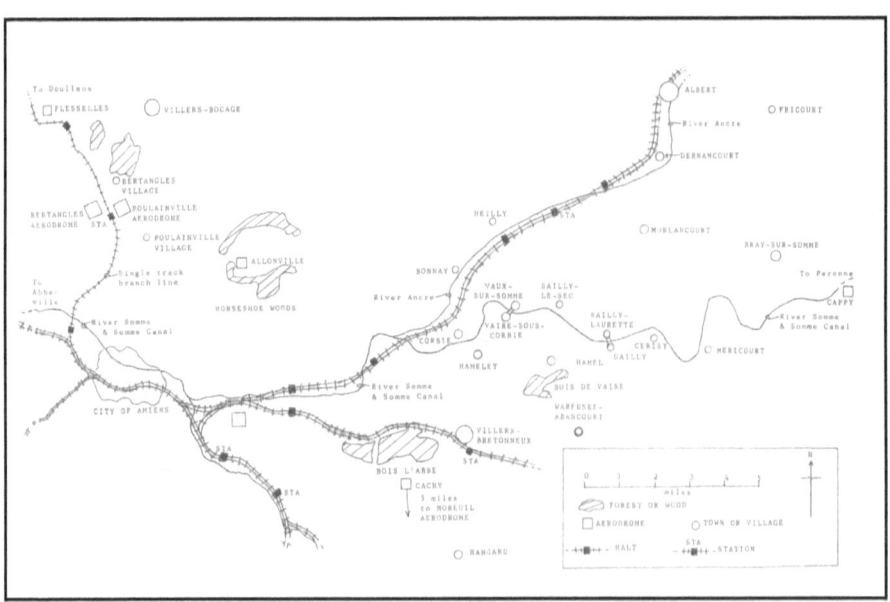

and railways are shown. Being mainly unmade, roads would not stand out clearly under the conditions of visibility from the air in April 1918.

The Somme and Ancre rivers had silted up centuries ago and had become marshland about half a mile wide. A canal, 30 metres wide, had been dug through the silt that had once been the River Somme, and barges could travel from Abbeville to over a hundred miles inland. The village of Vaux-sur-Somme on the north side of the Somme Canal is joined by a bridge to the village of Vaire-sous-Corbie on the south side; three miles upstream (east), the village of Sailly-Laurette on the north side of the canal is joined by a bridge to Gailly.

In the Somme Canal Vaux-sur-Somme and Vaire-sous-Corbie, and Sailly-Laurette/Gailly lie across similar looking bends in the Somme Canal, and on a day of poor visibility, a pilot could easily confuse one with the other. This could be dangerous because no man's land passed between them and on that part of the front there was little or nothing to mark it.

The marshland and the ponds alongside the canal, together with the high water table in the surrounding fields had made it impossible for either army to dig trenches. Furthermore, the German advance along the Somme Valley had been rapid and the fighting in any particular area had not been sufficiently prolonged for the familiar "moonscape" of no-man's-land to form. The buildings, trees and hedges were still standing and the crops were still in the fields. The respective fronts were defined by the villages and woods which were held by the opposing forces and this could not easily be determined from the air.

The weather was rotten all day, and the heavy guns of both sides thundered with loud voice all night.

10 April 1918.

10.4.18 - 09.00 AM - Camel B7270 - 30 mins - Albert to Hangard - Learning country.

10.50 AM - Camel B7270 - 85 mins - O.P. Albert to Hangard - Scrap with two-seater Albatros. Shot through petrol filter and was forced to land at Bois L'Abbe 1,000 yards behind lines.

Fortunately Bois l'Abbé was close to Cachy Aerodrome, which, although too close to the front for use as a station, still had emergency services and a telephone line to Bertangles. Arrangements were made to place a temporary patch on the damaged fuel filter after dark. The heavy guns of both sides continued firing all day.

11 April 1918.

11.4.18 - 07.25 AM - Camel B7270 - 20 mins - Bois L'Abbe to Bertangles - Mist and clouds 50 to 75'. Too low to fly over Amiens.

A replacement petrol filter for No. B7270 arrived that morning and while it was being installed, Roy used his flight's spare *Camel*, No. B6257, for his second patrol of the day.

11.4.18 - 02.00 PM - Camel B6257 - 140 mins - H.O.P. - Dived on 10 Albatros two-seaters. All of flight did not follow so could not attack. Chased four scouts but could not catch them. The two-seaters were bombing Amiens.

The railway station at l'Amiens was one of the principal German targets and had been shelled and bombed into ruins. The population of Amiens and the hospital had been evacuated some time earlier, and as a special pass was needed to enter the city, business was not good at Charlie's Bar or the Hotel du Rhin, the two restaurants and watering holes best known to the military.

Although 209 Squadron had suffered no losses in combat since the move to Bertangles, that afternoon Roy and his colleagues received another reminder that the sword of Damocles was suspended by a very fine thread. The charred remains of Lieutenant Miller were disinterred from the wood beside the airfield and reburied in a vacant section of Bertangles village cemetery which had recently been made available for airmen who had fallen in the defence of France. It would not be long before Miller acquired illustrious but in the eyes of the villagers, unwelcome company—the commanding officer of Jagdgeschwader (Wing) Nr.I, Rittmeister Manfred Albrecht Freiherr von Richthofen.

n this day, 11 April there occurred another of those incidents which throw doubt on official records. Royal Air Force Communique No. 2, covering 8-14 April 1918, gives Roy as sharing with Lieutenant Cedric George Edwards the combat victory of an enemy machine.

Lieutenant Edwards reported driving down an Albatros out of control over Albert at 5:00 p.m. on 11 April, but Roy's log book (above) contains no claim nor does it place him in the air at that time. At Alan Bennett's request, historian Stewart Taylor checked the 209 Squadron Record Book for 11 April and found it to be in agreement with Roy's log book. The entries indicate that neither Roy nor anyone in his flight was airborne after 4:20 p.m. on 11 April.

The research exercise was useful in that the squadron record book revealed what really did happen on that day. Between 3:30 and 5:45 p.m. Lieutenant O. W. Redgate was leading C Flight (in place of Captain Stearne Edwards), and Lieutenant C. G. Edwards had been one of his wing men. The combat report for C Flight, submitted by Lieutenant Redgate, described the action as follows: "I observed one E.A. sitting on Lieut. Edwards' tail. I fired on him making him turn. Lieut. Edwards fired into the bottom of his fuselage and I was firing at the same time. The E.A. was observed to fall over on its back and fall completely out of control (OOC). Lieut. Stovin observed this E.A. still out of control at about 2,000 feet." Lieutenant Redgate and Lieutenant Edwards shared the victory.

Bertangles and Poulainville aerodromes were bombed again that night. Flying at a high enough altitude to escape when it saw fighters taking off, and then returning every couple of hours and dropping an occasional bomb, a single enemy aeroplane could provoke the anti-aircraft guns into making enough noise to keep the Royal Air Force and Australian Flying Corps personnel awake most of the night—the main objective of the exercise.

THE MILITARY SITUATION IN MID-APRIL 1918

The German high command had moved a *Jagdgeschwader* (wing) of fighter squadrons to a recently captured, large aerodrome named Cappy situated beside the River Somme, two miles southeast of the town of Bray-sur-Somme. They were Jastas (Squadrons) 4, 6, 10 and 11, and together they formed Jagdgeschwader Nr. I (JG I), better known today as Richthofen's Flying Circus. The wing was equipped with Fokker Dr.I *Triplanes* and Albatros D.VAs and was under the command of Rittmeister (Cavalry Captain) Manfred Freiherr von Richthofen who normally led a *Kette* (flight) of Jasta 11 into battle.[19]

The Allied nickname "flying circus" for JG I came from its rapid mobility, and despite many tales to the contrary, it had nothing to do with the colour scheme of its aeroplanes. All the wing's hangars, stores and workshops were deliberately designed to be easily knocked down, transported and reassembled; just like a real circus, JG I could pack up and move overnight to a new location. The purpose of JG I's move to Cappy was to establish temporary air superiority in the Hamel-Corbie-Amiens area, where unpleasant things for the Allies were about to happen.

Before their advance on Amiens was halted, the German had captured and fortified the town of Hamel. The Allies were unaware of General Ludendorff's intention to cease a particular attack once the defence had hardened and then to transfer his assault troops to a new "soft" spot. On 9 April he had launched an attack in the area of La Bassée to the north along the River Lys, and when this slowed down, he began preparing an attack on the French in the Chemin des Dames area sixty miles to the southeast of Amiens. To keep the new objective "soft", he needed to hold the Allied reserves in the Amiens area, and the easiest way to achieve this was to deceive the Allied Supreme Command into believing he was preparing a renewal of the attempt to capture Amiens. An attack on Villers-Bretonneux 10, ten miles east of the city would do precisely that.

Along the north side of the Somme Canal, between Morlancourt and Corbie, stretches a long hill known as the Morlancourt Ridge. The German advance along the high, dry ground had been checked between Sailly-Laurette and Sailly-le-Sec, and Australian troops held the high ground to the west. From there, they overlooked the ground around Hamel where the German army had begun concentrating troops and supplies for General Ludendorff's diversionary attack, planned to begin on 23 April. The preparations were being hampered by Allied artillery fire; two batteries, the 53rd and 55th, which belonged to the fourteenth Field Artillery Brigade of the fifth Australian Division under Major-General Joseph John Talbot Hobbs, were a real nuisance. They were hidden out of sight behind the Morlancourt Ridge somewhere between Corbie and Vaux-sur-Somme, and at night these two batteries fired over the crest of the hill, dropping shells onto the German supply dumps and troop concentrations. Other field artillery batteries, such as the 108th, and a siege battery were also in the area, and when no specific targets were given, they all pasted the forests around the town of Hamel, where it was assumed that much was being hidden.

Manfred von Richthofen's command, JG I, had three tasks: (1) to protect the German troops and supply columns from the bombing and ground-strafing by Allied aeroplanes; (2) to enable two-seater photographic reconnaissance aeroplanes to locate Allied artillery batteries and follow troop movements; and (3) to prevent Allied daytime photographic reconnaissance aeroplanes from supplying the nighttime targets for the artillery hidden behind the Morlancourt Ridge. In short, the *Camels* of RAF 209 Squadron and the "Harry Tates" of AFC 3 Squadron were going to encounter strong opposition.

12 April 1918.

For the RAF 12 April was a glorious day; the weather was conducive to flying, and both sides took full advantage of it. Royal Air Force Communique No. 2 described the proceedings as follows:

The weather was fine all day and visibility was exceptionally good. A record number of flying was done, a record number of photographs taken, and a record number of bombs dropped for any 24 hours since the war started. A total of 45 tons of bombs were dropped. Enemy aircraft were active on the whole front, but particularly north of La Bassée Canal and in the neighbourhood of Hangard. 49 machines were brought down and 25 driven out of control. Two hostile machines were also brought down by A.A. and six balloons destroyed by our aeroplanes.

Roy's log book states:

12.4.18 - 07.30 AM - Camel B7270 - 120 mins - H.O.P. – Dived on 2 Fokker Triplanes. One did an Immelmann turn in front of me and I got in a good burst. He went down vertical and me after him. Burst in flame. Carried on vertical then pulled out and I left him at 500' gliding as if pilot was dead and machine naturally stable. Went down near Warfusee-Abancourt.

Roy shared this, his eigth, victory with Lieutenant F.J.W. Mellersh over a Fokker Dr.I near Warfusee-Abancourt. [20], [21] His conclusion that the Fokker Dr.I *Triplane*, which he had encountered for the first time, might be a naturally stable machine like the B.E.2C was incorrect. The wings of the Fokker *Triplane* had no dihedral angle, and there was no trimming wheel in the cockpit to adjust the tailplane; therefore, a pilot who spent too much time studying his map would soon find the horizon at a strange angle.[22] In the light of today's knowledge, Roy's statement indicates that the German pilot had control over his machine during the part of the glide that Roy had watched. Research by historian Stewart Taylor has indicated that the pilot was Leutenant Georg Wolff of Jasta 6, who was wounded in combat that morning in that area of France.

12.4.18 - 07.00 PM - *Camel B7270 - 55 mins - Protective Patrol - Protection to 65 Squadron who were shooting trenches during push at Hangard. No E.A. Wonderful barrage fire.*

It was on this day that Field Marshal Sir Douglas Haig issued his best remembered Order of the Day, part of which is quoted below:

> Many amongst us are now tired. To those I would say that victory will belong to the side which holds out the longest. The French Army is moving rapidly and in great force to our support.
> There is no other course open to us but to fight it out! Every position must be held to the last man: there must be no retirement.
> With our backs to the wall, and believing in the justice of our cause, each one of us must fight on to the end.

Bertangles and Poulainville aerodromes spent several hours under heavy attack from German bombers that day. Captain John Ingles Gilmour, DSO, MC with two bars, the senior flight commander of 65 Squadron, shot one down. He was later to became famous for shooting down five modern German fighters in forty-five minutes on the evening of 1 July 1918. The bombers returned after dark and in the moonless night dropped parachute flares in order to find their target. Bombs fell sporadically until 1 a.m. One "visitor" was caught by searchlights and brought down by anti-aircraft fire.

13 April 1918.

After an almost sleepless night, the pilots at Bertangles and Poulainville were able to sleep until midday on 13 April because of bad weather.

13.4.18 - 02.10 PM - Camel B7270 - 30 mins - Line Patrol - Showing new pilots position of lines.

Roy uses the euphemism "new"; the actual RAF term was "replacements." One of them was Lieutenant W.R. May, whose log book entry was: *"Line patrol with T.C. [top cover]. Visibility poor."*

In addition to the noisy nighttime "entertainment," the food situation had become difficult. The supply route from the British Army stores at Boulogne was now within German artillery range. Both road and rail traffic were disrupted by bombing, shelling and troop movements. Local food purchases became necessary, and the quality often left much to be desired. That day, Roy's noon meal was rabbit; he noticed that the taste was rather strong, but he put it down to the cooking spices. In the evening he was taken seriously ill, and it was probably Lieutenant G.E. Downs, RAMC, the 22 Wing medical officer, who ordered Roy to be transported from the station's sick quarters to hospital. From there Roy sent the regulation pre-printed field service postcard to his family: *"I have been admitted to hospital. I am being sent down to the base for a long time."* Roy had food poisoning; the rabbit meat had been contaminated.

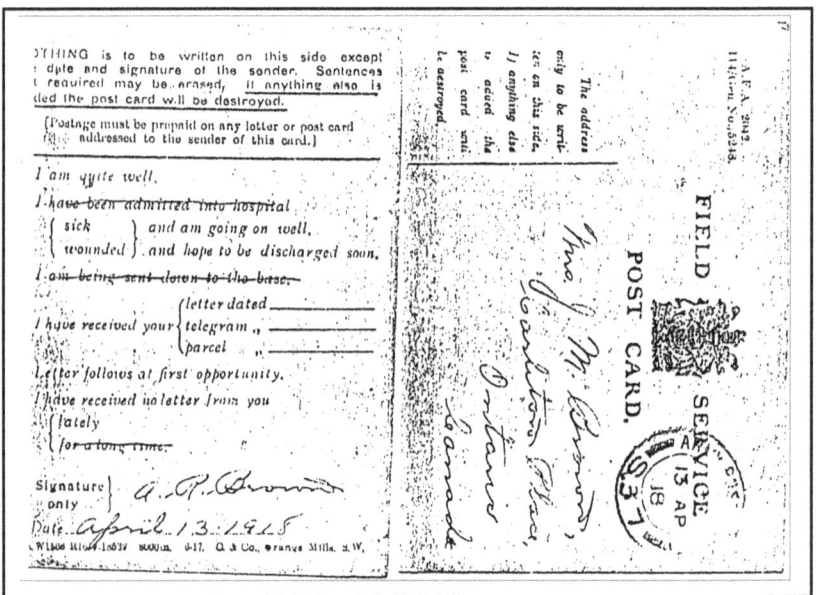

Field fervice postcard sent by Roy Brown notifying of his illness. The preprinted sentences, lined through, constitute the message.

The nearest hospital was 41 Stationary at Bertangles village and the short duration of Roy's absence from the Aerodrome (24 to 36 hours) suggests he was sent there. If a casualty card was made out for the incident, it no longer exists. All that Roy's daughter, Margaret, recalls of the incident is that never again in his life, under any circumstances, would her father eat rabbit.

The entrance to 41 Stationary Field Hospital at Bertangles was situated to the right of this pathway in a quiet pasture which had shade trees on three sides. On the fourth side, from which this photograph was taken, the view was clear but rather uninspiring. Directly behind the cameraman lies the village cemetery.

According to Mel Alexander of 210 Squadron, known previously as Naval 10, it was around this time that General Salmond discovered that the ex-RNAS squadrons in France had taken little or no action on his order concerning the removal of stripes, posters, names, red noses, et cetera, from his aeroplanes. He sent around a blisterer of an order, and most (but not all) of the affected squadron commanders began action that very day. Pots of regulation khaki paint were reluctantly withdrawn from the stores, and paint brushes were wielded even more reluctantly. Hats may have been removed also. Two squadrons are known to have ignored General Salmond's order. Photographs taken in May 1918 of the D.H.9s of 211 Squadron, commanded by Major Herbert Gardner Travers, DSC, depict them wearing black-and-white stripes; No. B7620 was still wearing them when it was written off on 27 June 1918. Major Raymond Collishaw, DSO and bar, DSC and bar, DFC, Croix de Guerre, of 203 Squadron went even further: not only did his *Camels* keep their decorative paintwork, but like Major Christopher Draper, DSC of 208 Squadron, he continued wearing his naval uniform until well after the end of the war.(23)

In the late 1950s, Captain Oliver LeBoutillier told author Dale Titler that the *Camels* in 209 Squadron had been among General Salmond's victims within the next day or so, the red engine cowlings of A flight were definitely repainted khaki before 21 April. Major Butler would have seen to that.

Roy took this photograph with his VPK camera and wrote on the back,
"*My flight at Bertangles.*"
The status of the 209 Squadron bar code, one before and two behind the roundel, varies from machine to machine, implying that repainting was in progress.
The stance of the second pilot from the front suggests that he is Wilfrid May.

A photograph of Roy and his *Camel*, No. B7270, also shows evidence of repainting, although the dark shiny paint on the cowling suggests that it was still cherry red at the time. The broad cherry-red V painted behind the cockpit had gone, but the V on the centre section of the upper wing was still there. The two round holes in the fuselage directly behind Roy's right shoulder provided access to the filler caps for the fuel tanks. The bottom end of the third white stripe of the bar code is just visible beneath Roy's right hand, but the roundel and the serial number B7270 are missing.

Roy Brown standing beside *Camel* No. B7270. Written on the back of this photograph in Roy's own hand is, "*My machine and myself at Bertangles north of Amiens.*" In many reproductions of this well-known photograph the small piece of the third white stripe of the bar code is very dim or cannot be seen at all.

Roy Brown with, "*My machine and the men who look after it.*" Lesser-known photograph on the same roll of film. Note the entire third stripe in this.

14 April 1918.

Due to strong winds and heavy rain there was no flying. German pilots called it "airmen's weather." Amiens was shelled again.

15 April 1918.

Roy was allowed to return to Bertangles, but aided by the continued "airmen's weather," he was grounded for a couple of days.

No. 209 Squadron R.A.F.
C/O G.P.O.
London
B.E.F.

April 15/18

Dear Dad,

I have been unable to write to you now for some time as we have been very busy. We have had two dud days now and I have been able to have numerous sleeps to catch up due to disturbed nights. Things are very serious here at present, more serious than ever before. Something will happen soon, though what it is I cannot say.

We have been right in the thick of it since coming out and have been very lucky. We are fortunate in having the best machine we could possibly get. We can still keep the Hun pretty well in his place in the air. His casualties in every way must be terrible. There is some satisfaction in being in the thick of it at the present time; to know you are doing useful work at the most critical stage.

There is very little to write at the present as it is all eat, work, sleep over and over.

I have got a new pilot in my flight who went to school with me in Edmonton. It is rather funny having him near me now. He is a good chap and will make a good pilot.

I receive the box mother sent and it surely is good to have my mouth full of coconut now, and so has Stearne. Everything arrived in perfect condition.

You don't need to worry as I am playing as safe as I can and do my job.

The serious matter to which Roy referred was the Germans' coming much closer to their goal of knocking the British Army out of the war; this was not admitted at the time, and the newspapers were certainly not allowed to print it. If the expected renewed attack on the city of Amiens were to succeed, the RAF would have to pull back to the supply depots near the Channel coast and would then be unable to provide close support to the army.

The new pilot from Edmonton was Wop May. Roy, of course, does not worry his father by mentioning illness as his reason for not having much to write about.

Lieutenant Wilfrid Reid May. His rumpled uniform shows the conditions under which 209 Squadron pilots were fighting, eating and trying to sleep in April 1918.

The German heavy artillery, which had the correct bearing, had not yet found the range for Bertangles and Poulainville aerodromes. The shells fired that night fell short but still served to disturb sleep.

16 April 1918.

Airmen's weather again, all day.

Daylight saving time came into effect in Germany, and accordingly, the German army, navy and air services advanced their timepieces one hour. (This was to cause some confusion in later years when German and Allied wartime reports were being compared for historical purposes.)

17 April 1918.

At 5 a.m. the German artillery opened fire on Bertangles and Poulainville aerodromes, and with the help of a two-seater wireless spotter, soon found the range.

By mid-morning Roy had recovered just enough from his illness to return to duty. Diarrhoea resulting from food poisoning was painful and inconvenient, but all experienced pilots, especially flight commanders, were urgently needed to prevent the success of the expected German advance towards Amiens.

17.4.18 - 10.30 AM - Camel B7270 - 125 mins - I.O.P. – Went in about 2,000 yards at 200' but could not observe any enemy to fire at.

On this date Brigadier-General L. E. O. Charlton, DSC, General Officer Commanding the RAF fifth Brigade, to which 209 Squadron belonged, submitted a memorandum to Royal Air Force Headquarters, supporting Major Butler's confidential report of 13 March on Roy. The memorandum said, "Recommended for promotion to Squadron Commander."

The position of an RAF squadron commander carried with it the rank of major, as in the old Royal Flying Corps.

During the night the Germans bombed and shelled Amiens and the aerodromes at Bertangles and Poulainville.

18 April 1918.

The next day dawned fine but the wind was strong, which were a pleasant change from the dull, rainy, and gusty weather of the past five days. Lieutenant Gould-Taylor (pilot) and Lieutenant Albert Lawrence Dean Taylor (observer) of AFC 3 Squadron attempted to take off on a bombing raid, but the strong wind caused the pilot to lose control and the R.E.8 turned over. The two men were not injured but the aeroplane was wrecked. That ended flying for the day at both aerodromes.

German bombers were overhead again during the night. One was caught by a searchlight, and anti-aircraft guns barked their loud objections, but the pilot twisted out of the beam and escaped.

19 April 1918.

Still suffering from the after-effects of food poisoning, which were now aggravated by lack of sleep, Roy was approaching physical exhaustion, but whishing not to let down his colleagues and the suffering Tommies, he did not report sick. He was living on milk and brandy, a diet that could not continue for many days.

The news that Roy Brown was ill and due to be rested reached his old RNAS friends. Major Raymond Collishaw, now the commanding officer of 203 Squadron, flew over to see him the next day and found the news to be true. The contaminated rabbit meal had left Roy with periodic intestinal cramps, and he did not look at all well.

Middle row, centre: Major Raymond Collishaw, DSO and bar, DSC and bar, DFC, Croix de Guerre, Commanding Officer of RAF 203 Squadron wearing RNAS blue uniform. Note the khaki RFC uniform *(rear, left)* and the assortment of Army and RNAS khaki uniforms.*

Major Collishaw advised Roy to confine himself to his ground duties until his resting order arrived. Unfortunately, Roy's commanding officer was Major Butler, not Major Collishaw, and even worse, it was known that the renewal of the German drive to capture Amiens would start any day now. Every pilot able to fly would urgently be needed in the air.

For similar reasons, the German ace fighter pilot Rittmeister Manfred von Richthofen, who had not yet fully recovered from his 1917 head wound, had returned to duty some weeks before. The following morning he and Roy would meet in the air.

Over the previous days Roy had been introducing his old school chum, Wop May, to the daily routine. On 20 April he twice took him across the lines, and during the morning patrol Wop fired his guns at the enemy for the first time.[24]

On this date, 9 Stationary Field Hospital began its move from St Omer to Étaples where 24 General Hospital (operated by the Order of St John) and 7 Stationary Hospital were located. Étaples, having a deep water harbour on the estuary of the River Canche, was directly accessible to hospital ships which could transport the serious cases to base hospitals in England.

It was a fine, moonlit night. German bombers flew over Bertangles and Poulainville every two hours, each time dropping sufficient bombs to provoke the anti-aircraft gun crews into working hard, and thereby kept the RAF and AFC personnel awake. After a night like that, the pilots had to rise before dawn and start work at 7:00 a.m.

Cleaning up after the "visitors" had departed. The overturned aeroplane was an R.E.8 of AFC 3 Squadron.

20 April 1918.

20.4.18 - 10.00 AM - Camel B7270 - 120 mins - H.O.P. – Dived on 7 triplanes. One I was firing on went over on its back side-slipping out and went down into clouds side-slipping and stalling.

Although this was Roy's fifteenth combat success, he was not credited with a victory because he did not see the enemy aircraft crash, nor were there any witnesses.

20.4.18 - 5.45 PM - Camel B7270 - 105 mins - I.O.P. – Nothing to report.

Margaret Brown Harmon recalls another of the few comments which her father made to his family concerning the war: some of the pilots who passed through the flights which he commanded were over-eager, and they created for him the unpleasant task of declining to endorse victories claimed on rather flimsy evidence. Basically it was a case of Roy following the general rule: no witness, no credit.

On the same day General Sir William Birdwood visited the squadrons at Poulainville. He was the commander of the Australian Corps until May 1918 when he was promoted and given the command of a newly created British Fifth Army. The Australian, General John Monash, was knighted by King George V on the field of battle and promoted to Australian corps commander.

The Germans continued with their plan to drain the energy of the pilots at Bertangles and Poulainville and mounted an air raid at 11:30 that night. One bomber was shot down.

21 April 1918.

21.4.18 - 9.30 AM - Camel B7270 - 90 mins - H.O.P. - (1) Observed 2 seater Albatross shot down in flames by Lieut. Taylor.

(2) Dived on large formation of triplanes and Albatros single-seaters. Two triplanes got on my tail so I cleared off. Climbed up and got back to scrap. Dived on pure red triplane which was on Lieut. May's tail. Got in good burst when he went down. Observed to crash by Lieut. Mellersh and Lieut. May. Dived on two more triplanes which were chasing Lieut. Mellersh. Did got them. Red triplane was Baron von Richthofen, confirmed by medical examination after being claimed by Australian RE8 squadron and 11th Australian Brigade.

The phrasing of the fifth sentence under Item 2 seems a little odd. Note that Roy had previously used the word "when" in the meaning of "*whereupon*" in his log book entry for 2:45 pm on 22 March 1918.

During Roy's chase of the pure-red triplane, he had noticed another *Camel* in worse trouble a couple of miles back to the northeast;

it was being attacked by two Fokker *Triplanes*. Accordingly, he did not spend time watching the red triplane until it struck the ground, but immediately made a U-turn and went to this second *Camel's* aid. This action of Roy's has not received much attention, but it was reported by three independent ground witnesses. The pilot of the second *Camel* Lieutenant Mellersh.

"*Did got them*" would appear to be a slip of the pen for "*Did not get them.*"

We know from Roy's previous reports and comments that he did not exaggerate and only he claimed a victory when he was absolutely certain. The red triplane's behaviour indicated that he had hit the pilot, who had thereupon collapsed onto his joystick. Roy's log book entry must have been made the following day because the medical officers of RAF 22 Wing did not begin their examination until nearly midnight.

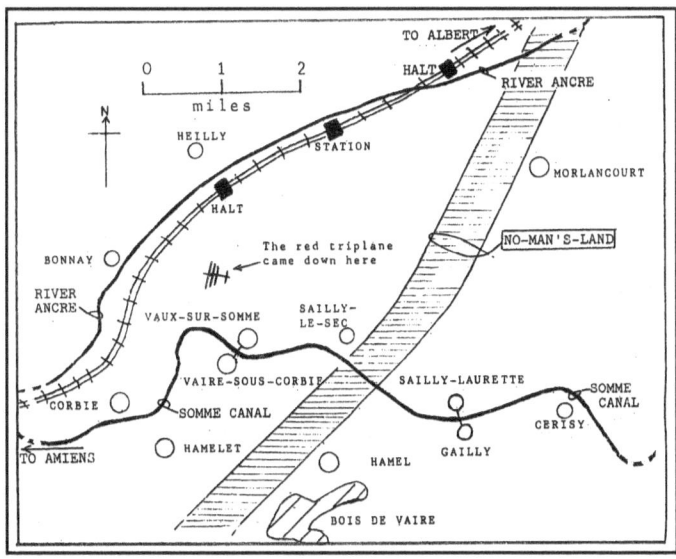

The place where the red triplane force-landed in relationship to no-man's-land and the nearby towns and villages.
It came to a halt with the nose facing west, towards Bonnay.

The fall of the red triplane was first reported by the Eleventh Australian Infantry Brigade; its field headquarters, hidden in a quarry on the east side of a wood shaped like a cow's tail, was only five hundred yards from where the triplane came to rest. The War Diary entries for 21 April 1918 of both the 11th Australian Infantry Brigade and the 14th Australian Field Artillery Brigade each state that one of its own machine-gunners brought down the red triplane. By word of mouth, it was known at Australian Corps headquarters that Sergeant Popkin of Eleventh Brigade (24 Machine Gun Company) had fired at the red triplane when it was on its way to the 53rd Battery and he had missed, but it was not known that he had fired again some thirty seconds after the triplane had left the 53rd Battery, and he appeared to have hit. Absent of this knowledge, by the evening of 21 April, the claim of Eleventh Brigade had been replaced by the claim of Fourteenth Brigade (53rd Battery) made by gunners Buie and Evans. Roy's naming of a claim by the *"11th Australian Brigade"* indicates how the impression of what had happened reversed twice with the passage of time. The paperwork for the Eleventh Brigade's claim covering Sergeant Popkin's second firing arrived at Australian Corps headquarters two days later.[25]

Although his combat success was disputed, Roy was officially credited victory by the RAF for the victory over a Fokker Dr.I near Vaux-sur-Somme.

Written immediately upon his return to Bertangles, Roy's combat report tells the same story but in fewer words, and therefore does not include the name of his victim or the claim by an Australian brigade, both being unknown at that time. The report was typed on plain paper, contained an alteration (three words added later) and was not signed by Roy; it was retyped on the official form and signed by him later that day. The spelling and layout of the body of the first report follow below. The three words *"and Lieut. May."*, which were squeezed in later below the end of a line, are shown in bold type.

(1)   At 10.35 a.m. I observed two Albatross burst into flames and crash.
(2)   Dived on large formation of 15-20 Albatross scouts D5 and Fokker triplanes, two of which got on my tail and I came out.

Went back again and dived on pure red triplane which was firing on Lieut. May. I got a long burst into him and he went down vertical and was observed to crash by Lieut. Mellersh. and Lieut. May.

I fired on two more but did not get them.

The number of enemy aeroplanes and their types are of interest. With the repetition of the tale, the total will increase and the mention of any Albatros DVs will disappear. The presence of the Albatros scouts suggests that Jasta 5 was involved. This unit, although not part of JG-I, was also stationed at Cappy and flew a mixture of Fokker Dr.Is and Albatros DVAs, normally in the standard German scout formation of ten machines. Counted together with the eight machines of Jasta 11, the total would be eighteen.

Roy's remarks on the colour of the triplane merit comment. Many German pilots decorated their aeroplanes with distinctive patterns, and Jasta 11 was no exception. Even an aeroplane that was not a flying work of art carried its pilot's identity marking in three places—on each side of the fuselage and along the upper surface of the top wing. There was also a squadron marking, which in the case of Jasta 11 was a white rudder. According to German propaganda, the British had placed a large bounty on Manfred von Richthofen's head; therefore, at the insistence of Lothar von Richthofen, the Baron's younger brother, several Jasta 11 triplanes were painted a basic red so that Manfred's machine would not be too readily identifiable by the enemy. Manfred's personal identification marks may be described in one word—none. Apart from the white rudder, the triplane (No. 425/17) which he flew on that day was a medium red all over, on top, sides and bottom. Triplane No. 425/17 also carried the latest nationality identification markings—the narrow Latin cross with a thin, white outline. Gone were the large white, rectangular panels previously used as background for the Maltese cross or the broad balken cross. Therefore, as far as appearances within the Jasta were concerned, No. 425/17 was pure red.[26] (Incidentally, the word "balken" has no connection with Balkan; it is derived from the appearance of a cross-joint between two balks of timber as used in the construction of a large hall or a barn.)

Lieutenant May's log book contains the following entry:

21.4.18 - Camel D3326 - 90 mins - Engaged 15 to 20 triplanes. Claimed one blue one. Several on my tail. Came out with red triplane on my tail which followed me down to the ground and over the lines on my tail all the time. Got several bursts into me but didn't hit me. When we got across the lines he was shot down by Captain Brown. I saw him crash into side of hill. Came back with Capt. We afterwards found out that the triplane (red) was the famous German airman Baron Richthofen. He was killed.

Although the layout of the land where Baron von Richthofen came down is correctly described, some years after the war Wilfrid May revealed that despite having watched the crash, he had had no idea whatsoever at the time where the hill was. He added that, contrary to several published stories, he personally had not seen Roy Brown attack the red triplane.

Weather permitting, the R.E.8s of AFC 3 Squadron had been conducting daily photographic flights to find targets for the Allied artillery batteries in the area. The task of any Allied fighter protection, intentionally or by good luck, was to keep German attackers occupied while the R.E.8 crews exposed their camera plates and made their escape. The duty of the R.E.8 crews was to return home immediately and not to become involved in anything which could cause the loss of the plates. That was the doctrine. On 21 April two R.E.8's were dispatched to photograph the forests near Hamel. These heavily wooded areas provided ideal shelter for supply dumps and troop concentrations and were suitably close to no man's land for the expected German attempt at capturing Villers-Bretonneux, as a prelude to crossing the Somme Canal.

An R.E.8 *Harry Tate* No. A4397 two-seater reconnaissance and bomber aeroplane of AFC 3 Squadron about to depart. Note the vane-type front sight on the observer's Lewis gun. This particular machine accumulated 440 hours 35 minutes of flight time over enemy-held territory.*

While the R.E.8s were taking their photographs, they were attacked by two Fokker *Triplanes*, both sporting large areas of red paint. After an exchange of fire, one desisted, climbed away and did not return. Moments later, the other dived away with the appearance of not being under perfect control, an indication of battle damage. When the news of the Rittmeister's forced landing and death was received, AFC 3 Squadron filed a claim, and soon the story reached 65 Squadron at Bertangles, but by that time it had suffered some changes.

The first version to make the rounds was that the Rittmeister had been shot down by a *corporal* on a *Harry Tate* of AFC 3 Squadron. This version reached General Sir John Monash, who repeated it in a letter to his wife a few days later, and thus appears to confirm the story. In reality, General Monash's letter merely confirms that it was quite some time before the truth was established.

Although corporal seems odd as an aircrew rank, corporals and even plain airmen were sometimes taken aloft as air gunners, especially in Bristol F.2A and F.2B *Fighters*. However, on operations where the duties of the second man required the schooling normally possessed by an officer, a trained observer was employed.

As the story spread, it changed with each retelling. A fourth or fifth version said that the aircraft of the Flying Circus surrounded the two R.E.8s and held them as helpless captives waiting for their leader to come and supply the death blow. Fortunately some Royal Air Force S.E.5As, *Camels* and SPADs saw what was happening and turned that way. The Baron, in his haste for one more easy kill was careless, and one of the R.E.8 observers, a corporal, shot him through the heart. As the triplane was diving to its doom, ground gunners opened fire and claimed to have killed him, but in reality he was already dead. The success of the British "hate the enemy" campaign can clearly be seen in the description of Baron von Richthofen's alleged method of running up a score. The sad part of the great propaganda success is that almost ninety years later, there are many who still do not know that such tales are far from the truth. Tragically, these tales find their way into serious history books, including some used in schools at the beginning of the twenty-first century.

Neither version mentions a claim by 209 Squadron on the other side of Bertangles Aerodrome, perhaps because at the time Roy's claim was believed to be for a different red triplane. Actually, it was the AFC claim 3 Squadron which was for a different red triplane, but more about that.

The responsibility for salvaging all wrecked aircraft, Allied or German, in the area covered by 22 Wing had been given to AFC 3 Squadron. Captain Roderick Ross, the squadron's technical officer, had delegated the task to Lieutenant. Walter Warneford, who recorded yet a third version:

> Von Richthofen down at sheet 62D J 19b 4.4. Salved [salvaged] the a/c and von Richthofen's body under their fire. Arrived back with body at 7:10 hrs and returned. Brought in the a/c getting back at 12:30 midnight. Later it was found that Gunner Buer of the Australian Artillery had shot him from the ground.

"Gunner Buer" was actually Gunner Robert Buie. The position specified by Lieutenant Warneford on British Army Map of France, Sheet 62D, is about three-quarters of a mile northwest of Vaux-sur-Somme. Co-ordinates 4.4 began life as an estimation; accurate measurements from fixed reference points were taken later that day.

A study of Roy's log book entry, Wop May's log book entry and the three versions of the last moments of Baron von Richthofen's life, all written within twenty-four hours of his death, reveals that only the following describe actions which the writer actually performed:

(a) Roy's two sentences; *"Dived on pure red triplane which was on Lieutenant May's tail. Got in good burst when he went down."*
(b) The first five lines of Lieutenant May's log book entry.
(c) The complete entry in Lieutenant Walter Warneford's diary.

This is a most important point, and this same criterion has to be applied to any other testimony when assessing its validity.

By the evening of 21 April the claim made by AFC 3 Squadron had been withdrawn; the time the two R.E.8s were attacked by two red Fokker *Triplanes* was too early. However, as no other red triplane had come down in that part of France, it was accepted that both Roy and Gunner Buie (together with his mate Gunner William John Evans) were claiming the same red triplane. Roy had attacked it from above and behind, whereas Gunners Buie and Evans had fired from below and almost directly in front. It should have been easy to decide which claim was valid, so the commanding officer of 22 Wing arranged for Lieutenant Downs, the wing medical officer, and his replacement, Captain Graham (who had already arrived), to examine the wounds in the Baron's body that evening and provide the answer.

The two claims had also worked their way up the chain of command to the headquarters of the Fourth Army, the ultimate authority in the region. General Sir Henry Rawlinson, its commander-in-chief, was faced with claims being vigorously pressed by the commanders of the RAF fifth Brigade and the Australian Imperial Force for the same victory. Although Roy had used identical ammunition (Mark VII rifle bullets) to that employed by Gunners Buie and Evans, their directions of fire had been almost completely opposite. The Fourth Army senior surgeon, Colonel Sinclair, and the senior physician, Colonel Nixon, made arrangements to perform an examination of the body on the following morning, 22 April.

The RAF 22 Wing medical examination began at 23:30 hours on the night of 21 April. The report, without mentioning names, unequivocally stated that only one bullet had struck the Baron and the direction from which it came (the rear, as shown by a sketch) eliminated the ground-fire claim. A careless paraphrasing of part of this report, in which the emphasis was shifted by omission of the front and rear aspects, was communicated to Major Butler, 209 Squadron and members of the RAF in general, and as a result that they understood the medical officers had determined that the bullet could only have been fired from the air. There being only one airborne claimant, Roy, who furthermore had attacked from behind, it was deemed obvious that he had fired it. A war correspondent filed the story, and Roy became famous overnight.

22 April 1918.

During the night of 21/22 April, the German Air Service continued its programme of keeping the Bertangles and Poulainville airmen awake, but this time one of the bombers was caught by searchlights over Bertangles Aerodrome, was damaged by anti-aircraft fire and had to make a forced landing in a field near Poulainville.

During the next morning, Colonels Sinclair and Nixon arrived at Poulainville and made their medical examination of the Rittmeister's body. Their report presented no conclusions or verdict concerning either of the two claims; it was simply an impartial analysis written in medical terms, stating that the direction of the wound matched neither the ground claim nor the air claim. The bullet had come from the side. When reduced to layman's language, it told Sir Henry that the shot could not have been fired by Gunner Buie, Gunner Evans or Roy, which explains why there was no immediate award of a medal or a citation. As this report contained no sensational revelations, it faded into the background and was either forgotten or ignored.

A third medical examination, which has received little publicity, was conducted later that morning by the senior medical officer of the Australian Corps, Colonel Barber, and his aide, Major Chapman, both of whom happened to be at Poulainville Aerodrome on other business. They agreed with the entry and exit points of the bullet given above, but in their opinion, the angle from which the bullet had struck could also imply a shot fired from the ground at the side of an aeroplane that was in a banked turn. They did not pronounce in favour of either claimant.

Essentially, all three medical reports (which are covered in detail in Part Two) revealed that only one bullet had struck the Baron and that it had come neither from the front nor the rear; it had passed sideways through his chest, from right to left. The entry point was inside his right armpit; the exit point was in his left breast just beneath and a little to the left of the nipple. All other marks on the body, stated by some to be wounds, were injuries acquired during the crash.

Unbeknownst to all directly concerned with evaluating the two claims, Sergeant Cedric Bassett Popkin of 24 Machine Gun Company had also filed a claim on 21 April, but the paperwork had not yet reached Fourth Army headquarters. His claim arrived on the heels of two dramatic developments in the war situation, both of which captured everyone's attention. The Royal Navy sank three blockships in the mouth of the Zeebrugge canal on 23 April, and the German offensive in the Somme Valley began again on 24 April. Sir Henry had more important things to worry about than a dead German airman.

A diagram gives an idea of the distances between the positions of those who filed claims for downing the red triplane. Statements made in the 1920s and later that Roy and the ground gunners had fired simultaneously will be seen to have little foundation. The diagram includes the Eleventh Brigade headquarters (an infantry brigade) mentioned in Roy's log book entry as the "*11th Australian Brigade,*" and the fourteenth Brigade headquarters (an artillery brigade), which had filed the claim to which Roy referred.

An examination of the positions of the Cow's Tail Wood and the summit of the Morlancourt Ridge (350 feet) indicates why Buie and Evans (at 330 feet) were unaware that Sergeant Popkin had also fired (and vice versa). The same summit also blocked Buie and Evans' view of the red triplane's forced landing. Sergeant Popkin and his crew had a similar problem in that the change in the gradient of the terraced hillside at the 330-feet level formed an intermediate brow which prevented them from seeing the forced landing.

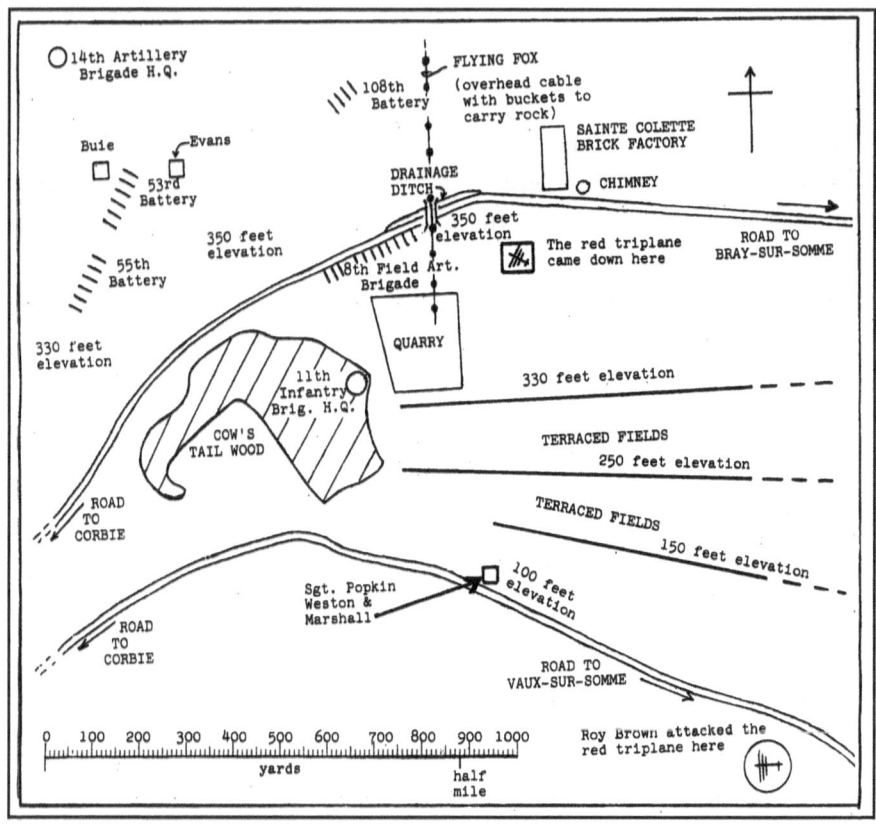

The relative positions of those who claimed to have shot down the Red Baron.

During Roy's lifetime, the original medical examination reports of RAF 22 Wing, the British Fourth Army and the Australian Corps were not released to the public, and Sergeant Popkin's claim remained relatively unknown. And thereby hangs a tale.

This tale is treated separately ,and in the detail required for proper understanding in Part Two herein.

The Royal Air Force announced Roy's victory in Communiqué No. 3 covering 15 to 21 April, which follows below. From the description of the weather given for 21 April, one would think that on that day the window used by the meteorologist at Fifth Brigade headquarters had faced a different direction from that of the one in Major Butler's office at Bertangles.

> April 21st. The weather was fine and the visibility good * 30 tons of bombs were dropped * Enemy aircraft were active but by no means aggressive. Two hostile machines were brought down by anti-aircraft fire - one falling in our lines - in addition to those brought down in combat.
> Capt M. von Richthofen, who is credited by the enemy with having brought down 80 Allied machines, was shot down and killed behind our lines near Corbie by Capt A.R. Brown, 209 Sqn.
> Capt A.R. Brown, 209 Sqn, dived on a red triplane which was attacking one of our machines. He fired a long burst into the E.A. which went down vertically and was seen to crash on our side of the lines by two other pilots of No. 209 Squadron.

Despite Roy's poor physical condition, he led his flight into action on the morning of 22 April.

22.4.18 - 8.30 AM - Camel B7270 - 120 mins - I.O.P. - Dived on 3 Albatross scouts attacking RE8 and drove them off but could not get them as guns jambed. Drove them off a second time with jambed guns. One bullet hole in lower left aileron from ground.

On this date, AFC 3 Squadron had undertaken another photographic reconnaissance flight over the forests near Hamel. The R.E.8 was No. C2270 with Lieutenant Thomas Latham Baillieu as pilot and Lieutenant Edward Fearnley Rowntree as his observer. While Lieutenant Rowntree was operating the camera, their R.E.8 was attacked at 3,000 feet over Bois de Vaire (a wood one mile southwest of Hamel). Their minds had been on more urgent things than making a precise count, and they later reported that three *Camels* had driven off the enemy scouts. The action is confirmed by 209 Squadron Record

Book, which names four pilots, Captain Brown and Lieutenants May, Lomas and Mellersh, as their saviours.

The page in 209 Squadron Record Book on which this event was typed (in triplicate) was dated 21 April at the top. The RAF administrative day ended at 4 p.m., and copies of the daily returns were sent to the wing at that hour. The page in question also recorded post-four o'clock entries for 21 April, as well as the first entry for 22 April. The presence of two different dates on the same page could easily have been overlooked, and this would appear to be the fountain from which an entirely fictitious air battle was accidentally created by Colonel E.A. Ewart. He worked for the Lecture Branch of the Aircraft Production Department and wrote articles for newspapers and trade magazines under the pen name of Boyd Cable. His speciality was providing stirring stories of the war in the air, the aim being to motivate aircraft factory workers and thereby boost production. According to Boyd Cable's combination of the two separate events, a flight of 209 Squadron pilots had intervened in an air fight between Baron von Richthofen's Fokker *Triplane* and two Allied artillery observation machines over Hamel on the morning of the 21 April, and their action had resulted in the death of the German ace. Boyd Cable's story, which was published in the London *Graphic* on 25 May 1918, is given in full in Appendix A of *The Red Baron's Last Flight*.

In the perverse nature of such things, a flaw in the carbon paper used with the 209 Squadron Record Book caused the change of date (from 21 to 22) part way down the page, not to be imprinted on the file copy at the RAF Historical Branch. Then to make matters worse, in 1925 an unknown researcher failed to notice that AFC 3 Squadron's records reported two separate encounters between Fokker *Triplanes* and R.E.8s over Hamel (21 and 22 April), and that when studied carefully, the 209 Squadron Record Book page dated 21 April showed that the encounter involving Roy Brown had been on the 22 April.

A quick reading of the final page for 21 April in the 209 Squadron Record Book appeared to confirm Boyd Cable's "stirring story," and it was not long before a description of a major air fight over Hamel flowed from his pen and was published in several newspapers. The unknown researcher's effort appeared as fact in part of a story known to historians as *"The Anonymous Account."* Over the intervening years, the fiction has gained a life of its own despite the absence of mention of any R.E.8s in Roy's 21 April log book entry or his combat report, and the equal absence of any fighters coming to their aid of the R.E.8 crews, in the letter's 21 April combat reports.

Progressive copying from article to article has turned an air fight which never happened into an accepted fact. This is somewhat surprising since maps of the area show that Hamel lies over one mile south of the Somme Canal, which places *"The Anonymous Account"* in conflict with Lieutenant May's story of being chased in a westerly direction just above the surface of the water near Sailly-le-Sec. The most recent appearance of what may be termed *"The Air Fight Which Never Happened"* is in a serious book on Canada's airmen in wartime written by the highly experienced author and aviation film producer Norman Shannon, entitled From Baddeck to the Yalu River and published in 2005.

23 April 1918.

On the night of 22/23 April the moon was almost full. German bombers arrived over Bertangles at 4 a.m. They did not stay for long, just enough to provoke the anti-aircraft guns into firing and to send everyone to the air-raid shelters. An hour later the bombers returned and woke everybody again. After a third performance, dawn came, whereupon the German aircrews went home to bed and the personnel at Bertangles went to work.

Roy did not fly on this day. The Remarks column in his log book contains: *"Sick, stomach trouble."*

A vacant tent-hangar was used on certain evenings as a cinema. This night was 48 Squadron's turn, but the silent picture show did not last for long; the German Air Service decided to provide sound effects, and the audience took to the air-raid shelters until midnight.

Judging by the descriptions of the noisy nights and the rotten weather which everyone at Bertangles and Poulainville aerodromes had to endure, it is a wonder that aircrew who were not sick still had the energy and the alertness to fly. After the war many were to pay for their stout-heartedness by dying young.

In a letter home dated 23 April 1918, Lieutenant

Arthur W. Aird wrote:

> *I am enclosing a piece of fabric of the Hun machine brought down by our Flight-Commander. It was the famous Hun airman Baron von Richthofen who has about 70 of our pilots to his credit. It has created quite a stir. The bringing down of the Baron was officially given to Brown, and Oh! What excitement.*

In a letter to a lady named Jean Brown (no relation to Roy) written this same week, Stearne Edwards said:

> *If any of your friends are not aware that you come from Carleton Place better tell them right now for C.P. is sure on the map now. You have no doubt heard of Baron von Richthofen, the famous German airman and in fact the greatest airman in the world. Perhaps you also noticed that just about this time he was shot down. Well, Roy Brown did the trick. Not so bad is it? And so Roy is now world famous, or should be if his name was only published. It is a big thing and means at least a D.S.O. and a good chance of a French and Belgian decoration. He will soon have a whole stick of rhubarb across his chest. He has been congratulated by Generals and all sorts of people and has made 209 Squadron R.A.F. envied by every other squadron in France.*

Note that neither A.W. Aird nor S.T. Edwards has a bad word to say about their late enemy. Like they, he had fought against the men and machines which opposed him at that moment. Post-war stories that Baron von Richthofen only attacked novices or crippled aircraft were like the armless-Belgian-baby and corpse-factory sensations—Allied wartime propaganda, nothing more, nothing less.

24 April 1918.

At 5:30 a.m. the German artillery subjected Villers-Bretonneux to a bombardment that shook the ground at Bertangles and Poulainville.

At 6:00 a.m. General von der Marwitz sprang two surprises: (1) Instead of crossing the Somme Canal between Corbie and Vaux-sur-Somme as expected, his troops, who had been hiding in the woods southwest of Hamel, advanced towards Hangard Wood and Villers-Bretonneux; and (2) for the first time in the war, German troops were supported by tanks.

Typical German tank of 1918, designed purely as a fighting machines, not as an armoured trench-crossing troop carrier.

The Allies assumed that the attack was a resumption of the advance on Amiens, which was the strategic road, canal and rail centre of the region, and with the Germans now employing tanks (their own and those captured from the British) the situation was cause for alarm. If Villers-Bretonneux were to be lost, the path to Amiens would be wide open. To delay the German advance, every available aeroplane (fighter, bomber or reconnaissance) was pressed into service in a ground-attack role. Sick pilots who could still fly were sent into action, and those whose aeroplanes became seriously damaged on such missions tried very hard to land as far away from their targets as possible.

24.4.18 - 3.25 PM - Camel B3329 - 65 mins - Special Mission - Bombing wood east of Villers Bretonneux and shooting troops in trenches. One bullet hole in top right aileron.

The official history of RAF 209 Squadron describes the special missions as follows:

> Bombs were carried and were directed against ground targets including enemy troop and machine-gun emplacements with good results. On the 24th Lieutenant Mellersh had just dropped his bombs near Gailly and was climbing into the clouds to avoid machine-gun fire, when he almost collided with an enemy two-seater.

The Australian Corps' fifth Division, commanded by Major-General Sir J.J. Talbot Hobbs, moved towards Villers-Bretonneux. The troops were mainly from the fifteenth Infantry Brigade, commanded by Major-General Harold Edward Elliott (nicknamed "Pompey"). With the aim of avoiding the bloodletting and butchery of an assault against prepared defensive positions, he decided that the cheapest way, in terms of human lives, to recapture the village would be a night attack before the Germans found time to consolidate.

As explained earlier, the German occupation of Villers-Bretonneux was but a feint to draw Allied attention and troop reserves away from the intended place of attack—Chemin des Dames, sixty miles to the southeast. The Australians brought in reinforcements, air power and tanks, and the first-ever tank-versus-tank battles occurred. In short, the deception worked. Two R.E.8s of AFC 3 Squadron were shot down. One returned later; the other, flown by Lieutenant Herbert (pilot) and Lieut. Sewell (observer), was posted as missing.

25 April 1918.

Heavy fighting took place all morning of 25 April in and around Villers-Bretonneux, with the Royal Air Force and the Australian Flying Corps providing all possible aid to the troops.

25.4.18 - 1.25 PM - Camel B7270 - 60 mins - Special Mission - Number of enemy massing east of Villers Bretonneux. Bullet lower main spar lower right plane. Returned sick.

That special mission was to be Roy's last flight in France. The night attack had been a spectacular success, and during the afternoon the Germans began to lose ground. The emergency was over; air power could be wound down. That evening the new medical officer of 22 Wing, Captain Norman Clotworthy Graham, decided he could now give Roy the rest from combat which he both deserved and needed.

Experience had shown that a hospital in quiet surroundings was the best place for those pilots who were suffering from physical as a result of too many hours at high altitudes, to recuperate their strength. If they were simply sent on leave to a place away from the fighting, the "rest" had been known to turn into "painting the town red," whereas at a military hospital with regular good-quality meals, beds with clean sheets, quiet nights and encouragement from friendly nurses, proper rest was assured. Military discipline made certain of that. Until the necessary arrangements could be made, Captain Graham grounded Roy.

At some time during the afternoon the papers containing Sergeant Popkin's claim finally reached fourth Army headquarters.

By nightfall most Germans had been ejected from Villers-Bretonneux, but sporadic fighting continued until dawn. At Poulainville and Bertangles the night was unusual; it was quiet.

26 April 1918.

During the morning of 16 April, Villers-Bretonneux and Hangard Wood were declared free of the enemy, and the work of the aircrews at Bertangles and Poulainville returned to normal. Major Butler sent the following memorandum to Lieutenant-Colonel T.A.E. Cairnes, who had taken over the command of 22 Wing from Lieutenant-Colonel F.V. Holt on 25 April. It consisted of excerpts from four of Roy's combat reports plus comments of his own; as a result, the narrative, switching between the first and third persons, may be a little difficult to comprehend at first reading.

> I wish to recommend the undermentioned Officer for immediate award for marked skill and gallantry in aerial fighting during the present operations, particularly on the occasions mentioned below.

Captain A R Brown, DSC

April 21st. Dived on formation of 15 to 20 Albatross scouts D5s and Fokker Triplanes, two of which got on my tail and I came out. Went back again and dived on pure red triplane which was firing on Lieut. May. I got a long burst into him and he went down vertical and was seen to crash by Lieut. Mellersh and Lieut. May. Engagement took place over Vaux-sur-Somme at about 11:00 a.m.

NOTE: This machine crashed in our lines and pilot was subsequently identified as Captain Baron Richthofen.

April 12th. Dived on two Fokker Triplanes over Warfusee-Abancourt followed by Lieuts. Mellersh, Mackenzie and Lomas. Lt. Mackenzie dived on one triplane and fired about 100 rounds. E.A. went down vertical and Lieut. Mackenzie lost sight of him. I observed it going down but could not watch him right down. Capt. Brown and Lieut. Mellersh dived on the other triplane. Each fired about 200 rounds. E.A. turned in front and we each got in a good burst. The E.A. then went down vertical and we followed him down. Lieut. Mackenzie and Capt. Brown observed burst of flame come out of him then. Followed him down to 500 feet when he came out of dive. Capt. Brown and Lieut. Mellersh opened fire again. E.A. carried on gliding and looked as if pilot was landing or was dead and machine gliding automatically.

NOTE: Confirmed in R.A.F. Communiqué No. 2, April 12th. 1 brought down and 1 driven down out of control.

March 22nd. Dived from 15,000 feet on 7 E.A. two-seaters. At first dived on one after another keeping E.A. from getting above us. Picked one and fired about 100 rounds into him at fairly close range. He did climbing left hand turns right in front of me while I was firing, then went into a vertical dive and I lost him under left wing.

NOTE: Engagement occurred N.E. of Foret d'Houthulst whilst escorting French Caudron. Confirmed by pilot of Caudron (as per Communique No. 18) to have crashed.

February 2nd. Dived on 2 Albatross two-seaters over Foret d'Houthulst and opened fire on one getting in about 100 rounds when the other two-seater began to get above me. I turned on him and fired about 350 rounds. The E.A. disappeared in the mist after I had turned to dive again.

NOTE: This officer was awarded the D.S.C. in October 1917 whilst with this squadron.

In his memorandum (above) Major Butler had not specified which award he would like to see conferred, but the footnote could be taken as hinting that a higher one than the DSC would be appropriate. His recommendation would need the agreement of Lieut.-Col. Cairnes and the endorsement of his superior officer, Brigadier General Charlton. It would then be reviewed by a staff officer at 4th Army HQ before being placed before General Rawlinson for final decision. In the case of a high award, several days would pass before it reached the general's desk.

In a letter home dated 26 April 1918, Lieut. M S (Sammy) Taylor wrote, "*I am sure you will be pleased to hear that the renowned Baron von Richthoven (sic) was bested by one of our chaps a few days ago. The victor was a Canadian boy who belongs to this squadron. All the credit goes to Brownie. I hope to be able to tell you about the scrap some day.*"

Sammy's hope was not to be. He was shot down and killed on 7 July.

27 April 1918.

To put it mildly, General Rawlinson had a problem on 27 April. Sergeant Popkin's claim, Gunners Evans and Buie's claim, and Major Butler's recommendation that Captain A. Roy Brown be honoured were all sitting on his desk awaiting action. Somebody deserved a medal, but who was it? In a wise move, he asked General Sir Talbot Hobbs to institute an enquiry. General Hobbs delegated the task to Captain Charles Edwin Woodrow Bean, the official war correspondent, who immediately began interviewing witnesses to establish precisely where the key people had been positioned, what they had seen and where the events had taken place.

209 Squadron R.A.F.
c/o G.P.O.
London B.E.F.

April 27/18

Show this letter to nobody but home, Uncle Clarence and Uncle Alex.

Dear Dad,

I am afraid I have not written for some time but it has not been my fault. We have been working so hard it has been impossible.

I feel just about all in today the way things have gone. My stomach has been very bad recently and the doctor says if I keep on I shall have a nervous break-down and has ordered me to stop active service flying. I am to have two weeks leave and then go up for a medical examination again. I have done everything in my power to come back to France after that but it does not look very hopeful. Both my C.O. and I have seen the Colonel about it and the Colonel is interviewing the General, but they all say I have to abide by the doctor's order. I am sorry that it should happen at the present time when there is so much work to do. I have just got my flight going beautifully now and I have all good chaps with me. What is more, we have been doing very good work. I have been congratulated by two Generals for what I have done, which is very pleasant.

Our best effort was on 21st when we fought Baron von Richthofen's Circus as they are called. I expect you will have read about them in the newspapers. There were eleven of us and twenty-two of them as nearly as we can make out. It was the most terrible fight I have ever seen in the air. I doubt whether there has been one like it before. We shot down three of their triplanes, which were seen to crash, and one that has not been confirmed as yet. Among these was the Baron whom I shot down on our side of the lines. We did not lose anyone in that fight. It is going to have a great effect on the war in the air as that fight was ordered by the Hun to give him a chance to do reconnaissance in the air and of course he was defeated. It is bound to have a great effect on the Hun especially when they lost their best fighter and their stunt squadron was defeated. That is one of the things we have done lately so you can plainly see I do not want to quit as there is such a wonderful opportunity at the present time to do effective work. We have a wonderful bunch of fellows in the squadron and I do hate to have to leave.

The doctor said he would give me leave to go to Canada but I refused as there is too much to do here at present. How it will all come out I do not know. I do not feel at all well at present but a couple of weeks rest I am quite sure will fix me all up again. The Colonel is to see the General this afternoon and then I shall go on leave. I shall write to you as soon I get on leave and let you know what has happened.

I received your letter dated Mar. 25 and I was very sorry to hear mother is sick and I hope by this time she is quite better again. If she would only not work so hard but there is no use saying anything. I am very glad to hear that Bess is not coming over. Try to persuade her not to come over at all. I hope she does not. Horace and I over here at once is quite enough.

It was rather funny about Richthofen being shot down. The infantry on the ground, the anti-aircraft and an Australian squadron put in reports that they had shot him down. All reports differed. They had a medical examination on the body and it was found that they were all wrong without the slightest of doubt. It is terrible when you think of it that they should examine a body to see who should have the credit of killing him. What I saw that day shook me up quite a lot as it was the first time I have ever seen a man whom I knew I had killed. If you don't shoot them they will shoot you so it has to be done.

The Colonel would have been Lieutenant-Colonel Cairnes, commanding officer of 22 Wing, and the General would have been

Brigadier-General Charlton, Commanding Officer of RAF fifth Brigade.

After the war, it was learned that only one Fokker triplane from Jasta 11 had been lost on that day—the one flown by the Baron. All the others returned safely to Cappy, although some sported a fine collection of bullet holes in the fabric. Therefore, the triplane with a blue tail, claimed by Lieutenant Mellersh, must have belonged to Jasta 5; it apparently force-landed, as no fighter pilot, other than Manfred von Richthofen, is listed among the German airmen killed in that area on that day. Lieutenant Mackenzie claimed one and Lieutenant May claimed one also, but no suitable victims are listed among the German casualties for the day.

The *"infantry on the ground"* was probably a reference to the report by Lieutenant Donald Lovat Fraser, the intelligence officer of the Eleventh Australian Infantry Brigade, that the pilot of the red triplane shot down by machine-gun fire from the southeast corner of La Queue de Vache (The Cow's Tail Wood) had been Baron von Richthofen. The *"anti-aircraft"* fits the claim of the 53rd Battery of the fourteenth Australian Field Artillery Brigade. The *"Australian Squadron"* was definitely AFC 3 at Poulainville.

It would be a while before the designations of the actual units involved would become generally known. Even at this early date, however, Roy had noticed that the importance of "who killed the Red Baron?" seemed to revolve more around reflected glory than any other reason. Over the years, the final remarks in his letter concerning seeing the Baron's body have been rewritten many times; one tear-jerking invention, which still finds believers among the many who have not seen the original, has him expressing regret at what he had done.

30 April 1918.

Captain Graham found a place for Roy at 24 General Hospital, Étaples, for treatment and rest. He was struck from the strength of 209 Squadron effective from 1 May. Other pilots would follow him as physical exhaustion from prolonged flying at high altitudes and the resultant splitting headaches took hold.

1 May 1918.

Form W.3121 from Brigadier-General Charlton arrived at fourth Army headquarters on 1 May. The text shows that the brigadier had taken Major Butler's hint and had recommended Roy for a higher award than the Distinguished Service Cross.

Lieutenant (Temporary Captain) Arthur Roy Brown, DSC, RAF
Recommendation for the award of the Distinguished Service Order.
For conspicuous gallantry and devotion to duty.

On April 21st, 1918, while leading a patrol of six of our scouts over Vaux-sur-Somme he observed a formation of hostile scouts led by a Fokker triplane with red wings, and black crosses, which answered the description of the machine flown by Baron Manfried [sic] von Richthofen.
Although his formation was numerically inferior to that of the enemy, he led it to the attack. First he engaged two Fokker triplanes, which he drove off. Then seeing that the Red Triplane was attacking and pressing hard one of our machines, he swooped upon it, firing the while, a long burst. Suddenly it went down diving vertically, crashing eventually North East of Corbie. When the machine was salved, it was found that the pilot was Baron Manfried von Richthofen.
He has also, since being awarded the Distinguished Service Cross, brought down four other enemy machines which were seen to be destroyed, and has shown great dash and enterprise in attacking, from low altitudes, enemy troops on

the ground, despite heavy fire from the enemy's anti-aircraft defences.

In the recommendation the location of the beginning of the air battle is stated incorrectly. It actually commenced over Cérisy, a village four and a half miles to the east of Vaux-sur-Somme and on the German side of no man's land. If the location had been Vaux-sur-Somme, there would have been about eight hundred enthralled witnesses.

The discussions between Sir Henry and his staff concerning this recommendation are unknown, but there was no doubt whatsoever concerning Roy's successful and courageous high-speed dive to rescue Lieutenant May or that this action had initiated the sequence of events which culminated in the death of the Baron. Roy's bravery and leadership in aerial combat over the preceding months of 1918 had also been amply documented. He deserved another Distinguished Service Cross for his work in general, but if Captain Bean's report should be in Roy's favour, the award of the Distinguished Service Order was a foregone conclusion.

2 May 1918.

The airmen's weather finally ended, and with flying again possible, AFC 3 Squadron received orders to move to Flesselles Aerodrome, about there miles to the northwest. The move was made two days later.

3 May 1918.

Lieutenant Oliver Redgate was promoted to temporary captain and placed in command of A Flight, where he inherited Roy's *Camel* No. B7270.

Rumour at fourth Army Headquarters said that Captain Bean's report was not going to be in favour of Roy Brown; therefore, Brigadier-General Charlton asked Major Butler to send him more details of what Roy, "Wop" May and "Tog" Mellersh had seen and done. Unfortunately Major Butler had little to add. Roy, who had fired on the red triplane, had not seen it crash; May and Mellersh, who had seen it crash and believed Roy to have been responsible, had not seen him attack it. Major Butler's possibilities of further enquiries were nil as Roy was fifty miles away, resting at Étaples hospital, and Mellersh had been posted to England. Feeling the pressure and urgently needing some answers for the "brass hats," Major Butler neither included a statement from, nor made any mention of, Captain Oliver LeBoutillier in his reply, although this officer was still flying with 209 Squadron at the time and was readily available to him. This is significant in view of a claim made nine years later by Oliver LeBoutillier that he had witnessed the entire event and had not been merely part of it. LeBoutillier's combat report for 21 April 1918 is of little help to his post-war claim; it places him several miles to the northeast of Vaux-sur-Somme at the time.

During the first week of May, Captain Bean's report was handed to Fourth Army Headquarters; its verdict was in favour of Gunners Buie and Evans. One conclusion from the text that Captain Bean had not seen any of the three medical examination reports, and had based his finding on the accounts of close witnesses to the final moments of the red triplane, none of whom had been in line of sight of Roy's attack. This was totally unacceptable to the Royal Air Force and not particularly helpful to Sir Henry, who had before him two written medical opinions, both of which disqualified Gunners Buie and Evans; by extension, they also disqualified Sergeant Popkin whose deposition indicated he had been firing frontally when the red triplane went temporarily out of control. Captain Bean's effort, entitled Official Report, was stamped "SECRET" and filed.

6 May 1918.

Major Butler handed over command of 209 Squadron to Major John Oliver Andrews, DSO, MC and bar, who was being given a rest from combat. One of the new commanding officer's victories had been over the much-decorated Oberleutnant Stefan Kirmaier (eleven victories), who was the commanding officer of Jasta 2, a high-grade squadron also known as Jasta Boelke in honour of its deceased commander. A few days later, when Lieutenant-Colonel Cairnes asked Major Andrews how he was settling in, the major answered that initially he had not understood what his officers wanted when they asked permission to go ashore; the whole squadron appeared to be run like a ship.

9 May 1918.
No. 24 General Hospital
Etaples
May 9/18

Dear Dad,

    Just a note to let you know I am getting along alright. I am off milk diet now and am getting eggs and fish. Tomorrow, if I am O.K. I shall get fowl, then it will not be very long before I shall be out of here. Wednesday next week I expect. I then go on leave to England. I was to go to the south of France but that has been changed as the place down there has been closed for the summer. What happens after that depends on how I feel, but I hope I shall be able to stay out here.

    There is nothing very interesting going on here. Stearne was along to see me one day to give me the squadron news. He is quite well and working hard, and good work too. I hope we do not get separated now. I shall write to you again when I get out of here.

P.S.
I am having all kinds of people coming around to shake hands with me and give me congratulations. They are funny and I can hardly keep my face straight sometimes.

While Roy was enjoying a well-earned rest in Étaples military hospital, his colleagues took a piece of fabric from the Baron's triplane, signed the reverse side and doped it to the middle of the Latin cross cut from the port side of the fuselage. There was obviously no doubt in 209 Squadron who had brought down the Baron. Note that faded paint makes it possible to discern the conversion from the factory Maltese cross to the broad balken cross and finally to the narrow Latin cross. In 1920 Roy donated the piece of fabric to the Canadian Military Institute in Toronto.

The twice-modified cross from the port side of the Baron's triplane bearing 25 signatures. Photograph taken by Wilfrid May.

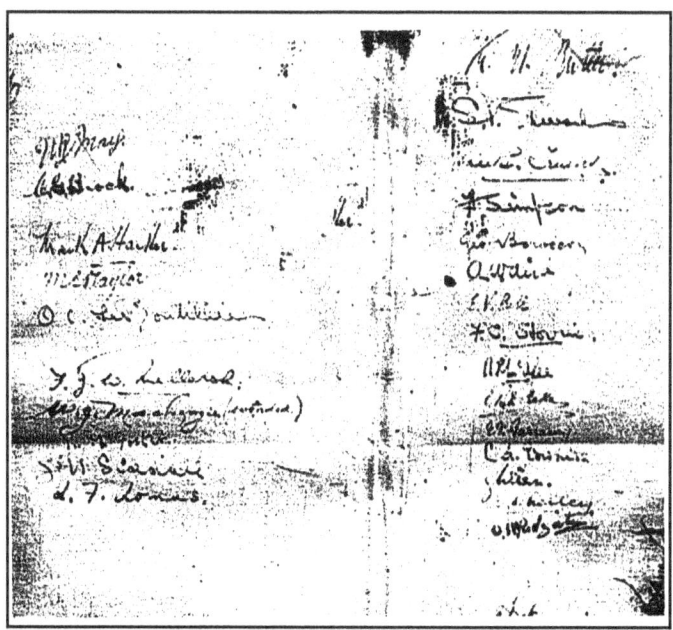

The 25 genuine signatures enhanced; a useful aid to historians.

The signatures, transcribed in the same order:

W R May	C H Butler
C G Brock	S T Edwards
Mark A Harker	Arthur Trudell
M S Taylor	F Simpson
O C LeBoutillier	Geo. Borocco
F J W Mellersh	A W Aird
W J Mackenzie (wounded)	E V Bell
R M Foster	F C Stovin
J H Sidall	A R McAfee
L F Lomas	E B Drake
	F F Garroway
	C G Edwards
	G Wilson
	A Shelley
	O W Redgate

As has been shown several times before, while on patrol or in contact with the enemy, Roy's loyalty to his colleagues took precedence over personal considerations. This is demonstrated once more by the aid which he gave to Lieut. Mellersh immediately following his rescue of Lieut. May on 21 April 1918.

Although the danger to Lieut. Mellersh's life was greater than that faced by Lieut. May, the former's predicament has not received the publicity it merits; probably because, unlike Lieut. May's adventure, it had no dramatic ending. When Roy took the decision to tackle the two triplanes attacking Lieutenant Mellersh, he forfeited his chance to watch the pure red one complete its descent and thus be able to state, from personal observation, what had happened to it. Although Captain Bean found plenty of witnesses, he did not find a single one who had seen a *Camel* make a diving attack on the red triplane and had then been able to keep his eyes on the latter all the way to the forced landing on the hillside. There appeared to be a time difference somewhere between one and two minutes between the two events. Could two red triplanes have been involved?

The gap in the testimony created a difficult situation for the 4th

Army staff officers who had to advise Sir Henry concerning Brigadier General Charlton's memorandum. The absence of a second downed triplane strongly suggested that the red Fokker Dr.I attacked by Roy, which according to him *'went down vertical'*, and the red Fokker Dr.I which force-landed on the hillside were one and the same, but the absolute certainty required for an award of the Distinguished Service Order, which ranks in military ceremonial precedence immediately below the Victoria Cross, simply was not there.

11 May 1918.

It must first be clarified to the reader that the conclusions reached by the Fourth Army Senior Surgeon (Colonel Sinclair) and Senior Physician (Colonel Nixon), when they examined the body of the late Rittmeister Manfred Freiherr von Richthofen, and the verdict of the Official Report written by Captain C.E.W. Bean (delivered to General Sir Henry Rawlinson by Major General Talbot Hobbs), were unknown at this time except to a few high-ranking officers. They remained 'buried' for several years. Both are given in full in PART TWO of this book.

General Sir Henry Rawlinson, who must have met Colonel Sinclair and Colonel Nixon almost daily in the senior officers' mess and trusted their judgement, reached a decision. Apparently he did not accept some of the contents of the OFFICIAL REPORT since he took no known steps over its verdict, but authorized the immediate award of a second Distinguished Service Cross to Captain A. Roy Brown. There could be no doubt concerning Roy's daring rescue of Lieut. May and then Lieut. Mellersh on 21 April, nor any argument over his brave and fearless leadership of his flight after receiving his first DSC. At least Sir Henry could do that much without stirring up a hornets' nest if the citation were worded carefully. His staff basically used the Distinguished Service Order recommendation written by Brigadier General Charlton, but without the Vaux-sur-Somme error or the two mentions of Baron von Richthofen. The paperwork would take two to three weeks.

15 May 1918.

In the morning, Captain Oliver Redgate scored his final victory, an Albatros D.V near Belloy-Pozières.

In the afternoon, 209 Sqn. tangled with JG I, ably led by Hauptman Wilhelm Reinhard, Rittmeister Manfred von Richthofen's successor. 2nd Lieut. O.J. Brittorous and Lieut. G. Wilson were killed and Oliver Redgate received a 'blighty one' - a nasty leg wound which sent him to hospital in England.

Captain Oliver Redgate, DFC standing beside Lieut. Mackenzie's *Camel*.

Oliver Redgate may have been fortunate since, unlike his four wingmen on 21 April; A.W. Aird, E.B. Drake, C.G. Edwards and J.H. Siddall, he survived the war. In July 1918 he was awarded the new RAF decoration; the Distinguished Flying Cross (DFC). Lieutenants Aird and Edwards are depicted in the following photograph.

From L to R: W.R. May, A.W. Aird, M.S. Taylor & C.G. Edwards. Only 'Wop' May survived the war. He was also awarded a DFC.

On the same day, Major J O Andrews put Lieut. May in Oliver Redgate's place as flight commander and recommended him for promotion to captain. This somewhat a surprise for 'Wop' who had expected Sammy Taylor, who was by far his senior, to be so honoured.

16 May 1918.

Roy was discharged from hospital at Étaples and sent to England on a fortnight's sick leave. The powers that be decided it was high time he received a long rest from the rigours of up to four hours a day spent in the freezing cold at 15,000 feet. Three, perhaps six months as an instructor at an advanced school for fighter pilots at the Home Establishment (H.E.) would profitably employ his talents and be beneficial to both parties. No.2 School of Aerial Fighting at Marske-by-the-Sea was just the place.

On the same day, Jean Brown, a lady in Ottawa who was not related to Morton Brown, sent the news from France to Bessie Brown, Roy's sister.

Department of Justice
Military Service Branch
Office of Commissioner of Police
Royal Bank Building

Ottawa 16th May, 1918

Dear Bess,-

    I hope you won't mind getting a letter written on the type-writer - it is probably the best way in the end for my writing is hard to read.
    This morning I received a letter from Stearne which reads in part as follows:-

"If any of your friends are not aware that you come from Carleton Place, better tell them right away for C.P. is sure on the map now.
    You have no doubt heard of Baron Von Richthofen, the famous German airman and in fact the greatest airman in the world. Perhaps you noticed it was just about this time he was shot down. Well, Roy Brown did the trick. Not so bad is it? And so Roy is now world famous, or should be if his name was only published. It is a big thing and means at least a D.S O. and a good chance of a French and Belgian decoration. He will soon have a whole stick of rhubarb across his chest. He has been congratulated by generals and all sorts of people and has made 209 Squadron R.A.F. envied by every other squadron in France."
    I expect you have heard from Roy and Horace by this morning's mail also, but I know there would not be as much in them about Roy as Stearne has told. I am so glad my name is "Brown", for I am sure everyone will at least think we are cousins.

Love to all,

Yours sincerely,
Jean

Roy's active service career in France terminated with 16 claimed combat successes which included 12 enemy aeroplanes which he believed to have shot down, 9 of which the RNAS or the RAF officially confirmed as destroyed. The 7 not confirmed were:

3 fighters shot down but which neither broke up in the air nor were seen to crash by another pilot.
2 observation balloons forced down.
2 two-seater aeroplanes forced to run for home with the observer killed or severely wounded.

Date	Aeroplanes Claimed Shot Down	Two-Seater Observers Disabled	Kite Balloons, Forced Down	Officially Confirmed Victories
RNAS Log Book	9	2	2	7
12 April 1918	1			
RAF Log Book				
20 April 1918	1			1
21 April 1918 (disputed)	1			1
RNAS + RAF	12	2	2	9

After the war, Roy assured his family and friends that he only put in a claim when he was personally quite certain the enemy had gone down. It was well known that one of the easiest ways of becoming a victim was to watch or follow one's adversary descending in order to make absolutely sure. Roy never made that mistake. This means that Roy's 16 successes in combat are closer to the true number of victories than the 9 officially confirmed.

Total Time in the Air: 257 hours.

23 May 1918

Captain Stearne Edwards was deemed by Captain Graham to be approaching physical exhaustion and in dire need of rest from combat. As in Roy's case, the M.O. found a place for him at No. 24 General

Hospital, Étaples, after which he could to expect to be posted to the Home Establishment for three to six months. By co-incidence, Stearne's destiny also lay at No.2 School of Aerial Fighting.

THE COURT OF ENQUIRY INTO THE DOWNING OF THE RED BARON

There is no record of a COURT OF ENQUIRY or a BOARD OF ENQUIRY ever being convened nor has anyone claimed to have served on it. The source of this myth is probably the perfectly true, post-war statement by Roy that, *"The claims were enquired into by a board."*

The only known gathering, or board, of officers to have conducted a type of inquest into the matter took place at Poulainville aerodrome on 22 April 1918 and is described in PART TWO of this book. It was composed entirely of Australians from 3 Squadron AFC and their verdict was in favour of Roy Brown, which neatly disposes of the second myth that the attitudes taken in the dispute in April 1918 were based upon nationality.

In some inexplicable manner Captain Bean's Official Report became confused with the earlier, unofficial investigation by 3 AFC. The situation became further clouded by a post-war story in which the 3 AFC investigation was 'promoted' to an Official Board of Enquiry which supposedly decided in Roy's favour.

Government regulations, at that time, required that official documents remain classified for 50 years. Roy had died before the precise contents of Captain Bean's investigation, the 4th Army and the RAF medical reports were released to the public. Colonel Barber's report has not yet been found.

THE MEDALS AND HONOURS AWARDED FOR THE DOWNING OF RITTMEISTER MANFRED BARON VON RICHTHOFEN

None was awarded. Hindsight suggests that General Sir Henry Rawlinson had no other choice. In that manner, all claimants were treated (or mistreated) equally.

ACKNOWLEDGEMENTS

The photographs of most complete aircraft and details of the RFC order on aircraft markings were most kindly provided by Mr. Stuart Leslie from the J.M.Bruce/G.S.Leslie collection.
The photographs of Roy Brown, his colleagues, their aeroplanes and aerodromes are from the Brown family collection.
The photograph of the S.E.5A in flight and the F.K.8 are by courtesy of Mr. Bain Simpson.
The photographs of Wilfrid May were supplied by his son, Denny Reid May.
The photograph of the Eastman Vest Pocket Kodak is published with the kind co-operation of the Royal Canadian Military Institute in Toronto.
The photographs of the 41st Field Hospital and the wrecked R.E.8 were contributed by Geoffrey Hine.
The aerial depiction of Bertangles and Poulainville aerodromes was assembled by Owen Brierley from three overlapping photographs.
The diary of Lieut. Warneford was kindly provided by his son John B Warneford.
Squadron Commander Butler's Confidential Reports were made available by the Fleet Air Arm Museum at Yeovilton.
Information on Artillery Batteries in the area and their equipment was provided by Colonel (retired) Andrew Pinion via Colonel (retired) David Storrie.
The description of 'night-life' at Bertangles and Poulainville aerodromes in April 1918 was taken from diaries kept by Air Mechanic 1st Class Morris Waldron and Air Mechanic 2nd Class Thomas Spencer of RAF 65 Squadron at Bertangles, and by Lieut. Walter Warneford of 2 AFC Squadron at Poulainville. The originals of the first two diaries and a copy of the third are in the RAF Museum Archives at Colindale, near Hendon, London, where they are available for study, by appointment.

ANNEX TO CHAPTER EIGHT

(1) THE CONSTANTINESCO-COLLEY HYDRAULIC MACHINE-GUN SYNCHRONIZING GEAR.

In 1916 a Romanian mining engineer, George Constantinesco (originally Gogu Constantinescu), was working at Aperton in England on his idea of operating rock drills by hydraulic impulses rather than blows transmitted mechanically. Major L.V.S. Blacker, who was looking into replacing the rods, pivots and links of the Sopwith/Kauper machine-gun synchronizing gear with a hydraulic system, heard of his work and decided to go and see him. Agreement was reached and a Vickers machine-gun quickly appeared on Constantinesco's doorstep. A little later that day a certain Major G.C. Colley, who thoroughly understood the Vickers, rang his doorbell. In less than two weeks this pair of engineers had produced a working prototype. A quick trip to the Patent Office in London was next on the agenda.

In August 1916 the CC Gear (CC stood for Constantinesco-Colley) was fitted to a B.E.2C and tested in the air. It worked properly first time and no shots struck the propeller.

In analogical terms; the CC system functioned like the hydraulic brakes on a car. A cam on the engine propeller shaft pushed the equivalent of the brake pedal at the appropriate moment. Oil in a copper tube transmitted the push, and a device, equivalent to the brake cylinder in a wheel, blocked the machine-gun firing lever while a propeller blade was in front of the muzzle. At all other points of the arc, the gun could fire freely. Most of the moving parts of the previous gun timing systems, together with their inertia, were replaced by this simple tube filled with a non-freezing oil. There were no moving parts to wear or metal rods to contract from the cold at high altitudes. The transmittal of the pulse was instantaneous, and the rate of fire no longer depended upon engine RPM.

The standard army version of the Vickers machine-gun fired 600 rounds per minute (10 per second), but a later style, with a return gas booster fitted to the muzzle, could fire at 840 rounds per minute (14 per second). The total improvement obtainable over the earlier Sopwith/Kauper system was a doubled rate of fire, and herein lies one of the reasons for the great success of the twin-gun Sopwith *Camel*. During the 1 to 3 seconds a pilot could hold an enemy aeroplane in his sights, he could fire four times the number of bullets than when flying a *Pup* or a standard *Triplane*.

If special springs were fitted to a Vickers, the rate of fire could be increased to 1,000 rounds per minute, but the rate of wear on the feed and extraction mechanism was high and jams were more frequent. This final uprating was principally used for ground strafing massed troops when the maximum effect for the minimum time over the target was required.

The CC system provided one extra task for a fighter pilot; he had to keep the hydraulic oil pressure pumped up otherwise his guns would not fire.

Gun timing marks on propeller.
This is a different aeroplane from the one in the photograph below.
The numbers indicate the Diameter and the Pitch in millimetres.

Gun timing mark on Clergêt engine of a Sopwith F1 *Camel*. The corresponding mark on the propeller is not visible in this photograph.

The serial number, G1302N80, of the propeller attached to the Clergêt engine decodes as follows: G = manufacturer, 1302 = factory production number, N = naval order, 80 = order number.

The other stampings on the propeller decode thus: AD = air department (of the Royal Navy), 644 = drawing number, RH = right hand rotation, D 2590 = diameter 2.590 metres, P 2650 = pitch 2.650 metres.

It is amusing to learn that when Constantinesco and Colley applied for a US Patent in 1918, the Patent Examiner was reluctant to grant one as he did not believe the system would work. They informed him by return post that in 1917 alone, over 6,000 had been produced, delivered, installed and were at that moment shooting down enemy aircraft. US Patent 1,372,944 was granted.

(2) THE ANTI-WAR MOVEMENTS.

General Ludendorff complained in his memoirs that by mid-1918 a disturbing number of Socialist Party members of the Reichstag were no longer supporting the war effort, and that Bolshevist agitators were active in the factories and in the armed forces.

In France, the situation was moving in the same direction. The French army was still recovering from the 1917 disaster at Chemin des

Dames and socialist agitators in that country were not too enthusiastic about the war either. In their view, German, French and British workers were killing one another simply because they had been ordered to do so by the rich and powerful. Now that the initial euphoria was over, the occasional rejoicing over battles won seemed not to be worth the price being paid in blood and destruction.

In England, the Independent Labour Party stated; *"We deplore the outbreak of war in Europe and the action of the British Government in embroiling the people in an international quarrel which can bring nothing but ruin and privation to the workers."* Spokesmen for several branches of the British Socialist Party proclaimed; *"t is our duty as socialists to refuse to murder one another."*

Conscription for military service had been introduced in the British Isles but the new army divisions thus raised were being retained in the south of England. The government believed if they were sent to France in advance of the 1919 campaign, the generals there would waste the soldiers' lives in another supposedly war-winning frontal assault on heavily fortified German defences. The costly failure of the 1917 attempt at Passchendaele in Belgium (the 3rd Battle of Ypres) had once more filled hospitals all over the country, and the extent of the two disasters could no longer be hidden from the public. One of the results was a sensational anti-war event on 18 September 1917. Protesters had hidden a thermite time bomb inside a crate of lifebelts about to be loaded onto the troopship *Onward* at Folkestone. As a precaution, they had carefully set the bomb to detonate before the troops embarked, and although the *Onward* went to the bottom of the harbour, no lives were lost. To the politicians, the message was clear.

At his trial for failing to register for conscription, English Socialist leader Arthur Gardiner claimed; *"I realize the interests of the workers of Germany are identical with those of the workers of England, and for that reason I cannot march against them and I will not."*

After the war it was learned that in the summer of 1917 a secret German Sailors' Union had been formed on the battleship *Friedrich der Grosse*, and that virtually every ship in the High Seas Fleet had anti-war agitators on board.

According to the memoirs of Sir Basil Zaharoff, also known as 'the armaments king', Socialist Party leaders from Germany and France, aided by Bolsheviks from Russia, met secretly in Switzerland in 1918 and began planning an end to the bloodbath. Other sources give hints that the plan was for armed groups of soldiers or sailors to eject the authorities in each German and French town, and take over the civilian and military buildings. Simultaneously all soldiers and sailors on active duty would cease hostilities whether their officers liked it or not. Soldiers' Councils would assume control at each level of the military and civil organizations, and the European brotherhood of man would be proclaimed. "*There would be no more wars to make the rich richer*, 'they said,' *and the poor to be forced to die for their profit.*"

The target date was the middle of November 1918 which meant peace by Christmas. The difficulty was how to organize it secretly. The shadow of a noose or a firing squad lay over each one of the delegates, but organize it, they did. On 1 November the clandestine German Sailors' Union acted, and by the 4th, the flag flying at all the ports used by the German navy was pure red. One week later when the armistice was announced, the secret German Soldiers' Councils at the front made common cause with the sailors, and the French delegates to the meeting in Switzerland heaved a sigh of relief.

When peace came, anti-war movements on both sides of the Atlantic Ocean strongly influenced public opinion and government policies up to the outbreak of the Second World War. The pacifists in England, the socialists in France and Canada, and the isolationists in the USA are examples.

(3) MACHINE-GUN JAMS CAUSED BY THE POOR QUALITY AMMUNITION BEING MANUFACTURED AT THIS STAGE OF THE WAR.

The 0.303" standard army Mark VII rifle cartridge was now being manufactured in many new factories, some being overseas. Sadly, for a few of the new factory owners profit was paramount, quality came second. In some factories the strength of the charge of cordite varied considerably, and so did the trajectory of the bullets manufactured there. The percussion caps (primers) which ignited the cordite often would not fire when struck. Some cartridge cases were out of round and would not slide easily into the breech. It was specifically for the latter that many pilots carried the wooden mallet (mentioned earlier) in the cockpit. Other cartridge cases were so thin that, after being fired, they would split into two pieces as the extractor claws pulled them from the breech block. One piece of the case would remain in the breech and the next cartridge would be forcibly telescoped into it. That mess could only be sorted out on the ground and a large part of the gun had to be dismantled in the process.

It was of little consolation that German pilots suffered from identical problems, and many, on both sides, pre-selected the rounds that their ground crews would later load into their weapons. That, at the least, eliminated those which externally appeared doubtful.

(4) THE DUTIES AND PRIVILEGES OF A FLIGHT COMMANDER.

ON THE GROUND

Each flight had air mechanics, riggers and armourers who worked under one or more sergeants. The sergeants reported to their Flight Commander, who was therefore the ultimate person responsible for the cleanliness, airworthiness and combat readiness of the aeroplanes in his flight. Pilots' complaints concerning the condition of their aeroplanes were made to him. Assuming five aeroplanes plus one spare per flight, the Flight Commander would have twenty to thirty airmen under his direct control. In addition, he was expected to keep an eye on the health, the behaviour and the expertise of his pilots.

Flight Commanders had priority at the de-briefing session after a patrol. He would provide a short description of the event for the Recording Officer, known today as the Adjutant, and then depart to his duties while the pilots individually made their reports. The Recording Officer would summarize and type the reports onto the official form, COMBATS IN THE AIR, and each pilot would sign his own. However, in the case of the Flight Commanders, who could be extremely busy organizing repairs to the aircraft when the squadron was heavily in action, some Recording Officers would not interrupt their work, but would imitate their signatures and send their report to the wing, together with all the others, at 16:00 hours. This was a useful convenience for the Flight Commanders, since the noisy maintenance workshops were usually at some distance from the administrative offices where quiet was appreciated.

When in his nineties, RNAS Flight Commander, later RAF Captain William Melville (Mel) Alexander, DFC, who married Roy's wife's sister, Clara Monypenny, reread his 1917 and 1918 COMBATS IN THE AIR reports. He commented they were marvels of understatement, and added that detailed or long-winded reports were frowned upon after early 1917.

IN THE AIR

Leading a flight required the ability to navigate accurately, to see tiny dots in the sky, and to decide whether they were enemy dots or friendly dots. On the tactical side, a Flight Commander had to decide when to attack or to retreat, and to play mother hen to the other pilots if a dog fight developed. After a period of furious combat, his final task was to bring his flight home. The last item was not so easy as it might seem; low clouds often hid the ground, and then the precious, many-jewelled watch on the instrument panel came into its own.

The Flight Commander would note the time and then use the aeroplane's compass to lead his flight in the homeward direction. After sufficient number of minutes had elapsed to be well inside Allied territory, he would descend and look for landmarks. As Captain Oliver LeBoutillier told author Dale Titler, it was at this point the really difficult part began: where the Flight Commander thought he might be, and where he actually was. These positions could be several miles apart in any direction. Great War air stories abound of competent pilots and famous aces who had to land to ask where they were. In his book AIR COMMAND, fighter ace, Raymond Collishaw, tells how, as he was taxiing towards the hangars on such a quest, he noticed the ground crew running towards him wore grey uniforms. He decided it would not be a good idea to ask them for directions.

A Flight Commander had always to bear in mind the three axioms of aerial combat:

> (a) The man with the height controls the fight.
> (b) Use the sun to hide from the Hun.
> (c) Get in close and shoot them down.

With two members of his flight charged with guarding his tail, a Flight

Commander was able to devote his attention to searching the sky for little black dots, studying his map and planning an attack. Many Flight Commanders considered the benefit to their health and well-being brought by the tail guards more than compensated for the heavy administrative work-load on the ground.

The Germans employed a similar system.

(5) THE AMALGAMATION OF THE RFC AND THE RNAS.

At the beginning of the war the RFC had been receiving its aeroplanes from the Royal Aircraft Factory (R.A.F.) and via direct purchases from French factories. The RNAS had a somewhat limited choice; it required seaplanes and flying boats and therefore had to go to suppliers who specialized in those. These were principally Short Brothers and Sopwith in the U.K., and Curtiss in the U.S.

When the RNAS saw the need for high performance landplanes, it approached the Sopwith Aviation Company from which it had earlier purchased some single-seater *Tabloid* seaplanes. The Sopwith *One and a Half Strutters* and *Pups* which it purchased proved to have performances superior to the landplanes designed by the Royal Aircraft Factory for the RFC. Unfortunately some types of engines were used both by the RNAS and the RFC, and competition between the respective purchasing departments for priority in deliveries then started causing problems; not only with the supply of engines, but of aircraft construction materials also.

On the subject of manufacturing quality, Mel Alexander once revealed that within the RNAS the Clergêt engines manufactured in France were believed to be of better quality than those manufactured under licence in England. He then told how he had arranged with the engine maintenance sergeant for any U.K. manufactured Clergêt engines found on the Sopwith *Triplanes* in his flight to be replaced with French ones from the other flights. The unholy row which occurred when the other two Flight Commanders, Raymond Collishaw and John Edward (Ted) Sharman, learned they had been robbed was beyond description.

In the long run, the RNAS did itself a disservice when it responded to the RFC's request for the loan of one, and then four more of its fighter squadrons. It gave some officials, who today would be known as long range snipers, the chance to allege that both services were doing the same job. An independent committee chaired by South African General, Jan Christian Smuts, decided that the quickest and best solution to all the aspects of the situation was to amalgamate the two services. The immediate results were beneficial, but the long term consequences were a disaster. When the Second World War began, no aircraft carrier version of the Spitfire or the Hurricane existed to protect ships once they came within range of the latest types of German bombers.

(6) THE ALLIED PLAN TO END THE WAR.

(7) THE BRISTOL F.2A *FIGHTER*.

The need for a Squadron Leader or Flight Commander to employ two tail guards was a clear indication of the weakness of single seater fighters. To a certain extent, the lack of a rearward firing machine-gun could be countered by the ability to make sharp turns; one reason why single combat tended to develop into a circling match.

Provided - and that is the key word - that a Sopwith *Camel* pilot saw an enemy on his tail in time, he could out-turn him and end up on his tail, but there was one exception; a Fokker *Triplane* could out-turn a *Camel*. Obviously there was a limit to the development of turning capability and these two aeroplanes appear to have reached it.

The original Sopwith fighter had a front and a rear gun; namely the two-seater version of the *One and a Half Strutter*, and with the advent of higher powered in-line engines, which did not weigh half a ton, a return to this concept seemed possible. Frank Barnwell, the chief designer of the British and Colonial Aeroplane Company, Ltd., designed a two-seater fighter around the newly developed Rolls Royce 12 cylinder water-cooled engine; the 190 HP Falcon. The pilot had a Vickers machine-gun, and the gunner had a single Lewis gun installation on a Scarff ring. It was known as the Bristol F.2A, and when flown as a fighter, could tackle anything the Germans had. Unfortunately, the rumour mill quite incorrectly said the Bristols were structurally weak and would collapse in a dog fight.

On 4 April 1917, Captain William Leefe Robinson, who had won the Victoria Cross for shooting down the Zeppelin L11 over

Cuffley, England, led six Bristol F.2A *Fighters* over the enemy lines. When attacked by Jagdstaffel 11 led by Baron von Richthofen, the Bristol pilots, who were new to this type of aeroplane, took the rumour seriously. They did not use the Bristols as fighters with a gunner to protect the tail, and instead of giving the Germans a hard time, they flew defensively. Four of the six were forced down inside enemy territory.

Once the weakness rumour was disproved, the value of the Bristol *Fighter*, nicknamed *Brisfit*, became obvious.

Typical Bristol F.2A *Fighter*.

An improved version, the F.2B, had a 275 HP Rolls Royce Falcon III engine, could climb to 10,000 feet in twelve minutes, and fly at 113 MPH at that altitude. With such power, speed, a Vickers machine-gun for the pilot and twin Lewis guns for the rear gunner, it could handle anything the Germans had in service and would but rarely be taken by surprise from the rear; almost 5,000 were built. With several upgrades, it continued in production until 1926.

(8) PASSING SHELLS AND SPENT BULLETS.
When an aeroplane collapsed in the air due to its structure having been weakened by enemy bullets, by over stressing, by having been left out in the rain, etc., a large piece would usually be observed to wave around and then fall off. Other nasty events would logically follow. However, pilots had occasionally noticed that an aeroplane in the formation would instantaneously disintegrate into matchwood for no apparent reason. Capt. A H Cobby of 4 Squadron, Australian Flying Corps, described such an event. *"[There was no black smoke,"* he wrote. *"No*

flame and no explosion; just hundreds of tiny pieces and three large objects where, seconds before, there had been an aeroplane. The three large objects were the engine, the fuel tank and the pilot."

One day, a pilot who had recently seen the aeroplane beside him disintegrate for no reason he could fathom, was intrigued to observe a tiny black dot in the sky ahead of him. The dot rapidly became larger. He dived immediately and then heard a roar like an express train as the dot passed overhead; it was a very large calibre artillery shell. The inexplicable was now explained.

The fuze in the nose of most artillery shells had adjustments which could be set to suit the range and type of target. A fuze, set to detonate the explosive charge shortly after a really solid impact, would not respond to the slight resistance of wood and fabric.

Major James McCudden wrote of a pilot (probably Captain Cecil Arthur Lewis, MC) in his squadron who saw a howitzer shell reach its peak height, watched its nose slowly turn over and then begin its journey downwards to earth carrying death and destruction.

Captain Arthur Gould Lee, MC, who later became an Air Vice Marshal, described how something dark approached and flashed by him at 8,000 feet altitude. He looked behind and saw what he assumed to be the rear end of a large shell on its way to Hunland. When he mentioned it in the mess, he learned that other pilots had seen such objects on previous occasions. In late summer 1917 the trailing edge of the port top wing of an R.E.8 of 2 Sqn. RFC, piloted by Lieut. Vernon Burgess, was grazed by a passing artillery shell. Fortunately the main spar was not broken and the aeroplane returned safely, but with a much shaken crew. At last there was tangible evidence of what many had suspected.

Lieut. Burgess's R.E.8. The main spar is exposed but fortunately still intact.

There is one documented case of an artillery shell striking something solid enough to cause it to explode; one could hypothesize that it struck the engine. Captain Guy Borthwick Moore, MC, a Canadian, was the victim. His colleagues, who witnessed the event, said that his S.E.5A suddenly turned into a huge cloud of smoke. There was no wreckage, just a mass of tiny fragments which drifted down to the ground. No mortal remains of Moore could be found.

Sometimes spent rifle and machine-gun bullets were also seen in the air. On 7 August 1917 the OTTAWA CITIZEN carried the following news item on page 3 column 7.

CATCHING BULLETS ON WING AVIATORS' SPORT

British Airman Calmly Pockets German Bullet
Reaching Maximum Height

LONDON, July 24 (by mail)

Flying over the German lines a British aviator was soon in the midst of a whining swarm of German bullets. The Germans in the trenches were firing straight up hoping to wing the flyer or pierce his fuel tank.

The aviator - a cool youngster - looked down and saw a bullet slowly ascending the last few feet of its maximum height. It stopped dead still for the smallest fraction of a second. The aviator reached quickly, grabbed the bullet and put it in his pocket.

There may be some truth behind the story, but it has changed somewhat in the multiple retelling. The aeroplane would be moving horizontally relative to the ground at anywhere between 60 and 120 MPH, depending upon the wind strength and direction, whereas the bullet, which had 'stopped dead still' in the vertical plane, would also be stationary in the horizontal plane. Therefore, at the moment the pilot allegedly stretched out his arm, his hand would have struck the bullet with an almighty whack. However, if the aeroplane had been flying at 3,000 to 5,000 feet altitude, and the bullet had been fired from a mile or so behind, the event could have occurred. It is far more likely the pilot had originally told of having seen a bullet in the air beside him, almost close enough to touch, which is something that really did happen to another pilot. Major James McCudden wrote that on 25 September 1915, during the battle of Loos, a bullet from the ground was seen as it passed slowly between the heads of a pilot, Sergeant Watts, and his observer, Corporal Roberts.

(13) The danger in which Roy stood in the few seconds before he was able to stop the engine may be gleaned from what happened to the German ace Max Immelmann, Pour le Mérite, 17 victories. Upon returning from a flight he complained that the engine of his Fokker

Eindecker (monoplane) was vibrating badly. The engine mounting was found to be cracked and had to be replaced. During an air fight with an F.E.2B, on the following day, the engine fell sideways as a mounting support fractured and the others bent and the Fokker cracked. There are two versions of the cause of the crash. The first one states that the original crack in the engine mounting had not been the cause, but the vibrations of the vibration on the previous day. The second one states that the synchronizing gear failed and Immelmann shot his own propeller to pieces, whereupon the engine oversped, causing its mounting to fracture. Immelmann was killed in the crash. The F.E.2B crew claimed a victory, but the wreckage of the Fokker indicated structural failure. Given the great flying experience of Max Immelmann, the authors feel he would immediately have recognized the change in the rhythm of his machine guns and ceased firing and/or stopped the engine. The first version would, therefore, appear to be the more likely cause of the crash.

(9) PILOTS WOUNDED OR KILLED IN THE AIR.

Manfred von Richthofen's brother, Leutnant Lothar von Richthofen (40 victories) and Captain A.H. Cobby both described in their memoirs how an aeroplane they were attacking had suddenly nosed up steeply which, they wrote, indicated their shots had hit the pilot. Captain A.G. Lee, in his book, NO PARACHUTE, describes five instances of the same thing within his own combat experience. What happened next would depend upon the painfulness and severity of the wound.

Medically speaking, the sudden nosing up, occasionally accompanied by a steep bank to the right, was the result of the general muscular contraction with which the human body responds to sudden, intense pain. The contraction of the pilot's right arm would jerk the joystick sharply back and sometimes to the right as well. The latter action would cause something like a climbing twist to the right, or what some would incorrectly describe as an Immelmann turn.

(10) THE DIFFERENCE BETWEEN A D.H.4 AND A D.H.9.

The D.H.9 was a development of the D.H.4 fast day bomber and very similar in appearance. The main difference constituted the location of the observer's cockpit. On the D.H.4 the fuel tank (positioned at the centre of gravity) had separated the crew members, and although the D.H.4 had a speaking tube intercommunication system (described below), it had been found that the noise of battle made messages inaudible at critical moments. During the design stage of the D.H.9, the fuel tank had been relocated and the observer's cockpit positioned directly behind the pilot's. The proximity of the two cockpits now made it possible for the observer to shout into the pilot's ear or use coded taps on his shoulders. In his book DOUBLEDECKER C333, Hauptmann Heydemarck, a German observer, wrote that he used similar means to communicate with his pilot.

The D.H.9 was intended to be a 'hot' performer, but unfortunately it's recently designed 300 HP Siddeley Puma engine suffered from serious problems in service and had to be derated to 230 HP. Even after the power reduction, the engine remained unreliable, and at Naval 5 and 6 squadrons the complete change-over from D.H.4s to D.H.9s was considerably delayed by problems of serviceability with the latter. So, although Roy calls the two-seaters D.H.9s, his remark that the flight could not not keep up with them suggests they were more likely to have been D.H.4s.

Thus the D.H.9 gained the doubtful distinction of having a performance considerably inferior to the type it was intended to replace. When later fitted with an American 400 HP Liberty engine, the D.H.9A or *'Nine Ack'*, as it became known, performed as intended and remained in service for many years after the war.

Typical Airco D.H.9 with Puma engine. The vertical object directly in front of the pilot and reaching up to the leading edge of the top wing is the engine cooling water tank. The radiator can be seen just ahead of the undercarriage. Note the two cockpits close together and the observer's Lewis gun, equipped with both ring and vane sights, mounted on a Scarff ring.

Typical Airco D.H.4 fast day bombers. These belonged to 202 Sqn. RAF (formerly Naval 2). Note the distance between the pilot and the observer caused by the fuel tank positioned at the centre of balance. From L to R: A7868, N5962, A7849. Photograph taken at Bergues.

The speaking tube intercommunication system on the D.H.4 was known as a Gosport Tube. The name was derived from the RNAS station, near Portsmouth, where it was invented. Left and right earpieces were fitted inside buttoned flaps on the student's leather flying helmet, and the instructor spoke into a small funnel at his end of the tube. As late as the Second World War, many simple types of two-seater primary trainers used the Gosport Tube system with great success on both sides of the Atlantic.

(11) GENERAL GOUGH'S REWARD FOR HIS EFFORTS.

Despite Field Marshal Haig's support, Lieutenant-General Sir Hubert Gough was relieved of his command by the former's political superiors in London who needed a scapegoat for public consumption. Haig suggested a Court Martial because this would reveal that the reinforcements, which both he and Gough had requested to face the impending German attack, had been retained in England. The request was denied by the Prime Minister, Lloyd George; the dirty laundry would have waved over the cabinet ministers who had held back the 300,000 soldiers and their reasons for doing so. Justice was finally done in 1937 when, in his first Birthday Honours List, a Royal Navy war veteran, who as a young man had fought in the Battle of Jutland, appointed Sir Hubert Gough a Knight Grand Cross of the Order of the Bath. The navy veteran was King George VI.

It is pleasing to know that Sir Hubert Gough had the last laugh; not only was he chosen by the army as a pall bearer for Sir Douglas Haig, but he outlived by several decades most of those who had 'shafted' him. He died in 1963 at the age of 93.

A similar set of circumstances occurred in the Second World War when US Admiral Husband E Kimmel, who commanded at Pearl Harbor in 1941, was denied the Court Martial which he had requested.

(12) TAKE-OFF AND LANDING ACCIDENTS.

Most aeroplanes of that era had no brakes: not a serious problem since landing speeds were slow compared to aeroplanes built ten years later. A fixed tailskid scraping against the turf-covered airfields created a braking force, and provided landings were made directly into the wind so that the aeroplane was not drifting to one side or the other, the system was adequate although certainly not ideal. If a pilot lost directional control before the ground crew caught the wing tips, his aeroplane would spin around once or twice like a dog chasing its own tail. The phenomenon is known as a 'ground loop' and was mentioned earlier in Chapter Four when Roy ground-looped Avro 504C 1480 on 1 April 1916. The Bristol F2A *Fighter* and all later versions left the factory with a major improvement in this area; a steerable tailskid. It was connected to the rudder pedals and gave the pilot some measure of control at low speed.

Take-offs were also made directly into the wind for similar reasons. The engine would be running at full power, thereby providing a strong airflow over the rudder, and cases of a pilot losing directional control were rare. However, problems occasionally occurred with the undercarriage. If a tyre burst or a wheel collapsed (some even fell off) during the last stage of the take-off run, the aeroplane would make a high speed ground-loop at full power, suffer serious structural damage and probably catch fire. With a fully armed and fuelled machine, the result was only too often fatal.

Lieut. Miller's fatal accident was of another only too familiar kind; engine failure shortly after take-off. Pilots had strict instructions not to turn back to the airfield unless they were at least 200 feet up at the time, but were to continue ahead into wind and make the best landing possible. This was safer by far as the danger of stalling and spinning during the U-turn was serious. From above 200 feet, such as in the case of Lieut. Miller, there was still danger but of a different variety. If the pilot's position relative to the airfield did not allow him to land into the wind, both the approach and touch-down would occur at ground speeds higher than usual. An inexperienced pilot, such as Lieut. Miller, upon seeing the ground passing by at an unusually high speed, could easily assume he had not slowed down enough. The result of correcting the 'error' would be a stall followed by a crash. Even in the case of proficient pilots, it was not unknown for a successful with-the-wind or a cross-wind touch-down without the help of engine power to result in a high speed ground-loop.

(13) MEL ALEXANDER'S ATTACK ON A KITE BALLOON.

Extract from the dialogue of a recorded interview with Mel Alexander when he was 90 years old.

"Did you ever get involved with attacking balloons?"

"Yes, I was on balloon strafes; two or three of them. On my last flight out there I was on a balloon strafe with another chap; Lieut. Payton. He and I were involved in attacking the balloons and the rest of the flight were protecting us. He went down on one; I went down on the other. These balloons were protected by what we used to call flaming onions. I don't know if you ever heard of them. A bunch of flaming rockets came up at you. The guns which fired them surrounded the balloons.

I went down on this balloon, Payton went down on the other. I was going down at a terrific speed and I happened to look over. I said, 'Holy Jumping! They're giving him the devil over there.' Those flaming onions were coming right up. I drove the balloon right down, and I think Payton did too. We never set them on fire.

When we got home, I said, 'Holy Jumping! You were getting a pasting. You were getting those flaming onions like nobody's business.' He said, 'I didn't see any, but you were getting them all around you.' We could see them around the other person but not around ourselves."

Flaming onions, was the nick-name given to a type of German gunfire which, as it climbed up into the sky, resembled the strings of onions which peacetime onion sellers carried over their shoulders as they hawked their wares through the streets of England, France and Spain. They were actually bursts of large incendiary bullets fired from Oerlikon heavy machine-guns and gave an appearance (incorrect) of being wired together. The bullets were 2.1 cm (almost 7/8") in diameter and 5 cms (almost 2") long. They were also known as flaming caterpillars.

One of the lessons to be learned from Mel's story is that even such highly illuminated ground fire is only visible if it is far enough away to grant the human eye sufficient time to record its passage.

Similarly, neither Mel Alexander nor Lieut. Payton would have seen any of the tracer bullets fired at them, but in their case, the reason is different. Due to stories, which purport to be history, in which characters see 'flaming tracers' fired from machine-guns in the daytime, it is little known that in 1914 - 1918 tracer bullets were only visible to a person positioned directly, or almost directly behind the weapon which was firing them. They appeared as pinpoints of blue light which left a faint trail of smoke. Such trails, appearing ahead of a pilot and receding into the distance, were an indication there was someone behind who objected to his presence.

Mel Alexander's PILOT'S FLYING LOG BOOK dates the balloon strafe (above) as having happened on 27 May 1918. His memory slipped a little in one aspect; it was not his last flight of the war. His Log Book indicates his actual last flight, which included combat with some Albatros D.VA scouts, occurred on the following day.

Captain William Melville Alexander seated in a Sopwith *Camel* of the Manston War Flight.

(14) HOW 'WONGA BONGA' EARNED ITS NAME.

RNAS Flight Lieutenants Arthur F Brandon and J Drake took off from Manston on 22 August 1917 to intercept a daylight raid by eleven Gotha bombers attacking Margate, Ramsgate and Dover. Both pilots stalked Gotha GIV/636/16 and caught up with the raider at 14,000 feet just off Margate, where they shot it down in flames. After this raid, in which three Gothas were brought down by the defences, the Germans changed to night bombing.

Lieut. Brandon, who was flying Sopwith *Camel* B3834 on that occasion, had been impressed by the rhythmic beat of the Gotha's two 260 HP Mercedes engines; they seemed to rumble; 'wonga-bonga, wonga-bonga', and that provided him with the idea.

Sopwith F1 *Camel* B3834 of Manston War Flight, wearing its new name. Behind it are a Sopwith *Triplane* and a *One and Half Strutter*.

(15) LIEUT. W R MAY'S PROWESS AS A TRAINEE PILOT.

Actually, Wop May was not so green as has been stated, restated and consequently believed by most for more than eighty years. Flying training had revealed Wop May to be a natural born pilot, which, together with his prowess in the various other subjects taught in flying training schools, gained for him a rare distinction. Along with his RFC Pilot's Certificate, he received an immediate advance in rank. On 5 April 1918 the *London Gazette* announced his promotion to 1st Lieutenant with effect from 28 February; the date of his graduation from No. 94 Higher Training Squadron at Hendon.

Royal Flying Corps - London Aerodrome - Acton, London - November 15, 1917
Lieut. W. R. "Wop" May 6th from the right - front row

An examination of Wop May's R.F.C. TRAINING TRANSFER CARD, in addition to giving the size of his gas mask, reveals that his gunnery was exceptional. In eleven tests, spread over one month, when firing Vickers machine-guns and Lewis automatic-guns on the ground at ground targets, he placed between 95 and 100% of his shots in the valid areas. On three other tests he scored between 85 and 90%. His air to ground gunnery scores were exceptional; on 16 and 22 March 1918 he fired a total of 300 rounds from a Sopwith *Pup* and scored 84%. According to Lt. Roland W. Richardson, an American who was training in France at the same time; "8% was considered pretty good for trainees." Wop's proficiency was not simply good luck, it came from his prior service in the Canadian Army where he had been a Master Gunner with the rank of Sergeant.

Sergeant Wilfrid May, in the centre of the photograph, giving machine-gun instruction in Canada.

If Wop May could avoid accidents due to engine failure, bad weather; etc., he stood a good chance of becoming an ace. This became true and he ended the war as Captain W.R. May, DFC, with 13 victories, plus 5 probables.

(16) THE GERMAN TITLE 'FREIHERR'.

Although Freiherr is normally translated as Baron, it actually signified that the holder was a free man; i.e. could not be taken to court without the approval of the Kaiser. The title was also conferred upon ladies; Manfred's mother was Kunigunde Freifrau von Richthofen, his sister was Elizabeth Freifraulein von Richthofen.

(17) THE IMMELMANN TURN.

Leutnant Max Immelmann devised a mean of giving an opponent a double surprise. If his diving attack from behind had been unsuccessful, he would use his speed to continue ahead and then pull up into a 180 degree stall turn and dive onto his quarry again. The enemy pilot, who had been shaken by his near escape, would be an easy target this time. The trick was to be far enough away when pulling up, otherwise during the low speed, stall turn; Immelmann would have presented himself as an easy target to his quarry. If, as happened with Roy on 12 April 1918, the attacker began an Immelmann turn too close to an enemy pilot who already knew from experience what would happen next, the biter stood a good chance of being bitten.

With the advent of stronger airframes, the first part of the manoeuvre became a half-loop, and when the aeroplane was upside down at the top, the pilot would roll it upright again and dive onto his quarry. That eliminated the dangerous, low speed portion.

(18) THE EFFECT OF DIHEDRAL ON THE STABILITY OF AN AEROPLANE.

The amount of dihedral, and the wings to which it is applied, exert great influence upon the manoeuvrability of a fighter aeroplane and its degree of stability in rough air. If an air 'bump' tilts an aeroplane to one side, it will begin to slip to that side. If the wings on the aeroplane in question have dihedral; i.e. they slope upwards like a shallow 'V', the sideways wind will press harder on the top of the raised wing than on the lowered one and will push the wings level again. If the wings have no dihedral, the sideways slip will continue until the pilot corrects it. A trained pilot will immediately know his aeroplane is slipping to one side as he will sense the sideways wind on his cheek. This is one reason why even today, some aerobatic pilots prefer to use an open cockpit machine for their displays.

Three wing arrangements are illustrated below.

Dihedral on upper and lower wings. Royal Aircraft Factory S.E.5A of 32 Sqn. RAF. Note 'B' Flight Commander's pennants on the tailplane.

It is worthy of comment that Captain William Carpenter Lambert, DFC, an American volunteer RFC pilot in 24 Sqn., had his riggers reduce the dihedral angle of his S.E.5A by 50%. He found a slight decrease in stability, a slight increase in manoeuvrability, but a most useful increase of 5 MPH in speed.

No dihedral. Super manoeuvrable Fokker *Triplane* F.I 101/17 overflying Adlershof aerodrome during type acceptance testing.

According to Anthony Fokker, the interplane struts were added to make the cantilever wings flex in unison during air turbulence. Apparently their independent motion had placed 'Schmetterlinge' in the stomachs of the test pilots. For those to whom German is a mystery, 'Schmetterlinge' means butterflies.

Dihedral on lower wings only. Sopwith *Camel*. Note 'C' Flight Commander's pennants on the interplane struts.

The absence of fabric on the upper wing centre section and the twin Lewis guns indicate this particular *Camel* was an RNAS night-fighter. For ease of manufacture, the upper wings were constructed as a flat, single piece. In compensation, extra dihedral was applied to the lower wings.

The following photograph illustrates how the wing dihedral arrangement can aid in the identification of distant aircraft. Air-to-air photography was rare in 1917/1918 so this photograph, taken at some time between April and July 1917, is a gem. The patrol was flying above the clouds at 17,000 feet, and the camera was a Vest Pocket Kodak using standard film. The propeller passed by while the shutter was open. Use the three preceding photographs to identify the type of aeroplane in this one. In case of doubt, item (24) at the end of this ANNEX provides the answer.

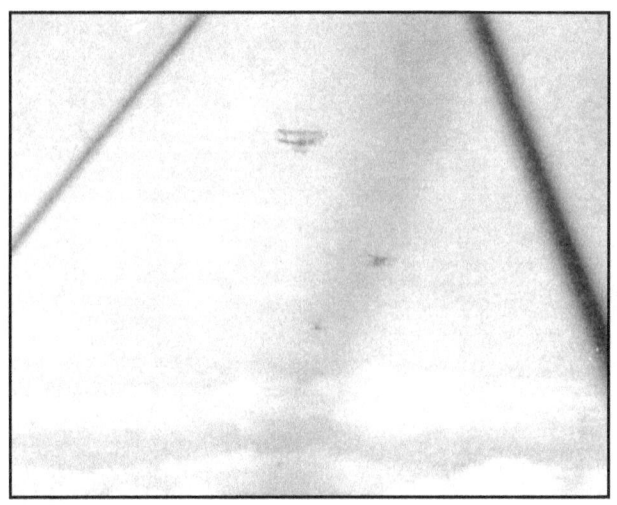

High altitude patrol.

(19) MEL ALEXANDER'S STORY ON THE UNEXPECTED RESULT OF REPAINTING 210 SQUADRON'S SOPWITH CAMELS.

Dialogue from a conversation between Mel Alexander and Air Vice Marshal Alfred William (Nick) Carter, DSC, OBE, MBE, recorded in 1970.

MEL. *"The fighting got pretty doggone strenuous as 1917 went on. We had superiority and started to paint our Camels up with stripes. It just happened that we were a pretty good squadron with pretty good pilots. You had to be good if you were going to be marked up like that and be recognized."*

NICK. *"We didn't have to apologize to anybody."*

MEL. *"Then the Royal Air Force came into being and Trenchard left. We now had Salmond. He came out looking at all his air force, his new squadrons and everything. He came down to our squadron, which was a pretty good squadron, a fine background, and by God! He saw those stripes. He was upset about that. No aeroplanes were to be painted with any other than the standard khaki colour plus the standard squadron markings."*

NICK. *"That's Right. Did we pay any attention to that?"*

MEL. *"No. We didn't."*

NICK. *"I don't think we did."*

MEL. *"Then he found out we had not done it. I think it was two or three weeks afterwards, and he really sent down a blisterer of an order and we had to take them off. I'll never forget the first time out with my flight without the stripes on. My God! The Huns were brave. They did not know we were this gang of hot stuff. By God! They started to fight back and acted quite brave."*

NICK. *"That made us mad. We'd just as soon they'd stayed away."*

On the left, Red and white striped *Camel* B6299 and others of 'B' Flight, Naval 10 Squadron. On the right, *Camels* of either 'A' (black and white stripes) or 'C' Flight (blue and white stripes).

Ringed *Camel* B3858 (mauve and green) of Naval 3 squadron. Captain Leonard Henry (Titch) Rochford, DSC & bar with *Camel* B3858 photographed at Walmer, Kent in November 1917.

On 5 February 1918 a broken connecting rod in the engine forced Lt. E (Pecker) Pierce to land B3858 as best as he could in a field full of shell holes. After a complete rebuild (and minus the coloured rings), it was issued to Lieutenant Robert Mordaunt Foster, DFC of 209 Squadron. He was flying it on Sunday 21 April 1918 during the action in which Manfred von Richthofen was killed.

(20) LIEUTENANT MAY'S INITIAL EXPERIENCES ON ACTIVE SERVICE.

In times of stress and intense excitement, seconds seem like minutes and minutes like hours. When no distinction is made between weekends and weekdays, all sense of time tends to become lost. It is not surprising that when Wop May gave a talk without notes to the 12th Calgary Boy Scout Troop on 19 February 1952 his memory betrayed him over a detail concerning his first experience of combat.

The entries in his Log Book for April 1918 (up to the 20th) are as follows:

09.4.18 - Reported to 209th Squadron April 9th. Flying Bentley Camels.

11.4.18 - Camel D3340 - 30 mins - Looking over ground & getting used to machine.

12.4.18 - Camel D3340 - 90 mins - Balloon patrol - Looking over the landmarks. Visibility good.

13.4.18 - Camel D3340 - 45 mins - Line Patrol with F.C. - Visibility poor.

(F.C. means Flight Commander. Roy Brown's Log Book for this day records that he was showing new pilots the position of the lines.)

16.4.18 - Camel D3340 - 30 mins - Target Practice.

17.4.18 - Camel D3340 - 60 mins - Target Practice.

20.4.18 - Camel D3326 - First time over the line. Flight got into scrap with triplanes - Got into scrap with 6   incl chap he crashed. I did not get a burst into them. Archied slightly.

Roy Brown, who was leading the flight, claimed a Fokker *Triplane* shot down in that engagement. One must assume that *"he"* in *"the chap he crashed"* refers to Lieut. May's Flight Commander.

20.4.18 - Camel D3326 - 105 mins - No E.A. seen. Line Patrol. Nothing seen.

The above entries indicate that Wop May's morning flight the next day would be his third venture into Hunland and his second involvement in an aerial combat.

(21) THE 11TH AND 14TH BRIGADE WAR DIARY ENTRIES FOR 21 APRIL 1918.

11th Australian Infantry Brigade

Partial entry. *"At 11.20 Baron Capt, von Richthofen was shot down by a 24 Aust M.G. Coy (Company) Sergeant firing a Vickers M.G."*

14th Australian Field Artillery Brigade

Partial entry. "*An enemy plane was brought down by Lewis gunners of 53rd Battery, the pilot who was killed proved to be Capt. Baron von Richthofen.*"

(22) THE COLOUR OF RITTMEISTER MANFRED VON RICHTHOFEN'S AEROPLANES.

Several of those who saw Fokker Dr.I 425/17 up close described it as being painted red, but not bright red. One Australian stated the colour was somewhere between Post Office red and the slightly bluish shade of red used on motorcycles manufactured in the USA by the INDIAN company.

From the time the Rittmeister adopted the bright red colour of his Uhlan regiment as his personal identification mark, he flew several aeroplanes representing the following types: Albatros DIII, Albatros DV, Halberstadt DI and Fokker Dr.I. Manfred von Richthofen received a brand new aeroplane as soon as a later design was released for service at the front, or wear and tear caused deterioration in the performance of the one he was using. The paint was applied at many different aerodromes and the colour was not always bright red. In 1918, the Germans were suffering from serious shortages of material, and Jasta 11 mechanics probably used whatever shade of red they could lay their hands on in occupied France.

Alan Bennett has seen many pieces of fabric from 425/17, both large and small, in England, Canada and the USA, and regardless of where or under what conditions of light, temperature and humidity they have been kept, they are all on the dark side of burgundy red. It is probable that the pigments on the surviving pieces of linen have darkened with age, but the presence of blue pigment in the paint is clearly discernable. Some pieces of fabric in the Pasquale Carisella collection are documented as having been cut from the underside of the wings or the tailplane. These all have two layers of paint; the one applied directly to the doped linen is sky blue, the top coat is red, thus confirming that unlike the Fokker *Triplanes* flown previously by the Rittmeister on which the underside was sky blue, 425/17 was red all over. Air Mechanic 1st Class Morris Waldron examined 425/17 on 22 April and his diary provides confirmation of the single colour.

(23) ROY BROWN'S SURVIVING COMBAT REPORTS FOR THIS PERIOD.

To find the matching Log Book entry, see the specified date in Chapter Eight. The lettering on the three reports below was unfit for reproduction. They have all been retyped following the original spacing, spelling, etc., and around the original signatures. The report for 12 April 1918 Roy indicates Roy has regained his RNAS Flight Commander (acting) status, but being now in the RAF, he lists himself as Captain (honorary).

```
                 COMBAT         REPORT.
                 ----------     ----------
     No. 9 Squadron                2nd February,1918
            Sopwith B.R.           2.20.p.m.
       B 7195
                                    Foret D' Houthulst.

     2 Syn.Vickers Guns            Offensive sweep.

     Flt Lt A.R.Brown              9.000 feet.


                2 Albatross two-seaters.


              I dived on two Albatross two-seaters over Foret
       D' Houthulst and opened fire on one getting in about 100
       rounds, when the other two-seater began to get above me.
       I turned on him and fired about 350 rounds. Both E.A.
       disappeared in the mist, after I had turned to dive again.


                                  [signature]
                                  Flight Lieutenant.

                                  [signature]
                                  SQUADRON COMMANDER


   Retyped 12 March 2002
```

COMBAT REPORT.
---------- ----------

No. 9. R. N. A. S. February 6th 1918.
        Sopwith F 1 10. 20 a.m.
B 3919. B 6289. 10 miles to sea North of
                                                   Ostende.
Two Vickers Syn. Guns. S. L. P.

Flt.Lt's. Brown and Wood.
                                            1.000 - 500 feet.

    One large seaplane carrying torpedo and two small seaplane scouts. Also three other similar machines following at a distance of about a mile.

    Observed 3 seaplanes about 10 miles to sea North of Ostende going to usual position occupied by Fleet. I dived on them followed by Flt. Lt. Wood and drove them into Zeebrugge harbour. Guns jammed in No. 3 position about every 20 or 30 rounds so did not get the E.A.
    The machine I was flying has just arrived from No. 10 Squadron and there has been no time to overhaul guns.
    Three other seaplanes came up behind us which were attacked by Flt. Lt. Wood but he could not get long enough bursts to shoot them down.
    850 rounds were fired in all.

                                                              J. R. Brown.
                                                              Flight Lieut.

                                                              Flight Lieut.

Retyped 12 March, 2002
                                                           Squadron Commander

                    209 R.A.F.   April 12th 1918.
                         Sopwith BR
         B 7270, B 3326, B 7245, B 3340.   8.30 a.m.
                                                Warfusee - Abancourt.
                    Two Vickers Syn.Guns.
                                                H.O.P.
                    ~~xxxx~~ Captain Brown and
                    flight.   4,000 feet.

                    2 Fokker Triplanes.

        (1)   Dived on two Fokker Triplanes over Warfusee-Abancourt
        followed by Lieuts. Mellersh, Mackenzie and Lomas.
                 Lieut. Mackenzie (on Sopwith Camel D 7245) dived on
        one triplane and fired about 100 rounds.   E.A. went
        down vertical and Lieut. Mackenzie lost sight of him. I
        observed it going xxx down but could not watch him right
        down.

        (2)   Captain Brown (on Sopwith Camel D 7270,2 Vickers) and
        Lieut. Mellersh(on Sopwith Camel D 3326, 2 Vickers) dived
        on the other Triplane.   Each fired about 200 rounds.
        E.A. turned in front and each got in a good burst.   The
        E.A. then went down vertical and we followed him down.
        Lieut.Mackenzie and Captain Brown observed burst of flame
        come out of him then.
                 Followed him down to about 500 feet when he came out
        of dive.   Captain Brown and Lieut.Mellersh opened fire
        again.   E.A. carried on gliding and looked as if pilot
        was landing or was dead and machine gliding automatically.

                                    A. R. Brown.
                                         Captain

Retyped 12 March, 2002

(24) THE ANSWER TO THE QUESTION AT THE END OF ITEM (18) ABOVE.

The air-to-air photograph is of three Sopwith Camels on patrol. The pilots are O C 'Boots' LeBoutillier, unknown and E 'Pecker' Pierce. The photograph was taken by A.T. Whealy.

Author Dale Titler received the print from from Oliver LeBoutillier in the 1960's, and generously provided a copy for this book.

ACKNOWLEDGEMENTS

The photographs of the machine-gun timing marks and the cable synchronized Maxim LMG 08/15 twin machine guns are published by courtesy of the Royal Air Force Museum at Hendon.

The photograph of the R.E.8 struck by a passing artillery shell was supplied by Air Vice Marshal Peter Dye of the RAF.

The photographs of the other aircraft in the ANNEX were most kindly provided by Mr. Stuart Leslie from the J.M. Bruce/G.S. Leslie collection. Mr Leslie also provided the information on the Constantinesco/Colley hydraulic machine-gun synchronizing system.

The photograph and memoirs of Mel Alexander were supplied by his sons David and Hugh.

The extract from Lieut. W R May's PILOT'S FLYING LOG BOOK, his RFC Acton Training School group photograph and the machine-gun instructor photograph are by courtesy of his son Denny.

The aerial photographs and Combat Reports are from Captain A Roy Brown's documents and papers.

CHAPTER NINE

REST, CRASH & DEMOBILIZATION
(16 May 1918 to the end of 1928)

On 16 May, Roy was discharged from No. 24 General Hospital at Étaples and sent on a fortnight's sick leave. He travelled to London and checked into the Savoy Hotel. One presumes he attended the 'Five O'clock Standby' in the bar where the ex-RNAS officers learned of one another's presence in town.

Roy's officially recognized success in leading his flight and then the squadron while Stearne Edwards was on leave, plus the fame acquired from the air battle on 21 April, had placed him in a good position for promotion to the command of a fighter squadron in France when a vacancy arose.

Savoy Hotel
London W.C.2

May 17. 18
(Friday)

Dear Dad, -

At last I am out of hospital again and am glad of it. My stomach is feeling fairly good now although I feel pretty washed out as yet.

Stearne expects to be on leave the beginning of the week and we are going to take a canoe trip up the river. It is the best thing I know to make me fit again. I hope I am alright when I have to go back as I do not want to quit just at the present time. There is a pretty fair chance of getting a squadron now. I should have a pretty good chance if I am able to go back to France and carry on. If I am not fit, I shall not try it.

I hope the next letter I write will be from somewhere on the river.

Love to all
Roy

Stearne's arrival was delayed. As mentioned in the previous chapter, Lieut. Downs, the 22 Wing Medical Officer, had sent him to No. 24 General Hospital for a rest from combat in pleasant, but disciplined surroundings, to be followed by a fortnight's leave.

While Stearne was enjoying peace and quiet, good food and comfortable accommodations at Étaples, Roy found himself unable to shake off the combined effects of the contaminated rabbit and the many hours he had spent at temperatures well below freezing at high altitudes where the oxygen shortage was a serious health hazard.

R.A.F. Gen. Hosp.
Hampstead
May 28.18
(Tuesday)

Dear Dad. -

Well I am back in hospital again. I came on leave alright but I have been feeling so rotten that I decided my leave was doing me no good, so I reported and have been sent here. I do not know what they are going to do with me as I have not seen the medical officer yet.

This is a splendid hospital with an excellent situation. It is on a hill close to Hampstead Heath which gives it lots of fresh air. It seems to be very well run from the little I have seen. They do a lot of research work here into the different kinds of troubles which are peculiar to flying people. It is purely for R.A.F. officers so they get lots of material to work on. It is a very good idea having a hospital like this as in an ordinary hospital they do not know how to treat the troubles of flying people.

What they will have me do, I do not know but I am certainly not nearly as fit as I thought I was and shall not be able to go back to France for *an indefinite time.*

I shall let you know when I get some kind of definite news. I shall be quite alright. All that is really the matter with me is that I am just tired out.

Love to all
Roy

Mount Vernon Hospital, as it was named, would not have been so quiet during a German air raid on London; anti-aircraft guns and searchlights were located on a level portion of a hillside not far away. Otherwise, there were paths to follow through the fields, shade trees with benches, hungry London sparrows to feed and ponds where ducks begged for pieces of bread. It was an ideal place to pass peaceful days. Roy was diagnosed as suffering from 'Stress of Service' and was discharged with four weeks' sick leave ending on 3 July. The date suggests he left hospital on 6 June, or thereabouts, which is in tune with the probable date of Stearne's arrival in London.

It was on this day, 28 May 1918, that General Sir Henry Sir Henry Rawlinson promulgated the award of a second Distinguished Service Cross to Roy.

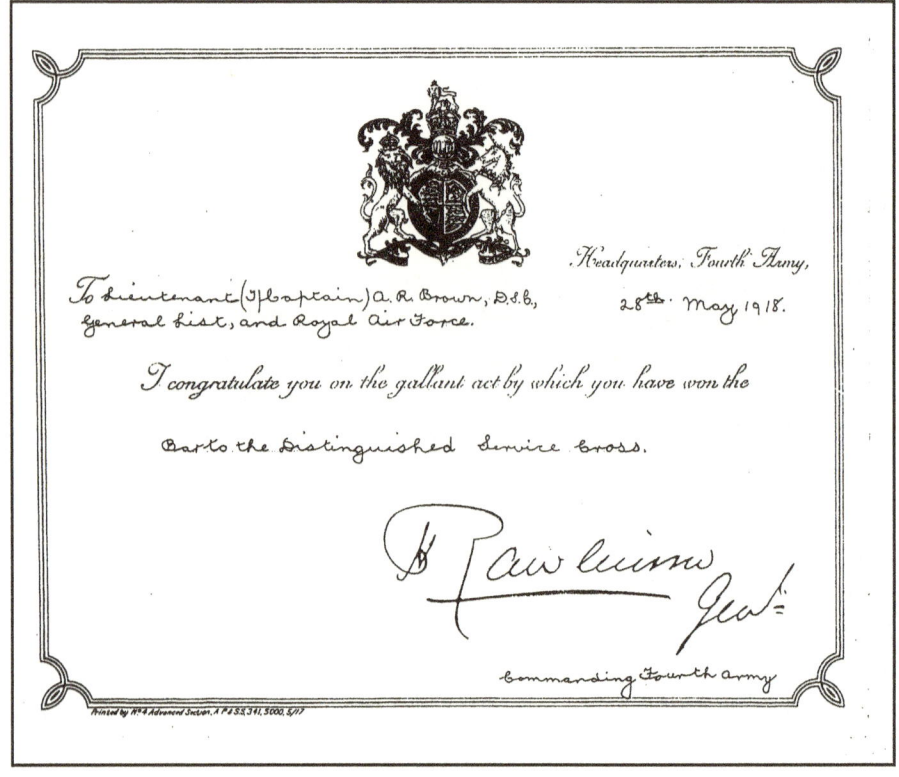

Roy Brown's award certificate for his second DSC.

Roy would not receive a second medal but instead be presented with a bar to be attached to the ribbon of the DSC he had won on 10 October 1917.

The award of a bar to the DSCs worn by Captain Arthur Treloar Whealy and Captain Stearne Tighe Edwards was announced a fortnight later. Roy and his two colleagues were to receive their bars from H.R.H. the Prince of Wales in a public ceremony scheduled for July. Arthur Whealy will appear again in a later chapter; he was best man at Roy's wedding.

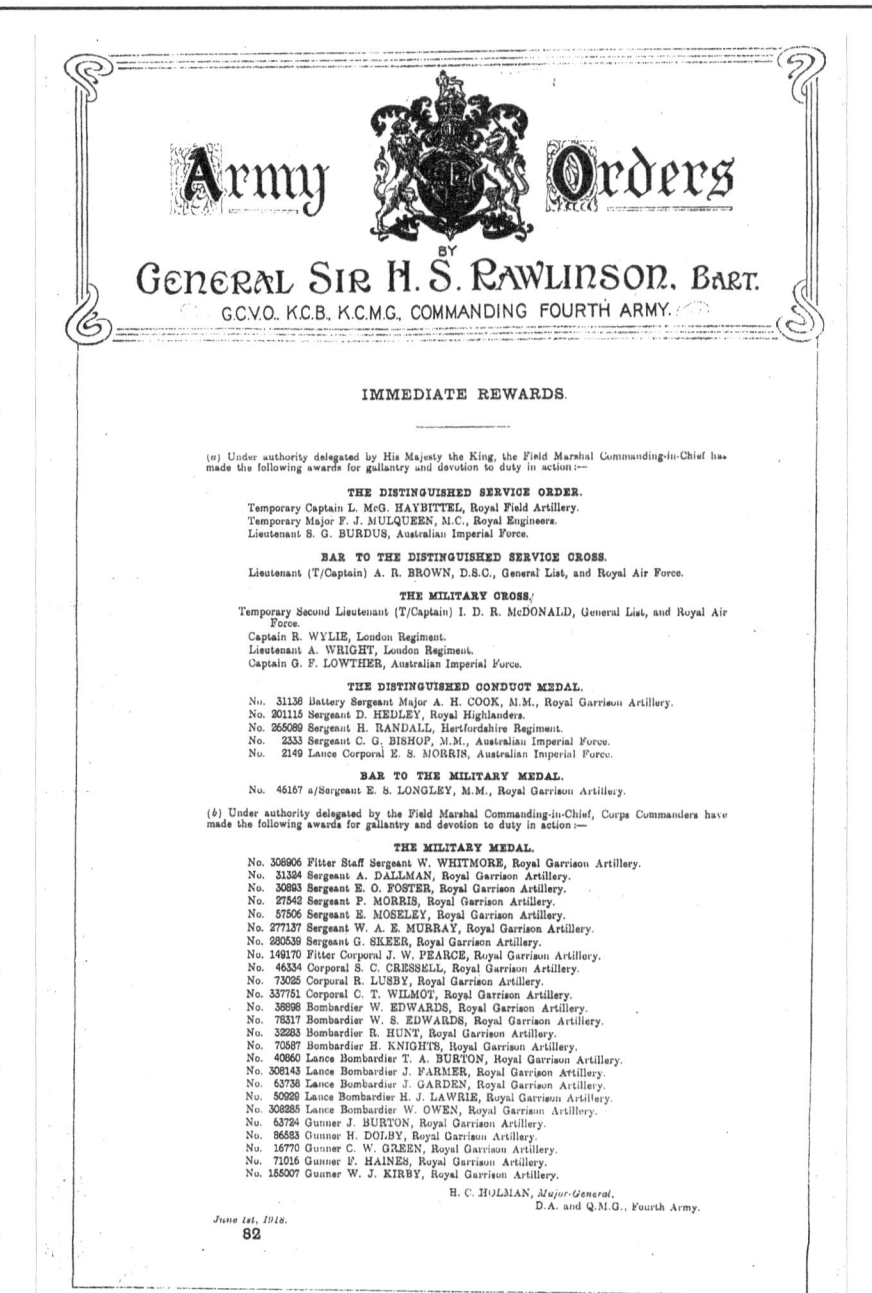

Army Orders 1st June, 1918.
The Field Marshal Commanding-in-Chief was Sir Douglas Haig.

The Supplement to the London Gazette, dated 21 June 1918, included the following:

HONOURS FOR OFFICERS LATE OF THE ROYAL NAVAL AIR SERVICE

The KING has been graciously pleased to approve the award of Bars to the Distinguished Service Cross to the undermentioned officers late of the Royal Naval Air Service:-

To receive a Bar to the Distinguished Service Cross

Lieut. (tempy. Capt.) Stearne Tighe Edwards, D.S.C., R.A.F.

For conspicuous bravery and most brilliant leadership of fighting patrols against enemy aircraft. On the 2nd May, 1918, whilst leading a patrol of four scouts, he encountered a hostile formation of eight enemy scouts, and drove down one machine completely out of control. Soon afterwards he engaged another formation of six enemy scouts, driving down one to its destruction whilst his patrol accounted for another. He only broke off the fight owing to lack of ammunition. He has destroyed or driven down out of control many enemy machines since he was awarded the Distinguished Service Cross and has at all times shown the greatest gallantry and a fine offensive spirit.

Lieut. (Hon. Capt.) Arthur Roy Brown, D.S.C., R.A.F.

For conspicuous gallantry and devotion to duty. On the 21st April, 1918, while leading a patrol of six scouts he attacked a formation of 20 hostile scouts. He personally engaged two Fokker triplanes, which he drove off; then, seeing that one of our machines was being attacked and apparently hard pressed, he dived on the hostile scout firing the while. This scout, a Fokker triplane, nose dived and crashed to the ground. Since the award of the Distinguished Service Cross he has destroyed several other enemy aircraft and has shown great dash and enterprise in attacking enemy troops from low altitude despite heavy anti-aircraft fire.

Lieut. (Hon. Capt.) Arthur Treloar Whealy, D.S.C., R.A.F.

For conspicuous gallantry and devotion to duty. He has proved himself to be a brilliant fighting pilot. Under his able and determined leadership his flight has engaged and accounted for many enemy machines, he himself being personally responsible for many of these.

Savoy Hotel
London W.C.2
June 23. 18.

Dear Dad, -

Just arrived here this morning from Scotland. Stearne and I have been on leave together. We report again on July 3.

In Edinburgh I saw Dick Simmot on the street. He was on draught leave, going over to France the end of this week. Doug. Findlay was in Edinburgh also. He was up there on duty. He was to fly a machine from there to his station, a flight of about five and a half to six hours.

We were up the River Thames for a dandy trip. Got a canoe, the same as Skeet and I did two years ago, and paddled up the river staying wherever we liked. In all we paddled over 100 miles, which certainly made me feel a lot better than I was. We were up the river as far as Reading. Passed all kinds of historical places.

Stearne and I had our pictures in the papers yesterday. Getting right up in society now.

We are going to stay in town a few days and then may go down to the south of England. Moving around and seeing all these places is about as good thing as we can do. It makes us fit as well as gives us a chance to see the country, although it is fearfully expensive. I do not know what I shall do after my leave is over. I am not going back to France and what kind of a job they will give me here I have not the faintest idea. I expect I shall get tired of England very soon and ask to be sent back to France. Flying in England does *not appeal to me very much. When you have to take a soft job you do not want it.*

I have had one letter from home in the last, I don't know how long. It was the one after you had received the news about the Baron.

I have a couple more letters to write now and must get busy.

Love to all
Roy

The London newspapers which reported the presence of two RAF aces in town that week and printed their photographs were the Daily Sketch and the Daily Mirror dated 22 June 1918. The latter gave its readers the following exciting glimpse of a fighter pilot's life in France.

Lieut. (Hon. Capt.) Arthur Roy Brown on April 21, while leading a patrol of six scouts, attacked a formation of 20 scouts.

He personally engaged two Fokker Triplanes, which he drove off. Seeing that one of our award of the D.S.C. he has destroyed several other aircraft.

At the end of his leave, Roy was classified as fit for Home Service flying duties and was given a post on the staff of No. 2 School of Aerial Fighting and Gunnery at Marske-by-the-Sea, Yorkshire. His orders were *machines was hard pressed, he dived on the hostile scout which nose-dived and crashed. Since the* to report there on 6 July 1918. At some time towards the end of the month he would have to journey down to London to receive the bar to his DSC from His Majesty King George V.

Marske-by-the-Sea had been an RNAS Flying Training Station since 1 November 1917 and had connections with the newly formed RAF North-Eastern Flying Instructors School at Redcar, also an ex-RNAS station.

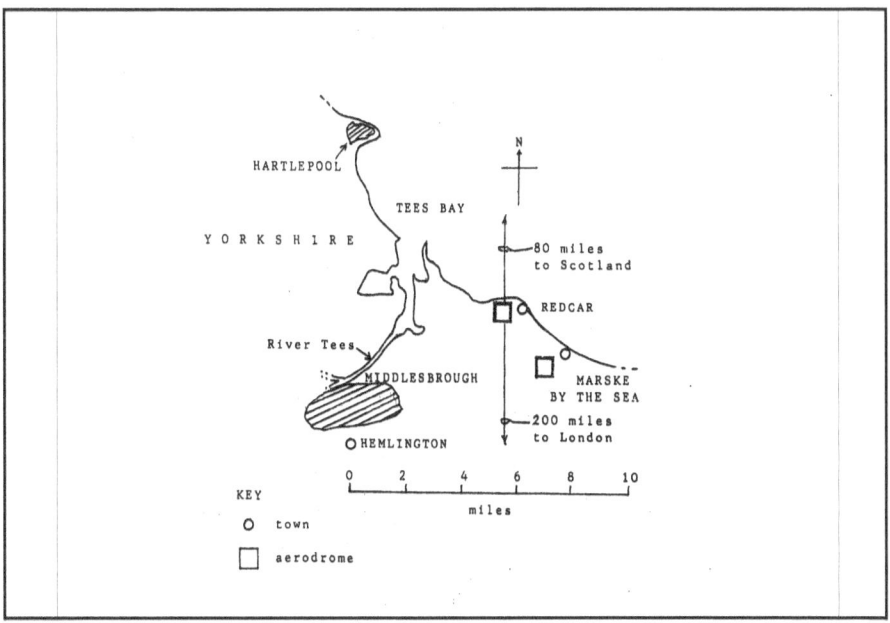

The locations of Marske-by-the-Sea and Redcar aerodromes. Note their proximity to Hemlington where there was a hospital equipped to handle severe injuries.

The aerodrome at Marske-by-the-Sea.

Logically, both Roy and Stearne first had to receive guidance on the syllabus and how to conduct mock combats in a safe manner. Among the 'old hands' at Redcar was Captain Austin Frauenfelder, an Australian, who bore the nickname of 'Fritz'. He had begun the war as an infantryman in the Australian Imperial Force, risen to Lance-Sergeant, and while in France, had obtained a transfer to the RNAS for pilot training. Upon graduating at Redcar, he had received a commission, and being a capable pilot with a pleasant personality, was retained there as a flying instructor. At a post-war gathering of RFC/RNAS/RAF pilots he mentioned, among other things, he had been Roy Brown's instructor. Being that 'Fritz' Frauenfelder never flew in France, and that prior to July 1918, Roy was never stationed in England further north than Freiston-on-Sea, and this must have been at the Redcar/Marske complex. The point assumes importance relative to a newspaper report given prominence in Canada in the year 2003, and will be covered in PART TWO of this book.

No. 2 Fighting School
Marske by the Sea
Yorks.

13. 7. 18

Dear Dad, -

You will be wondering what has happened to me as it is over two weeks since I have written. I was sick as a dog with Spanish influenza which everyone has been having. I had quite a temperature for a while but I am better again.

I reported here on 6th but went on the sick list immediately and have been kept in bed until yesterday. I feel much better today. I shall try to get started at work tomorrow if I do not feel too shaky.

Stearne and I are both here as fighting instructors. Our duties are to teach pupils how to fight single seaters and how to attack two seaters with single seaters. We also have to teach them how to fly formation and the methods of attacking troops on the ground. The work should be very interesting. How long we shall be here I have not the faintest idea. This place seems to be quite a backwater. Once you drift into it, you are apt to stay in it for some time.

> While I was on leave I heard that some changes will take place soon for Canadians in the R.A.F. What they are, I do not know but I am anxious to hear as it must mean something important. Whatever the change is, when it does take place I am going to try to get a permanent commission. If a Canadian service is formed, I shall certainly try to get it in that, otherwise in the R.A.F. The present situation of the war, as far as I can see, points more than ever to a much longer struggle than we forsaw a year ago.
>
> We seem to have a fairly good mess here as the meals which have been brought to me have been quite good and the cooking is exceptionally good. Stearne and I are in the same cabin. There is not much furniture in it at all. All we have is a bed and a cupboard for our clothes. Once we get settled in we shall get a table and some chairs and make things more comfortable.
>
> My mail is still going everywhere but where I am, and Stearne's seems to be even worse.
>
> Shall write again soon and tell you what I can about my work.
>
> Love to all
> Roy

Typical RNAS officer's cabin with electric light on a permanent station. Note the small round object hanging from a hook in the wall in front of the pillow; it was much safer there than left in his aeroplane. Photo taken at RNAS Coudekerke.

Typical Officers' Mess. Photo taken at RNAS Petit Synthe.

The Spanish influenza to which Roy referred was the first outbreak. There were to be two more of increasing intensity. At the end of the final epidemic, more people had died in Europe than during the Black Death (the Bubonic Plague) 250 years before.

To help teach fighter pilots and observers to estimate the proper aiming point when diving on or flying past a stationary object on the ground, camera guns were used together with marked targets.

A Sopwith F.1 *Camel* equipped with a camera gun.

One of the ground targets at Marske-by-the-Sea.

The camera guns were most effective in teaching the deflection angles required for aerial combat. The instructors' aeroplanes were painted white but occasionally there were casualties when a pupil failed to break away in time. Some instructors claimed they felt safer fighting experienced German pilots than teaching trainees; the Germans knew how to avoid a mid-air collision. When air-to-air marksmanship with live ammunition was practised, targets towed on rather long cables behind other aeroplanes were employed. Among the 'old favourites' used at the school were Sopwith *Pups* and *Triplanes*.

Sopwith *Triplane* N 5912 wearing No.2 Flying School number 94. Note the two LIFT HERE signs at the rear of the fuselage.

It was at Marske-by-the-Sea that Roy suffered an almost fatal flying accident. Despite ample documentation of the crash, a totally incorrect cause, first published in the 1920's, has been repeated so many times that the truth may come as a surprise to most. Fortunately, Stearne's letters have survived, and if anyone truly knows what happened and what he personally did, it is Stearne himself.

Before beginning work at Marske, Roy and Stearne had to learn to recognize the surrounding area from the air. At about 11 a.m. on 15 July, Roy climbed into Sopwith F1 *Camel* C175 to make his second local familiarization flight. Stearne Edwards, who was standing near the hangars, watched Roy taxi out to the field, turn into wind and begin his take-off run. The *Camel* left the ground, levelled off slightly to gain speed and then began to climb away from the field. As Stearne watched, it continued to gain height, then he saw the rotation of the propeller slow down and heard the noise of the engine cease. Actually the two events took place in reverse order, but light travels faster than sound. Roy, who was over telegraph wires and trees, judged he had sufficient height to glide back to the aerodrome, so he pushed the nose down and began a 180 degree turn. Stearne watched him cross the aerodrome boundary and had begun to breathe again when, in the last part of the turn, the *Camel* stalled and fell sideways from the air. It struck the ground about 100 feet from the station hospital.

Sopwith F1 *Camel* No. C175, 140 HP Clergêt 9BF, at the crash site near Marske-by-the-Sea RAF station hospital.

See (1) in the ANNEX to this chapter for more information on engine failure during take off.

A horrified Stearne ran across the field arriving at the hospital where he found two orderlies with what they assumed to be a dead pilot on a stretcher. It has been said they were headed for the mortuary or had even arrived there, but that may not be so. Stearne noticed the 'corpse' was bleeding; the presence of blood pressure meant Roy was still alive. The Medical Officer arrived, but after a short examination he decided Roy had only a few hours to live and that treating his injuries would gain nothing. Stearne Edwards did not accept that diagnosis, and in the belief, "while there is life there is hope", he intervened personally.

The RAF station hospital at Marske-by-the-Sea.

Margaret Harmon remembers her father giving the following description of what happened next;

"*Stearne borrowed a motorcycle, and leaving me in the care of the nurses who were dealing with the shock and the external bleeding, he rode into town to find a doctor and bring him back to the aerodrome.*" (This was more easily said than done since by military regulations civilian doctors were not permitted to enter a military base to treat servicemen.) "*Stearne found one*" (whom or where her father did not recall) *and made the following proposal to overcome his reluctance to break the law;* "*If you do not come with me right now to work on my colleague, I shall start work on you even sooner.*"

How Stearne secured the doctor's admittance to the base is unknown; the aerodrome was a large field and he may simply have driven through a gap in a hedge, but their combined efforts were successful and Roy's condition was stabilized. Since the patient obviously could not be moved, arrangements were made for a military doctor, a specialist in accident cases, to come to the aerodrome later that day. Logically, the accident had to be reported which meant that such indiscipline on Stearne's part could not be quietly forgotten; there were going to be consequences.

CASUALTY CARD F.S.Form 559 dated 15.7.18 from the RAF Museum, Hendon.

For those who may have difficulty with 1918 abbreviations and handwriting, the card states that Roy's accident had been reported by telephone from Marske-by-the-Sea. Among the information in the various columns is to be found:

NATURE AND CAUSE OF ACCIDENT. On taking off, engine failed, and turning to re-enter aerodrome side slipped and nose dived.

See (2) in the ANNEX to this chapter for a surprising statement made in 1961 by the RAF Historical Branch on Roy's accident.

The military hospital covering that area was the Territorial Army 1st Northern General Hospital in Newcastle. A 130 bed auxiliary of this hospital was located in a wing of the North Riding Infirmary at Hemlington in the town of Middlesbrough. This was the closest medical facility to Redcar/Marske, and the senior surgeons and the senior physicians there had been given temporary army rank to enable them to treat military cases. The surgeons were Lieutenant-Colonel William

Stewart Dickie FRCS, OBE and Captain James Donaldson. The physicians were Captains W.W. Williams and J. Brownlee.

The North Riding Infirmary at Middlesbrough.

Which of the four specialists went to Marske to examine Roy is unknown, but whoever it was, decided the patient had a chance of survival. He ordered Roy not to be moved for the while and specified round the clock care. Three nurses were assigned to the task; one of them being the station adjutant's wife. According to Margaret Harmon, about the only thing her father remembered in later life about this stage of his treatment was that every day a nurse poured a small bottle of iodine into each of two holes in his chest. However, he did recall being informed some time later about the consequences of Stearne's actions on the day of his crash. The inevitable investigation had drawn attention to the less than professional manner in which the Medical Officer at Marske-by-the-Sea aerodrome had handled some earlier serious cases, and as a result, he was severely reprimanded and replaced.

Most readers who have heard before about Roy's accident may already be wondering whether the cause stated above can possibly be true. That is not surprising because, as far as Alan Bennett and his colleague historians are aware, all previously published stories have given a totally different reason for Roy's crash. Unfortunately such 'creativity' does not end there. As in the case of Roy's accident at RNAS Chingford, his injuries have been changed and grossly exaggerated. Proper documentation of the truth now follows.

The first news to reach Mr. & Mrs. Brown arrived in a letter from Mrs. Bridget Earle, the wife of the Adjutant (formerly known as the Recording Officer) to the C.O. of No. 2 Aerial Fighting and Gunnery School.

No. 2 Fighting School
Marske-by-the-Sea
Yorkshire

Friday July 19th, 1918

Dear Mr. Brown

Your son asked me to write to you and tell you that he has had a crash but is getting on very well. At present his memory is bad and he cannot remember very much about anything, but I think I can safely assure you that all danger is now, humanly speaking, past, and I can't tell you how glad I am. His face is badly cut about and he has a bad shoulder wound, but both are healing up very well.

From all accounts his engine "conked" and he took a spinning dive into the ground. The Staff Sergeant here pulled him out just in time, and since then he has been in this hospital, but I am doing the best I can to nurse him back to health.

You have all my deep sympathy over your gallant son, and I hope you will rest assured that all is being done that can be done, and that there is no cause for anxiety.

Yours sincerely

Bridget Earle

P.S. I am your son's adjutant's wife. Please forgive this awful paper but I can find nothing else.

In the front row of the following photograph, the seven ladies wearing white collars have the appearance of nurses. The three who attended Roy should be amongst them. The officer in charge of the Women's Royal Air Force (WRAF) at Marske-by-the-Sea is clearly distinguishable in the middle of the front row. Seated immediately to her right (her left when looking at the photo) might well be the head nurse.

The WRAF personnel at Marske-by-the-Sea aerodrome in 1918/1919.

Two days later Stearne Edwards sent more details. His letter confirms the cause of the accident.

No. 2 Fighting School
Marske, Yorks

July 21, 1918

Dear Mr. Brown.

Long before you get this it will be one thing or the other with Roy. I hope you will forgive me for not having cabled you immediately but I could not do it for up till two days ago they expected every minute to be his last and I could not bring myself to send you news of that sort. He was mostly kept under the influence of drugs, and even when conscious, could not understand anything said to him.

He was just getting off the ground on his second flight here. At about 200 feet his engine stopped and since there were trees and telegraph wires in front of him, he tried to turn back to the aerodrome. He lost his speed on the sharp turn and he fell from about 60 feet vertical to the ground. Luckily the ground was soft, but it was bad enough. The engine somehow was thrown on the top of the wreckage, although it was a Camel he was flying, and its weight was more or less on his head and back. I saw it all from where I stood and thought he must be killed instantly. The Red Cross hut was not 100 feet away and no time was lost. Both collar bones are broken, four ribs I think, one of which pierced his lung. His jaw may or may not be broken. There is a cut, or rather a hole, in the inside upper corner of his eye, which they thought at first had pierced the brain, but it has not and probably will not be serious. There is also a cut on his forehead and of course many smaller cuts and bruises on his face and body.

The station doctor gave up all hope for him immediately and I brought a specialist down who arrived that evening and said the same thing, so you see things looked pretty blue. However he has gradually improved and it is the opinion of three doctors that he will pull through. He is being well looked after and has three nurses for himself.

He was quite rational in his mind for a while yesterday but wandered quite a lot. The nurse told me he had gotten her to write you (see Bridget Earle's letter above).

Today he was better than ever and could talk quite well. He is in no pain at all except that he sometimes insists on moving his arm and then his shoulder hurts. He has been talking all day and keeps the nurses laughing, so he is in good spirits.

As soon as he is fit, they will move him to a hospital.

Well, it has been a very anxious week but I think the worst is over now, though of course he has a long way yet to go.

Anyway, here's hoping for the best.

Goodbye

Stearne Edwards

Stearne's words, '*although it was a Camel*' refer to the position of the engine, which despite being at the front of the fuselage, had ended up on Roy's back. This is something which often happened to the pilot of a D.H.2, an F.E.8 or an F.E.2, which all had the engine at the rear, but is difficult to imagine happening with a Sopwith *Camel* and thus supports a statement in another document that Roy's *Camel* struck the ground sideways.

As in the case of Wilfrid May, the induction papers and other RNAS/RAF documents for Stearne Edwards misspell his first name and have confused historians for decades. Stearne's hand-written letter, kept by Mary Brown and only discovered in 1998, contains a clearly written signature and thus eliminates any doubt.

Captain Stearne Tighe Edwards, DSC and bar in RNAS uniform.

Roy's recovery was semi-miraculous but not sufficient for him to attend the ceremony in London for the investiture of the bar to his DSC. Within a fortnight of his accident he had improved enough to write a long letter home. The hand-writing is strong and clear until the fifth page whereupon it starts to straggle a little.

North Riding Infirmary
Middlesbrough

Aug 1. 18

Dear Dad, -

I do not know how far I shall get writing this or whether you will be able to read it or not, but at any rate I shall make a start.

The last two weeks and a half must have been a rather worrying time as you could not know what kind of word Stearne would be able to send you.

I certainly did my very best to kill myself and from what they have told me I nearly succeeded. They gave me up for hopeless three or four times. I do not remember anything about what happened to myself at all. What I write now is what they told me. I crashed at about eleven something in the morning; cause unknown. It was very bad crash; everything being smashed up rather badly. I have not heard full particulars of how I hit and what happened to the machine. They did not think I would be alive when they went to get me out. However, I fooled them and have done so several times since.

My clothes had to be taken off me and burned as everything was soaked full of blood. The serious result was my chest. My right lung was crushed in badly, surgical emphysema resulting in a very bad way; I was blown up like a ball all over. Three ribs broken also, but that or anything else that happened was not serious, but my lung was nearly fatal. No complications set in, however, which was very fortunate as if that had happened I do not suppose I would have pulled through. I had a rather large hole in my chest, round fairly well to the side somewhat under my arm. I also had one on the left side almost over my heart, but it did not amount to anything.

I fractured the right clavicule rather badly and from the way things look now, my right shoulder will have a small droop in it. It is the chief reason why I have not been able to write to you sooner as my right arm is very awkward and movement has been somewhat painful. It does not seem to hurt so much to write as I thought it would. I also had concussion of the brain from a wound on the left side of my forehead just over the left eye. It will leave a rather nasty looking scar.

Part of my left eyebrow has been shoved up onto my forehead and will look rather strange after I get properly healed up. My teeth, both upper and lower, went through my lower lip meeting on the outside, which makes two cuts on the inside meeting one on the outside. It will not leave much of a scar but it is still rather painful, although it is all healed up now. It has been really marvellous the way the different places have healed, I only have three dressings now. The two places on my chest and a boil which appeared on the back of my right shoulder.

My head is not quite right yet, it aches rather badly all the time and my memory is not very accurate. No matter what I feel like I am certainly fortunate to be alive at all. I hurt my back again too, although not at all seriously. I am not allowed out of bed yet.

Have rested for a while to see if my head would improve, but writing makes it ache too much to write more. Please let Alice know you have heard from me as I may not be able to write again for a few days.

Love from
Roy

Stearne Edwards then supplied further details.

No. 2 Fighting School
Marske-by-the-Sea
Yorks

Aug 5. 18

Dear Mr. Brown.

Roy tells me he wrote you himself a few days ago so there is not much need of this.

I see him quite often of course as he is in Middlesbrough hospital which is only a few miles away. I was in last night and he says he expects to be moved soon to Newcastle - a military hospital, No. 1 General. He has certainly fooled everyone by the way he has improved in the last two weeks. To see him now it is hard to realize how bad he was two weeks ago. He hardly realizes yet himself what a serious condition he was in. His wounds have almost healed. His jaw, which at first we thought was broken is O.K. again. The air which had got under his skin almost all over his body from the pierced lung is normal again. The hole in the corner of his eye proved not to be serious, but the cut on his forehead affected his brain for some time. The doctors were afraid. It appeared to me that it might be serious but that is also O.K. now. His memory is still a little weak, that is he forgets a good many things that I tell him, but he has stopped talking of things which never happened and it is easy to see that he is improving fast. I am afraid there will be a bad scar but that is not important.

The only thing at present that is a little unsatisfactory is that his knee and his back have both been bruised in places that gave him trouble before. They are all he complains of now. I think that they will be all right, that is no worse than before this accident.

The doctors seem to think now that he did not have pneumonia, though they told me once that he did. They say that he could not have had it and lived. Your wire asking me for details found me five days after you sent it. It was posted to me from London. I put the address of this place on each of the wires I sent you but perhaps the telegraph company did not send it through.

Well, as far as anyone can tell, there is no fear at all now of everything not going well. It is going to take some time, I should think, before he is allowed from hospital to a convalescent home, and as far as flying again, it is hard to say whether or not he will be allowed. But anyway, he is going to be all right and all he needs is time.

Goodbye
Yours sincerely
Stearne Edwards

On 14 August 1918 Roy was transferred to the parent hospital about fifty miles away, the 1st Northern General at Newcastle, where better facilities were available. Once there, he improved so rapidly that he was sent to an officers' convalescent hospital in a beautiful setting beside the River Thames. The nearest town was Staines which lies midway between London and Windsor; about ten miles from each.

Telegrams:
Prince of Wales's
Jamnagar, Staines
Hospital for Officers

Aug 23/18

My dear mother, -

    As you see I have been moved again. This a very nice place and everyone is exceptionally good and thoughtful with me. My night nurse and the sister who is here during the day have both been in Canada which makes it pleasant.
    This one of my fed-up days. I do not sleep very well of course, and last night I could not sleep until four o'clock. While I was awake the nurse came in and I did not hear her till she was quite close to my bed. When I heard her I jumped and was as frightened as a baby. After that every little noise made me jump and frightened me the same. My head was pretty bad at the time. Please excuse me writing and telling you all this, I must unburden myself some time. I cannot understand why I acted as I did, but after what I have had, I should not be surprised at anything which may result. My head and back are still pretty painful and of course my chest is sore if I take a long breath or cough. I spend most of my time reading but not for very long at a time.
    This hospital is right on the banks of the Thames. All the chaps who are fit spend most of their time on the river. I hope to be able to get in a boat soon and have someone row me about. From what I can see the grounds must be very pretty. This place is financed in everyway by an Indian Nizam. It was a private home originally.
    It has taken a while to write this letter, I can only do a bit at a time.

Love from
Roy

India's war effort from 1914 to 1918 was much greater than was generally realised in the late 20th century, or even today. The Nizam of Hyderabad presented many aeroplanes to the RFC, which explains the name HYDERABAD seen often in photographs of F.E.2Ds and D.H.4s. He later donated the entire complement of D.H.9As (15 plus 3 reserve) for RAF 110 Squadron. The part of India ruled by the Nizam who totally financed the hospital at Staines may be gleaned from the telegraphic address at the head of Roy's letter.

Roy had his daily ups and downs but the base line continued to improve.

Canadian Pacific R'y Co.'s Telegraph
Staines, Sept 3

Mortimer Brown
Carleton Place, Ont.

Improving nicely convalescent home six months. Roy Brown.

Roy's friends continued to visit him when they could obtain 48 hours' leave, and Douglas Findlay sent his good impressions to Mortimer Brown.

Waldorf Hotel
Aldwych, London

Sept 14th, 1918

Dear Mr. Brown.

I've spent most of the last two days with Roy and as it is the first I have seen of him since his crash I thought you might like to have my opinion of his condition.

I had formed a fair opinion of what his condition must have been immediately after the accident from what Stearne and Horace have told me and I really expected to see a battered and maimed man. But this is far from the case because with the exception of a slight limp and a fairly perceptible scar over his left eye brow, he looks as well as he ever did.

Of course, his whole system must have suffered a terrific shock and it will take time to get over the tired and nervous state so brought about.

He says that his back, knees and head are his chief troubles, but as regards his head, you'll be able to judge for yourself from his letters that it is quickly becoming normal.

I don't know how seriously his back and knees are injured but I think that with proper care and time they will become as strong as could be expected; i.e. that he'll be absolutely independent, though he'll not be able to stand much manual work for a long time.

Now, I've only given you my simple opinion for what it is worth, and I think that all that can be done for him till he is strong enough to stand the trip home is to write him cheery letters and keep up his spirits.

Of course he is a Spartan as regards pain, and his determination to get well has been and is doing wonders even where the doctors feared to tread.

I'll do all I can to help him along.

Yours very sincerely
Douglas Findlay

Captain David Douglas Findlay.

Trouble never comes singly. Roy's sister Bessie was involved in a road accident; she was thrown through the windscreen of the car in which she was riding and for the rest of her life suffered from painful headaches.

Telegrams:
Prince of Wales's
Jamnagar, Staines
Hospital for Officers

Sept 14/18

Dear Bess, -

I am very sorry to hear of the rotten time you have been having. Your poor head will be better when you get rid of it so it seems. I have been having some fun along similar lines all to myself. My back is the only thing that will keep me company for ever. They have never given me an X-ray yet but are going to next week. Imagine, five certain fractures and probably a fractured skull with not one X-ray. It's certainly good.
I might possibly get home about the spring but do not know yet. Up to the present, I could not stand the trip as it would do me more harm than good. It's lots of fun being so much trouble to yourself I don't think.
Hope you are much better by the time this reaches you.

With love to all
Roy

Although Roy's letter dated 1 August lists four fractures; his right collarbone and three ribs, the letter above states five. The nature of the fifth has proven impossible to identify, Roy never mentions it again. Apparently the fifth fracture was either not serious or possibly a mistaken belief on his part.

Over the years, Roy's injuries have also grown and grown like the little girl named Topsy. The only ones mentioned by Roy, Stearne Edwards, Bridget Earle and Douglas Findlay may be summarized in non-medical terms as follows:

A broken right collar-bone
Three broken ribs (one or more had pierced he skin)
A perforated right lung (punctured by one of the three ribs)
A deep cut on the left side of his chest
A blow on the head which caused severe cerebral concussion.

Horton War Hospital
Epsom, Oct 9. 18

Dear Dad, -

Shall only be able to write a little as I am not supposed to write at all, this being a special concession.

I have been moved here for X-ray for my head which has been giving me a lot of trouble. I do not sleep well. For example, it was five o'clock this morning before I slept, then I awakened at eight. My head is really much better than it was. I am not allowed up at all, no visitors, reading only head lines of newspapers and ten minutes reading at a time. So all together I am having a good time. Treatment is very drastic but I am improving.

Shall write again when allowed but may not be for some time. Been here about three weeks now.

Love to all
Roy

As though the accident to Bessie were not enough, Horace suffered one in England. He had been pedalling along on his bicycle when a horse and cart, showing no lights, had carelessly been driven through a gap in a hedgerow. The driver had then turned the cart onto the wrong side of the road and the horse had run into Horace. Northern France, where people had learned to watch out for hidden danger, appeared to be safer than anywhere else.

Horton War Hospital
Epsom, Oct 15. 18

My dear Mother. -

    This is the best day in every way which I have had since I have been here. I received four letters today, all from Canada, and Doug Findlay has been to see me. Doug is certainly a good friend to have. He went to see Horace, who is in hospital at Ilford, then came here to tell me that Horace was all O.K. and nothing serious. Horace had an accident while on a bicycle, he ran into a horse and cart in the dark. A shaft struck him on the chest. They thought he was going to have pneumonia at first but he is all O.K. now and will soon be up and around again. Nothing serious and absolutely nothing to worry over.
    More good news. My head is very much better. It seems now to have taken a definite turn for the better at last. It has only been aching a very little this afternoon. If it gets worse again and I cannot write, I shall have someone write to you. My worse problem now is monotony. I am so very restricted in what I am allowed to do.
    The letter I received from you was Sept 18 enclosing one from Aunt Blanche. Do not think of sending things to me. As far as eats are concerned I have very little appetite, I am doing so little. What I want are good home-cooked things, but they are one of the easiest things to wait for. It will be at least another two or three months before I can get leave to go home.
    This is a real hospital where they do everything to make a patient fit and take some interest in his case. It has 5,000 beds and some of the best doctors in the country, so be assured that everything that can be done is being done. They are doing nothing but treat my head, everything else can wait. I hope it will not be long now.
    Really must not write more now though I should like to.

Love from
Roy

From Roy's letters one can see he had been putting a brave face on things, but the apparent over-optimism at the 1st Northern General and the shuffling between hospitals seem somewhat strange. Stearne Edwards was concerned by this also.

38 Training Depot School
Tadcaster, Yorks
Oct 17. '18

Dear Mr Brown.

I do not know whether Roy has been writing you often but in case he is not allowed to write letters I think I had better tell you all I know of his case.

After he left Marske they sent him to hospital at Newcastle. The doctors there must have been fools for they discharged him from hospital to a convalescent home in Staines on the Thames. He was there for some weeks and was allowed short leave & all the excitement he could get, which, I have been told, is very bad for concussion of the brain. I think he got steadily worse all the time he was at Staines. I could tell by his letters and I got 48 hours leave to see him. He had been moved back to hospital at Epsom the day I got there.

I went to Epsom with Horace and after some trouble we were allowed to see Roy. He seems quite all right as regards his head, but the doctor considered it a very serious case. I do not mean to make it worse than it is, but the doctor certainly scared me. He said that a lot of damage had been done by sending Roy to a convalescent home, which he would try to repair, but unless every care was taken, Roy would be affected for life. I asked about his back but he said no other troubles could be considered serious compared to his head, and when that was better it would be time to think of the others. He would have to be kept perfectly quiet and could not read, write, talk or anything else.

Well, that was about three weeks ago. Yesterday I had a letter from Roy written on the Q.T. and I am sure he is getting on well. It is not at all like the previous ones. He says he is trying to live up to all the restrictions they put on him so as to get better quickly, and as long as he realizes that he must do that, I am sure he will be all right in time. I asked him for his doctor's name so that

I might write him but Roy does not want me to, so I will have to do without the doctor's opinion.

I wish I could get away again to see him but it is so very hard to get leave, I told Roy if there was anything for me to do, to let me know and I would try to get away somehow. I do not think there is anything to be done just now more than they are doing. The doctor seemed a very capable man. I think he knew what he was doing.

I know I ought to have written sooner but it is rather hard to write when things are going badly. However, I think from now on he will improve.

I received your two letters some time ago and I wish you did not think it necessary to thank me for anything I have tried to do for Roy.

Sincerely
Stearne Edwards

See (3) in the ANNEX to this chapter for an evaluation of Roy's condition and treatment in the light of 21st century medicine.

Horace was back in hospital with complications from his bicycle accident. A blow from the cart shaft had been almost exactly on the place of his earlier, serious bayonet wound. How unlucky can one be?

The war situation had improved dramatically, Bulgaria and Turkey had been knocked out of the war, and Austria had thrown in the towel. Germany was now alone and there were signs that the projected 1919 Allied spring offensive might not be required. Food was short in Germany, arms and munitions workers had staged strikes, and the anti-war movement was gaining popularity. The German government realized that battles won on the western front were not bringing final victory any closer. The U-boat campaign had failed, and with the American entry into the war, an unfavourable end was only a matter of time. The 'time' might be a year away, but why wait that long and incur another 250,000 dead when the final outcome was now certain? General Ludendorff began looking for a way to halt the fighting while politicians negotiated a peace treaty. President Wilson's Fourteen Points sounded promising, however, there was a catch not fully realized in Germany; America was not one of the Allies, she was a co-belligerent.

Her peace terms were hers alone.

Roy's letters home for the next three weeks indicated his recovery had reached a plateau and more time would be required. The following one shows that his spirits have improved.

Horton War Hospital
Epsom, Nov 9. 18

Dear Dad, -

Just a note as there is really nothing to write of except that Horace is much better and should be out of hospital soon now. Uncle Harry did find me eventually after hunting all over the country. He looks well and was surprised to see me looking so well. Nobody believes from looking at me what I have had. My scars do not show at all now.

I am not allowed up yet as my head is very slow in coming to order again. If it does not get any worse than this, it does not matter much.

Doug Findlay got to see me yesterday. The fellows have been very good in coming here. I never knew I had so many real friends. They are very good in the hospital too. The sister in this ward just worries herself all the time about what she can do for me. Don't let mother worry about me as I am alright.

Love to all
Roy

Uncle Harry was his mother's brother and was in the Canadian Army in England.

The end to the fighting was set for 11 a.m., Allied time (midday German time), on Monday 11 November. The German High Command still had 146 army divisions in the field, and the retreat had not yet reached the German border, but for the German soldiers, the cease fire was the end of their misery and hardship. The Soldiers' Councils emerged from the shadows and declared themselves in charge. The 146 divisions just melted away as the troops demobilized themselves and headed home, some groups carrying the red flag of the socialist revolution. The German population was thunderstruck; after all the great victories on land and sea which they had celebrated during the preceding four years, what had happened? General Ludendorff's plan of negotiating a peace treaty from a position of strength collapsed overnight. With the army gone and the navy controlled by mutineers, Germany had no cards left in its hand. The armistice turned into surrender, and the legend of the stab in the back was born.

See (4) in the ANNEX to this chapter for more information on 'the stab in the back'.

There were celebrations in France and England, and on the Tuesday 12 November at No. 38 Training Depot Station (TDS) Tadcaster, Stearne Edwards took off in Sopwith *Pup* N4181 just to have something to do. An earlier date is sometimes given for the flight, but 12 November is the correct one. Unfortunately Stearne did what both Roy and the late Rittmeister had always warned against; low level aerobatics. During the recovery from a slow roll, a wingtip brushed the ground and Stearne was severely injured. One of his injuries was a compound fracture of a leg. He appeared to be making a good recovery, but quite unexpectedly infection set and he died in hospital at York on 22 November.

See (5) in the ANNEX to this chapter for Major Mulholland's letter to Stearne's mother describing the accident.

Horton War Hospital
Epsom, Nov 23. 18

Dear Mother, -

This has been the hardest day I have ever spent in my life and I don't expect I shall ever spend such another again. I cannot write how I feel as words are too feeble. Stearne has been so much to me since coming over here, more than anyone ever has been before or will be again. I have no particulars, just a telegram from a mutual friend saying that he is dead. Please give his mother my sympathy and let her know how I feel about it.
I can write no more.

Love from
Your son
Roy

Stearne's crash cannot be blamed upon revelry the day before as he neither smoked nor drank. Captain Oliver Redgate apparently saw the accident and was of the opinion that Stearne had misjudged his height. Once again, a training school in England had proved to be more dangerous for an ace pilot than active service in France.

See (6) in the ANNEX to this chapter for a medical opinion on the possible cause of Stearne's unexpected death.

The war, which was expected to end in the spring of 1920, was now over, and the heavily indebted governments of France and England were desperate to economize. Contracts issued by the Air Ministry were abruptly cancelled, and manufacturers, who had planned for production until the end of 1919, were left with factories full of material to build aeroplanes, engines and accessories for which there was no longer a buyer. Sopwith, Clergêt, Grahame-White and others went out of business. Hospital budgets were examined very carefully; cuts were the order of the day.

Horton War Hospital
Epsom,
Dec 2. 18

My dear Dad, -

I have at last reached a decision as to what I am going to do about getting fixed up in this hospital. I am not receiving the treatment the doctor orders for me and I cannot eat enough of the food we get here to build me up again. The only solution is for me to say I am fit enough to leave here for a convalescent home. Then, when I am fit enough, to travel home where I can have an environment to help me. Nearly everyone in this ward is deciding to do the same thing. I am not the only one who views the situation this way.

Tomorrow I shall start telling lies so that I can get out. Please do not show this letter to mother, I know she would worry more than is necessary.

Love to all
Roy

Apparently Roy's plan met with success.

Horton War Hospital
Epsom 14. 12. 18

My dear people at home, -

This should just about reach you at Christmas now that the boats are leaving regularly again. I expect to spend Christmas at Marske-by-the-Sea with Mrs. Bridget Earle and her husband, the Adjutant. She was the first nurse I ever had. From what Stearne told me, I would not have lived but for her. She is very nice and I shall be very well looked after as she is extremely good to me. I am getting much stronger now and shall soon be fit enough to go to a convalescent hospital.

I hope you will all have a happy Christmas and New Year and that I shall be able to spend the next one at home with you all.

Love to all
Roy

Something happened to change Roy's plans. Instead of going to the Earles' for Christmas, he travelled to London where by pre-arrangement he met Horace and Douglas Findlay. All three made plans for a quiet week in the countryside.

Savoy Hotel
London WC2
31. 12. 18

Dear Dad, -

Just got half an hour before I have to go back to hospital so shall spend it writing as much as I can about the place we spent Christmas.
Mr. Morris is a large chocolate manufacturer and has a business making the machines used in chocolate factories. He has travelled the whole world and is about the most broad minded man I have ever met. He is married, with three young girls and three boys, the youngest being a baby.
His home is a beautiful old place built in Tudor architecture and is very comfortable. It is on a farm where they grow all their own supplies and have the best cream I ever tasted. He drives a white Sunbeam racing car to and from home to business, which is about 35 miles. They have beautiful gardens, greenhouses, etc., just the kind of place that is absolutely ideal. In fact, he has what to me would be an ideal life. Enough city life to get tired of, and enough country life to make a man appreciate both.
They were all as good to us as they could possibly be. We drove to Eastbourne (a seaside resort on the south coast) for two days and had a splendid time there. His car is great.
Horace and Doug drove with him to Sheerness (a naval base on the Isle of Sheppey at the mouth of the River Thames) to see his oldest son back to the destroyer which he is on. I did not go that day as I felt I had done just about as much as I could do. Being there has done me a world of good and I have a standing invitation to spend leave with them. I wish there was something I could do to return his kindness.
I think I had better leave now for the hospital. How I love it, I don't think.

Love to all
Roy

Douglas Findlay wrote to Mrs. Brown about their holiday. His letter completes the story of Roy's Christmas holiday.

No. 5 Training Depot Station
Royal Air Force

Stamford. Lincs.
January 3rd, 1919

Dear Mrs. Brown:

As Roy, Horace and I spent Christmas together, I thought I'd write to you and say what I think of Roy's condition because I had a really good chance to judge it.

We arranged to meet in London and spend a quiet Christmas in some country town hotel where we could be our own masters and lie in bed as late as we liked: but all our plans went astray.

We met in London and got busy hunting up reports of south coast towns and hotel accommodation then we finally decided to go to Wales.

But, happily for us, a friend of Roy's, Major Huskinson, knew how we intended spending our Christmas leave. He introduced us to an English gentleman by the name of Edgar Morris, who very kindly and insistently asked us to spend Xmas with him at his home in Ashurst near Tunbridge Wells.

He was such a good sport and so different from the average aristocratic Englishman that we went and we had the most homelike time since I left home.

We motored to his place from London in his car and lived on the very best of homelike food. Every day for nearly a week we went for a long ride in the car and came home to all the best comforts one could ask. I know that I went to bed every night as tired as could be.

This pace proved too much for Roy after his long rest in hospital so he spent one day in bed. He took it easy the next day and was O.K. for the two days before we left for London again.

He walks quite well now with the help of a stick but is not much for distance as he tires easily, but that is bound to improve with time. His back is *the main trouble because it is still so weak and that is where I think it will take some to set things right.*

He still complained of headaches but says that his head is not nearly so bad as it was.

All things considered, I think he should be in fit condition to try the voyage home by spring and I know he is looking forward to it. He is optimistic about his condition.

Yours very sincerely
Douglas Findlay

The Major Huskinson mentioned in the letter was Major Peter Huskinson, MC & bar, the C.O of RAF 19 Squadron, which was equipped with Sopwith 5F.1 *Dolphin* high altitude fighters.

Douglas Findlay's impression was correct, and Roy's condition continued to improve. A true friend to all; Douglas Findlay worked hard seeing that Stearne's back pay, pension and gratuity would be transferred to his mother. The task was finally completed on 10 February when he dispatched Stearne's effects home. The full story of Douglas Findlay's efforts is to be found in WE ARE THE DEAD, by historian Larry Gray of Carleton Place.

The toilet paper I.O.U.s were not among the items shipped home; at some point following Stearne's death the wad had disappeared. Be that as it may, one debt is known to have been paid. In early 1919 Mrs. Edwards received a cheque for $300.00 dollars from RAF Major Ronald Redpath, who, like Stearne, had served in 3 Wing (naval), 6N and 11N, but had not been favoured by the goddess of fortune at the poker table.

Horton War Hospital
Epsom. 16. 1. 19

Dear Dad, -

Received your letter of Dec 19. I am getting along splendidly now and really beginning to feel fit again and get my strength back.

I hardly limp at all now and soon shall walk quite alright. My head is fairly good as long as I remain quiet enough. My knee will soon be alright again. My back does not prevent me from walking erect but has no strength in it, and when I use it, it gets worse. They have found that two vertebrae have been injured but time is the only thing as there is nothing which can be done for them.

I shall be sent to a convalescent home soon. I expect to be there for about two months or so.

Love to all
Roy

Roy was being somewhat optimistic. On 22 January, the hospital doctors had reported him as being unfit for General Service for six months and unfit for Home Service for 1 month. In early February he began to feel unwell again and the Central RAF Hospital at Dollis Hill, Hampstead diagnosed him as suffering from 'concussion & pneumonia'. The entry on his Casualty Card (depicted earlier in this chapter), dated 18 Feb. 1919, was made after he had left.

While Roy was at Dollis Hill, his brother, Horace, was caught by the third and the worst wave of the Spanish influenza, and was sent to the RAF Officers' Hospital at 82 Eaton Square, London SW. This was the greatest European viral plague in history and from October 1918 to February 1919, 20,000,000 people succumbed; twice the total of those killed (or later died of wounds) on all the battlefields of the world in the four years of fighting. Some idea of the severity of the three epidemics may be gleaned from a simple statistic; of the 110,000 American Expeditionary Force members who died from all causes during the war, 50,000 were victims of what became known as the 'Spanish Flu'.

RAF Officers' Hospital, 82 Eaton Square. The entrance can be seen just round the corner of the building.

On Saturday 15 February 1919, Roy was transferred from Dollis Hill to 82 Eaton Square and was shocked to find his brother there, critically ill. He sent a cable home:

HORACE INFLUENZA PNEUMONIA CRITICAL RECEIVING PERFECT ATTENTION

On Monday 17 February, he cabled again:

HORACE'S DANGER OVER

The good news was premature for on Wednesday 19 February, he had to advise:

HORACE DIED TUESDAY. ADVISE INTERMENT HERE. CABLE INSTRUCTIONS 82 EATON SQ LONDON.

Roy was with his brother when he died. No better proof exists for the strong friendship uniting the Carleton Place airmen than Douglas Findlay's 18 February diary entry upon learning of the death of Horace; *"Poor old Horry and Roy."* Part of his entry for the 22nd reads; *"It's funny how all my friends have gone. Old Horry."* Again, the full story is to be found in WE ARE THE DEAD by Larry Gray. See ACKNOWLEDGEMENTS at the end of this chapter.

Upon instructions from the family in Canada Horace's body was embalmed and prepared for return to Canada in a sealed, lead coffin.

Roy went before the Central RAF Hospital medical board at Dollis Hill on 22 February and was classified as being unfit for any duties for 3 months. The board recommended he be granted 3 months' leave in Canada. The entry on his Service Record is dated 24 Feb. 1919. Plans were made for Horace's body to travel on the same ship as Roy.

On 3 March 1919, Douglas Findlay cabled Mortimer Brown:

ROY FULLY CAPABLE TRAVELLING HAS GOOD COMPANIONS

On Saturday 8 March, Roy sailed from Liverpool on the S S *Minnedosa* for St. John, New Brunswick, but without Horace's body; it had not arrived at the dockside in time. Roy arrived home at Carleton Place by train on Tuesday 18 March, and Horace's body followed a week later.

A military funeral for Horace was held on Saturday 29 March; Major W.H. Hooper, Horace's old army C.O. led the cortège. The service was conducted at Zion Presbyterian Church in Carleton Place by the Rev. W.A. Dobson (to whom Roy had written a long letter on his life in the RNAS on 2 July 1917). Horace was buried in the family plot in the Saint Fillans section of the United Cemetery in Beckwith Township, where, despite the bitterly cold weather, there was a large crowd of mourners. Bill Andison, who was a member of the firing party, told W. Brian Costello in 1970 that the weather was so cold that, during the three volleys, some of the rifles failed to fire.

On 5 April, Douglas Findlay was authorized to leave for Canada. He sailed at the end of the week.

Roy spent part of his leave in Toronto, receiving treatment at the military hospital. While he was there, his mother and his uncle, Dr. Clarence, paid him a visit.

Officers' Convalescent Hospital
460 Jarvis Street
Toronto

22. 4. 19

Dear Uncle Clarence, -

I am sorry I missed you all when I went to get the X-ray plates. I thank you very much for saying whatever you did to Lt.- Colonels McVic and Starr. They have been, both of them, most kind to me.

Lieut.- Colonel Starr says as far as he can see there is nothing in the way of bone injury on my skull. There is nothing that can be done for my back except a certain amount of massage. After that, all there is for me to do is to build up my general health and strength again. I expect I shall be here until the end of May and then home.

I am having a very busy time amusing myself at present.
There are a number of fellows I know very well in the city at present and as a result I am asked all over the place.

Give my kindest regards to Aunt Mamie and I hope that Alice's health is improving again.

Your nephew
Roy

The massage treatment Roy received was to cause a major change in the direction of his life.

See (7) in the ANNEX to this chapter for more information on Alice Pickup.

On 29 May 1919, Roy was called before a medical board. The physical examination revealed his height to be one and a half inches less than when Admiral Kingsmill had accepted him for pilot training.

The board classifed his health as Category 'D' and recommended he be admitted to hospital for an unspecified operation.

On 28 July 1919, Roy again went before the medical board. He was re-classified as Category 'C'. Accordingly, he abandoned his idea of taking a permanent commission in the RAF or the RCAF and returning to flying. In fact, never again would he be permitted to act as pilot-in-command of an aeroplane.

Roy was advised that arrangements were being made for him to receive the bar to his DSC, either from the Governor General or from H.R.H., Edward, Prince of Wales who was planning a tour of Canada later in the year.

Royal Air Force
Records & Recruiting Office
George and Duke St.
Toronto, Canada

July 31st 1919.

Capt. A.R.Brown
Carleton Place
Ontario

Proceedings of Medical Board held on your case in Toronto 28-7-19 received at this Headquarters.

As you are in Service Category, you are eligible for demobilization and will be recommended to the Air Ministry for demobilization with effect from 1-8-19, from which date you are at liberty to accept civilian employment.

Demobilization papers will be prepared by the Air Ministry and forwarded to this headquarters for re-addressing to you.

Anitoyle Seymour

Major for,
Officer Commanding,
Royal Air Force, Canada

On 1 August 1919, Roy was transferred to the unemployed list and permitted to retain the rank of Captain (Flying). His release from the RAF was promulgated in the London Gazette dated 20 April 1920.

The Prince of Wales's tour of Canada took place as planned at the beginning of November and Roy was invited to Parliament Buildings in Toronto on Tuesday 4 November 1919. In a ceremony, which began at 3 p.m., H.R.H. the Prince of Wales invested him with the bar to his Distinguished Service Cross. Roy's 16 year old brother, Howard, watched the proceedings from the beginning to the end through a window in an empty room above the reception area. Before Howard could leave, H.R.H. and a well-dressed lady entered the room. As Howard departed in a hurry, he remembered the prince enquiring what he was doing in there alone.

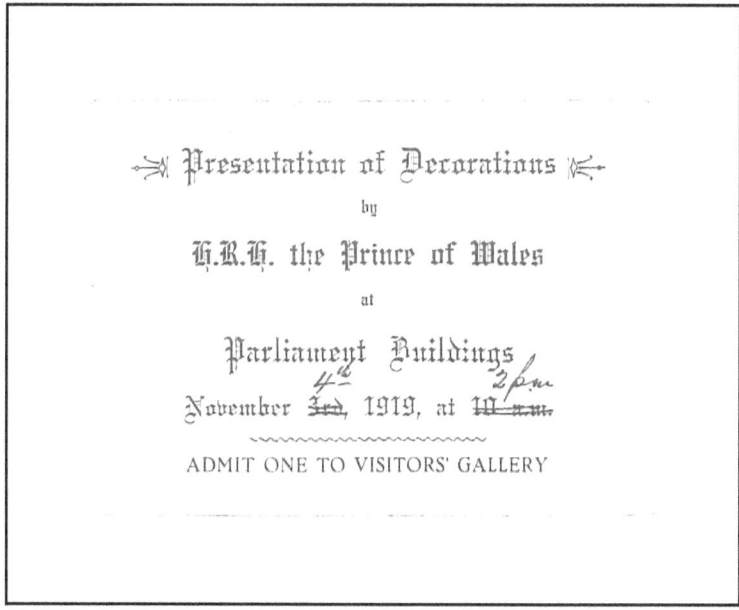

Howard Brown's invitation to the ceremony.

On 5 November, 1919 *The Toronto Globe* newspaper reported that on the previous afternoon, 270 persons had personally received decorations from the Prince of Wales which had been awarded for deeds of valour performed during the war. The Prince was accompanied by his Honour the Lieutenant Governor, Sir John Hendrie, and the presentations were made in the Legislative Assembly chamber. It was an entirely formal affair, interspersed with suitable music played by an orchestra. Even though admission was by ticket only, every available seat on the floor of the House and in all the galleries was occupied by the recipients-to-be and their families. When Captain Arthur Roy Brown's name was called, he stepped forward, the Prince shook hands with him and pinned the award to his breast.

Roy's awards and medals may be described as follows:

The **Distinguished Service Cross and bar** are made of silver; the ribbon is dark blue with a white stripe down the middle.

The **British War Medal**, for service overseas between 1914 and 1920, is also made of silver. The obverse is King George V as depicted on a 1 crown coin. The reverse depicts St. George on horseback with the horse standing on an enemy shield. From both edges the ribbon changes from blue, black and white to a gold middle stripe.

The **Allied Victory Medal** (British version), for service in an active theatre of war, is made of bronze. The obverse depicts the winged figure of Victory. The reverse is an oak leaf cluster surrounding the inscription, THE GREAT WAR FOR CIVILISATION 1914 - 1919. From both edges the ribbon progresses from mauve through shades of blue, green, yellow and gold to a red middle stripe.

Captain Roy Brown

Roy's Distinguished Service Cross; obverse side only.

Roy's Allied Victory Medal (British version) and British War Medal: obverse side.

Reverse side.

That same evening the Prince departed by rail to Ottawa where on 12 November *The Ottawa Citizen* newspaper reported he had learned that infirmity due to war service had prevented Captain Leonard Askwith from attending the investiture ceremony in Toronto. Accordingly the Prince went to Captain Askwith's home on the 11th, and in a private ceremony, he invested him with the Military Cross.

After the awards ceremonies were finished, Roy's life settled down again, and in a manner described in a later chapter by his daughter, Margaret, he became quite friendly with the volunteer nurse who was administering his massage treatment. She was Edythe Lois Monypenny, the daughter of Thomas Flavelle Monypenny, the Chairman of the National Military Committee of the YMCA, and one of the owners of the *Imperial Varnish and Color Company* in Toronto. It was not long before they began going out together.

The wedding took place at 3 o'clock in the afternoon of 19 February 1920 at the Monypenny residence at 57 Langley Avenue. The Reverend W E Baker performed the ceremony; Roy's RNAS pilot friend Arthur Whealy was best man.

Unfortunately no good print of the wedding photograph exists; the best one available is reproduced below.

Captain and Mrs. A Roy Brown.

The happy couple were not exactly flush with money and set up their home in a rather small apartment. It was not long before furnishings usurped the space occupied by Roy's souvenirs from the Great War, so he donated the seat and the inscribed piece of fabric from Rittmeister Manfred Freiherr von Richthofen's triplane to the Canadian Military Institute, 426 University Avenue, Toronto, where they were placed on display in a function room. Included in the display was a walking-stick carved from the triplane's propeller by the sergeant fitter (the highest grade of mechanic) of Oliver LeBoutillier's flight. It was on temporary loan and was later returned to its owner. There being no 'paper trail', the owner's identity became lost in the mists of time, but there was a suggestion, which turned out to be erroneous, that 'Boots', himself, had placed it there. The story of the search for the stick and the discovery that it had a 'brother' is told in PART TWO of this book.

In the photograph below, note how the successive layers of paint used to change the original Maltese cross to a Balkan Cross, and then finally to a Latin cross have flaked off in some places.

One part of the Roy Brown display at the CMI; the inscribed piece of fabric and the walking-stick.

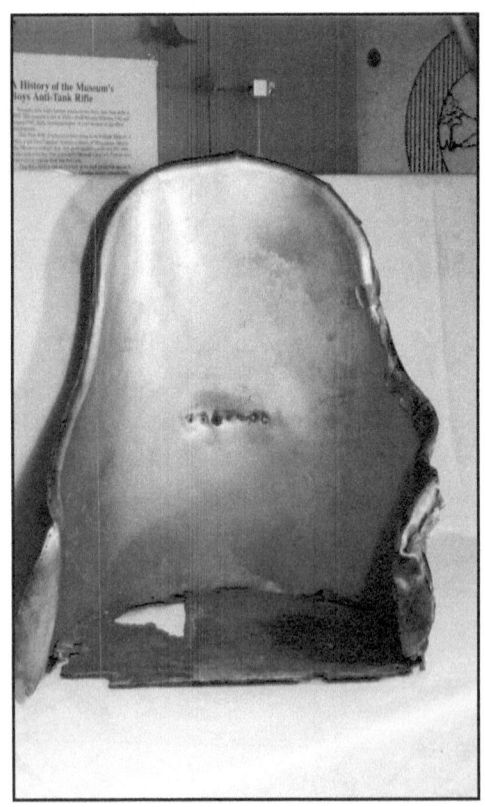

The other part of the display; the seat.

A commemorative placard was placed beside the seat. In 1977 the Curator (Lieut.-Colonel W.G. Heard) of the re-named Royal Canadian Military Institute, advised historian, Frank McGuire, that the origin of the wording thereon was a short statement dictated by Roy for an Ontario Board of Education grade 8 History of Canada textbook published by Coppe, Clarke and Company. The history book and the placard are historically important, being the only unedited, written statements known to exist of what Roy personally understood, in the 1920s, to have happened on 21/22 April 1918.

> This case contains the seat of the Fokker triplane of Baron M. Von Richthofen regarded as the most distinguished of the German airmen in the Great War, having 82 Allied planes to his credit. He was shot through the heart by Captain A. Roy Brown, D.S.C. and bar, Royal Air Force, of Carleton Place, Ont., in an air engagement over the Somme Valley, 21st April 1918. Captain Brown was flying after Richthofen, and while slightly above and behind him on his left rear brought him down by the shot mentioned.
>
> When the German triplane reached the earth, a claim was made by the crew of a machine gun, and also by an anti-aircraft battery, that they had fired the shot which ended the career of Richthofen. These claims, and the statement of Captain Brown were enquired into by a Board, and the evidence adduced by those firing being somewhat conflicting, the evidence of the surgeon who examined the dead and gallant airman, proved that the course of the bullet through the body showed that it could only have been fired from an aeroplane in the position of Captain Brown, and a finding was made accordingly.
>
> Captain Brown having been given this trophy and memento, has kindly deposited it in the Museum of The Canadian Military Institute.

The commemorative placard.

The seat was later placed inside a glass case for protection. Shadows from the indirect lighting made the seven 4mm (0.157 inch) rivet holes in the backrest appear considerably larger than their true size. In the coming years this was to cause much argument as their origin. The subject is covered in detail in PART TWO.

Other souvenirs found homes, both temporary and permanent, with relatives and military museums. As of this writing, the year 2005, several items are on public display at the Canadian Military Heritage Museum at Brantford, Ontario. Roy's RNAS Pilot's Licence (photograph in Chapter Four), the pocket watch presented to him by his father (photograph in Chapter Two) and the hub of the propeller from one of his Sopwith *Camels* (depicted immediately below) are among them. The propeller blades, sawn off by Roy, are in the possession of relatives.

The laminated construction employed in the manufacture of propellers, stands out clearly in the photograph below. The inscription reads:

SOPWITH F1
130 HP CLERGET
AD 644 RH
D 2590 P 2650

A decoding of the last two lines of the inscription is to be found under Item (1) in the ANNEX to Chapter 8.

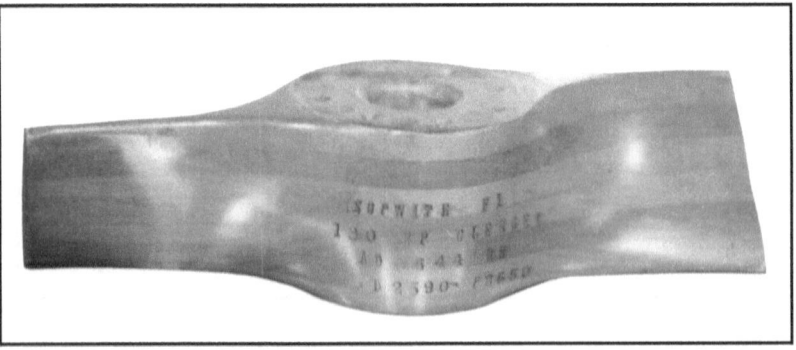

Propeller hub from one of Roy's Sopwith *Camels*.

Captain Roy Brown 617

After Roy's marriage, he began work in the sales department of his father-in-law's company, *Imperial Varnish and Color Co.*, but as his health improved, his eyes turned towards the sky. Although he would never be pilot-in-command again in his lifetime - the after-effects of his head injuries at Marske-by-the-Sea and the long hours spent in the bitter cold at 17,000 feet still remained with him - he could **own** an aeroplane. There was an adventurous living to be made by charter flying miners and mining equipment to isolated places where existing methods of travel took days, sometimes weeks. An aeroplane, which could operate on skis, floats or wheels as the seasons changed, would be required, and there were plenty of good ex-RNAS pilots around in need of a job. He began discussions with friends and colleagues on how to raise the necessary funds.

At an unknown date in the 1920's, Arthur Whealy, Roy's RNAS pilot friend, had suggested to his relatives that Roy's two pre-war years at the Willis School of Business could be of use to the family enterprise, a rapidly expanding company named Regal Bakeries. Roy was appointed to the board of directors and the extra income became of great use in planning his new venture. For how long he served in that capacity is unknown.

On 2 December 1925, the WINNIPEG EVENING TRIBUNE and the OTTAWA CITIZEN published a story of the air battle on 21 April 1918 told by a person who described himself as having been a pilot in 209 Squadron. The pilot was not named, which was bad enough, but worse yet, the story, known to historians as *The Anonymous Account*, had been exaggerated to the point that anyone who believed it, would believe anything. The increased circulation due to the resulting furore was noticed by the staff of more than one publication, and the hypothetical well from which such nonsensical tales were drawn soon began to overflow.

The Anonymous Account is reproduced below exactly as printed in the OTTAWA CITIZEN:

> *Fifteen of our planes were patrolling along the lines. Captain Brown was leading his squadron of five machines parallel with the second squadron, and some distance above the third and leading squadron.*
>
> *We had not gone far when we saw above us two or three R.E.8s out*

on artillery observation, and attacking them were several German triplanes. At that time we were at an altitude of 15,000 feet, and the enemy planes were flying quite low.

Captain Brown, without hesitation, dived, the others following. Within a few minutes we were in the middle of a dog fight. We discovered we were attacking 22 enemy machines. Fortunately the speed of the onslaught threw the enemy off guard, and the old R.E.8s were able to get away undamaged.

Captain Brown, as leader of the squadron, was keeping an eye on the entire fight. He had one pilot, Captain 'Wop' May of Edmonton, who had never before taken part in an air battle and quite naturally he paid particular care to the new man. Captain May dived with the rest, engaged with a German, and after bringing him down, made towards our lines in accordance with instructions.

No sooner had he become detached from the others than Richthofen made after him and opened up heavy fire. Fortunately Captain Brown had been watching this turn of events and immediately followed after Richthofen. His first bullets ripped through the fuselage of the enemy plane. We saw him elevate his fire slightly. Richthofen collapsed in his seat and the plane plunged to the ground.

GOT EIGHT ENEMY PLANES

When the battle was over, we discovered that we had accounted for eight enemy planes, and we had received no damage at all.

Richthofen was usually successful because he invariably followed any plane which had become detached from the fight. I question whether he ever realized that he in turn, was being followed. He was killed instantaneously by the first burst of bullets and his machine was riddled.

The story is 75% fiction, distortion and exaggeration woven around 25% fact. In the first paragraph, the alleged pilot does not know the difference between a flight and a squadron, a confusion which does not exactly inspire confidence in what follows. The second and third paragraphs include an event which occurred on the following day. This is the fiction mentioned in Chapter Eight shortly after Roy's Log Book entry for 22 April. The 'GOT EIGHT' enemy planes statements are double the claims made by the 209 squadron pilots, of which only two were confirmed - Roy's and Mellersh's. The *'we had received no damage at all'*, statement makes it difficult to explain Lieut. Mackenzie's wound, or that his *Camel* had been so badly shot up, that it had to be transported by rail to No.2 Aircraft Depot for a complete rebuild. It was issued to 213 Sqn. in June. The AIRCRAFT DAMAGE REPORT for Lieut. Mackenzie's *Camel* is reproduced below.

```
              A I R C R A F T   D A M A G E   R E P O R T
              -----------------------------------------

  209                    22                   April 21st  1918.
                         Sopwith B.R. B 7245.
         1-150-509.      WD 36941.
      Lieut. W.J.Mackenzie.

                         ___
         H.O.P.


                         Vickers Syn. Guns Nos. C 7874 & C 5110.
                  No.
                  No.
                         2" Aldis Sight No. 76890.


                         Fuselage and 3-ply shot through, strut
                         sockets to engine bearer shot away.
                         Ribs in planes and longeron shot
                         through.  Total flying time 33 hours
                         40 minutes.

  Returned to No. 2 A.S.D. 21/4/18.

  Engine  -  serviceable  -  removed  from  machine  before  being
  returned.

                                                    [signature]

  Retyped 13 March, 2002                            209
```

Lieut. William John Mackenzie at Bertangles. Photograph from his personal album via Ida Bridges (his sister) and Stewart Taylor.

A detailed rebuttal of *The Anonymous Account* is to be found in APPENDIX B of THE RED BARON'S LAST FLIGHT.

What Roy thought about the article is unknown, but it would serve as the basis for later fantasies which were to cause him much aggravation.

The 'five o'clock standby' habit died hard. The ex-RNAS pilots had occasional get-togethers at the home of one or the other. Roy's daughter, Margaret, recalls that towards the close of an evening, things could become a bit noisy. They also met, but more formally, at Armistice Day ceremonies. It was to one such event that Roy's wife, Edythe, invited her younger sister Clara Flavelle Monypenny.

Clara Flavelle Monypenny at age 19.

Edythe introduced Clara to Mel Alexander, Roy's good friend from Naval 10 squadron; romance blossomed and on 27 February 1927 they became man and wife.

The occasional, informal meetings developed into something more substantial and in early 1932 the 'Comrades of the Royal Air Force Association, Canada Branch No. 40' came into being. All war-time pilots and observers, whether RNAS, RFC or RAF were invited to join. The chairman was C.B. Stenning (ex-56 Sqn. RFC) and Roy was one of the vice-chairmen. On 2 April 1932 the first reunion of what the members called the Canadian Comrades Association was a dinner at the Royal York Hotel in Toronto where General Airways had an office. Roy, who had arranged the catering, was the toastmaster. The banquet was a great success and the members decided to hold a similar event in a year's time. It took place at the same hotel on Armistice Day 1933, Roy organized it and the toastmaster was Air Commodore R.H. Mulock.

For reasons now unknown, the next meeting was not held until 1938, at which time Roy was the president. It began at the King Edward Hotel in Toronto in the evening of 30 August, and helped by live entertainment, the banquet lasted well into the wee hours of the following morning. Among the attendees who drove past the milkman on their way home were Mel Alexander and Gerry Nash. Roy did a little more than that; he drove his car into the rear of a milk cart that was not showing any lights. Some bottles were broken, but fortunately, neither the milkman nor the horse suffered injury. The last meeting of the Canadian Comrades Association was held at the Royal York Hotel on 7 April 1958 by which time Roy had been dead for 14 years.

Returning to 1927, Roy's efforts to raise capital moved slowly but in the right direction, then came disaster. A city in South America needed to finance some major projects, and to encourage investors it issued bonds with an unusually high yield. Roy put much of his money into these, but after two or three years, a sudden, major devaluation of that nation's currency occurred, and he lost most of his investment. This was quite a setback to the charter air service plan, but a year or two later, the Goddess of Fortune smiled upon him from an unexpected direction.

An author, named Floyd Gibbons, decided to write a biography of Rittmeister Manfred Albrecht Freiherr von Richthofen. In order to portray the Rittmeister's death in battle as accurately as possible, Gibbons approached the RAF Historical Branch in London. With whom he dealt is unknown, but the accuracy of much of the information he received was on a level with Brigadier General Charlton placing the Cérisy air battle over Vaux-sur-Somme. From the multitude of errors and impossibilities which Gibbons was told; three, which need no discussion, are given below:

(1) Lieut. May came from Melbourne, Australia.
(2) It was Lieut. Mellersh who salvaged the red triplane.
(3) Roy Brown's *Camel* had been badly shot up low down near Vaux-sur-Somme and he had flown it 12 miles back to Bertangles with only three cylinders working in his nine-cylinder engine.

See (8) in the ANNEX to this chapter for more information on the effects of non-working cylinders on the flight of an aeroplane fitted with a rotary engine.

How could such things happen? The answer could be that the correct information was buried in the several tons of records the Historical

Branch was working valiantly to classify and organize. The staff members did the best they could, but stories they had read on that subject in newspapers and magazines were still fresh in their minds. Thus, outside sources somewhat more oriented to increasing the readership than expounding the truth, overshadowed the little documentation they had found inside up to that date.

In mid-1927 the first of twenty-four parts of THE RED KNIGHT OF GERMANY, by Floyd Gibbons, appeared in the LIBERTY magazine, published in New York, NY. When parts 22 and 23 appeared on 12 and 19 November 1927 respectively, they created quite a sensation, which, in view of what is written above about the sources Gibbons had used and trusted, is not surprising. Excerpts were published in newspapers in Canada, England and Australia, and 'Letters to the Editor' began to fly. In November 1927 THE RED KNIGHT OF GERMANY, with some parts rewritten, appeared in book form, and the uproar in Australia surrounding some of the historical inaccuracies, geographical misrepresentations and mechanical impossibilities repeated therein became intense. Gibbons was unaware that the downed triplane had been filmed for a newsreel and photographed for the press, and that his most sensational and dramatic revelation; namely, the presence of a bullet hole in the back of the pilot's seat, was demonstrably false.

Gibbons had been taken in by *The Anonymous Account*, which when supplemented by the flawed information obtained from the RAF Historical Branch, was to carry him even further away from the truth. Not only did he accept the fictional rescue of the two R.E.8s on 21 April 1918 as true, but he provided a thrilling, three-page, detailed description which has been bouncing around ever since. The event, as described, might well be termed *The Air Fight That Never Happened*.

See (9) in the ANNEX to this chapter for more information on The Air Fight That Never Happened.

The following condensed excerpt from the book form of THE RED KNIGHT OF GERMANY should be read carefully; part of it will shortly reappear in a paraphrased and expanded form under another title, every word being attributed to Roy.

For a second time, the reader is invited to sit down with a cup of refreshment, then to make a mental note of any statements which seem odd.

> 'The Australian machine-gunner aimed forward and upward. So close was Richthofen on May's tail that he dared not fire. Another Lewis gunner beyond the ridge sprayed a stream of lead upward. He saw splinters flying from the woodwork of the German plane. Brown had arrived at the end of his dive. His last drum of ammunition was in place. He pressed the trigger. He watched the tracer bullets going into the red triplane from the right side. They hit the tail first. A slight pull on the stick - a fractional elevation of the Camel's nose and his line of fire started to tuck a seam up the body of the Fokker. Richthofen, with his spurting Spandaus still trained on May, was unaware of this new attack from the rear.'

The main points of divergence from the truth are:

AA.   The sequence of events is reversed; Roy's attack occurred first. He had turned back to help Mellersh long before May and the Baron came into the range of the machine-gunners on the ground.

BB.   Roy's *Camel*, not being a high altitude night fighter, had two belt-fed Vickers machine-guns.

CC.   Roy said that he attacked from the left.

DD.   The cinema newsreel and press photographs taken of the triplane from several angles do not show bullet holes anywhere in it. The tail and the top of the fuselage appear clearly in some scenes.

EE.   Bullets hitting taut fabric produce an extremely loud noise.

In a later edition Gibbons corrected the *'last drum of ammunition'* slip; he changed it to *'last belt'*. Unfortunately, he was unaware that the 400 round belt could only be installed on the ground. A photograph and a description of the installation are to be found under item (3) in the ANNEX to Chapter Six. This episode demonstrates the dangers which await an author who uncritically accepts information derived from other sources.

When LIBERTY magazine learned that Captain Roy Brown was living in Toronto, the Editor approached him for his story. The outcome was that Roy agreed to write six articles on air fighting in the Great War for which he would be paid handsomely. Overnight Roy's idea of owning a charter air service changed from a remote possibility to a distinct probability.

In the 1960's Roy's brother, Howard, told historian Frank McGuire that LIBERTY magazine engaged Frederick Griffin, a reporter from THE TORONTO STAR to interview Roy, and he certainly took careful notes as can be seen from some of the details published. However, between the note taking and the publishing a lot can happen, especially when sensation means sales. Apparently someone in New York noticed that the notes concerning Roy's encounter with the Rittmeister did not include lots of the action that had been described in detail by Floyd Gibbons and others. The gaps were filled in by a copywriter who was again unaware that the downed triplane had been photographed for the press and filmed for a cinema newsreel, and that due to his additional dramatization there were now two more points which were demonstrably false. The story was named MY FIGHT WITH RICHTHOFEN and misleadingly subtitled 'As Told by the Man who Shot him Down'.

In 1971 the Editors of LIBERTY magazine checked the 1928 records and concluded that the story submitted by Roy's interviewer *'might have been ghost-written; certainly it must, at least, have been heavily edited and rewritten'*. The bones of Roy's true story are clearly discernable, but when the trails of the additions and changes are followed back to their sources (via the repetition of certain phrases and factual errors), it can be seen that many first saw the light of day in *The Anonymous Account*. Then, accompanied by ideas from the RED KNIGHT OF GERMANY, they found their way into MY FIGHT WITH RICHTHOFEN.

On 11 January 1928 the CHICAGO TRIBUNE reported from London:

A fierce ten year old controversy as to who gets the honor of bringing down Capt. Baron Manfred von Richthofen, the famous German flying ace, in April 1918, was revived today by war mates of the Canadian flyer, Capt. A. Roy Brown. These protest that he received and is entitled to full credit instead of Gunner W.J. Evans of the Australian field artillery, as claimed by the Australian forces.

The struggle is reopened as a result of a news dispatch from Australia reporting General Rawlinson's alleged support of Gunner Evans' claim, as well as the "unfavorable reception" given Capt. Brown's claim.

The records clerk of Capt. Brown's squadron, as well as Capt. Brown's former buddies, today produced official records to the effect that Capt. Brown was given full credit at the time, receiving an additional bar on his Distinguished Service Cross as well as the engine of the "Red Knight's" plane, while his comrades received souvenir trophies of the plane, thus confirming the story recently published in Liberty magazine.

The claim that official 209 Sqn. records had been consulted seems rather doubtful since Roy received one bar to his DSC, not two, and it was the pilot's seat he received as a souvenir, not the engine.

In 1999, Howard Brown told Alan Bennett that his brother, Roy, was not happy with what had been published, but he had signed a contract which permitted editing, had accepted payment, and had already spent the money on aeroplanes and equipment. Although Roy's understanding of the term 'editing' did not exactly include what had happened, there was not much that he could do about it.

General Airways was formed in June 1928 with A Roy Brown as president. It would be three months before it took to the skies and its story is told in the following chapter.

THE CHICAGO SUNDAY TRIBUNE, which in early 1929 had already published THE RED KNIGHT OF GERMANY in twelve episodes, now published MY FIGHT WITH RICHTHOFEN (with a few changes of an editing nature) in five. The two-year gap between the LIBERTY and TRIBUNE presentations tended to hide that the latter was a rewrite of the former. Historian Frank McGuire has pointed out instances in which more than one reputable writer has cited the 1929 TRIBUNE articles in support of a disputed item from the 1927 story in LIBERTY, which brings to mind the story of the Antwerp Church Bells related under Item (7) in the ANNEX to Chapter Three.

Thus it can be seen that several mutually supportive, incorrect items found in accounts published between 1925 and 1950, only agree because they have a common source. Even the statement made by the RAF Historical Branch, mentioned in the reply to Wing Commander Manning on Roy's accident at Marske-by-the-Sea [see Item (2) in the ANNEX to this chapter], is traceable back to *The Anonymous Account*, which puts the authorities in the unenviable position of endorsing make-believe, albeit with the caveat of not having the actual documents available at the time.

MY FIGHT WITH RICHTHOFEN begins with an expanded version of Roy's Log Book entries from the beginning of March 1918. The only variation of significance is in the style of prose used, which is the natural result of the editing to heighten the drama, and in some instances the humour. There are some slips concerning details that Roy would have stated correctly, but nothing serious. No-one can really quarrel with the first part of the story without being termed a 'nit-picker'.

A sudden change occurs on 21 April 1918; here the heavy editing; i.e. the rewriting begins. Some statements are completely out of character for Roy. Others are positively slanderous, which the reader will recognize as not being Roy's style at all. The sequence in which some events occurred is altered and their locations changed; geography is turned upside down, and participants are mixed up. Roy's rescue of an R.E.8 of 3 Squadron AFC on 22 April, and his encounter with Jasta 11 on 21 April, are rolled into one fictitious event which bears a striking resemblance to *The Air Fight That Never Happened* as published earlier in THE RED KNIGHT OF GERMANY. The tale continues from there with nasty remarks about an Australian airman (probably Lieut. Alfred Victor Barrow), who had quite honestly filed a legitimate claim for a victory in an air fight which did happen, and concludes with complaints concerning the awarding of medals. Lieut. Barrow's story is told in Chapter 16.

Logically, there was another uproar in Australia, which resulted in letters to the press and further investigation by Dr. C E W Bean. Details are to be found in THE DAY THE RED BARON DIED, by Dale Titler and WHO KILLED THE RED BARON? by Pasquale Carisella and James Ryan. It is surprising that the pilots of 3 Squadron AFC and

Major Leslie Ellis Beavis of the army did not begin a libel action.

In footnote #4 on page 694 of THE AUSTRALIAN IMPERIAL FORCE IN FRANCE, the Official Australian Historian, Dr. C E W Bean, wrote, *"Captain Brown, on being asked in 1935 if the narrative in the Chicago Sunday Tribune was correct, was unable to confirm it or otherwise, not having read the paper at the time."* It is what the Australians would call a 'left-handed answer', but in view of the acrimonious circumstances, what could he have said without creating a storm in the USA and possibly being sued as well?

The true story, as contained in his Roy's Log Book and letters, plus RAF and Army documents in their original form, was overwhelmed by the sensational presentation of what many assumed to be his personal memoirs. In the eyes of those who knew the landscape and the true sequence of events, the easily demonstrable falsehoods seriously damaged Roy's perfectly valid claim to have shot down the Red Baron. If his claim to victory depended on that story, the circumstances had to be rather shaky, to say the least.

See (10) in the ANNEX to this chapter for Gunner Robert Buie's comment on the Chicago *Sunday Tribune* story.

For those who would like to read the six articles, there are a surprising number of public libraries around the world which have the magazine LIBERTY (published in New York, NY, USA by Macfadden Publications) in their microfilm vault, or can obtain the microfilm upon request. The same applies to the CHICAGO TRIBUNE. The SUNDAY edition is usually on the same reel.

The titles of the articles and the dates on which they were published in LIBERTY are as follows:

>My Fight with Richthofen, Part 1 - 26 November 1927
>My Fight with Richthofen, Part 2 - 3 December 1927
>My Fight with Richthofen, Part 3 - 10 December 1927
>My Fight with Richthofen, Part 4 - 17 December 1927
>Dirty Work at the Crossroads - 24 December 1927
>Nighthawks, True Tales of Flying Bombers - 31 December 1927
>Luck on the Wing - 9 June 1928

Bishop of the Eagle Eye - 27 Sept. 1930
My Fight with Richthofen, a reprinting of Parts 3 & 4 - Volume 1, No. 2, Autumn issue, 1971

See (11) in the ANNEX to this chapter for information on how Roy's name became confused with that of another writer.

As has been revealed by Roy's letters in earlier chapters, he was a calm, polite person who did not write in an emphatic or exaggerated manner, nor did he make derogatory comments about others. RNAS/RAF ace fighter pilot Mel Alexander, who has been mentioned several times already, described him as *"a quiet reticent chap."* Roy's neighbour in Stouffville, Ontario, Mr. Earl Brillinger, described him as *"a quiet and courteous man."* He also said, *"Roy Brown was a gentleman and it would be difficult to find a finer man than he was."*

In the excerpts from MY FIGHT WITH RICHTHOFEN which follow, quite apart from the statements not sounding anything like Roy's style of writing or self-expression, each of them differs radically from what he would have known to be true. The object of the *"heavy editing and rewriting"* seems to have been to apply the most melodramatic amplification and spin that Roy's original words would bear.

EXCERPT AA.
Richthofen's end was little different from the fate of his fourscore victims. He had the ill luck to find himself at the wrong end of a machine-gun spraying tracer bullets. That finished him. For the greatest of them all - Boelke, Ball, Guynemer, McCudden - died like the poorest dub when an enemy pilot spewed a straight burst at the right moment.

THE FACTS.
Most, if not all RAF pilots were well aware that the super aces Ball, Boelke and McCudden had died in flying accidents. The fourth, Guynemer (54), was believed at that time simply to have disappeared without trace. Roy had obviously mentioned these names as examples of how the capricious hand of fate could strike down even the best.

EXCERPT BB.

On that March morning when the Hun began his last tremendous effort to smash through to the Channel ports, we of the 209th Squadron, Royal Air Force, were at that time at the middle aerodrome. This was about half way between Bray Dunes and the Belgian Frontier.

THE FACTS.
On that date the RAF did not exist. Roy belonged to Naval 9 and was proud of it. He undoubtedly said he was at Middle Aerodrome, the actual name of an RNAS station. The person who dramatized his words 'corrected' what he took to be a syntax error and added the wrong squadron details.

EXCERPT CC.
I noticed two of our own R.E.8s down low over the Somme near Cerisy. Two enemy aircraft were attacking them. It was a moment which called for hesitation, the two had become twenty-two. Frankly I did not know what to do. The squadron formation had disappeared. Behind me were only the members of my flight - five of us altogether - and back of them a few other Camels. Attack in the face of such odds was plain suicide. Something snapped inside me: "You-cold footed pup! Save those R.E.8s. Go in and smash those Huns." Down I flung, full out at the tripe attacking the nearest British bus. All I recall of him was his blue tail. Mellersh was right beside me, firing too. It was he who got the credit for him.

THE FACTS
Here begins a re-write of *The Air Fight That Never Happened*, as published in THE RED KNIGHT OF GERMANY, but to make an encounter with 209 Sqn. more plausible, the R.E.8s have been moved from Hamel to Cérisy.

EXCERPT DD.
I thought of Wop May. At last I sighted him, up toward Corbie, north of me. Out of the haze I saw a red triplane go darting after him. I dived toward the tail of the red plane. That was the moment May gave up. He heard my guns. He flashed a look. "Thank God its Brownie!"

THE FACTS.
All 209 Sqn. *Camels* were identically painted.
Corbie was due west of Roy's position.
May neither heard nor saw Roy's rescue attempt.

EXCERPT EE.
Bullets ripped into the triplane's elevator and tail plane. The flaming tracers showed me where they hit. A little short. The stream of bullets tore along the body of the all-red tripe. Its occupant turned and looked back. I had a flash of his eyes behind the goggles. Then he crumpled. It was an affair of seconds, faster than the telling. The triplane went down. It was a quick descent, 300 feet. May saw it, I saw it and Mellersh saw it.

THE FACTS.
Paraphrased, with additions, from THE RED KNIGHT OF GERMANY. The major points which diverge from reality are:

    1918 tracer bullets did not flame in daylight.

    There were no bullet holes in the elevators, nor the tailplane, nor along the body of the triplane.

    If the Rittmeister had decided to attempt suicide in combat that day by looking around behind, and did in fact see a *Camel* there, it means he knew he was being attacked from the left. In which case, why did he turn the wrong way (to the right) to escape the shots being fired at him?

    The top of Vaux-sur-Somme church tower is 60 feet above ground level. Witnesses saw both May and the Baron swerve to avoid hitting it seconds before the second *Camel* attacked the latter.

    The so-called crash occurred one minute later, but Roy did not see it. He was a mile or two away to the NE returning from rescuing Mellersh from the two triplanes which had sought the latter's hide.

EXCERPT FF.
Limping like a lame duck I returned to Bertangles. Only three cylinders were hitting. The propeller was scarcely turning over. But I made the drome.

THE FACTS.
The reader will recognize this tale. It was presented a few pages earlier

in this chapter under the 'errors and impossibilities to be found in THE RED KNIGHT OF GERMANY. Its origin was *The Anonymous Account* of December 1925 also given earlier in this chapter. It was copied into the 'Summary on Brown' which Floyd Gibbons received from the Public Record Office in London. This supposedly historical document reads like an article taken from a magazine offering thrilling stories for boys. For the full text of the Summary on Brown, see APPENDIX C in THE RED BARON'S LAST FLIGHT.

Lieut's May and Mellersh accompanied their flight commander on the 12 mile flight home. Neither mentioned any abnormality, nor did Roy.

The writer obviously knew little about aeroplanes. The effects upon flight of damaged or defective engines have been presented several times in previous chapters, therefore the technical impossibility and absurdity of the description of Roy's engine and propeller need no comment. The following photograph (shown once in an earlier chapter) will remind the reader of the damage which can occur if a severely vibrating rotary engine is not shut down immediately.

Sopwith *Pup* which successful forced-landed in a field after the engine became unbalanced in flight. In this case, a cylinder parted company from the crankcase.

The narrative continues with some negative comments about the Australian troops and 3 Squadron AFC. A description of an interview with an Australian Major then follows.

EXCERPT GG.
The 11th Brigade commander sent for the Major who was in charge of that part of the line. The major had his story pat. He had witnessed the triplanes' attack on the R.E.8s and they had seen the Camels jump on the tripes and engage them heavily. A red-nosed Camel had broken loose from the fight and had been immediately dived on by an all-red triplane. The pair of them, one chasing the other had come so close and low that he ordered his machine-gunners to open fire on the enemy flier. I spoke only once. "And what," I asked, "did the red-nosed Camel behind the all-red tripe do?" The major hesitated, flushed, stuttered. "He-he-b-but there was no red-nosed Camel behind." On the way out I told Cairns, "That Major is a bloody liar." I pointed out that he could not have missed seeing my Camel on the tail of the tripe. "But," I said, "after we inspect the body, I suggest we look at the machine. I won't say any more now."

THE FACTS.
The front line was nowhere near there. The major who was in charge of that part of the line (almost three miles to the east) was not the one who commanded the 53rd Field Artillery Battery to which the machine-gunners belonged.

The Air Fight That Never Happened appears again, but the new site (Cérisy) of that fictious event has been shifted to an even newer site five miles west of the first one, where it was *"witnessed"* by the un-named major.

The red noses had been painted khaki during the previous week.

According to Gunner Buie and Bombardier Seccull in separate interviews, there was quite a long discussion.

After rescuing Lieut. May at Vaux-sur-Somme, Roy had turned back to help Lieut. Mellersh. At the time cited above, Roy was half a mile, or more, to the east of the red triplane.

Note the misspelling of 'Cairnes', Roy's wing commander, whose name he must have seen written several times on orders.

The episode of the *"bloody liar"* occurred the other way around. It was one of Major Beavis's officers who defamed Roy during the meeting. The event is described in PART TWO of this book.

The narrative continues with Lieut.-Colonel Cairnes and Roy stepping outside the 11th Infantry Brigade HQ where they encounter the Baron's body. Actually the body was near the 53rd Battery position half a mile away on the other side of the hill. While still (supposedly) at the 11th Brigade HQ, they decide to look at the downed triplane, but the itinerary given reads more like a departure from the 53rd Battery commander's dugout.

EXCERPT HH.

"Let's get out. We'll go and see the machine. We walked towards the place where the triplane lay. It was possibly a mile and a half away. A road ran part of the distance. Then we entered the reserve trenches, but the triplane was still 100 yards away. In a flash I was over the edge of the trench and running to the plane."

THE FACTS.

Unlike Roy, who had been shown the crash site from about a quarter of a mile away, the person who wrote this paragraph had not the foggiest idea where it was. Even the main highway from Corbie to Bray, which ran close by, is described incorrectly.

See (12) in the ANNEX to this chapter for more information about the fictitious trench adventure.

EXCERPT II.

"I saw what I wanted to find. Starting at the elevator bullets had ripped their way along the fuselage; bullets fired from above and behind. They had travelled right along to the cockpit. There were holes in the cockpit. Blood spattered the seat. There was a hole in it."

THE FACTS.

The scene is paraphrased from THE RED KNIGHT OF GERMANY, with the dramatic addition for good measure, of an imaginary bullet hole in the seat. The seat was Roy's personal souvenir and he was well aware that every hole in it had been made at the Fokker factory.

The narrative now spends some time insulting and deriding the Australian R.E.8 observer (mentioned earlier) for shamelessly claiming the victory after the risks, which according to *The Air Fight That Never Happened*, Roy's flight had taken to save him. It then continues with more complaints.

EXCERPT JJ.

I was given neither recognition nor award, although two Australian Tommies were credited with receiving Distinguished Conduct Medals for their unsuccessful shooting from the trenches. Cairns went on to say that the Australians had demanded the decorations aforesaid. It had become a kind of complication within the British Empire - Canada versus Australia. The British authorities, bowing before the ruckus raised by the Australian command, had thought it wise to make no recognition of my part in it, lest the Australians be offended.

No medal or citation of any kind was issued to any Australian.

There is no mention anywhere in the files of England, Canada or Australia of a demand for decorations.

EXCERPT KK.

I finished my month's leave of absence with Stearne Edwards and was flying in England preparatory to going back to the front when I crashed and broke my back. Long before I was able to walk the war was over. So was my flying.

THE FACTS.

Both Roy and Stearne Edwards were posted to Marske-by-the-Sea for an indefinite period as aerial combat instructors.

Roy did not break his back. In 1971 LIBERTY reprinted the article, shortened a little by omitting some paragraphs. At the same time, the 'broke my back' error was 'corrected' by changing the word 'back' to read 'neck', but as the reader will recall from Roy's medical treatment detailed earlier in this chapter, he did not break that either.

In late August 1918, Roy was allowed to go on a short leave. On 14 September, Douglas Findlay informed Roy's parents that their son's only visible disability was a slight limp. The war ended two months later.

If the reader is wondering how such a mixture of truth, distortion and outright fabrication could ever have been taken seriously or accepted as written by Roy, it must be emphasized that most of the letters, diaries and some of the documents contained in this book have never before been published in any form whatsoever. Several were not known to exist, others were not widely known in their original phrasing. Story writers for magazines were often faced with having to decide which of several versions of an event was the most likely to be true, but how the obvious nonsense concerning the engine and propeller passed unchallenged by them defies imagination. Books and articles by researchers, such as Dale Titler, Pasquale Carisella, James Ryan and Frank McGuire, who made their own investigations and found THE RED KNIGHT OF GERMANY and MY FIGHT WITH RICHTHOFEN to be deeply flawed, were reviewed by the press and soon forgotten.

Roy Brown's letters home, when considered together with the discovery of the exact positions of the 1918 Sainte Colette brick factory chimney, the drainage ditch, the overhead transporter cable and the place where the red triplane slid to a halt, provide benchmarks around which true information must logically fit and therefore become a firm basis for judgement.

It is probably most apt now to quote Colonel (retired) Fletcher Prouty of the U.S. Air Force who wrote;

During this 20th century, there has been a flood of creative and interpretive history that has been inadequately researched, totally misguided, replete with the omission of crucial facts, strongly biased and just generally of poor quality.

What is even more damaging is that these fabricated historical presentations have misled later generations of students and their teachers.

During the later part of the international argument provoked by the Chicago Sunday Tribune publication of MY FIGHT WITH RICHTHOFEN, Roy heard that Major Beavis had supplied his version of the event to the ARMY QUARTERLY, a magazine published in London, and wrote to him requesting a copy. The major, who was serving there at the time, replied immediately complying with Roy's request. The tone of both letters was remarkably polite in view the circumstances. Possibly Major Beavis, who had met Roy on 21 April, knew his character and his polite way of talking, suspected what had happened to his memoirs between the telling and the printing.

See (13) in the ANNEX to this chapter for Roy's exchange of letters with Major Beavis.

Roy and 'Wop' May were interviewed several times by newspaper reporters between 1919 and 1931. Logically they could only tell what they knew, which included what they had been told by Major Butler in April 1918. He, in turn, only knew what he had been told by his superiors about the results of the examination of the Baron's body by 22 Wing medical officers. The two medical examinations conducted separately by two pairs of highly qualified army physicians and surgeons appear to have been unknown or not acknowledged by the RAF. From Lieut.-Colonel Cairnes downwards, knowledge of the 'damage' to the Baron's body came mainly from a paraphrasing of the 22 Wing report in which the emphasis had been shifted, or from a retyping (still present in some archives) which placed the entrance wound on the 'left' side of the Baron's chest instead of on the 'right'.

On 9 July 1919 The EDMONTON BULLETIN interviewed 'Wop' May. He told the reporter:

"In about an hour we heard for sure that it was the Red Baron. He had been shot through the heart and instantly killed. The bullet had entered his shoulder and went down through his heart thus establishing beyond doubt that it same from above and was fired by Captain Brown."

On 1 December 1925 the TORONTO STAR reported that Roy had stated;

"It was definitely established that Richthofen had been shot from the air. One bullet entered the left shoulder, passed through the heart and came out through the abdomen."

On 2 December 1925 the OTTAWA CITIZEN added a little more;

> "There was an enquiry and it was found that the bullets had been fired from above. It was definitely established that Richthofen had been shot from the air. One bullet entered the left shoulder, passed through the heart and came out through the abdomen."

On 5 February 1931 the OTTAWA CITIZEN contained the following report;

> In the Mount Royal Hotel last night Roy Brown was questioned about who had brought down the crack enemy airman. He answered: I have no bones to pick with those who think they brought him down, they were quite right in believing what they did. Their guns were in the ground and trained up at an angle. They saw him coming, they fired and he fell. But the autopsy revealed the bullets had hit from above and behind. The Royal Air Force recognized me as the man who brought him down. I was right on his tail at the time I shot. Therefore, either Richthofen was flying upside down and backwards, or else I brought him down."

Note the contrast between Roy's polite assertions and the abrasive style which LIBERTY magazine employed in MY FIGHT WITH RICHTHOFEN. Note also that neither Roy nor 'Wop' knew that the bullet had crossed the Baron's chest sideways from right to left, and that Roy firmly believed the entry wound had been in the *"left shoulder"* and that the bullet had followed a steeply downward path.

Roy's final interview quoted above took place during the period when Dr. C.E.W. Bean and Dr. H.A. Jones were co-operating on writing their respective histories of the A.I.F and the R.A.F., and logically the matter of MY FIGHT WITH RICHTHOFEN assumed some importance. To avoid accidental shifts of meaning or emphasis imposed by paraphrasing or summarizing, Bean's letter to Jones is fully and faithfully transcribed below. It will be seen that, contrary to allegations made in later years that the Australians 'ganged up' to steal Roy's victory, Dr. Bean was bending over backwards to be fair, and the same might also be said of Dr. Jones. Apparently they finally agreed to differ in what they published, but appear privately to have been in fairly close agreement.

3 Oct 1932

Dear Jones,

I have received your chapters and have skimmed through them. I have noted one or two points that may be useful to me, and one or two on which I think we may be able to help you. I will dig into these a little deeper and will write to you again in a fortnight. I hope that is not too late.

But it has occurred to me that, in the interest of both our histories, I should lose no time in writing to you about a vexed point that you will encounter in your next volume, the controversy over Richthofen's death. Here is an outline of what I know about the affair.

Shortly after Richthofen was shot down, I received a message from the 5th Australian Division to the effect that the published version, that he had been shot down from the air by Brown, was incorrect. General Talbot Hobbs, G.O.C. 5th Aust. Div., said that his division claimed that its machine-gunners had shot down Richthofen, and that the men were very much annoyed at the publication of an incorrect story, which was tending to bring the air service into contempt in the division etc., (or other arguments to that effect).

It seemed to me that the matter was a trivial one, if machine-gunners on the ground had brought Richthofen down, the credit to them was slight, or at least was slight in comparison with that of bringing him down from the air. It seemed a very small matter to make a fuss about. I personally was not at all enthusiastic about touching on the subject, and hoped that the air story was true. However, I was told that Hobbs wanted me specially to go out and probe his men's story, as they were not contented to leave things as they were, and I accordingly did so.

I went out to the 5th Divisional Artillery, and interviewed the two Lewis Gunners whose guns had been firing at him and were said to have caused his crash; and there was no doubt that they and other members of their gun crews, and their officers who had seen something of the incident, told a very convincing story. Without going into all the details, it was as follows.

The battery was bivouacked with other Australian infantry and artillery close behind the lines on the hills immediately bordering the Somme.

Air fighting had been going on over the front, some miles away, pretty high up, affording a more or less distant side-show for the camps. Next, the attention of a great many officers and men in the neighbourhood was attracted by the roar of engines, and two planes were seen approaching the hills on which the troops were camped. The planes were so low that some who watched from the flank told me that they thought they might crash into the hilltop unless they altered their course. As they approached, it was seen that the two were a German machine pursuing a British, the German being almost on the other's tail and slightly higher. The German was firing, and it looked as if his opponent was dead meat. They skimmed the hilltop, and the two Lewis guns in the battery lines ahead and slightly apart from one another opened together at short range. The British plane was almost screening the German, but the gunners could see their bullets knocking chips or fabric from the German plane, and it now suddenly banked, swerved, and crashed on the hilltop some distance away at the flank of the guns.

This came from a large number of witnesses, and, as to the general details - the position of the two planes, the swerve and crash of the German etc. were confirmed by the infantry camped on the same hill, among whom I had personal friends. It was, I thought, almost conclusive. There might be a theory that Richthofen had been hit in the air fighting with the other planes over Villers Bretonneux way, and had fainted a few minutes later when pursuing this opponent close to the ground. I put this to some of those who saw the incident, or rather, I asked them if they thought Richthofen was in full possession of his powers when he was chasing the English plane. They said that Richthofen was fighting hard, obviously intent upon killing the Englishman; there was nothing in his action which would lead you to think he had been previously badly hit, quite the reverse.

I heard later that a machine-gunner of the 13th Brigade (the infantry on the same hill) thought that it was he who had hit Richthofen and that some of the officers there, including a friend of mine, thought that this was the case.

On the strength of all this I wrote the report which caused the authorities to hedge in the subsequently published communique. At that stage I pulled out of the controversy - I had never much wanted to be in it; I personally felt that it was a trifle ghoulish.

However, years after the war the matter was resuscitated by the publication of an article by Captain Brown, who pitched into the Australians in a way that did not seem to be quite cricket. As far as I knew we had never done him any harm but had merely told the truth as we saw it. I had never forgotten that there might be three explanations of his story consistent with his honesty:-

(1) He might have shot someone else and thought it was Richthofen.

(2) He might have hit Richthofen in the dogfight that was going on high in the air, and - though it seemed far-fetched - Richthofen might afterwards have fainted in this subsequent fight.

(3) He might have been the pilot of the plane which Richthofen was pursuing, and, in spite of all the witnesses, the machine might have been a two seater with an observer firing over its tail, who had got in a lucky shot.

The third was practically an impossibility, and so I expected that when Brown's narrative came to hand (we only had a resume by cable) we should have his version of how he shot Richthofen at several thousand feet and saw him afterwards crash. But when his article came to hand we found that he put in quite a different claim. He said that his plane was following Richthofen's in the same way as Richthofen's was following the English plane, the three almost on top of one another, and that he had shot Richthofen close to the ground and had seen him immediately crash.

This was a story that was never dreamt of by any one here before Brown's article arrived. I have heard many accounts at the time and since, and all mentioned only the two planes. Some said that there was no other plane within half a mile at least. The narrators include my own friends and I cannot believe that a third plane could have been on Richthofen's tail, or any where near him, without almost some of these mentioning it at the time. They would have been only too glad to give the credit to an airman if there had been a third plane anywhere in the picture. But those that I have asked since Brown's story arrived are emphatic that there was no third plane that could have been even remotely connected with the incident.

I understand that another airman said that he saw Brown crash Richthofen, and I am aware that medical officers were of opinion that the bullet had traversed the body in a direction which showed that it could not have been fired from the ground. Colonel Barber, of the Australian medical service, who has been quoted as having given this verdict told me that his opinion had been misquoted; that he held that the bullet could have been fired from the ground. I can only interpret all this in the light of the fact which I know beyond doubt, that scores of witnesses who gave me or have written or spoken their accounts of the incident obviously know nothing of any third plane, and that they could not have helped seeing it if Brown's version was true.

I realise that it follows that Brown's story must be romance. I wonder if you have read it - the style does not impress me with any great confidence. Moreover, I believe that in his first report there is a natural implication that his opponent was shot down from some height. Also the first German communique said, I believe, that Richthofen was shot from the ground, and I remember that, when I noticed this, it occurred to me that it was published before there could have come from our side, the suggestion that he had been shot from the ground, and I attributed it to some German airman who had seen him leave the fight in the high air. I have not however had time to check these times and dates, and may be quite wrong in this inference.

This is a resume of the story as I know it, written off hand. I have no doubt, myself that only two planes were involved, Richthofen's and his quarry's. Everyone described them in detail. If Brown's story had been consistent with this in any way at all, I would have believed that there was a mistake or the remote possibility of a previous wounding. But Brown has nailed down his assertion in his article, definitely, with much detail, and has accused an Australian witness of - for some reason - knowingly lying when he said there was no third plane in it. The truth is that no witness that I have spoken to ever dreamt that it would be suggested that there were more than two planes. I cannot believe that a score of them would deliberately lie about it, and they include some of whom I know that any such suspicion would be absurd.

You may be able to unravel the other side of all this. I suppose the death of a great opponent is a matter of such historical importance, whatever one thought of the controversy at the time, that it should be settled with all possible care. If you wish for detailed evidence, I will get for you what I can. If you find any strong evidence conflicting with this, I would be grateful if you would let me have it.

Yours sincerely,

(signed) C.E.W. Bean

The mention of the 13th Infantry Brigade might be a mistake for 11th; the troops on the hill belonged to the latter. However, the 24th Machine-gun Company may actually have belonged to the 13th Brigade but been on temporary attachment to the 11th at that time of crisis.

There was a much shifting around of small detachments for which no permanent documentation was made.

As a result of the reports in the Australian newspapers and Dr. Bean's published requests for witnesses, several Australian soldiers came forward. Lieut. R A Wood told of a British aeroplane diving on and firing at a German triplane which was chasing another British Aeroplane. Lieut. John Murdock Prentice and Gunner George Ridgway, specifically stated that the third aeroplane, after attacking the second, turned to the north and flew away. It is understandable that the members of the 53rd Battery had not seen Roy's attack on the red triplane down in the misty valley a mile to their south-east; visibility in that direction was blocked by the crest of the hill which hid their guns from the Germans. The view of the sky to the south-east was not particularly good either; the sun had only risen 26 degrees above the horizon and was shining from that direction.

The third aeroplane which had been described to Dr. Bean as being *"half a mile away at least"* could well have been Roy on his way to help Mellersh. Being half a mile to the east of the viewer(s) and heading away from them (i.e. heading east), who would connect this aeroplane with the two right in front of their eyes which were flying towards them (i.e. heading west)?

Dr. H.A. Jones's reply written in November 1932 went as follows:

> *About Richthofen. I agree with you that it is a pity there should be a controversy. This has given me a good deal of trouble and I have been into the question from every angle. As you will see, the conclusion I come to is that the likeliest explanation is that Captain Brown shot Richthofen down. There is no doubt in my mind that the machine-gunners of the 53rd Battery can be ruled out. The evidence is that the triplane was in trouble before these gunners opened fire, and there is the further difficulty that from the relative positions of the machine-gunners and of Richthofen's aeroplane, the bullet fired by the 53rd gunners could not have entered Richthofen's body from the right. This latter difficulty also seems to rule out the 24th Machine Gun Company. If you plot, as I have done, the positions of the various machine-gun posts, etc., and read the evidence of the eye-witnesses with the plan in front of you, you cannot fail to come to the conclusion that the bullet fired from the*

machine-gun of the 24th could not have entered Richthofen's body from the right and made the sort of wound which, as we know, caused the pilot's death. This, of course, is assuming that the medical evidence about the wound is correct, and the body was examined by four medical officers who all agreed with the entrance and exit particulars.

All the same, I would hesitate to say that there is no element of doubt, and it is unlikely that the exact cause of Richthofen's death will ever be resolved. I have even thought that it is not entirely out of the question that some unknown Australian infantryman, perhaps in the reserve trenches, seeing the aeroplane suddenly appear above, took a chance shot at the German triplane and scored a hit.

Dr. Jones had apparently not heard of the medical examination made by Colonel Barber and Major Chapman of the Australian Imperial Force. He was aware of the claim by the Sergeant Popkin of the 24th Machine Gun Company but had only his short report, dated 24 April 1918, to go by. Three years were to pass before a reopening of the investigation caused Dr. Bean to write to Sergeant Popkin requesting full details. The correspondence is given in PART TWO of this book.

Dr. Bean replied that Jones was not alone in his musing, and then commented:

> Major Blair Wark, VC, the second-in-command of the 32nd Battalion, who had watched the last part of the Baron's flight was of the opinion that the fatal shot came from another machine-gun other than those with the 53rd Battery and the 24th M.G. Company, but definitely from one firing from the ground. A number were firing at the 'plane.

From the above it will be noted that Dr. H.A. Jones and Dr. C.E.W. Bean, who had the best resources ever to provide a definite answer, were both privately uncertain.

THE VERDICTS GIVEN IN THE OFFICIAL HISTORIES OF THE WAR IN THE AIR.

(1) The Royal Air Force Opinion.
In the Official History of the Royal Air Force, published in 1935, in

Volume IV, Chapter VIII, Page 393 of THE WAR IN THE AIR, BEING THE STORY OF THE PART PLAYED IN THE GREAT WAR BY THE ROYAL AIR FORCE, H A Jones, the official historian, credits the fatal bullet to Captain A Roy Brown as follows:

> "The gun firing the bullet, said the reports, must have been situated 'roughly in the same plane as the long axis of the German aircraft and fired from the right', and the medical officers were agreed that the entrance and exit wounds were such that they could not have been caused by a bullet fired from the ground. After a careful examination of these and of all other reports, the official decision was that Richthofen was killed by a bullet from the machine-guns of Captain A.R. Brown."

Note that H A Jones presents Lieut. Downs and Captain Graham's dismissal of the one and only ground fire claim they investigated as applying to all other ground fire claims which were presented to the authorities in April 1918.

See (14) in the ANNEX to this chapter for comments on other pages in H A Jones's description of the events of 21 April 1918.

In the 1920's when RAF squadron badges were being designed, 209 Squadron chose an eagle falling. The eagle is depicted in red.

(2) The Canadian Air Force Opinion.
In the Official History of The Royal Canadian Air Force; Volume One, Canadian Airmen in The First World War, published in Toronto in 1980, Prof. Sydney F Wise wrote:

> "The fledgling RAF, well aware of the propaganda value of having the great German ace shot down by one of their fighter pilots, was quick to report; 'Captain M. von Richthofen... shot down and killed behind our lines near Corbie by Capt. A.R. Brown.' Popular histories crudely but vigorously supported the RAF claim after the war and it was subsequently given scholarly recognition in the British official history (by H.A. Jones). Australian official historians, understandably, have taken a different view and more recent research and analysis have confirmed beyond a reasonable doubt that one or

other of the machine-gunners on the ground fired the actual bullet that killed Richthofen."

(3) The Australian Opinion.

The Official History of the Australian Imperial Force in France was first published in 1937. In Appendix No.4, Page 700, of the 1943 reprint, C E W Bean, the official historian, who had now changed his mind, still does not totally commit himself. He wrote:

> "It will be seen that Richthofen, before reaching Vaux, was dived on by Captain Brown, who thought he had killed him; that Captain Brown's immediate report that Richthofen 'went down vertical' was mistaken, and shows that Brown saw nothing of the chase that followed; that Richthofen actually went on chasing Lieutenant May for almost exactly a mile, attempting to follow his manoeuvres and firing bursts from his machine-gun."
>
> "It is also clear that Sergeant Popkin's gun, when first fired, and those of the 53rd Battery cannot have sent the fatal shot - since it came almost directly from the right and from below the aviator - although they may well have caused him to turn; but scores of other men were firing and, when Richthofen banked and turned back, Sergeant Popkin (who now opened again) was in a position to fire such a shot as killed Richthofen."

(4) The German Air Force Opinion.

In 1921 the memoirs of General Ernst Wilhelm von Hoeppner, the Commanding General of the German Air Force, DEUTSCHLANDS KRIEG IN DER LUFT, were published. Their title, in the 1994 English translation by J. Hawley Larned, was 'Germany's War in the Air'. On page 149 the general credited ground fire as follows:

> "The hope that our most brilliant fighter pilot might be spared to us was not realized for he was mortally wounded on April 21, 1918. In the pursuit of an opponent who was flying at low altitude behind the enemy's front, he had apparently been caught in the defensive machine-gun fire of an Australian battery. We suffered an irreparable loss in the death of this heroic and inspired leader."

Roy's opinion on the official verdicts was solicited and he replied as follows:

"As far as I am concerned, I know in my own mind what happened, and the war being over and the job being done, there is nothing to be gained by arguing back and forth as to who did this and who did that. The main point is that, from the standpoint of the troops in the war, we gained our objective."

General Sir Henry Rawlinson who had badly needed a simple answer in May 1918 never received one, and it was here that the matter rested during Roy's lifetime.

ACKNOWLEDGEMENTS

Larry Gray for permission to quote from his book WE ARE THE DEAD, published in 2000 by General Store Publishing House, Burnstown, Ontario, Canada.

Hugh Alexander for information on his father, W'm Melville Alexander and for the photograph of Clara Monypenny before she became Mrs. Alexander.

The Board of Directors of the Royal Canadian Military Institute, Toronto for access to the Roy Brown display, and for the aid of the Museum Curator, Gregory Loughton, in taking the photographs.

F A Beardmore for the photographs of Marske-by-the-Sea aerodrome.

Phil Philo, Old Hall Museum, Kirkleatham, for information on aerodromes in the area of Marske-by-the-Sea.

Michael J Charterisfor extensive newspaper research in Australia.

W. Brian Costello for photographs of pilots from Carleton Place.

Lambis Englezos for the correspondence between C.E.W. Bean and H.A. Jones.

Stuart Leslie for photographs of aeroplanes and aerodromes.

Stewart Taylor for information on the Canadian Comrades Association.

Leslie K. Redman of the Canadian War Museum, Ottawa, for locating the J. Horace Brown file, his service record and the notes he took during his flying training course.

ANNEX TO CHAPTER NINE

(1) ENGINE FAILURE DURING TAKE-OFF.

The 130 HP Clergêt engine of Roy's Sopwith F1 *Camel* had two completely separate ignition systems. Before take-off it was mandatory to verify that both were working; individual switches being provided for this purpose. Self-preservation being a strong motive, it is highly unlikely that Roy would have failed to make this simple, easy check.

The fuel supply to the engine was also duplicated as was explained in item (6) of ANNEX 6. A supply failure from the main tank at any altitude created an enervating situation for a pilot, time being required for the new fuel to reach the engine after he changed tanks. Safety lay in having adequate height above ground to glide until power was restored. Fortunately, the large diameter, low RPM propellers used in those days functioned as windmills and kept the engines turning during the interval.

At low altitude, such as shortly after take-off, pilots had a choice between two evils and a large poster was displayed at all training schools to help them decide. It illustrated the danger of attempting a U-turn back to the airfield from less than 500 feet height above ground; namely stalling, spinning and dying in the process. In large, heavy block letters it exhorted all pilots, **"IN CASE OF ENGINE FAILURE DON'T TURN BACK - PUT HER NOSE DOWN AT ONCE AND MAKE SOME SORT OF LANDING AHEAD."** This direction, being into wind, provided the additional benefit of reducing the aircraft's speed relative to the terrain below. Therein lay the greater chance of survival.

The legends say:

> 1st position. Machine climbing, engine failing.
> 2nd position. Pilot decides to turn back and endeavouring not to lose height, stalls the machine.
> 3rd position. Machine out of control, spin commencing.
> 4th position. Spinning nose dive.
> 5th position. Crash.

Roy's engine stopped as he climbed away from the airfield. Unfortunately, it is unclear from Stearne's description whether the propeller came to a complete standstill or continued 'windmilling', which opens a wide range of possibilities as to the cause. With trees and telegraph poles obstructing a forced landing into wind straight ahead, and having gained about 200 feet above ground, Roy decided to make a U-turn back to the aerodrome close behind him. There was nothing wrong with this decision, his situation being far more favourable than the heavier, fully-loaded R.E.8 two-seater shown in the poster. A *Camel* had a lower wing loading (its weight relative to its wing area) than a loaded R.E.8, and therefore had a shallower gliding angle which placed the field well within reach.

With his *Camel* headed back towards the field and being helped in that direction by the air mass which supported the wings (the wind), Roy's speed relative to the ground was the sum of the wind speed **PLUS** his own speed through the aforesaid air mass (his air speed). This was opposite to a normal landing (into the wind) in which his ground speed was his air speed **MINUS** the wind speed, and was therefore an unfamiliar situation. To explain the matter from another angle: on a day with a 15 MPH wind, the ground, a pilot's focus of attention during a landing, would be approaching 30 MPH more quickly than he was accustomed to seeing, and thus give a false impression of vastly excessive air speed. Roy was but a few seconds from completing the turn and a making a safe landing when he allowed his air speed to decrease too much. The wings on the inside of the turn stalled and the process illustrated on the poster began. Fortunately his *Camel* was not high enough for a spin to develop, nor did it flick upside down, and that saved his life.

The reason why Roy's engine stopped is not stated in any of the currently known letters or documents which mention the accident.

The following photograph depicts a similar accident. It was taken on 25 June 1918 at Vendôme Training Depot Station (205 TDS) shortly after Flight Cadet J E S Denham stalled the inside wings of Sopwith 2F.1 *Camel* N6628 during a turn at low altitude. Before he had time to take any corrective action, it flicked upside down and struck the ground inverted. Great War squadron records and casualty forms currently available to the RAF Museum, Hendon, do not reveal the fate of the pilot.

Sopwith F.1 *Camel* N6628 with a 130 HP Clergêt engine. Photograph taken by Horace Brown. Note the position of the Rotherham wind-driven pump.

Most modern civilian single-engined training aeroplanes have a higher wing loading than a *Camel* and require about 500 feet altitude for a safe return.

Chad Wille, who currently (2005) flies a replica Sopwith F.1 *Camel* with a 160 HP Gnôme rotary engine at air shows and has been mentioned in previous chapters, provided significant help from personal experience on the subject of forced landings in Sopwith *Camels*. During his career as a pilot of Great War aeroplane replicas, he has also flown a Sopwith *Pup*, a Sopwith *Triplane* and a Nieuport 11 with an 80 HP Le Rhone rotary engine. In a telephone conversation with the author he gave his opinion that in flying characteristics the *Triplane* was the best Sopwith of them all.

Chad Wille and his 160 HP Gnome rotary-engined Sopwith F.1 *Camel* painted in the colours of 'B' Flight, Naval 10 Squadron.

(2) EXTRACT FROM THE REPLY OF THE AIR MINISTRY IN LONDON TO AN ENQUIRY FROM THE CANADIAN WAR MUSEUM, OTTAWA, CANADA.

Air Historical Branch
London S.W.1

25th October, 1961

Dear Wing Commander Manning,

    Thank you for your letter dated 26th September, 1961.
    It is not quite so easy as it once was to obtain personal details about our first world War pilots, especially as much of our material for that period is in the course of transfer to the Public Record Office.
    I think we have found most of the information you asked for:
    (a) According to his record Roy Brown was sent to No. 24 General Hospital. A brief biography in our possession says that apparently the day after his fight with Richthofen he collapsed suffering from some kind of stomach trouble accentuated by nervous strain.
    (b) Brown did not see action again, and after his recovery became an instructor. On 15th July, 1918 he took an aircraft up for a practice flight and fainted in the air. His aircraft crashed from about 300 feet and he suffered severe injuries including, I believe, a fractured skull.
    I hope these facts will help you to complete your record of Brown. I cannot vouch for all of them, but since some were taken from a report of an interview with him, I do not think anyone is likely to dispute them.

Yours sincerely

(signature illegible)

COMMENTS.
(a) The brief biography of Roy Brown to which the writer referred is probably the assembly of truth, half-truths and fiction which so badly misled Floyd Gibbons. No other is known to exist in the RAF files in any location.

(b) Roy did not collapse. On the evening of 25 April, four days after his encounter with the Rittmeister, the Wing M.O. grounded him to prevent that from happening.

(c) The proper cards and forms concerning Roy's crash were filled in at the time and they still exist. They all give engine failure during take-off as the cause. The truth would not have been difficult to find within their own archive.

(d) The *'Report of an Interview'*, cited in the final paragraph of the letter above, was filed in two parts. Both are seriously flawed. Some sections appear to have been lifted from newspaper reports, together with the attendant journalistic hyperbole. Other sections closely resemble stories shown by later research to have been based upon pure guesswork. For examples: the report incorrectly states that Major Butler led 209 Squadron into battle on 21st April 1918, that Lieut. May was wounded in the engagement, and that it was Roy Brown, himself, who went into the field at Sainte Colette to recover the Baron's body.

(e) The so-called interviews, which are both unsigned and undated, are to be found verbatim in Appendices C and D of THE RED BARON'S LAST FLIGHT.

(3) ROY BROWN'S MEDICAL CONDITION AND TREATMENT EVALUATED IN THE LIGHT OF YEAR 2001 MEDICINE.

Alan Bennett and Roy's daughter, Margaret, began the task by trying to locate any surviving records of Roy's July 1918 crash. They learned that after the war all military hospital records had been sent to the Ministry of Pensions to substantiate war claims, and once compensation had been determined, the records (they weighed 200 tons) were destroyed.

The RAF Museum at Hendon succeeded in locating Roy's RAF CASUALTY CARDS for 1918/1919. Definite dates and locations were given for many events described in letters by Roy, Douglas Findlay and Stearne Edwards.

The Historical Branch of the Royal Army Medical Corps

(RAMC) identified the hospitals in the Middlesbrough area which might have been involved in saving Roy's life, but a major hurdle remained; how was a civilian specialist allowed to enter an RAF station and treat a military patient there?

Alan Bennett made contact with the Tyneside municipal authorities who suggested consulting Dr. Geoffrey Stout, a retired general practitioner (family doctor) who was writing a history of medical services in that area. Dr. Stout was able to provide details of the 1918/1919 medical staff of the hospitals in question. The RAMC was then able to check these names against a list of civilian doctors who had been given temporary commissions to enable them to treat military patients. A match was obtained exactly where it was needed.

Dr. Stout put considerable time, effort and enthusiasm into studying Roy Brown's case (including consulting colleagues with expertise in the effects and treatment of concussion), and kindly consented to his comments being included in this book. Unfortunately he did not live to see its publication.

Comments by Dr. Geoffrey Stout.

"In retrospect, Stearne Edwards' action in seeking a second opinion was crucial as the surgeon's favourable opinion gave hope to all those concerned with Roy's care and undoubtedly contributed to his miraculous recovery. The Royal Air Force "FS Form 558 Casualty Card" records Roy's accident as occurring on the 15 July 1918, and lists the injuries in an entry dated the 16th:

Injured very seriously (Aeroplane Accident)
Compound fracture left ribs 3 + 4, pleurisy, deep wound nasal side, left eye, condition dangerous, improved.

Of these serious injuries, Roy's head injuries were to prove the most damaging to his future. Loss of memory, as happened to Roy, following a period of unconsciousness is devastating. It deprives a person any chance of recollecting actions in the period leading up to the accident. Perhaps this is nature's way of shielding the person from a feeling of guilt. The longer the period of unconsciousness, the longer the loss of memory. Loss of memory affects the events immediately before the accident and to a limited extent, after the accident. The nature of his crash, falling to the ground from sixty feet, no head protection against the aeroplane engine which landed on top of his head and neck, would cause severe skull and brain injury. The skull might well be fractured.

How Roy's surgical management could have been undertaken in the primitive station hospital over the first few days after his life-threatening injuries is incredible. Stearne Edwards' letter of Sunday 21 July 1918 paints a horrific picture.

"....up till two days ago they expected every minute to be his last... He was mostly kept under the influence of drugs, and even when conscious, could not understand anything said to him. (On Saturday the 20th) he was quite rational in his mind for a while... but wandered quite a lot. (On Sunday) he could talk quite well... and kept the nurses laughing..."

The medical officer and the three nurses, all under the direction of a specialist from the military section of the North Riding Infirmary at Middlesbrough, had coped with unconsciousness, severe head injuries, fractured ribs puncturing one lung and severe blood loss. Today a multi-disciplinary team in an acute reception unit would be stretched to deal with such a casualty.

Roy described how his body was: "...blown up like a ball all over." This condition - surgical emphysema - is a complication where air from a punctured lung escapes beneath the skin causing swelling over the face, trunk and limbs except the scalp, palms and soles. Such an escape of air may not necessarily cause more problems, but it gives the skin a cold puffy feeling as if something bubbly is there underneath, plus a deathly pallor. Roy's appearance must have been frightening as the pallor would have contrasted with the multiple bruising.

The use of the term 'Pleurisy' in the entry on 16 July is puzzling; it means inflammation of the pleura - the lining of the lung. Pleurisy is a complication that would take a few days to develop; one can only speculate that the term was used non-definitively to describe his severe pain rather than implying an inflammatory state. Roy's open chest wound, his fractured ribs puncturing the pleura, damaging his left lung and allowing air to escape, was associated with partial collapse of his left lung - a condition known as pneumothorax. As there was considerable associated bleeding, the diagnosis would be haemo-pneumo-thorax. His open chest wound might even seal over in its depths and allow pressure to build up inside the chest, a condition known as tension pneumothorax.

There are no further data for Roy's period at Marske by the Sea station hospital. He had recovered sufficiently to be transferred on Tuesday 23 July to the military beds at Middlesbrough. This was an auxiliary to the 1st Northern General Hospital at Newcastle and was located in a wing of the North Riding Infirmary. Middlesbrough had a lot of heavy industry, including ironstone mining and iron and steel works, therefore it had the medical facilities to deal with serious industrial accidents. The two major hospitals, the North Riding Infirmary and the North Ormsby Hospital had active surgical units and X-ray departments, but it is unlikely that there would be portable facilities to undertake skull or chest X-rays off the premises at that time.

Until 1900, the hospitals of provincial, non-university towns were not served by specialists as today. The general practitioners in a town acted as honorary physicians and surgeons. By and large they did not possess higher qualifications; e.g. FRCS (Fellow of the Royal College of Surgeons), but carried out the routine operations needed in day-to-day practice. The university centres, Newcastle or Leeds, provided secondary specialist opinions and undertook major operations.

Around the turn of the century, specialist surgeons started to appear in smaller towns distant from university centres of excellence. William Stewart Dickie, FRCS came to practise in Middlesbrough in 1903 and joined the staff of the North Riding Infirmary. Dickie had a strong personality and built up a reputation throughout the North of England. In January 1916, when a wing at the North Riding Infirmary was taken over as an auxiliary to the 1st Northern General Hospital at Newcastle and allocated to military casualties, he was commissioned as a Temporary Major so that he could carry out surgical work on servicemen. In January 1918 he was promoted to Temporary Lieut.-Colonel and allowed to remain in Middlesbrough.

Unfortunately no admission registers for the time of the Great War survive from the North Riding Infirmary. Despite trying many sources and an appeal to the 'Remember When' feature, run by Terry Gilder in the local Evening Gazette, no positive identification of the surgeon who attended Roy has been made. Probability would indicate W.S.Dickie.

According to Roy's Casualty Record Card, he was moved from Middlesbrough to Lincoln General Hospital, but neither Stearne Edwards nor Roy mentions Lincoln. This would appear to be an erroneous entry since we know from Roy's letters that he was sent to the 1st Northern General Hospital at Newcastle. The latter, being the parent to the Middlesbrough auxiliary, would be the more logical.

Roy's recovery from serious multiple injuries was remarkable - a tribute to his character and will to overcome these. Sadly, despite his physical recovery, his systems had paid a price which imperilled his responses to the post-concussional patterns of headache and other complications. Post-concussional headache may be constant, varying between a dull ache and unbearable pain. As Roy wrote to his mother, "I told the nurse that I was tired of being in pain all the time." The headache may be exacerbated by noise, excitement, exertion or head movement. Roy's description, in the same letter, of being startled by a noise when half-asleep is a classic description of such a condition. His restriction to bed, to shield him from stimuli which could provoke headache, would aggravate muscle wasting and weight loss which would lead to depression. His loss of blood - both externally and from internal bruising - must have been considerable, leaving him anaemic. The coupling of depression to loss of weight and anaemia would lead to the poor appetite which Roy complained about. His poor concentration and the restrictions on reading meant he found it difficult to fill his time.

Concussion of the brain is a condition caused by violent blows to the head, and tends to be followed by varied troublesome symptoms - including headache, dizziness and irritability - suggesting disturbance of many brain functions. These symptoms are subjective and difficult to measure, therefore, like backache, controversy over their nature has arisen. In years past, unsympathetic doctors have even queried their genuineness.

Until well after the Second World War, the only identifiable damage was gross tears of brain substance, and theories were postulated that pressure disturbances in the closed fluids which bathe the brain inside the skull were damaging brain cells. However, no consistent pattern of brain cell damage was noted.

Only in recent decades has the nature of the brain damage involved been established. Microscopic examination has identified widely scattered areas of damage to minute groups of cells which later develop scarring and degeneration. The technical term for this is Diffuse Axonal Injury (D A I). It explains how the pattern of symptoms after concussion - headadche, dizziness, tinnitus (ringing in the ears), lack of concentration, depression, personality changes, impairment of memory, disturbance of sleep - is so varied. Even a minor blow on the head can result in D A I.

> *Tinnitus and dizziness are due to damaged hearing and balance areas. Mood changes may appear as depression, lack of concentration and irritability. Sleep disturbance is controlled by yet another brain area. The pattern of post-concussional symptoms, especially their long duration, is disruptive to patient behaviour, and causes much human misery, broken relationships and poor employment. The management of patients suffering from concussion is thus complex, depending on multi-purpose rehabilitation skills and drugs.*
>
> *Looking at modern rehabilitation programmes - early ambulation, physiotherapy and occupational exercises - nearly all the steps taken in Roy's post-concussional management were ill-conceived, if not adverse. It is easy to sit in an armchair in this year 2001 and criticise what happened, but 80 years ago knowledge how to treat such cases was in its infancy."*

Dr. Stout possibly came very close to learning more about Roy's case when he learned that Dr. W.S. Dickie's daughter had practised as a physician and surgeon in Middlesbrough and was living there in retirement. Unfortunately, she had died a few weeks earlier. Dr. Stout then provided these additional comments:

> *"From the remarks made to Stearne Edwards by the doctor at the Horton War Hospital ("Roy's was a very serious case… a lot of damage has been done"), it would appear that Roy's astonishingly rapid recovery from physical damage at the North Riding Infirmary worked against him in the long term. The doctors at the Newcastle parent hospital apparently did not realize that brain concussion might be lurking beneath the bright exterior, and instead of prescribing a long period of peace and quiet under their observation, they sent Roy to a convalescent hospital which also took an optimistic view and allowed him to go on leave. Today, doctors are well aware of delayed after effects in cases of concussion, but in 1918 that was uncharted territory.*
>
> *Roy suffered from headaches for the rest of his life. In an attempt to relieve them he underwent surgery to block a nerve. No details have survived, except that no improvement resulted. In the light of today's knowledge that brain damage from concussion occurs over scattered areas, it would appear that more than one nerve block would be required; assuming that today's technology would be able to identify where."*

(4) THE STAB IN THE BACK.

During the Second World War the Allies took great care to prevent a repetition of the 'Stab in The Back' legend. Approaches from groups of Germans opposed to Hitler were ignored and attempts at a negotiated peace rejected. This time all Germans were to be made to understand that the German armed forces had unquestionably been defeated in battle on all fronts.

(5) MAJOR MULHOLLAND'S LETTER TO MRS. EDWARDS.

Royal Air Force
Tadcaster
Yorks

Saturday 28th December, 1918

My Dear Mrs. Edwards

This is the most difficult letter ever written in my life. I want to cry when I think of poor Stearne. My heart goes out to you in this, your time of trial. I have put off writing to you because I felt certain I would be able to write and tell you how well your dear son was getting along.

I feel certain you would like to know things fully. On Tuesday morning, the 12th, Stearne went up in the air in his favourite aeroplane (Sop. Pup) and was just flying around the aerodrome amusing himself. He put the machine into a spin and was just coming out of it when his wing tip touched the ground.

He was unconscious when we lifted him out of the machine and was taken into hospital in York right away. The following day when I went in to see him he was not in pain. His only worry seemed to be that he had crashed one of my machines.

He picked up strength from day to day, but on Thursday, the 21st, it was found necessary to amputate his leg below the knee. The shock was too much for him and he never gained full consciousness after the operation. He died at 5.15 on Friday morning.

He is being buried at Tadcaster with full military honours on Monday morning at 10 o'clock.

He was the outstanding character in the station, always doing more than his share of the work and helping along the backward ones. As you probably know, he was in command of the American Group at this station, and was so proud of it because he had worked it all up from the beginning himself, and had received congratulations from General Beck on three separate occasions. I think he would have been promoted to Major in a few weeks time.

It must be a comfort to you to know that your son played such a noble part in this great war of ours, and the sympathy of every man and woman on this station goes across the dark waters to you in your time of great sorrow.

I will write again and send you some photographs, and all Stearne's belongings will be sent safely to you.

Yours very sincerely
Douglas Mulholland, Major

At some time long ago an incorrect date was given to the authorities in Canada for Stearne's accident. It appears on a memorial plaque in Carleton Place, in some publications on his life, and on his tombstone in England where the error may have begun. Occasionally one finds his first name mispelled as well. The confusion comes from other members of his family who bear the same name but spell it differently. The dates and the spelling given in Major Mulholland's letter (above) are the correct ones.

The grave of Stearne Tighe Edwards at Tadcaster, Torkshire.

(6) A YEAR 2001 REVIEW OF THE MEDICAL CONDITION OF STEARNE EDWARDS.

The Carleton Place Herald, dated 26 November 1918, reported the death of Captain Stearne Tighe Edwards, aged 25 years. He had broken both legs and fractured his skull in a flying accident on Tuesday, the 12th. He had begun a good recovery, but for reasons presently unknown, the doctors decided that it was necessary to amputate one leg. The operation was performed on the 21st. Quite unexpectedly, Stearne did not recover consciousness and died on Friday, the 22nd.

Dr. Geoffrey Stout was again asked for guidance as what might have happened. It is of significance that at the time Dr. Stout wrote the following comments he was not aware of Stearne's skull injury.

Dr. Stout wrote,

"In view of the dearth of details concerning Stearne's injuries, to comment was a difficult task. Stearne being found unconscious in the wreck would suggest head injuries, as would his relapsing into unconsciousness after the leg amputation.

The usual reason for amputation in 1918 would have been infection - either streptococcal or gas gangrene, of a compound leg fracture - to prevent the spread of infection or blood poisoning (septicaemia). The term gas gangrene has no connection with poison gas warfare but refers to gas generated in muscular tissue by a certain type of infection. Another possibility would be blood vessel damage - endangering the arterial or venous circulation.

The possible causes of his death 24 hours after the amputation range from infection to a stroke. In the latter case, a well-known complication of orthopaedic conditions is a fat embolism in which fat emboli reach the brain with little warning.

In 1918, the combination of head injury, serious leg injury, shock and blood loss would be a platform for such a tragic loss."

(7) ALICE PICKUP.

This is the last mention of Alice Pickup in any of Roy's letters. His friendship with her dwindled after he returned to Canada in 1919, but it would not be appropriate to leave the reader wondering what the future held for her.

She married Gurney Little, the brother of Richard Little, a world famous comedian and impersonator who performed at Las Vegas Theatres, and some years later appeared in American television programmes.

During the Second World War, when Roy's daughters Margaret and Barbara were at Rockcliffe Barracks with the RCAF Women's Division, they saw Alice and Gurney quite often.

(8) THE EFFECTS OF NON-WORKING CYLINDERS ON A ROTARY ENGINE.

In the first place, with only three out of nine cylinders working, the severe power loss would not have permitted Roy's *Camel* (at 1,000 feet altitude when it happened) to maintain sufficient height above ground to fly the twelve miles back to Bertangles aerodrome. However, that would have been the least of his problems.

Rotary engines on all aeroplanes had no exhaust system; each cylinder had a short stub of pipe which discharged the hot gases into the atmosphere. In the case of Sopwith *Camels*, the stubs discharged into the engine cowling and out through the bottom of it. The un-burned fuel from non-working cylinders would collect inside the cowling and then run along the underside of the fuselage creating the conditions for a fire. Pilots were instructed that if their engine began misfiring, they should give the 'dud engine' signal by repeatedly dipping the nose of their machine and pulling it up again. Then they should immediately return to base at reduced power or make a precautionary landing in a field, preferably on the Allied side of the front, before flames appeared around their feet.

The severe engine vibration from the uneven firing was equally dangerous - sooner or later it would cause the engine mountings to fracture. The engine would thereupon fall off or just possibly hang down in a crazy position.

The tale, known to historians as *The Anonymous Account*, from which the story originated, said that only two of the nine cylinders were still working. Apparently Gibbons found that too difficult to believe; he increased the number to three.

In some squadrons, pilots gave the 'dud engine' signal by firing a green cartridge from their Very pistol. See **(15) VERY PISTOL SIGNALLING** in this Annex for more information.

(9) THE AIR FIGHT THAT NEVER HAPPENED.

Weather permitting, 3 AFC had been conducting daily photographic flights to find targets for the artillery batteries in the area. The town of Hamel was of particular interest since it was a suitable starting point for an attempt to capture Villers-Bretonneux and then force a crossing of the Somme Canal. On 21 April two R.E.8s were dispatched to the Hamel area in an attempt to locate the German supply dumps and troop concentrations for the impending attack. The nearby forests provided ideal shelter and were suitably close to no-man's-land, hence the particular attention paid to them by 3 AFC. Once the plates had been exposed, the crews under orders were to return home immediately. Hundreds of army lives, possibly thousands, would depend upon the analysis of the information they were bringing.

The crew of R.E.8 No. E52 of 'B' flight, 15 Sqn. Note the map fixed to the pilot's instrument panel and the double drum on the observer's Lewis gun. The pilot is Lieut. Gerald Gomez Fonseca, a Canadian, and the observer is Lieut. Jackson. Photograph taken in July 1918.

As was explained in Chapter Eight, the confusion began when the 209 Squadron morning flights on 22 April were entered in the Squadron Record Book directly beneath the post 4 p.m. flight made by Lieut. G. Wilson on the 21st. A flaw in the carbon paper caused the '22' in '22:4:18' not to be imprinted on the copy, and the entry appeared to refer to the 21st. A careful reading of 209 RAF and 3 AFC Squadron Record Books and Pilots' Combat Reports clarifies the dates.

An air-to-air photograph of an R.E.8 in flight. Note the observer's excellent field of fire. The enemy would try to creep up on an R.E.8 from behind and below where the observer's view and field of fire were obstructed.

The tale of *The Air Fight That Never Happened* progressed through two major retellings, and like the story of the Antwerp church bells, it both grew and changed dramatically. In the final version the R.E.8 crews were castigated for not remaining to lend a hand in the battle, but diving away with their tails metaphorically between their legs and leaving the heavily outnumbered *Camels* to face the hornets' nest they, themselves, had stirred up. The theme of the story, that the cowardly AFC crews abandoned their gallant RAF saviours in their hour of need, becomes obviously false once the nature of photographic operations is understood.

(10) ROBERT BUIE'S COMMENTS ON THE CHICAGO SUNDAY *TRIBUNE* STORIES.

The December 1959 edition of *Cavalier* magazine contained an article by Dale Titler reporting an interview with Robert Buie on the events of 21 April 1918. Although Buie saw neither the beginning nor the end of the action, he participated in the middle portion and was present when Roy visited the 53rd Battery. His opinion on stories published between 1927 and 1929 went as follows:

> "*During the past 42 years I've read some strange accounts of what was supposed to have taken place during the action, and each has been more fantastic than the preceding one. But by far the most incorrect versions are contained in Gibbons' THE RED KNIGHT OF GERMANY and Quentin Reynolds' THEY FOUGHT FOR THE SKY.*
> *Quentin Reynolds - - - drew heavily from Gibbons' faulty material and completely ignored the ground action. Their information is all wrong, as is Captain Brown's personal account which appeared in several American and Canadian newspapers under the title MY FIGHT WITH RICHTHOFEN.*"

Note that Buie refers to MY FIGHT WITH RICHTHOFEN as Roy's personal account. This confirms that even late in 1959, it was generally taken that every word had been written by Roy, which in view of the misleading subtitle 'As Told by the Man who Shot him Down', is not surprising.

In another part of his account, Buie confirms that Roy had seen the Baron's body as it lay on the stretcher, but gives the impression this occurred when Roy arrived, at about one o'clock. Buie reveals that after some discussion, Major Beavis, Lieutenant Albert Bruchiaux Ellis and he showed Roy and Lt.-Col. Cairnes where the red triplane came down. Buie does not say they walked over to it, nor does he say they examined the wreck; both would be rather unlikely due to the ever present danger of a shell or two arriving if the German artillery observer in the Hamel church tower saw a small group of people on the road. On the other hand, to point out the site from the crown of the hill would be simple; the brick factory chimney is the most prominent landmark for miles around, and both the field and the drainage ditch are in clear view. Confirmation that neither Roy nor Lt.-Col. Cairnes examined or even went near the red triplane comes from two sources. Roy never mentioned meeting Lt. Warneford's men who were working on it, and they never mentioned a visit by Roy or Lt.-Col. Cairnes, for both of whom they would have to stop work, stand to attention and salute.

The following two excerpts from THEY FOUGHT FOR THE SKY are of interest. The reader will recognize the first one; it has appeared twice before.

"His tracers tucked a seam along the body of the Fokker."

The second one illustrates another way that 'borrowing' may be detected.

"The plane landed just beyond the gun pits of the Thirty-third Australian Field Battery."

In Gibbons's book a typing error had changed '53rd Battery' into '33rd Battery' at about the same place in the story.

(11) THE MUDDLING OF ROY'S NAME.

In the middle of the *Liberty* magazine series of Roy Brown stories, on 19 January 1929 to be precise, there appeared a depression era boy meets girl tale entitled 'Love with a Dash of Whisky'. The writer was a lady named Royal Brown, and although a quick scan through the text revealed it was a love story which had nothing to do with aviation, it was not long before word flashed around that Roy's true name was Royal. As late as 1999, some articles on the events of 21 April 1918 were still declaring this to be so. Fortunately, a concerted effort by Margaret Brown Harmon and Alan Bennett succeeded, for the while, in correcting the situation.

For those who might wish to read the story and form their own opinion, the necessary data are:

Love With a Dash of Whisky - published in *Liberty* magazine, Macfadden Publications, New York, NY, on 19 January 1929. Avaliable on microfilm at many public libraries and newspaper libraries around the world, or on inter-library loan from most others.

(12) THE RESERVE TRENCH ADVENTURE FROM 'MY FIGHT WITH RICHTHOFEN'. COMMENTS ON THE DIVERGENCES FROM THE GEOGRAPHICAL, CHRONOLOGICAL AND DOCUMENTED CIRCUMSTANCES.

The statement that Roy saw the the Baron's body somewhere on the hill; i.e. not beside the red triplane or at Poulainville, is a most important point. When considered together with Lieut. Warneford's diary entries, it establishes the time frame of the event; namely, while Lieut. Warneford was in the area. Also, it confirms that Roy and Lt.-Col. Cairnes visited the 53rd Battery of the 14th (Australian Field Artillery) Brigade, not the 11th (Australian Infantry) Brigade as stated in the narrative. From other testimony, it is known that Bombardier Seccull and Gunner Buie met Roy, but Lieut. Warneford did not. At the time, he had been with the salvage crew down on the road organizing the retrieval and the dismantling of 425/17. After the war, Lieut. Warneford mentioned he had heard that the pilot, who claimed to have shot Richthofen down, had been at the battery.

As mentioned in item (10) above, according to Gunner Buie, Roy and Lt.-Col. Cairnes were shown where the red triplane had come down. From the crown of the hill they could see the aircraft quite clearly, so there was no need to expose themselves to shellfire by going any further. The piece of the narrative describing their journey to the triplane is an addition to the true story. The person who rewrote Roy's original words obviously earned his pay.

Roy and Lt.-Col. Cairnes supposedly continued over the crown of the hill and walked down the slope to the road. It is at this point the geographical discrepancies begin. The road did not stop there; it ran all the way to Bray-sur-Somme. Furthermore, it still does. There were no trenches of any kind between the road and the triplane; aerial photographs taken before and after 21 April confirm this. The long, single, reserve trench first appears in photographs taken in May. It crosses the field from north to south 300 yards east of the place where the triplane slid to a stop. It may well have been there on 21 April, but no photographic proof of that exists. The writer borrowed the scene from THE RED KNIGHT OF GERMANY which presents the red triplane as having come down between the Allied front line and reserve trenches (plural).

To follow the route as described, Roy and Lt.-Col. Cairnes would have walked 400 yards east along a road under sporadic shell-fire, entered the trench and followed it south for about 100 yards. They then would have climbed out into the clear view of the Germans and run 300 yards back west to within 100 yards of their starting point.

The route supposedly followed by Roy and Lieut.-Col. Cairnes.

PART TWO of this book contains more 1918 aerial photographs of the field, the road and the trench.

There is an additional complication. By the time Roy and Lt.-Col. Cairnes arrived, the red triplane was in the process of being moved from the field on the south side of the road to the drainage ditch on the north side of the road, and they would have walked right past it on their way to the trench. As stated earlier, for Roy and Lt.- Col. Cairnes to manage all this WITHOUT any member of the salvage crew remarking their presence, nor they noticing the work of the salvage crew, would be quite an achievement.

The above analysis of the supposed route followed by Roy and Lt.-Col. Cairnes is based upon accurate knowledge of the position of the red triplane plotted on April 1918 maps; i.e. to the west of the brick factory and on the south side of the road. If August 1917 maps are employed, the plot still places the red triplane to the west of the brick factory but moves it to the north side of the road. If the rewriting of what Roy saw from the hilltop is believed, the red triplane came down to the east of the brick factory and on the north side of the road; i.e. somewhere to the NE of the storage yard beside the factory.

To understand the situation, look again at the photograph above, and once more imagine you are following the road east to the reserve trench. This time, turn left (north) and walk along the trench for 150 yards where it skirts the perimeter of the brick factory storage yard. Then jump out and run east for 100 yards., This will place you in the area which, based upon this part of MY FIGHT WITH RICHTHOFEN, has several times been given as the Red Baron's crash site between the reserve and the front line trenches. How the German artillery observers could see the red triplane through their range-finders in that location behind the crown of the hill has never been explained.

The photograph above also shows clearly that a real walk from the 11th Brigade HQ, where Roy and Lt.-Col. Cairnes allegedly met the brigade commander (unnamed) and *'the major in charge of that part of the line'* (also unnamed), to the resting place of the red triplane would not match the description given for their supposed route. There is neither a road nor a trench, and most of the trek would have been through a field in clear view of the German artillery observer in Hamel church tower. Three other points worth pondering are:

(1) Captain Edgar Copley Adams, Lieut. Donald Lovat Fraser and Lieut. George Maurice Travers from 11th Brigade HQ, who were all heavily involved and later extensively interviewed on the events of the day, never mentioned meeting Roy. Their stories are told in PART TWO of this book.

(2) The only army major known to have discussed the red triplane at a meeting with Roy and Lieut.-Col. Cairnes was Major Beavis of the 53rd Artillery Battery. Roy knew his name so there was no valid reason to omit it. This was the occasion when Major Beavis ordered Lieut. Ellis to apologize to Roy for having called him a liar.

(3) The front line was two miles away to the SE at the closest point. Furthermore, *"The major in charge of that part of the line."* would have belonged to an infantry brigade not an artillery brigade.

The event would appear to have been constructed around Roy's Log Book entry for 21 April which erroneously cites the 11th Infantry Brigade as having made the claim. As for a brigade commander having been present, neither Brigadier General James Harold Cannan, commander of the 11th Infantry Brigade, nor Major General Francis Plumley Derham, commander of the 14th Artillery Brigade, ever mentioned what would have been a memorable meeting. Here, as in the case of Roy's Sopwith *Camel* supposedly flying home with only *"three (out of nine) cylinders hitting and the propeller scarcely turning over"*, we see the hand of someone, not only totally ignorant of how an aeroplane would behave under such conditions, but also of the military organization and the key landscape features of the area where the events took place.

The serious flaws mentioned above make it highly unlikely that Roy had any hand in the sensational adventure created from the information he had provided.

(13) ROY'S EXCHANGE OF LETTERS WITH MAJOR BEAVIS.
The following letter written in 1932 by Roy to Major Leslie Beavis, who was in command of the 53rd Australian Field Artillery Battery in 1918, supports Mel Alexander's description of his demeanour.

8 Morse Street
Toronto 8
Ontario

January 7,

Major L.E. BEAVIS
Australian Staff Corps,
Australia House,
London, Eng.

Dear Sir,

In November 30th issue of 'Reveille' published in Sydney, Australia, edited by W.J.STAGG, on page 43 there is a note that you make a very good and logical case for the Australian Lewis Gunner challenging the claim of the Royal Air Force for shooting down Baron von Richthofen.

I was not fortunate enough to get an opportunity of reading your very good article and presentation of the case and would appreciate it very much, if you have a copy of your presentation, if you would send it to me as I am rather particularly interested having been a pilot of His Majesty's Royal Air Force and received official credit for the downing of our gallant opponent, Baron Von Richthofen.

Yours truly
(signed) A. Roy Brown

The Australian magazine *Reveille* was commenting on a letter from Major Beavis to the U.K. magazine, *The Army Quarterly* (issue #31, published in London, July 1931), in which he had written that during the time Gunners Buie and Evans were firing at the red triplane, "*there was no third plane in the vicinity - certainly not within a radius of at least 2,000 yards, in fact there was none to be seen nearer than the fight still going on over Sailly-Laurette.*" He also said hundreds of soldiers had been witnesses and there was no doubt about it.

A paraphrasing of Major Beavis's statement in the book VON RICHTHOFEN AND THE FLYING CIRCUS credited him with saying, *"the nearest aircraft when von Richthofen crashed was a Camel some 2,000 yards away"* and his veracity as a witness was challenged on such precise identification with the naked eye. Major Beavis countered by pointing out that the original text, both as written by him and published in the magazine, was considerably different in phrasing and meaning. Furthermore, as the reader may verify by returning to the previous paragraph, Major Beavis did not specify the type of aeroplane.

Incidentally, the initial capital letter applied to the word 'Gunner' in paragraph one in Roy's letter (above) is possibly the source of the canard, mentioned in a previous chapter, that the 'murderer' of Manfred von Richthofen was a soldier named Lewis Gunner.

In the second paragraph Roy presented his claim in a very low key manner, which does not justify it being loosely paraphrased decades later into a complaint the Australians were trying to steal his victory. IN PART TWO of this book the reader will encounter further instances of paraphrasings or retellings which alter the original meaning to a significant degree. In one case, a statement by Colonel Barber, the original meaning is reversed.

Major Beavis replied towards the end of the month as follows:

A. Roy Brown Esq.,

Dear Sir,

I am enclosing a copy of the letter which was published in the July 1931 issue of the 'Army Quarterly'. Some minor alterations of a grammatical nature only were made before publication: the substance remained the same as in this copy.

A copy of this letter was sent to Mr. C.E.W. Bean, the Australian Official Historian who, in acknowledging its receipt, stated that the contentions made therein are amply borne out by a mass of evidence of Australians.

You will understand of course, that there is no suggestion of disparagement of the magnificent work done by our Royal Air Force pilots, including that of your squadron on 21st April, 1918.

Yours truly,

(signed) L.E. Beavis

(14) COMMENTS ON OTHER PAGES IN H A JONES'S DESCRIPTION OF THE EVENTS OF 21 APRIL 1918.

Page 390 of H.A. Jones's introduction to the death of Richthofen will appear strangely familiar to one who remembers the content of item (9) above - it is a retelling of 'The Air Fight That Never Happened', an invention which first saw life in THE ANONYMOUS ACCOUNT (given in full in Chapter Eight), and found its way into MY FIGHT WITH RICHTHOFEN. Perhaps it should be renamed 'The Air Fight That will Not Die'. In the year 2005 it was recycled as fact in two serious publications; one in Australia and one in Canada.

Page 391 will also seem familiar. It is a retelling of another part of MY FIGHT WITH RICHTHOFEN. At the foot of page 392, Jones confirms his source by advising the reader that *"a detailed account of the fight, written by Captain Brown, appeared in the American publication, LIBERTY, of Dec. 10th, 1927."*

In 2002 Alan Bennett sent historian Frank McGuire a copy of H A Jones's November 1932 letter to C.E.W. Bean. McGuire replied that when he was in England in 1961, Mr. Nearney, an aide to Jones, had mentioned that pressure had been applied to his chief to support the official decision by the RAF Fifth Brigade. No mention is made that the ultimate authority in that part of France; i.e. the British Fourth Army Headquarters, had remained unconvinced.

It is somewhat difficult to believe that H.A. Jones, who was no fool and had many RAF pilots to advise him, could have read the description of Roy's return to Bertangles without realising that the author of MY FIGHT WITH RICHTHOFEN had never flown an aeroplane in his life.

It is possible that Jones included the footnote as a left-handed way of revenge upon those who had forced him to use that information and had thereby put him in the position of officially confirming pure invention. It is obvious that any aircraft pilot, military or civilian, who took the trouble to follow his advice and read the recommended text, would immediately notice an absolute aeronautical impossibility presented as fact; that is the part about flying home with only three out of nine cylinders firing and the propeller only just turning over. Furthermore, anyone who visited the Royal Canadian Military Institute in Toronto, Canada, could see for himself/herself that there is no bullet hole in the backrest of the pilot's seat from Fokker Dr.I 425/17.

Pages 394 through 397 tell the story of Manfred Freiherr von Richthofen's service career in a pleasant manner, unlike some other publications which take a negative 'hate the enemy' tone. H.A. Jones presents him as courteous and without any ill will towards those of his victims who became prisoners of war. He was popular with his own pilots, being a natural leader and careful with their lives. The prose is H A Jones at his best and the style supports the contention that he was not happy when told to accept MY FIGHT WITH RICHTHOFEN, a story written on the *'three thrills per page principal'*, as historical fact. Pages 394 through 397 are well worth reading and their content should be remembered. Between them may lie the reason why he could not bring himself to take the life of an obvious novice, Lt. May, but decided to capture him instead.

(15) VERY PISTOL SIGNALLING.

Edward W. Very (the correct spelling), a US Navy officer, invented a system for signalling by means of firing coloured flares (generally known as 'Very lights') into the sky in pre-arranged sequences. The system involved a pistol with a large diameter barrel, and cartridges which looked as though they belonged to an oversize shotgun. The cartridge holder was often mounted outside the cockpit, in an easy to reach position, and can be seen in several photographs in this book.

In the Great War, flight commanders carried a Very pistol and cartridges of the colours of the week. Two common signals were:

(1)   'Regroup'; i.e. a command to pilots who had been scattered during combat to reform on the flight commander.
(2)   The 'washout' command; i.e., *"Let's all give up and go home."*

In some squadrons, pilots also carried a Very pistol. Typical uses would be to call for help, or to advise, *"Dud engine. I am going home."*

In the first years of the war, when artillery observation aircraft were not equipped with Morse code transmitters (wireless telegraphy), observers used Very lights to signal range and bearing corrections to artillery batteries. A good exposition on the subject is to be found in 'Cross and Cockade International' magazine, Volume 23, No. 3, published in 1992.

ACKNOWLEDGEMENTS

Margaret Bell RN, historian, for providing a list of the Great War military Hospitals.
Sarah Paterson, Imperial War Museum, for showing the way to learning about the Great War military hospitals in the north of England.
Patricia Sheldon, Newcastle City Library, for advice on whom to consult on the Great War military hospitals in the area.
David Tyrell, Teesside Archives, Middlesbrough Borough Council and Elizabeth Rees BA DAS, Tyne and Wear Archives, for providing information on the rôle of the hospitals in the area during the Great War.
R.L. Barrett-Cross MRSH, RAMC, for identifying the Middlesbrough hospitals involved in treating Roy Brown after his crash at Marske-by-the-Sea.
Dr. Geoffrey Stout, M.B., Ch.B., for detailed information on the history of the hospitals in the Middlesbrough area, and on the effects of the injuries suffered by Roy Brown and Stearne Edwards.
Terry Gilder, 'Remember When' column, Middlesbrough Evening News, for seeking information from the general public on Roy Brown's hospitalization.
Ian Marsh, Bsc, FIDiagE, engineer and aviation enthusiast for information on the fuel systems employed with rotary engines.
Stuart Leslie, aviation history and photographs of aeroplanes.
Chad Wille, pilot of a Sopwith *Camel* with a 160 HP Gnôme rotary engine and a Nieuport 11 with an 80 HP Le Rhône rotary engine.
Gordon Leith, for help from the RAF Museum Archives, Hendon.
Mrs Mary Baxter for information and photographs of her mother, Alice Pickup.
Frank Mcguire, for information on his visit to the RAF Historical Branch in 1961.

CHAPTER TEN

GENERAL AIRWAYS
(1928 to 1939)

"*Coming home.*" Painting by Denny May of Fokker Super Universal CF-AEW of General Airways returning to its base at Rouyn/Noranda during the warm season.

According to information attributed to the Canadian Department of National Defence in Ottawa, by the end of the Great War, one third of the fighter pilots serving with the RAF in France were Canadians. As they returned home the eyes of some turned towards the skies; others never wished to fly again. In both categories few talked about their wartime experiences; they wished to forget close friends who had been killed in aerial combat, or roasted alive in flying accidents in front of their eyes. Equally bad were the memories of the indiscriminate slaughter when they had machine-gunned German soldiers in their trenches and horses pulling carts along the roads during the desperate times of 1917 and 1918. In the latter year, the critical rôle of the RFC and RNAS squadrons in helping, possibly enabling, the 23 infantry and 3 cavalry divisions of Lieutenant-General Hubert Gough's Fifth Army to slow down and then halt the advance of 76 German divisions along a 40 mile front is not particularly well-known. For some obscure reason, possibly because the airmen involved numbered but a few hundred whereas the ground forces were measured in hundreds of thousands, their story and their achievement have not received sufficient recognition in history.

See (1) in the ANNEX to this chapter for more information on the use of aircraft against enemy ground forces.

In 1919, large numbers of Canadian and US-built Curtiss Jenny trainers and De Havilland D.H.4s, no longer required by the armed forces, were offered to the North American public at give-away prices. Many were purchased by demobilized pilots who believed that a living could be made giving joy-rides to the public and staging air shows. The age of the 'Barnstormer' had begun.

It was also in 1919 that the Laurentide Pulp and Paper Company found a new way to deal with an old problem. For a long time it had needed to know the status and the extent of the forests upon which it depended for pulp, but ground surveyors, quite truly, could not see the forest for the trees. Aerial photography might just be the answer; it had developed into a useful art during the war, and government surplus cameras, specially made for the purpose, were available. There were no open spaces where an aeroplane could land, but there were plenty of lakes where a seaplane or a flying boat could alight.

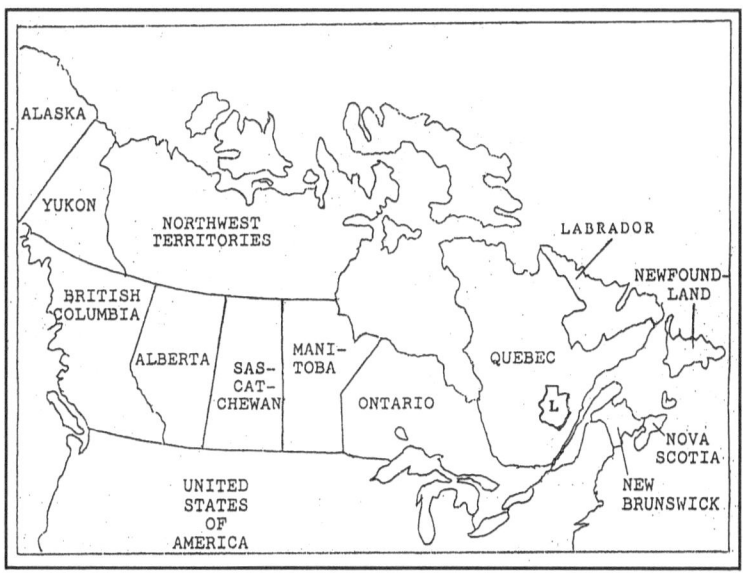

1930 map of Canada. The Laurentide region in the province of Quebec, with its network of rivers, lakes, forests and meadows, is marked 'L'.

The long range, ocean-going Felixstowe flying boats, jointly designed by Glenn Curtiss and John Porte during the war and built in England for the RNAS, were a proven technology, but they were rather on the large side for use on lakes and rivers. Again government surplus held the answer - the Curtiss H2-SL single-engined flying boat, designed in 1917 for anti-submarine patrol and used in action by the US Navy. It was a three-seater with a 375 HP Liberty engine and carried fuel for six hours' flight.

Once aerial surveying began in June 1919, it was quickly realized that regular patrols could detect illegal logging and quickly pin-point forest fires. The Laurentide Air Services company was born and it was not long before staff and internal mail were being carried by air to, from and between remote locations.

Two Curtiss H2-SL flying boats at a lakeside base.

Aircraft were frequently in the news in 1919, not because of horrendous crashes but due to sensational achievements; the world appeared to be shrinking week by week. Naval Curtiss No.4 (NC-4) flying boat of the US Navy, under Lt. Commander A.C. Read, left Long Island on 8 May 1919. With seven intermediate stops it reached Lisbon, Portugal on the 27th and Plymouth, England on the 31st. The NC-4 is on display at the Sarasota, Florida Naval base. On 14 June John Alcock and Arthur Whitten Brown flew non-stop from Newfoundland to Ireland in a Vickers Vimy landplane. They arrived on the 15th after 16 hours in the air. The Vimy is on display at the South Kensington Science Museum in London. On 2 July the airship R34 (a copy of Zeppelin L33 which force-landed in Essex in 1916) captained by Major G.H. Scott, left East Fortune, Scotland and arrived at Long Island, New York on the 6th. It began the return trip on the 9th, arriving at Pulham in Norfolk, England after a flight of 75 hours. Unlike its winged predecessors, the R34 is not on display; it was totally destroyed at Howden (near Kingston-on-Hull), England by a storm on 28 January 1921.

The Atlantic had been conquered by a flying boat, a landplane and an airship; all in the same month and without the loss of a single life. Travel by air caught the imagination of the public, world-wide, and a number of wartime pilots who wished to fly again saw commercial possibilities. Only a solo, non-stop trans-Atlantic flight was needed for further motivation, and that should not be long delayed. Unfortunately, it was not to be so; there would be a wait of nine years, plus a long list of dead or missing aviators during the interval.

The formation of the Canadian Air Force was authorized on 18 February 1920. It became the Royal Canadian Air Force on 15 February 1923 and it was around this time that the US Army Air Force began flying mail between major American cities. The air mail idea looked attractive to the Canadian air staff as a way to justify the existence of the RCAF during the government cost cutting after 'the war to end all wars', and a Commercial Operations Branch was established to carry mail and government officials.

The first problem was that the necessary aerodromes at many of the Canadian major cities had yet to be built, and to complement them, a series of intermediate airfields for refuelling and emergency landings would be required. The second problem was that coast-to-coast and intercity mail were both carried quite efficiently by the Canadian Pacific and Canadian National Railway companies. Until aeroplanes with longer range and the ability to operate both at night and in bad weather came into service, no guarantee existed that a more costly airmail letter would arrive far sooner than an ordinary one. Mail contracts being quite lucrative, the two transcontinental railway companies were not exactly thrilled at what the near future appeared to hold if the delivery time for a coast-to-coast letter could be reduced from two weeks to four days when carried by air.

As aircraft engines with equivalent horse power became both lighter in weight and more reliable, several pilots investigated the possibility of earning a living by carrying paying passengers from cities to remote towns and mining settlements. Access by land to many of these places was measured in days, even weeks, and there would be profit for both parties if the time could be reduced to hours. If a remote settlement had wireless telegraphy equipment, a message could be sent over the air in Morse Code requesting an aeroplane to fly a sick person to hospital or to bring supplies. The aeroplanes would need to be able to operate on wheels, floats or skis to accommodate the seasonal conditions, therefore considerable preparation would be required and the aircraft types carefully selected. It was not long before small private companies serving particular areas of Canada came into being.

Logically, when the word was out that an aeroplane was about to fly to a remote location, the pilot would be asked to carry letters and small packages as a favour. The Post Office was not concerned for the moment about this; it was not providing service to such places - yet. The Post Master General actually gave permission for some companies to sell stickers for the purpose. Each company set its own price, which varied between five and ten times that of an ordinary postage stamp, and personal favours were replaced by a system which generated revenue. Once flights acquired some regularity, the income from the stickers often exceeded that from carrying passengers. This did not escape the notice of the RCAF or the Post Office.

As the profitable business of joy rides and air shows for the public declined, more private aerial transport companies came into being. Again, each one specialized in a particular area of Canada. Some grew to a considerable size, often aided by mergers. As the possibility of regular flights between some cities became a reality, the Post Office began to sell its own airmail stamps and started paying the private companies to carry the letters. Business was good; therefore to obtain the greatest profit, the Post Office began a system of tenders. The lowest bidder for a particular route received the contract and the system of privately issued stickers soon came to an end. Unfortunately, there was no guarantee that a company, which had invested time and money in providing facilities for handling mail and was thus performing well, would receive a renewal of its contract the following year.

Roy Brown was one of those whose eyes turned towards the sky, and realizing that 'what the Post Office giveth, the Post Office taketh away', decided the future lay in air freight first, passengers second, and mail a distant third. He would carry sacks of mail as cargo of opportunity, but not under contract, This was a wise move as competition between the several companies, both large and small, for the initially lucrative Post Office airmail contracts rapidly drove the bids down. The law, as it then stood, did not require the Post Office to select the lowest bidder and in some instances political patronage appeared to be the governing factor.

On 20 May 1927, the world was electrified to hear that Charles

Lindbergh, flying a Ryan monoplane named *Spirit of St. Louis*, had made the long awaited solo, non-stop crossing from New York to Paris. He had departed on the 19th and the flight had taken 33 1/2 hours. In addition to his great 'first', he had become the 92nd person to cross the Atlantic Ocean by air. The *Spirit of St. Louis* is on display at the Smithsonian Institution in Washington, DC. Commercial aviation received much benefit from the flight, the publicity surrounding it, and especially from Lindbergh's words, *"The year will surely come when passengers and mail will fly every day from America to Europe. Possibly everyone will travel by air in another fifty years."* If we regard 'everyone' as signifying 'most people', the advent of the jet engine made Lindbergh's trans-Atlantic prediction came true twenty years sooner than he had predicted.

In early July 1927, an accident to a steam turbine at a place named Flin Flon revealed the advantages that air transport could provide. The turbine drove a mill which crushed rock, and the entire ore processing plant came to a halt. Western Canada Airways flew a General Electric service engineer from Winnipeg to Flin Flon in one day. He found that a shaft was broken and sent a telegram to the GE factory in Massachusetts. A new shaft was immediately sent by rail to Winnipeg, and on the morning it arrived there, it was immediately transported by air the final 385 miles to Flin Flon.

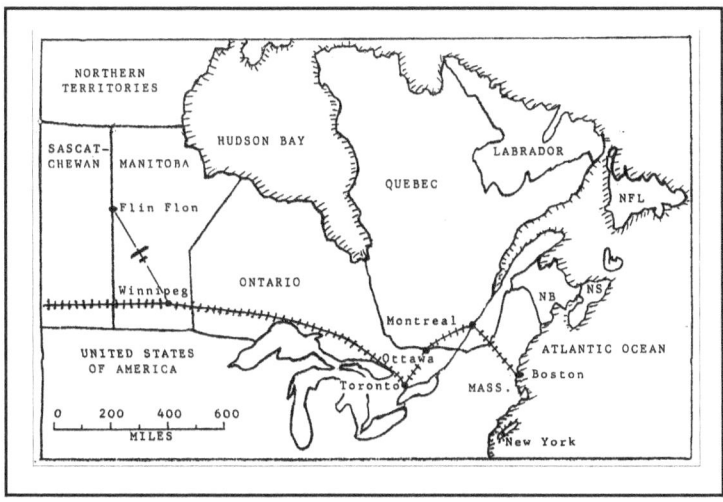

The rail and air route from Massachusetts to Flin Flon.

Within one week of the breakdown, the mill was again in operation. When the cost of chartering the two aeroplanes is equated to the two weeks' lost production, which would have resulted from transporting the shaft overland from Winnipeg (the route ran 150 miles east before turning north), the expenses incurred were a bargain. Word spread and considerable interest in air freight to remote locations was thereby generated. The 'bean counters' soon realized that when all associated costs were factored in, sending tools, machinery, fuel and even dynamite by air to places where access was only by pack animals, was the cheapest method. Better yet, if a decent patch of snow could be provided, aeroplanes fitted with skis could continue to operate after the rivers had frozen.

A month before the accident happened at Flin Flon; June 1927 to be precise, Roy had already filed the papers for the incorporation of 'National Airways Limited' as a company. The Secretary of State objected to the name as it suggested Canadian Government involvement. Roy then suggested 'General Air Transport Limited', which was rejected due to similarity with an existing registered business. Roy then submitted three names:

General Airways Limited
Air Transport Limited
Airways Corporation Limited

Giving the first listed as his preference. It was accepted, and on 8 March 1928, a private company, 'General Airways Limited', located in Toronto, Ontario, came into existence. It was capitalized at $50,000 in 1,000 shares and Roy immediately began organizing bases, staff and equipment. A pilot named Wilson Harold Clarke, who had originally learned to fly at Camp Borden - the Canadian government training school - and now held Canadian commercial licence No. 248, was looking for employment. He approached Roy, who unfortunately had no vacancy for a pilot, but did need an assistant mechanic. Wilson Clarke had good mechanical knowledge of aircraft so Roy accepted him and found his enthusiasm to be contagious. Roy allowed Wilson Clarke leave of absence for a refresher course at Camp Borden, and upon his return hired him as a pilot. Camp Borden appears later in this chapter on the map showing the location of Big Cedar Point on Lake Simcoe.

In June 1928 General Airways began operations from Amos, Quebec with two aeroplanes:

    G-CAJJ, Fairchild FC-2 built in USA
    G-CATJ, De Havilland 60X Cirrus Moth built in England

The 'G-C' part of the registration letters decodes as Great Britain - Canada. The two aeroplanes were painted an orangey-red colour to make them stand out against the snow, and for everyone on board, each carried enough food and survival gear to last for ten days.

G-CATJ, De Havilland 60X Cirrus Moth together with G-CAJJ, Fairchild FC-2 beached in front of the General Airways base at Amos, Quebec on 12 October 1928. National Aviation Museum photograph.

G-CAJJ, Fairchild FC-2 beside the landing at the foot of the stairway to Tom Monypenny's summer cottage at Big Cedar Point on the west side of Lake Simcoe, Ontario. National Aviation Museum photograph.

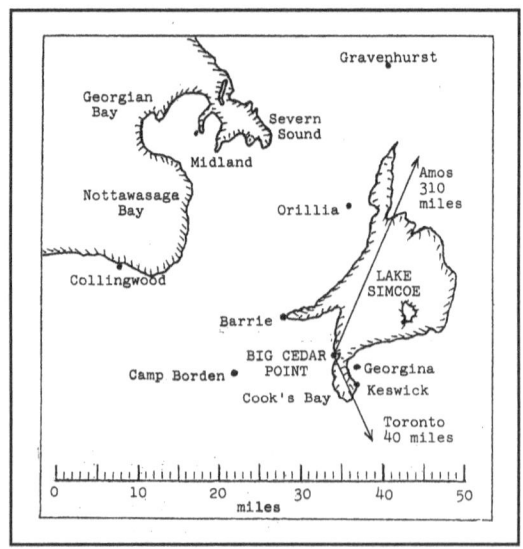

The location of Big Cedar Point on Lake Simcoe.

Due to the shape of the top of the fuselage behind the cabin, the Fairchild FC-2 soon acquired the nick-name 'Razorback'. It had a 200 HP Wright J-5 engine and could carry a ton at 103 mph for 6 hours. The cabin had seats for four passengers.

As business prospered, a base with offices and a maintenance hangar was established at the twin settlements of Noranda and Rouyn, Quebec, both shown on the General Airways route map later in this chapter.

In the summertime; G-CAJJ, Fairchild FC-2 on floats, moored on the lake at Noranda/Rouyn.

In the wintertime; G-CAJJ, Fairchild FC-2 on skis, taxiing across the snow-covered ice on the lake at Noranda/Rouyn.

The DH 60X Cirrus Moth was used when just one passenger or a only small load was available. With its 85 HP Cirrus II engine it could carry a third of a ton and could fly for over three hours at 85 mph on 19 gallons of fuel. Not very many two-seater light aeroplanes designed since then have a better performance. Like the B.E.2C on which Roy trained at Chingford, when the Cirrus Moth was flown solo, the pilot sat in the rear cockpit to maintain proper fore and aft weight balance. The 'X' after the '60' in the type designation means there is no spreader bar between the wheels of the undercarriage; the two legs are independently sprung.

On 31 August 1928 the FINANCIAL POST reported;

General Airways Limited, with flying base at Amos, Quebec was organized in June of this year.

Operations commenced with one four passenger Fairchild cabin monoplane and since then the company has added a 'Moth' plane. To date the Fairchild has flown 100 hours and the 'Moth' over 50.

The company's planes serve the Abitibi District and that section of the north extending from Cochrane on the west, east to Amos and Montreal, and south to Ottawa. Negotiations are under way for a mail contract.
Rates: Haileybury to Amos $40.00; return trip $75.00. Planes may be hired by hour or special trips arranged.

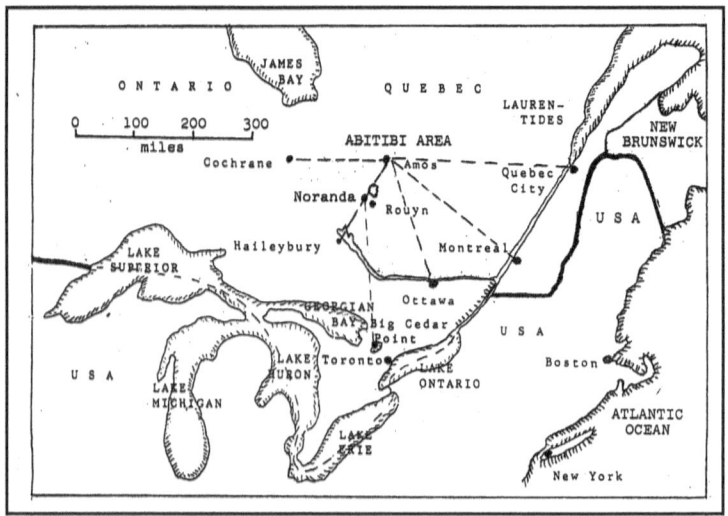

The routes flown by General Airways from Amos, Quebec.

A company emblem was designed. It featured a Fokker F-VII/3m, the latest version of the well-known F-VII, but equipped with three engines for greater safety and increased load carrying capacity. As things turned out, General Airways never acquired any aeroplanes of that type.

The company emblem. The colours were red, black, light blue and white.

The General Airways pilots developed a simple method of solving a complicated problem; preventing a combination of fuel, passengers and freight from causing over-loading when operating on floats. Each aeroplane was placed in the water, loaded to the legal maximum weight and a Plimsoll line, as used on ships, was then painted on the floats.

On 28 January 1929, a new international code for aircraft registration came into force. Canada became CF-***, and remained so until 1 January 1974, when it became C-****. Thus G-CAJJ, Fairchild FC-2 became CF-AJJ, then finally C-FAJJ.

In 1929 Roy added a Fokker Super Universal (CF-AEW) built in the USA. It was fitted with a 420 HP Pratt & Whitney Wasp engine and could carry six passengers and/or cargo, up to a total of one ton, for six hours at 118 mph. Like the earlier Dr.I triplane and D-VIII parasol monoplane, Anthony Fokker had made the wings so strong that neither bracing wires nor struts were needed. The tank for the engine oil was beneath the pilot's seat where it provided him with a source of warmth in winter and annoyance in summer.

In the same year the De Havilland 60X Cirrus Moth (G-CATJ) was sold and replaced with the more powerful De Havilland 60M Gipsy Moth (CF-ADR). One reason was that parts for the Cirrus engine - based on a design by Renault in France - were becoming difficult to acquire, whereas the 100 HP Gipsy I engine was a De Havilland design and in steady production. Unfortunately, no photograph of CF-ADR can be found. In general appearance a Gipsy Moth was identical to a Cirrus Moth; the difference lay in the engine fitted, plus one or two internal improvements. The DH 60X and 60M were both variants of the DH 60 Moth. When floats were used in place of wheels or skis, there was a load penalty of 25 pounds and a decrease in cruising speed of 12 MPH.

On 3 May 1929, The Financial Post reported;

GENERAL AIRWAYS PROVES GREAT AID TO NORTH COUNTRY
Company completes successful year serving isolated mines.

General Airways in June 1929 will have completed its first year of flying, with a number of notable flying achievements to its credit. This company, operating with Amos, Quebec as its base, has done much to speed up mining development in the North Country. The company's planes serve the Abitibi-Harricana mining district, and that section of the north country extending from Cochrane on the west, east to Amos and Montreal, and south to Ottawa, including the Porcupine, Kirkland Lake, Larder Lake, and Cobalt mining camps in Ontario, and Rouyn, Val d'Or, Malartic, Senneterre, and adjoining districts in Quebec.

The company's service was inaugurated with a four-passenger Fairchild-Wright cabin monoplane and a De Havilland Moth. These were later equipped with heated compartments for winter flying and despite severe winter conditions General Airways kept the outlying mining camps in close touch with the outside world from freezeup in the fall to break-up in the spring.

This service meant much to such mines as the Graham-Bousquet, Thompson-Cadillac, and O'Brian in Cadillac township, the Malartic in Fournière, and the Siscoe and Greene-Stabelle on the upper reaches of the Harricana.

Amos, the nearest railhead, lies from forty to sixty miles away. In summer it may be reached by canoes equipped with "kickers", in from five to eight hours, but in winter when dog teams are the sole means of communication, the trip takes a day and sometimes longer.

During the past winter travellers were flown in from Haileybury to

Greene-Stabelle and back in three hours, a trip that would otherwise have required nine days.

In this matter of winter flying, Pilots W. H. Clarke and G.C. Dingwall acquired a reputation for always being on the spot.

During the winter the company undertook a bi-weekly mail service to the Graham-Bousquet mine in Cadillac township, and the Siscoe mine on the Harricana. Of all these flights only two had to be postponed to the following day, the others being carried out on schedule, despite unfavourable weather conditions.

Some of the longer flights undertaken were: Amos to James Bay, and Amos to Mattagami Lake. Flights from Amos to Haileybury were made frequently.

During its season of operations the company carried 1,600 passengers, 3 1/2 tons of express matter, and 1,638 pounds of mail. 1,000 single trips were made without an injury to passengers, goods, or aircraft.

A total of 400 hours were flown during the winter season.

Safety being the company's first consideration, no stunts were allowed even during the instruction of several students, two of whom have made their first solo flight. The instructions were carried out from the company's large and spacious hangar at Amos.

A great deal of the company's success has been due to the organization of its general manager Brett Pliske, who made the preliminary flights over country hitherto unvisited by aeroplane and subsequently built up the personnel that constitute the General Airways present flying force.

The company has a capitalization of $50,000 divided into shares of $100 at par value.

Directors: president, Apt'd A. Roy Brown, Toronto; vice-president, W.M. Brawley, Toronto; managing director, Brett Pliske, Amos, Quebec.

The settlements, towns and cities mentioned in the press report above are capitalized on the two route maps which follow. In the 1930s the land routes shown on the maps were not suitable for wheeled traffic in the winter. Note how Amos is well positioned for future service expansion to the east.

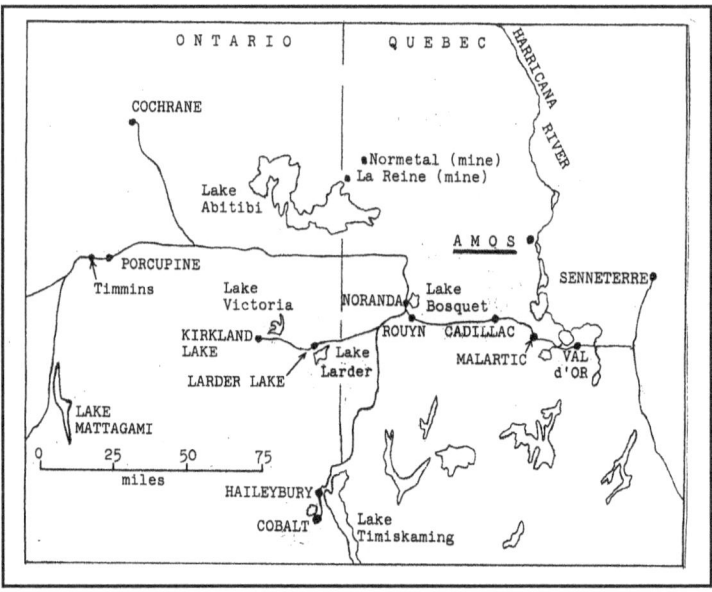

The shorter routes regularly flown by General Airways during its first year; June 1928 to June 1929.

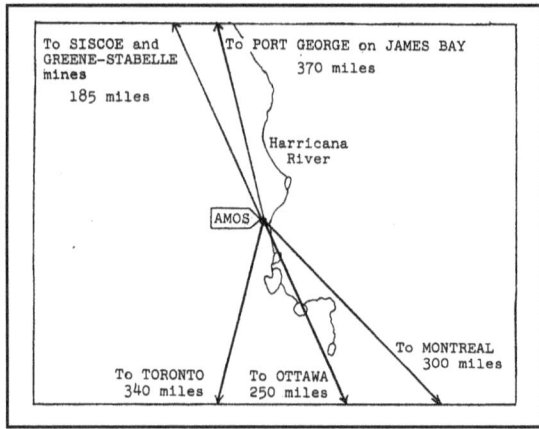

The longer routes frequently flown by General Airways during its first year; June 1928 to June 1929.

In the summer of 1929, General Airways began service to the mines and settlements east of Amos from Lake Waswanipi to Lake Chibougamau. Shortly after it began, an influenza epidemic struck the Lake Gwillan, Lake Opemiska and Lake Doré areas. The Indians, who had little if any resistance to that type of illness, were in dire straits and many needed immediate hospitalization in Amos. General Airways operated a dawn to dusk ambulance service and 'Clarkie', as Wilson Clarke was known, became a local hero. By coincidence, Wilfrid Reid (Wop) May, Roy's RAF 209 squadron colleague, was involved in a similar but considerably more dangerous venture in another region of Canada later that year.

See (2) in the ANNEX to this chapter for more information on Wop May's perilous mercy flight.

The lakes and settlements mentioned above are capitalized in the map which follows. Oskelaneo, which appears in the next paragraph, is also included. The other lakes shown were less frequent destinations.

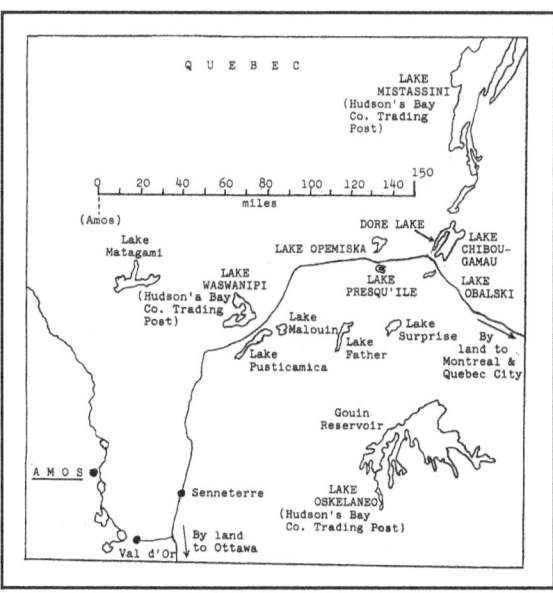

The new routes east of Amos inaugurated in summer 1929, including the influenza epidemic area.

That winter, Clarke flew mining engineer, Leo G. Springer, in the Gipsy Moth (CF-ADR), to examine the land between 100 and 200 miles north of Oskelaneo (see map above) where the Hudson's Bay Company had established a trading post. Springer found extensive copper deposits in the Lake Opemiska area; he also found gold.

The following photograph of CF-AEW parked for the night illustrates the procedure followed for all aircraft during the winter. The lubricating oil was first drained from the engine and taken to a warm place (some pilots took the can of oil into their quarters and placed it inside their sleeping bag), then a canvas shroud was fitted over the engine. In the morning, that part of the shroud seen hanging down, became a chimney for a naphtha-burning heater. Once the engine had been pre-heated, the lubricating oil was poured back in and the engine started. Note the shroud over the engine. Note also the exhaust pipe alongside the bottom of the port side of the cabin and that the wing has no bracing struts. The large, vertical shock absorber attached to the ski on the port side stands out clearly.

CF-AEW, Fokker Super Universal on winter skis parked on the frozen Lake Doré (Lac aux Dorés) near Lake Obalski in the Chibougamau area.

In spring, the Fokker Super Universal (CF-AEW) was put back on floats and made many trips to the Hudson's Bay Co.'s trading post beside Lake Waswanipi. The post is shown in the two photographs which follow.

The Hudson's Bay Co.'s trading post (see lower right) on an inlet of Lake Waswanipi as seen from 4,000 feet in the winter. Note the snow covering the frozen surface of the lake.

G-CAJJ, Fairchild FC-2 being beached at the Hudson's Bay Co.'s trading post beside Lake Waswanipi.
The bracing struts for the wings easily distinguish it from Fokker CF-AEW.

The large Fokker Super Universals possessed the strength to carry heavy loads and the size to carry light but bulky ones, however, they suffered from an operational problem in the northern climate. The wings, which were manufactured as an immensely strong single-piece, were difficult to handle away from a roomy, heated, base workshop. If a mishap occurred to one wing, it, alone, could not be removed for repair.

In the following photograph of Fokker Super Universal CF-AEW, note how the single-piece wing forms part of the roof over the cabin. Note again the exhaust pipe running back along the fuselage to beyond the cabin door, and the absence of wing bracing struts. The bracing strut on the wing of the other aeroplane identifies it as a Fairchild.

CF-AEW, Fokker Super Universal (left) and G-CAJJ, Fairchild FC-2 (right) being loaded from the surface of frozen Lake Presqu'Île near Opemiska Copper Mine in 1929.

CF-AEW, Fokker Super Universal being unloaded at the Hudson's Bay Co.'s trading post beside Lake Mistassini.

After the unloading comes the hard work; Fairchild G-CAJJ being refuelled via a hand pump.

In 1930 the Fokker Super Universal (CF-AEW) was destroyed when an engine problem caused the exhaust pipe to emit flames during take-off and the fuselage caught fire. Roy replaced the Fokker with a 300 HP Bellanca CH-300 (CF-AOL), a later design than the 420 HP Fokker Super Universal. This machine had almost equivalent performance to the Fokker but on less power. It used less fuel, had separate port and starboard wings, and was therefore both more economical to operate and easier to repair.

CF-AOL, Bellanca CH-300 at Lake Swayze during the 1931 - 32 gold rush.

General Airways was now one of the five major aviation companies in eastern Canada. The others were International Airways, Canadian Transcontinental Airways, Fairchild Aviation and Canadian Airways. The picture changed at the end of the year when a holding company named the Aviation Corporation of Canada was formed with strong financial backing. It purchased outright or acquired the major holding of shares in Roy's competitors with the sole exception of Canadian Transcontinental Airways. Not to scare customers away, the component divisions were allowed to continue operations under their old company names.

Despite organized competition, business for Roy's company continued to increase during 1930 and he declined a buy-out offer from the Aviation Corporation of Canada, Canadian Airways division.

The private air transport companies in the east and west of Canada had developed what today is known as 'hub and spoke' systems but there was a problem; the spokes rarely linked the hubs. Therefore, due to lack of aerodromes along some parts of the route, it was not possible to fly across Canada from one coast to the other. If the RCAF wished to send aircraft from Ottawa to Vancouver, the machines had to be dismantled and dispatched by rail. Four weeks would pass before they could take to the air again.

A change of federal government occurred at this time and a number of politicians who favoured socialism found themselves in power. They were faced with the joblessness created by the Great Depression and sought the means to rectify the situation. The result was the Unemployment Relief Project in which the government hired labour to perform public works. Under this plan, General McNaughton was authorized to recommence work on the Trans-Canada Airway. This was a line of aerodromes with intermediate emergency landing grounds to the north of the Canada/USA border whose construction had earlier been stopped as an economy measure. Radio stations to transmit navigation signals were part of the project.

See (3) in the ANNEX to this chapter for more information on the Trans-Canada radio navigation system.

In those times of heavy demands upon the government's

shrunken purse, the RCAF had to justify its existence. The old idea of carrying airmail resurfaced and the RCAF was asked to take over a number of routes. Once operations began, the air staff soon realized that the elaborate requirements for winter flying to remote locations in the north detracted from the RCAF's real purpose - the defence of Canada - and bowed out. Regions where special equipment was not required were another matter, and the RCAF continued to carry mail, politicians, government officials and personnel over the more southerly routes.

In 1930, the Aviation Corporation of Canada underwent internal change and took the name of one of its holdings, Canadian Airways Ltd. In light of hindsight, the choice of name did not portend well for the future of the other air transport companies.

In 1931, Roy's last independent competitor, Canadian Transcontinental Airways, was bought out by Canadian Airways Ltd. The question then became for how much longer General Airways could avoid a similar fate. The answer turned out to be eight years; General Airways had no air mail contracts, cargoes or routes which Canadian Airways Ltd. coveted. Roy's business decisions over the years had been sound, but unfortunately, the good profit generated from the routes flown by General Airways attracted undesirable attention.

Roy with some of General Airways staff in 1931. L to R: Wilson Clarke, Dixon, Roy, Earl Jellison and Kelly Edmison. National Aviation Museum photograph.

On 10 June 1933, General Airways Limited became a public company. A statement, in lieu of a Prospectus, filed on 2 February 1934, listed A. Roy Brown, Frederick O. Mitchell and L.E. Blackwell as company directors. Capitalization was to be increased to $100,000 by a further issue of shares.

General Airways purchased five more aeroplanes. The De Havilland 60M Gipsy Moth (CF-ADR), now too small, was sold. The new aeroplanes were:

>CF-ATN, Bellanca CH-300 (1932)
>CF-AND, Bellanca Pacemaker (1932)
>CF-API, De Havilland 83 Fox Moth (1933)
>CF-AEC, Bellanca CH-300 (1934)
>CF-AWO, Stinson SR-5A Reliant (1934)

CF-AWO, Stinson SR-5A Reliant on its way to General Airways. Note the straight edges to the wings and the small cabin door.

The De Havilland 83 Fox Moth was developed from the Gipsy Moth. The design intent was an inexpensive aeroplane which could carry the maximum possible payload on a 120 HP Gipsy III engine. The cost saving came from the use of wings already in mass production for the DH-82A Tiger Moth, a pilot training aeroplane for the RAF and other air forces around the world. It carried four passengers in a heated cabin but the pilot was not quite so lucky. The prototype G-ABUO was sent to Canada in 1932 for evaluation on wheels, floats and skis by Canadian Airways Limited, which improved the lot of the pilot by placing an enclosed canopy over his cockpit. The British registration was changed to CF-API shortly after Roy purchased it. CF-API flew under various owners until 1950 when it was retired due to general fatigue in the airframe; not an uncommon fate for an aeroplane of wooden construction employed in an environment with large changes of temperature and humidity.

G-ABUO, De Havilland 83 Fox Moth, which later became CF-API, moored at Big Cedar Point, Lake Simcoe near the summer cottage used by Roy and his family. The canoe belonged to Roy's son Donald.

CF-ATN, Bellanca CH-300 being met by a 'reception committee' at Big Cedar Point. The young girl is Roy's daughter Margaret.

By June 1934, General Airways had grown to the point whereby its business required Roy's complete attention. On the 15th of the month he tendered his resignation to Imperial Varnish and Color. The company continued in business until the mid-1960s when it was acquired by DuPont Industries.

On 22 September 1934, The Financial Post reported;

Chibougamau is fast taking its place as an important Quebec mining area. The latest entry into the field is Consolidated Mining and Smelting Co., which recently acquired control of Consolidated Chibougamau Goldfields and is directing development operations.

The plan to exhaustively develop the property can be seen in the announcement that in excess of 150 tons of equipment and supplies are being transported to the property of Oskelaneo, Quebec, by airplane. The transportation job is being rushed by General Airways Ltd. in order that all freight will be moved in before the freeze-up, which comes about October 15 in the Chibougamau country.

By 1935 Wilson Clarke had become the Chief Pilot and General Manager. The six pilots who reported to him were; Kelly Edmison, 'Bun' Paget, Stuart Hill, Curt Bogart, Tim McCoy and 'Gath' Edward. The mechanics and radio operators numbered twelve.

Often the cargoes and the people carried to isolated locations were rather unusual, which might have been one factor behind the lack of perseverance shown by Canadian Airways Ltd. in acquiring the routes flown by General Airways. The cargoes included sleds, complete with dog teams; explosives; steel for constructing buildings (this sometimes affected the magnetic compass); drums of fuel; freshly killed fish, and canoes. Among the people carried were to be found injured miners; dead bodies and prisoners awaiting trial in town. General Airways transported anything which could be loaded into the cabin or lashed to the skis, floats or struts outside.

In reasonable weather, just before the monthly payday occurred at a distant mine or some other enterprise, it often happened that three or four enterprising ladies of the night would charter an aeroplane and load it with alcoholic refreshments, camping gear, food and a cash box. They would then set off on a highly profitable business trip during which no receipts were asked or given. All was grist which came to General Airways' mill.

Much of the cargo was small in size but extremely heavy, such as gold in sealed boxes and diamond-tipped drill bits. To carry such loads in quantities acceptable to the customers, a more powerful aeroplane soon became necessary. Bellanca had the answer; the Senior Pacemaker. It was a freighter version of the popular Pacemaker featuring a stronger floor and a 450 HP Wright Whirlwind engine. In 1935, Roy purchased one (CF-ANX) but unfortunately no photograph can be found.

Several more small, specialised air transport companies were formed in the mid-1930's. In 1934 a Western Airways pilot named Francis Roy Brown resigned his position, and together with pilots Milton Ashton, Edward Stull and Jack Moar, founded an air transport company named Wings Limited. They acquired some WACO cabin biplanes with de luxe upholstery and carried their passengers in unusual comfort for those times.

See (4) in the ANNEX to this chapter for information on the confusion between Arthur Roy Brown and Francis Roy Brown.

In 1935 Canadian Airways Ltd. again approached Roy proposing a buy-out. This time he was prepared to agree, but on one condition, that he be given the post of General Manager of the combined enterprise. This was unacceptable to the directors of Canadian Airways Ltd. and the matter was dropped.

General Airways now operated from four bases in Quebec; Amos, Rouyn/Noranda, Senneterre and Oskelaneo, and was carrying good loads of passengers and freight into the settlements surrounding Lake Chibougamau and Lake Rose. A fifth base had been established at Hudson in Ontario (650 miles east and 150 miles north of Amos) providing similar service to the settlements at Red Lake and Pickle Crow. The Albany River, which discharged in James Bay, contained sturgeon aplenty and the local Indians sold their catch to the Baillie-Maxwell company. An air service from the lakes along the riverside to the company's fish processing and caviar extracting plant at Nakina was exactly what all parties needed. The Hudson's Bay Co. also benefited from the deal; Baillie-Maxwell gave the Indians vouchers which they could convert into goods at the company's Ogoki and Lake Saint Joseph trading posts.

The mining companies in Quebec and Ontario were now so aware of the money to be saved in the long run by using air freight, that a request to deliver a hundred tons of cargo would make neither Wilson Clarke nor Roy blink. The record for the amount of cargo delivered to one particular customer during 1935 is said to have been 600 tons. The carrier was Canadian Airways Ltd.

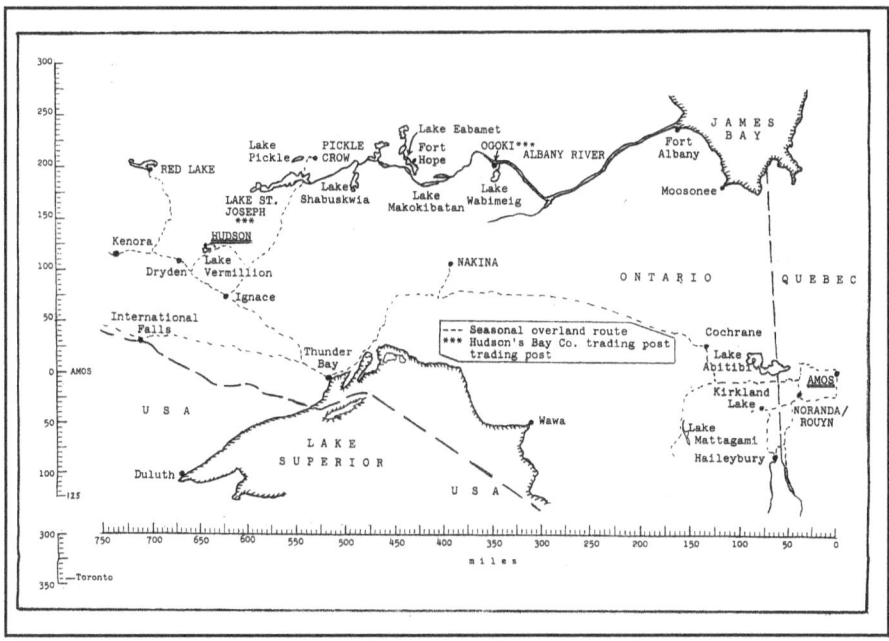

The principal places in Ontario served by General Airways from Amos and Hudson in 1935. Both mileage scales are zeroed on Amos.

Aerial surveys were another highly profitable business for Roy. A prospector could accomplish in a couple of hours what would previously have taken a month. Upon finding a site which required closer examination, the aeroplane could alight on a nearby lake or a river and bring into action the canoe lashed to its float struts or beneath the fuselage. General Airways had been carrying geologists on such surveys since mid-1928 and they had located a large number of commercially attractive sites. Twelve of them contained sufficient minerals - including gold - for mining to be undertaken. Wilson Clarke took Leo Springer on several surveying trips and they became good friends.

General Airways was prospering; the company's assets were now in excess of $300,000 and its fleet consisted of seven aeroplanes. These were:

Bellanca CH-300:- CF-AOL, CF-ATN, CF-AEC
Bellanca Pacemaker:- CF-AND
Bellanca Senior Pacemaker:- CF-ANX
De Havilland 83 Fox Moth:- CF-API
Stinson SR-5A Reliant:- CF-AWO

General Airways now operated the largest fleet of Bellancas in private hands; only the RCAF had more.

General Airways Bellanca shrouded and tied down for the night.

From L to R: Two Bellanca CH-300s and CF-API Fox Moth moored at Noranda/Rouyn. National Aviation Museum photograph.

Roy had been pleased with the performance of Stinson Reliant CF-AWO and was interested in purchasing more of this type if a hatch could be installed in one side of the fuselage to permit bulky cargoes to be loaded and unloaded. Stinson improved on this idea by basically replacing one side of the cabin with a large door. When closed, it added to the structural strength of the fuselage; when open, the cabin space was accessible from the floor almost to the ceiling. According to the Toronto GLOBE AND MAIL, dated 1 February 1936, Stinson had found this feature highly marketable and the US government had ordered sixteen of what were known inside the factory as 'Roy Brown Specials'.

General Airways began providing scheduled service to places as far west as Winnipeg. When cargo or passengers appeared, which was quite frequently, flights were made as far as Reindeer Lake (200 miles beyond Flin Flon) where the Indians caught trout for the inhabitants of Winnipeg. To the east, service was provided along the east bank of James Bay to Eastmain on the Riviére Eastmain (River Eastmain) and on to Fort George at the mouth of La Grande Riviére (The Great River). The service was soon extended to Cape Jones, to Kuujjuarapik at the mouth of Grande Riviére de la Baleine (Great Whale River) terminating 500 miles north of Amos at Lac Guillaume de Lisle on Hudson Bay.

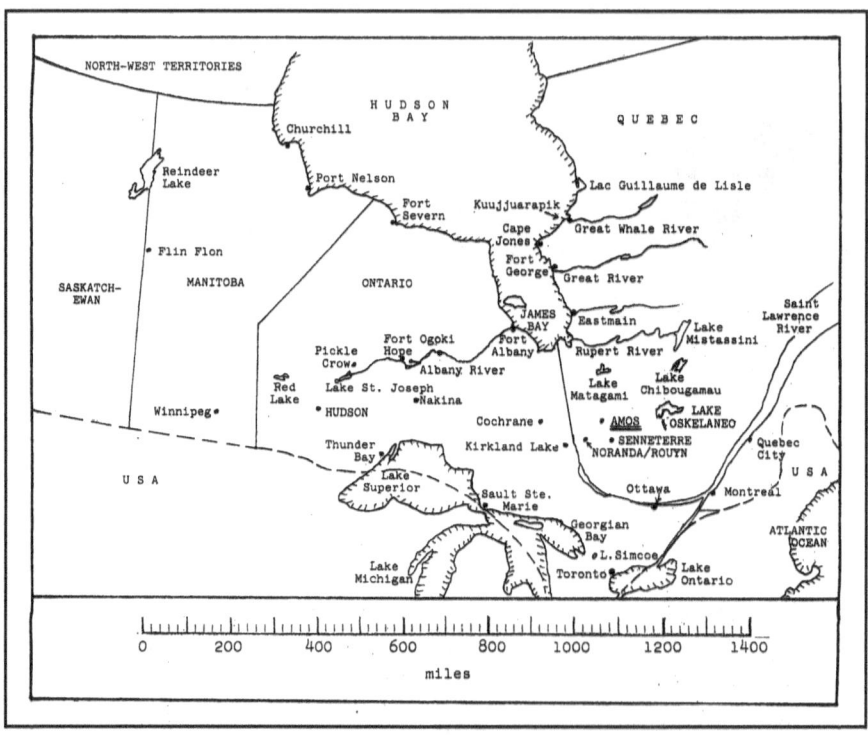

The principal localities serviced by General Airways Ltd. in 1936.
The five bases are capitalized.

When the lakes, rivers, towns and settlements serviced by General Airways with regular or charter flights are considered in relation to Canada as a whole, the company was running quite a large operation. Some destinations had scheduled service, others were seasonal; flights further afield were made upon request. This intense activity, together with the profitability of the routes, was noticed by some in Ottawa who remembered the federal, one could say the taxpayers' money spent to complete the Trans-Canada Airway under the Unemployment Relief Project a few years earlier.

The map which follows places the one above into context relative to the total size of Canada.

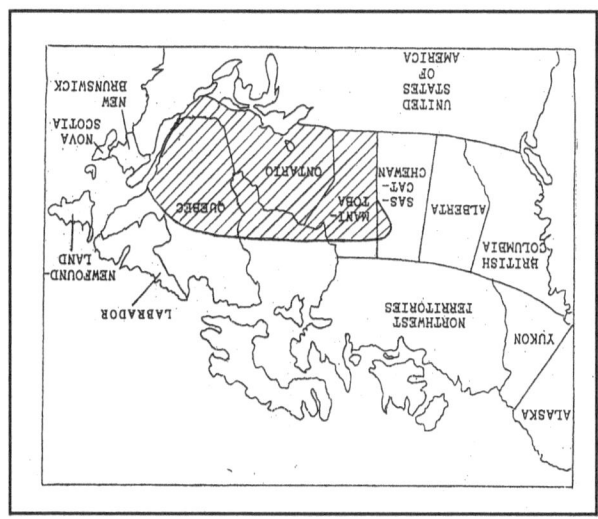

Map of Canada showing the area within which General Airways operated. It covered 600 miles N/S and 1,400 miles E/W.

Logically, operating aeroplanes under the weather conditions of the snowy north had resulted in occasional incidents and accidents. In early 1935 CF-AJJ, the Fairchild FC-2 Razorback, caught fire as the engine was being pre-heated prior to being started. The charred remains were not worth repairing.

The engine of CF-AJJ, Fairchild FC-2 ready for pre-heating. The heater would be placed on the ground inside the bottom of the canvas shroud. Wilson Clarke is standing on the left.

In 1936, CF-AWO, the Stinson SR-5A Reliant, attempted flight all by itself, but not having had any practice at doing this, it climbed too steeply, stalled and crashed. The pilot, Stuart Hill, had left the engine running while he walked over to the Siscoe Mining Company office. It was cold outside, so he had allowed the passenger to stay on board in the warm cabin. Unfortunately, while stretching, the passenger knocked the throttle lever wide open whereupon the engine let forth a mighty roar and CF-AWO began moving. The passenger, not realizing what he had done, exited the cabin with the utmost alacrity and watched his suitcase, which had suddenly become 'unaccompanied baggage', take to the skies. Perhaps the Stinson's registration should have contained one more letter; CF-AWOL.

Utter disaster struck on Saturday 23 May 1936; Bellanca CF-AOL disappeared on a return flight from Lake Presqu'Île to the General Airways base at Rouyn. Wilson Clarke, the pilot in command, was giving a final check ride to George Millham, a General Airways mechanic who had completed pilot training and was on the verge of taking over that route. One of the passengers happened to be Clarke's customer friend, L H Springer, the President of Ceres Exploration Ltd. and a major shareholder in the Opemiska Mining Company. All that was known concerning the return journey was that an intermediate stop at Lake Father was intended. The weather was so bad on Sunday that no search could be launched, but on Monday morning 'Gath' Edward took off for Lake Presqu'Île in Bellanca CF-ATN, expecting, while on the way, to find CF-AOL anchored on a lake with some mechanical problem. He maintained a close watch along the route and saw what he first took to be a red tent on the ground near an unnamed lake not shown on the 1936 maps of the area. On his way back, he looked more closely and did not like what he saw. The red colour of the tent-like object was close to an orangey-red, and that was the colour of the aircraft owned by General Airways. He felt a sinking feeling in the pit of his stomach. He circled overhead for a better look, then alighted on the lake. He had found the wreckage of CF-AOL.

Bellanca CH-300, CF-ATN in flight.

The unnamed lake in question was situated one mile east of Lake Pusticamica (also known as Lake Puskitamika), and the wreckage lay on the ground facing north, 500 feet beyond its north shore. He found Wilson Clarke's body outside on the ground; he had been thrown 6 feet through the windscreen. The bodies of George Millham and five others were still inside the fuselage; he touched nothing. Upon reaching Amos, 'Gath' Edward reported what he had observed and an aeroplane flew to the site carrying Roy Brown, an official accident investigator and some other officials. Roy flew back to Senneterre where he telephoned for two more aeroplanes to bring rescue workers.

The ill-fated Bellanca CF-AOL on Lake Bosquet, east of Noranda. The pilot is steadying it by holding the wing strut. Note the easy access for cargo provided by the large cabin door.

Roy and the officials found seven people on board CF-AOL instead of the six (including the pilot) the aircraft was authorized to carry. The Bellanca had left Lake Presqu'Île with two pilots, two passengers and some cargo on board and had alighted at Lake Father to collect three more passengers. However, it is certain that before take-off from there, a pilot of Clarke's experience would personally have verified the gross weight was within limits and the load was properly distributed in order that the fore and aft balance of CF-AOL was correct. If anything had been amiss (weight, balance or engine power), Clarke would certainly have noticed it during the departure from Lake Father and would not have continued the journey to Rouyn.

See (5) in the ANNEX to this chapter for information on the behaviour at take-off of an overloaded seaplane.

The crash investigators weighed the cargo found in the wreckage and checked the fuel load on board when CF-AOL left Lake Presqu'Île. Calculations established that at the time CF-AOL left Lake Father, the total weight on board (fuel, cargo, two pilots and five passengers) did not exceed gross; i.e. the maximum permitted to be carried. In plain

English; CF-AOL was not overloaded. It was, however, in an illegal condition, aggravated by the omission of the General Airways maintenance chief to sign the Technical Log Book that morning certifying its fitness to fly.

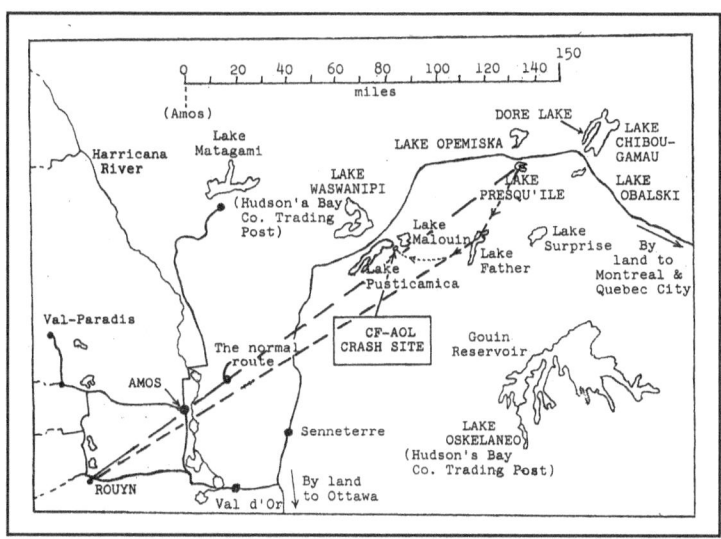

The normal route from Rouyn to Presqu'Île and return, plus the diversion made by CF-AOL via Father Lake.

The inquest was held at Amos on 27 May 1936. Roy Brown testified he had an idea concerning what had transpired. He explained that if Wilson Clarke had simply flown into the ground, the aeroplane would have gone forward several hundred feet and the trees would have cushioned the impact. The accident looked like the result of a phenomenon dreaded by all airmen; 'crazy air', which he had personally experienced during the war. According to the TORONTO STAR on 28 May 1936, he told the following story:

"I took off normally one day then levelled out to gain speed before climbing, then without any action on my part, my machine went into a left vertical bank. Although I had the controls jammed hard over to the right, my left wing tip was within a foot of the ground. Had I hit an ant-hill, I would have spun right over. My first thought was that spies had tampered with the controls of my machine and that I might just as well say goodbye; there were

trees at the end of the aerodrome and I was heading straight for them. Just a short distance from the trees the aeroplane righted itself and leaped 100 feet into the air, but I still had no control. Up above I got into normal air again and my controls behaved normally. It was something like that which drove Clarke to earth."

He further explained that at Amos, the day before, an old prospector had told him about a lake in the Pusticamica area which the Indians refused to cross in their canoes. On stormy days, the wind at one end of it blew strongly in one direction, but at the other end, the wind blew even more strongly in the opposite direction. Roy then added;

> "I am satisfied that the aeroplane was completely beyond Clarke's control. I regret the disaster more than I can say but I cannot accept, on his behalf, any blame."

The investigation established that during flight in a northerly direction at low level under conditions of poor visibility, the spreader bar between the floats of CF-AOL had cut the tops off two tall poplar trees. CF-AOL had not gone down nose first, but had hit the ground extremely hard in flying attitude. The marks of the two floats on the ground began twenty-four feet to the north of those two trees (i.e. beyond them) and were clear and easily interpreted. After striking the ground there had been little forward movement; no more than five to six feet in a northerly direction. In other words, CF-AOL, while in a normal, horizontal position, had descended close to vertically. The impact had concertinaed the fuselage of CF-AOL upwards from bottom to top.

When the investigators examined the instrument panel, they noted the clock had stopped at 11.35 and the magneto selector switch was in the OFF position. Confirmation that Clarke had turned the switch at some time prior to contact with the ground was provided by the propeller; blade damage indicated it had only been turning slowly (windmilling) at the time of impact. The switch position indicated that Clarke knew that a crash was coming as any pilot trying to clear tree-tops would have been seeking every horse power he could obtain from the engine - not the reverse. Turning the switch OFF is a normal precaution against fire, but how would Clarke have been able to do this while subjected to the violent deceleration from the impact with the tree-tops?

Two of the many photographs taken by the investigators are shown below.

Tracks made by the pontoons seen from behind. The wreckage of Bellanca CF-AOL is in the top right corner. The camera is facing north.

A closer view of the wreckage. The camera is facing north.

The accident investigators' report, which accompanied the photographs, described the wreck as follows:

"Six passengers and pilot on last flight. (Aircraft licensed for five passengers

and pilot). No proof of overloading in lbs (pounds). Evidence of fuel and oil. As far as could be established all control operating devices and control surfaces had been operating normally. No evidence of structural failure. Engine switches "off". Condition of airscrew blades indicated a slowly revolving or stopped airscrew (propeller) on impact. Pontoons badly damaged at forward ends but still attached to fuselage on buckled and swept back undercarriage struts. Left wing torn off, badly wrecked and lying to port (left) quarter of fuselage. Right wing badly damaged and lying parallel to right side of fuselage. Evidence of pontoon marks in ground indicate right wing low on impact. Engine broken from mountings and badly smashed. Four longerons fractured immediately aft of cabin section and lying immediately ahead of and at slightly more than right angles to rear section of the fuselage. Lower longerons fractured in tension."

Item 4 of the Final Report issued by the Board of Enquiry stated:

"Where the aircraft first made contact with the ground the only marks discernable were those of the pontoons. There was no sign of the engine or other parts of the aircraft striking the ground at this point. The right pontoon mark was six feet long and the left five feet, the right mark being slightly deeper. These marks were such as to indicate that, although the aircraft had struck the tip of a tree 24 feet immediately previous to contacting the ground, the aircraft had at the last moment been pulled up, but too late to avoid contact with the ground especially if the pilot had been flying under blind conditions and the trees were his first indication of his close proximity to the ground. Had the aircraft struck at an angle of 40 or 45 degrees, it might well be assumed that the aircraft would have remained more or less where it had struck, but in any case the pontoons would probably have been torn completely off, or at least some parts of the pontoons or aircraft would have been found at the first point of contact. The engine switches were definitely off and the condition of the air screw (propeller) conclusively indicated that it had been revolving very slowly or had assumed a stationary condition on impact, and it is quite reasonable to believe that the pilot had switched off pending a possible accident or that engine trouble had developed. Whichever condition prevailed does not alter the opinion of the Board in that the aircraft was in gliding flight and struck the ground in that position. Had flying conditions been good there is little doubt but that a normal landing could have been made on the body of water close *at hand even had engine trouble been present. There is the alternative that the aircraft might have landed on the nearby lake due to bad weather and had taken off when the weather had cleared and had crashed due to engine failure almost immediately after take off. This is not probable for as the take off at Presqu'ile Lake was reported as 10:40 hours and a landing apparently made at Father Lake, an air line distance of approximately 32 miles, and the flight then continued to the place of the accident a further distance of approximately 40 miles, and as the aircraft clock had stopped at 11:35 hours, sufficient time would not have elapsed to permit a landing on the lake near the accident. The possibility of an accident after take off may therefore be wholly or in part eliminated. Should engine trouble have developed at a time when the aircraft was not within reach of a suitable landing place, it is highly possible that a landing could have been made in that type of country which normally might have caused considerable damage to the aircraft but might not have been so disastrous to the crew and passengers. There was no indication that a forced landing in scrub timber country by a seaplane had been attempted. The only reasonable conclusion that can be arrived at is that the pilot, while in steep gliding flight in adverse weather conditions, approached too close to the ground and was not able to manoeuvre the aircraft in time to prevent contact with the ground."*

It must be clarified that the '*adverse weather conditions*' cited above could have caused a large error in the height indicated by the altimeter in CF-AOL, thus Clarke, enveloped in low cloud, could have been much closer to the ground than he believed.

See (6) in the ANNEX to this chapter for more information on aircraft altimeter error.

In its findings, dated 3 June 1936 and signed by Inspector T G Stephens, the Board of Enquiry stated, "*The cause of the accident is difficult, if not impossible to determine.*" It named eight possible causes, and selected two as the most probable; namely, "*weather conditions and engine trouble.*" Of the two, it placed considerably more emphasis on the weather which it described as having been, "*poor with little visibility, a low ceiling, and, at times rain*". 'Gath' Edward had testified at the hearing that on the 23rd "*the ceiling at its highest was not more than 1,500 feet and* that only in spots. There were rain squalls and at times the ground was entirely blotted out by rain and low clouds."

Under such conditions, low flight to follow landmarks would have been the norm, and Wilson Clarke was a renowned expert at that. Today, what Roy termed *"crazy air"* is known by a different name; it is officially termed wind shear. He would have had no means of knowing the presence of the dreaded *"crazy air"* on the far side of the lake until he felt its effect. However, a question that was not asked is why, at the time of the crash, Clarke was heading in a northerly direction when his destination lay to the south?

See (7) in the ANNEX to this chapter for more information on wind shear.

The Board's final comment was, *"The weather conditions appear to have been conducive to carburettor icing."* This is a serious matter; ice can accumulate with surprising rapidity in the carburettor air intake under certain conditions of temperature and humidity. If Wilson Clarke had noticed too late that ice was forming in the carburettor, the accumulation could have caused the *"engine trouble"* suggested by the Board.

A document entitled SUMMARY REPORT of the Board's conclusions went as follows:

"On May 22nd, 1936, pilot W.H. Clarke took off from Rouyn, Quebec, in Bellanca aircraft CF-AOL with two passengers and freight aboard for a general routine flight, the first on pontoons following the spring (surface ice) break-up. The aircraft landed at Guillam Lake and the pilot reported by radio that everything was fine except the weather. The aircraft was reported leaving Guillam Lake at 0940 on May 23rd, and leaving Presq'Ile Lake at 1040 for Father Lake. No further communication was received from the aircraft. Weather in the area was reported to have been overcast, ceiling aproximately 1500 (feet), rain squalls, poor visibility.

No particular anxiety was felt by personnel of General Airways, Limited, when the aircraft did not show up on the 24th, as it was presumed the pilot was waiting for an improvement in the weather. On the 25th, a General Airways pilot located the aircraft a short distance inland from the north shore of an unnamed lake. It was obviously a major crash and there was no sign of life or movement in the area.

An official enquiry was initiated. It was found that the pilot and six passengers had been fatally injured. The aircraft was written off. The aircraft was licensed to carry pilot and five passengers only.

It was not possible to determine the exact cause of the accident. It can only be deduced that while flying in poor weather and restricted visibility, the pilot manoeuvred the aircraft too close to the ground and was unable to prevent the accident."

As usually tends to happen, by the time the result of the enquiry was released, the public and the press had lost interest in the crash. Therefore those, who are either unaware of the enquiry or do not have access to its conclusions, may easily be misled by the news reports of 26, 27 and 28 May 1936, in which three different lakes are named as the crash site, and the descriptions of the wreckage vary widely. Some of the reports contain the erroneous suggestion, *for which there was not a single shred of evidence other than gossip and speculation*, that the cause of the accident was overloading.

The first question which still remains unanswered is why CF-AOL had been 18 miles away from the direct path between Father Lake and Rouyn. A sound, practical reason could be Clarke had decided to fly west (see the map above) until reaching his normal Rouyn - Lake Presqui'Île - Rouyn flight path and thus be able to make his way home following a series of familiar landmarks. Another reason, suggested by Roy, was that Clarke was diverting around one of the rain squalls present on that day. The answer to the question might well be a combination of the two reasons suggested, plus a short wait on the lake until the squall had passed by.

The second unanswered question concerns the accident itself; namely, the reason why Clarke had placed the engine switches in the OFF position (i.e. he had switched off the two magnetos which provide the sparks for ignition). The direction of the float tracks; namely, into the 10 knot wind, conforms with an attempted forced-landing due to engine trouble. Gliding down in that direction would reduce the speed of CF-AOL relative to the ground and make the eventual encounter, with whatever kind of surface was below, a little less dangerous.

Otherwise, why was CF-AOL headed away from its destination (Rouyn) to the SE? Under such circumstances, even with a dead engine, switching off both magnetos to reduce the danger of fire is mandatory in the aviation world. The OFF position of the magneto switches points to engine failure rather than pilot error.

The reader may have noticed that the location of the crash and the direction of flight at the time conform to a typical take-off accident due to engine failure. In this case, wind shear and icing may also have been involved. When an aeroplane, which took off in marginal weather, disappears on route, the searchers first look for it within a mile of the end of the runway from which it departed. It being that for Clarke to attempt a U-turn at low altitude and at low speed would have been tantamount to committing suicide, to slow down as much as possible and drop the aeroplane into the timber scrub, as mentioned in Item 4 of the FINAL REPORT issued by the Board of Inquiry (above), would have been Clarke's least hazardous choice of action. Unfortunately, wind shear occurred... there were tall trees directly in front... the rest is history.

The Board of Inquiry did not favour engine failure during take-off as being the cause of the accident. To the members, the elapsed time of 55 minutes between the time of departure of CF-AOL from Father Lake (10.40 hrs) and the time indicated on the dashboard clock (11.35 hrs), when matched to the distance between the two locations (40 miles), was insufficient for a precautionary alighting, a wait for a squall to pass and then a take-off. However, if the strong tail wind enjoyed by CF-AOL on that flight is taken into account, a different picture appears. The cruising speed (the most economical flying speed) of a Bellanca CH-300 on floats is 110 MPH, and with a 10 MPH tail wind, probably about 20 MPH above 2,000 feet altitude, it would cover 2 miles per minute relative to the ground. The elapsed time 'en route' would have been 20 minutes, thus allowing 35 minutes for two take-offs, one alighting and waiting time on the water. Depending upon the manoeuvring involved in lining CF-AOL up for an alighting and take-off at the un-named lake, there would have been between 20 and 30 minutes waiting time available.

As in most serious accidents, the combination of a number of problems and events probably lies behind the tragic result. The bad weather appears to have been the root cause in that it facilitated both wind shear and engine failure and prevented Wilson Clarke, whatever he was attempting to do, from seeing the two tall trees early enough to pass to one side.

Voluminous correspondence between various government agencies and departments took place. The Superintendent of Air Regulations, although recognizing that the irregularities were not the cause of the accident to CF-AOL, wished the Controller of Civil Aviation to take legal action against General Airways to impress upon air transport companies in general that breaches of Air Regulations would not be tolerated. The Deputy Air Minister, the Civil Aviation Branch, the Ontario Mining Association, the Minister of Mines, the Minister of Railways and Canals, and the Minister of National Defence all became involved, each one appearing to hope that one of the others would take action. Finally, the Judge Advocate General ruled that the case fell under the jurisdiction of the Department of Transport, but as that had not yet come into official existence, the case remained with the Minister of Defence. The Minister of Defence did not agree that action lay with him, and there the matter ended.

The crash was the worst accident in the twelve years of what had become known as 'bush flying' and dealt a severe blow to General Airways. Roy's General Manager, a trained mechanic and five passengers had been killed and his company's eight year record of safe flying in bad weather had vanished overnight. A sad Roy re-arranged the staff of General Airways but he could not replace the ebullient, hard-working 'Clarkie' whose competence and personality had been a major attraction to customers.

During 1936 Roy took delivery of four Stinson 'Roy Brown Specials'. They were;

>   CF-AYW, Stinson 7RB Reliant
>   CF-AZH, Stinson 7RB Reliant
>   CF-AZZ, Stinson 8DM Reliant
>   CF-BAG, Stinson 8DM Reliant

These aeroplanes had wings shaped like those of a seagull; they were more efficient than the straight wings on earlier models. The 'Roy

Brown Specials' could carry four passengers in comfort, plus baggage, to a total load of 1,300 pounds. With 500 pounds of fuel in the tanks, they could fly at 140 mph for four and a half hours.

Stinson 7RB Reliant CF-AYW. Note the gull wings.

Stinson Reliant CF-AYW being refuelled at night. Roy is sitting on the wing holding a chamois leather filter which also serves as a funnel.

Four Stinson Reliants and two Bellancas at Noranda.
National Aviation Museum photograph.

Companies which operated the gull-winged Stinson 7RB and 8BM Reliants had noticed symptoms of metal fatigue at the attachment points of the wings to the fuselage and had reported this to the manufacturer. Roy was aware of this potential hazard and careful, periodic inspections were made.

In 1937 he sold Stinsons CF-AYW and CF-AZH and replaced CF-AYW with Stinson 9EM Reliant CF-BEI a later design from the same factory. Before accepting delivery, he made certain that the Stinson engineers' design modifications to prevent metal fatigue from occurring at the wing attachment points had been performed. No photograph can be found of CF-BEI.

Roy replaced Stinson CF-AZH with a Canadian aeroplane designed and built for bush flying. This was a Noorduyn Norseman Mk IV (CF-BAN).

The Norseman had a Pratt & Whitney Wasp 550 HP engine, cruised at 150 mph, and could carry a ton and a half for four hours. This aeroplane was a great success, and remained in production until 1960. Many were used in the Second World War by the USAAF, RCAF and RAF as communications aircraft. No photograph can be found of CF-BAN.

Troubles rarely come singly. The feared results of the federal government having spent public money on the Trans-Canada Airway and the sale of airmail stamps by the Post Office now began to appear. There was feeling among federal ministers with socialist opinions that the airways belonged to the people and should not be used, they termed it 'exploited', for private profit. This particularly applied to Canadian subsidiaries of American companies, which were seen as the thin end of a wedge by which American business interests would eventually dominate Canada's air services. Some of these subsidiaries, wholly-owned by the American parent company, even bore names which gave the impression they were 100% Canadian enterprises.

Several ministers felt the national objective should be to form a people's airline with a government mandate to link Canada from east to west. Such an airline would be able to provide every service the nation required, and, as a non-profit organization, do so far less expensively than the existing private companies. The people's airline was formed in mid-1937 and took its name from the government-built airway which the private companies had been using and expected to continue using. Like the Post Office earlier; the government giveth; the government taketh away.

The people's airline was registered as Trans-Canada Air Lines and began with a silver spoon in its mouth; government funds. It offered salaries and wages higher than those the private companies could afford to pay, plus a measure of job security. As a direct result, many of the most highly qualified pilots and mechanics in the private sector changed employers. Then, for good measure, the RCAF closed its Civil Operations Branch and government departments gave their business to Trans-Canada Air Lines. Many of the small operators either amalgamated or folded their wings.

General Airways Ltd. and the conglomerate, Canadian Airways Ltd., now had a branch of the Canadian federal government as a competitor. Worse yet; a department of that same government set the rules, the rates and arbitrated disputes.

Within the private sector operations, the dozen or so small companies still in existence did not present serious competition to General Airways. Indeed, where the aerodromes and airfields used by General Airways formed part of the routes of the other small companies, relations were friendly between the pilots. However, competition between the management of these small companies for cargo and airmail contracts caused undesirable friction. There was also the question of proper equipment in the air and on the ground for safe operation. Some organizing was obviously required.

The following report in The Financial Post on 6 February 1937 describes a move made by three private operators to organize their services and combine their needs. One of these was Wings Ltd., Francis Roy Brown's company, so there must have been some confusion from time to time between the two Roys.

3 AIR FIRMS UNITE SERVICE
New Company Controlled by Wings, General and MacKenzie

The formation of United Air Services Ltd. under Dominion charter marks a combination of interests of three air transport firms, Wings Ltd.,

Mackenzie Air Service, and General Airways Ltd.

The three operating companies will control United Air Services which has an authorized capital of $400,000, with no par value common shares. One objective is to integrate extensive flying services.

General Airways operates from Rouyn and north-western Quebec to Montreal and other eastern points. Wings Ltd. operates from Winnipeg principally to mining areas in north-western Ontario and north-eastern Manitoba. MacKenzie Air Service has its headquarters in Edmonton and serves Fort Smith and northern areas.

It is expected that United Air Services will provide cross-country services, but the initial objectives are to pool purchases of aircraft and equipment, and to obtain group insurance coverage.

The Canadian government in Ottawa also decided the private companies needed organizing, but its idea of organization was somewhat different from the usual meaning of the word. The government began by instituting a route licensing system for determined periods. Then, in an intra-government branch arrangement, the Post Office began awarding airmail contracts to Trans-Canada Air Lines without following the tender process. The squeeze on the private sector had begun.

In 1938 the squeeze tightened. The government route licensing authority declined to renew a number of route licences which had expired, and it was not long before the private companies realized Trans-Canada Air Lines seemed to have a say in the 'Yea' or 'Nay' part of the renewal process. This time General Airways Ltd. was among those affected; the licences for it to operate some of its more profitable routes were not renewed. The reason is not difficult to understand. The nationalization programme had to start somewhere, and the most profitable routes of the most profitable private companies were a good place to begin. Roy did not need a crystal ball to see what was coming next and decided it was time to ease out of the air transport business. He slowly began to relinquish the remaining routes licensed to his company and to sell some of his aeroplanes.

1938 was also the year of General Airways Ltd's second fatal accident. On 12 January CF-BEI, Stinson Reliant 9EM shed a wing in flight killing Tim McCoy, the pilot. This was the very machine which the Stinson factory had modified in 1937 to cure the fatigue problem. Sometimes it is difficult for a manufacturer to find the true cause of a random failure, and the strengthening of one area may transfer the load, torsion or tension to another thereby adding to stresses already there. Such may have been the case.

In the first months of 1939, the route licensing authority gave the screw yet another turn; it restricted the days when some of the remaining routes licensed to General Airways could be flown, and Roy could see the company books shortly moving into the red. He waited no longer and sold the remainder of his aeroplanes except Stinson SR-8DM Reliant, CF-BAG. On 10 March he closed and locked the hangar doors. CF-BAG was sold in early 1940 and General Airways Limited ceased to exist, even on paper.

See (8) in the ANNEX to this chapter for lists of the aeroplanes operated by General Airways Limited, and of the staff who managed, flew or maintained them.

In the 1940's a series of small airline mergers with Canadian Airways brought Canadian Pacific Airlines into being. In 1965 the government airline, Trans-Canada Air Lines, changed its name to Air Canada and in the 1990's Canadian Pacific Airlines became Canadian Airlines International. This arrangement only lasted a few years, and as the century ended, Canadian Airlines International merged with Air Canada. Several well-known companies disappeared in the process; among them were Nordair, Northwest Territorial Air, Pacific Western Airlines, Wardair and Canada 3000.

Currently (2006) there are 41 small aviation companies listed as operating out of Yellowknife into the North West Territories, Nunavut and the Yukon; some providing regular passenger flights as well as charter and helicopter services. Roy's experience suggests they would do well to remain small.

In later years, whenever Roy was asked about the demise of his airline, he would reply, *"General Airways was put out of business by the government in Ottawa."*

ACKNOWLEDGEMENTS

The information on air transport in Canada in the 1920's and 1930's was derived from Roy Brown's papers and Denny May's knowledge of Canadian airlines, supplemented by extensive research on aeroplanes of the period made by the late Theodore Crayston.

Thanks are given to Mr. Owen A Cooke for his help in locating the Department of Defence file on the accident to CF-AOL.

The photographs are from Roy Brown's personal album, except where otherwise indicated.

ANNEX TO CHAPTER TEN

(1) THE EMPLOYMENT OF AIRCRAFT AGAINST ENEMY GROUND FORCES, PLUS THE ADVENTURES OF FLIGHT SUB-LIEUTENANT GERRY NASH AND OBERLEUTNANT KARL ALLMENRÖDER.

Since the summer of 1917, some German Staffel commanders had been quite upset at this new use, or mis-use in their eyes, of aircraft. Machine-gunning troops, who were quite unable to defend themselves whilst marching in columns or standing between the walls of their trenches, and deliberately killing horses, whose only offence was to be pulling a cart, was not their idea of the way to conduct war in the air. In July 1917 Oberleutnant Hermann Göring (21 victories), during a visit to Jasta 11, had gone as far as proposing to decapitate prisoner-of-war, Flight Sub-Lieutenant Gerald Ewart Nash from Naval 10 squadron, and drop his head over the lines with a message attached saying that unless his colleagues ceased this butchery, all future prisoners from Naval 10 would be treated the same way. It is eternally to the credit of the Rittmeister that he refused to consider Göring's idea of using threats against captured pilots, who, after all, had to obey orders or face serious consequences, and he absolutely forbade such action by anyone under his command.

Gerry Nash, as he was known, came from Stoney Creek, Ontario, Canada. He was an ace pilot in Raymond Collishaw's flight in Naval 10 Squadron and had scored six victories in May and June, three of them being Albatros D-III fighters. Naval 10 was equipped with Sopwith *Triplanes* on which the fuselage from the cockpit to the nose, the wheel covers and the tail fin (but not the rudder), had been painted in distinctive a colour to indicate 'A', 'B' or 'C' flight. In Acting Flight Commander Collishaw's 'B' Flight the colour was black, and each machine had been given a suitable name; Gerry Nash had chosen *Black Sheep*. Mel Alexander, who has appeared in previous chapters, flew N5487, *Black Prince*. Gerry normally flew N5492, which he considered to be his lucky machine.

According to Gerry Nash's post-war recollections, on the evening of 24 June, there had been a party at the Officers' Mess. The following morning, just for a prank, another pilot took N5492 before Gerry could reach it and apparently took Gerry's good luck with him. Gerry was obliged to take N5376, a brand new triplane which had only been flown in action once since delivery to Naval 10 from the RNAS AD (aircraft depot) on 16 June. Many years later, Raymond Collishaw revealed the identity of the prankster. While Gerry was on leave in England from 10 to 23 June, Collishaw had damaged his own triplane, N5480, and 'borrowed' Gerry's N5487. He liked it so much that when Gerry returned he did not wish to part with it, and it would appear that at take-off time on 25 June, he reached it before Gerry.

That morning, when Gerry Nash force-landed the battle damaged N5376 inside German-held territory, he became the 29th victory of Oberleutnant Karl Allmenröder, second in command of Richthofen's Jasta 11, the holder of the Pour le Mérite and several other high awards. Gerry was able to set fire to N5376 before being taken prisoner and sent to the nearest German Air Service aerodrome. In this case it was where Jasta 11, commanded by Rittmeister Manfred von Richthofen, was stationed. As mentioned above, Oberleutnant Hermann Göring, the C.O. of Jasta 27, was there on a visit when Gerry was brought in, and both he and the Rittmeister began to question the prisoner. Being apprehensive of what the future might hold for one who had shot down seven German aeroplanes, Gerry pretended to be a novice, but the Rittmeister, who spoke excellent English, was not to be fooled. He took Gerry over to his red Albatros D.V and pointed to some well-placed bullet holes in the fabric. He said, *"No novice could do that. You are an expert."*

Flight Sub-Lieutenant Gerald Ewart Nash in classic pose beside *Black Sheep*, his lucky Sopwith *Triplane* N5492.

In 1917, General Hermann von der Lieth-Thomsen, the commander of the German Air Service, decided to group Jastas 4, 6, 10 & 11 into a wing (Geschwader). It was named Jagdgeschwader Nr. 1, which is generally known by the abbreviated form 'JG I'. On 26 June the Rittmeister took command of JG I and thereupon made Oberleutnant Karl Allmenröder the C.O. of Jasta 11. The Rittmeister's former deputy was destined to have but one day to enjoy his new status.

After the party at Jasta 11, on the evening of the 26th, for a gallant foe captured unharmed, Gerry Nash was sent, together with some cigars, bottles of wine and a hang-over, to the nearby town of Marcke where he spent a couple of days awaiting transport to a POW camp. On the morning of the 28th, he heard a nearby church bell tolling slowly and his guard informed him that his victor, Oberleutnant Karl Allmenröder, had been killed in action the previous day. When the news of Allmenröder's end reached Naval 10 a few days later, Collishaw recalled that on the 27th at about 18:00 hours, as he disengaged from an air battle, an Albatros D.V fighter, which at a quick glance appeared to be painted like the one usually flown by Allmenröder, had crossed his path about 100 yards away. In his book AIR COMMAND,

Collishaw describes how he fired at it, not really expecting to hit anything at that range, but saw the Albatros jerk upwards, fall into a spin and then disappear from view. At the time he had assumed the manoeuvre had been evasive action but now it looked as though he might have shot down the new C.O. of Jasta 11, an ace with 30 victories. The affair being rather doubtful, Collishaw did not file a claim.

In the 1920s and 1930s the Collishaw's story surfaced, and with each retelling, not only did the colours of Allmenröder's Albatros change radically, but the story grew until it became an elaborate blow-by-blow description of a prolonged, desperate battle between the two super aces, Collishaw and Allmenröder. In the grande finale, Collishaw fired into the Albatros at point-blank range and down it went. This second air fight which never happened was still appearing as fact in publications as late as 1965.

The truth is that Karl Allmenröder's Albatros crashed in no man's land at 0945 hours on 27 June 1917, and the German army commander of the sector waited until dark to retrieve the pilot's body. This means that when Collishaw chanced his long-range shot, Karl Allmenröder had already been dead for eight hours. The cause of his crash is unknown; it is thought that he may have been hit by anti-aircraft fire. Gerry Nash spent the rest of the war in the Holzminden and Clausthal prisoner-of-war camps in the Harz mountain region, where he was allowed parole and was thus able to enjoy the scenery from time to time.

Parole card issued to Flight Sub-Lieutenant G.E.Nash at Clausthal prisoner-of-war camp on 18 October 1918

Gerry Nash has one more claim to fame. On one occasion he was forced to dive his Sopwith *Triplane* dangerously low to escape from the foe. His story could not be doubted; the ground crew found a washing line with the remains of a farmer's wife's laundry, trailing from the undercarriage.

2. In late December 1928, a case of diphtheria was identified among the staff of the trading post at the settlement of Little Red River in Northern Alberta. Pilots Wop May and Vic Horner volunteered to deliver antitoxin serum by air. They departed on 2 January 1929 in Avro *Avian* No. G-CAVB, a small, open cockpit 75hp two-seater biplane (on wheels) built for flight instruction. In four days they successfully completed the 1,200-mile round-trip journey, in temperatures down to -36°C (-33°F). They landed on the frozen Peace River near Fort Vermillion and delivered the serum to Dr Harold Hamman who was awaiting their arrival. He conveyed it overland to Little Red River, and was able to prevent an epidemic among the local Cree Indians who had little or no resistance against such diseases. The full stories of the flight, and its re-enactment on 21 June 1979 using Fleet Finch Serial No. 1001,

are told in *Wings of a Hero* by Sheila Reid (Vanwell Publishing Ltd., Ontario, Canada).

3. Each aerodrome on the Trans-Canada Airway had a radio navigation station with two pairs of highly directional antennas. One pair transmitted in the precise direction of the aerodrome located to the east of the radio station, and the other pair in the precise direction of the aerodrome located to the west of the radio station. Within each pair, one antenna broadcast Dots, the other broadcast Dashes, and when an aeroplane was exactly in the middle of the airway, the pilot heard a continuous tone in his earphones. If he drifted too far to one side or the other, the Dots or the Dashes would become distinguishable. The pilot would then correct his direction of flight until the tone once more became continuous. The system was an aid to visual navigation at night, or in daytime when the terrain was covered with snow. The final part of a flight required the pilot to recognize flashing electric beacons at his destination aerodrome.

4. Some philatelists who have purchased first-day covers which were autographed *"Roy Brown"* to commemorate the inauguration of air mail routes in the bush have been disturbed to find that the signature does not even remotely resemble the one on Captain A. Roy Brown's combat reports. There were two Roy Browns-Arthur Roy and Francis Roy. Both were Canadians, and their respective wives had rather similar names. Each served in the Royal Air Force as a fighter pilot in the Great War, and in the 1920s each became interested in aerial transport as a livelihood.

Francis Roy Brown was born in Stockton, Manitoba, in 1896. When war broke out, he joined the Canadian Cycle Corps and served in the battles of Ypres, Vimy Ridge and Passchendaele. He transferred to the Royal Flying Corps in 1917 and took pilot training in England. He was posted to RAF 204 Squadron (previously Naval 4), and just prior to the end of the war his *Camel*, No. D8218, was hit by anti-aircraft fire over Belgium. He succeeded in making a forced landing just inside Allied territory, but completely wrecked his machine in the process. In 1928 Francis Roy Brown joined Western Canada Airways as a pilot and rose to be in charge of its airmail service at Moose Jaw.

On 9 September 1929 Fokker Super Universal No. G-CASK of Western Canada Airways and Fairchild FC-2 No. CF-AA0 of Dominion Explorers, carrying officials from a mining company, failed to arrive at their destination in the Northwest Territories, bad weather had forced them to land, and they had become stuck due to lack of fuel. Francis Roy Brown and eight other WCA pilots participated in the search operation, during which his own aeroplane also became a casualty and he was marooned on a frozen lake for twelve days. The rescue party first found Francis Roy Brown and then the mining officials and their pilots. They all reached safety on 2 December without any lives being lost.

In 1934, Francis Roy Brown and three other pilots started a bush flying company called Wings Limited, and he became well known all over western Canada. Between 1937 and 1939, Wings and General Airways were parts of United Air Services Ltd., but whether the two Roys actually met is unknown. In 1942 when United Air Services was absorbed by Canadian Airways Ltd., Francis worked for MacDonald Brothers Aircraft in Winnipeg as a test pilot.

Francis Roy Brown.

When Arthur Roy Brown died in 1944, Mrs Edith Brown (note the spelling of "Edith"), the wife of Francis Roy Brown, was surprised to receive a phone call consoling her on the death of her husband, who was standing right there beside her. She was to receive many more calls and a large number of cards that week. Heart problems terminated Francis Roy Brown's flying career in 1954, and when he died in 1960, Arthur Roy Brown's widow, Edythe, received dozens of letters and cards of condolence.

Confusion between F. Roy Brown and A. Roy Brown sometimes occurs in deeply researched books on Canadian airlines. The error usually appears in the index where the adventures of Roy Brown the bush pilot are listed under A. Roy Brown the airline owner. However, once the reader becomes aware of the different types and areas of activity of A. Roy Brown and F. Roy Brown, it is not difficult to distinguish between them. One such book also lists a Roy A. Brown but provides no further information on his identity or activities.

A brief summary of the careers of the two Roy Browns reads as follows:

> **A. Roy Brown** served in various Royal Naval Air Service squadrons and finally in Royal Air Force 209 Squadron. After the war, he founded and was the principal shareholder of General Airways Limited, but he never piloted any of its aeroplanes. General Airways carried freight and people, but no airmail, over a large part of eastern Canada. He signed his name "A.R. Brown".
>
> **F. Roy Brown** served in Royal Air Force 204 Squadron. After the war he was hired by Western Canada Airways Limited as a pilot. In 1934 he left that company and co-founded Wings Limited. He was an active pilot in this company, which carried airmail and people all over western Canada. He signed his name "Roy Brown."

There is no evidence that anyone named Roy A. Brown existed in the airline world at that time.

5. Overloading can be ruled out as the cause of the accident since No. CF-AOL had made a successful departure from Lake Father. Seaplanes are notoriously sensitive to excess weight. Halfway along the undersurface of the floats there is a "step." During the takeoff run of an

overloaded seaplane, the floats will not lift onto the step; their entire length remains in the water, creating too much drag for the seaplane to reach flying speed. At the time of the accident, the gross weight of No. CF-AOL would have been less than at departure from Lake Father. The takeoff and climb-out, plus the forty-mile journey to Lake Pusticamica, would have consumed 8–10 gallons of fuel, thereby reducing the gross weight by 64–80 pounds.

6. Unless it is the radio type which sends a pulse signal to ground and receives the echo, an aircraft altimeter is basically a barometer with a dial calibrated in feet or metres. If barometric pressure changes during flight, a pilot who has neglected to apply the necessary correction will not be flying at the height indicated on his altimeter. When weather is deteriorating, the barometric pressure generally decreases, which means an altimeter will read high. Therefore, unless compensation is applied, the aeroplane will be flying lower than the indication on the cockpit altimeter. The error can easily be of 500 feet; 1,000 feet is not uncommon. 2,000 feet is not unknown. An uncompensated decrease in barometric pressure of 1.1 inches of mercury—for example, from 30.1 (fair weather) to 29.0 (rain) — will cause an altimeter to indicate 1,000 feet above true. Measured on a metric barometer, the equivalent pressure change would be 35 millibars.

Prior to takeoff a pilot turns the barometric-pressure- adjusting knob on his altimeter to match the barometric pressure at his airfield of departure. To be certain his altimeter is indicating the correct height above ground while he is en route, a pilot will radio for the barometric pressure at intermediate points and shortly before reaching his destination. When he is flying over uninhabited territory, en-route altimeter compensation settings are not available; therefore, a pilot will maintain a safe margin of height above ground. However, on a day with a heavy layer of very low cloud, a pilot with engine trouble could easily fly into tree-tops as he descended.

7. The term "wind shear" means a sudden, unexpected reversal of the direction from which the wind is blowing. Ever since the crash of a large passenger jet at Pittsburgh airport in the 1970s, the presence of wind shear of any degree of severity in the vicinity of an airport has been

communicated to pilots who are about to arrive or depart. When severe wind shear is detected, airport operations are suspended until it ceases. The danger occurs as described below.

Aeroplanes takeoff and land into the wind so that the speed of the wind adds to the speed of the aeroplane through the air. If the direction of a 10mph wind suddenly reverses, 20 mph is instantaneously subtracted from the airspeed with a consequent, immediate loss of lift. In an aeroplane of the size of the Bellanca flown by Clarkie, such a wind shear encountered at cruising speed en route would produce nothing more than an uncomfortable downward bump, commonly termed an air pocket. However, just after take-off, when an aeroplane is still close to the ground, or during a landing approach, a sudden 20mph reduction in speed through the air can be exciting. In the case of the sudden reversal of a 20mph wind (40 mph wind shear), an aeroplane which has just taken off or is on final approach to a landing may drop far enough to strike the ground before the pilot can regain control. The sensation may be compared to a chair collapsing. The descent is so sudden that the seated person has no time to stiffen his or her knees to avoid hitting the floor.

8. The General Airways fleet consisted of the following aircraft over the years. The list was compiled by Denny May.

      G-CATJ   de Havilland 60X Cirrus Moth, 1928–1929. Sold.
      G-CAJJ   Fairchild FC-2 *Razorback*, 1928–1935. Destroyed by fire during pre-heating of engine.
      CF-AFW   Fokker Super Universal, 1929–1930. Destroyed by fire during takeoff.
      CF-ADR   de Havilland 60M Gipsy Moth, 1929–1934. Sold.
      CF-AOL   Bellanca CH-300, 1930–1936. Destroyed in a crash at Lake Pusticamica just after take-off. Pilots Clarke and Millham and all six passengers killed.
      CF-ATN   Bellanca CH-300, 1932–1938. Sold.
      CF-AND   Bellanca Pacemaker, 1932–1939. Sold.
      CF-API   de Havilland 83 Fox Moth, 1933–1937. Sold.
      CF-AWO   Stinson SRE-5A Reliant, 1934–1936. Destroyed in a runaway crash at Siscoe Mine. No-one on board at the time.

CF-AEC   Bellanca CH-300, 1934–1939. Sold.
CF-ANX   Bellanca Senior Pacemaker, 1935–1939. Sold.
CF-AYW   Stinson SR-7B Reliant, 1936–1937. Sold.
CF-AZH   Stinson SR-7B Reliant, 1936–1937. Sold.
CF-AZZ   Stinson SR-8DM Reliant, 1936–1938. Sold.
CF-BAG   Stinson SR-8DM Reliant, 1936–1940. Sold.
CF-BAN   Noorduyn Norseman Mk IV, 1937–1938. Sold.
CF-BEI   Stinson SR-9EM, 1937–1938. Destroyed in a crash after shedding a wing in flight. Pilot Tim McCoy was killed.

General Airways staff, over the years, included the following people. Their pilot's licence numbers, where known, are given in parentheses. The names were provided by Denny May and the late Theodore Crayston.

Baillie, Frank	- pilot
Baker, Ross	- engineer
Berrie, Cyrus	
Bogart, Curt	- pilot
Brown, A. Roy	- company president
Brown, Howard	- Noranda base manager
Brown, Norman	- engineer
Bruneau, Tony	- engineer
Casey, Peter	- radio operator
Clarke, Wilson	- chief pilot (248) and general manager
Crump, Bert	- radio operator
Dingwall, Gordon	- pilot (267)
Dixon, (unknown)	
Edmison, Kelly	- pilot
Edward, G.K. (Gath)	- pilot
Fisher, Frank	- pilot (496)
Gunter, Dick	- pilot
Hill, Stuart	- pilot
Jellison, Earl	
Jones, Jack	- engineer
Langford, Harold	- pilot (253)
Mahon, Tom	- pilot

McCoy, Tim — pilot
Millham, George — engineer and trainee pilot
O'Brien, Geoffrey — pilot (386)
Paget, "Bun" — pilot
Phillips, "Bert" — engineer
Pliske, Brett — pilot (302) and Amos base manager
Pope, George — radio operator
Sarsfield, "Red" — mechanic
Stalport, Aimé — engineer
Turner, Bill — engineer
Twist, Pat — pilot
Ward, George — pilot

ACKNOWLEDGEMENTS

The photograph of Flight Sub-Lieutenant Gerald E. Nash, the story of his capture, and his parole card were provided by his son, Gerald A. Nash, LL.B.

The photograph of Francis Roy Brown was supplied by the late Theodore Crayston.

End of Volume 3 of 6 volumes, ebook edition.

CHAPTER ELEVEN

EARLY FAMILY MEMORIES
(1919 to 1939)

After the war, on Tuesday, 18 March, 1919, Captain Roy Brown had returned to Carleton Place to begin his demobilization leave. He was still under medical treatment for the injuries suffered in his crash at Marske-by-the-Sea and was to have physiotherapy at Christie Street Veterans' Hospital in Toronto. In those days this was mainly massage.

Margaret Brown Harmon continues his story. Some friends from Ottawa invited my father and his mother to dinner. Mrs Emma Cummings was also invited, but (and this is where fate stepped in) her brother-in-law, Tom Monypenny, was unable to take her there in his car. So with some difficulty, she managed to persuade Tom's daughter, Edythe, to drive her there and to join them all for the festivities.

Edythe Monypenny was working as a volunteer masseuse with the Red Cross, at Christie Street Veterans' Hospital. She was known by the interesting nickname of "Sister Cash." During the evening Edythe was introduced to a Royal Air Force officer, Roy Brown. Finding the name familiar, she asked him whether by any chance he was the "Roy Brown" who had missed every single appointment made with her for massage treatment. My father admitted that he was one and the same! This, however, did not discourage him from inviting her out for dinner and dancing at the Brant Inn, a fashionable supper club some twenty miles from Toronto. She enthusiastically accepted the invitation but told him she could only borrow her father's car on very special occasions. This apparently was not one of them, so Roy was forced to hire a car. This was very upscale and expensive: in those days a hired car came with a driver; rental cars were still far into the future.

Expense and all, the evening must have gone well, for on 19 February, 1920 they were married with all the bells and whistles. The best man at the wedding was Arthur Whealy, the flight commander who upon going home on leave to Canada in mid-1917 had been ordered to hand his Sopwith Camel over to my father. Unfortunately, when Whealy returned to France, his pride and joy was no more; my father had worn it out on the long, twice-daily patrols over enemy territory.

The happy couple moved into an apartment in Toronto, and due to its small size my father's souvenirs from the Red Baron's triplane had to go. He gave the pilot's seat and the autographed black cross to the Canadian Military Institute in Toronto. The piece of a wing tip and the fabric covering from the left side of the rudder were given to Billy Bishop, who hung them on a wall of his office. Times were hard in those days, and it was fortunate for them that Grandfather Monypenny was one of the owners of Imperial Varnish and Color Company. To survive, my parents had many a nourishing meal with the Monypennys.

There is an amusing story in connection with Grandfather Monypenny's purchase of a Gray Dort car a year or two earlier. In those days, driving licences were not required; car salesmen had to teach their customers how to drive. Just before one particular lesson Grandfather asked my mother, Edythe, to come along with him to learn a little more about driving. After the lesson he drove with the salesman and Edythe to the factory, and as he turned into the driveway, Grandfather slammed the accelerator to the floor, having confused it with the brake. The salesman tried with all his might to pull my grandfather's leg off the pedal. The salesman lost the contest, and with the accelerator still floored, the car crashed into a tree. Grandfather said not a word. He stepped out of the brand–new scratched and dented car, walked into the factory and returned with a can of varnish and a paintbrush. Then to everyone's astonishment, he calmly proceeded to varnish the damaged parts of the tree. He wished to protect it from all sorts of destructive worms and insects. Edythe wished that the earth would open up and swallow the car, the salesman and even her father.

The Gray Company of Chatham, Ontario, Canada, a manufacturer of marine engines, produced the Dort car from approximately 1920 to 1930.

Roy Brown returned to his accounting and business management studies, but the severe head injuries, and especially the concussion, which he had suffered in the 1918 plane crash, prevented him from continuing. Thanks to a little nepotism, he obtained a post at the Imperial Varnish and Color Company as manager of sales promotions. He worked in the head office in Toronto for twelve years, eventually rising to office manager.

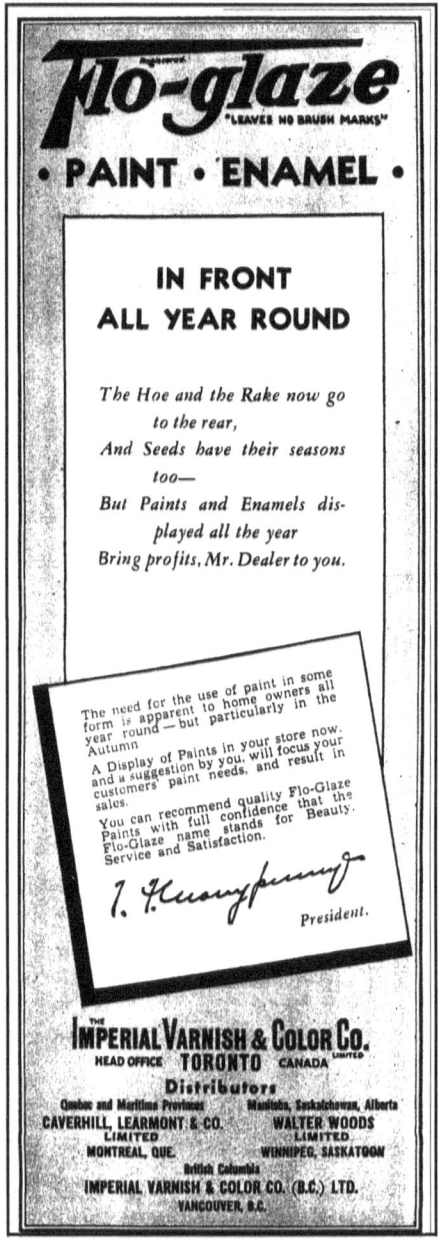

A trade magazine advertisement for Flo-glaze paint.

In the 1920s there was such a need for aerial communications in the far-flung, snowy north of Canada that several wartime pilots decided to start small, private air–transport companies to service the widely separated mining communities. "Wop" May and Francis Roy Brown (whose wife was named Edith) are two who come to mind. To my father, despite his terrible injuries, the pull of the air was still strong and his thoughts often turned to profitable ventures up there in the skies.

Two events enabled him to turn his thoughts into reality. The first was a sad one. On 25 November 1926 his father, Morton, died from the delayed results of injuries suffered a year or two earlier, and Dad inherited his share of H. Brown & Sons. The second event was the publication of Floyd Gibbons' book the *Red Knight of Germany* which carried a detailed account of the life of the German air ace Baron Manfred von Richthofen. Coincidence played a part here, for the Great War air ace Archie Whitehouse, who worked for the American magazine *Liberty*, was simultaneously presenting a series of thrilling air–combat adventure stories obtained from other pilots. Archie had little trouble acquiring their stories since *Liberty* not only paid for them but paid well. A little editing here and there made the heroes' super heroic and the enemy not too courageous. Intrigued by Floyd Gibbons' book, in which Captain A. Roy Brown played a starring role, Archie decided to make a proposition to my father—to acquire his story. The funds derived from the two events described above were sufficient for my father to found a company, General Airways Limited.

The accident in which my grandfather Morton Brown was injured deserves explanation. In his capacity as church warden he had been up on a ladder, inspecting a heavy snowfall on the roof of the Presbyterian Church at Carleton Place. Unfortunately the sun had been shining for a while and the adhesion of the snow to the tiles had weakened. The snow began to slide and to push against the top of the ladder on which Grandfather Brown was standing. The snow, the ladder and my poor grandfather crashed to the earth. He recovered from the shock of his sudden meeting with terra firma but was never the same man again.

My grandfather seemed to be accident prone. Another close call occurred in his boathouse on Lake Mississippi near Carleton Place.

Grandfather Monypenny, who was on his way from Toronto to Ottawa, stopped in for a chat with Grandfather Brown. He found him in the boathouse, working beneath his boat as it hung by just one sling from the rafters. He suggested that Grandfather Brown add a second sling as a precaution. Then they went to lunch. Fortunately Grandfather Brown took his advice. Shortly afterwards, the original sling broke. Where was Grandfather Brown? He was under the boat.

To continue the story: I was born in May 1922. After seeing me, my parents thought they could do a lot better, and so my sister, Barbara Joan, was born in May 1923. My brother, Donald, came along three and a half years later to complete the family, and he was the apple of their eye.

From left to right: Roy Brown's children, Barbara Joan, Donald Morton and Margaret Elizabeth (circa 1928).

In 1928 General Airways Ltd. began operations, and aircraft were acquired one by one as routes were added. Father never piloted any of his aeroplanes although he often flew as a passenger. He remained in the paint business until his new company had grown to the point that it would support his family. In 1934 he left Imperial Varnish and Color and transferred all his activities to the General Airways company offices in downtown Toronto.

As children we loved his secretary, Miss Pritchard, and she reciprocated wholeheartedly. Our family only had one car so we children were frequently taken to the office when Mother drove there to pick up my father, and we would have wonderful visits with this delightful lady. One day Miss Pritchard commented to my two-year-old brother, *"Donny, you look so pale. Are you all right?"* He replied, *"I always look a little puny, but I feel fine."* He was an adorable blond, curly-haired boy, however, very pale complexion.

My father was always having health problems. Thirty-two broken bones caused by various escapades and accidents during his life, some of them quite serious, had their cumulative effect, he was also subjected to many surgeries. It was, however, the final flying accident in England that really ruined his health. I remember one serious health problem that arose while we were still living at 97 Garfield Avenue in Toronto. Dad had an emergency appendectomy, which in those days carried an extremely high risk. After convalescing at home for some weeks, the great day finally arrived when he was allowed to go down the stairs, albeit very slowly and very carefully. A celebration was in order, so my Aunt Doris, grandfather and grandmother were invited to dinner. The meal over, we children were sent upstairs to play in the den where there was a cosy fireplace with tall, leaded casement windows on each side.

Not having much to do, we shortly became bored. Then inspiration struck! We concocted a plan to liven things up a bit, but with no idea of how dire the consequences would be. Barbara and I hid our "puny," by then four-year-old brother in a closet and ran to the head of the open staircase, calling down that Donny had fallen out of the window. It was a plausible tale, for both windows opened over the gravel driveway one-and-a-half storeys below.

Pandemonium ensued! My father, who until that moment had only been allowed to hobble around and even then with assistance, sped down the stairs and out the door. Not finding the apple of his eye there, he ran into the backyard to check the other windows. Only one person present, my aunt Doris, did not panic. She was suspicious, for being a paediatrician she knew the tricks that children could dream up. She marched straight up the stairs and into the den, where she immediately found Donald in the closet. Unfortunately I was the eldest and to this day I will never forget the spankings I received from each and every loving relative present. I am happy to report that my father suffered no severe ill effects from his sprint down the stairs.

My brother, Donald, as a child seemed to have a sixth sense—intuition, mental telepathy, whatever you care to call it. Many children have this ability when they are young but lose it as they grow older. On one occasion, when Donald was about five years old, my father had gone to New York City on a business trip. At bed-time Donald became very agitated and repeatedly asked my mother, *"Have you called Daddy?"*

"No. Daddy will be home tomorrow."
"You must call Daddy. He's very sick."

Mother tried to assure him that Daddy was fine and he would be home the next day. Even after Donald was in bed, he kept calling to her over and over again, asking the same question. My mother became a little annoyed, but luckily for my brother, he fell asleep. First thing in the morning, Donald was still asking her to call Daddy who, he insisted, was very sick. Around eleven o'clock in the morning the phone rang; it was a call from a New York hospital saying that my father was in the emergency room *"very ill with ptomaine poisoning."* How Donald knew this is truly a mystery!

My brother continued to have many more such experiences. On one occasion Grandfather Monypenny called my mother to say that Grandmother had suffered some sort of terrible attack and that a doctor was on his way. Mother left hurriedly, telling the three of us that Grandmother was sick and that we should stay in the house and behave ourselves; she promised to call us as soon as she could. When she called, Donald answered the phone, and as soon as he recognized her voice he said, *"Grandmother's dead, isn't she, Mommy?"* It was true. She had died from a heart attack.

My father away on business much of the time; however, when he was home, he was very, very "home." He came into our lives in a big way, joining us in all sorts of activities, such as sandlot baseball. Normally the children with the greatest ability at sports were the first to be chosen when teams were being picked; this placed me either last or second to last. When my father was there, it was a great day for me:

I was chosen much earlier. A real feather in my cap! Dad encouraged us in all kinds of activities—baseball, skating, hockey, swimming, diving and even the lowly game of marbles. We played all kinds of card games, but my father drew the line at teaching us to play poker, experienced though he was!

The family home at 97 Garfield Avenue, Toronto, many years after the Browns' departure.

With all this activity going on, scraped knees were common. Mother would apply iodine liberally to knees or any other part of our anatomy she deemed necessary. Loud screaming and yelling would accompany the procedure. At some point in our young lives Dad told us the story about being in the hospital for a very long time after his terrible crash in England. Amongst his many injuries he had had two holes in his chest, one on each side, and every morning a nurse had poured a small bottle of tincture of iodine into each hole. This story effectively stopped any whining whatsoever from us, no matter where the iodine was daubed. Some pretty clever psychology was applied there as well as iodine.

Mother brilliantly changed the criminal way of life that my sister and I had chosen. For some years Barbara and I had been a little "light-fingered". We would check Mother's purse, and if she had enough change, we took whatever we thought would be undetectable. Mother, who was the treasurer of the Big Sisters Association, a charitable organization, had become suspicious but was never able to catch us in the act of thievery. One day she left a nickel on her desk. Normally we would never bother with such small change; we were into the "big time"! I scooped up the coin, and we headed for the popcorn wagon at the end of the street, where we bought two candy apples for a nickel. As we walked along McClennan Avenue, Mom and Dad drove by in the car. This meant *trouble*, for they did not allow us to buy candy apples from that particular vendor and, worse than that, they knew we had no money! No sooner had I taken a bite than a worm crawled out of my apple, so I promptly threw it away. We thought nothing of the stolen nickel; for us, that was small time.

That afternoon, just before school closed, there was a knock at the classroom door. It was Mother, holding Barbara by the hand. She said to the teacher, *"Would you have Margaret Brown get her coat, because I would like her to come with me."* Having forgotten about the earlier minor crime, I was all excited and asked my mother, *"Where are we going? Are we going downtown?"* She replied, *"No, you are going to jail. You stole a nickel which belonged to the Big Sisters. That was theft and there is no way to repay it."*

Our feet dragged all the way to the car where Donald awaited us, and off to the police station we went. I remember the location so well that to this day I could show you exactly where it is. Not saying a word, my mother went into the police station alone. (This should have, but did not, "tip us off.")

Donald was elated to see his older sisters getting into trouble and gleefully tormented us about our fate while we waited for Mother. She returned and took Barbara and me inside. Instantly Barbara was on her knees begging for mercy. I, being older, made a valiant effort to maintain some composure. The policeman said to us, *"You have stolen a nickel. This is a very serious matter. That nickel was to help poor people."*

I admitted the crime. More wails from Barbara.

"Do you want to see the cell where you will be locked up if you ever steal again?" asked the policeman.

By now, even I had butterflies, and we of course had no desire to see the cell. Relentlessly he took us down a dark corridor and showed us what threatened to be our new abode. Barbara and I assured him that we would never, ever steal again. He took us back to his office and asked us if we would like to see the whip from which we would receive one lash for every nickel we stole. That had even less appeal for us than visiting that barred cell! What he would have done had we replied, "Yes," I will never know. What I do know is that Mother's wisdom brought our criminal careers to a screeching halt! From that day to this, although far from perfect, I have never stolen a red cent.

From Left to Right: Barbara, Donald and Margaret (circa 1932).

One more example of my parents' use of psychology took place when we were older. Dad knew that we would be coming into contact with young people who drank, so one day he casually asked us if we would do him a favour: *"If you ever want to have a drink, would you have your first drink with me?"* So when high-school friends thought the smart thing to do was to drink, Barbara and I were not in the least interested because we knew we could drink at home any old time. Consequently we did not "bend our elbows" until years later after we had joined the air force.

It seems to me now, as I look back, that the success of General Airways allowed us to live in the lap of luxury. We had a lovely house in Toronto, went to private school and spent our summers at one of my Grandfather Monypenny's cottages on Lake Simcoe—all this during the Depression. Summers were a happy time, even exciting, especially when one of the General Airways seaplanes came in on the lake. In the 1930s that was quite a novelty. Boats from miles around would gather so fast, and so many of them, that the plane often could not touch down until they were frantically waved away by people on the shore. My father was not always on the plane, but no matter; we knew and liked all the pilots. They often had a swim or took us for a "flip." sometimes staying for dinner. Clarkie ("Mr Clarke" to us) was Dad's chief pilot. I well remember him taking us up for a ride late one afternoon. What aerobatic stunts he performed I'll never know because I could not see; my head was down between my knees, almost to the floor, and hard as I might try, I could not sit up. It was embarrassing for an eight-year-old. So until I was able to pull my head up, I tried to act as though this was quite normal and I was looking around on the floor for something of interest. I later learned that he was probably in a steeply banked turn.

My mother often joined my father on business trips and in 1936 they went to Dayton, Ohio. My father knew that Orville Wright, a confirmed bachelor, was still living there; his brother Wilbur had died of typhoid fever in 1912. Orville had owned the school where Dad had learned to fly, and he wondered aloud to Mother whether he should pay him a visit. Before she could answer, Dad demurred, saying that a man of Wright's station and stature would certainly not be interested in seeing a student from days gone by. My mother encouraged him, saying that Mr Wright might be lonely and would really enjoy a visit. Somewhat reluctantly my father approached Orville Wright's mansion, my mother not allowing him any other course. When the housekeeper answered the door, my father asked her to inform Mr Wright that Roy Brown was there and to enquire whether Mr Wright would like to meet him briefly for old times' sake. As it turned out, Orville, by then quite elderly, could not have been more delighted. Not only did he have time for a visit, but he insisted that it be a long one. My mother and father stayed with the legendary man well into the night and left with his best wishes ringing in their ears.

My mother told me this story and added that Orville seemed a charming old man, leading a lonely life with his housekeeper. Mother had managed to disappear for quite a while during the visit so that Orville and Dad would not feel that they should restrict their conversation to subjects in which she could participate. This visit had an unexpected, pleasant corollary.

In 1937 the Early Birds, an organization of people who had learned to fly before 17 December, 1916, arranged for the Edison Institute to purchase the Wright Brothers' workshop and the Wright family home in Dayton, Ohio. Both buildings were moved to Greenfield Village, an outdoor collection of historical buildings open to the public and situated near the Ford Museum at Dearborn, Michigan. On 16 April 1938, the anniversary of Wilbur Wright's birth, Henry and Edsel Ford presided at a ceremony in which the two buildings were dedicated in honour of Orville and in memory of his late brother.

Orville Wright was the guest of honour, and he obviously had had a hand in the selection of some of the guests. It would appear that he remembered the flyboy student who had taken the trouble to visit him for old times' sake, for my father was not merely invited but placed at the head table of the banquet which followed the ceremony. Beside him was seated his close friend Lloyd Breadner, then a senior officer in the Royal Canadian Air Force; and but a chair away sat Walter Brookins, one of his 1915 flying instructors who, in 1910, had become the first American civilian to be taught to fly by the Wright Brothers. There must have been much talk of the early days, of old comrades and of sleeping in the leaking hangar with the aeroplanes for company. All who attended the banquet received a commemorative book which had as its frontispiece a print, made directly from the original glass plate negative, of the Wright Brothers' first successful powered flight. I still have that book.

The Dedication Banquet at Greenfield Village. *Counting from the right*: (2) Walter Brookins, (4) A. Roy Brown, (5) Lloyd Breadner, (7) Edsel Ford, (9) Orville Wright, (10) Henry Ford.

Also present at the banquet was my father's old 1918 colleague from the Royal Air Force 209 Squadron, Wop May, who was a well-known bush pilot in northern Canada and now managing the Alberta operations for Canadian Airlines Ltd. in Edmonton.

By 1936 there had been a lot of talk between the owners of private airlines about combining into groups to prevent a new, well-financed company from eating them up one by one, but nothing much came of it. There had also been tentative moves by Members of Parliament in Ottawa towards legislation to establish such an airline but one that would be owned and operated by the government.

Wilfrid R. May and A. Roy Brown at Greenfield Village, Michigan, on 16 April 1938. The appearance of both Wop May's right eye and Roy Brown's raised left eyebrow resulted from surgery following injuries. Wop May had suffered an accident while machining a part on a lathe.

On Sunday evening, 24 May 1936, Dad drove us all home from a weekend at the cottage, and as he approached the house we noticed a beautiful, long, yellow convertible parked at the curb. We recognized it instantly: it belonged to Boaden (Bo) Burns, a business friend of my father's. Instead of coming into the house, Dad went over to talk to him. Moments later I saw Dad leaning his head up against the garage door, looking as though he were very ill. Obviously something terrible had happened. When Dad came back into the house, he told us, *"There has been a terrible crash. Clarkie and his passengers have all been killed."* This crash took place shortly before the political rhetoric intensified in favour of a single government-owned airline, covering all of Canada.

By the beginning of 1938 my father realized that a Canadian "Official" airline, with Treasury funding and the compulsory powers of the government behind it, was inevitable and that it would eventually take over all air transport within Canada. He decided not to wait for that to happen and in a gradual process withdrew his aircraft from the routes and sold them. It was a clever move; it would have been foolish to hang on and then be forced into a fire sale. Trans–Canada Airlines had been formed, and the routes which could be flown by the private airlines were progressively restricted until many operations became totally unprofitable.

In 1939 my father closed General Airways, which had a major effect upon our lives. He joined a stockbrokerage house owned by Jack Cameron, and we then had to cut our cloth according to our new, reduced income. Dad sold our lovely home on Garfield Avenue, and we moved into a very nice rental house on Alexander Boulevard in North Toronto, near Grandfather Monypenny's home. My sister and I had to leave Havergal College so fast it would make your head spin, and we transferred to Lawrence Park Collegiate, a brand new, state-of-the-art high school.

During all these years there was one subject my father preferred to avoid and that was the death of the Red Baron or any part he may have played in it. Initially he freely and pleasantly replied to reporters' questions, but when he saw the published versions of the interviews, he hardly recognized them. As a result he later absolutely refused to comment to reporters, but he found that this tended to create the very situation he was trying to avoid. Not all the would-be interviewers had the courage to return to their superiors with an empty notepad, so for self-preservation some would rewrite tales, true or false, which they had read elsewhere and submit their "story." After many such experiences, Dad decided to satisfy them with some actual facts rather than remain silent, but he could not win; some of the interviewers simply took my father's words as a basis and proceeded to fabricate from thereon.

One example of how things can get twisted occurred in 1929. *Liberty* magazine published a fictional adventure story submitted by a lady named Royal Brown. Lo and behold, the word spread that father's true name was Royal! To this day some people still believe it.

CHAPTER TWELVE

LISNACLIN FARM AND THE ROYAL CANADIAN AIR FORCE, WOMEN'S DIVISION
(1939 to 1945)

Dad's health had been slowly deteriorating. Constantly working inside offices, breathing polluted air, was not conducive to good health. In 1939 doctors gave him one year to live if he did not move from the city to the fresh air of the countryside. Quite aware of his physical condition, my father agreed with the doctors and immediately he and my mother, despite being city-born and bred, moved lock, stock and barrel to a farm. They found a bargain, a 176–acre farm near Stouffville, Ontario, which they purchased for payment of back taxes from a man named March. This farm had a creek, four houses for hired men and their families, to say nothing of a barn, chicken house, and piggery. There was also an apple and pear orchard, and all this only twenty-three miles from the city limits of Toronto. However, the property was in a state of ill repair; it was obvious that Mr. March had let more things go than just his taxes. My parents named the farm "Lisnaclin" after the farm where my grandfather had been born in Ireland.

Many repairs were made, especially to the main house and the barn. My parents proceeded to acquire a milking herd, horses, pigs, chickens, dogs, cats to catch the rats, and George, a huge bull—one of the largest bulls ever known to mankind. Many crops were planted on many acres. My sister and I hated the whole operation, whether it was digging potatoes, collecting eggs, working in the hayloft or cleaning out the pigsty. Luckily for me, I had only one year left of high school, so I was soon off to college and city life. My brother and sister did not fare so well; they were younger and stayed on the farm until high–school graduation.

Lisnaclin Farm, *left to right*: the sheds, the barn and the family house.

My father, armed with his measuring tapes and every government pamphlet ever issued on Holstein cattle, scoured the countryside, carefully selecting his herd. Little did we then know of the success that would come from his new found skills. He had chosen a cow, Doncrest Pegtop Burke, that a few years later would break the world's record for the amount of milk and butterfat content on two milkings a day. In one year she produced 3,120 imperial gallons (3,747 U.S. gallons; 14,184 litres) of milk. Sadly, my father died less than a year before his achievement would be recognized. My mother and brother were wined and dined in Toronto at receptions and dinners where they were presented with trophies and even an engraved silver tray. Mother sold this $250 cow to a Canadian buyer for $5,000; she was later offered $10,000 by American buyers.

Doncrest Pegtop Burke and Sam Adams the herdsman on prize-giving day, 6 February, 1945.

As he scoured the country for cattle, he made a particular selection that was not at all successful—it was a goat. Goats were supposed to keep all the cows in a highly euphoric state so they would give even larger quantities of milk. Our "Billy" wandered freely throughout the barn. At every opportunity, whatever Dad's position was—just as long as his back was turned—the goat would sneak over quietly, then taking the last few steps in a rush, he butted, bunted or rammed my father! It didn't take Billy long to seal his own fate. I guess the poor goat ended up in the stew pot.

In February 1943, my father was offered a position by Maclean's Publishing as editor of a magazine named *Canadian Aviation*. He replaced Ronald Keith who was on war service. This endeavour did not last more than a year for two reasons: it was not what the "doctor ordered," and it left Mother with too much responsibility. By then there were three hired men and lots of work to oversee. Once, her duties even included having to deliver a baby for the wife of one of the hired men—

a very unnerving experience!

One morning each fall, ten or more hungry farmers would descend upon Lisnaclin at some unearthly hour, such as five o'clock, for breakfast. The bill of fare was hearty indeed—fruit, juices, hot and cold cereals, bacon, sausage's, steak and eggs, toast, sweet rolls, pies. Then they worked for hours threshing the grain. Only one farmer in the area owned a threshing machine, and he hired it out as required. By one o'clock all the men returned to the house, where the table groaned with the sumptuous mid-day meal. One can imagine the frantic cooking that must have gone on for weeks ahead as the big day approached. However, everyone went home tired, happy and exceedingly well fed; "doggy bags" were not allowed. I am sure the farmers' wives must have collapsed in a heap after their turn to feed all these calorie-burning men; we certainly did.

Donald Morton Brown with his red setter, Timmy, in 1941.

Practically all these hardworking people who farmed in our neighbourhood were Mennonites. There was a Mennonite church up the gravel road from us, right before the store. The store was owned by the Smiths and, complete with its wood-burning, pot-bellied stove, was a welcoming, cosy meeting place for everyone. As sophisticated city transplants, we were quite amazed at the different life style of the

Mennonites. Their church had an entrance for men and another one for women. In their home's, no newspapers could be read, no radios could be listened to, and yet they would question my father at great length about world news and the war with Hitler. This puzzled us all. Every once in a while, a male Mennonite delegation would be sent to visit "he new people on the block." On the first occasion they requested that my mother stop wearing shorts. She agreed that in deference to them she would not be seen in shorts "off the farm," but she intended to wear them when and where she wished on her own property. No doubt, mother would be sitting in her favourite chair, with a drink in one hand and maybe a cigarette in the other, as they tried to straighten out her life.

Another time, a delegation asked us to sign a petition to dismiss the teacher who taught in the one–room schoolhouse nearby. It happened that Mother liked this particular teacher very much and they had become quite friendly. The teacher was to be fired in a hurry because she had been caught "huggin' and kissin'" the janitor down in the basement by the furnace. Mother's reply was, "I really don't know whether or not I would like to hug and kiss the janitor down in the basement by the furnace because I have never met him but if she enjoys hugging and kissing the janitor, that is her business and hers alone." I am sure that effectively took care of whether or not she would sign the petition.

With my father going off daily to Mclean's Publishing and my Mother having to keep track of what she wore and where, she decided she needed a little help in the house, so she hired a maid; unfortunately the girl was not too bright. One day after lunch, Mother was sitting in her favourite chair by the living–room window, sipping her coffee, when the maid came up beside her and spent a great deal of time peering through the windowpane at the scenery. First she looked up, then down and then around and then did it all over again. Mother looked at the girl, and then she too stood up and looked all around outside, trying to discover what this girl saw. Finally curiosity got the better of her and she asked, "What in the world do you see out there?" The girl replied in a monotone, "Don't look like Wednesday, do it?"

In 1942 my sister and I joined the Royal Canadian Air Force, Women's Division. Barb was just out of Aurora High School, and I had completed one year at the University of Toronto. We enlisted as the lowest of the low (airwoman second class) choosing radar as our trade. We had never even heard of the word "radar"; the technology had been kept hush-hush since 1938, and we only chose the trade because it required four years of high school, the highest qualification on the list. We were sent to Rockcliffe Air Force Base near Ottawa, Ontario, for basic training and spent six long weeks confined to barracks. We washed dishes and scrubbed floors; we learned to march and to salute anything that moved. We were given physicals and shots galore; TABTs were particularly deadly and landed me in the hospital for over a week. Even there, when I was beginning to think I might rejoin the human race, I had to gather trays from the rooms, wash dishes and perform lots of KP (kitchen policing). This was not exactly what I had signed up for. So, life could only improve, and it did.

Wearing smart, new uniforms, Airwomen Second Class Margaret (left) and Barbara Brown.(right).

Barb and I graduated from basic training and then were off to a six-week radar course, also in Rockcliffe. We moved up one notch, becoming airwomen first class.

Finally the great day arrived when we had acquired sufficient radar–plotting skills to be posted to Eastern Air Command in Halifax, Nova Scotia. We lived in overflowing barracks on a Halifax Royal Canadian Air Force station, which was overcrowded with personnel waiting to go overseas. However, life was busy and interesting; it didn't hurt at all that the men greatly outnumbered the women.

One morning as we were leaving Eastern Air Command, three of us were asked if we would cross the harbour to the air force base at Dartmouth to have pictures taken for a recruiting campaign. The next thing I knew, I was wearing a flying suit, boots and gloves that were all ten sizes too large and I had a weighty parachute strapped to my back. I was then told to climb up onto the wing of a Bristol Bolingbroke, the Canadian version of the Blenheim medium bomber. This was not even in the realm of possibility, for I could scarcely walk under my own steam, so I was given a good boost onto the wing of this huge plane. I shall never forget Pilot Officer McWilliam asking me, with some concern in his voice, "What's my wife going to say when she sees these pictures?" I never found out because I only ever saw him again after they were published.

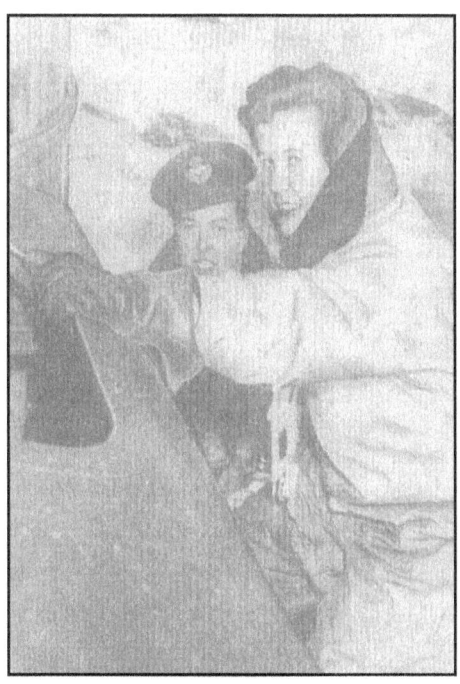

"We serve that men may fly" is the motto of the RCAF Women's Division. Off duty, however, the women sometimes take "familiarization flights," and here Airwomen First Class Margaret Brown of Stouffville climbs into a plane with the help of Pilot Officer R.P. McWilliam of Montreal. She inherits the air force tradition: her father was one of Canada's great aces of the last war.

Margaret Brown returning from her flight (of fancy).

Then "the cat was out of the bag," and everyone found out that my sister and I were the daughters of Captain A. Roy Brown. It was not long before headlines in the Toronto papers read: "Air Force Bags Daughters of A. Roy Brown."

It does not take much imagination to insert a comma between the words "bags" and "daughters." These headlines caused my mother to wonder where she fitted into the scheme of things. We had also moved up one more notch; we were now leading airwomen. My sister and I later were commissioned and worked in Halifax as officers in the filter room, where the signals from radar stations were cross-confirmed (filtered) to eliminate duplication and echoes; the results were then placed on a plotting table.

The air force was an interesting and exciting three-year education. There was always a memorable experience around the corner. To mention but a few: an afternoon spent on the battleship *Renown* - sister ship to the *Repulse*;, stunt flying in a Harvard at the air

Leading Airwomen Barbara and Margaret Brown at the launching of a Victory Loan drive in Halifax. The RCAF officer is Flight Lieutenant C.F.W. Burns, chairman of the loan committee.

base in St John's, Newfoundland, and then being grounded there by dense fog for the next two weeks; many parties on corvettes, English submarines and destroyers; and VE Day spent amidst mounds of ticker tape in Times Square, New York. Thanks to the air force, I certainly became a more tolerant person and learned to get along with people from many walks of life.

Section Officer Margaret E. Brown in 1943.

CHAPTER THIRTEEN

THE SECOND WORLD WAR AND THE 1943 PROVINCIAL ELECTION (1939 to 1944)

When the Second World War started, Roy Brown wanted to do his part, but his health was so poor that he failed the Royal Canadian Air Force medical examination. His daughter Margaret recalls one morning when he was talking to her he swayed and quickly had to grab the back of a chair; his severe head injuries from the crash in 1918 still sometimes affected his balance. She laughingly said, *"Drunk again,"* and Roy just quipped, *"Yes, and the sun isn't yet over the yardarm."*

As a result of the physical wear and tear caused by daily high–altitude patrols which lasted from one to two hours and were conducted without oxygen to breathe and at temperatures below zero degrees Fahrenheit, he looked like a man of sixty-five although he was twenty years younger. The thirty-one broken bones, later to become thirty-two, which he had incurred in various accidents, plus frequent severe headaches, did not help either. He was in no condition to serve in the RCAF, and it is not surprising that the doctors said no.

Roy had hopes of helping with the British Commonwealth Air Training Plan, but some of his public remarks on the conduct of the war appear to have upset high political authority and his services were declined. He was disappointed and is reported to have said, *"There should be some place for former pilots to tell new ones what to expect, what to avoid and thereby to save lives. The tools are different but the rules are the same."* The manner in which he fell into disfavour had revolved around newspaper and radio interviews concerning Canada's air arm.

To reassure the public on the status of the Royal Canadian Air

Force and the progress of the British Commonwealth Air Training Plan, the Canadian government led by William Lyon Mackenzie King had issued some rather optimistic statements. Roy Brown took issue with them publicly, and speaking at St Thomas, Ontario on 24 March 1940, he challenged the assertion that Canada had more than 300 modern aircraft. The truth, he claimed, was a total of 270 of all types including the ancient ones in storage. He said that the training aircraft and facilities of the air force were still on the pre-war level, and the maximum number of pilots that could be trained that year was 25 to 30, whereas 5,000 were needed. Concerning a government announcement that army co-operation squadrons had been stationed on the east and west coast's, he stated that they were squadrons in name only; each one had but two aeroplanes. In answer to a question on the equipment which had accompanied the first squadron of Canadian fliers to be sent overseas, he said, *"They had no aircraft, no tools to work on aircraft. In short, they had absolutely nothing."*

Roy informed his audience:

"The government has finally taken steps for manufacture of the primary training aeroplanes for which the need has been known for six months. Four hundred Tiger Moths have been ordered from de Havilland Canada and four hundred Fleet Finches from Fleet Aircraft of Canada, both with delivery to be completed by the end of 1941. This means that not until two and a quarter years after Canada's declaration of war can we hope to have the means to train the required number of pilots."

The De Havilland 82C Tiger Moth. Note the enclosed cockpit for protection against the bitter winter temperatures. When flying solo, the pilot occupied the rear seat to maintain the centre of balance within design limits.
Photographed by Denny May at Grande Prairie in 1974.

Many Canadian-built de Havilland 82C Tiger Moth's were fitted with a 125–hp Menasco Pirate D4 engine imported from the United States in place of the original 130–hp Gipsy Major engine. The two different types of engines introduced a problem. As seen from the pilot's seat, the de Havilland engine rotated anti-clockwise and required immediate application of left rudder to hold the aeroplane straight. The Menasco engine rotated clockwise and required right rudder. A trainee pilot who forgot the difference and applied compensation the wrong way as he opened the throttle was in for a second or two of excitement until his instructor took action.

Typical Fleet Finch, Serial No. 1001. Denny May is flying from the rear (pilot's) seat; Bob Horner is in the front. Photographed by David May in 1979.

Roy answered a question on the duties of Honorary Air Marshal W.A. Bishop by stating, *"Bill Bishop, as far as the last war is concerned and far as fighting airmen are concerned, is the greatest airman living today in what he has accomplished, but the government in Ottawa has not seen fit to give him a command."*

Concerning the claim that the British Commonwealth Air Training Plan had been inspired by the Mackenzie King government, he said, *"The claim is completely false; prior to the outbreak of war they opposed it. I have come to the conclusion that the government in Ottawa has no sincerity in its war effort."*

The immediate shortage of aeroplanes described above by Roy was overcome by large shipments from England of single-engined aircraft for pilot training and some twin-engined aircraft for aircrew training. Instruction began on 29 April 1940. As the programme gained momentum, additional aircraft for training pilots and aircrew and for combat training of fighter pilots were manufactured in Canada or purchased from the United States.[1] Two of the Royal Flying Corps, Royal Naval Air Service or Royal Air Force pilots from the Great War who served as civilian instructors or administrators were Roy's colleague Captain Wilfrid May from 209 Squadron and Captain F. Roy Brown from 204 Squadron, his namesake in the airline business.[2]

Roy's public statements aroused ire in Ottawa, and retaliation occurred. In early March 1940 a British government film entitled *the Lion Has Wings*, depicted the activities of the Royal Air Force in the war and was being shown in cinemas across Canada. Roy was asked to speak about it over a nationwide radio station link. A day or so before the broadcast the producer regretfully informed him that under Defence of Canada Regulations his talk had been banned by the Ottawa government. Roy did not accept this rebuff easily, and in a broadcast from Toronto on 11 March he stated:

> *I have had the honour of holding a commission from the King and of wearing the King's uniform, and I gave three years of my life to upholding the ideals of the Empire and democracy. Today government ministers in Ottawa are using their power to stifle those ideals. No-one can speak frankly today on the radio, but must beware of the censor and the Defence of Canada Regulations, which might have been better named the Defence of Mackenzie King Regulations. I would like to know what he has done for his country in the face of the enemy to entitle him to impose restrictions on the freedom of speech. Before the dark days of this war are past, we are going to have to make sacrifices such as we never knew before, and to do this we must have sincere, capable and honest leadership. In my opinion this can only be accomplished by a national government.*

The idea of an all-party national government, which would come to pass in England one month later under Winston Churchill, had already been suggested in Canada. The concept was not adopted, and Roy remained *persona non grata* with the powers that be. The years 1940 and 1941 passed by and the Liberal Party continued in power in Ottawa. Although many of his old RNAS and RAF colleagues had long been serving overseas with the RCAF or the RAF, or in Canada with the British Commonwealth Air Training Plan, Roy's services in Canada's war effort remained unrequired. He was not happy.[3]

In late November 1942, Canada's most famous Second World War ace, Pilot Officer George (Buzz) Beurling, DSO, DFC, DFM and bar, was back home recovering from burns and wounds incurred when he was shot down over the sea near Malta on 14 October 1942. He had scored 27 victories in the short period of four months during the successful defence of that beleaguered Mediterranean island. The Royal Air Force squadrons on Malta had been facing the best fighter and attack aircraft that Germany and Italy had in service, and Beurling's score was a notable achievement. When describing an air action, he had the habit of calling his opponent a "screwball," so it was not long before that became his nickname out there. Prior to being posted to Malta he had shot down two German aeroplanes over northern France; therefore he had a total of 29 victories by November.

In March 1943 Roy returned to Maclean's Publishing with a part-time position as an associate editor for the magazine *Canadian Aviation*. His function was to edit and contribute patriotic articles on the war in the air. The first article published under his name was an interview with Pilot Officer George Beurling, who was aiding government war bond sales campaigns by attending public meetings and telling the audience about the activities of the RCAF and the RAF in the air attacks against Germany and Italy. Roy interviewed Buzz at the magazine office in Toronto and then invited him out to the farm. Buzz arrived, accompanied by a number of newspaper reporters and a photographer, and was greeted by Roy, Edythe and Margaret. After the press had left, Roy and Buzz retired to the living room and had a long conversation comparing the tactics used in air combat in the 1940s with those of the Great War. After Beurling had left, Roy sadly remarked to his wife and daughter, *"He takes too many chances and is going to get himself killed."*[4]

Roy Brown at home with George (Buzz) Beurling and holding a model of a Handley Page Hampden bomber. Photograph from the Brown family collection.

Roy still felt strongly that there had to be some way in which he could contribute to Canada's war effort. If he could not join his old friends, perhaps he could support them in other ways. An opportunity occurred the when a provincial election was held in Ontario.

Right from the beginning of the Second World War the Canadian political scene had been somewhat unusual. Both the Canadian federal government and the Ontario provincial government were in the hands of the Liberal Party, but there the similarity ended. Prime Minister, Mackenzie King, had to consider the feelings in those provinces where the majority of the citizens were of French origin, and many did not wish to be sent overseas to fight in a war declared by a government composed mainly of Canadians of English origin. The Ontario provincial government, led by Premier Mitchell Hepburn took a different view, and as a result, relations between Mackenzie King and Mitchell Hepburn could hardly have been worse. By October 1942 the ailing Mitchell Hepburn, whose unpredictable attitudes and vitriolic outbursts against Mackenzie King had become a liability to the Liberal

Party, resigned and Gordon Conant took his place. The April 1943 Liberal Party Convention elected Harry Nixon as the new leader and on 30 April he took office as premier of Ontario. Unfortunately for Harry Nixon, a provincial election was already one year overdue, and despite the war situation he found himself obliged to call one.

Several of the cabinet ministers in the government of Ontario, and in particular some who had participated in Mitchell Hepburn's administration, were unpopular with the electorate to the degree that even traditional Liberal voters were unlikely to wish them back in office. In an attempt to overcome this handicap, Harry Nixon decided to tap patriotic sentiment by presenting a number of well-known war heroes as Liberal candidates for Parliament. As Roy owned an apartment building in the Woodbine electoral district of Toronto, he was entitled to vote and stand for election in that district. The local Liberal Party leaders invited him to be their candidate, and he accepted.

In 2001 Howard Brown told Alan Bennett that his brother's political leanings had always been conservative in nature, and for him to stand as a Liberal Party candidate was somewhat out of character. Roy's father-in-law, Tom Monypenny, advised him not to become involved, explaining that even if he were to be personally successful in the Woodbine riding, it was most unlikely that sufficient Liberals would be elected across the province to form the next government. Therefore, his influence upon the conduct of the war would be minimal.

Harry Nixon went on a speaking tour of Ontario in support of the local Liberal candidates. He emphasized that thirty-four of them had either served in the Great War or were currently serving in the armed forces and that they would help Ontario pressure the federal government into a more vigorous prosecution of the current conflict. To encourage women to vote Liberal he promised one cabinet position would be given to a female candidate. On Thursday, 29 July, at 8:30 pm he and Arthur Slaght, KC, MP addressed a meeting at Massey Hall, where Roy appeared together with those candidates for the various ridings in Toronto and York who were being presented to the public.

With the workload of electoral canvassing now added to that of running the farm, Roy had less time available for driving to the magazine office in Toronto several days a week. In July he relinquished his position as associate editor and became technical adviser. His contribution was reduced to a patriotic column entitled "Contact" in which he commented on the war in the air.

On 4 August the voters of Ontario gave their verdict: it was a landslide defeat for the Liberal Party, which until then had held 61 of the 90 seats; seven of the eleven cabinet members lost their seats. The results were Progressive Conservatives, 38 seats; Co-operative Commonwealth Federation, 34 seats; Liberals, 14 seats; and others 4 seats. George Drew, the leader of the Progressive Conservatives, became premier. In the Toronto and York ridings, where the Liberal Party had held 9 of the 17 seats prior to the election, not a single Liberal candidate was elected. The Progressive Conservatives captured 7 seats, the Co-operative Commonwealth Federation (Socialists) won 8, and Labour and Independents took the remaining 2 seats. In the Woodbine riding the results were: Bertram E. Leavens Co-operative Commonwealth Federation, 8,436; Goldwin C. Elgie Progressive Conservatives, 6,954; A. Roy Brown Liberals, 2,295. The result was not directed personally against Roy; he had achieved a higher percentage of votes cast than the Liberal candidates in many other ridings. Tom Monypenny had been right: however strong Roy's own case, he should not have tied his boat to a sinking ship.

Roy, who had been suffering from jaundice, continued with Canadian Aviation until mid-September when he found the drive to Toronto too demanding.[5] "Contact" appeared for the last time in the October 1943 issue; the main topic was an interview with Wing Commander Guy Penrose Gibson, VC, DSO and bar, DFC and bar. In May, Gibson had led the famous bouncing bomb attack on three large hydro-electric dams in Germany, and war production in the Ruhr was seriously disturbed for some months.

ACKNOWLEDGEMENTS

Neil McKenty kindly provided help in researching the 1943 Ontario provincial election.

ANNEX TO CHAPTER THIRTEEN

(1) THE BRITISH COMMONWEALTH AIR TRAINING PLAN.

Prior to 1936 much of the world had not perceived the directions in which the authoritarian governments of Germany and Italy were heading. It is said that 'nothing succeeds like success' and when the first adventurous steps of the Fuehrer and the Duce were unopposed by The League of Nations, except by talk, the way seemed clear for further action. This was noted in Paris and London, and the expansion of the French and British armed forces began. However, there was a major difference between 1914 and 1936; the Zeppelin and Gotha raids in 1916 - 18 had brought with them the realization that the English Channel and the Royal Navy no longer shielded the cities and towns of the United Kingdom from foreign attack. The aerodromes, where Royal Air Force flying training schools were based, would certainly be prime targets during what the doomsayers termed a 'knockout blow' delivered the moment war was declared, if not an hour or so before. The December 1941 attack on Pearl Harbor was that theory translated into practice by the Japanese.

The story of the British Commonwealth Air Training Plan began with RAF Group Captain Robert Leckie. When the Great War ended this ex-RNAS flying boat expert was seconded to Canada to help the Canadian Air Council organize government sponsored civil aviation. At that time, there were more conveniently located lakes than aerodromes near the centres of population, and it appeared that flying boats, both large and small would be the preferred means of air transport over long distances. Leckie remained there until 1922. In 1936 when the subject of expanding the RAF arose, he drew the attention of the Air Ministry in London to the possibilities offered by Canada. He informed the Air Staff that, although the extremes of Canadian weather were harsher than the English variety, the skies were clearer, and on a per annum basis there were more than twice the number of suitable days for primary flying training than in England. In the case of advanced flying training, Canada's vast prairies would provide the means for navigation and long range bombing exercises. Best of all, training schools located there would be exempt from enemy action. Another attractive aspect was that both in England and throughout the Dominions, anti-war sentiment kept military budgets small and it made sound economic sense to concentrate all flying training in one place.

In 1937 The Empire Air Training Scheme (EATS) was conceived under which airmen from Australia, New Zealand, Canada and the United Kingdom would all be trained in Canada. The Royal Air Force would transfer its instructors to Canada and Canadian factories would build the aircraft. The forty government-owned aerodromes and emergency landing fields, built from one end of the Canada/USA border to the other as Unemployment Relief Projects during the depression, already existed. Here, begging for greater use, were the homes for the Empire Air Training Scheme. The RCAF, still tight for money, was delighted; all this and heaven too, but the euphoria was to suffer a severe blow. Prime Minister McKenzie King of Canada realized that the RAF gift horse, plus the financing it would bring, was a two-edged sword. To the dismay of the RCAF, he looked the horse in the mouth and saw that his political opponents would immediately accuse him of committing Canada to fight at England's side should war break out in Europe.

It must be explained that in the 1930's the anti-war movement exerted great influence on both sides of the North Atlantic Ocean and in the Antipodes. Many returned veterans' organizations, together with a number of political parties which followed socialist philosophy, took a strong anti-war stance. The shell-shocked, the armless, legless and those unable to work due to lung damage from poison gas were still a familiar sight in the streets. Their presence exerted so much power at the polls that many voters said, *"Never again."*

In France the cry was, *"Not a soul for arms."* In England a group of university students publicly declared unwillingness to fight for their country in another war, and some socialist leaders exhorted British workers to refuse to manufacture munitions or weapons. In the USA, and to some extent in Canada, isolationism came into vogue; *"If the Europeans wish to fight again, this time we shall watch."* What became known as the 'shameful surrender at Munich' when in September 1938 the British and French governments agreed to the Sudetenland being returned to Germany, was in a large part due to the virtual total absence of domestic and international voter support for a firm stand which many believed would lead to a major European war that very month. To postpone was perhaps to avoid; unfortunately the reverse proved to be the case. The declarations in Paris and London of *"Peace in our time"* caused the German General Staff to cancel the plan to overthrow the Hitler regime that very night. As General Franz Halder asked his judges at the Nuremberg Trials, *"How can you depose a successful politician?"* Adolf Hitler suspected something had been in the wind and replaced the top leadership of the army with younger men. The prime minister of Canada, Mr. McKenzie King, was not the only one with problems.

McKenzie King's solution was a plan to change the nature of the air training programme. He would make it 100% Canadian and then invite England, Australia and New Zealand to join on his terms. One of his ideas was a new name; The British Commonwealth Air Training Plan (the BCATP). Unfortunately, in 1938 the RCAF did not possess the means to implement such a programme and the invitees were not prepared to wait. The RAF expanded in England, and the RAAF (Australia) and the RNZAF (New Zealand) sent trainees there. The BCATP fell into a kind of limbo and the RCAF had to live within its peacetime means for the next two years.

On 1 September 1939 the German army entered Poland and the Second World War began. Canada declared war on Germany on the 10th and it became politically possible for McKenzie King to start negotiations with England, Australia and New Zealand to activate the BCATP. When the Ottawa government realized the size of the funding required if the enterprise were to be 100% Canadian, the previously unwanted gift horse began to look rather attractive. An agreement between the four countries was signed on 17 December 1939. Such is politics.

Four aircrew training commands were established:

No. 1 with HQ in Toronto
No. 2 with HQ in Winnipeg
No. 3 with HQ in Montreal
No. 4 with HQ in Regina/Calgary.

Using round numbers, the total of aircrew trained at RCAF schools during the war was 132,000 and of these 50,000 were pilots. The latter were distributed as follows; RCAF 26,000, RAF 18,000, RAAF 4,000 and RNZAF 2,000.

In addition to the Canadian programme, six flying training schools for the RAF were quietly established in the USA prior to the Japanese landing at Kota Bharu in Malaya and the attack on Pearl Harbor (the Kota Bharu landing was actually the first of the two, but being on the 'day later' side of the International Date Line and in a different time zone, at a quick glance it appears to be the second). When RAF training was later phased out, the civilian-run Polaris Flight Academy, operated by the California Aero Corporation at War Eagle Field, Lancaster, California was established under contract to the US Army. In charge of flight operations in one of the training squadrons was a Canadian who wore RAF wings and active service ribbons on his shirt. He was said to have been a fighter pilot in the Great War and was known to his students as Captain Brown. When the trainees noticed that his fellow officers called him 'Roy', word flashed around the squadron that it was their officer who had downed the famous German ace, Baron Manfred von Richthofen. Few would notice that 'their officer' signed his name F. Roy Brown, and of those who did, apparently none knew the significance of the 'F'.

The aeroplanes shipped over from England to start the BCATP comprised the following types:

De Havilland 82A Tiger Moth G-AHIA with a 130 HP Gipsy Major engine. This is an example of the type supplied to Canada in 1940. Photograph taken at Cambridge Flying Group, England in July 1991 with Willam Willink (the instructor) in the front seat and Alan Bennett in the pilot's seat.

Typical Fairey Battle Bomber with Rolls-Royce Merlin engine. Typical of those supplied for training bomb aimers and air gunners.
For the latter purpose the rear portion of the original long, glazed crew compartment was replaced with a gun turret.

Avro Anson Mk.I N4877. Typical of those supplied from England for bomber pilot training and for use as a flying classroom for wireless operators and navigators. Note the 'blisters' around the engine cowling to provide clearance for the cylinder heads of the 350 HP Armstrong-Siddeley Cheetah IX engines. The gun turret was removed upon arrival in Canada.

Detailed information on the BCATP is to be found in: THE AERODROME OF DEMOCRACY by F.J. Hatch, published in English and French by the Canadian Government Publishing Centre Supply and Services Canada, Ottawa, Ontario, Canada, K1A 0S9.

Many commercially published books on the subject are also available and are generally catalogued under The British Commonwealth Air Training Plan. Three known to the present author are:

    WINGS FOR VICTORY by Spencer Dunmore
    THE PLAN by James N. Williams
    BEHIND THE GLORY by Ted Barris

(2) WILFRID REID MAY IN THE SECOND WORLD WAR.

'Wop' was prevented from joining the RCAF by the post-war loss of an eye in an industrial accident. He was given the task of managing BCATP Air Observer School No. 2 at Edmonton, Alberta.

W R May in BCATP uniform talking to the Duke of Kent at No.2 A.O.S. in spring 1942.

Wilfrid May (front row, centre) with some of his Edmonton staff and pupils in front of an Avro Anson flying classroom.
The 'blisters' on the engine cowlings identify it as a Mark I.

L - R: 'Con' Farrell, Wilfrid May, Harry Winney, Matt Berry, unknown, Herbert Hollick-Kenton, Walter Gilbert, unknown, at #2 A.O.S, Edmonton in 1944.

In the photograph above, the different shaped engine cowling (compare with the Mark I shipped from England) indicates this Canadian-built Anson has American engines. The shape of the propeller blades indicates they ran in the opposite direction to the Armstrong-Siddeley Cheetahs on the Mk.I. As in the case of the Tiger Moths, which could have either a DeHavilland Gipsy Major or an American Menasco Pirate D4 engine, a trainee pilot, who did not remember this difference when he opened the throttles for take off, could easily part company with the runway horizontally instead of vertically, and scare a few cows in the process.

An interesting design feature of all Avro Ansons is well illustrated in this photograph of Avro Anson Mk. II at 33 Flying Training School at Carberry, Manitoba. The landing wheels, even when fully retracted, would bear the weight of the entire aeroplane; a useful asset in a pilot training school.

(3) THE SERVICE CAREERS OF THE 'GANG' FROM CARLETON PLACE AND SOME OF ROY'S RAF COLLEAGUES DURING THE SECOND WORLD WAR.

THE GANG

ABBOTT, Robert Franklyn Preston, did not participate. He died in 1931 due to the after effects of high altitude flying in sub-zero (F) temperatures.
BREADNER, Lloyd Samuel, remained in the RAF after the Great War. He transferred to Canada where he rose in the RCAF to be Chief of Air Staff and then Chief of the RCAF Overseas. He retired in 1945 as Air Chief Marshal.
FINDLAY, David Douglas, joined the RCAF when WW-2 began, and became the C.O. of several air stations both in Canada and overseas. He was demobilized in 1945 with the rank of Group Captain.
GALBRAITH, Daniel Murray Bayne, did not participate. He was demobilized from the RAF in 1919 and returned to Canada where he joined the Canadian Air Force, the predecessor of the RCAF. He became the first CAF member to lose his life when he was killed in a motoring accident on 29 March 1921.

EX-RNAS/RAF COLLEAGUES

From 10(N) Squadron:
COLLISHAW, Raymond, remained in the RAF and held senior operational commands during the first half of WW-2. He retired in 1943 as Air Vice-Marshal.
NASH, Gerald Ewart, joined the RCAF when WW-2 began and became the C.O. of the Manning Depot at Aylmer, Ontario. He was demobilized in 1945 with the rank of Group Captain. His wife aided the war effort by packing parachutes at Beamsville, Ontario.

From 9(N) Squadron:
FOSTER, Robert Mordaunt, remained in the RAF and held senior commands throughout WW-2. He retired as Air Chief Marshal Sir Robert Foster.
MELLERSH, Francis John Williamson, remained in the RAF and held senior commands throughout the war. As Air Marshal Sir Francis Mellersh, he was killed in the mid-1950's when a helicopter fell on him.

From 10(N) Squadron:
ALEXANDER, William Melville, did not participate.

EX-RFC/RAF COLLEAGUES

From 48 Squadron:
PARK, Keith Rodney, the C.O. of the Bristol F2B *Fighters* stationed at Poulainville in April 1918, remained in the RAF after the war. He became famous as Air Officer Commanding No. 11 Group of Fighter Command during the Battle of Britain. He retired to his native New Zealand as Air Chief Marshal Sir Keith Park.

From 209 Squadron:
MAY, Wilfrid Reid. See (2) above.

FLYING HOURS, A COMPARISON BETWEEN TWO WARS

One day in 1970 Mel Alexander and Nick Carter were reminiscing about their adventures in the Great War. Mel had just returned from the Air Ministry in Ottawa where he had learned that very few WW-2 fighter pilots achieved more than 400 hours of combat flying. During the Great War Mel's total was 600 hours and Nick's 700. There were two reasons for this. First, to reduce combat fatigue, a system of tours of combat duty had been introduced. A tour was anywhere between 150 and 200 hours, and despite closed cockpits and the provision of oxygen for high altitudes, not many pilots performed three tours. Second, WW-2 aeroplanes cruised at somewhere between twice and thrice the speed of a Sopwith *Camel*, which meant the equivalent reduction in flying hours over the same distance.

(4) PILOT OFFICER GEORGE "BUZZ" BEURLING.

"Buzz" Beurling was not happy talking about the war, he wanted to return to active service and made no bones about it. In July 1943, just after his interview with Roy Brown for the magazine CANADIAN AVIATION, the RAF returned him to Britain where he taught marksmanship and deflection shooting at training schools for three months, then transferred to active service in the RCAF. He achieved two more victories in the skies over France, but was unable to accept counsel that times had changed and that if he continued making lone patrols against an enemy that was now operating in groups of 40 or 50, he would soon join most of his victims. In May 1944, after considerable friction with his superior officers, he resigned his commission, and with a grand total of 31 combat victories, became a civilian again. In 1948 he and three companions were killed in a take-off accident at Rome airport while on their way to join the Israeli Air Force as mercenary pilots.

The secret of "Buzz" Beurling's success in combat was identical to that of the German Great War ace, Manfred von Richthofen; namely, first class marksmanship coupled with accurately estimated deflection shooting. While his Spitfire was turning, Beurling could bring down an enemy aeroplane which was also turning, and achieve this with but a few shots. In the book WINGED VICTORY, his Malta C.O., Wing

Commander P B (Laddie) Lucas, CBE, DSO, DFC describes how, during one encounter, Sergeant Pilot Beurling shot down three enemy fighters in such a manner. The last was an Italian Macchi Mc 202 which was obliged to force land on Gozo. When Beurling was taken to see it, he noticed his cannon fire had struck between the cockpit and the tail. According to Lucas, Beurling seemed a little unhappy and murmured, *"Dammit. I was quite sure I had hit that Screwball up in the engine."*

(5) 'CANADIAN AVIATION' MAGAZINE.

For those who wish to read Roy Brown's contributions to CANADIAN AVIATION magazine, they are available in the public libraries in most Canadian Provincial capitals, definitely in Toronto. Photostat copies may be ordered.

March 1943 - Volume 16, No. 3
Roy Brown's appointment as an Associate Editor was announced on the Editorial Index page following the advertisements.

April 1943 - Volume 16, No. 4
Pages 47, 48, 49 & 112, **"Tools are different... Rules the same"**. Roy's interview with George Buerling.

July 1943 - Volume 16, No. 7
Pages 37, 38, 39, 96 & 97, **"Crash and Die, Live to Fly."**

September 1943 - Volume 16, No. 9. Roy Brown was listed as Technical Adviser.
Pages 56, 57, 58 & 79, **"Contact"** The Victory Aircraft Plant at Malton.

October 1943 - Volume 16, No. 10
Pages 65 & 138, **"Contact"** Roy's interview with Guy Gibson.

ACKNOWLEDGEMENTS

With the exception of the De Havilland Tiger Moth at Cambridge (courtesy of Daphne Poynter), the photographs above are from the J.M. Bruce/G.S. Leslie collection and the May family archive.

The story of Polaris Flight Academy at Lancaster, CA was kindly provided by Harold Jordan, who trained there as an aviation cadet in 1943.

CHAPTER FOURTEEN

A QUIET DEPARTURE
(1944 TO 1965)

Margaret Brown Harmon remembers that on 9 March 1944, having just finished his lunch, her father reminded her mother that he had stopped smoking a year ago to the day and he certainly had it "beat" this time. His health being poorer than usual, he was slightly jaundiced and he went upstairs for a nap. Edythe, who never napped, for some reason decided she would go up and have a short one as well.

Margaret continues this story: I don't know how long she had been up there when Dad had some sort of attack and died very quickly. It was diagnosed by doctors as a heart attack, but no autopsy was ever performed. My mother, who in her nursing days had seen many deaths from heart attack's, did not think he looked like a heart attack victim. She thought, *"Something went wrong in his head;"* - maybe it was a stroke or an aneurysm. He was just fifty years old.

I was on duty in the filter room when Mother called me with this horrifying news. Barb and I were able to book on Trans–Canada Airlines on 10 March. The morning dawned bright and clear, and we were at the airport early—only to find out that the flight had been cancelled due to mechanical problems. To go by train would take much too long, so we went right to the top of Eastern Air Command for help. The Air Vice Marshal was kind enough to have us flown in a small plane to Moncton, New Brunswick. It was absolutely freezing cold, and we were sitting in the back on the floor of "the shell" of an aircraft. The second, longer flight took place in a much larger aircraft, which turned out to be just a much larger shell. Off we flew to Montreal, absolutely frozen stiff the whole way. My sister could not even talk, her jaw chattered so violently, but we did thaw out on the train trip to Toronto. Believe it or not, way back then, all this took the better part of twenty-four hours. It really was one of the most gruelling and sad experiences of our young lives!

My father was buried in the cemetery in the town of Aurora on 13 March. Air Vice-Marshal A.T.N. Cowley represented the Chief of Air Staff at the funeral. A number of years later his body was disinterred to be cremated as had been his wish and his ashes are now in a mausoleum in Toronto, Ontario. This was a very sad time in our lives. My sister was discharged from the air force on compassionate grounds to return home; my brother left the university in Guelph, Ontario, to help Mother run the farm; and I stayed in the Royal Canadian Air Force.

My mother and brother successfully managed the farm for many years. To do so, they changed from general farming to specialization, first in broilers (frying chickens) and then in laying-birds. Fifteen women were employed just to grade the eggs. These operations were very profitable until, with both specializations, they were put out of business by government price controls. Mother found it regrettable that the Canadian government had put our family out of business on three occasions—first the airline business, then the broiler business and finally the egg business. She maintained that the degree of control which the government exercised over private enterprise made the Russian system of communism appear to be just slightly pink.

Edythe Brown and another entrepreneur at a Canadian Manufacturers' Convention.

In the late 1950s, Mother sold the farm to a developer who used the acreage as the main part of a golf course called Rolling Hills. The barn was converted into a curling club. Mother reserved some land, built her home overlooking the golf course and lived there happily with her flowers and gardens until she moved to Toronto in the late 1960s.

Edythe Brown's new house at the extreme left, the curling club barn in the middle background, and the farmhouse to the right.

EPILOGUE CHAPTER 15

Few members of Roy Brown's family are alive today. His brother, Horace, survived the wounds, accidents and illnesses of World War One only to succumb in England to the third and severest European influenza epidemic of all time. He died in Eaton Square Hospital in London, on Tuesday, 18 February, 1919. Had there been space on a ship returning to Canada, even a week earlier, he probably would not have contracted the flu and might have lived to a ripe old age—a very sad and unlucky turn of events.

Roy's sister Margaret, nicknamed "Reta," was a registered nurse working and teaching in the United States. Margaret Brown Harmon tells how she was killed in a nasty car accident in 1933 near Rochester, New York. Reta's car had a flat tire, and the repairman from Rochester had just finished changing it when a truck came speeding along the highway. The driver, who was hopelessly drunk, weaved onto the wrong side of the road and hit the repair truck, pinning Reta between the two vehicles. She was still alive but so badly injured that she suffered terribly and later died in a Rochester hospital.

Roy's other sister Bessie lived in the family home at 146 Judson Street, never marrying but following her career as a registered nurse. Unfortunately she suffered from headaches caused by a car accident in which she had been thrown through the windshield. In her later years she was secretary to the Carleton Place Library Board. Bessie died in 1971, and the family home in Carleton Place was sold.

Donald, Roy's son, was married in 1955 to Barbara Davidson, and they had two daughters, Frances in 1956, and Catherine in 1958. They lived for the next five years in the Lisnaclin family home, after which they moved to Woodstock in about 1960. Donald was killed in a tragic car accident on 1 November, 1963. Some young, high school students on Halloween night had removed a Stop sign at a blind intersection. Driving along the next day in unfamiliar territory, Donald naturally thought he had the right of way, but he was hit by a soft-drink truck and killed instantly. He was only 36 years old, with two very young pre-school children.

Margaret's sister, Barbara, joined the Young Women's Christian Association shortly after being discharged from the air force. She was sent to a large air force base in Pat Bay, British Columbia, to be in charge of entertainment, crafts and parties. There she met Squadron Leader Phillip Brodeur, and they were later married in Toronto in 1945. They lived in many places in Canada and then for four years in Germany as Phil was in the permanent Royal Canadian Air Force. They had two children, Diane and Donald; Don was also a pilot in the RCAF and spent two years in the Snowbirds, Canada's aerobatic team. Barbara died of ALS, known in the United States as Lou Gehrig's Disease, at the age of 67.

Roy's father-in-law, Tom Monypenny, died on 29 March 1948.

Edythe Brown lived until she was just two months shy of 93. Margaret Brown Harmon recounts: she lived by herself in an apartment, determinedly independent, until I had to trick her into moving to a nursing home. There she spent fourteen rather unhappy months. However, she never lost her sense of humour, even after losing her highly valued independence. There is an amusing story about my mother's almost indecipherable handwriting. She had attended private school and then changed to public school at the time she was learning to write. The public school taught a style of penmanship considerably different from that of the private school. She was totally confused, and it was obvious in the way she signed her name. When writing "Edythe," she did not connect the "y" to the "t" which followed, so her name looked like "Edy the." After my father died, Mother signed Christmas cards with her name only, and for a now-forgotten reason she abbreviated "Brown" to just the letter "B." She was somewhat surprised when her closest friends, the Longfellows, said nothing about having received a particularly beautiful card. Almost a year later, Mother was talking to Mrs Longfellow when the subject of the card came up. Mrs Longfellow exclaimed, *"That does it! All year long Ed and I have been puzzling about who in the world Edy the B is!"*

My father's youngest brother, my Uncle Howard, often referred to his *"unlucky family,"* and he had good reason to do so. Of his parents and the five siblings, only his mother and he had not suffered serious or fatal injury in a violent accident or been the victim of an epidemic. None of that bad luck seemed to have rubbed off on him, as he lived to the ripe old age of ninety-six and a half. His wife, my Aunt Connie, celebrated her hundredth birthday on 14 January, 2005 as a very bright and alert little lady. So now I, Margaret Brown Harmon, am the matriarch on both sides of my family; let's hope it lasts for a few years to come.

End of Volume 4 of 6 volumes, ebook edition.
End of Part One of Two parts.

For sales, editorial information, subsidiary rights information
or a catalog, please write or phone or e-mail
Brick Tower Press
1230 Park Avenue
New York, NY 10128, US
Sales: 1-800-68-BRICK
Tel: 212-427-7139
www.BrickTowerPress.com
email: bricktower@aol.com.

www.ingram.com

www.ingramcontent.com/pod-product-compliance
Lightning Source LLC
Chambersburg PA
CBHW021239240426
43673CB00057B/616